# SURVEY
# OF
# SOCIAL
# SCIENCE

# SURVEY OF SOCIAL SCIENCE

## PSYCHOLOGY SERIES

Volume 1
1-466
A—Brain-Stem Structures

*Edited by*

# FRANK N. MAGILL

*Consulting Editor*

JACLYN RODRIGUEZ
OCCIDENTAL COLLEGE

SALEM PRESS

Pasadena, California      Englewood Cliffs, New Jersey

∞ The paper used in these volumes conforms to the
American National Standard for Permanence of Paper
for Printed Library Materials, Z39.48-1984.

**Library of Congress Cataloging-in-Publication Data**
Survey of social science. Psychology series/edited by
Frank N. Magill; consulting editor Jaclyn Rodriguez
  p. cm.
  Includes bibliographical references and index.
  1. Psychology—Encyclopedias. I. Magill, Frank Nor-
then, 1907     . II. Rodriguez, Jaclyn.
BF31.S79   1993                                    93-34708
150′.3—dc20                                            CIP
ISBN 0-89356-732-9 (set)
ISBN 0-89356-733-7 (volume 1)

Second Printing

PRINTED IN THE UNITED STATES OF AMERICA

# PUBLISHER'S NOTE

The *Psychology Series* is the second set in the *Survey of Social Science*. The six volumes of the *Psychology Series* follow the *Economics Series* (1991, five volumes) and will in turn be followed by series on sociology and on government and politics. All are designed to provide the general reader with insight into topics in the social sciences that are often accessible only to academicians and experts in the field. The *Survey of Social Science* supplies information in a quickly retrievable format and easy-to-understand style, providing the nonspecialist with views of essential areas that are increasingly important to the layperson as well as the specialist.

The 410 articles of the *Psychology Series* follow the familiar Magill format. Averaging six pages in length, they begin with ready-reference information that states the type of psychology and particular field (or fields) of study to which the article's topic belongs. A brief, italicized summary describes the topic's significance; key terms are then listed and defined. To aid the reader in finding the information sought, the main text of each article is divided into three sections: "Overview," "Applications," and "Context." The "Overview" section introduces and explains the topic. "Applications" then describes how the topic is put into practice, including examinations of laboratory or field experimentation as well as a look at how it may be applied to everyday life. "Context" locates the subject within the context of psychology as a whole, relates it to relevant historical or cultural currents, and notes its implications. An annotated "Bibliography" follows these sections; it directs the reader to other sources that have been selected for their accessibility to the nonspecialist—the student and the general reader. Finally, "Cross-References" lists related articles (giving their page numbers) that appear elsewhere in the *Psychology Series*.

The *Psychology Series* is broad in scope, examining topics from eighteen major areas of psychology. Ten articles introduce historical perspectives, discussing such early twentieth century concepts as functionalism, and present overviews of psychology's principal fields, such as behaviorism, cognitive psychology, and psychoanalytic psychology. Each of these fields is also covered in greater detail by many articles focusing on particular specialties and concepts within them. The thirty-nine articles on specific aspects of developmental psychology, for example, address topics ranging from prenatal development to the cognitive and physical changes of old age. Aspects of infant and childhood development include reflexes in infants, moral development, and the formation of gender identity; articles on adolescence include sexuality and identity crises; adulthood issues covered include career change and divorce. Retirement and grandparenthood are among the aspects of aging that are examined. Major contributions by influential theorists are highlighted in individual articles; here, for example, one finds articles on the work of Jean Piaget and Erik Erikson.

The physiological bases of behavior are examined in twenty-four articles that look closely at the workings of the endocrine and nervous systems, including such topics as hormones and behavior, brain specialization, and reflexes. Articles that treat cognition include discussions of problem solving, concept formation, and artificial intelligence. Consciousness is explored in articles on topics such as dreams, levels of consciousness, and altered states of consciousness. Aspects of emotion discussed include the cognitive and physiological interactions involved, the functions of emotion, and cultural variations. The concept of intelligence and its relation to ability and intelligence testing are addressed in topics ranging from creativity and intelligence to college entrance examinations to bias in intelligence testing. Twelve articles look at aspects of language and language acquisition, such as the developmental sequence of language use and speech disorders. Learning and memory are two topics that have interested psychologists since the discipline began. Pavlovian (classical) conditioning and instrumental conditioning are specifically covered here in eight articles; other topics include observational learning and learned helplessness. Fourteen articles explore the workings of memory, describing such concepts as short-term and long-term memory, memory enhancement, and the physiology of memory. Motivation, including physical motives such as hunger and social motives such as aggression and work motivation, is treated in twenty-one articles.

The related areas of personality, psychopathology, and psychotherapy represent a part of psychology that fascinates the expert and the layperson alike. Thirty articles detail aspects of personality, including theories of personality, concepts such as the collective unconscious and ego defense mechanisms, and the tools of personality assessment. The models of major theorists, from Sigmund Freud to Karen Horney to B. F. Skinner, are presented in sixteen articles. Articles on psychopathology cover topics such as phobias, hyperactivity, depression, suicide, Alzheimer's disease, psychosomatic disorders, schizophrenia, sexual dysfunction, obsessions and compulsions, and the addictive personality. Psychotherapy topics include cognitive behavioral therapy, electroconvulsive therapy, psychosurgery, drug therapy, the effectiveness of psychotherapy, couples therapy, group therapy, classical versus modern psychoanalysis, and person-centered therapy. The field of social psychology is represented by forty-two articles addressing topics that range from the effects of violence and sexuality in the mass media to cognitive dissonance theory, from consumer decision making to theories of attraction, and from self-esteem to the effects of prejudice. Articles cover twenty-nine aspects of sensation and perception, including speech perception, optical illusions, pain, and techniques for measuring perception. Stress is explored in a range of articles that discuss its causes and effects as well as methods of predicting and coping with stress. Eighteen articles describe particular methods psychologists use in their research, including case-study methodologies, survey research, animal experimentation, and the use of statistics.

The field of psychology is constantly evolving, and new concepts and issues are always coming into focus; this process is reflected in the *Psychology Series.* "Feminist Psychotherapy," for example, looks at the attempts to free psychotherapy from societal influences affecting its views of women. "Bilingualism: Acquisition, Storage, and Processing" examines the ways people learn and use two languages. Articles are devoted to such widespread and complex problems of our time as substance abuse and anorexia nervosa. The problem of bias in "impartial" ability tests is addressed, as are the relationship between psychology and law and the debate over the reliability of eyewitness testimony.

Readers can locate information on a particular topic in a number of ways. The series is arranged alphabetically by article title, so looking for "behaviorism," for example, will bring the reader to the article "Behaviorism: An Overview"; the cross-references at the end of that article refer the reader to related articles, such as "Radical Behaviorism: B. F. Skinner." Each volume begins with a contents list of the volume and ends with an alphabetical listing of the contents of the entire set, followed by a listing of the contents grouped by category. Two other features that will aid the reader in understanding and locating information are found at the end of volume six. A glossary defines more than five hundred important terms, and a comprehensive, cross-referenced index directs the reader to topics, personages, terms, and concepts.

Salem Press gratefully acknowledges all the academicians and professionals who contributed their time, talents, and expertise to *Survey of Social Science: Psychology Series.* A list of these individuals and their affiliations appears on the following pages. We would especially like to thank Consulting Editor Jaclyn Rodriguez of Occidental College for her invaluable contributions to the series.

# CONTRIBUTORS

Christopher M. Aanstoos
*West Georgia College*

Norman Abeles
*Michigan State University*

Steven C. Abell
*Loyola University of Chicago*

Richard Adler
*University of Michigan—Dearborn*

Mark B. Alcorn
*University of Northern Colorado*

Charles N. Alexander
*Maharishi International University*

Dan Hawkmoon Alford
*California Institute of Integral Studies*

Jeffery B. Allen
*University of Mississippi*

Tara Anthony
*Syracuse University*

Eileen Astor-Stetson
*Bloomsburg University of Pennsylvania*

Richard P. Atkinson
*Fort Hays State University*

Bryan C. Auday
*Gordon College*

Stephen M. Auerbach
*Virginia Commonwealth University*

Bruce E. Bailey
*Stephen F. Austin State University*

Marie T. Balaban
*Harvard University*

Stephen R. H. Beach
*University of Georgia*

Donald G. Beal
*Eastern Kentucky University*

Alan J. Beauchamp
*Northern Michigan University*

Brett L. Beck
*Bloomsbury University*

Bill E. Beckwith
*University of North Dakota*

Susan E. Beers
*Sweet Briar College*

D. Alan Bensley
*Texas Wesleyan University*

Barbara E. Brackney
*Eastern Michigan University*

Nyla R. Branscombe
*University of Kansas*

Barbara A. Bremer
*Pennsylvania State University Harrisburg*

Christiane Brems
*University of Alaska*

Bruce Bridgeman
*University of California, Santa Cruz*

T. L. Brink
*Crafton Hills College*

John T. Burns
*Bethany College*

Joan Bartczak Cannon
*University of Lowell*

Michael D. Chafetz
*University of New Orleans*

Paul J. Chara, Jr.
*Loras College*

Garvin Chastain
*Boise State University*

Carl D. Cheney
*Utah State University*

Rebecca M. Chesire
*University of Hawaii—Manoa*

Barbara Clark
*Michigan State University*

Linda Collins
*Memphis State University*

Allen L. Combs
*University of North Carolina at Asheville*

ix

Richard G. Cormack
*Independent Scholar*

Lincoln G. Craton
*Trinity University*

Salvatore Cullari
*Lebanon Valley College*

Kenneth G. DeBono
*Union College*

Jack Demick
*Suffolk University*

James R. Deni
*Appalachian State University*

Karen M. Derr
*Airport Marina Counseling Service*

Thomas E. DeWolfe
*Hampden-Sydney College*

George Domino
*University of Arizona*

Roger A. Drake
*Western State College of Colorado*

Dana S. Dunn
*Moravian College*

Ted H. Eilders
*American Psychological Association*

Russell Eisenman
*McNeese State University*

David G. Elmes
*Washington and Lee University*

Carolyn Zerbe Enns
*Cornell College*

Charles H. Evans
*LaGrange College*

Lawrence A. Fehr
*Widener University*

Julie A. Felender
*Fullerton College*

John H. Fleming
*University of Minnesota—Minneapolis*

Roy Fontaine
*Pennsylvania College of Technology*

Karen Anding Fontenot
*Louisiana State University*

Michael J. Fontenot
*Southern University*

Margaret M. Frailey
*American Association of Counseling
and Development*

Robin Franck
*Southwestern College*

Donna J. Frick
*North Carolina A&T University*

Lisa Friedenberg
*University of North Carolina at Asheville*

Jerome Frieman
*Kansas State University*

Jim Fultz
*Northern Illinois University*

R. G. Gaddis
*Gardner-Webb College*

Judith L. Gay
*Chestnut Hill College*

Alan K. Gibson
*Southern California College*

Albert R. Gilgen
*University of Northern Iowa*

Virginia L. Goetsch
*West Virginia University*

Doyle R. Goff
*Lee College*

Sanford Golin
*University of Pittsburgh*

Jeff Greenberg
*University of Arizona*

Laurence Grimm
*University of Illinois at Chicago*

Lonnie J. Guralnick
*Western Oregon State College*

John P. Hall
*Texas Wesleyan University*

Leonard W. Hamilton
*Rutgers University*

Ruth T. Hannon
*Bridgewater State College*

Phyllis A. Heath
*Central Michigan University*

## CONTRIBUTORS

Jean S. Helgeson
*Collin County Community College*

James Taylor Henderson
*Wingate College*

Oliver W. Hill, Jr.
*Virginia State University*

Peter C. Hill
*Grove City College*

Robert A. Hock
*Xavier University*

David Wason Hollar, Jr.
*Rockingham Community College*

Brynda Holton
*St. Mary's College of Maryland*

Sigmund Hsiao
*University of Arizona*

Timothy L. Hubbard
*Eastern Oregon State College*

Tiffany A. Ito
*University of Southern California*

Jane A. Jegerski
*Elmhurst College*

Craig Johnson
*Syracuse University*

Eugene R. Johnson
*Central Washington University*

Mark E. Johnson
*University of Alaska, Anchorage*

Robert D. Johnson
*Arkansas State University*

Jonathan Kahane
*Springfield College*

Laura Kamptner
*California State University, San Bernardino*

William B. King
*Edison Community College*

Debra King-Johnson
*Clemson University*

Terry J. Knapp
*University of Nevada, Las Vegas*

Arlene Confalone Lacombe
*Chestnut Hill College*

R. Eric Landrum
*Boise State University*

Kevin T. Larkin
*West Virginia University*

Ellen Lavelle
*Teikyo Western University*

Joseph C. LaVoie
*University of Nebraska at Omaha*

Leon Lewis
*Appalachian State University*

Scott O. Lilienfeld
*State University of New York at Albany*

Charles J. Long
*Memphis State College*

Gary T. Long
*University of North Carolina at Charlotte*

Richard D. McAnulty
*University of North Carolina at Charlotte*

Jasmin T. McConatha
*Westchester University*

Deborah R. McDonald
*New Mexico State University*

Nancy E. Macdonald
*University of South Carolina at Sumter*

David S. McDougal
*Plymouth State College of the
    University System of New Hampshire*

Salvador Macias, III
*University of South Carolina at Sumter*

Paul D. Mageli
*Independent Scholar*

Amy Marcus-Newhall
*Occidental College
University of Southern California*

Linda Mealey
*College of St. Benedict*

Linda E. Meashey
*Pennsylvania State University Harrisburg*

Laurence Miller
*Western Washington University*

Laurie S. Miller
*University of Illinois at Chicago*

# PSYCHOLOGY

Norman Miller
*University of Southern California*

Rowland Miller
*Sam Houston State University*

Joseph R. Mobley, Jr.
*University of Hawaii—West Oahu*

Fathali M. Moghaddam
*Georgetown University*

Brian Mullen
*Syracuse University*

Julie Nelson
*University of Illinois at Chicago*

John W. Nichols
*Tulsa Junior College*

Steve A. Nida
*Franklin University*

Annette O'Connor
*La Salle University*

Nancy Oley
*City University of New York,*
*Medgar Evers College*

Don R. Osborn
*Bellarmine College*

Randall E. Osborne
*Phillips University*

Shirley A. Albertson Owens
*Southern California College*

Linda J. Palm
*Edison Community College*

Beverly B. Palmer
*California State University,*
*Dominguez Hills*

Keith Krom Parker
*Western Montana College of the*
*University of Montana*

Vicky Phares
*University of Connecticut*

Anthony R. Pratkanis
*University of California, Santa Cruz*

Judith Primavera
*Fairfield University*

R. Christopher Qualls
*Emory and Henry College*

Timothy S. Rampey
*Victoria College*

F. Wayne Reno
*Mt. Vernon Nazarene College*

Paul August Rentz
*South Dakota State University*

Ronald G. Ribble
*University of Texas at San Antonio*

Richard J. Ricard
*Texas A&M University*

Cheryl A. Rickabaugh
*University of Redlands*

Loretta A. Rieser-Danner
*Pennsylvania State University, Ogontz*

Edwin S. Robbins
*New York University Medical Center*

Lillian Cukier Robbins
*Rutgers University—Newark*

Jaclyn Rodriguez
*Occidental College*

Míchaél D. Roe
*Seattle Pacific University*

René R. Roth
*University of Western Ontario, Canada*

Daniel Sachau
*Mankato State University*

Denise S. St. Cyr
*New Hampshire Technical College*

James D. St. James
*Millikin University*

Frank A. Salamone
*Iona College*

David Sands
*Maharishi International University*

John Santelli
*Fairleigh Dickinson University*

Rosemary Scheirer
*Chestnut Hill College*

Samuel B. Schnitzer
*Indiana State University*

Michael F. Schober
*New School for Social Research*

# CONTRIBUTORS

Elliott Schuman
*Long Island University*

Pennie S. Seibert
*Boise State University*

Susan J. Shapiro
*Indiana University East*

Matthew J. Sharps
*California State University, Fresno*

Michael F. Shaughnessy
*Eastern New Mexico University*

Bonnie S. Sherman
*St. Olaf College*

Harold I. Siegel
*Institute of Animal Behavior,*
*  Rutgers University*

Marilyn N. Silva
*California State University, Hayward*

David D. Simpson
*Carroll College*

Sanford S. Singer
*University of Dayton*

Lesley A. Slavin
*Virginia Commonwealth University*

Charles V. Smedley
*Charleston Southern University*

Stephanie Smith
*Indiana University Northwest*

Janet A. Sniezek
*University of Illinois at*
*  Urbana-Champaign*

Sheldon Solomon
*Skidmore College*

Gerald Sperrazzo
*University of San Diego*

Michael A. Steele
*Wilkes University*

Stephanie Stein
*Central Washington University*

Joseph E. Steinmetz
*Indiana University Bloomington*

Lloyd K. Stires
*Indiana University of Pennsylvania*

Leland C. Swenson
*Loyola Marymount University*

Richard G. Tedeschi
*University of North Carolina at Charlotte*

Lori L. Temple
*University of Nevada, Las Vegas*

Thomas J. Thieman
*College of St. Catherine*

Harry A. Tiemann, Jr.
*Mesa State College*

C. Robin Timmons
*Drew University*

Derise E. Tolliver
*DePaul University*

James T. Trent
*Middle Tennessee State University*

Marlene E. Turner
*San Jose State University*

John V. Urbas
*Kennesaw State College*

Susana P. Urbina
*University of North Florida*

Mary Moore Vandendorpe
*Lewis University*

Lois Veltum
*University of North Dakota*

Scott R. Vrana
*Purdue University*

Elaine F. Walker
*Emory University*

Daniel L. Wann
*Murray State University*
*University of Kansas*

Jennifer A. Sanders Wann
*Murray State University*

Ann L. Weber
*University of North Carolina at Asheville*

George I. Whitehead, III
*Salisbury State University*

Edward R. Whitson
*State University of New York,*
*  College at Genesco*

# PSYCHOLOGY

Michael Wierzbicki
*Marquette University*

David A. Wilder
*Rutgers University*

Mark A. Williams
*University of Mississippi*

Bradley R. A. Wilson
*University of Cincinnati*

Gregory L. Wilson
*Washington State University*

Adam Winsler
*Stanford University*

Stephen L. Wolfe
*University of California, Davis*

Karen Wolford
*State University of New York,
  College at Oswego*

Edelgard Wulfert
*State University of New York at Albany*

Frederic Wynn
*County College of Morris*

Taher Zandi
*State University of New York*

Debra Zehner
*Wilkes University*

# CONTENTS

# PSYCHOLOGY

# SURVEY
# OF
# SOCIAL
# SCIENCE

# ABILITY TESTING: INDIVIDUAL AND GROUP

*Type of psychology:* Intelligence and intelligence testing
*Field of study:* Ability tests

*Ability tests measure human performance in a wide variety of areas and encourage test takers to perform as well as they can. They have been used for thousands of years not only to select individuals with specific abilities but also to classify, screen, and counsel persons for a wide range of reasons.*

*Principal terms*
> ABILITY: the capability of an individual to perform in a certain area
> ACHIEVEMENT: a knowledge or skill that a person has attained in a specific area or domain
> ASSESSMENT: the process of collecting information about an individual in order to make predictions and inferences
> INTELLIGENCE: the ability to learn and understand; often associated with a person's skill at dealing with new or unfamiliar materials
> RELIABILITY: the ability of a test to measure information consistently over time
> STANDARDIZATION: the administration, scoring, and interpretation of a test in a prescribed manner so that differences in test results can be attributed to the testee
> TEST: a sample of behavior from which other behaviors can be predicted or inferred
> VALIDITY: the ability of a test to measure what it is supposed to measure

## Overview

There are nearly as many types of ability tests as there are tasks that a human being can perform. Within ten minutes of birth, an infant has been tested twice. The test utilized, the Apgar, named after its developer, Virginia Apgar, measures the newborn's ability to adjust to its new environment outside the womb. Throughout an individual's life, continual ability testing will be encountered in both individual and group settings. Public school systems are one of the largest users of ability tests, assessing students not only in traditional academic areas such as reading and math, but also in specialty areas such as physical prowess and the ability to build and maintain interpersonal relationships. Ability testing does not end at graduation, as individuals are assessed further by other interested organizations, including the armed forces, employers, and even by the Internal Revenue Service.

Ability tests are found in two major formats: individual and group. Individual tests are developed to be administered by a highly trained examiner (a psychologist or doctor) during a one-on-one testing session. A strength of this format is that it allows the examiner to question and probe the testee when ambiguous responses are given. Questions may vary from verbal inquiries designed to see how well an individual can solve a specific problem, such as determining how long it will take a train traveling at a particular speed to travel from point A to point B, to having the testee sort objects into a logical, predetermined sequence. Questions can also be devised to tap very specific abilities, and may require a testee to type excerpts from a manuscript or to run 100 meters as fast as possible. The particular test format used is selected to meet the requirements of the test user. Individually administered ability tests are time-consuming and costly to the user; however, the results obtained often have high validity.

One of the most widely utilized individual ability tests is the Wechsler Intelligence Scale for Children-Revised (WISC-R). Through the administration of twelve subtests covering a wide range of topics, three intelligence quotient (IQ) scores are obtained: verbal IQ, performance IQ, and full-scale IQ, a combination of the verbal and performance scores. Example items similar to those found on verbal subtests of the WISC-R might be "In what ways are tea and milk alike?" or "What is the thing to do if you cut your foot?" Nonverbal test items include putting together puzzles and arranging a series of pictures in a meaningful sequence. Results from the WISC-R are often used to determine eligibility for special education programs within the public schools.

Group tests of ability, as the name would imply, can be administered to a large number of individuals at the same time. Instructions are given to an entire group simultaneously, and the test takers are then required to complete the test items on their own. A multiple-choice question format which requires the testee to read a question and then select an answer from numerous possible answers is most often utilized; however, as with individually administered tests, various question formats are available to the test user to meet specific needs. Group tests are cost efficient while retaining the capability of providing valid results. Should the testee not understand a question or a written instruction, however, this format does not allow for probing or clarification by the examiner.

The Scholastic Aptitude Test (SAT) is a widely used group instrument designed to measure skills and diligence required in college work. The test comprises two sections, verbal and quantitative. The verbal portion is designed to measure verbal reasoning and comprehension, while the quantitative section addresses reasoning with numerical materials along with basic principles from geometry and algebra. The SAT is required by most private colleges for admission and placement. Testees can also use their results to help them select colleges to which to apply.

## Applications

In the broadest sense, ability tests, whether they be administered individually or in a group, are used to measure performance in order to make decisions. Tests are generally given to meet the needs of the user (for example, an educational system or an employer). Most often, ability test results are used in the process of selection. Test results are utilized to select students to participate in specific classes or programs. Employers reward employees with promotions and salary increases based on ability test results. Students who obtain the highest scores on college entrance examinations are selected first by colleges and universities. Similarly, an employer with one position to fill may select from fifty candidates based on ability test scores. Although there is controversy involved with the utilization of ability tests in a variety of situations, tests have gained considerable acceptance by experts and the public because they are viewed as being more objective than other techniques.

While ability test results are often used in selection decisions, many other uses remain. Ability tests are frequently called upon in situations in which a diagnosis is needed. Doctors and educators alike utilize tests to identify specific maladies, whether they be appendicitis, flu, or a learning disability. Ability tests have been developed to measure specific traits (or lack of such traits) so that test users can compare a person's results to a specific set of characteristics found in persons with specific difficulties. For example, a student with a learning disability typically has a discrepancy between ability and level of academic achievement. That is, the student is not achieving at his or her potential. Other characteristics may include difficulty with coordination, poor peer relationships, and even behavioral problems. To diagnose a learning disability, educators administer a series of ability tests designed to measure general ability and to pinpoint specific problems. Specific performance patterns are noted and interpreted by the test user.

Often, a quick form of an ability test known as a screening is utilized by test givers. While most tests of ability are designed to take hours or even days, the intent of a screening is to assess large numbers of individuals quickly in order to identify those individuals who require more in-depth testing. Screening devices are frequently used by employers to determine which employees may have the potential to benefit from further training or education. It is also common to enter a grocery store or shopping mall and find teams of professionals quickly screening individuals for high cholesterol or high blood pressure. Screenings are also used in the educational setting to test large numbers of students to determine which are potentially at risk for having learning, social, or health problems.

Classification is another important use of ability tests. It is not uncommon for an employer to have a number of job vacancies available in a variety of skill areas. In this situation, ability tests are used to measure applicants' skills and match them with a specific area. The armed services have made extensive use of ability tests to place recruits in positions ranging from fighter pilot to desk clerk. Ability tests can measure specific skills in areas such as mechanics, scientific knowledge, and even the performing arts. The information gained provides the user with the specific information necessary to make appropriate classifications.

While the needs of the test user motivate much ability testing, ability testing is also dictated by the needs of the testee. Ability test results are utilized in guidance and career counseling situations. Results from an ability test battery can help direct an individual in making changes in his or her life which could enhance career and educational possibilities. Numerous ability tests focus on interests that an individual may have. By identifying areas of interest, an individual can make career choices which will reflect his or her skills and wishes.

## Context

The history of ability testing can be traced back to around 2200 B.C. There is evidence that the ancient Chinese used various tests of proficiency to measure an individual's ability and level of education. Later, the tests became part of the Chinese civil-service system. More recently, ability testing gained momentum during the late nineteenth and early twentieth centuries. The early works of Sir Francis Galton and James McKeen Cattell focused on the assessment of individual differences. Many scientists of the time had noticed that people react differently to various physical stimuli. For example, one person was capable of seeing a fainter light than another. Similarly, some individuals could follow a moving object with a pointer more accurately than others. The early measurement of these individual differences paved the way for today's ability tests. These early scientists discovered that not all people had the same abilities; they also found that people had varying degrees of ability in different areas. For example, a person could possess excellent skills in the area of public speaking but poor abilities in spelling.

At a time when most scientists focused their attention on the measurement of sensory-motor abilities, Cattell began to look at a wider range of personal abilities, and was the first person to use the term "mental test." At this same time, Alfred Binet, a French psychologist, was commissioned by the French government to develop a test instrument to assess students in school. Binet's charge was to develop an instrument capable of identifying those students who would benefit from special education. Over the next several decades, Binet and his colleagues constructed and modified numerous versions of his ability test. Updated forms of his initial instruments continue to be widely utilized in the United States today. As a result of his work, Binet is generally considered the "father of the intelligence test."

While individual ability testing was gaining impetus in the early twentieth century, group testing was also growing in popularity. During World War I, the United States government needed quick and efficient techniques which would allow it to make decisions about new recruits entering the armed forces. The Army Alpha and Army Beta tests were developed and designed to screen large numbers of recruits to provide information for placement into a wide range of categories. It is reported that before the end of World War I, more than one million men had completed the Army Alpha test battery alone.

With the advent of compulsory education at the beginning of the twentieth century, ability tests were needed to assist in the educational process for growing numbers of students. Ability tests were required to measure student progress, determine areas in which students needed remediation, identify handicapped students, and provide information which would be beneficial in evaluating educational programs. In addition, individual and group ability tests were needed to assess academic achievement in all academic areas. To meet this need, large testing programs were developed by numerous publishing companies which provide tests to school districts nationwide. Many districts routinely test their students once each year. The results assist in measuring the effectiveness of educational programs as well as in monitoring student progress. Because of the magnitude of these testing programs, results can be compared to schoolwide, statewide, regional, and even national populations.

As with education, the employment market continues to evolve and grow, thus necessitating the data collected by ability tests. Computer technology increases the need for individuals with specific skills in the marketplace. As specific skills arise, new assessment instruments are developed to identify individuals with the specific skills to fill such positions.

With technological and educational advances, it is reasonable to believe that ability testing will remain an important endeavor in the field of psychology for years to come. As society continues to evolve, so will the development and implementation of ability tests designed to meet the changing needs of the test user and testee. Tests will continue to provide the necessary information required to make decisions.

## Bibliography

Brown, Frederick Gramm. *Principles of Educational and Psychological Testing.* 3d ed. New York: Holt, Rinehart and Winston, 1983. Covers a wide variety of topics surrounding educational and psychological testing. Specific content areas deal with a wide range of testing instruments along with their usage.

Cronbach, Lee J. *Essentials of Psychological Testing.* 4th ed. New York: Harper & Row, 1984. A definitive text in the area of psychological testing. Provides an in-depth assessment. Test construction as well as a variety of testing instruments are reviewed.

Graham, John Robert, and Roy S. Lilly. *Psychological Testing.* Englewood Cliffs, N.J.: Prentice-Hall, 1984. Provides information pertaining to the history and development of psychological testing, as well as an overview of many of the major tests utilized in the 1980's.

Thorndike, Robert M., and David F. Lohman. *A Century of Ability Testing.* Chicago: Riverside, 1990. Chronicles the development of ability testing in the twentieth century. Provides an in-depth look at ability testing through the eyes of many famous test developers.

Weiner, Elliot A., and Barbara J. Stewart. *Assessing Individuals: Psychological and Educational Tests and Measurements.* Boston: Little, Brown, 1984. Looks at a variety of assessment instruments utilized in testing individuals. Chapters center on instruments designed to assess specific areas.

Wigdor, Alexandra K., and Wendell R. Garner, eds. *Ability Testing: Uses, Consequences, and Controversies.* Washington, D.C.: National Academy Press, 1982. Presents the work of a team of psychologists and educational specialists brought together as a committee on ability testing by the National Research Council. The result is a technical but in-depth look at ability testing from a modern-day perspective.

*Eugene R. Johnson*

## Cross-References

Bias in Ability Tests, 7; Ability Tests: Design and Construction, 13; Ability Tests: Reliability, Validity, and Standardization, 21; Ability Tests: Uses and Misuses, 27; College Entrance Examinations, 598; Intelligence Tests, 1341; Interest Inventories, 1349; Testing: Historical Perspectives, 2540.

# BIAS IN ABILITY TESTS

*Type of psychology:* Intelligence and intelligence testing
*Fields of study:* Ability tests; general issues in intelligence

*Ability tests are sometimes described as objective and fair tools for identifying individuals' strengths; however, many people have criticized them as being biased against African Americans, Hispanics, women, and other groups. Because of the increasing use of ability tests in the decisions made about people's daily lives, it is critical to understand how they might be unfair.*

### Principal terms

ABILITY TEST: a standardized test designed to measure aptitude, school achievement, intelligence, or any number of specific skills
ACCULTURATION: becoming conditioned or adapted to the customs, values, beliefs, and patterns of a different culture
COGNITIVE STYLE: a person's preferred way of knowing or of solving problems
CULTURAL GROUP: a group of people distinguishable by their shared attitudes, values, customs, symbols, art, experiences, and rules
FAIR: free from prejudice and discrimination
HEREDITARIAN: a person who believes that intelligence is an inherited trait
TEST BIAS: a situation in which the meanings of test performance are not the same for members of different groups; aspects of a test that discriminate against certain people taking it

## Overview

Ability tests play a significant role in American society. Intelligence and achievement tests are used for many purposes in education: to evaluate a student's progress, to identify areas of weakness, and to help define teaching goals. They are a major component in the decision to place students in special classes or to admit students to universities and colleges. Some occupations also utilize ability tests to determine qualifications for employment, entrance into training programs, and promotions. With such widespread use, it is imperative that these tests be fair.

Test bias is a systematic error that disadvantages the performance of one group over another. Although lower scores are not always indicators of bias, various aspects of a test can affect performance and lead to incorrect beliefs about the abilities, knowledge, and characteristics of an individual or group.

Critics identify several sources of bias in test items. Most important, they note that tests are biased toward the culture in which they are developed. Those developed in the United States, for example, generally have been written by middle-class males who have had Anglo-American life experiences. Their attitudes, beliefs, and values are subtly built into their tests. The information that these individuals have acquired and used within their own cultural experiences will determine what they think is important to know. Therefore, the content presented in the test may be culturally inappropriate for someone who has not been reared in the same cultural situation as the test developer. For example, an American child would not be expected to know what a shilling is, although a British child would. Asking a child who lives in the barrio about polo may be equally unfair as asking an American child about shillings, since neither the term nor the experience is familiar to the child.

Psychologist Robert Williams believes that items on ability tests do not measure general abilities, aptitude, or intelligence for everyone who takes them. Instead, he says, they require the test taker to "tell me [the test producer] what you know about my culture." Not only must the test takers know the "correct" answer, they also must respond in a specific way in order to get credit for their knowledge. The scores on these tests, then, will be as much measures of acculturation and income as they will be measures of ability or skills. The test takers' own cultural experiences will determine what the "correct" answers are for them. These will not always correspond to what the scoring manual says is correct.

People's cultural backgrounds influence how they perceive the environment; their experiences of their culture affect what they see and how they see it. For example, city children might readily recognize the shapes of squares and rectangles as representing houses; however, for other children, a triangle or a semicircle might be closer to the shape of the structure they recognize as a place to live. Therefore, a test item that requires the association of a square with a house might be missed by someone who does not see things that way. Again, the more familiar the individual is with the material presented in the test item, the more likely he or she is to give the correct response.

Language has been identified as a major source of bias in ability test items. Test takers may not adequately understand the wording of items because they are not written in their native language, or because items may be phrased in an unfamiliar way. Psychologist Ernesto Bernal points out that even with translated tests or the use of interpreters, the language bias is not always eliminated, because the meaning of a word in one language, dialect, or region may not directly correspond to a word or phrase in another language, dialect, or region. A related type of bias results from the differences in meanings of words, which may be related to cultural background, gender, or income. For example, to some children, the word environment refers to home, people, or surroundings. To others, it may be associated with air, pollution, or the Earth. Although both uses are correct, only one may be acceptable on a test.

Sometimes the type of question asked or task required may interfere with a test taker doing his or her best. Researchers have discovered that people have different cognitive or information-processing styles. That is, they have preferences for the ways they learn, remember, and solve problems most effectively. Some do well with understanding bits of information that have meaning by themselves. Others will learn and remember things as they are related to other information. Asa Hilliard refers to these as analytical and relational styles, respectively. It is important to note that these are differences in styles, not abilities. If the ability-test item is written in such a way that it restricts certain test takers from using their preferred ways of processing information, they are more likely to do poorly on the test. In fact, most tests assume that everyone will or should use the style that is seen primarily among middle-class or upper-middle-class white males. If they do not, they are penalized for using a "nonstandard" problem-solving approach.

There is also research that suggests that test takers tend to score better when they identify with the situations and subjects covered by the test items. Researcher Paula Selkow found that women and men sometimes respond differently to male-oriented and female-oriented content. The timed format of some tests may also be a source of bias.

## Applications

Several examples can illustrate how items on ability tests may be biased and there-fore affect the performance and scores of test takers.

Some standardized intelligence quotient (IQ) tests contain a section designed to measure social reasoning and knowledge of socially acceptable ways of behaving. A child who has been taught different cultural values and/or has life experiences that do not mirror those of the test developer will be at a serious disadvantage when taking this part of the test. For example, consider the question, "What is the thing to do if you lose a ball that belongs to one of your friends?" The "best" answer, according to the scoring guidelines in the test manual, is to buy a new one and pay for it. A poor child, however, may not be able to buy a new ball, and may not see that as an option. The "next-best" answer is to look all over for the ball. Yet if the ball is really lost, would it not be a waste of time to continue to look for it? If it were possible to find it, however, it might very well be better to look for it than to buy a new one. A child may have been taught that it would be best to apologize for losing the ball. The test taker would not receive credit for this answer.

Another section of a popular IQ test requires the test taker to put together picture cards in the correct order to tell a story that makes sense. One eighteen-year-old African-American female from inner-city Detroit put together the story of a burglar who gets caught, goes to jail, then appears before the judge. According to the scor-ing manual, the correct order would have the thief sentenced by the judge before going to jail. In reality, some people who are picked up for suspicion of a crime are detained in jail before they have the opportunity to go before a judge. Although the answer given was realistic and was consistent with her experience (and that of many other inner-city residents), the young woman received no credit for her alternative response.

When value-based questions such as the ones above are scored, an assumption is made that the test taker lacks the knowledge to answer the question correctly. It would not be clear, however, without further questioning, why an individual actually missed the question.

There could be other reasons for poor performance on a test. Did the test taker understand the language in the question? Was the situation described unfamiliar to the test taker? Did the item have a common meaning to all who were examined? Did the individual have enough time? If any of these questions could be answered no, a test taker's true ability may be underestimated. Scoring procedures do not generally allow for the possibility of alternative correct answers. The test assumes a common cultural perspective that may not be shared by all test takers.

Another type of ability-test item asks for general information, such as "What is the shape of a house?" The wording of such questions often implies that everyone should clearly understand what is being asked. If the test asks, "When was Washington born?" without additional information, is it correct to assume that everyone will know that the item refers to George Washington? Not necessarily, especially if there were other individuals named Washington who are more prominent in the mind of the test taker.

Some tests require that the examinee respond to or respond with information that is decontextualized. That is, the information is taken out of the situation that makes it relevant. This is consistent with an analytical cognitive style and is the type of training that is likely to be emphasized by middle-class whites and the traditional education system. For example, many vocabulary tests require a strong memory for specific facts and details. Relational learners may have difficulty defining words that are presented to them outside a meaningful context, such as a picture, a sentence, or a paragraph. They may "talk around" the definition and receive no credit for their knowledge.

Suppose a test question were "What is a sentence?" A person using an analytical style might respond that a sentence is a group of words stating, asking, commanding, or exclaiming something. This would be considered the correct answer. Relational people, on the other hand, are likely to respond with an actual sentence. They would not receive credit, even though they might be able to distinguish among a sentence, a phrase, and a word by giving examples of each. There are many forms of bias that may exist in the content and structure of ability-test items. When this bias occurs, it limits how much can validly be said about the meaning of test scores.

## Context

Concerns about test bias have existed since the beginning of the psychological testing movement. At various points in history, European immigrants to the United States, African Americans, and Hispanics have been discriminated against by those using results from ability tests as evidence of their supposed inferiority. Native Americans, Asians, and Jews have also been affected by the misuse of tests.

Alfred Binet developed the first usable IQ test in 1905, as a way to diagnose low-achieving French students. He argued against the notion that intelligence was a fixed quantity. Lewis Terman, however, who provided the major adaptation of Binet's intelligence test from French to English in 1916, stated that the questions on the test did indeed provide a measure of innate intelligence. He believed that his revised test proved that the Eastern European immigrants of the day, as well as people of African descent and the poor of all colors, were genetically inferior to whites. He did not include test items that were consistent with the language and other cultural experiences of these groups.

The personal and political views of social scientists have contributed to the biased use of tests. This is seen in the fabricated data that was reported by Sir Cyril Burt, whose many twin studies from the 1940's to the 1970's were used as support by the hereditarians. So strong were some psychologists' beliefs that men were smarter than women that they threw out IQ test questions on which men scored lower than women. More recently, psychologist Arthur Jensen has widely published articles and books since the 1960's that support the view that intelligence is an inherited trait. Most often cited as evidence are the large differences between the average IQ scores of whites and other groups. He opposes the notion that these differences are attributable to item bias.

The large differences in average IQ scores between whites and almost every other group have concerned other psychologists, who do see this as an indication of test bias. They note that many individuals who are not proficient in English have been subjected to IQ tests in that language. Also problematic for them are the social consequences for groups that have already suffered educational and vocational disadvantages, as well as discrimination. According to these psychologists, IQ testing often leads to further negative political and educational consequences.

In the 1920's and 1930's, studies conducted by African-American educators and psychologists Horace Mann Bond, Martin Jenkins, and Howard Long demonstrated that environmental factors, such as socioeconomic status and amount of rapport with the examiner, had a major effect on IQ test performance. By the 1940's, the general social science community began to take seriously the objections to the hereditarian perspective. Anne Anastasi, in 1950, suggested that test instruments should be developed based on behaviors that represent intelligent behavior within specific cultures. In keeping with this suggestion, Williams has developed a culture-specific test using items that tap the experiences of African Americans.

As long as ability tests continue to be used in making major decisions in society, it is important that biases inherent in them be detected. If biases are found, they must be eliminated. This is an important step toward developing meaningful and fair tests for everyone.

## Bibliography
Hilliard, Asa G., III. "IQ Testing as the Emperor's New Clothes: A Critique of Jensen's *Bias in Mental Testing.*" In *Perspectives on Bias in Mental Testing*, edited by Cecil R. Reynolds and Robert T. Brown. New York: Plenum Press, 1984. Presents a critique both of Jensen's work and of the notion that IQ tests measure intelligence. Hilliard provides a very detailed account of the shortcomings he sees in Jensen's book. References to empirical work that supports his own position are included. Clear and easy to read.

Jensen, Arthur Robert. *Bias in Mental Testing.* New York: Free Press, 1980. An attempt to deal comprehensively with the issues of IQ testing and bias. He challenges the criticisms against IQ tests and offers research to support his view that group differences in IQ test scores are not attributable to bias.

_____. "Test Bias: Concepts and Criticisms." In *Perspectives on Bias in Mental Testing*, edited by Cecil R. Reynolds and Robert T. Brown. New York: Plenum Press, 1984. Responds to the Hilliard critique of his book. Jensen argues against test bias as a reason for the differences between racial groups in IQ test scores. Provides theoretical and research evidence to support his position.

Kamin, Leon J. *The Science and Politics of IQ.* New York: Halsted Press, 1974. Discusses the political nature of the role psychologists have played in support of IQ testing. The role of psychologists in the eugenics movement and in education is discussed. Includes strong critiques of the work done by Burt and Jensen.

Williams, Robert, and Horace Mitchell. "The Testing Game." In *Black Psychology*, edited by Reginald Lanier Jones. 3d ed. Berkeley, Calif.: Cobb & Henry, 1991. Argues that testing is a biased game. The roles of various players (for example, students as pawns) are detailed. The authors' novel approach helps the reader better understand the position of opponents of IQ testing.

*Derise E. Tolliver*

**Cross-References**

Ability Tests: Design and Construction, 13; Ability Tests: Reliability, Validity, and Standardization, 21; Ability Tests: Uses and Misuses, 27; College Entrance Examinations, 598; Intelligence Tests, 1341; Race and Intelligence, 2031.

# ABILITY TESTS: DESIGN AND CONSTRUCTION

*Type of psychology:* Intelligence and intelligence testing
*Fields of study:* Ability tests; intelligence assessment

*Ability tests designed by psychologists are used extensively in schools, government, industry, and psychological clinics for classifying, guiding, placing, evaluating, and counseling people. An understanding of the basic principles of ability test design and construction is vital for a fuller understanding of ability test uses, limitations, social and ethical consequences, and controversies.*

*Principal terms*

ABILITY TEST: a test which measures demonstrable knowledge or skills

ACHIEVEMENT TEST: a test which measures the extent to which an individual has acquired certain information or mastered certain skills as a function of specific instruction; measures acquired knowledge

APTITUDE TEST: a test designed to predict future learning or performance; measures ability to profit from further training or experience

FACTOR ANALYSIS: a statistical procedure for analyzing the correlations among tests to determine the minimum number of dimensions needed to explain the correlations

ITEM ANALYSIS: a statistical procedure used to determine the quality of individual test items; usually includes analyses of item discriminability and item difficulty

NORMS: the statistical summaries of the performance of a group of individuals upon which a test is standardized

PSYCHOMETRICS: the theory or technique of psychological measurement; the measurement of psychological differences among people and the statistical analysis of those differences

RELIABILITY: the extent to which a score or measure is free of measurement error; test scores must be consistent both among items and across time

STANDARDIZATION: the administering of a scientifically constructed test to a large representative sample of people under uniform conditions to determine norms for comparing the performance of future test takers

VALIDITY: a characteristic of a good test, ensuring that the test truly measures what it purports to measure

## Overview

A scientifically designed ability test provides objective, systematic, standardized samples of performance of a task. It allows one to measure differences between individuals or between the behavior of the same individuals on different occasions and to specify the degree of accuracy of the measurement.

There are many kinds of ability tests in existence. Among those most widely used are individually administered tests (such as the Wechsler Adult Intelligence Scale and the Stanford-Binet test), which involve oral questioning by a highly trained test administrator, and group-administered, computer-scored tests such as the Scholastic Aptitude Test (SAT), the American College Test (ACT), and the Professional and Administrative Career Examination (PACE). A distinction is often made between aptitude tests (designed to predict what a person can do with training) and achievement tests (designed to measure present accomplishments), but it is more useful to think of ability tests as falling along a continuum of the dimension of a person's present and potential abilities.

A second useful continuum along which ability tests vary is that of specificity versus generality of relevant prior experiences needed to excel on the test. Some ability tests are designed to measure a very narrow domain of specific content (for example, a test of musical aptitude); others are intended to be relatively independent of prior experiences and tap broader content domains (for example, the SAT).

There is a wide range of human abilities; accordingly, ability tests have been developed to measure such diverse attributes as sensory-motor skills, manual dexterity, mechanical ability, vocational interests, reading, personality, learning abilities, foreign-language aptitude, music and art aptitude, intelligence, creativity, and driving ability. Most psychologists contend that these tests do not measure a fixed or inherent component of an individual and that ability tests measure abilities as they exist at a given moment in time.

The amount of effort involved in constructing a psychological test depends on the type of test and the purposes for which it is intended. In designing a test which will be used to screen applicants for a job, one must first conduct a detailed analysis of the activities that make up the job so that test situations can be devised to predict performance. Often, one will attempt to identify "critical incidents"—behaviors vitally related to successful performance or to failure. In the developing of achievement tests, an attempt is made to specify instructional objectives clearly and to develop items related to those objectives.

Commercial constructors of ability tests, such as the Psychological Corporation or the Educational Testing Service, employ as item writers persons highly knowledgeable about subject matter and item writing who must follow a relatively complex set of procedures. The first step is to define carefully the attribute to be measured. This definition should specify what behaviors and responses would most likely indicate the existence of the attribute of interest.

The second step is to develop a large pool of items. Sometimes, test developers arrive at this pool of items by choosing those which seem to be logically or intuitively related to the dimension of interest. Other times, the test developers may attempt to find items on which the responses of people in a given group are known to differ from those of people in general (method of empirical construction). Sometimes, this pool of items is chosen by using a complex statistical procedure called factor analysis to identify the fundamental dimensions (factors) measured by other tests which claim to measure the attribute of interest. The test developers then attempt to write test items or rewrite items from other tests which best correlate with the factors revealed by the data analysis.

A third step in test construction involves administering this large pool of items to a large sample of subjects. The responses of these subjects play a vital role in the refinement of the original item pool. A statistical procedure called item analysis is often used to determine objectively which items should be selected for the final version of the test. Item difficulty is usually defined by the percentage of subjects who answer an item correctly; test developers usually select items with a range of difficulty. The most frequently computed item discriminability index measures the extent to which each potential item is related to performance on the whole test. Test developers often select only test items which the highest-ability students consistently answer correctly and which the least able students consistently answer incorrectly. All items are carefully examined, and items which are too difficult, too easy, ambiguous, fail to distinguish between the least and most able test takers, or are least related to the domain of interest are either deleted or rewritten. This revised test is then administered to new samples of subjects to standardize the test and to determine the test's reliability, validity, and normative responses.

Standardization is important as it provides a basis for later interpreting test scores. The revised test is therefore administered to a large group of people who are representative of the population for which the test is designed. The test developers must determine how test performance scores are distributed—the range of score performance and the average performance—and from this information create test norms describing the proportion of individuals scoring at or below each possible score level. A test score on the final version of the test in most cases will be interpreted by comparing it with this normative group (norm-referenced testing); in a few cases, however, an individual's score may instead be compared to some predetermined cutoff score (criterion-referenced testing).

Two necessary conditions which must be met by all standardized tests are that they must be both reliable and valid. A test is reliable if its results are reproducible and consistent. Research investigating the reliability of a test determines whether test items are internally consistent (that is, they measure the same thing), and whether test scores are stable across time. Special statistical formulas and procedures have been developed to answer these questions. A test is considered valid if it can be demonstrated that it indeed measures what it is intended to measure. Test developers will often conduct studies to demonstrate a test's construct validity (How well does the test representatively sample the domain of interest?), its criterion-related validity (How well does the test relate to present performance or predict future performance?), and its construct validity (How well does the test relate to the concept described by theory?). Test items need not have face validity—that is, they do not have to resemble closely the behavior which they are designed to predict.

Once all these standardization, norm development, and reliability and validity studies have been completed and the final instrument is ready, the test developers then write a test manual which provides information essential for administering, scoring, and interpreting a particular test. Included in the manual are full and detailed instructions for uniformly administering the newly developed test, a scoring key, and normative data concerning test interpretation, validity, and reliability. Most professional test developers follow the guidelines spelled out in the 1985 publication *Standards for Educational and Psychological Testing*, prepared by a joint committee of the American Educational Research Association, the American Psychological Association, and the National Council on Measurement in Education.

## Applications

Ability tests used at the elementary and secondary school level are often referred to as multiple-level test batteries because they consist of overlapping difficulty levels of tests that allow the measurement of developed school abilities across different grade levels. One such widely used ability test is the Cognitive Abilities Test (CAT).

The CAT is a revision of the Lorge-Thorndike intelligence tests originally developed by Robert L. Thorndike and Elizabeth Hagen in 1964. One of the two test batteries is designed primarily for children in kindergarten through third grade; the other is for grades three through twelve. The three sections of the test (verbal, quantitative, and nonverbal) are intended to measure cognitive reasoning. Norms for the 1978 version of the test were based on the performance of approximately eighteen thousand students from each school grade representative of the United States school population. A student's raw score is converted to a universal scale which in turn allows comparisons by age and grade level. This test is highly reliable and an excellent predictor of academic achievement and of intelligence quotient (IQ).

The Differential Aptitude Test (DAT), published by the Psychological Corporation, is a second widely used standardized group ability test. First published in 1947 and revised several times since then, the DAT was designed to provide a well-standardized procedure for measuring the multiple aptitudes of students in grades eight through twelve. The test measures eight aptitudes: verbal reasoning, numerical ability, abstract reasoning, clerical speed and accuracy, mechanical reasoning, space relations, spelling ability, and language usage. The normative sample for the 1980 revision consisted of some sixty-two thousand students in grades eight through twelve, selected from sixty-four public and private schools representative of the United States population of high school students. Students who take the test receive an individual report form showing their raw score (number correct), performance relative to the normative groups, and a graphic profile of their aptitudes which highlights their relative strengths and weaknesses. The validation and reliability studies which are reported in the test manual convincingly document the reliability of the test and its usefulness for predicting high school grades and other achievement test performance. A plethora of well-written and informative interpretive materials are provided to counselors, students, teachers, and parents. Both the CAT and the DAT are reviewed favorably by test construction experts, and they epitomize the highest standards and guidelines for test design and construction.

A third widely used ability test is the General Aptitude Test Battery (GATB). One of the first test batteries developed by using the statistical procedure of factor analysis, the GATB was developed by the United States Employment Service and is used primarily for employment counseling in government offices and for vocational and rehabilitation counseling in government agencies. The entire test battery, which requires two and one-half hours to complete, consists of twelve tests which measure nine different aptitudes: intelligence, verbal aptitude, numerical aptitude, spatial aptitude, clerical perception, form perception, motor coordination, manual dexterity, and finger dexterity. These nine aptitudes were originally identified through extensive factor-analytic studies of existing tests. The GATB is designed to reflect different levels of aptitude across a large number of potentially job-related aptitudes.

The GATB was originally standardized in 1952 on a sample of four thousand people representative of the United States in terms of geographical distribution, education, occupation, gender, and age. One of the major ways that GATB test scores are used is to create minimum multiple cutoff scores above which, research suggests, there is a greater probability of success in certain occupations. The GATB is also part of a coordinated career counseling system which attempts to match a person's strengths with occupations known to use those strengths. Although considerable information is reported in the GATB manual concerning validity studies (including validation studies for minorities) and reliability, several test experts, such as Anne Anastasi (1982) and Bruce Walsh and Nancy Betz (1985), have criticized the test for out-of-date norms and for the use of multiple cutoff scores.

## Context

The English scientist Sir Francis Galton strongly influenced the direction of the development of ability tests when he began a program of research to identify and measure biological differences predictive of high ability. In 1884, Galton, a cousin of Charles Darwin, set up an anthropocentric laboratory in London, where, for a number of years, visitors for a small fee could be measured on a number of basic motor skills and sensory abilities Galton believed related to intelligence. He also developed a statistical procedure, subsequently refined by Karl Pearson in 1920, to quantify the correlations among these variables and to predict performance. In addition, Galton observed that the distribution of many of the human traits he measured closely resembled the normal curve developed by the Belgian statistician Lambert Quetelet. The rise of the notion of measurable individual differences, application of that notion to prediction, and knowledge about the frequency distributions of human performance provided a framework for relating the performance of an individual to that of a population of individuals—that is, to a normative standardization group. At the same time as these fundamental developments in mental measurement were occurring, there were concurrent developments in the social values and needs in Europe. The growing industrial economy resulted in increasingly diverse job needs, formal education was spreading among the population, and there was a growth in governmental bureaucracy. The stage was set for the development of standardized tests rather than the use of intuition or social class as criteria for personnel selection and decision making.

The ability test as it now is known was developed in France in 1905 by Alfred Binet and his assistant Theodore Simon. In 1881, the French government passed a law requiring school attendance by all children—including slow learners who traditionally had been kept at home. Binet and Simon's test, which, unlike Galton's sensory tests, measured psychological abilities such as comprehension, memory, and reasoning, was designed to identify children not profiting from school as much as they should. The American psychologist Lewis Terman translated and standardized the test for American schoolchildren in 1916.

The prototype of virtually all scientifically developed, group-administered, pencil-and-paper ability tests was the Army's Alpha Test. Written in a form which could be administered to a large number of individuals simultaneously, and designed to eliminate unfit recruits and to identify officer candidates, this test was a product of a number of prominent psychologists, including Terman, Arthur Otis, and Edward Thorndike, who became leaders in the development of ability tests for education, government, and industry after World War I. The pervasiveness of ability testing today in schools, government, psychological clinics, and industry for the counseling, placement, and selection of people has resulted in psychological measurement becoming a big business; it has also raised numerous important issues concerning the validity, use, interpretation, and ethics of ability testing.

## Bibliography

Aiken, Lewis R. *Psychological Testing and Assessment.* 4th ed. Boston: Allyn & Bacon, 1982. A clearly written introduction to all aspects of psychological testing. The first part of this college-level text deals with the methodology of assessment, the second part with cognitive tests, the third with affective tests, and the fourth with progress in psychological assessment. Includes exercises and suggested readings at the end of each chapter.

American Educational Research Association, American Psychological Association, and National Council on Measurement in Education. *Standards for Educational and Psychological Testing.* Washington, D.C.: American Psychological Association, 1985. This important reference work provides—succinctly but comprehensively—the criteria widely used for the evaluation of tests, testing practice, and recommended practices in constructing tests based on the contemporary state of knowledge in the field. Among the kinds of guidance provided are suggestions about what information pertaining to norms, reliability, validity, and other test characteristics should be included in the test manual. Most professional test-construction companies follow these recommendations closely.

Anastasi, Anne. *Psychological Testing.* 5th ed. New York: Macmillan, 1982. A widely used college text which provides extensive information about test construction and evaluations of specific tests. Included among the appendices are suggestions for evaluating tests, a list of publishers' addresses, and a list of representative tests and where to find recent critical reviews.

Buros, Oscar Krisen, ed. *The Mental Measurement Yearbooks.* Highland Park, N.J.: Gryphon Press, 1938-1972. One of the most important sources of reviews of tests, this series of yearbooks was originally edited by Oscar K. Buros as a kind of *Consumer Reports* of psychological tests. The volumes cover practically all commercially available educational, psychological, and vocational tests published in the English language. Each yearbook covers tests published during a specified period. Included are critical reviews by test experts, information about publishers, and a thorough list of studies which examine each test.

Fancher, Raymond E. *The Intelligence Men: Makers of the IQ Controversy.* New York: W. W. Norton, 1985. Provides an extensive portrayal of the history of intelligence testing. Addresses controversial issues surrounding intelligence tests regarding their validity and the nature-nurture debate. Includes many photographs of the key figures in the history of intelligence testing.

Gardner, Howard. *Frames of Mind: The Theory of Multiple Intelligences.* New York: Basic Books, 1983. Based on a neuropsychological analysis of intelligence, this author rejects the notion of one overall intellectual ability in favor of seven independent intellectual domains: linguistic, logical-mathematical, spatial, musical, bodily-kinesthetic, intrapersonal, and interpersonal.

Gould, Stephen Jay. *The Mismeasure of Man.* New York: W. W. Norton, 1981. A well-written, engaging, and highly critical review of intelligence testing. Gould delineates how tests have repeatedly been misused and abused.

Sternberg, Robert J. *The Triarchic Mind.* New York: Viking Press, 1988. This readable and accessible presentation by a highly influential psychologist offers many real-life applications of many different kinds of intelligence, with suggestions for how to improve one's problem-solving skills. Sternberg's information-processing approach argues that there are three distinct types of intelligence: componential (the "school smarts" necessary for effectively processing information); experiential (the insight and ability to think analytically and creatively, and to make routine a new skill); and contextual (practical, "street-smart" intelligence).

Walsh, W. Bruce, and Nancy E. Betz. *Tests and Assessment.* Englewood Cliffs, N.J.: Prentice-Hall, 1985. This college textbook is oriented toward students in undergraduate and graduate courses in counseling psychology, industrial psychology, vocational psychology, and educational psychology, and toward disciplines in which assessment is important. Views assessment of a person as incomplete without an assessment of the environment. Chapters 1 and 2, which deal with the history of assessment and test construction, respectively, and Chapter 14, which discusses social issues surrounding assessment, may prove of particular value to the assessment novice.

Wigdor, Alexandra K., and Wendell R. Garner, eds. *Ability Testing: Uses, Consequences, and Controversies.* Part 1, *Report of the Committee.* Washington, D.C.:

National Academy Press, 1982. This first volume of a two-volume report describes the conclusions of a blue-ribbon panel of the U.S. National Research Council on ability testing. Provides a readable, nontechnical overview of ability testing issues, produced by a multicultural, multidisciplinary group which includes a lawyer, an educator, a historian, and a psychologist. Addresses the nature, impact, and incidence of ability testing practices, and the policy questions raised by standardized testing.

*David D. Simpson*

## Cross-References

Ability Testing: Individual and Group, 1; Bias in Ability Tests, 7; Ability Tests: Reliability, Validity, and Standardization, 21; Ability Tests: Uses and Misuses, 27; College Entrance Examinations, 598; Intelligence Tests, 1341; Race and Intelligence, 2031.

# ABILITY TESTS: RELIABILITY, VALIDITY, AND STANDARDIZATION

*Type of psychology:* Intelligence and intelligence testing
*Fields of study:* Ability tests; intelligence assessment

*Any measuring instrument, including psychological tests, must meet certain criteria to be useful: A test must be reliable, or consistent; it must be valid—that is, it must in fact measure its stated objective; and it must be standardized—there must be uniformity in its application.*

### Principal terms

CONSTRUCT VALIDITY: a type of validity that assesses what a test measures, both from a theoretical and an applied perspective
RELIABILITY: consistency of measurement
STANDARDIZATION: the uniformity of procedure, from administration to the meaning assigned to the test score
TEST-RETEST RELIABILITY: a common way of determining consistency, by administering the same test twice to the same persons
VALIDITY: the extent to which an instrument really measures the intended variable

## Overview

Every measuring instrument, whether it be an intelligence test, a depression inventory, a questionnaire about one's political views, a speedometer, or a bathroom scale, must meet two requirements: It must yield consistent measurement (that is, it must show reliability) and it must in fact measure what it purports to measure—it must have validity. In addition, the measuring instrument must be used according to certain guidelines; there must be uniformity of procedure or standardization. The determination of these three aspects involves considerable technical detail.

Measurement must first of all be consistent. Suppose a man is 6 feet 2 inches tall, but his yardstick indicates that on Monday he is 5 feet 9 inches, and on Tuesday he is 6 feet 6 inches. Assuming that it is not his body that is expanding so rapidly, one would question the consistency of that measuring instrument. In everyday physical measurement, consistency is ordinarily not much of a problem. One may dispute the police officer's report that one was going 57 miles per hour, but unless the speedometer is broken, one usually assumes a correspondence between the values shown and the actual velocity. In psychological and educational measurement, consistency is of greater concern, since psychological variables such as intelligence, depression, and self-esteem tend to be multi-faceted and imprecise; it is important that the measuring instrument in fact be consistent.

Reliability can be determined by administering a test or questionnaire twice to the same persons and statistically analyzing whether the responses or scores change substantially. This is known as test-retest reliability, and works quite well, except when boredom, fatigue, or other aspects might interfere with the second administration.

Another form of reliability is called alternate-form reliability. Here, two forms of the same measuring instrument are used, for example, two sets of fifty multiple-choice vocabulary items. The two forms should be different from each other yet equivalent. The two forms are administered to the same persons and the results compared statistically to see if indeed there is consistency. An important consideration with both test-retest reliability and alternate-forms reliability concerns the amount of time that elapses between administrations. If the time is too great, there may have occurred real changes, and thus "inconsistency" may in fact reflect a real change. The same would be true of stepping on a bathroom scale today and then again a year from now after completing a rigorous diet.

A third type of reliability is called split-half reliability, because the one test form that is administered gives two scores, one for each half of the test. For example, a multiple-choice vocabulary test with one hundred items might yield two scores per person, one based on the odd-numbered items and one based on the even-numbered items.

Finally, there is a fourth type of reliability, called inter-item consistency. This is a logical extension of the split-half reliability and in effect says that if one can divide a test into two halves, one can also divide it into as many parts as there are items, so that each item can be used to estimate reliability.

In addition to these four basic types of reliability, there can be concern about the consistency of the examiner and/or scorer, at least with some tests. In the case of a multiple-choice test in an American history class, the role of the instructor may not be crucial from the viewpoint of consistency, since the test can be administered and scored fairly objectively. There are some tests, however, such as the Rorschach ink-blot test, whose very administration and scoring are fairly subjective; thus, different results may be obtained by different examiners.

The validity of a test is established by obtaining evidence that the test indeed measures what it is supposed to measure—for example, that a test of American history is indeed a test of American history, rather than a test of memory, of the ability to outguess the teacher or to follow instructions, or of general intelligence. The establishment of the validity of a test is a complex endeavor, involving many different procedures. A good place to start, especially with achievement tests, is to analyze the contents of the test, to make sure the test adequately covers the intended area. An achievement test of fifth-grade arithmetic should cover all four basic arithmetic operations and also fractions, decimals, percents, and so on. A test of depression should ask not only about depressing feelings, but also about disturbed sleep, alterations in food intake, suicidal thoughts, and so on.

Having content validity is a beginning but is not enough. It must be shown that scores on a test are indeed related to other ways of measuring the same dimension. The developer of a new test of intelligence needs to show that scores on the new test are related to other ways of measuring intelligence. These other ways are called criteria; the test must be shown to have criterion validity. Yet there is wide disagreement as to what may be considered criteria of intelligence. Academic achievement as measured by grade point average, income, erudition of vocabulary, knowledge about the world, rapidity in the solving of problems, and many other criteria have indeed been used, but none is really completely satisfactory.

Finally, there is construct validity, an umbrella type of validity that covers all other types of validity. Most of what social scientists measure, such as intelligence, depression, or self-esteem, are dimensions or traits that do not exist in the same way as a tree or a house exists, but are theoretical constructs, dimensions that are useful to use and assess. Determining the validity of such a construct involves gathering much information dictated or related to the theory about the construct. For example, a researcher may have a theory about depression—about its nature, its manifestations, its relationship to age and gender, and so on. The researcher develops a test of depression and, once its reliability has been established, collects information on its construct validity, to see whether in fact his or her theoretical position can be supported.

A test must also be standardized. This means that the procedure for administering the test—directions, time limits, number of items, oral versus written administration, and so on—must be uniform. Scoring must also follow uniform guidelines, as must the meaning attributed to the scores. Usually this meaning is obtained by establishing norms: information based on a large representative sample concerning the distribution of scores and the meaning attached to them. Thus, standardization, or uniformity of procedure, is an important aspect of psychological testing.

## Applications

The development of a test is a complex endeavor requiring both an artistic touch—the application of creative thinking, originality, and imagination—and the precision of scientific thinking—that is, thorough knowledge of human behavior, sampling techniques, research methodology, and statistical analyses. Such endeavors are more and more the result of collaborative efforts among many individuals, often in the context of a commercial company that can provide not only the marketing for the future product but also the facilities and technical expertise for its development.

Although this article has only scratched the surface of this topic, the fact that a properly constructed psychological test must meet some rather strict specifications in terms of reliability, validity, and standardization is evident. That is why the "tests" that are found in popular magazines, which purport to assess how depressed a person might be, or the degree of leadership ability a person shows, or how sensitive a spouse the reader might be, typically leave much to be desired from a technical viewpoint and, though amusing, are essentially worthless.

Since a test cannot be valid if it is not reliable, reliability comes first; but the question of reliability is relatively easy to answer in comparison to the complex question of validity. Consider again the example of an intelligence test. Intelligence is a very complex construct, and not all psychologists agree as to its definition, basic composition, developmental nature over the life span, and so on. Imagine that a new intelligence test in the form of a multiple-choice vocabulary test is developed. Vocabulary seems to be a major component of intelligence, at least in traditional Western cultures, and multiple-choice tests are convenient to administer and score. Assume that evidence already has been collected showing that the test is reliable. Now it must be proved valid. To that end, scores on the test must be statistically compared with scores on some other measure of intelligence. If the subjects are college students, their test scores could be compared with their grades. Their grades, however, may not really be evidence of intelligence. In some classes, merely being physically present will guarantee a high grade, while in other classes, a high grade may not be possible even after herculean study efforts. Equalizing the demands made in an organic chemistry course for premedical students with a less demanding, general course in remedial writing presents a problem. So does explaining the difference, for example, between "John" and "Bill," both of whom have fallen madly in love; but whereas John's grades have deteriorated hopelessly, Bill is using his romance to scale new heights of academic achievement. Even if these issues could be taken into account, academic performance may not really be a good reflection of intelligence. There are individuals who have made outstanding contributions to society or have been financially successful in business, but did relatively poorly in school. Should income then be a criterion of intelligence?

The validation of a test presents many challenges that often do not have easy answers. Since the real world rarely provides clear-cut, well-defined criteria for those psychological dimensions which tests often seek to measure, the establishment of validity for a particular test is not an all-or-none phenomenon, but a continuing effort in which multiple answers are sought. One example of such an effort can be found in the California Psychological Inventory (CPI), a widely used personality test developed by Harrison Gough. Several thousand studies have been done on the CPI to assess the validity of its scales, and such work continues. Another test that has also received much attention, but is more controversial, is the Rorschach inkblot test. The Rorschach continues to be widely used, though it has been severely criticized on a number of dimensions.

## Context

Psychological testing is a central topic in the field of psychology, both in its own right, as a way of assessing individuals for various purposes, and as a methodology that underlies much of psychological experimentation.

Psychological testing, and especially ability testing, is a recent phenomenon closely interwoven with twentieth century American culture; yet the use of systematic procedures for comparing and evaluating individuals is quite old. Around 2000 B.C., for example, the Chinese used a rather elaborate system of examinations for public officials. These tests covered areas such as writing, music, archery, and knowledge of ceremonial rites, and the results were used either to promote or to dismiss those who held public office. The Old Testament also contains a description of what might be termed the first situational test. In the Book of Judges, when Gideon, a hero of the Israelites, is about to wage war, his army of enthusiastic volunteers is too large. God advises Gideon to take the prospective soldiers to the river for a drink; those who lap the water while holding their swords are to be accepted, but those who kneel to drink and hence expose their backs to a potential enemy are to be rejected. Of the ten thousand volunteers, it is said, only three hundred passed this test and went on to victory.

The more modern beginnings of testing can be found in the work of the Frenchman Alfred Binet, who in 1915 developed the first practical test of intelligence; in the many contributions of the British psychologist Sir Francis Galton, who launched psychological testing; and in the efforts of the American professor James McKeen Cattell, who was the first, in 1890, to use the term "mental tests," and attempted to predict the academic achievement of Columbia University undergraduates through a series of tests.

Psychological testing has gone through various cycles. It has received accolades for meeting vital needs in World Wars I and II, when tests were used to screen recruits, to identify those with specific aptitudes, talents, or psychiatric problems. Substantial criticisms have reflected fear of a "Big Brother" syndrome, of the misuse of tests by people in authority to make important but unfair decisions.

Psychological testing is here to stay, if for no other reason than that decisions need to be made, and tests can provide valuable and objective information on which to base those decisions. The ubiquity of the computer in contemporary culture, the need to make informed decisions about large groups of people, and the preference for rational, objective, and democratic methods, all assure that the use (and misuse) of psychological tests will continue for a long time to come.

## Bibliography

Anastasi, Anne. *Psychological Testing.* 6th ed. New York: Macmillan, 1988. Probably the best introduction to the field of psychological testing and to the topics of reliability, validity, and standardization. Written by a psychologist who has been a leader in the profession and who was awarded the National Medal of Science by President Reagan in 1987 for her work.

Cronbach, Lee J. *Essentials of Psychological Testing.* New York: Harper & Row, 1990. Another excellent introduction to the field of psychological testing. Chapter 5 discusses validity, chapter 6 reliability, and chapter 2 standardization.

Ghiselli, Edwin Ernest, John P. Campbell, and Sheldon Zedeck. *Measurement Theory for the Behavioral Sciences.* San Francisco: W. H. Freeman, 1981. For the reader who wants a more statistical introduction to the concepts of reliability and validity, and who is comfortable with (or at least not made highly anxious by) formulas and their derivations. An excellent, brief book, but not one to be read for entertainment value.

Lyman, Howard B. *Test Scores and What They Mean.* Englewood Cliffs, N.J.:

Prentice-Hall, 1963. A well-written, brief book aimed at readers who may not have a background in testing but need to understand some of the basic issues. As the title indicates, the focus is on the meaning of test scores. Chapter 3 covers both reliability and validity.

Tyler, Leona Elizabeth. *Tests and Measurements.* Englewood Cliffs, N.J.: Prentice-Hall, 1963. Another short book that takes a complex topic and tries to simplify it. Part of a series of such booklets aimed at college students taking introductory psychology. Oversimplifies many topics, but still provides a valuable introduction to the topic of psychological testing. Chapter 3 covers the topics of reliability and validity.

Weiner, Elliot A., and Barbara J. Stewart. *Assessing Individuals.* Boston: Little, Brown, 1984. A condensed, paperback version (209 pages) of the more standard-length introduction to the field of psychological and educational testing, but it is interestingly written, and the authors' involvement in the topic comes through clearly.

*George Domino*

## Cross-References

Ability Testing: Individual and Group, 1; Bias in Ability Tests, 7; Ability Tests: Design and Construction, 13; Intelligence Tests, 1341; Interest Inventories, 1349; Race and Intelligence, 2031; Testing: Historical Perspectives, 2540.

# ABILITY TESTS: USES AND MISUSES

*Type of psychology:* Intelligence and intelligence testing
*Fields of study:* Ability tests; intelligence assessment

*Ability tests can quickly and economically provide useful information for a variety of applications. At one extreme, some tests measure specific abilities such as typing skill; at the other extreme, some measure the most general of aptitudes, intelligence. Like all tools, these tests can be used well or badly.*

### Principal terms

ABILITY: a presently available skill

APTITUDE: the potential to develop an ability with training and/or experience

DIFFERENTIAL VALIDITY: validity that varies across subgroups of test takers; for example, an employment test might rate high for inexperienced applicants but low for experienced workers

MODERATOR VARIABLE: an identified factor (for example, age or experience) that lets a test user anticipate and adjust for differential validity

UNFAIR DISCRIMINATION: the making of erroneous test-based judgments of ability or aptitude, often because of low test validity or differential validity

VALIDITY: the extent to which a test measures what its author(s) and user(s) intend to measure

## Overview

Ability tests are samples of behavior that can provide information that otherwise would be much more time-consuming and expensive to gather. To ensure that they indeed provide useful information, reputable tests are standardized, and their reliability and validity are assessed before they are put to use. Standardization is accomplished by giving a test under development to a large number of respondents similar to those for whom it is intended to be used later, in order to judge the effectiveness of the instructions for the tests, the appropriateness of time limits, and so on, and to calculate performance norms.

Reliability refers to a test's consistency, sometimes internal consistency from one question or section to another, but more often consistency over time, as measured by repeated administrations to the same respondents. A highly reliable test is like a yardstick that will give the same measurements next year as it does today, or did last year. Reliability is essential for a test to have reasonable validity—that is, for it to measure what its authors and users intend it to measure. This is the essential quality that a test must possess. Using a psychological test lacking validity is like using a barometer (a pressure gauge) to measure the temperature in a room.

If a test is designed to assess a concrete ability, judgments by experts familiar with that ability can validate it. For example, math teachers could, simply by reviewing a test intended to assess a child's ability to carry out long division, decide whether it measured what was intended. Content validation, as this process is called, is simple and straightforward, and may generalize fairly well from one setting to another.

If a test is designed to forecast complex performance, criterion-related validation must be carried out to determine how closely test takers' scores are related to those same individuals' standings on some criterion. For example, to validate a test of aptitude for success in college, a test developer would need to administer the test to a large number of prospective students, then at some later time (perhaps graduation) compare their test scores with the grades they had earned. Criterion-related validation is in principle a simple procedure, but in practice is often complex and troublesome. Problems with the nature of the criteria to be used in validation research, and problems of differential validity, make it so.

In the above example concerning the prediction of success in college, grade point average at graduation is a definitive success criterion. For most settings, however, several possible criteria might be used, and deciding which is preferable complicates test validation. For example, to validate a test used to hire people for sales positions, the researcher might compare test scores of the newly hired employees with their grades in a training session, with their first quarter's sales, or with their average sales over a five-year period.

Using a test that lacks validity is a serious misuse of testing, one that becomes even more serious if some readily identifiable subgroups, such as racial or age groups, score low. A test that is not valid forecasts nothing, so it is, in a sense, unfair to everyone. If low scorers on the meaningless test are denied employment, however, they have become victims of silent discrimination.

Another misuse of tests occurs if a test on which decisions are based is valid for some respondents but not for others. Differential validity attracted much attention among professional psychologists, and even in the popular press, in the late 1960's because of the fear that test use might inadvertently be supporting racial discrimination. While the differential-validity concept was not new among testing experts, in earlier decades its possible consequences had been of less concern to society. Although it does not eliminate the problem, the concept of a moderator variable provides a practical way of dealing with differential validity. A moderator variable is an identified factor—such as age, experience, race, or gender—that lets a test user anticipate and often adjust for effects of differential validity.

If validation research does not examine the possible influence of moderator variables on obtained validity, it may provide a very deceptive picture of a test's practical value. Reasonably high validity may conceal serious differences of validity among those tested. For example, validity for white applicants from the middle socioeconomic classes might be very high, and validity for black applicants from a lower socioeconomic class very low; average scores for the two groups might be very similar despite the validity differences. If only a few black applicants are tested among a large number of whites, the forecasting success for whites masks the lack of success for blacks. Hiring decisions concerning African Americans based on the test scores will be haphazard, harming many applicants and the employer.

Knowing that a particular test poorly forecasts success of black applicants gives the test user a clear justification not to use it for blacks, but rather to seek another test or procedure that gives a reasonable forecast. Such alternatives are controversial, but often far fairer than ignoring validity problems.

## Applications

Lee J. Cronbach, in the fifth edition of his classic text *Essentials of Psychological Testing* (1990), lists four uses for tests: classification, promoting self-understanding, evaluation and modification of treatments or programs, and scientific inquiry.

Classification refers to assigning a test taker to one category rather than another. Often the outcome of this assignment is quite important to the person (for example, being accepted in a college program). Well-crafted tests are available to estimate a college applicant's likelihood of success in undergraduate study in general, and even of success in several basic fields of study. For example, with the American College Testing Program ACT test, an overall score (composite) is provided along with scores for English, mathematics, natural sciences, and social sciences. Similar tests are available to estimate success in graduate education, again both in general study and in the many disciplines and subdisciplines for which formal college programs exist.

Evidence-based self-understanding can be a great help to the person who is seeking it. To know how one's intellectual level compares to that of other people might only satisfy a test taker's curiosity, but it can often help a person realistically set goals and plan for the future.

Program evaluation shifts the focus of test use from the individual to some activity intended to benefit participants. For example, an ability test given at the end of an academic class can, beyond telling something about the students, tell something about the quality of the teaching. Scientific inquiry can be about almost any topic and can cut across the other uses Cronbach lists. Where objective information that other researchers can verify is needed, tests can be very useful tools. Interestingly, tests are often used as tools to produce new tests.

Criticisms of ability testing have focused on classification more often than on any of the other three applications discussed. Almost always, being put into certain categories is more desirable than being put into others. Being hired is better than being rejected; being placed in an advanced class is better than being placed in one for slow learners, and so on. When the outcome of an unfavorable classification is important, scrutiny of its reasonableness by those affected is all but guaranteed.

Tests are frequently in the unfortunate position of being messengers delivering unpleasant news, and often they are accused of being the causes of what they report. When a low test score keeps a person from being hired, for example, it is far more comfortable to accuse the test of being wrong than it is to grant that the test has revealed a personal weakness. For at least two reasons, tests are especially vulnerable to such criticism, even when the information they convey is essentially correct.

First, even the most reliable test, validated for the desired application and given under the very best of circumstances, is far from infallible. Because tests are not perfect, obvious misclassification is common enough that most people can think of a time when it happened to them or to someone they know, and it is easier to remember the occasional time when testing was wrong than the frequent times when it was correct. Second, tests are very often misused, most often by people who are unaware that, for the particular purpose and/or the particular people involved, the test they have administered is inappropriate and the scores it has generated are meaningless.

From the mid-1960's on, there have been frequent attempts to remove testing programs that have led to unfavorable classifications. If what seem to be unreasonable numbers of African Americans, Hispanics, women, or the aged are being denied access to something because of their test scores, a call is heard to cease such testing. Yet such a solution is likely to be the proverbial "jumping from the frying pan into the fire." Tests were heralded by their earliest developers as objective means of improving upon subjective, personal judgments, and reputable tests used for the purposes for which they are validated meet those developers' expectations quite well. If an employment test is dropped from the hiring sequence, for example, something else must serve to classify applicants into "hired" and "rejected." Virtually any other decision-making procedure imaginable has a greater potential than tests for reflecting the decision makers' biases and prejudices.

Over most of the history of testing, tests were administered by having someone question, listen to, and observe a respondent in a one-on-one setting or, more commonly, by having respondents in groups answer questions printed in booklets. Since computers have become common in society, remarkably versatile methods of testing have become possible. Computers can substitute for test administrators, presenting questions or other test stimuli on a monitor, tallying and organizing a test taker's responses as they are made, and preparing them for immediate feedback to the individual. When there are concerns that the content of a test may become known, compromising its value, computers can be used to customize tests; for example, they can construct from a bank of questions a unique test for each person to be tested. The application of computers to testing seems likely to allow advancements yet to be imagined; however, it also may make it even more tempting for people to give tests rather than seek more appropriate sources of information.

## Context

Although ability tests were used about three thousand years ago in China to judge applicants' qualifications for civil-service positions, present-day ability tests are nearly all descendants of an intelligence test devised by Alfred Binet in 1904. Commissioned by the French government to sort school children according to their potentials for academic success, Binet wrote a series of questions that could be used to assign "mental age." By his definition, the number of questions correctly answered by the average five-year-old indicated a mental age of five, the number correctly answered by the average six-year-old a mental age of six, and so on. A number of psychologists, especially in the United States, began developing tests based on Binet's model, and when William Stern suggested dividing mental age by chronological age to allow mental comparison of children of different ages, the "intelligence quotient" soon became the favored way of reporting intelligence.

Binet was quite cautious in his use of intelligence testing. He insisted that the results were nothing more than an indication of where a student stood among his peers at present. Within a decade of Binet's initial success, however, others were beginning to think about intelligence measures and beginning to use them in ways that are still creating problems.

First, they began to contend that the IQ was a genetically determined, unchangeable part of a person, not merely a measure of present standing. This led to evaluating people according to IQ, often in ways that helped psychologists and educators keep tidy records, but at the expense of those being labeled. Those with IQs between 90 and 110 were "normal"; those below were "morons," "imbeciles," and "idiots"; those above were "the gifted" or "geniuses." The early, insulting labels for the subnormal were later replaced with kinder ones, but the idea of a person's IQ being comparable to the karat marking on a piece of gold remains.

Second, users after Binet began to extend their intelligence testing far beyond academic settings for which it was designed and reasonably valid. As identified by the tests, more-intelligent children did succeed better than less-intelligent ones in school, so many people believed that the more intelligent should also make the best policemen, the best soldiers, or the best employees. What seemed a reasonable possibility in the early decades of testing proved to be in most cases wrong, but widespread use of intelligence tests far beyond the classroom persists.

Conscientious test authors, publishers, and users have long worried about the misuse of tests and have tried to control it through strategies ranging from recommending self-regulation by users to enforcing experience and education standards for those who may purchase tests. Control remains at best only partial, however, and both those who use test results and the test takers who provide them need to remain wary of misuse.

## Bibliography

American Educational Research Association, American Psychological Association, and National Council on Measurement in Education. *Standards for Educational and Psychological Testing.* Washington, D.C.: American Psychological Association, 1985. Although probably not for the casual reader, this brief technical publication describes the standards for testing the experts have established for their own use, and it well illustrates the concern they have that testing must be done responsibly.

American Personnel and Guidance Association. "Responsibilities of Users of Standardized Tests." *Guidepost* 21 (October 5, 1978): 5-8. A companion piece to the references above and below, this article is directed explicitly at users of standardized tests.

American Psychological Association. *Guidelines for Computer Based Tests and Interpretations.* Washington, D.C.: Author, 1986. A companion piece to the two references above.

Buros, Oscar Krisen. *The Mental Measurements Yearbooks.* Highland Park, N.J.: Gryphon Press, 1938-1972. Two or more experts critically review each of the many tests listed in these volumes. Few tests escaped Buros' scrutiny, and his reviewers showed no timidity in addressing questionable uses of tests. *The Ninth Mental Measurement Yearbook*, listed below without annotation, is edited by James V. Mitchell, Jr., who is carrying on Buros' work after his death.

Cronbach, Lee J. *Essentials of Psychological Testing.* 5th ed. New York: Harper & Row, 1990. A sophisticated introduction to testing. Published as a text for college courses in psychological testing, but remarkably accessible, even interesting, to an average reader. Appendix A, "Selected Publishers and Test Distributors," and Appendix B, "Classified List of Tests and Inventories," can serve as first sources to check for the sort of information they list; although brief, they contain much useful information.

_____. "Five Decades of Public Controversy over Mental Testing." *American Psychologist* 30 (January, 1975): 1-30. Published in a journal found in most college and public libraries, this classic article is worth pursuing for its excellent review of testing controversies. Clearly illustrates that often they are essentially social and political ones, expressed as dissatisfaction with psychology's efforts.

Hilgard, Ernest Ropiequet. *Psychology in America: A Historical Survey.* San Diego: Harcourt Brace Jovanovich, 1987. Chapter 13, "Intelligence: Measurement and Controversy," offers an excellent account of the field's development, from mid-1800's attempts to understand individual differences, through testing as a major commercial application of psychology. Material in several other chapters, especially those on industrial/organizational psychology and social psychology, helps place ability testing in the context of its parent discipline.

Mitchell, James V., Jr. *The Ninth Mental Measurements Yearbook.* Lincoln: University of Nebraska Press, 1985. A continuation of the famous set of yearbooks published by Oscar K. Buros, annotated under his name above.

*Harry A. Tiemann, Jr.*

## Cross-References

Bias in Ability Tests, 7; Ability Tests: Reliability, Validity, and Standardization, 21; College Entrance Examinations, 598; Intelligence: Definition and Theoretical Models, 1328; Intelligence Tests, 1341; Race and Intelligence, 2031; Testing: Historical Perspectives, 2540.

# ABNORMALITY: BEHAVIORAL MODELS

*Type of psychology:* Psychopathology
*Fields of study:* Behavioral and cognitive models; models of abnormality

*Behavioral models of abnormal behavior use principles of learning to explain how maladaptive behaviors develop. Learning-based explanations have proved useful for both conceptualizing the development of abnormality and developing effective treatments for abnormal behaviors.*

### Principal terms

ABNORMALITY: a pattern of behavior that is maladaptive for the individual or society

BEHAVIOR THERAPIES: treatment approaches for abnormal behavior that are derived from principles of learning

CLASSICAL CONDITIONING: a learning principle used to explain how emotional and physiological responses can be learned

EXTINCTION: a process by means of which the probability of a behavior occurring is decreased; applies to both classical and operant conditioning and involves the unlearning of a response

OPERANT CONDITIONING: a learning principle used to explain how voluntary behavior can be learned; states that behavior is a function of its consequences

STIMULUS GENERALIZATION: the ability of stimuli that are similar to other stimuli to elicit a response that was previously elicited only by the first stimuli

## Overview

The behavioral model asserts that normal as well as abnormal behaviors are acquired through learning. Unlike biomedical or psychodynamic models, which view abnormal behavior as symptoms of underlying pathology (biochemical disturbance and psychological conflicts, respectively), the behavioral model does not postulate underlying causes.

Behavioral explanations state that behavior is determined by the environment. Genetically or biologically determined variations in abilities are accepted. Apart from this, however, the behavioral model asserts that specific behavioral characteristics are acquired through learning experiences. Therefore, the same individual has the potential to develop numerous different characteristics. For example, the factors that determine whether one will become a criminal or a priest are the learning experiences one has.

Behavioral models of abnormal behavior have emerged from two basic learning processes: classical conditioning and operant conditioning. Classical conditioning is typically used to explain how emotional and physiological responses can be brought under the control of cues in the environment. For example, the emotional (for example, fear) and physiological (for example, increased heart rate) responses elicited by the presentation of a dog to an individual with a dog phobia (an extreme, unrealistic fear of dogs), can be explained by classical conditioning. "Voluntary" behaviors, however, such as running away when a dog is seen, can be explained by operant conditioning.

The classical conditioning model states that by pairing a neutral stimulus with a stimulus that produces an unlearned emotional or physiological response (called the unconditioned response), the neutral stimulus (now called the conditioned stimulus) can take on properties that allow it to elicit a response (called the conditioned response) that is similar to the unconditioned response. Stimulus generalization is said to occur when stimuli that are similar to the conditioned stimulus take on the ability to elicit a conditioned response. Principles derived from the study of classical conditioning have led to the development of useful conceptualizations of fear-based abnormal behaviors.

Whereas the classical conditioning model has been useful in demonstrating how "nonvoluntary" (emotional and physiological) reactions can be learned, principles of operant conditioning have been useful in explaining goal-directed, "voluntary" behaviors. The basic assumption of the operant conditioning model is that behaviors are controlled by their consequences. Positive reinforcers are consequences that, when presented following the performance of a target behavior, result in the increased occurrence of that target behavior in the future. Negative reinforcers are consequences that allow the escape from aversive situations and result in an increase in avoidance and escape behaviors in the future. Punishers are consequences that result in the decreased occurrence of the punished behavior in the future. The operant conditioning model views the consequences of behaviors as responsible for shaping behavior, both normal and abnormal.

Behavioral explanations have been presented to explain nearly all classes of abnormal behaviors. The usefulness of this model in accounting for the etiology of the vast range of abnormal behaviors is, however, varied. Behavioral explanations have been most useful in accounting for maladaptive behaviors characterized by relatively discrete, overt responses that are considered abnormal because of their excessive, deficient, or inappropriate expression. Examples include phobias, psychophysiological disorders (abnormal physical responses not caused by physical pathology), paraphilias (abnormal sexual arousal toward nonhuman objects), and conduct disturbances (such as oppositional or delinquent behaviors). Empirical evidence exists that demonstrates the process of learning and unlearning these abnormal responses.

Abnormal behaviors that are characterized by abnormal covert processes, such as disturbances in attention, perception, thought, and emotion, do not lend themselves to behavioral explanations. For example, schizophrenia is an abnormal behavior characterized by the presence of bizarre behavior, unrealistic thoughts, auditory or visual hallucinations, and inappropriate emotional expressions. The biomedical model, which postulates underlying brain pathology, provides a more useful general explanation for the development of schizophrenia than that provided by the behavioral model.

Although the behavioral model is not useful as a general explanation for the development of some disorders, it is helpful in explaining individual differences in overt behavior across all types of abnormality. Despite the likely contribution of biological factors in the formation of some classes of abnormal behavior, environmental-learning factors also continue to be influential. Principles of classical and operant conditioning are just as responsible for shaping the behaviors of schizophrenics as they are for shaping the behaviors of everyone else. Although the environment affects persons differently (partly as a result of biological differences between individuals), it does not cease to control behavior. Thus, in many cases behavioral models offer good general explanations for abnormal behaviors, while in other cases behavioral explanations must be combined with other models to produce useful explanations.

## Applications

The behavioral model of abnormal behavior has probably been credited most with providing a useful explanation for the development of phobias. A phobia is defined as a strong, persistent fear that is out of proportion to any real threat that may be present.

To explain the development of phobias, the behavioral model uses both classical and operant conditioning principles. Take, for example, the development of a dog phobia. According to the classical conditioning model, the presence of a dog becomes associated with an extremely frightening situation. One such experience may be enough to cause the dog to become a conditioned stimulus for a fear reaction. A child who has never touched a dog before and who has the unfortunate experience of attempting to pet a dog that barks ferociously may develop a dog phobia. The dog's ferocious bark represents the unconditioned stimulus that, without prior learning, elicits a fear response (the unconditioned response). The dog (conditioned stimulus) is the primary neutral stimulus that becomes associated with the frightening situation. The next time the child sees the same dog, he or she may respond with extreme fear even if the dog does not bark ferociously.

The principle of stimulus generalization accounts for the observation that the child has developed a phobia not only for the ferocious dog that initially frightened the child but also for all dogs and perhaps even other furry creatures such as cats and squirrels. This explanation of the development of phobias has received much empirical support. On average, 60 percent of phobic individuals can recall a traumatic event that precipitated the development of their phobia.

The second aspect of phobias that any model must explain is the fact that they tend to be persistent. The classical conditioning model predicts that the phobic response should extinguish (gradually weaken) after a few trials of facing the dog (conditioned stimulus) in the absence of ferocious barking (unconditioned stimulus). In order to explain the absence of extinction (or persistence of the phobia), the principle of negative reinforcement is used.

The principle of negative reinforcement states that any behavior that is immediately followed by escape from or avoidance of an aversive consequence will be
strengthened. Phobias are persistent because individuals actively avoid or escape
from situations in which the phobic object is present. The fear reduction that escape
and avoidance behaviors produce results in these behaviors being strengthened in the
future. Therefore, extinction trials are not given an opportunity to take place.

Behavioral therapies for phobias are also derived from learning principles. The
most common therapies involve procedures that are designed to make the phobic
individual face the feared object in the absence of any real danger so that extinction
can take place. One procedure, which is called modeling, involves having the phobic
individual observe another person (the model) performing the feared tasks. In the
case of a dog phobic, the model would pet the dog in the presence of the dog phobic.
As the phobic individual becomes less frightened, he or she approaches the dog
until eventually he or she is able to interact with the dog without being overwhelmed
by fear.

The behavioral model has also been useful in explaining disorders of conduct,
such as juvenile delinquency. Most treatment programs for conduct disorders are
based upon behavioral principles. These programs provide delinquent youths with
structured environments that are designed in such a way that prosocial behaviors are
reinforced and antisocial or delinquent behaviors are punished. These programs have
demonstrated that, by systematically controlling the consequences for prosocial as
well as problem behaviors, delinquent behaviors can be controlled. Unfortunately,
when the child is returned home, the old behavior-consequence contingencies may
still be present, and as a result, the old behavior patterns will return.

Behavioral models have been used in combination with other models to explain
the etiology of some abnormal behaviors. For example, autism, a disorder that is
first expressed in childhood, is characterized by disturbed language development, a
lack of interpersonal responsiveness, odd and repetitive behaviors, and resistance to
changes in the environment. Although little is known about the specific etiology of
this disorder, the most promising model currently is the biomedical model. This
model accounts for autism by referring to disturbed neurological functioning. The
behavioral model has been useful in demonstrating that, despite the presence of an
apparent neurological disturbance, principles of learning also apply to these individuals. The most effective treatments for autism (as of the early 1990's) have been
based upon principles of classical and operant conditioning. For example, language
skills and appropriate social behaviors have been effectively taught by systematically
using such operant-conditioning principles as positive and negative reinforcement.

## Context

Behavioral models of abnormality began to gain a following in the academic arena
in the 1920's, after John B. Watson, commonly referred to as the "father of behaviorism," published a series of works on behaviorism. Watson argued that the focus of a
scientific psychology should be overt behavior. He rejected the study of mental en-

tities such as thoughts as useless, because such entities cannot be measured objectively and reliably. Watson proposed a model for understanding behavior that was based upon Ivan Pavlov's principles of classical conditioning. During the same decade, Pavlov published reports on what he called "experimental neurosis." In these reports, Pavlov explained how "neurotic" or abnormal behavior could be taught to dogs by using the principles of conditioning.

Two psychologists, John Dollard and Neal Miller, published a book entitled *Personality and Psychotherapy: An Analysis in Terms of Learning, Thinking, and Culture* (1950), which used principles of conditioning to explain how abnormal behavior develops and how it can be changed. This book was important in expanding the behavioral influence outside academic circles and into the applied areas of case conceptualization and treatment. At the same time that behaviorism was becoming a powerful force among academic psychologists, clinical psychologists, who were in great demand, began to provide treatment for disturbed individuals. The role of treatment provider had previously been restricted to psychiatrists. The influx of psychologists into treatment was followed by an increased influence of behavioral psychology on conceptualizing and treating abnormal behavior. In the 1950's, new treatment approaches based upon learning theories began to multiply. These treatments are referred to collectively as "behavior therapies."

Behavioral models of abnormality provide useful explanations for the etiology and treatment of numerous types of abnormal behaviors. The experimental methodology from which behaviorism has developed has also influenced other models of abnormality. This has been seen, for example, in the increased interest among psychoanalytic theorists in developing empirical tests to evaluate their theories.

Behavioral models will continue to be developed and evaluated. It is likely that interdisciplinary models will become more common in the future. For example, behavioral models have recently been combined with models from developmental psychology. Developmental psychologists study the psychological development of normal individuals across the life span. Knowledge gained from developmental psychology about the abilities and characteristics of children at different ages has been helpful in refining behavioral therapies for children. This trend shows promise for the development of more effective treatment interventions for children and adolescents.

## Bibliography

Dollard, John, and Neal E. Miller. *Personality and Psychotherapy: An Analysis in Terms of Learning, Thinking, and Culture.* New York: McGraw-Hill, 1950. This classic work was very influential in bringing behavioral theories into the applied realm of explaining and treating abnormal behaviors. Phenomena such as defense mechanisms, which are concepts from psychoanalytic theory, are examined and explained within a behavioral framework. This book should be read only after the reader has gained a basic knowledge of psychoanalytic and behavioral models of abnormality.

Masters, John C., et al. *Behavior Therapy: Techniques and Empirical Findings.* 3d ed. San Diego: Harcourt Brace Jovanovich, 1987. Provides an exhaustive review of behavioral therapies. Theoretical explanations as well as reviews of empirical findings are presented. This text offers an introductory yet complete presentation of behavior therapy. Useful as a reference text for specific behavior therapies.

Rosenhan, David L., and Martin E. P. Seligman. "The Environmentalist Model: Behavioral and Cognitive Approaches." In *Abnormal Psychology*. 2d ed. New York: W. W. Norton, 1989. This chapter provides an easy-to-read introduction to behavioral models of abnormality. The basic assumptions of behavioral models are discussed, and interesting case conceptualizations from a behavioral perspective are given. This is a good source for the reader who is interested in a brief yet informative presentation of behavioral models of abnormality.

Skinner, Burrhus Frederic. *Science and Human Behavior.* New York: Free Press, 1953. This book is considered a classic among behavioral psychologists. Skinner presents the principles of operant conditioning and then uses them to explain human behavior at the private, social, and cultural levels. The depth of presentation precludes this book from being a good reference book. For the serious student of behaviorism, however, this is required reading.

Wolpe, Joseph. *Psychotherapy by Reciprocal Inhibition.* Stanford, Calif.: Stanford University Press, 1958. Wolpe's development of a treatment technique called systematic desensitization led to a rapid acceptance of behaviorally based interventions. In this book, Wolpe provides a learning-based explanation for abnormal behaviors. Clinical and experimental support is given for behavioral interventions. The chapters are arranged in such a way that the book can be used as a reference for varying principles in the behavioral model.

*Mark A. Williams*

## Cross-References

Abnormality Defined, 89; Aversion, Implosion, and Systematic Desensitization Therapies, 368; Avoidance Learning, 375; Behaviorism: An Overview, 401; Escape Conditioning, 985; Instrumental Conditioning: Acquisition and Extinction, 1315; Learning: Generalization and Discrimination, 1437; Operant Conditioning Therapies, 1714; Pavlovian Conditioning: Theoretical Foundations, 1764; Punishment, 2016.

# ABNORMALITY: BIOMEDICAL MODELS

*Type of psychology:* Psychopathology
*Field of study:* Models of abnormality

*Biomedical models of abnormality examine the roles of medical, neurological, and biochemical factors in creating psychological disturbances. Psychologists have come to realize that many disturbances have a significant biomedical component or are, in some cases, primarily organic. This has led to the development of more effective biomedical therapies, such as drug therapies, for these disorders.*

### Principal terms

ANTIDEPRESSANT DRUGS: drugs such as iproniazid, imipramine, and amitriptyline that are used to treat depression

ANTIPSYCHOTIC DRUGS: drugs such as chlorpromazine and clozapine that alleviate the symptoms of schizophrenia; also called neuroleptics

BIOGENIC AMINES: a class of neurotransmitter chemicals in the brain, including dopamine, norepinephrine, and serotonin

CEREBROSPINAL FLUID: a fluid, derived from blood, that circulates in and around the brain and spinal cord

DIFFERENTIAL DIAGNOSIS: distinguishing between two or more illnesses that have the same or very similar symptoms

LIMBIC SYSTEM: a system of structures in the brain that regulates emotional responsiveness and plays a role in learning and memory

NEUROTRANSMITTER: a chemical that is secreted from one nerve cell and stimulates receptors on another nerve cell, thus transmitting a message between them

PRIMARY DISORDER: the principal disorder, not the result of some other medical condition, as opposed to a secondary disorder, in which the disorder and its symptoms result from some other medical condition

TRANQUILIZERS: drugs such as Librium and Valium that are used to treat anxiety disorders; also called antianxiety drugs or anxiolytics

## Overview

The study of biomedical bases for mental illnesses and their treatment is called biological psychiatry or biopsychiatry. A basic premise of biopsychiatry is that psychiatric symptoms occur in many conditions—some psychological and some medical.

Inherent in this viewpoint is a new outlook on mental illness. Faced with a patient who is lethargic, has lost his or her appetite, cannot sleep normally, and feels sad, traditional psychotherapists may diagnose him or her as suffering from one of the depressive disorders. Usually, the bias is that this illness is psychological in origin and calls for treatment with psychotherapy. Biopsychiatrists, however, see depression not as a diagnosis, but as a description of the patient's condition. The task of diagnosing—of finding the underlying illness—remains to be done.

After examining the patient and doing a battery of medical tests, the biopsychiatrist, too, may conclude that the condition is a primary mood disorder. Further tests may reveal whether it is caused by life stresses, in which case psychotherapy is called for, or by biochemical imbalances in the brain, in which case drug therapy—perhaps in concert with psychotherapy—is called for. The medical tests may indicate that the depression is secondary to a medical condition—such as Addison's disease or cancer of the pancreas—in which case medical treatment of the primary condition is called for.

An important distinction must be made between psychiatric conditions resulting from the psychological stress of having a serious illness and psychiatric conditions resulting from chemical imbalances or endocrine disturbances produced by the illness. For example, the knowledge that one has pancreatic cancer can certainly lead to depression. This is a primary mood disorder that can be treated with psychotherapy. According to Mark Gold, a leading biopsychiatrist, however, depression occurs secondarily to pancreatic cancer in up to three-quarters of patients who have the disease and may precede physical symptoms by many years. In such a case, psychotherapy not only would be pointless but also would actually put the patient's life at risk if it delayed diagnosis of the underlying cancer.

According to Gold, there are at least seventy-five medical diseases that can produce psychiatric symptoms. Among these are endocrine disorders, including diseases of the thyroid, adrenal, and parathyroid glands; disorders of the blood and cardiovascular system; infectious diseases, such as hepatitis and syphilis; vitamin-deficiency diseases caused by niacin and folic acid deficiencies; temporal-lobe and psychomotor epilepsies; drug abuse and side effects of prescription drugs; head injury; brain tumors and other cancers; neurodegenerative diseases such as Alzheimer's, Huntington's, and Parkinson's diseases; multiple sclerosis; stroke; poisoning by toxic chemicals, such as metals or insecticides; respiratory disorders; and mineral imbalances.

After medical illnesses are ruled out, the psychiatric symptoms can be attributed to a primary psychological disorder. This is not to say that biomedical factors are unimportant. Compelling evidence indicates that the more severe psychotic disorders are caused by biochemical imbalances in the brain.

The evidence of genetic predispositions for schizophrenia, major depressive disorder, and manic-depressive disorder is strong. The function of genes is to regulate biochemical activity within cells, which implies that these disorders are caused by biochemical abnormalities.

Research suggests that schizophrenia, in most cases, results from an abnormality in the dopamine neurotransmitter system in the brain. All drugs that effectively treat schizophrenia block the action of dopamine, and the more powerfully they do so, the more effective they are therapeutically. Furthermore, overdoses of drugs, such as amphetamines, that strongly stimulate the dopamine system often cause a schizophrenia-like psychosis. Finally, studies show that, in certain areas of the brain in schizophrenic patients, tissues are abnormally sensitive to dopamine.

In major depressive disorders, the biogenic amine theory is strongly supported. Biogenic amines, among which are dopamine, norepinephrine, and serotonin, are neurotransmitters in the brain that are concentrated in the limbic system, which regulates emotional responses. Biogenic amines were originally implicated by the observation that drugs that deplete them in the brain, such as reserpine, frequently cause depression, whereas drugs that stimulate them, such as amphetamines, cause euphoria. Studies of cerebrospinal fluid have revealed abnormalities in the biochemical activity of these amines in some depressed patients. In many suicidally depressed patients, for example, serotonin activity in the brain is unusually low. In other depressed patients, norepinephrine or dopamine activity is deficient. These patients often respond well to antidepressant medications, which increase the activity of the biogenic amine neurotransmitter systems.

Less severe neurotic, emotional disturbances may also have biochemical explanations in some patients. Research suggests that mild or moderate depressions often result from learned helplessness, a condition in which the person has learned that his or her behavior is ineffective in controlling reinforcing or punishing consequences. Experiments show that this produces depletion of norepinephrine in the brain, as do other psychological stressors that cause depression. These patients also are sometimes helped by antidepressant drugs.

Finally, many anxiety disorders may result from biochemical imbalances in the brain. Drugs that alleviate anxiety, such as Librium (chlordiazepoxide) and Valium (diazepam), have powerful effects on a brain neurotransmitter called gamma-aminobutyric acid (GABA), as do other tranquilizers, such as alcohol and barbiturates. GABA is an inhibitory neurotransmitter that acts to keep brain activity from running away with itself, so to speak. When GABA is prevented from acting, the result is agitation, seizures, and death. Positron emission tomography (PET) scans of the brains of people suffering from panic attacks show that they have abnormally high activity in a part of the limbic system called the parahippocampal gyrus, an effect that might be caused by a GABA deficiency there.

## Applications

Understanding the biomedical factors that cause illnesses with psychiatric symptoms leads directly to improved diagnoses and subsequent patient care. Numerous studies have shown that psychiatric disorders are misdiagnosed between 25 percent and 50 percent of the time, the most persistent bias being toward diagnosing medical problems as psychological illnesses. A study published in 1981 by Richard Hall and colleagues found that, of one hundred psychiatric patients admitted consecutively to a state hospital, eighty had a physical illness that required medical treatment but had not been diagnosed in preadmission screening. In twenty-eight of these patients, proper medical treatment resulted in rapid and dramatic clearing of their psychiatric symptoms. In another eighteen patients, medical treatment resulted in substantial improvement of their psychiatric conditions. In an earlier study, Hall and colleagues found that 10 percent of psychiatric outpatients—those whose conditions were not severe enough to require hospitalization—had medical disorders that caused or contributed to their psychiatric illnesses.

Psychiatric symptoms are often among the earliest warning signs of dangerous, even life-threatening, medical illnesses. Thus, proper physical evaluation and differential diagnosis, especially of patients with psychiatric symptoms not obviously of psychological origin, is critical. In other cases, psychiatric illnesses result from biochemical imbalances in the brain. In any case, patients and therapists alike must be wary of uncritically accepting after-the-fact psychological explanations. A psychological bias can all too easily become a self-fulfilling prophecy, to the detriment of the patient's health and well-being.

Hall et al. found that a medical workup consisting of psychiatric and physical examinations, complete blood-chemistry analysis, urinalysis and urine drug screening, electrocardiogram (EKG), and electroencephalogram (EEG) successfully identified more than 90 percent of the medical illnesses present in their sample of one hundred psychiatric patients. The authors recommend that such a workup be done routinely for all patients admitted to psychiatric hospitals.

E. Fuller Torrey makes similar recommendations for patients admitted to psychiatric hospitals because of schizophrenia. He recommends that a thorough examination should include a careful and complete medical history and mental-status examination, with assistance from family members and friends if necessary. Physical and neurological examinations are also recommended. A blood count, blood-chemical screen, and urinalysis should be done to reveal conditions such as anemia, metal poisoning, endocrine or metabolic imbalances, syphilis, and drug abuse. A computerized axial tomography (CAT) scan may be necessary to clarify suspicions of brain abnormalities. Some doctors recommend that a CAT scan be done routinely to detect conditions such as brain tumors, neurodegenerative diseases, subdural hematomas (bleeding into the brain resulting from head injuries), viral encephalitis, and other conditions that might be missed upon initial neurological screening. Torrey also recommends a routine examination of cerebrospinal fluid obtained by lumbar puncture, which can reveal viral infections, brain injury, and biochemical abnormalities in the brain, and a routine electroencephalogram, which can reveal abnormal electrical activity in the brain caused by infections, inflammations, head injury, or epilepsy.

If any medical disorder is discovered, it should be treated appropriately. If this does not result in clearing the psychiatric symptoms, Torrey recommends that antipsychotic medications be given. If the initial drug trial is unsuccessful, then the dosage may have to be adjusted or another drug tried, since a patient's response to medication can be quite idiosyncratic. About 5 percent of patients react adversely to medication, in which case it may have to be discontinued.

Mark Gold makes parallel recommendations for patients with depressive and anxiety disorders. In patients who have depressive symptoms, tests for thyroid function are particularly important. Perhaps 10 to 15 percent of depressed patients test positive for thyroid disorder. Hypothyroidism, especially before the disease is fully developed, may present only psychiatric, particularly depressive, symptoms. Hyperthyroidism may be indicated by depression, mania, or psychosis. Blood and urine screens for drug abuse are also indicated for patients with depression.

Patients who are found to have a primary mood disorder may be candidates for antidepressant drug therapy. Since responses to these medications are highly idiosyncratic, careful monitoring of patients is required. Blood tests can determine whether the drug has reached an ideally effective concentration in the body.

In some cases, even biological depressions can be treated without drugs. Seasonal affective disorder (SAD), also called winter depression, may be treated with exposure to full-spectrum lights that mimic sunlight. Studies suggest that this alters activity in the pineal gland, which secretes melatonin, a hormone that has mood-altering effects. Similarly, some depressions may result from biological rhythms that are out of synchronization. Exposure to lights is often helpful in such cases, as is sleep deprivation.

In anxious patients, tests for endocrine function, especially hyperthyroidism, are called for, as are tests of the cardiovascular system and tests for drug abuse. In patients in whom no primary medical disorder is identified, the use of antianxiety medications may be indicated. Patients on medication should be closely monitored. Psychotherapy, such as behavior therapy for avoidant behaviors engendered by panic attacks and phobias, is also indicated.

As the public becomes more knowledgeable about the biomedical factors in psychiatric illnesses, malpractice lawsuits against therapists who misdiagnose these illnesses or who misapply psychotherapy and psychoactive drug therapy are becoming more common. In the future, it is likely that all manner of mental health providers will have to become more medically sophisticated and rely more on medical testing for the purpose of the differential diagnosis of illnesses presenting psychiatric symptoms.

## Context

Theories of abnormal behavior have existed since prehistoric times. At first, these centered on supernatural forces. Behavior disturbances were thought to result from invasion by evil spirits. Treatment was likely to consist of trephining—drilling a hole in the skull to allow malevolent spirits to escape. The threat of trephination must have motivated many psychotic individuals to stay out of public view or to comply as nearly as possible with social expectations.

In the fourth century B.C., the Greek physician Hippocrates proposed the first rudimentary biomedical theory. He proposed that illnesses, including mental illnesses, resulted from imbalances in vital bodily fluids. His break with supernatural explanations resulted in more humane treatment of the mentally ill. Unfortunately, this trend proved to be abortive. By medieval times, theories of abnormality had reverted to demonology. Mental illness was often attributed to demoniac possession, and "treatment" was sometimes little less than torture.

The Renaissance, with its revival of learning and interest in nature, initially saw little change in this attitude. People whose behavior was considered peculiar were often accused of witchcraft or of conspiring with the devil. As knowledge of the human organism increased, however, superstitions again gave way to speculation that "insanity" resulted from physical illness or injury. The mentally ill were consigned to asylums where, it was hoped, they would be treated by physicians. In most cases, unfortunately, asylums were essentially prisons, and medical treatment, when available, was rarely effective.

Two historical movements were responsible for restoring humane treatment to the mentally ill. The first was a moral reform movement ushered in by such individuals as Phillipe Pinel in France, William Tuke in England, and Dorothea Dix in America.

The second was continuing research in chemistry, biology, and medicine. By the nineteenth century, the brain was recognized as the seat of human reasoning and emotion. Once thought to be a place of supernatural happenings, the brain was finally revealed to be an organ not unlike the liver. Like the liver, the brain is subject to organic disturbances, and the result of these is similarly predictable—namely, psychological abnormalities. Discovery of diseases, such as advanced syphilis, that cause brain deterioration and are characterized by psychological symptoms, supported this organic model.

By the mid-twentieth century, little reasonable doubt remained that some psychological disturbances have biomedical causes. Interest centered especially on schizophrenia, major depressive disorder, and manic-depressive psychosis (later called bipolar disorder). Genetic studies strongly indicated that organic factors existed in each of these illnesses, and research was directed toward finding the biomedical fault and effecting a cure.

Paradoxically, effective treatments were found before medical understanding of the disorders was achieved. Therapeutic drugs were developed first for schizophrenia, then for depression, and finally for anxiety. These drugs proved to be important research tools, leading directly to discovery of neurotransmitter systems in the brain and helping to elucidate the biochemical nature of brain functioning. Much neuroscience research is still motivated by the desire for a better biomedical understanding of psychological disorders, which will ultimately lead to more effective treatments and patient care for these conditions.

## Bibliography

Andreasen, Nancy C. *The Broken Brain: The Biological Revolution in Psychiatry.* New York: Harper & Row, 1984. An excellent introduction to biopsychiatry for the general reader. Andreasen's summary of brain structure and function, and their relationship to mood and behavior, is one of the best in a book of this type. Highly recommended.

Gold, Mark S. *The Good News About Depression: Cures and Treatments in the New Age of Psychiatry.* New York: Random House, 1986. Written in a light, easy-to-read style, this book discusses the myriad biomedical conditions that can lead to depression and describes how they can be diagnosed and treated. Especially valuable for someone who is contemplating psychiatric treatment for depression or who has a loved one who is.

_____. *The Good News About Panic, Anxiety, and Phobias.* New York: Random House, 1989. Written for the nontechnical reader, this book offers a good general summary of anxiety disorders, their diagnosis (and misdiagnosis), and their treatment. The second half deals specifically with the biopsychiatric approach to anxiety. Gold's books also include extensive bibliographies and state-by-state listings of experts in the field.

Gottesman, Irving I. *Schizophrenia Genesis: The Origins of Madness.* New York: W. H. Freeman, 1991. An excellent, well-written resource on the causes of schizophrenia that can be understood without a technical background. Highly recommended.

Torrey, E. Fuller. *Surviving Schizophrenia: A Family Manual.* Rev. ed. New York: Perennial Library, 1988. An excellent book for the general reader on schizophrenia. It should be read by everyone interested in the disorder, including every mental health worker. Many libraries have only the first edition. Read the revised edition if possible.

Willner, Paul. *Depression: A Psychobiological Synthesis.* New York: John Wiley & Sons, 1985. This book was written for the specialist in the field but is not beyond the reach of readers with a solid background in science, especially chemistry (but keep a medical dictionary close by). The bibliography is very extensive.

*William B. King*

## Cross-References

Anxiety Disorders: Theoretical Explanations, 272; Bipolar Disorder, 422; Depression: Theoretical Explanations, 789; Madness: Historical Concepts, 1492; Neurotransmitters, 1673; Psychoactive Drug Therapy, 1891; Schizophrenia: Background, Types, and Symptoms, 2129; Schizophrenia: Theoretical Explanations, 2141; Seasonal Affective Disorder, 2155.

# ABNORMALITY: COGNITIVE MODELS

*Type of psychology:* Psychopathology
*Fields of study:* Cognitive processes; models of abnormality

*The cognitive perspective on psychopathology asserts that faulty thinking in the form of irrational or illogical thought processes leads to abnormal behavior; although the cognitive approach has been criticized for overlooking biological or genetic influences, it has led to effective treatments for anxiety and depression.*

*Principal terms*
APPRAISAL: a short-term cognitive process; an automatic evaluation of an event based on past experience
ATTRIBUTION: a short-term cognitive process in which the cause of an event is attributed to someone or something
COGNITIONS: thoughts believed to lead to certain behavioral responses
COGNITIVE BEHAVIOR THERAPY: therapy that integrates principles of learning theory with cognitive strategies to treat disorders such as depression, anxiety, and other behavioral problems (smoking, obesity)
COGNITIVE BIAS: the particular way in which one sees the world and forms a basis for interpreting or misinterpreting events from a certain perspective
COGNITIVE EXPECTANCY: the belief that something done by oneself or others will lead to a certain outcome
COGNITIVE PROCESSES: the processes a person uses to become aware of events or things and their mental representations: learning, memory, images, reason, and problem solving
NEGATIVE COGNITIVE TRIAD: the view that the present, past, and future are all hopeless; a pattern of thinking seen as a root cause of depression
RELAPSE: returning to problem behaviors (such as drinking or binge eating) at the level of impairment observed before treatment

## Overview

Cognitive models of abnormality assume that the way a person interprets and evaluates experience through his or her thoughts leads directly to emotional and behavioral consequences. These units of thought are called cognitions. Activities involving reasoning, memory, imagining, problem solving, and decision making form the mental representations of events in one's life and are called cognitive processes. Short-term cognitive processes are referred to as "expectations, attributions, and appraisals," and long-term cognitive processes are called "beliefs." When viewing psychopathology (the study of abnormal behavior) from a cognitive perspective, illogical, erroneous, or irrational thoughts are seen as the cause of the maladaptive behavioral responses.

Behaviorists believe that maladaptive behavior is learned through the principles of conditioning and reinforcement; however, cognitive psychologists note that phobias, fear reactions, or aggressive behavior can be acquired through observation or modeling alone, without any direct experience, as Albert Bandura demonstrated in the case of aggression. Bandura conducted a study in which children observed and then imitated adult "parental models" whom they viewed punching and kicking an inflatable "Bobo" doll. It became increasingly apparent that strict behavioral explanations for abnormal behavior were inadequate. Cognitive psychologists began to look for the intervening variable and proposed that the key to behavioral responses is the way people think about and perceive events. The children who imitated the parental models probably thought, "If a grown-up can kick and punch that doll, then I can too."

Dissonant cognitions and their contribution to anxiety disorders or neurotic behavior was explained by Carl Rogers in the early 1960's. Rogers believed that the stronger the magnitude or perception of threat, the more likely it is that a person will resort to denying or distorting the event. This happens as the person attempts to cope with information that is dissonant (does not fit) with his or her expectations. As a result of this process, Rogers suggested, one's self-image lowers as coping strategies for anxiety begin to fail.

Aaron Beck and Donald Meichenbaum have both developed comprehensive theories regarding the influence of cognitive processes on the onset and maintenance of psychiatric disorders such as anxiety and depression. Beck systematically studies the illogical or negative thought processes of an individual that occur in response to stimuli through a process called "rational analysis." He sets up a series of homework assignments, designed to be accomplished easily, to assist the client in changing maladaptive thoughts and behaviors. By encouraging the client to engage in behaviors they have previously avoided, Beck demonstrated the ability to change the irrational beliefs that had inhibited those behaviors in the first place. Beck's cognitive interpretation of anxiety disorders is the following: Such a disorder has occurred when a person has a negative, distorted view (schema) of some event, thing, or person and responds with anxiety when exposed to the feared situation or stimulus because of this distorted view. These cognitive errors are thought to be based on early experiences, and they lead to negative attributions, such as "I did not get promoted because I cannot handle any stress," or to negative appraisals, such as "I am a nervous person." Expectations are other forms of short-term cognitions; they include "outcome expectations" that refer to the desired outcome and "efficacy expectations" that refer to whether the person has the capacity to accomplish a behavior that produces a desired outcome. Attributions, or automatic explanations for events, can be global ("I am a failure at everything") or specific ("I am not good at football"). They can be stable (fixed), as in "I will always be unhappy," or unstable (changing), as in "I am having a bad day but tomorrow will be better," and can be internal, as in "It is my fault I had an accident; I should have seen the car coming through the stop sign," or external, as in "The other person ran the stop sign and hit my car." A cognitive therapist tries to get clients to adjust their attributions to be specific, unstable, and external in order to improve problems such as anxiety.

Beck uses the cognitive model to understand how depression arises and is maintained. He proposed the existence of a "negative cognitive triad" that consists of negative thoughts about the present, the past, and the future. This negative triad forms a vicious circle of thinking that leads to the hopelessness and helplessness associated with depressive disorders. A cognitive therapist would intervene at any point in the triad to change the pessimistic outlook and to help the client increase involvement in positive rewarding experiences.

Donald Meichenbaum, a cognitive therapist, explores a client's illogical beliefs and uses an interview style he calls "Columbo style interviewing," in which the therapist encourages the client to assist in solving the mystery of why illogical thoughts are allowed to influence the client's behavior. Meichenbaum, in a supportive but gently confrontational manner, engages the client in the therapeutic task. Most cognitive psychologists use techniques such as "thought substitution" and "behavioral substitution" to replace negative thoughts and behaviors with more appropriate behaviors. The process of changing the negative or illogical thought processes has been called "cognitive restructuring." For example, Meichenbaum might say to a client, "Maybe you think you have no friends or that no one likes you, but that cannot be true, because you just named six people with whom you socialize regularly. I wonder if you can help me figure this puzzle out?"

Albert Ellis uses a form of cognitive therapy he calls "rational-emotive therapy" to accomplish the corrective process. Ellis uses a technique called "disputation" to help a person replace damaging thoughts such as "I should always be perfect" or "Everyone must always love me" with more realistic ideas. Ellis' belief that people are ruled by their "shoulds" and "musts" and need to become aware of this to live happier and fuller lives led to his treatment approach.

Cognitive processes have been examined as contributors to childhood psychopathology. Developmental psychologists focus on cognitive functions as organizing capacities for children's ego functions. This model uses an information-processing analogy for the various ego functions (reasoning, problem solving, and so on). As the child progresses developmentally and cognitively, the cognitive information-processing functions become more complex and sophisticated. Individuals who have difficulty with these cognitive functions may be more vulnerable to experiencing psychopathology, since their ego functions are not as flexible or adaptive as those of a person who has achieved higher developmental levels of cognitive functioning. Children who have major psychiatric disorders such as schizophrenia may have immature, egocentric ego capacity, compared to mentally healthy children. This cognitive information-processing model has been expanded to adult psychopathology by Michael F. Basch in his book *Understanding Psychotherapy* (1988).

## Applications

David Shapiro applied the theory of different levels of cognitive organization to personality styles. His book *Neurotic Styles* (1965) illustrates with intriguing examples the psychopathological forms of experiencing, perceiving, and relating to the world that accompany depressive, obsessive-compulsive, paranoid, and other personality styles.

Many other types of psychiatric problems have been addressed by the cognitive model. Alan Marlatt has used the cognitive approach to explain the addictive cycle of alcohol "craving" and chronic drinking. A person's cognitive expectancy that alcohol will reduce anxiety or help him or her get through a difficult social situation fuels the person's desire for alcohol or other addictive substances. Marlatt's work has been utilized in the treatment of obesity, in which the addictive substance is food, and the process of craving and cognitive expectancy is thought to be in some ways similar to that of alcohol abuse. If a person who is obese can change the automatic negative thoughts that accompany a lapse (a temporary reversion to maladaptive habits), such as "I binged once this week; therefore I am a failure at managing my weight, so why bother trying to lose any more weight?" to more positive thoughts, such as "Well, I have only binged once this week, I can compensate with more exercise," it allows him or her to regain control over his or her behavior and resume positive weight-management strategies. If an obese individual does not regain control cognitively and behaviorally over his or her eating habits, the risk of relapse becomes greater.

Cognitive-behavioral approaches have been applied in group settings with eating-disordered populations and in couples therapy for marital problems. Meichenbaum has applied the cognitive approach to stress management in a treatment approach he outlined in his book *Stress Inoculation Training: A Clinical Guidebook* (1985). In this application, he developed a short manual designed to help a therapist take a person through the steps of preparing for and coping with various stressors.

Self-help programs are available and are increasing in popularity for individuals who have discrete problems such as having difficulty relaxing or difficulty with smoking cessation, test anxiety, stress management, or chronic headache. These programs, often on audiotapes or in books, utilize cognitive strategies to address negative thought patterns associated with these problems and substitute more appropriate thoughts and behaviors in a process called "cognitive restructuring." In addition, these self-help programs use practice homework assignments—daily logs or journals to document and record behavior change toward the targeted goal.

A set of audiotapes, developed in 1991 by Thomas Cash, utilizes cognitive strategies to identify cognitive distortions and correct distorted body image. He found a total of twelve cognitive errors that people make that affect body image negatively, such as "magnification of flaws," "overlooking assets," and "comparing oneself to more beautiful others." Cash's research found that as many as 40 percent of normal-weight women and 30 percent of normal-weight men are dissatisfied with some aspects of their physical appearance. If normal-weight individuals have difficulty with body image, then one can imagine the problems someone with an eating disorder has with accepting his or her body. In fact, one of the most difficult aspects to treat in individuals with eating disorders is the cognitive problem of body-image distortion.

## Context

The cognitive model was born out of a dissatisfaction with models of "radical behaviorism" of the 1950's. Cognitive psychologists believed that there was more to understanding abnormal behavior than just looking at the connection between an environmental event or stimulus and the resulting behavior—the approach used by the most prominent behavioral psychologist at the time, B. F. Skinner. In other words, cognitive psychologists believe that understanding the way people interpret or evaluate events in their lives is the key to correcting faulty thinking and abnormal behavior. The cognitive psychology movement in relation to understanding and treating psychopathology is relatively new, starting sometime in the early 1960's; many important studies were conducted in the 1970's and 1980's.

Aaron T. Beck began publishing his work on the cognitive aspects of depression in the 1960's. Continuing that line of research, he expanded it into the cognitive understanding of anxiety disorders and their treatment. Beck's studies on hopelessness and suicide spanned the decades from the 1970's to the 1990's. He found that the single best predictor for future suicide was the cognitive variable of hopelessness, and he developed the Beck Depression Inventory (BDI) to measure the cognitive, behavioral, motivational, and physical aspects of depression. Treatment of personality-disordered individuals from the cognitive perspective was introduced by Beck in his book *Cognitive Therapy of Personality Disorders* (1990). For a long time, many in the helping professions thought that individuals with personality disorders (long-standing maladaptive ways of perceiving and behaving) were untreatable. There have been some effective approaches for understanding and treating characterological problems with psychodynamic methods, but these have been criticized for being time-consuming and expensive. Beck's cognitive therapy for personality disorders holds the promise of utilizing briefer forms of treatment for people with personality disorders.

Donald Meichenbaum published *Cognitive-Behavior Modification: An Integrative Approach* (1977) and has presented numerous workshops on the cognitive treatment of depression to professional therapists and counselors from virtually every mental health discipline. Arnold Lazarus developed the multimodal approach to treatment in the 1970's, which consists of the following components, referred to as the BASIC ID: behavioral, affective, sensation, interpersonal, cognitive, imaging, and drugs (for psychotropic medication). Lazarus has demonstrated success with his multimodal comprehensive treatment approach for individuals with severe disorders such as schizophrenia. Lazarus and Alan Fay have applied the cognitive-behavioral approach to the treatment of couples in marital therapy and have written a number of useful books on this subject. Some are designed for the general public as self-help reference tools to be used as an adjunct to therapy.

Wallace Wilkins, like Beck, has applied cognitive psychotherapy principles to the treatment of mood disorders. He uses an approach that he calls "personal empowering strategies for improving moods," which works on the principle of increasing self-enhancing thoughts to improve mood and behavior. Wilkins outlines a three-step process: building a foundation, identifying self-limiting thoughts, and perishing thoughts. His list of perishable thoughts is long and includes black-or-white thinking; catastrophic thinking; shoulds, oughts, and musts; perfectionistic evaluation standards; and many others. He helps clients change two critical processes: externalizing causes for success and internalizing causes for failure.

In the late 1980's and into the 1990's, the area of developmental psychopathology gained a foothold and a new momentum in the study of abnormality. This discipline represents the marriage of clinical and developmental psychology in the joint effort to understand the development and maintenance of psychiatric disorders. New models for comprehending abnormal psychology, particularly in children but also in adults, have been generated from this approach. Philip Cowan developed the "nine-cell model," which represents a three-by-three matrix for the conceptualization of psychopathology. He has incorporated biological, environmental, and interactive aspects on the horizontal axis, with individual, psychological (cognitive), and relationship aspects on the vertical axis. The resulting framework of nine cells allows the reader to understand the interrelationship of multidimensional contributors to psychopathology and shows the many ways one can intervene in any of the cells to begin the corrective treatment process. Each cell contains a theoretical cause for the disorder and a proposed treatment. In the future, comprehensive models such as Cowan's nine-cell model may further clarify the interconnection of cognitive processes with behavioral, biological, interpersonal, environmental, and genetic variables.

## Bibliography

Beck, Aaron T., and Gary Emery. *Anxiety Disorders and Phobias: A Cognitive Perspective.* New York: Basic Books, 1985. This book gives the reader a more in-depth understanding of the specific cognitive aspects that are involved in the development and maintenance of anxiety disorders. There is a focus on phobias, one of the most common types of anxiety disorders experienced by both children and adults in Western society.

Beck, Aaron T., A. J. Rush, B. F. Shaw, and Gary Emery. *Cognitive Therapy of Depression.* New York: Guilford Press, 1979. One of the most helpful resources in bringing the reader to an awareness of how specific types of cognitive-behavioral therapeutic interventions can be utilized to treat depression. Depression has been called the "common cold" of emotional disorders and has affected as many as one out of every ten to twenty people in the United States.

Holmes, David S. "Theoretical Perspectives." In *Abnormal Psychology.* New York: HarperCollins, 1991. Holmes reviews the major theoretical perspectives and models that aid in understanding abnormal psychology in this abnormal psychology textbook. Provides a critique of cognitive and other models and gives examples that illustrate the models.

Meichenbaum, Donald. *Cognitive-Behavior Modification: An Integrative Approach.* New York: Plenum Press, 1977. Explains the process and technique of cognitive-behavioral therapy in an easy-to-understand way. The author presents illustrative examples and is able to bring to life the types of problems that people are likely to have and the corresponding interventions from which they may benefit.

_____. *Stress Inoculation Training: A Clinical Guidebook.* New York: Pergamon Press, 1985. This brief, concise manual covers the areas of stress reactions and outlines the strategies that can be used to intervene or to prevent negative reactions to stressful experiences.

Willerman, Lee, and D. B. Cohen. *Psychopathology.* New York: McGraw-Hill, 1990. Provides a general introduction to psychopathology with a more sophisticated discussion of theoretical facets of abnormality, psychiatric disorders, and their treatments.

*Karen Wolford*

## Cross-References

Abnormality Defined, 89; Cognitive Behavior Therapy, 546; Cognitive Social Learning: Walter Mischel, 580; Cognitive Therapy, 586; Personal Constructs: George A. Kelly, 1784; Rational-Emotive Therapy, 2052; Reality Therapy, 2059; Transactional Analysis, 2584.

# ABNORMALITY: FAMILY MODELS

*Type of psychology:* Psychopathology
*Field of study:* Models of abnormality

   *Dysfunctional family communications and structures have been regarded as contributing to psychopathology of family members. These faulty communications and structures can lead to the scapegoating and labeling of vulnerable family members. In certain families, significant psychopathology in either or both parents can lead to disturbed family communications including double-bind messages, denial or injection of meaning, and distortion of meaning.*

   *Principal terms*
      DOUBLE-BIND COMMUNICATION: a statement that contains two
         independent and contradictory messages; results in a "no-win"
         situation for the recipient of the communication
      DYSFUNCTIONAL FAMILY: a family grouping that is characterized by the
         presence of disturbed interactions and communications; an abusive,
         incestuous, or alcoholic family
      EXPRESSED EMOTION (EE): hostile or negative communications by family
         members; they have been identified as contributing to high relapse
         rates, particularly in people with schizophrenia
      FIELD THEORY: a view that interpersonal interactions in the family
         system create conditions for a child's psychopathology, and that this
         pathology fulfills a specific function in the system
      PSYCHOANALYTIC THEORY: in this context, a theory which holds that
         parental pathology and conflicts are mirrored or represented in the
         offspring, and that negative emotions and fantasies are reexperienced
         in the family interactions
      SCAPEGOATING: the targeting of one member of a family, usually a child,
         by the other members as the "problem child" or "identified patient"
      SCHISMATIC FAMILY STRUCTURE: a disturbed family structure that is
         created when there is marital hostility and the child or children are
         forced to mediate between the parents or choose sides in the marital
         problem
      SCHIZOPHRENOGENIC: a term that refers to a parent whose
         communication style is dominated by double-bind or contradictory
         communications to the child
      SKEWED FAMILY STRUCTURE: a disturbed family structure formed when a
         parent is mentally ill and the other parent and members of the family
         "adopt" the distorted view of the mentally ill parent to keep peace in
         the home

SYMBIOTIC RELATIONSHIP: an overprotective, often enmeshed relationship
   between a parent and child
SYSTEMS THEORY: a concept in which the family grouping is viewed as a
   biosocial subsystem existing within the larger system of society;
   intrafamilial communications are the mechanisms of subsystem
   interchange

## Overview

A certain amount of conflict, stress, and disagreement is common in most family systems. It has even been jokingly suggested that no one has been reared in a "functional family." Yet there are a significant number of families in the United States whose family structures or systems are definitely thought to be pathological, or dysfunctional, when viewed by standards set by mental health professionals or representatives of other social agencies. Families in which significant substance abuse is present, such as alcoholic family settings, are an example of where pathological family dynamics would be likely to occur. In addition, families in which child abuse (emotional or physical), incest, or other forms of victimization and scapegoating occur are also described as dysfunctional.

Family models of abnormality include those studied in relation to the hypothesized development of schizophrenia. Most researchers now regard schizophrenia as a biological disease, a major psychiatric disorder which is caused by a biochemical imbalance or structural brain disorder. In the early views of investigators who studied family interaction, certain family structures were thought to foster psychosis. Three early family models thought to contribute to schizophrenia were schizophrenogenic, schismatic, and skewed family structures.

Schizophrenogenic referred to settings in which parents (usually the mother) communicate to their children using "double-bind" messages. A double-bind message refers to communication containing two contradictory, opposing messages. An example is when a mother says to a child, "Come here and give me a hug and show me you love me," and then, when the child complies, pushes him or her away and says, "Don't touch me, you'll mess up my clothes." One can easily see that a child who complies with such a communication is in a "no-win" situation in which anything the child does will meet with dissatisfaction. Another double-bind communication is when the parent makes a comment such as "You should not do that," but says it in a tone of voice that is permissive. The child is left in a state of confusion about the real message and what is expected of him or her.

A second type of disturbed family structure is referred to as a schismatic family structure. Schismatic families are those in which there are significant marital problems that are not being addressed within the marital dyad. Instead, the children are triangulated into the marital relationship and often serve as go-betweens for marital communication. There may be an attempt on the part of one parent to get the child to align with that parent against the other parent. This results in confusion and guilt in the child, who is forced to choose sides and align against a parent.

The third disturbed family structure is the skewed family. In this family, one member, usually one of the parents, has a major mental illness. The rest of the family adopts the disturbed view of the world in order to keep peace at home. For example, in the case of a family in which the father has chronic paranoid schizophrenia, the family members, including the healthy spouse, assist in not letting others into the home, keep the drapes closed, and generally do not trust outsiders. All of this is designed to keep the fears of the disturbed parent at a minimum. Additional pathological communications found in disturbed families include messages in which one person tries to tell another how the other person thinks or feels. Denial of meaning, for example, refers to one person telling another that the other person is not really angry or depressed when in fact the person is. Distortion of meaning occurs when the first person tells the second person that the second person really *means* to say something other than what the person has said; injection of meaning is telling someone else what he or she thinks.

Margaret Mahler, a psychoanalytic theorist, studied childhood and family development in the early 1950's and proposed a developmental stage theory for the healthy development of the self. If parental behaviors and communications are disturbed, the child's development can be adversely affected. This can be manifested in enmeshed, symbiotic relationships in which the mother intrudes on her child and literally invades the child's autonomy or development of the self. A mother who develops a symbiotic relationship with a child may not give adequate room for the child to develop or adequate privacy and respect to the child's own ideas. A child in this type of relationship will not learn to trust his or her own ideas and may remain dependent on the parent into the adult years.

Theodore Lidz, who studied family interactions in the 1960's, also found that the parents' personalities and the marital coalition strongly influenced the effectiveness of their children's ability to negotiate the outside world. In some cases, the child's mental illness can appear to have been learned from the parent's mental illness and pathological behaviors. Both chaotic families, which lack a stable figure with whom the child can identify, and rigid families, which permit only superficial, stereotyped communications and behaviors, have been the breeding grounds for disturbed children, particularly children with schizophrenia; however, many normal children have also come from these homes. Research is increasingly focusing on these resilient children, those who are able to emerge from pathological families relatively emotionally intact.

## Applications

Applications of the knowledge that has been gathered regarding disturbed family systems and family communications have been plentiful. One area has been the development of a parental support group called Parents Anonymous. This program has been developed on the twelve-step approach of Alcoholics Anonymous (AA). Often, these groups are sponsored by an agency and may have a professional counselor as a leader. Parents Anonymous has been successful in helping some parents gain advice, support, and understanding of their parenting behaviors. It is a proactive approach that assists all parents, and especially parents who feel that they may harm their children either emotionally or physically. Along this line of prevention, child abuse hotlines and family crisis daycare centers have been established in many communities. Parents who are under stress can call for assistance or go to a crisis center and receive counseling while someone else takes over the child care.

Thomas Gordon wrote a book that has been widely read entitled *Parent Effectiveness Training: The Tested New Way to Raise Responsible Children* (1972). This is a guide for all parents that presents positive alternatives for discipline and scheduling of family activities. Communication patterns are suggested that do not negate the child but make the desired behaviors clear and easy to understand. The book has been used as an aid to family therapy and for adjunctive parent counseling of parents whose children may be in therapy.

Family therapy itself has been a growing area. Multigroup family therapy has also been developed to bring families together in this process. Filial therapy was developed as a unique approach established on the principle of using parents as therapists for their own children. Lawrence Hornsby and Alan Applebaum expanded on the approach in the late 1970's to involve the parents in therapy themselves as well as in the play therapy with their own children. Hornsby and Applebaum then supervise the direction of the play therapy. Six to eight sessions are conducted to train the parents, who then continue the play therapy in their home on a weekly basis.

PROMISE, a support group for parents and relatives of the mentally ill, has been a growing presence in communities in the United States. This group provides support, referral, and advocacy for its members and their offspring. The group has been active in informing politicians about the need for mental health services for the severely mentally ill.

In the 1990's, there has been an increasing focus on the nuclear family structure and on the single-parent family. These family structures have disadvantages that can lead to increased stress on the parents and the children. Without an extended family network of support, many times the focus on maintaining a career competes with the needs of the children. Third parties such as day-care centers, schools, churches, and babysitters become key influences on the development of the children, and parents have been cautioned to choose such settings and caregivers wisely. Research has suggested that quality programs and caregivers can enhance the child's development; however, there have been numerous problems with unqualified, overburdened, or even pathological third-party caregivers who may contribute to disturbed child development.

The rise of addiction as a major form of pathology has also led to applications of family work with the complementary components of AA such as ALANON, ALATEEN, and ACOA (Adult Children of Alcoholics) support groups. There are now also support groups for victims of anorexia and bulimia and their family members. Most clinical treatment programs for these addictive or habit disorders require the family to be involved in the treatment and healing process. Survivors of sexual abuse and incest victim support groups can aid members in overcoming the devastating effects of growing up in a pathological, abusive environment.

## Context

Margaret Mahler, Frieda Fromm-Reichmann, Theodore Lidz, and other dynamic theorists noted the difference between normal and pathological family communications and structures in the mid 1900's. Faulty communications between child and parent, as well as disturbed family structures, have been correlated with disturbance in some offspring. The majority of children coming from pathological homes remain intact, however, which suggests these are not causal factors in mental illness but may be contributing factors. Some children may be vulnerable to such dynamics or may be singled out or scapegoated for abuse. For example, Lidz and others, in the mid 1950's, wrote about the effect of a remote or distant father on the subsequent development of schizophrenic or homosexual behavior in some children. Role reversals in family structure in which there is a weak, ineffective male model and a strong, overbearing female model have also been linked to variations in development of sexual identity in children.

Family therapy itself has been a growing area in the decades that followed. Salvador Minuchin, Virginia Satir, Jay Haley, Murray Bowen, and Carl Whittaker all made significant contributions to the field of family therapy and family systems theory in the decades that followed. Minuchin is credited, because of his work at the Philadelphia Child Guidance Center, with leading the movement toward family therapy during the decade of the 1970's. His "structural family therapy" approach uses systems theory to resolve family pathology. If the family system is changed, Minuchin feels, then the individual family members will also change and take on more adaptive roles within the new system.

Haley has focused on the particular meaning of certain communications and wrote extensively in the 1970's about techniques for therapeutic intervention in disturbed family interactions. Haley and his colleagues often prescribe homework and specific exercises designed to break through family resistance to change. In fact, Haley will sometimes direct a family *not* to change in hopes that "going with the resistance" will eventually lead to effective improvement in the family interaction. This type of intervention has been called a paradoxical approach because of its ambiguous nature. Haley believes that an individual's psychopathology is a key component in the family system and that the individual's disturbance and symptoms cannot change unless the family also changes. From this understanding, the term "identified patient" was derived, which refers to the identification of one problem member in the family as being a symptom of the family pathology.

In the late 1960's, Virginia Satir's popular approach to family therapy was called conjoint family therapy. In order to develop a family system that better met the emotional needs of the family members, Satir focused on improving impaired communications and interactions as well as impaired relationships among family members. Also in this time period, family therapist Carl Whittaker demonstrated his intergenerational approach to family therapy in a film entitled *A Different Kind of Caring*. In this demonstration, Whittaker works with an entire family, focusing on both the parents and their needs and on the children, and on how the two generations influence each other. Whittaker often shares his own observations, using humor and anecdotes to "break the ice." Family therapy work is often difficult, and many therapists undertake it with a cotherapist to balance the therapeutic interchange.

In the late 1970's, Peter Steinglass studied the effects of specific communications and relapse rates of schizophrenia. His work, published in 1980, highlighted the importance of what Steinglass termed high expressed emotion (EE). EE refers to negative, hostile, often rejecting communications of the family directed toward a mentally ill (usually schizophrenic) member. Relapse rates have been 40 percent higher for clients returning to these types of hostile households after psychiatric hospitalization. Family work to educate the members about the effects of these types of communications is necessary to prevent relapse. If the family is so dysfunctional that it does not change to improve the home environment, alternate living arrangements for the client may be pursued.

Family dynamics, communication, and structure are key components in attempts to alleviate psychopathology. This work, although challenging, is expected to grow and continue to benefit both families and society well into the future.

## Bibliography

Arnold, L. Eugene. *Helping Parents Help Their Children*. New York: Brunner/Mazel, 1978. Outlines general principles of parent guidance. Details are provided about family therapy, including filial therapy (Hornsby and Applebaum's approach). Specific problems of children, such as mental retardation, learning disabilities, hyperactivity, and so on are addressed, as are specific problems of parents, such as the abusing parent, teenage motherhood, adoptive parenthood, and more.

Bowen, Murray. *Family Therapy in Clinical Practice*. New York: Jason Aronson, 1978. Bowen is well respected as a family therapist and presenter of workshops. Here he shows his application of family therapy in the clinical setting.

Brown, Fredda Herz, ed. *Reweaving the Family Tapestry: A Multigenerational Approach to Families*. New York: W. W. Norton, 1991. Gives an overview of the work done by the Family Institute of Westchester. This approach is important not only from the multigenerational perspective, but also because extremely important issues of race, class, gender, and ethnicity are incorporated into clinical analysis and treatment.

Figley, Charles R., ed. *Treating Stress in Families*. New York: Brunner/Mazel, 1989. In today's stress-focused society, this book makes an important contribution. Observations are provided from scientific studies of families regarding how they not only cope with but also produce stress and react to stress. Interventions for prevention are explored.

Minuchin, Salvador. *Families and Family Therapy*. Cambridge, Mass.: Harvard University Press, 1974. A leader in family therapy interventions and techniques writes about his work and experiences treating families at the Philadelphia Child Guidance Center.

Ramsey, Christian N., Jr., ed. *Family Systems in Medicine.* New York: Guilford Press, 1989. A landmark book that expands what is known about family dysfunction and its effects on family members to the field of medicine. Reviews family systems theory, including a family stress model developed by Joan M. Patterson. Family systems research, immunology, endocrinology, biology, health, chronic illness, and behavioral disorders are all covered thoroughly. Suggestions for future directions of research are offered.

Skynner, A. C. Robin. *Systems of Family and Marital Psychotherapy.* New York: Brunner/Mazel, 1976. A systems approach to marital and family communication that integrates gender and role as well as relationship and sexuality to complete the picture of the influence of the marital relationship on the family.

*Karen Wolford*

### Cross-References

# ABNORMALITY: HUMANISTIC-EXISTENTIAL MODELS

*Type of psychology:* Psychopathology
*Fields of study:* Humanistic-phenomenological models; models of abnormality

*The humanistic-existential approach views psychopathology as stemming from feelings of meaninglessness, valuelessness, and alienation; lack of commitment, will, and responsibility; and failure to grow and to realize potentials. This paradigm has led to therapies that emphasize awareness, authenticity, free will, choice, integration, human growth, and fulfillment.*

*Principal terms*
EXISTENTIALISM: a viewpoint emphasizing human existence and situation in the world, and giving life meaning through the free choice of mature values and commitment to goals
HIERARCHY OF NEEDS: a sequence of basic human needs, including (from more to less powerful) physiological needs, safety and security, love and belongingness, esteem and respect, and self-actualization needs
HUMANISTIC PSYCHOLOGY: a branch of psychology that emphasizes the human tendencies toward growth and fulfillment, autonomy, choice, responsibility, and ultimate values such as truth, love, and justice
INCONGRUENCE: the possession of false aspects of the self-concept; lack of genuineness
PHENOMENOLOGY: an approach that stresses openness to direct experience in introspective or unsophisticated ways
SELF: the unified and integrated center of one's experience and awareness, which one experiences both subjectively, as an actor, and objectively, as recipient of actions
SELF-ACTUALIZATION: a constructive process of functioning optimally and fulfilling one's potential; characterized by acceptance, autonomy, accurate perceptions, creativity, high ethics, personal growing, and societal contributions

## Overview

Humanistic-existential models provide a way of understanding psychopathology that is an alternative to those offered by the biological, psychoanalytic, and behavioral and social learning paradigms. In contrast to explaining abnormal behavior through biological or physiological defects or anomalies (the medical or illness model), or through unconscious intrapsychic conflict and unresolved psychosexual developmental issues from the first six years of life (the psychoanalytic model), or as a result of past conditioning or reinforcement history or observational learning (the learning paradigm), humanistic-existential models essentially maintain that abnormality reflects and results from a failure to grow and to realize one's potentials.

The humanistic viewpoint emphasizes that all people have the human potential to grow and the capacity for full functioning; given the proper conditions for growth, people will be self-determining, will exercise choice and responsibility, and will fulfill their potentials and be self-actualizing.

Abnormality is the failure of such growth and development to be realized. Thus, in the humanistic model, health is not necessarily the absence of disease, but is instead something positive. Whereas the medical or illness model has traditionally stressed movement or change from sickness to normalcy, the humanistic model emphasizes change from normalcy or deficiency in growth to full functioning. The humanistic model also maintains that people must develop values and make their choices freely, based on their own experiences. If a person blindly accepts others' values and choices, then the person will lose a sense of self and become incongruent. Such incongruence is equivalent to abnormality.

The self is a central theme for humanistic psychologists. Carl Rogers postulated that all people have an actualizing tendency to maintain and enhance themselves, including their self-concept. Rogers described an organismic valuing process: What is experienced as satisfying is consistent with the actualizing tendency, and what is unsatisfying is not in accord with this tendency. When people distort or even deny experiences into conscious awareness, they have given up using their self or their organismic valuing process. Instead, they adopt conditions of worth that have been imposed by parents or other significant people. By becoming what others want them to be, or evaluating according to others' perceptions or experience, they obtain the positive regard and caring that is so important but they sacrifice accurate and efficient perception of reality, and ultimately lose their true self.

Failure to satisfy basic needs leads to deficiency and is another source of psychopathology. Abraham Maslow's motivational theory described a hierarchy of basic needs. Ranging from the more powerful to the less prepotent higher needs, these are physiological requirements, safety and security, love and belongingness, esteem and regard, aesthetic and cognitive, and self-actualization needs. In healthy, self-actualizing individuals, all the lower needs in the hierarchy are or have at one time been adequately satisfied; thus, these individuals can express more of their self-actualizing needs and motives (which include values such as truth, justice, beauty, and wholeness).

People are not self-actualizing if they are motivated primarily by lower deficiency needs, such as for safety, belongingness, or esteem; the self-actualization or growth motivation is the weakest of all the needs in the hierarchy. Maslow and other humanistic psychologists have identified other reasons why so few individuals may be self-actualizing. The force of habit, the tendency to stay where one is (inertia), and the fear of becoming all that one can be (which Maslow called the Jonah complex) are some psychological forces that conspire against growth. The misfortunes of poverty, poor parenting, or other sociocultural barriers can prevent growth motivation from being central. The tremendous power of culture, which can greatly inhibit deviation from the norm, or societal sanctions that can punish (socially or otherwise) those who stray too far beyond what society dictates as normal or acceptable prevent many from realizing their true self-expression and potentials. Certain political free-doms are also basic requisites for human fulfillment.

According to Maslow, when a person does not function according to growth moti-vation and the various self-actualization needs (truth, beauty, justice, and others), then he or she suffers from various kinds of spiritual disorders such as cynicism, nihilism, or emptiness. Spiritual or existential disorders are also highlighted by the existential perspective. All humans must have the courage, commitment, and will to use their freedom to choose values that guide life, give life its meaning, and empha-size obligations to others. Failure to choose, to create one's essence, or to deal with normal guilt (awareness of not fulfilling potentials) or normal existential anxiety (stemming from challenges to one's values and from awareness of one's ultimate death or nonbeing) results in existential despair and frustration. An existential disor-der or crisis is often a reflection of perceived meaninglessness, isolation, alienation, or valuelessness.

Both Rogers and Maslow characterized the actualizing tendency or self-actualization need as positive, constructive, rational, trustworthy, and in the direction of growth and harmony. Existentialists, not quite so optimistically, place additional emphasis on irrational forces and the potentiality of evil in the normal human personality.

Optimal health, full functioning, self-actualization, or existential being can be difficult to realize; Maslow spoke of the "psychopathology of the average," meaning that most normal people are content to be adjusted to their social group of society, and do not truly grow and realize their full potentials as human beings. Indeed, Maslow suggested that perhaps only 1 percent of the American population might be self-actualizing. Existential crises, problems of values and meaning, stunted growth, and lack of fulfillment are not uncommon among materially comfortable people.

## Applications

Humanistic and existential models are appropriately applied in situations in which clients desire not merely symptomatic relief, but also to become more aware of self and of existential conflicts and to achieve greater personal growth. Indeed, the hu-manistic paradigm has been particularly dissatisfied with pathology-centered con-ceptualizations, which have several disadvantages. One problem is that the illness model stresses the need (rather than the desirability) for treatment; the decision concerning need for therapy is often made by someone other than the person herself or himself. A second disadvantage is that therapists tend to be elevated above the patient, often in an authoritarian, parent-type role, rather than functioning in a more egalitarian therapeutic relationship. A third problem involves reinforcing the belief that people are sick and cannot really care for themselves or take an active and responsible role in their treatment. The humanistic model presents an alternative, one which would increase client choice and responsibility and focus on positive goals of fostering strengths rather than simply getting rid of illness or weakness. Humanistic theorists have observed that the goal of much counseling and psycho-therapy is more than eliminating pathology and achieving a state of normalcy.

Humanistic and existential therapists place great emphasis on the nature of the therapist-client relationship. Existential thinkers such as Martin Buber and Karl Jaspers stressed the tremendous importance and impact of therapists providing a full human presence, an authentic encounter, an "I-Thou" relationship with their clients. Such a deep encounter of intimacy and authenticity allows clients to gain access to their inner worlds through the unfolding of their real feelings, experiences, and potentials. Buber emphasized "unfolding" as the desired approach for both therapists and educators.

One of the leading existential analysts was Viktor Frankl, who developed an approach that he called "logotherapy." By examining each person's unique way of "being there," in relation to the physical world, social world, and self, and by engaging in intimate, open, authentic therapeutic encounter, the logotherapist allows clients through their basic freedom to take responsibility for creating a life with meaning. Frankl emphasized techniques such as de-reflection and paradoxical intention. De-reflection involves taking attention away from oneself and one's problems and symptoms and focusing instead on activities that could be done, on experiences that can be enjoyed, and on other people. Paradoxical intention involves the client's engaging in and even exaggerating symptoms; by thus magnifying and even ridiculing the symptoms, the client can understand his or her control over the neurotic behaviors and symptoms, and can choose different responses. Logotherapy, like most humanistic-existential approaches, stresses authenticity and working with immediacy on issues and experience in the present; it is especially useful for people dealing with existential crises or boundary situations (such as confrontation with one's own death, major changes in life that highlight one's ultimate aloneness, or situations that challenge one's values or that give one a feeling of meaninglessness).

Gestalt therapy, developed by Fritz and Laura Perls, is yet another approach that is phenomenological and existential in form and process. Centrally important are awareness and dialogue, using the direct phenomenological experience of therapist and client. Process (what and how) in the present (here and now) is amplified and experienced through contact and existential dialogue, and clients are able in such an environment to assume responsibility for their choices and values. Gestalt therapists help patients focus on present experience, reexperience emotions or enact feelings or thoughts in the present, visualize, act out elements of a dream or parts of a conflict, exaggerate gestures or bodily symptoms—all to increase client self-awareness and integration through organismic self-regulation. Various specialized Gestalt techniques to increase awareness, to resolve splits or conflicts within the self, and to achieve integration have been developed; the therapist balances frustration and support to achieve these goals. This approach is particularly useful for people who tend to live in the past or the anticipated future, and for those who overemphasize intellectual functions and restrain or neglect their feelings and bodily experiences.

The person-centered approach is perhaps humanistic psychology's most practiced and influential system of psychotherapy. Developed as a process of counseling troubled individuals, it has extended to groups, to human relations training programs, and even to institutional change. The emphasis of the approach is squarely on the relationship. Grounded in trust, and with the therapist providing the necessary facilitative conditions of genuineness, unconditional positive regard for the client, and accurate empathy (deeply listening and reflecting the client's feelings and meanings without interpretation or judgment), the client may become more genuine and use the self as the basis for evaluating experience and behavior. The negative feelings, discouragement, and conflicts typically experienced in early therapy sessions give way to increased hope and self-acceptance and ultimately to reaching out to others and living a more flexible, adaptable, existential, constructive, full-functioning life. This approach is particularly helpful for those who seem to have lost their sense of who they are, or who are troubled because of external or internal blockages of their growth.

Rogers, Perls, Maslow, and other humanistic psychologists contributed greatly to the growth of the human potential movement, which promoted sensitivity training, encounter groups, and other forms of growth groups and workshops. Such notions and emphases as the self, growth, free will, choice, autonomy, commitment, responsibility, awareness, positive self-regard, integration, congruence, authenticity, immediacy, encounter, and human potential are also common to group and institutional applications of the humanistic-existential approach.

## Context

The biological or medical model of human health had rapidly gained ascendance during and after the Renaissance, and it dominated psychopathology during the 1800's. This medical approach continues to be a well-established and even entrenched model; types of maladjustment or problems in living such as depression, anxiety disorders, eating disorders, and alcoholism are often viewed essentially and sometimes exclusively as diseases, notwithstanding limited evidence of biological factors in many instances of these disorders.

Within contemporary psychopathology, the first comprehensive psychologically oriented approach for conceptualizing abnormality was Sigmund Freud's psychoanalysis. This model, like the medical model, sees the person as a patient, is pathology centered, implies little free will, and offers limited responsibility and choice. It has been criticized as being reductionistic (a person is reduced to drives and intrapsychic conflicts), mechanistic (a person is viewed as a machine would be), deterministic (a person has little freedom in creating himself or herself), and pessimistic (a person is motivated by irrational forces, including instincts for aggression, unrestrained sexuality, and self-destruction). The psychoanalytic approach inadequately accounts for human potentials or existential concerns. Yet until the humanistic-existential approaches developed, the psychoanalytic was the predominant psychotherapy system available.

The classical conditioning work of Ivan Pavlov, the tremendous influence of John B. Watson, and B. F. Skinner's subsequent monumental contributions in instrumental learning led the behavioral approach to rival the psychoanalytic in explaining abnormality. Viewing psychopathology as the failure to learn adaptive responses or the learning of maladaptive ones, behaviorists utilize the scientific method with precise theoretical formulations and careful observation and measurement to test and advance their views. Their experimental approach, however, is also reductionistic (a person is reduced to stimulus-response bonds or a product of reinforcement history), mechanistic, and deterministic; Skinner disavowed freedom and even the possibility of dignity.

The humanistic-existential paradigm presented an alternative: a holistic, organismic, optimistic approach emphasizing innate growth tendencies, potentials, and freedom. Many instances of abnormality were viewed as failures to grow, and as resulting from perceived isolation and alienation in an increasingly technological and bureaucratic world, or as problems concerning values and meaning. In these cases, applying the other paradigms meant that people simply were not being understood or helped.

The humanistic-existential model emerged as a significant contemporary paradigm for explaining and treating psychopathology during the 1940's and 1950's, and became increasingly influential during the next two decades. Carl Rogers formulated client-centered therapy during the 1940's as an alternative to psychoanalytic techniques. Abraham Maslow devoted much of his professional life to the study of self-actualization. Ludwig Binswanger developed existential analysis during the 1940's; Rollo May and Irvin Yalom became highly influential developers of existential therapy. Fritz Perls's first book was published in the 1940's. Thus, both the humanistic and existential branches of this approach were developing simultaneously as coherent, interrelated perspectives.

Many humanistic and existential writers believe that their approach will be successful to the degree that their notions, emphases, and procedures are incorporated into the underlying attitudes, techniques, and approaches of the other major models. If this be the measure, then humanistic-existential writers have already been quite successful. From behavioral medicine to contemporary psychodynamic approaches to cognitive-behavioral strategies, many theorists and therapists have broadened their conceptualizing and enhanced the therapy process by incorporating at least some of the insights, concepts, techniques, and approaches championed by the major humanistic and existential writers. Given that the true origins of these insights and notions undoubtedly go back to the philosophers and religious leaders of antiquity, this important model has achieved another measure of success by penetrating to a large segment of the lay community. This paradigm points to and confronts dimensions of each person's existence and humanity that had previously been ignored by the other perspectives; in these ways, the humanistic-existential model has enhanced people's understanding of normality and abnormality, and of themselves.

## Bibliography

Fagan, Joen, and Irma Lee Shepherd, eds. *Gestalt Therapy Now.* Palo Alto, Calif.: Science and Behavior Books, 1970. Contains articles by several leading Gestalt therapists, who discuss the theory of this therapy approach, various Gestalt techniques, and applications. Includes a bibliography of Gestalt books and materials.

Frankl, Viktor Emil. *The Doctor and the Soul: From Psychotherapy to Logotherapy.* 2d expanded ed. New York: Alfred A. Knopf, 1965. Highlights how the spiritual and existential domains have been neglected by psychoanalysis and earlier therapeutic systems. Focusing on the "will to meaning," Frankl discusses the meaning of life, death, suffering, work, and love. Examines existential analyses of several types of psychopathology, and presents the therapeutic technique of logotherapy.

May, Rollo. *Power and Violence: A Search for the Sources of Violence.* New York: W. W. Norton, 1972. An existential analysis of power, self-affirmation, self-assertion, aggression, and violence. May argues that feelings of impotence, powerlessness, and insignificance underlie aggression and violence, and argues strongly against innocence and for power in terms of psychological and spiritual valuing of self, assuming responsibility, and acknowledging people's potentiality for evil.

May, Rollo, Ernest Angel, and Henri F. Ellenberger, eds. *Existence: A New Dimension in Psychology and Psychiatry.* New York: Basic Books, 1958. A historically important book that helped initiate existential psychology in America. The first two essays and some case studies (including that of Ellen West) are quite readable and rewarding, but some articles may be rather difficult reading.

Perls, Frederick S. *The Gestalt Approach and Eye Witness to Therapy.* Ben Lomond, Calif.: Science and Behavior Books, 1973. One of the better-written and more accessible of Perls's efforts to describe Gestalt therapy. Describes foundations, theory, and techniques; offers verbatim excerpts of filmed transcripts of introductory Gestalt work. Provides a good description of Perls's style and approach.

Rogers, Carl Ransom. *Client-Centered Therapy.* Boston: Houghton Mifflin, 1951. Rogers' first book on the person-centered approach to therapy is very readable and affords a good introduction. Includes discussion of the necessary therapist characteristics, the nature of the therapy relationship and the therapeutic process, theory of therapy, training of therapists, and applications in counseling, teaching, and administration.

Yalom, Irvin D. *Existential Psychotherapy.* New York: Basic Books, 1980. A clinically oriented book that describes abnormality in terms of how one deals with one's own mortality, isolation, lack of fulfilling potential, feelings of meaninglessness, and freedom. Also applies theory to clinical practice and examines implications of the approach.

*Edward R. Whitson*

## Cross-References

Abnormality: Cognitive Models, 46; Abnormality: Sociocultural Models, 82; Existential Analysis and Therapy, 999; Gestalt Therapy, 1088; Humanism: An Overview, 1203; Humanistic Trait Models: Gordon Allport, 1210; Person-Centered Therapy, 1777; Personology: Henry A. Murray, 1810; Self-Actualization, 2168.

# ABNORMALITY: LEGAL MODELS

*Type of psychology:* Psychopathology
*Field of study:* Models of abnormality

*The law assumes rationality. Abnormality is a departure from this rationality, including the incapacity to have criminal intent (insanity) and the inability to understand legal responsibilities (incompetence). The law protects citizens from those who are dangerous and protects harmless incompetents from themselves; psychological research has influenced a broadening of the "insanity" rule and a limitation on involuntary commitment.*

### Principal terms

CIVIL LAW: law that pertains to disputes between private individuals

CRIMINAL LAW: law that relates to offenses against the public order and punishment for such offenses

INCOMPETENCY: the legally established lack of sufficient knowledge and judgment to perform a given right or responsibility

INSANITY: the condition of having a mental disease or defect so great that criminal intent or responsibility and punishability are not possible

M'NAGHTEN RULE: the traditional insanity rule, which holds that a person incapable of knowing the nature, quality, and wrongfulness of his or her act is legally "insane"

MENS REA: the possession of intent to commit a crime; intent must be present as well as the legal offense itself before a punishable crime exists (literally, "guilty mind")

PARENS PATRIAE: the power of the state to act as guardian of those people who cannot take care of themselves (literally, "parent of the country")

POLICE POWER: the inherent responsibility of the state to protect the public from danger to persons and property

PSYCHOSIS: a mental condition involving distortion of universal assumptions about time, space, cause and effect, or "reality"

RATIONALITY: the capability of thinking logically so that one is aware of the consequences (rewards and costs) of actions

## Overview

In the United States, three broadly based legal principles and their elaboration by judicial interpretation (case law) and by legislatures (statutory law) reflect the law's core assumptions about normal and abnormal behavior. These principles are rationality, the protection of the incompetent, and protection from the dangerous.

The first of these concerns is the importance of rational understanding. The normal person is, the law assumes, sufficiently rational that the person can base his or her choices and actions upon a consideration of possible consequences, of benefits and costs. In the civil law, two people making a contract or agreement are expected to be "competent" to understand its terms. In the criminal law, a destructive act is deemed much worse and punishable if it is intentional and deliberate. Concern about motivation extends through the normal range of illegal acts, and offenses resulting from malice (that is, intentional offenses) are generally dealt with more harshly than those that result from mere negligence. Under the civil law, those incapable of understanding simple business transactions with ordinary prudence may be deemed "incompetent." Under the criminal law, in a principle that dates back to Roman times, persons who are deprived of understanding are considered incapable of intent and the corresponding guilty mind (*mens rea*). In the words of the 1843 M'Naghten rule (named for Daniel M'Naghten, also spelled McNaughton), if the accused is laboring under such a defect of reason from a disease of the mind as not to know the nature and quality of the act he was doing, or, if he did know it, he did not know what he was doing was wrong, then this accused person is "insane" and cannot be found guilty.

Two other basic legal principles justify society's special attention to helpless people and to dangerous people. The doctrine of *parens patriae* as early as 1324 authorized King Edward II of England to protect the lands and profits of "idiots" and "lunatics." Under this doctrine, the state may appoint a guardian for the harmless but helpless mentally ill—that is, those incapable of managing their ordinary business affairs. Since the mentally incompetent cannot make an informed decision about their need for treatment, the protection of the state allows the "commitment" of such people to hospitals, regardless of their own wishes.

The third doctrine which has been applied to the abnormal is the "police power" of the state. Inherent in the very concept of a state is a duty to protect its citizens from danger to their personal safety or property. This duty is considered to include the right to remove from society those abnormal people who are dangerous and to segregate them in institutions. In the United States, the laws of all fifty states authorize the restraint and custody of persons displaying aberrant behaviors that may be dangerous to themselves or others.

These principles of law, all based upon logically derived exemptions from assumptions concerning rational intent and understanding, have changed slowly in response to influences from the public and from the mental health professions. In institutionalization decisions, the *parens patriae* power of the state became more widely used beginning in the mid-nineteenth century as judges and the public became more accepting of the mental health enterprise. Hospitals were considered protective, nonstressful environments where the harmless insane would be safe.

In the decade of the 1960's, the arguments of critics of these views became widely known. Psychiatrist Thomas Szasz argued that mental illnesses were little more than crude metaphors for "problems in living," myths that were used, harmfully, to deprive individuals of their feelings of responsibility. Erving Goffman charged that institutionalization was a degrading, dependency-producing process. As a result of these criticisms, the institutionalization of individuals for their own welfare (*parens patriae*) became less common. Dangerousness became the major reason for involuntary commitment.

The insanity exemption from legal responsibility also has been adjusted and modified. The central concern of the professionals was that strict M'Naghten-rule "insanity" included only the small minority of offenders who had no understanding whatsoever that their offense was unlawful, the sort of offender who shot the victim thinking he was a tree. An offender could be mentally ill by psychiatric standards but still be considered sane. As a response to these criticisms, new legal tests that expanded the meaning of insanity were somewhat experimentally adopted by a few courts. The "irresistible impulse" rule, stating that a person would not be considered responsible if driven by an impulse so strong it would have occurred had there been "a policeman at his elbow," supplemented the M'Naghten rule in some states. In 1954, the federal courts, in the case of the *United States v. Durham*, adopted an even simpler rule: Insanity involves simply the illegal act being "the product of mental disease or defect." This Durham rule was quickly attacked for turning a legal decision over to mental health professionals, some of whom seemed to consider virtually all deviancy a disease. Stung by such criticisms, the federal courts, along with twenty-six states, adopted a rule proposed by the American Law Institutes (the ALI rule) that seemed to incorporate aspects of each of the preceding rules: Because of mental disease or defect (Durham rule), the defendant lacks the substantial capacity to appreciate the criminality of his or her conduct (a softening of M'Naghten "know"), or to conform this act to the requirements of law (the substance of the "irresistible impulse test").

As a result of public fears that manipulative villains would use the insanity defense as a way of escaping punishment, some states have adopted the alternative of allowing "guilty but mentally ill" verdicts or abolishing the insanity plea entirely.

## Applications

Abstract models of abnormality represented in the law often present many complexities when applied to an actual case. Before such concepts as insanity or dangerousness can be implemented, many commonsense and often implicit assumptions are added to the legal definitions.

Studies of the deliberations of mock (simulated) juries and the decisions of real juries in various types of cases suggest that a successful insanity plea would have a number of characteristics. The offender would have a record of psychiatric contact before the offense, preferably hospitalization. His or her offense would not seem to make sense—that is, it would involve a trivial reward and poor or no planning. His or her stated reasons for the offense would sound fantastic to others. He or she would initially be found incompetent to stand trial. The crime with which he or she was charged would not be murder and especially would not be seen as a heinous offense. Curiously enough, most of these factors are considered by juries regardless of the legal rule in effect. Most of the factors are involved in the 80 percent of all successful insanity pleas which seem sufficiently clear that they are not contested by the prosecution. Most defendants found not guilty by reason of insanity remain in mental institutions as long as they would have otherwise served in prison if convicted.

A case that displays most of the ambiguities that sometimes occur in the process, and that shifted public opinion against the legitimacy of the insanity plea, was the trial of John Hinckley, a young man who attempted to assassinate President Ronald Reagan and gravely wounded Reagan's press secretary. Hinckley's act had many of the elements of an "insane" one. Hinckley identified very closely with a character in a popular motion picture, a loner who stalks the president and engages in a rescue attempt that ends in a bloody gun battle. So involved was Hinckley with the film that he seemed controlled by his fantasy and unaware of his own identity. Diagnosed a schizophrenic, a condition in which fantasies cannot be separated from reality, he had wandered aimlessly for years and had consulted psychiatrists. On the other hand, he had clearly planned the act, bought special bullets, and given every indication he knew the act was illegal. Under strict M'Naghten-rule standards, he would probably have been found to "know" right from wrong. Under the more liberal ALI standard, however, it was felt that he both had a mental disease and was driven to the act by his fantasy; he lacked the capacity to conform his behavior to the law. He was found "insane" and committed to locked facilities in a hospital.

Aside from illustrating the complexity of an actual case at law, the Hinckley case illustrates an implicit assumption of the public: A notorious offense against a popular leader seems to justify punishment. In other famous cases, the offenders appeared clearly schizophrenic as well, but "insanity" was not used successfully as a defense. Serial killer David Berkowitz received instructions from a dog; Herbert Mullin killed at random whenever instructed by mysterious voices. Both were found sane in spite of obvious symptoms. Heinous crimes seem to require punishment regardless of the mental state of the offender.

The investigation of the meaning of the term "dangerousness" offers an example of how a term can be operationalized by experience. This term has been elaborated by the laws of the various states. It usually includes dangerousness against oneself as well as others. It can include threats against the property of others or even, sometimes, unintended harm caused by incompetence. A retarded person wandering onto a busy highway might be a case of this last condition. Often the word "dangerousness" is used in connection with other aberrant behavior.

John Monahan, refining the word "dangerousness" to imply the prediction of future violent behavior, has reviewed several studies that have spoken to the question of the accuracy of such predictions. If one excludes that minority of such individuals who have already committed violent acts, the post hospitalization rate of violent acts of former mental patients seems approximately similar to the rate of violent acts in the public in general. In a typical study, offenders at a Massachusetts facility were evaluated for dangerousness by clinical examinations and by the careful construction of their life record. Of 435 released patients during a ten-year period, approximately 50 were evaluated as dangerous. The rate of commission of a new violent (assaultive) act was 35 percent among those predicted dangerous but only 8 percent among those judged nondangerous and ready for release: There was sufficiently more violence among the predicted group. This research was interpreted to indicate that such predictions could be made for groups. Nevertheless, two-thirds of those predicted as dangerous failed to commit another violent act during the five-year follow-up period. But for a judicial order, they would have been incarcerated for what a team of mental health evaluators had to say about their potential—for what they were expected to do in the future. It should be added that among the most valid predictors was the presence of overt violent acts in the past.

## Context

Legal models of abnormality were formulated in Western civilization many centuries before psychology existed as a science. The models were based upon principles concerning human beings that evolved in folk wisdom and in religion. The normal person was expected to be able to undertake important actions intentionally and to be aware of the consequences. Abnormality was any condition that involved the incapacity to make intentional decisions with awareness of the consequences. There was, by necessity, a sharp dividing line between the normal and abnormal, as a lack of competence made an agreement invalid. The degree of rationality needed was a minimal one involving only an understanding of the direct and immediate consequences of an act. The rest of the law concerning abnormality involved two additional considerations: the protection of the harmless insane, and protection of citizens from those who were "dangerous." For centuries, the legal system merely fine-tuned these basic principles: The M'Naghten rule expressed proof of the lack of criminal intent more precisely; state laws often provided in greater detail just what was meant by dangerousness.

The legal model evolved as a separate system and was little influenced by the academic psychology of the early twentieth century. Since about 1950, the legal model has been influenced by some general insights from the behavioral sciences. The broadening of the insanity rule and the narrowing of the justification for institutionalization were the direct effects of such influences.

Psychological models of abnormality, in contrast to legal models, tend to be less narrowly focused on thinking processes, look for causes and consequences that are hidden or far removed, and see abnormality as a matter of degree. Almost inevitably, psychological models are biased against seeing a criminal action entirely as the result of a decision made a few minutes before and in favor of determination by external events. A few psychologists have publicly extended the concept of mental illness to cover such conditions as "television intoxication." Public reactions to broadening the concept of abnormality, along with the Hinckley case, have led to pressures to eliminate the insanity defense altogether.

Psychology is well positioned to continue its contributions to legal models by helping to make clear the meaning of legal terms which sometimes imply predictions or refer to quantifiable dimensions. The skills involved in "competence to stand trial" or "legal responsibility" have been quantified in standardized interviews that yield numerical scores. This can bring greater objectivity to a process that has largely been intuitive. A better than chance prediction of future violent acts can be made only for those who have already committed violent acts. Further study of these violent actors might advance understanding of motivational factors that lead to the repetition of violence.

Psychological criticism of the legal system is sometimes little more than disguised criticism of the assumption of free will and responsibility on which the law is based. Psychology (and other behavioral sciences) generally looks for causes of external events that are far removed from the point at which individual decisions are made.

The law, on the other hand, assumes that an individual can at any given moment exercise a choice, "free will." Any foreseeable consequences that come from that choice are "caused" by the individual who makes it. The assumption of free choice and responsibility found in the law is an assumption necessary to an ordered system of justice. For this reason, rational intent will continue to be an intrinsic part of the law, as will special treatment for those who lack the capacity to make this choice.

## Bibliography

Bartol, Curt R. *Psychology and the American Law.* Belmont, Calif.: Wadsworth, 1983. Reviews both the criminal law and the civil law as they deal with concepts of competence, dangerousness, and legal responsibility. Contains a thorough presentation of the historic origin of the rules pertaining to civil commitment. Chapters 4 and 5 are particularly relevant. Written on an introductory level.

Golding, S. L., and R. Roesch. "The Assessment of Criminal Responsibility: A Historical Approach to a Current Controversy." In *Handbook of Forensic Psychology*, edited by Irving B. Weiner and Allen K. Hess. New York: John Wiley & Sons, 1987. Traces the history of the "guilty mind" requirement for criminal responsibility and finds that recurrent public pressures to restrict the insanity defense follow well-publicized and dramatic cases at widely different historic periods.

Monahan, J. "The Prediction of Violent Behavior: Developments in Psychology and Law." In *The Master Lecture Series: Psychology and the Law*, edited by C. James Scheirer and Barbara L. Hammonds. Vol. 2. Washington, D.C.: American Psychological Association, 1983. Reviews the arguments for psychologists to play a role in predicting violence, and the evidence on how well this can be done. The conclusion is that predictions of violent behavior tend to predict a considerable amount of violence that never occurs. Relevant because "dangerousness" is the primary reason for involuntary commitment.

Slovenko, R. "Civil Competency." In *Handbook of Forensic Psychology*, edited by Irving B. Weiner and Allen K. Hess. New York: John Wiley & Sons, 1987. Reviews the legal requirement of competency to sign a contract, consent to a medical procedure, make out a will, serve as a witness, and stand trial. As important as competence is in the civil and criminal law, treatments of the topic in a basic work are rare.

Szasz, Thomas Stephen. *Law, Liberty, and Psychiatry.* New York: Macmillan, 1963. A discussion of what Szasz considers the "psychiatrization" of the law. Argues that due process protections and responsibility are eroded by loose "mental illness" standards. Well written, one-sided, somewhat polemical in style. Very readable and informative.

Weiner, Irving B., and Allen K. Hess, eds. *Handbook of Forensic Psychology.* New York: John Wiley & Sons, 1987. Twenty-six chapters, each written by an expert in the variety of areas related to psychology and the law. In addition to chapters cited separately here, chapters on the competence of juries, competency to stand trial, diminished responsibility, predicting violence, and psychotherapy with criminal offenders are relevant. Sometimes heavy going, but worth it.

Wrightsman, Lawrence S. *Psychology and the Legal System.* Monterey, Calif.: Brooks/ Cole, 1987. Contains a review of the legal rules concerning insanity, placed in a historical context, and the rules pertaining to civil commitment. Particularly strong in summarizing a number of court cases in which the insanity defense was employed and in reviewing current arguments for and against this defense. Written on the level of a college introductory text.

*Thomas E. DeWolfe*

## Cross-References

Abnormality: Behavioral Models, 33; Abnormality: Biomedical Models, 39; Abnormality: Humanistic-Existential Models, 60; Abnormality: Psychodynamic Models, 74; Abnormality: Sociocultural Models, 82; Abnormality Defined, 89; Law and Psychology, 1413.

# ABNORMALITY: PSYCHODYNAMIC MODELS

*Type of psychology:* Psychopathology
*Fields of study:* Models of abnormality; psychodynamic and neoanalytic models

*Psychodynamic models of psychopathology contribute much to the investigation of abnormality and to the study of personality in general. The psychodynamic view pivots around the strong influence of the unconscious and internal psychological conflict on human emotions and behavior and in the development of psychiatric disorders. Neoanalytic models such as ego analytic, ego psychology, and self/object relations models have gained increasing popularity.*

### Principal terms

CONVERSION DISORDER: a disorder in which unconscious conflicts are transformed into physical symptoms such as blindness, loss of function, or paralysis

DEFENSE MECHANISMS: coping strategies that distort reality to some degree and are used to deal with anxiety aroused by internal conflict

EGO: the fundamental part of the mind that mediates among the reality of the world, id forces, and superego forces

FIXATION: an inability to progress to the next level of psychosexual development because of overgratification or undergratification of desires at a particular stage

ID: the part of the mind that operates on the pleasure principle: contains unconscious biological drives for sex, hunger, and aggression

IDENTIFICATION: the internalization of parental or societal values, behaviors, and attitudes

NEUROSIS: a disorder caused by internal conflict generated by the conflicting internal forces of id, ego, and superego; also called anxiety disorder

PSYCHOSEXUAL STAGES: the stages of psychosexual (personality) development; they are the oral, anal, phallic, latency, and genital stages

REGRESSION: a coping strategy or defense involving the return to an early, more primitive developmental stage

SUPEREGO: the process in the mind that is commonly thought of as one's conscience

## Overview

Psychoanalytic theory forms the basis for the psychodynamic model as developed by Sigmund Freud in the early 1900's. Freud and the other psychodynamic theorists of his time believed strongly in the principle of psychic determinism. This principle is founded on the belief that men and women are not free to choose their behaviors;

rather, behaviors, both normal and abnormal, are determined or caused by a combination of intrapsychic forces, which Freud named the id, ego, and superego. These processes interact in the execution of internal mental activities that are both conscious and unconscious. Unsuccessfully resolved conflicts within the mind can lead to abnormal behavior. The ego, which operates on the reality principle, must negotiate between the desires generated by the id, the controls of the superego, and the demands of the real world. Successful negotiation can be illustrated by the following example. An ice cream truck drives through Michelle's suburban neighborhood every day at dinner time. Michelle's parents have forbidden her to buy a Popsicle, however, because it will ruin her appetite. Michelle approaches her parents and says, "Can I buy a Popsicle now and put it in the freezer until after dinner? I promise I will clean my plate." In this example, the ego has arrived at an acceptable compromise between the id, which operates on the pleasure principle ("I want the Popsicle now") and the superego or conscience ("Mom and dad will be angry at me unless I wait until after dinner"). Partial or incomplete resolution of internal conflicts are thought to lead to psychopathology.

In 1905, Freud proposed that personality development progresses through a series of "psychosexual stages." Disorders such as schizophrenia, according to some psychoanalytic theorists, are thought to be a result of an individual's "regression," or return to an earlier, more primitive level of psychosexual development, such as the oral stage. This regression can signal that the patient is not ready to cope with the demands of adult sexuality or responsibility and may be unconsciously designed to elicit caregiving or nurturing from others. Some psychoanalysts have advocated a type of "reparenting therapy" to encourage resolution of early conflicts about being cared for and to encourage the patient to return to higher developmental levels of functioning. In the case of schizophrenia, symptoms such as symbolic language and bizarre gestures may represent the patient's distorted attempt to communicate the underlying conflict or trauma. Some patients who have experienced schizophrenic regression and withdrawal and recovered have reported that they knew people were talking to them but could not respond or look at them because of overwhelming fears, such as that the world would end. The intense, overwhelming anxiety and the accompanying difficulties in being able to communicate with others often make it more difficult to reach out to the individual who is suffering. The book *The Eden Express* (1975), by Mark Vonnegut, presents a personal account of the experience of developing schizophrenia and recovering from the disorder.

Many professionals believe that some major psychiatric disorders such as depression and schizophrenia result from both internal psychological conflict or trauma and biochemical changes or abnormalities. Combination treatments that utilize psychotropic medication to calm the overwhelming anxiety or treat the depression can often make the patient better able to benefit from psychodynamic therapies. Depression, according to psychoanalysts, may result from anger turned inward on the self. The self forms a love attachment to an idealized other in a close relationship; when the relationship is over, that part of the self that identified and internalized the image of the other turns the anger of rejection in on those parts of itself. Psychodynamic interventions would seek to help the depressed person release this anger in appropriate ways rather than internalize it.

The development of some personality disorders or traits are thought to have origins in the early (pregenital) psychosexual stages. Freud hypothesized that toilet training that was too harsh or too lax could lead to "fixation" in the anal stage. If someone became fixated at this or any other pregenital stage, Freud believed that he or she would be thwarted in achieving mature personality development. He proposed the "anal character" (such as the obsessive-compulsive personality) to describe an adult who may be excessively sloppy or neat, depending on the nature of the toilet training the person experienced. Similarly, the oral character is a person who was fixated at the oral stage and may show symptoms such as chain smoking, overeating, or other excessive oral habits. Although this idea is intriguing, there has been little empirical support for these hypotheses.

Some of the anxiety disorders are thought to originate in the phallic stage. For example, a little boy who develops a phobia or irrational fear of adult men might have been thought to have displaced the castration anxiety he had experienced from his father to all adult men. The internal conflict related to sexuality results in anxiety and avoidance. If the central conflict of this period was resolved successfully, the child would progress to the next stage of development, the latency period. Partial resolution of any of the conflicts associated with the stages could lead to other psychiatric disorders. Freud believed that conflicts over sexuality and traumatic experiences would be repressed or eliminated from conscious awareness because they were too unpleasant and caused too much tension and anxiety if the person became conscious of these memories or thoughts. This reliance on repression can lead to dissociative disorders such as fugue states or multiple personality disorder, in which entire periods of a person's life are blocked out of conscious awareness. Although there is controversy over the existence of multiple personality disorder, a dissociative disorder in which alternate identities are formed through dissociation and a form of self-hypnosis as a defense against abuse or trauma, many clinicians believe they have treated individuals with this disorder.

Freud's last stage of development, the genital stage, represents the highest level of psychosexual development. Adults who have successfully negotiated the tasks of this stage are able to sublimate sexual and aggressive energy. Sublimation refers to the ability to channel these energies into socially acceptable activities. In this stage, mature sexuality and altruistic (nonselfish) love evolve. Persons who can function normally are thought to have reached this level of development; however, Freud believed that even emotionally healthy people use defense mechanisms to cope with anxiety.

Anna Freud, his daughter, further developed and refined the list of defense mechanisms that were originally proposed. Each time one uses a defense mechanism, however, one gives up or distorts a little of the true reality one experiences. For example, a college student fails to attend class regularly, thinking he or she can pass the course anyway, but flunks the first test. The student then says to his or her roommate, "I would have passed the exam if the professor had given a fair test." In this example, the student uses the defense of denial, essentially disregarding his or her failure to attend class as a contributing factor in the poor academic outcome. It also demonstrates rationalization, or making up an excuse that is not accurate but is acceptable to one's self-esteem.

Freud treated the neurotic or anxiety disorders exhibited by his patients with the method of psychoanalytic psychotherapy. Clients, or patients, as they were referred to then, would lie on a couch, with Freud seated at the head, looking away from the client. Then the first step of psychoanalysis, called free association, would begin; the patient was encouraged to say anything that came to his or her mind. Each thought or memory was believed to trigger subsequent memories and tap into the stream of unconscious thought. During the free association period, early childhood experiences were relived and their anxiety was released in a process called catharsis. This represented a cleansing of the mind through the release of repressed (forgotten) traumas. Repression, previously mentioned, is a defense mechanism that has a central place in psychodynamic theory; it is thought to occur at the unconscious level to block memories that are too painful for the person to remember. Freud used the psychoanalytic technique to treat a common disorder of the times, which was then called "hysteria." This disorder was thought by Freud to be caused by repressed memories that led to the expression of various symptoms such as temporary loss of vision, temporary paralysis, and anxiety.

The psychoanalytic model and the method of psychoanalysis have been criticized for several reasons. Neo-Freudians considered the psychodynamic model to be too focused on psychosexual development, determinism, sexuality, and aggression; however, most did believe that the model was viable for explaining the development of various psychiatric disorders. Psychoanalysis, as a method of treatment, has been criticized as being too time-consuming and expensive, often taking years to accomplish its goal. Proof of its effectiveness as a therapeutic approach has not been unequivocally documented by outcome research. Neoanalytic theorists (or ego psychologists, as some have been termed) developed psychodynamic theory further to focus more on the development of the self. Important contributors to modified versions of psychodynamic theory were Carl Jung, Alfred Adler, Karen Horney, and Harry Stack Sullivan. Important ego psychologists included Heinz Hartmann and Erik Erikson. Margaret Mahler, Heinz Kohut, Melanie Klein, James Masterson, and Otto Kernberg have also been contributors to self or object relations theory, another psychodynamic stage theory that refers to the development of mental representations of one's emotional attachments to significant others.

## Applications

Psychoanalytic models have had widespread influence on the field of psychology and have strongly influenced contemporary thinking, especially in the area of marketing to consumers. Although there has been mixed empirical support for the advertising technique referred to as "subliminal persuasion," this technique has been used to market products to consumers in the form of subliminal messages flashed on television screens, subliminal audio messages played over piped-in music in stores, and pictures secretly embedded in magazine ads. Subliminal persuasion is designed to influence the unconscious mind in order to get people to purchase certain products without their conscious or direct awareness. Subliminal messages are also used in self-help programs produced on audio cassette tapes to help people relax or to raise their self-esteem. The unconscious subliminal messages are embedded in background sounds such as music and are not audible to the listener.

The most direct applications of the psychodynamic model have been in the ability to understand psychopathology and personality development. The use of this model to develop forms of short-term psychodynamic psychotherapy has played a significant role in the area of psychotherapy. Short-term therapy refers to a treatment approach that is more focused and goal-oriented than traditional, classical psychoanalysis, with a maximum time limit of twenty sessions or six months. This approach has been popular with third-party reimbursement agencies such as insurance companies, who often impose limits on reimbursement.

The following case example illustrates the use of short-term psychodynamic treatment of a conversion disorder. Michael had been playing ball with a friend when the friend ran out into the street to retrieve the ball. The friend was hit by a car and became paralyzed and confined to a wheelchair. After a few weeks, Michael, who had been traumatized by witnessing the event and who felt guilty about having thrown the ball, lost the function of his legs and became unable to walk. Physical examination showed no organic cause for his paralysis, and he was referred to a psychodynamic therapist. A complete history was taken, which included recent events. His parents reported the incident with his friend; Michael, however, had repressed it and did not recall what had happened. One day in a therapy session, Michael noticed a picture in the office of a famous baseball player. He then remembered for the first time witnessing the accident (a memory he had previously found too anxiety provoking). After several more sessions in which Michael expressed his guilt and remorse over the accident, he began to realize that he did not intentionally want his friend to be hurt. Sometime later, Michael regained the use of his legs. The treatment took two months, with weekly one-hour sessions. In this case, the symptom of paralysis of Michael's legs represented the unconscious conversion of his intense internal anxiety into a physical symptom. The memory lapse for the incident represented repression and dissociation.

Art therapists have used psychodynamic models to understand the meaning underlying artwork created by emotionally disturbed children. This application is often referred to as art therapy or expressive therapy. The "kinetic house, tree, person" drawings and "draw a person" tests utilize principles of art therapy based on psychoanalytic theory as the basis for interpreting the drawings and discovering the developmental level and psychological defenses of the child. Determining the presence of unconscious conflicts such as a child's difficulty with aggressive or sexual impulses has also been accomplished with these interpretive methods.

Hilde Bruch studied eating disorders, particularly anorexia nervosa and bulimia nervosa, for three decades and was a proponent of the ego-analytic approach to explain the underlying problem central to eating disorders. Bruch believed that the central problem in individuals with eating disorders was the failure to develop an autonomous self. According to her theory, women with anorexia seek to control their bodies as a substitute for their lack of control in making their own decisions and because they have not been able to develop mature ego functions as a result of parental overprotection or domination. Bruch's work has had a significant influence on the successful treatment of clients with eating disorders and represents a lasting contribution to the field of psychology.

## Context

Sigmund Freud has been described as the father of psychoanalysis, the forerunner of modern psychotherapy. He originally studied hypnosis and trained under Josef Breuer. Freud was educated as a physician, with a specialty in neurology; he was also influenced by the theories of Charles Darwin, particularly *The Descent of Man* (1871). Freud's heritage was Jewish, and he was originally from Germany. He fled Germany to escape the Nazis, an event that undoubtedly had a strong influence on his perspective. He settled in Vienna, Austria, which became the seat of development of many psychoanalytic theoreticians of late Victorian times; however, because of the social setting (upper-middle-class Vienna) and the time period (Victorian), Freud's theories met with strong objection. Particularly offensive was his focus on infant sexuality as well as adult sexuality. During this period, society in Vienna was very strict and repressive regarding sexuality. Women, especially, were discouraged from expressing or even acknowledging sexual desires and impulses. The society was strongly patriarchal, with the male head of the household holding a dominant position of authority, under which the wife and children were seen as possessions. Thus, Freud's theory was not popular with the public; in fact, it was originally rejected by other professionals as well.

The Neo-Freudians, dissatisfied with the deterministic approach of psychoanalytic theory, began to branch out and broaden the psychodynamic perspective. Carl Jung, a Swiss psychiatrist, believed that Freud's theory was too negative and narrow. Jung proposed that the mind houses a "collective unconscious" that consists of archetypes, which are symbols of the experience common to all humans. In addition, Jung's therapy operated on the integration of conflicting or opposite aspects of the self, such as masculinity and femininity.

Another contemporary and colleague of Freud, Alfred Adler, disagreed with the part of drive theory that emphasized sexuality. Adler preferred to emphasize the ego, or the self, and one's relationships to others and society. He believed that humans suffer from feelings of inferiority, and thought that the important drive determining actions is a drive for dominance over others. In the early and mid-1900's, Harry Stack Sullivan and Karen Horney continued this emphasis on the importance of social relationships, specifically the importance of the parenting relationship. They suggested that poor parenting during early childhood leads to anxiety and poor self-concept in later adult years.

In this same period, Heinz Hartmann, credited with being the founding father of the contemporary school of ego psychology, proposed the existence of the "conflict-free sphere" of ego functioning. Hartmann believed that the ego not only negotiates between the opposing forces of the id and superego but also has independent, free functions of its own. Erik Erikson developed a theory of psychosocial development that outlined and defined the formation of "ego identity" achieved through a conflict resolution of crises presented at eight stages of development. For example, in the first stage, from birth to age two, the child has to learn whether it can trust its caretakers. If not, the child will have a basic mistrust that will influence subsequent development and relationships.

Margaret Mahler has been one of the most influential object relations theorists. Object relations are defined as the mental representations of one's emotional attachments to significant others. Mahler developed a stage theory that outlines the development of the psychological birth of an individual. The stages are autism, symbiosis, separation-individuation, and on-the-way-to-object-constancy. The end product of the progression through these stages is an individual who can function independently and hold mental representations of others as whole persons with both good and bad qualities. Mahler's separation-individuation stage has been one of the most important contributions to object relations theory; children who do not complete the tasks of the stage will never develop into fully independent adults. Object relations approaches and short-term psychodynamic therapy are widely used to treat individuals who suffer from personality disorders.

## Bibliography

Bootzin, Richard R., and Joan Ross Acocella. *Abnormal Psychology: Current Perspectives.* 5th ed. New York: Random House, 1988. This abnormal psychology text reviews the psychoanalytic perspective in clear, understandable terms with meaningful examples. In the section on psychiatric disorders, the contribution of the psychodynamic model to underlying cause and to treatment of certain disorders is explained.

Bruch, Hilde. *The Golden Cage: The Enigma of Anorexia Nervosa.* Cambridge, Mass.: Harvard University Press, 1978. Bruch explains the central dilemma in anorexia as a failure in the autonomous or independent development of the self. Her work is based on clinical experience, and the case examples show the reader the reality of anorexia and its impact on individuals and their families.

Vonnegut, Mark. *The Eden Express.* New York: Praeger, 1975. A personal description of the experience of developing schizophrenia. Gives readers insight into the dynamics underlying some cases of the disorder.

Wertheimer, Michael. *A Brief History of Psychology.* New York: Holt, Rinehart and Winston, 1970. Provides a brief historical overview of various approaches to psychological study including gestalt, behavioral and psychodynamic. The facts regarding the history of each movement are concise and interesting.

Willerman, Lee. *Psychopathology.* New York: McGraw-Hill, 1990. Provides a general introduction to psychopathology, with a fairly sophisticated discussion of theoretical facets of abnormality, psychiatric disorders, and their treatments.

*Karen Wolford*

## Cross-References

Abnormality: Behavioral Models, 33; Abnormality: Biomedical Models, 39; Abnormality Defined, 89; Behavioral Assessment and Personality Rating Scales, 387; Borderline, Histrionic, and Narcissistic Personalities, 441; Feminist Psychotherapy, 1025; Psychoanalytic Psychology: An Overview, 1905; Psychosexual Development, 1969.

# ABNORMALITY: SOCIOCULTURAL MODELS

*Type of psychology:* Psychopathology
*Field of study:* Models of abnormality

*A sociocultural approach to abnormal psychology examines how cultural factors determine what behavior is labeled abnormal within different societies; in addition, it investigates how societal values promote certain types of psychological abnormality.*

### Principal terms

CROSS-CULTURAL RESEARCH ON ABNORMALITY: a comparison of different cultures' practices of labeling behavior as abnormal
CULTURAL FACTORS: the standards and expectations of a particular society that influence the labeling of behavior as abnormal
PSYCHIATRIC DIAGNOSIS: the label applied to an individual whose behavior is thought to be the result of a specific mental disorder
STEREOTYPIC GENDER ROLES: a society's expectations of individuals' behavior based on their gender
STIGMATIZATION: the practice of discrediting or discriminating against someone because of a past or present psychological disorder

### Overview

A sociocultural viewpoint of abnormality is one of several approaches used in attempting to explain the causes of abnormal behavior. Unlike other approaches to abnormality, this perspective places great emphasis not only on the causes of abnormality but also on the reasons behind why certain behaviors are labeled abnormal. Supporters of this approach assert that cultural factors are at work within each society determining why certain behaviors are considered normal while others are not. Therefore, a sociocultural perspective uses research from areas such as anthropology, sociology, and political science as well as psychology in studying abnormality.

There is a large range of opinion regarding what should be considered abnormal behavior even among those who take a sociocultural viewpoint. Certain investigators consider the concept of psychological abnormality to be a complete myth. Thomas Szasz and R. D. Laing, both psychiatrists, are two examples of such individuals. Szasz, in *The Myth of Mental Illness* (1961), rejected the idea that people have mental illnesses in the same way that individuals have physical disorders such as cancer or heart disease. Szasz contended that behavior said to be the result of mental illness is nothing more than an individual's way of managing the problems of living.

R. D. Laing expressed a similar viewpoint and extended it to the condition of schizophrenia. Considered by most mental health professionals to be one of the most severe psychological disorders, schizophrenia is characterized by symptoms which include auditory or visual hallucinations (hearing voices or seeing visions of people or things not physically present), delusions (beliefs not based in reality), and deterioration in areas such as work or school, interpersonal relationships, and hygiene. Laing asserted that certain individuals enact these schizophrenic symptoms as a reasonable response to an unreasonable living situation. That is, individuals who are diagnosed as schizophrenic perceive their current environment as unlivable and face it by adopting schizophrenia. Laing concluded that these individuals are diagnosed as schizophrenic because of their violation of particular social standards, not because they have an underlying physical disease that causes their behavior (Richard Evans, 1976).

Most investigators who endorse a sociocultural view of abnormal behavior are not as radical as Szasz or Laing. More moderate advocates of a sociocultural perspective do not deny the existence of factors other than societal standards (for example, biological influences) that cause the development of abnormality. The goal of sociocultural researchers, however, is to illustrate how societal standards dictate what behavior is labeled abnormal.

Cross-cultural investigations are one way of examining the influence that societal factors have on determining the behaviors which are considered abnormal. Cross-cultural research has shown that societal factors are important in determining not only what is diagnosed as psychologically abnormal, but also what is labeled physically abnormal. For example, dyschromic spriochaetosis, a disfiguring disease characterized by multicolored spots on the skin, is so common among members of a South American tribe that those who do *not* have it were long considered abnormal. To a greater extent, societal standards also determine which behaviors are considered psychologically abnormal. For example, until recently, every winter near the southeastern Canadian region of the Saint Lawrence River, male residents of all ages engaged in a yearly ritual of clubbing to death baby seals for their pelts. Even though more humane ways were available to kill the seals, citizens of this region viewed clubbing the seals to death as normal because of the tradition surrounding the practice. This treatment of animals within most parts of American society would be considered cruel, and it is likely that those who participated in it would be labeled as abnormal. In summary, cross-cultural studies demonstrate that what is considered abnormal behavior differs across societies depending on the values and customs of a particular culture.

The sociocultural approach proposes that, across different societies, there are certain types of action likely to be viewed as abnormal. One type of conduct that is likely to be viewed as abnormal is behavior that violates societal expectations. Each society has expectations about what is appropriate and inappropriate behavior for a given setting. For example, if in the middle of a college lecture a student were to strip down to a bathing suit, most Americans would believe that this behavior was the result of a psychological disorder. If the same student were to undress in a similar fashion on a public beach, however, minimum disruption would occur, and few, if any, fellow sunbathers would consider this conduct abnormal. This example illustrates how a particular society's expectations regarding what is appropriate behavior for a particular situation determine what is considered normal or abnormal.

A second type of behavior likely to be termed abnormal is behavior that is disturbing enough to others that they want it changed (Leonard Krasner, Author Houts, and Leonard Ullmann, 1992). Children who are diagnosed as having attention-deficit hyperactivity disorder (ADHD) would fit this criterion. In the classroom, ADHD children have difficulty remaining seated and waiting their turns, often blurt out answers, talk excessively, and do not follow instructions. These behaviors are often so disturbing to their peers and teachers that children who engage in them are frequently referred to mental health professionals because they are considered abnormal and in need of treatment.

A final type of behavior that is likely to be labeled abnormal is behavior that appears irrational, self-defeating, or maladaptive. For example, imagine the reaction most people would have if they were to view a man walking along a downtown street, shabbily dressed and foul smelling, and talking to himself about Martian invaders sent to Earth to steal his mind. It is likely that most observers of this individual would consider him to be crazy. In this connection, persons who exhibit the symptoms of schizophrenia, as illustrated in this example, seem to most observers to be engaging in actions that are irrational and maladaptive.

## Applications

Researchers who advocate a sociocultural perspective are very concerned with the potential weaknesses and misuses of labeling certain people abnormal. Psychiatric diagnoses are obtained through a psychiatrist's or other mental health professional's labeling of someone as having a mental disorder based on that person's reported or observed behavior. In practice, diagnosing involves taking the reported and observed behavior of an individual and comparing it to the conditions listed in the American Psychiatric Association's *Diagnostic and Statistical Manual of Mental Disorders* (rev. 3d ed., 1987, DSM-III-R). The manual contains a sanctioned system for diagnosing behavior. A now-classic study conducted by David Rosenhan, "On Being Sane in Insane Places" (1973), demonstrated several potential problems with correctly diagnosing people as psychologically abnormal. In Rosenhan's experiment, he and seven associates from Stanford University presented themselves to mental hospitals under false identities and complained of hearing voices saying "empty," "hollow," and "thud." All eight were admitted to the hospitals; seven were diagnosed as schizophrenic, and the eighth person was diagnosed as having another severe psychological disorder. After being admitted to the hospital, the pseudopatients behaved as normally as they did before their admission and stopped complaining of hearing voices.

During their hospital stay, some of the patients recorded information in notebooks. This note-taking behavior, as well as other normal behavior, was listed in their medical records as further evidence of their mental disorder. In spite of their normality, the average patient was hospitalized for nineteen days and typically released with the diagnosis of "schizophrenia in remission." That is, although the pseudopatients did not exhibit schizophrenic behavior at the time of their discharge, they were labeled as having an underlying psychological disorder that could recur in the future. Rosenhan's study illustrates several potential limitations to declaring people abnormal. First, people are often labeled as abnormal with insufficient supporting evidence. Second, once a person is designated as abnormal, much of his or her behavior, whether otherwise normal or not, is seen as part of his or her abnormality. Third, the label of being abnormal is difficult to discard. That is, even though the pseudopatients were discharged, they were released carrying psychiatric diagnoses.

In addition to the potential problems with accurately diagnosing abnormality, the label of abnormality is often intentionally used to harm or discredit individuals. One graphic example of how the concept of psychological abnormality has been misused is the practice of leaders in some countries diagnosing political dissidents as mentally ill in order to banish them to psychiatric hospitals for "treatment," thus silencing their protests. Andrei Sakharov, regarded as a prominent nuclear physicist within the Soviet Union until he began to criticize the Communist party, wrote about how political opponents of the Communist government were often diagnosed as schizophrenic and sent to mental hospitals. Once hospitalized, these dissidents often were given powerful psychiatric medications and kept from the public as a means of quieting their protesting.

In America, individuals diagnosed with psychological disorders such as depression may be refused access to benefits such as health insurance and employment. In addition, those diagnosed as having mental disorders are often stigmatized. Stigmatization is the practice of discrediting or discriminating against someone because of having a past or present psychological disorder. An example of stigmatization occurred in the 1972 presidential campaign, when Democratic vice-presidential candidate Thomas Eagleton was pressured into withdrawing from the race because of the revelation that he had received treatment for depression.

In addition to pointing out the potential misuses of labeling someone as abnormal, sociocultural investigators are interested in identifying the larger societal influences responsible for creating behaviors that are labeled abnormal. Among these suggested sociocultural causes of abnormal behavior are factors such as stereotypical gender roles and poverty. Stereotypic gender roles are the types of behaviors and attitudes that are expected from individuals because they are either males or females. Each society has its own set of stereotypic gender roles. These expectations based on gender place both males and females at higher risk for exhibiting different types of abnormal behavior. For example, males are at much higher risk to develop pedophilia, a disorder characterized by recurrent sexual arousal toward children, and frequently accompanied by attempts to have sexual relations with children. A sociocultural perspective on pedophilia would highlight the cultural factors that promote pedophilia, such as society's frequent depiction of men as dominating women and children, and the belief that men have a right to satisfy their sexual desires even at the expense of others.

Women also are at greater risk for developing certain psychological disorders as a result of particular cultural factors. For example, women are approximately nineteen times more likely than men to develop anorexia nervosa. Anorexia nervosa is an eating disorder in which the individual is extremely underweight because of self-imposed starvation, sees herself as fat even though she is underweight, and is fearful of becoming obese. One prominent sociocultural factor that is suggested as making women more vulnerable to developing anorexia is society's emphasis on women being thin in order to be considered attractive. A study by David Garner and colleagues, published in 1980, illustrated this increased emphasis on thinness within today's society by analyzing the weight of women depicted in *Playboy* centerfolds from 1959 to 1978. The results of this analysis revealed that the average weight of the centerfolds decreased significantly over the twenty-year period. This finding indicated that the ideal woman, as defined by Western society, has become thinner even as the weight of the average American woman has continued to rise. Supporters of a sociocultural viewpoint state that these contradictory events have placed women under pressure to be thin even at extreme costs to their health and happiness.

Poverty is another sociocultural factor that places particular members of society at greater risk for developing psychological disorders. For example, children reared in impoverished environments experience an increased number of stressful events such as witnessing violence. This high level of stress increases the likelihood that these children will develop psychological disorders such as post-traumatic stress disorder (PTSD). PTSD develops as a reaction to a traumatic stressor (for example, witnessing the murder of one's parents) and consists of symptoms such as experiencing recurrent nightmares regarding the traumatic event, withdrawing from one's family and friends, and having difficulty concentrating.

## Context

The sociocultural approach to examining abnormal psychology was spurred on by criticisms made by Szasz and Laing in the early 1960's. Both these men had personal reasons to react against the practice of labeling people as psychologically abnormal. Laing was aware that some of his own personal experiences would be considered by many to be abnormal. For example, Laing reported that he was able to sleep one hour a night for a week's time, without the use of drugs, by altering his own state of mind. Laing also described his participation in mystical experiences of altered consciousness which he regarded as similar to a schizophrenic's hallucinations. Because of his own experience of altered states of mind and his realization of his normality, Laing was adamant in his denunciation of assigning labels to people whose behavior is different from that of the typical person.

More recently, those offering a sociocultural perspective on abnormality have grown concerned over the increase in the number of labels available to diagnose someone as having a mental disorder. From the introduction of the first edition of the *Diagnostic and Statistical Manual of Mental Disorders* in 1952 to its 1987 edition (DSM-III-R), the number of psychiatric labels roughly tripled, from approximately one hundred to three hundred. Not by coincidence, sociocultural advocates contend, the number of mental health workers has increased fourfold during the same approximate time period. This suggests that the rapid expansion of diagnostic labels has greatly added to the number of people who can be labeled abnormal, thus creating an increased market for more mental health professionals.

As a consequence of the proliferation in the number of diagnostic labels, the number of people being diagnosed as suffering from a mental disorder also has increased. Sociocultural advocates are concerned with this trend, given the possibility that someone may be discriminated against because of being diagnosed mentally ill. The potential stigmatization that could occur as a result of being labeled mentally ill should give all reason to reflect on the usefulness and validity of the current practice of psychiatric labeling.

In addition to its important criticism of the manner in which people are often diagnosed as abnormal, the sociocultural approach is useful in that it alerts individuals to societal pressures that might promote psychological disorders. An awareness of these societal pressures allows for the initiation of efforts to prevent the development of certain psychological disorders. For example, if it is acknowledged that society's overemphasis on thinness for women is behind certain women developing anorexia nervosa, then steps such as educational efforts within school systems can be taken to challenge the attitude that women must be thin to be attractive.

## Bibliography

Bayer, Ronald. *Homosexuality and American Psychiatry: The Politics of Diagnosis.* New York: Basic Books, 1981. A thorough examination of the politics involved in the removal of homosexuality from the official guide of psychiatric diagnoses (DSM-III). An important illustration of how political processes become involved in determining what behavior, in this case homosexuality, is designated normal or abnormal. Very readable work.

Brumberg, Joan Jacobs. *Fasting Girls: The Emergence of Anorexia Nervosa as a Modern Disease.* Cambridge, Mass.: Harvard University Press, 1988. Brumberg, a historian, presents the history of anorexia nervosa from a sociocultural perspective. This book provides an in-depth examination of how societal values operate to increase the prevalence of a specific psychological disorder. A well-researched and very readable book.

Evans, Richard Isadore. *R. D. Laing: The Man and His Ideas.* New York: E. P. Dutton, 1976. A series of discussions with Laing regarding his views on the concept of mental illness. In this readable work, Laing outlines his objections to the diagnostic and treatment approaches of the mental health establishment.

Krasner, Leonard, Author C. Houts, and Leonard P. Ullmann. *A Psychological Approach to Abnormal Behavior: Invention and Discovery.* Englewood Cliffs, N.J.: Prentice-Hall, 1992. This textbook differs from other abnormal psychology texts in that it examines each category of psychiatric disorders from a sociocultural perspective. Provides an excellent historical overview of the development of the concept of psychological abnormality. Also examines the politics involved in the decision-making process by which behaviors are labeled abnormal.

Offer, David, and Melvin Sabshin. "Culture, Values, and Normality." In *Normality and the Life Cycle*. New York: Basic Books, 1984. Provides an excellent sociocultural perspective on abnormality; it gives numerous examples from ancient and modern times regarding the influence of societal standards in dictating which behavior is labeled abnormal. A readable chapter.

Rosenhan, David L. "On Being Sane in Insane Places." *Science* 179 (January 19, 1973): 250-258. Provides the findings of a classic study investigating the pitfalls of labeling people as abnormal. Extremely well written, and easily understood even by psychological novices.

Szasz, Thomas S. *The Myth of Mental Illness*. New York: Dell Books, 1961. A classic work in which Szasz provides his objections to the concept of "mental illness." An ageless critique of the practice of psychiatric diagnosis; for the advanced reader.

*R. Christopher Qualls*

## Cross-References

Abnormality: Behavioral Models, 33; Abnormality: Biomedical Models, 39; Abnormality: Family Models, 53; Abnormality: Psychodynamic Models, 74; Anorexia Nervosa and Bulimia Nervosa, 259; Emotion: Cultural Variations, 887; Feminist Psychotherapy, 1025; Madness: Historical Concepts, 1492; Social Psychological Models: Erich Fromm, 2318.

# ABNORMALITY DEFINED

*Type of psychology:* Psychopathology
*Field of study:* Models of abnormality

*Abnormality means behavior, thinking processes, or feelings deemed undesirable and therefore subject to control or change. Differing points of view about theoretical orientation, tolerance for deviance, where to draw the line between normal and abnormal, and the use of labeling lead to differences in the criteria used for definitions. Important criteria include subjective discomfort, disability or inefficiency, and deviance, especially bizarre or reality-distorting deviance.*

### Principal terms

ANXIETY: a chronic fearlike state that is accompanied by feelings of impending doom and cannot be explained by a threatening object or event

BEHAVIORAL VIEW: a perspective that emphasizes understanding a person in terms of his or her objectively measured behavior; normal, in this view, is functioning well

DEVIANCY: the quality of having a condition or engaging in behavior that is different from the typical in a social group and is considered undesirable

DISTORTIONS OF REALITY: beliefs that distort universally accepted assumptions such as those about time, space, cause and effect, or life and death; delusions

MEDICAL MODEL: a view in which abnormality consists of a number of diseases which originate in bodily functions, especially in the brain, and have defined symptoms, treatments, and outcomes

NEUROSIS: a mild abnormality accompanied by moderate discomfort and impairment in functioning; a consequence of anxiety and rigid, play-it-safe behavior

PHENOMENOLOGICAL VIEW: a perspective that emphasizes understanding a person from his or her own viewpoint; normal, in this view, is feeling satisfied with oneself

PSYCHODYNAMIC VIEW: a perspective that emphasizes understanding a person in terms of how he or she copes with unconscious feelings and conflicts; normal, in this view, is understanding and controlling the feelings and conflicts

PSYCHOSIS: a severe abnormality accompanied by distortions in reality and breakdown of functioning

STATISTICAL DEFINITION: a definition of abnormality as a condition that is different from the average or mean of the characteristic or trait

## Overview

Abnormality is a term applied to behaviors, thinking processes, or feelings that are viewed by the individual and/or by society as undesirable and requiring control or change, and viewed as deficits which may or may not have a clear etiology but which should be compensated for by the individual and society. Psychologists or other mental health professionals are enlisted to test and/or interview individuals to determine whether a condition is abnormal, and to facilitate change or advise in delineating compensation. There are three typical standards, or criteria, that are used by mental health professionals to decide whether the condition is abnormal: discomfort, disability, and deviance.

The first two of these criteria have some similarity to the general indicators of a physical disease. Just as physical disease may be marked by pain, the major symptom that brings most private patients to a psychotherapist is a chronic psychological pain or discomfort. Just as a physical impairment, such as a broken leg, usually leads to problems in daily living, so the second condition that defines abnormality is some sort of difficulty in functioning, a disability or impairment. Both discomfort and disability are often evaluated by one's personal standards. One is feeling discomfort because of problems one knows best oneself, or one is inefficient compared to what one expects of oneself.

The third major criteria for abnormality, deviance, is based not on personal standards but on the standards of society. Deviance is behavior that is undesirably different from social expectations; such behavior is most likely to be considered psychologically abnormal if it is unpredictable, bizarre, or dangerous.

Each of these three major criteria that collectively define psychological abnormality can range greatly in quality and degree, and each summarizes a large number of symptoms and conditions. Any deviancy or discomfort is more likely to be defined as abnormal if disability or impairment in function is present. The impairment can be judged based on the typical performance of others, or it can be judged based upon the individual's own potential or subjective expectation. The impairment may sometimes be based on a physical condition such as retardation or brain injury. Even if the condition itself cannot be changed, a psychologist can help determine the degree of the problem and help facilitate useful compensations.

Although one can catalog the suggested criteria for abnormality, there are broad theoretical disagreements about which of these criteria should be emphasized in practice. For example, there are phenomenologists who argue that problems do not exist unless they are perceived by the individual and reflected in personal distress. There are behaviorists who argue equally vehemently that only overt behavior should be treated. Such theoretical differences are a primary reason for differences in definitions.

A second core issue is the quantitative one, the question of how much deviance, bizarreness, inefficiency, or distress constitutes "abnormality." Many of those who use the medical model assume a dichotomy between those who have a specific mental disease and the vast majority of normals who are disease free. An alternative view is that the dimensions defining illness are continuous ones ranging from abnormality through mere adequacy to equally rare degrees of supernormality.

Defining categories of deviancy as "abnormal" presents the particularly thorny problem of the relativity of cultural standards. The actions society considers deviant seem limited to particular cultures at particular times. For example, in Victorian times, young women who had children out of wedlock were sometimes committed to hospitals for the "morally insane." Such deviant actions of one generation may later be ignored or even approved by society. A common solution to this dilemma is to distinguish deviancies requiring correction and treatment from others. Deviancies that are dangerous, harmful to others, or accompanied by personal distress are examples.

A final issue pertains to the value placed on the defining process itself. According to the medical model, the definition of abnormality is all-important, central to understanding the cause of the disease and to planning treatment. Any disease should be diagnosed as soon as possible. A sharply contrasting view, held by some sociologists, is that defining, or labeling, has mostly harmful effects. Not only does labeling a person as abnormal relegate him or her to the stigma of being undesirably different, but the label itself creates a self-fulfilling prophecy as others pay particular attention to symptoms of the person's deviancy. The process is also challenged because it focuses on symptoms of the individual that may really result from difficulties in the family, the community, or even the society.

## Applications

Each criterion for abnormality referred to above can be applied to many varieties of abnormality, differing in quality and degree. One important feeling of discomfort is sadness, which is called "depression" when it is considered abnormal. Another typical feeling of discomfort is anxiety: a chronic, vague, fearlike feeling of impending doom. When depression or anxiety is chronic, intense, and interferes with functioning, it is much more likely to be considered abnormal than when it is the temporary or mild feeling everyone has from time to time. These feelings are also much more likely to be considered abnormal if there is no real-life stress or crisis to explain them.

Another major criterion of abnormality is deviance, characterized by a condition or behavior that is undesirably different from that of the significant cultural group. This is not necessarily the same as being statistically different from the average of the group, as one can be statistically different in unimportant or even desirable ways. (Wolfgang Amadeus Mozart and Albert Einstein were statistically different from the average.) Rather, deviance is always different in some significant way and is undesirable.

To classify conditions as psychologically abnormal simply because they are deviant is an expansive use of the concept of abnormality that is highly controversial. There are, nevertheless, particular types of deviants that are practically always thought of as abnormal, particularly those that seem bizarre.

The key discriminator, bizarreness, involves behavior, thoughts, or feelings that do not seem consistent with any recognized social role. The deviant individual may distort reality in that he holds beliefs that violate universal assumptions about time, space, selfhood, and cause and effect. Belief in bizarre plots, seeing things that are not there, or hearing imaginary voices are all examples of such distortions. It should be pointed out that this sort of behavior seems to be accepted as abnormal in practically every known culture, although some cultures have valued such bizarreness as religious experiences.

Definitional questions are involved whenever a psychologist considers the question of whether a patient is suitable for treatment and, if so, what sorts of treatment are appropriate. Typical cases sometimes involve the referral of a case that fits only one of the criteria above. A successful lawyer, married, with an attractive family, sees his career as one of only playing silly games. Adequate and conforming, he is abnormal only by the standard of subjective discomfort. A student promoted to the fourth grade seems conscientious and hardworking, but cannot seem to do much more than first-grade work. A psychologist finds that she tests within the retarded range of intelligence. Her problem is an impairment in functioning. A youth who has wounded an owner of a jewelry store during a robbery is interviewed by a psychologist in a detention center. He explains that he did not do anything wrong, really, because the store owner could have simply collected from his insurance company and should have minded his own business. This young man, who can easily rationalize almost any behavior, feels good about himself. He is abnormal in the sense of being deviant and dangerous.

Psychodynamic or phenomenologically oriented psychologists would consider the first patient ideal; behavioral psychologists might help the second develop useful compensations. The approach to the deviant would be largely a matter of external controls.

Most cases seen by psychologists would be abnormal by more than a single criterion. A young man who cannot start the day without a couple of shots of vodka begins developing family problems and staying away from work. He is both a deviant (alcoholic) and shows an impairment in functioning. A woman in a deep depression considers herself worthless and feels she is guilty of unforgivable sins. She also moves very slowly and has stopped eating. She experiences discomfort, shows impairment, and her feelings of guilt seem to distort reality. A middle-aged accountant becomes preoccupied with the fact that he feels estranged from his wife. He thinks so much about this that his performance ratings drop. Like most of the milder cases seen by mental health professionals, subjective discomfort here results in an impairment in efficiency.

Many symptoms that could be diagnosed from a psychiatric manual may not really be considered significant or abnormal if they do not interfere with the individual's functioning. A phobia concerning flying would not be significant for those who never travel; such a phobia might be highly significant for someone who has to travel in work.

Definitional questions are also involved in collective decisions of the American

Psychiatric Association (APA) when they revise their *Diagnostic and Statistical Manual of Mental Disorders* (DSM), first published in 1952. At each revision, new syndromes are proposed and borderline ones discussed. As the third edition was being prepared, homosexuality became the focus of a major controversy. Some psychodynamically oriented psychiatrists argued that homosexuality involves an impairment in mature sexual functioning, and so is inherently abnormal. The argument that homosexuals function adequately and sometimes extremely well in important areas of life and that any discomfort is largely the result of discrimination, however, prevailed. Homosexuality was removed from the DSM-III (1980) as a mental disorder.

## Context

Many professionals of the late twentieth century deal with an enormously varied assortment of problems. Definitions of abnormality offer a guideline as to what conditions should be treated in whom. In contrast, the pioneers of the mental health professions served limited groups of dramatically different populations in different settings.

One such limited group was the hospitalized psychotic population on which the medically oriented Emil Kraepelin, about 1900, commenced his work of classifying the behavior of patients. He hypothesized discrete diseases, each of which presumably had a specific course, outcome, and cause within the brain. Advocates of the medical model still hold that real abnormalities are brain conditions. Even in cases of such real brain impairment, it is usually behavior that reveals the abnormality.

Sigmund Freud, a pioneer of psychodynamic theory and a contemporary of Kraepelin, saw ambulatory middle-class patients who were suffering from anxiety and irrational rigidity in their behavior. Freud identified the causes as impulsive desires with various defensive strategies to keep these from awareness. The defining symptoms that brought the patients to Freud, however, were the anxiety (subjective discomfort) and the rigid, defensive behavior (impairment).

Around the middle of the twentieth century, phenomenologist Carl Rogers identified the basic problem of many of his bright young college students as a lack of self-esteem. This was caused, he believed, by the client's adopting of the artificial, unrealistic standards of others. Rogers paid attention to the client's subjective comfort, or inner attitude toward self. To the phenomenologist, a person, however deviant, who knows and likes himself, is normal. Rogers, like Freud, had faith in insight into oneself and the world "as it really is" as the key to normality.

About the same time in mid-century, the behavioral psychology of B. F. Skinner developed in the animal laboratory, and was applied to the treatment of humans. To Skinner, abnormality consisted of adjustive behavior that had not been learned (impairment) and maladjustive behavior that had been learned (deviance). Inner torment was not, to the behaviorist, a problem.

Definitions of abnormality allowed the practitioner to know the conditions appropriate for treatment and clarified the differences among practitioners. In the last years of the twentieth century, criticism from several sources has led to a fine-tuning of these definitions. The tendency to extend the illness model to many conditions when there is no hard evidence of brain pathology and to assert medical control over these conditions was challenged by Thomas Szasz. Sociologists pointed out the negative effects of labeling as well as the relevance of family and community problems that are defined by psychologists as individual abnormality. In contrast to widely held assumptions, research by Shelley Taylor and associates suggested that the most robust, altruistic people were not the most "realistic" and open to experience, but were rather biased toward a belief in their own good traits and good fortunes. Research and new technology in the field of medical psychology has led to an understanding of genetic or physiological components in conditions previously known only by behavior.

The mental health professions have begun to absorb this research and technology to extend an understanding of abnormalities outward to the community and inward toward underlying genetic or brain pathology. Criteria for the conditions which they define within the domain of psychology will remain the same: discomfort, disability, and deviance.

## Bibliography

Altrocchi, John. *Abnormal Behavior.* New York: Harcourt Brace Jovanovich, 1980. Practically every textbook of abnormal behavior contains a discussion of the definitional problem. Altrocchi's chapter 1 offers a particularly thorough discussion, put in the historical context of alternative nonmedical approaches to abnormal conditions. Written on the introductory college level.

Archer, D. "Social Deviance." In *Handbook of Social Psychology*, edited by Gardner Lindzey and Elliot Aronson. 3d ed. Hillsdale, N.J.: Lawrence Erlbaum, 1985. Chapter 26 presents a general review of deviance from the perspective of several sociologists. A discussion of the variety of conditions which are defined as deviant at different times and places, and the negative consequences of labeling. Puts the issue in a sociological perspective. Heavy going but worth it.

Jahoda, Marie. *Current Concepts of Positive Mental Health.* New York: Basic Books, 1958. Reviews and classifies the many different views of mental health, with an emphasis upon those offered by psychotherapists. Argues for attention to "psychological health," which Jahoda views as a "positive striving," not the mere absence of illness. Good as a review of the early literature on the specific problem of definition. Thorough, but some knowledge of personality theories helps.

Phares, E. Jerry. *Clinical Psychology: Concepts, Methods, and Profession.* 3d ed. Homewood, Ill.: Dorsey Press, 1988. Chapter 4 of this text for college psychology students contains a thorough description of standards for judging normality. These are discussed from the viewpoint of famous psychologists and applied to problems in psychological diagnosis. Cases of the sort found in clinical practice illustrate and help the reader comprehend the issues. Quite readable by the introductory-level student.

Wechsler, Henry, Leonard Solomon, and Bernard M. Kramer, eds. *Social Psychol-*

*ogy and Mental Health.* New York: Holt, Rinehart and Winston, 1970. Each of the first ten papers in this edited volume consists of arguments for one of the alternative definitions of abnormality, each by a leading proponent. The papers, particularly those for and against the medical model, are classics. One would otherwise have to comb many journals to find so many important papers from a variety of perspectives.

Widiger, T. A., and T. J. Trull. "Diagnosis and Clinical Assessment." In *Annual Review of Psychology* 42. Stanford, Calif.: Annual Reviews, 1991. This article applies a consideration of definitions of abnormality to the continuing problem of specifically what sorts of disabling or distressful conditions should be included in the APA's revised diagnostic manual. Shows that psychiatrists take the definitional issue seriously.

*Thomas E. DeWolfe*

## Cross-References

Abnormality: Behavior Models, 33; Abnormality: Biomedical Models, 39; Abnormality: Cognitive Models, 46; Abnormality: Family Models, 53; Abnormality: Humanistic-Existential Models, 60; Abnormality: Legal Models, 67; Abnormality: Psychodynamic Models, 74; Abnormality: Sociocultural Models, 82; Clinical Interviewing, Testing, and Observation, 527; Madness: Historical Models, 1492; Psychological Diagnosis and Classification: DSM-III-R, 1925.

# ACHIEVEMENT MOTIVATION

*Type of psychology:* Motivation
*Fields of study:* Motivation theory; personality theory; social motives

*The study of achievement motivation examines crucial ingredients in the accom-
plishment of desirable goals. Studies have included a wide variety of domains, and
new insights have been gained into factors involved in areas of accomplishment such
as academic achievement, economic and other work-related achievement, gender
differences regarding achievement orientation, and individual personality differences.*

*Principal terms*

ACHIEVEMENT MOTIVE: the tendency to strive for success or attain a
desired end
EXPECTANCY-VALUE THEORY: the perspective that achievement motivation
is predicted by expectancy of success in relation to expectancy of
failure, with consideration of values associated with each expectancy
EXTRINSIC MOTIVATION: engaging in activities for external reward
INTRINSIC MOTIVATION: engaging in activities for internal reward such as
enjoyment or satisfaction
PSYCHOANALYTIC THEORY: a set of theories conceived by Sigmund Freud
which see the roots of human behavior in unconscious motivation
and conflict
TRAIT THEORY: a way of conceptualizing personality in terms of
relatively persistent and consistent behavior patterns manifested in
a wide range of circumstances
UNCONSCIOUS BEHAVIOR: an activity in which an individual engages
without knowing the reason or motive for the action

## Overview

Achievement motivation can be understood simply as the tendency to strive for
success or the attainment of a desirable goal. Embedded within this definition are a
number of important implications. First, it is suggested that achievement motivation
involves an inclination on the part of the individual. Usually, this includes a consideration of the individual's personality and how that personality influences a motivational state given the presence of certain environmental factors. Second, achievement usually involves a task-oriented behavior that can be evaluated. Third, the task
orientation usually involves some standard of excellence that may be either internally
(by the person) or externally (by others) imposed.

Henry A. Murray, in his influential book *Explorations in Personality* (1938), conceived of personality as a series of needs which involve a "readiness to respond" in
certain ways under specific conditions. Largely influenced by Sigmund Freud's psychoanalytic theory of personality, Murray considered these needs to be primarily

unconscious. One of these needs is the need for achievement. Because these needs are largely unconscious, Murray decided that he could not use standard techniques such as questionnaires to measure them directly. He therefore developed the Thematic Apperception Test (TAT). The test involves relatively ambiguous pictures that should evoke from individuals, when asked to provide interpretations, themes reflecting underlying personality needs or characteristics.

With regard to achievement, four pictures are used (for example, one shows a boy looking into space with a violin on a table in front of him). Some interpretations are indicative of a high need for achievement (for example, "The boy is taking a break from his usual hard work of becoming an accomplished violinist"), while others indicate a low need for achievement (for example, "The boy wishes he were outside playing with his friends instead of having to practice"). The test itself, however, is not a particularly valid and reliable indicator of need for achievement and has therefore been frequently replaced by other techniques of measurement.

John Atkinson refined the concept of achievement motivation in 1957 by proposing the expectancy-value theory. This theory maintains that the strength of the achievement motive is determined by two opposing inclinations: a tendency to approach success and a tendency to avoid failure. The first tendency is manifested by engaging in achievement-oriented activities, while the second tendency is manifested by not engaging in such activities. Atkinson further specifies on what basis the strength of these two opposing tendencies can be determined. He suggests, first, that the expectancy, or perceived probability, of success or failure of the action is important. Second, he suggests that the incentive value of success and failure must be taken into account. By this, he means that the degree of pride in accomplishment versus the degree of shame in failure must be considered.

Several modifications were subsequently offered by Atkinson and others. For example, an important distinction between extrinsic motivation (engagement in a task for an external reward, such as a school grade or a pay raise) and intrinsic motivation (engagement in a task as a pleasure in its own right, with some standard of performance as a goal in itself) was developed to explain why some people may still engage in achievement activities, such as attending school or accepting a demanding job, even when their tendency to avoid failure is greater than their tendency to approach success. Though modifications have been necessary and some detailed predictions of the model have not been supported, the general expectancy value model has been helpful in understanding the achievement motive.

The concept of intrinsic motivation has particularly interested psychologists and has been the focus of work by Janet Spence and Robert Helmreich. They were concerned that the earlier work of psychologists on achievement motivation was too unidimensional, and suggested that intrinsic achievement motivation may be something more complex than simply a striving toward excellence for its own sake. Their thinking, based upon some initial research involving statistical analyses of collected data, was that achievement motivation is best conceptualized in terms of three dimensions: work orientation, mastery, and competitiveness. Spence and Helmreich also developed the Work and Family Orientation Questionnaire (WOFO) to measure each of these factors. Work orientation, the first factor, refers to the amount of effort one is willing to put in on a task to do a good job. People who strongly agree with statements such as "There is satisfaction in a job well done" or "It is important for me to do my work as well as I can, even if it isn't popular with my coworkers" from the WOFO would score high on this dimension. The mastery factor reflects a preference for an internally prescribed standard of performance and for difficult, challenging tasks. A person who would strongly disagree with statements on the WOFO such as "I would rather learn easy, fun games than difficult thought games" would score high in achievement motivation on this factor. The competitiveness dimension describes the enjoyment in interpersonal striving, such as the desire to be "number one."

Like Murray had in the 1930's, Spence and Helmreich reflected the mind-set of many psychologists in suggesting that the achievement motive should be considered in terms of general personality traits. Unlike Murray, however, who maintained that the need for achievement was a single need (or trait), Spence and Helmreich thought that achievement motivation consists of three traits (work orientation, mastery, and competitiveness). The idea that these are general personality traits is an important one because it means that the person should somewhat consistently reflect these traits regardless of the situation. Also, if these are personality traits, then people will normally not show sudden changes or major shifts as they grow older.

## Applications

Achievement motivation is an important psychological concept and is useful in explaining why some people are more successful in attaining goals than are others. In general, people with a higher need for achievement do better than their counterparts with a low need for achievement.

With regard to academic achievement in college students, it has been found that people with higher need for achievement have higher grade point averages (GPAs). In terms of the three dimensions of achievement recommended by Spence and Helmreich, the correlation between achievement motivation and GPA is a function of the work orientation and mastery factors. In one study, high-GPA students scored high on these two dimensions but surprisingly low on the competitiveness factor. Low-GPA students scored low on all three factors. The same pattern of results was found with fifth- and sixth-grade students in another study. Those with higher standardized achievement test scores were also higher on work orientation and mastery, but lower on competitiveness. Thus, it appears that, at least in relation to academic achievement, not all components of a high need for achievement correspond to better performance.

David McClelland and his associates have studied the relation of achievement motivation to vocational performance. His conclusion is similar to what is commonly found in much of the achievement literature: High achievement is generally a desirable trait that leads to more successful performance. In particular, it appears that entrepreneurs require a high need for achievement to function successfully. Again, however, a broad conclusion such as this may need to be qualified. Spence and Helmreich again question whether a competitive spirit is necessary or even helpful in attaining goals. For example, they found that highly competitive individuals, especially if they are also high in work orientation and mastery, make lower salaries than less competitive colleagues. While salaries may not be a complete measure of success, these results further imply that a competitive characteristic may actually result in lowered performance. Whether discussing academic or vocational performance, one must draw conclusions such as these cautiously since the underlying causes for this relationship are not yet fully understood.

One of the most interesting applications in the study of achievement motivation has involved gender differences. Achievement motivation in women may be a considerably different experience than it is for men. Most of the research conducted by McClelland and Atkinson during the 1950's and 1960's was with men only, in part on the basis of the belief that men need success and women need approval. With women's changing roles in society, however, the study of achievement motivation in women has flourished since the late 1960's.

Early research indicated that women show less need for achievement than do men. One explanation was derived from Atkinson's expectancy-value model, which suggested that women fear success out of concern for the negative social consequences they may experience if they achieve too much. An example would be a girl who lets her boyfriend win when they play tennis. In part, she may be concerned about his feelings, but she may also believe that she will be better accepted (by him and others) if she loses. While it is clear that some people, especially some women, may not find as much delight in winning as do others, subsequent research has suggested that some of the original conclusions may have been overstated. In fact, in terms of Spence and Helmreich's three-factor model of achievement motivation, it appears that the structure of men's and women's achievement motives are more similar than they are different. When sex differences do emerge, women tend to be slightly higher than men in work orientation, while men seem to be slightly higher in mastery and considerably higher in competitiveness.

McClelland has also attempted to demonstrate the potential benefits of increasing achievement motivation in certain populations. Through various educational programs, increasing achievement motivation has helped raise the standard of living for the poor, has helped in the control of alcoholism, and has helped make business management more effective. McCelland has also developed, with apparent success, an elaborate program designed to increase achievement motivation among businesspeople, especially in Third World countries.

## Context

The study of achievement motivation grew out of two separate perspectives in the study of personality. The first perspective is the psychoanalytic tradition of Sigmund Freud. Henry Murray was a committed Freudian in his theory of personality, stressing an unconscious dynamic interaction of three personality components: the id, the ego, and the superego. Psychoanalytic thought stresses the similarity of motives among all people by focusing on these driving forces from the unconscious domain of the personality. Murray's contribution to the psychoanalytic tradition is the concept of need, which is understood as an entity that unconsciously organizes one's perception of and one's action orientation toward the world. One of these needs is the need for achievement.

The second major perspective is the trait, or dispositional, tradition in personality theory. This perspective assumes that there are measurable individual differences between people in terms of their needs and motives; that these individual differences are relatively stable over time and manifest themselves in a wide variety of behaviors; and that motives (including the achievement motive), as dispositions within people, provide the basis of behavior. Thus, the emphasis within the trait tradition is on individuals' differences of motives. The psychoanalytic and trait approaches intersect in Murray's theory, which is one reason why his theory is so important in psychology.

In addition, developments in industrial and postindustrial twentieth century societies made the time ripe for the study of achievement. McClelland has suggested that achievement motivation may explain economic differences between societies. In his book *The Achieving Society* (1961), McClelland attempted to predict the economic growth of twenty-three countries from 1929 to 1950 on the basis of images of achievement found in children's stories in those countries in the decade of 1920 to 1929. He found that those societies which emphasized achievement through children's stories generally experienced greater economic growth. While direct cause-and-effect relationships could not be established in a study such as this, subsequent research using experimental studies provided some support for McClelland's position.

Finally, developments in academic achievement testing and vocational performance testing since the early part of the twentieth century have provided a natural setting for measuring attainment in these domains. As more and more tests were developed, and as they became increasingly sophisticated in measuring achievement, it became readily apparent that a conceptual model of achievement was necessary.

## Bibliography

Alschuler, Alfred S., Diane Tabor, and James McIntyre. *Teaching Achievement Motivation: Theory and Practice in Psychological Education.* Middletown, Conn.: Education Ventures, 1970. An immensely practical book that briefly discusses achievement motivation and psychological growth, and then describes in considerable detail the ten sessions of an achievement motivation workshop for teachers. The final chapter discusses achievement motivation training for students as well. Can easily be read by individuals at the high school level.

Atkinson, John William, and D. Birch. *An Introduction to Motivation.* 2d ed. New York: Van Nostrand, 1978. Very readable; does an effective job of discussing motivational concepts in general. Because of the first author's interest and research, a heavy emphasis is placed on achievement motivation, focusing particularly on elaborations of the expectancy value model.

Atkinson, John William, and Joel O. Raynor, eds. *Motivation and Achievement.* New York: Halsted Press, 1974. Reprints some of the most important research on achievement motivation. Many of the articles are too technical for the nonprofessional, but chapters 1, 2, 15, 19, and 20 are readable for the college student and are outstanding reviews of prior theory and application to academic achievement and career striving.

DeCharms, Richard. *Enhancing Motivation in the Classroom.* New York: Irvington, 1976. Designed primarily for teachers, with applications at all levels. Nicely incorporates prior research on achievement motivation. More than a "how-to" book; provides a challenge to the reader to think about factors involved in differing levels of achievement motivation in students.

McClelland, David Clarence. *The Achieving Society.* Princeton, N.J.: Van Nostrand, 1961. Considered by many a classic. Applies the methods of the behavioral sciences to provide a psychological basis for evaluating economic, historical, and sociological explanations of the rise and fall of civilizations. The achievement motive is a key to McClelland's theory. Readable by the general reader at the college level and beyond. Highly recommended.

Spence, Janet T., ed. *Achievement and Achievement Motives: Psychological and Sociological Approaches.* San Francisco: W. H. Freeman, 1983. Applies theoretical developments in achievement motivation to topics such as gender differences, children from one-parent households, social mobility, and cultural differences. Though scholarly and thorough, this excellent book is readable by the general audience at a college level, but not without effort.

*Peter C. Hill*

## Cross-References

Birth Order and Personality, 436; Motivational Constructs, 1616; Personality Theory: Major Issues, 1804; Personology: Henry A. Murray, 1810; Sport Psychology, 2363; Work Motivation, 2654.

# ADDICTIVE PERSONALITY AND BEHAVIORS

*Type of psychology:* Psychopathology
*Fields of study:* Attitudes and behavior; critical issues in stress; substance abuse

*The effects of an addictive personality are harmful to the afflicted individual and are often harmful to others. Addictive behaviors seem to be at least partly caused by a need to self-medicate and by low self-esteem; study of these behaviors involves attempts to identify, predict, and treat them.*

*Principal terms*
ADDICTION: a condition of slavery to a habit, or a very strong inclination concerning it
COMPULSION: an impulse that is difficult to resist
DEPENDENCY: the state of relying on another for support or existence
OBSESSION: a compelling idea or feeling, usually irrational, over which a person has little conscious control
PERSONALITY: the total physical, intellectual, and emotional structure of an individual, exhibited through consistent patterns of behavior
SYMPTOM: a sign or indication of a problem; it is not necessarily noticeable to the untrained individual

**Overview**

Fascination with the idea of an addictive personality and related behavior dates back to 950 B.C., to the works of Homer, the Greek poet, and perhaps before that to the writings of Lao-tzu, a Chinese philosopher and imperial adviser. These men studied human nature and sometimes wrote about the uncontrollable allure of certain desires which led to behaviors that were likely to cause personal and cultural destruction.

Some researchers have asked whether there is a single psychological predisposition or a multilevel series of complications involved in the addictive personality—or whether virtually any personality is vulnerable. Researchers administering the Minnesota Multiphasic Personality Inventory, an objective personality test, to addicted individuals have found that they have distinctive personality traits; sometimes these traits precede the addiction, and sometimes they seem to be caused by or exacerbated by the addiction. These findings are highly controversial and have fueled many heated discussions.

A surplus of aggressive energy seems to be at the core of most addictions. Indulgence in the addictive behavior is accompanied by the release of aggressive impulses, resulting in a feeling of euphoria. This feeling of relief is then associated with the outlet used, and it seduces the user to attempt a duplication of the original process, thus reexperiencing the euphoria.

Inadequate self-esteem is another psychological predisposition thought to be a common source of imperceptible pain, and the inability to handle the pain can lead to striving for a pain-reducing outlet. The addictive personality seems to have the desire to control the pain but lacks the necessary social, psychological, and biological tools to follow through. Other symptoms of the addictive personality that show up early enough to allow preventive measures to be taken include poor impulse control; intolerance and low frustration level, leading to a need for control; a strong sense of denial in everyday situations; and rigidness and extremes in action and thoughts.

Psychic and/or physical dependence on a release can occur. This dependence can take the form of an addiction to drugs, food, work, sex, gambling, exercise, or any number of other compulsive behaviors. Problems such as manipulation, denial of responsibility, displacement of emotions, and general dishonesty in life-style may provoke the process. The addictive process can be periodic, cyclic, sporadic, or continuous, depending upon a person's life patterns.

Different personality theories have conflicting ideas on addiction, adding to the controversy surrounding this topic. The psychoanalytic group believes that the addictive personality is a result of unconscious conflicts and of fixation on the pleasure principle, which states that one's energy in life is directed toward reducing pain and that one's innate drives control one's actions. Although some neo-Freudians disagreed with the cause of the pain, most agreed with the basic concept. Social learning and behavioral psychologists believe that an addictive personality is molded through shaping—the slow and continual development of a behavior, with continuous reinforcement along the way, based on the social mores prevalent when the individual grew up. The need to be accepted becomes the driving force.

The cognitive group holds that an addictive personality is formulated by the way a person receives, processes, stores, and retrieves information received through the senses. If the action taken produces a positive effect, then the person is likely to repeat the process so that the effect can be duplicated. In essence, people become addicted to the pleasurable results before they become addicted to the particular path taken to achieve them. The humanistic group concentrates on the here and now, focusing on the fact that people have choices, yet many people do not know how to make them because of a trauma they experienced while growing up. To the humanist, the idea of the family becomes very important, particularly how love was expressed and experienced, because through love, a person can believe in himself or herself enough to be able to make a positive choice. The proponents of trait theory contend that people are born with certain tendencies and preferences of action, which may or may not be genetic; the evidence is inconclusive. Trait theorists seem to agree, however, that society and the family have a strong influence on people and that some people are predisposed toward compulsive behavior from an early age.

Biological studies have been conducted to explore the suspected link between addictive behavior and genes, suggesting that, at least in part, the addictive personality may be inherited. Studies suggest that certain people may have inherited an impaired neurological homeostasis, which is partly corrected by their addiction—

such as to alcohol. The sons of alcoholic fathers have a higher "body sway" than do nonalcoholics; it decreases when they are intoxicated. Sons of alcoholics have a higher rate of addiction than do daughters, no matter which parent reared the children.

People with "familial essential tremor," an inherited disorder, have less tremor when drinking and have a higher rate of alcohol dependence. Also, while alcohol-dependent people do not have higher levels of arousal at rest, they become more aroused when stressed, as measured by heart rate, and are slower to return to rest.

Other studies have suggested that people who are at high risk have abnormal brain-wave activity, suggesting an inability to concentrate or a reduced brain capacity. High-risk people have shown normal to slightly above normal intelligence quotient (IQ) test scores, but low scores on verbal subscales and attention. They also show delayed language development. Moreover, they seem to produce a heroinlike tranquilizing substance which is released and soothes the person when using an addictive substance or pursuing addictive behavior.

The majority of controlled scientific studies on genetics have been conducted on the alcoholic population; because of this, they are inconclusive when discussing the addictive personality overall. They do, however, add evidence to the possible link between biology and behavior.

## Applications

It seems clear from the research that addiction is a multilevel problem with complex roots, dispersed throughout psychology, sociology, biology, and genetics. A look at three of the symptoms of this disorder will help provide a clearer picture of the observable behavior that results from whatever combination of earlier experiences and inherited traits causes it. Among the symptoms of addictive behavior are a strong need to self-medicate, low self-esteem, and a tendency toward excessiveness.

A strong need to self-medicate, or to stop the pain, seems to be found in most addicts. Whether the pain is real or perceived does not seem to matter; most addicts have both a low tolerance and a strong need to get their way, which reduces the pain for them.

This tendency can be traced back to childhood and used as a warning sign so that an effort can be made to alter the child's first impulse and slowly, over time and with much positive reinforcement, show the child alternative, acceptable behavior. When the child can be taught to achieve the self-medication in a positive way, according to his or her society, there is a better chance for positive achievement as an outcome. Sigmund Freud called this mechanism sublimation—the rechanneling of a socially unacceptable trait or feeling into a socially acceptable outlet. As an example of self-medication, Alice, a five-year-old child in a typical suburban community, is experiencing considerable anxiety because of going to school for the first time. She is swinging her legs back and forth while she sits in her chair as her mother speaks to the teacher on the first day. Her fingers encircle her thumbs and her head is down. The swinging of Alice's legs is a form of self-medication to relieve the anxiety of starting school; it is perfectly normal in this situation and is appropriate for a child of Alice's age.

If this same self-medicating style shows up in other areas of Alice's life, however, in less appropriate situations, then it becomes a symptom and deserves to be watched. At this time, steps can be taken to help Alice feel more confident, which could relieve much of the anxiety and could reduce the need to self-medicate. Children's body language can tell much about their inner feelings and give adults time to alter a potential problem before it gets out of control.

If it is not addressed at this time and Alice is allowed to get into the habit of self-medicating in this relatively harmless way, she may develop a tolerance for this behavior; as she approaches puberty, she might change her habits to include more powerful self-medicating forms such as alcohol, sex, or overeating, which may also be more popular with her age group. She would then need to be taught socially appropriate tools to handle her anxiety. As one can readily see, the deeper the anxiety, the more powerful the self-medicating outlet, and the more difficult it is to turn around.

Another warning sign that seems to appear most of the time in addictive people is low self-esteem. Research has shown that self-esteem is based on a gradual shaping of many small experiences into a general feeling of power—the ability to have a positive effect on one's environment and the people within it. The addictive person translates a feeling of powerlessness into pain, and then must self-medicate to alleviate this condition.

The channel taken to ease the pain may be the one that is easiest to reach or that is most acceptable in the social group that surrounds the individual or that the individual wishes to enter. Therefore, the addictive personality may reach out through work, gambling, sex, eating, dieting, substance use, exercising, competition, or many other ways that can eventually get out of control and lead to destructive patterns of behavior. Self-esteem, or a general feeling of worth, begins at birth. (Some say that it begins while the child is still in the womb, around the sixth or seventh month, but this idea is controversial.)

Children seem to pick up the behaviors and concepts shown them by the society in which they grow up. Socially, a child becomes what society teaches him or her to become. Sarah, for example, is one of three children being reared by an upwardly mobile family interested only in what is best for their children. All her life, Sarah has received a double message: "I love you when you do what I want, and I am disappointed with you when you do what you want to do."

Sarah, like any healthy child, wants to please her parents, so she concentrates on doing what they want; however, it does not seem to be enough, and over the years she begins to numb herself from the pain of rejection and failure. She begins to believe that she is not worth loving, except when she does what others want—and when she does, it is not enough, so she does not see why she should bother. She looks for a group outside her home that will accept her for who she is, or she withdraws or becomes defiant in order to get attention. Sarah is now vulnerable to any self-medicating outlet that comes her way, as she seeks to relieve the pain of her perceived rejection. It does not matter if the pain is justified or is falsely perceived; to the addictive personality, it is real and must be soothed. Sarah's siblings may not experience their family or surroundings in the same way and therefore may not have the need to self-medicate; not all children in an addictive family follow addictive behavior patterns.

Another precursor to addictive behavior seems to be an ever-growing need to get a little more from whatever task is giving one pleasure at the time; this has been called "excessiveness," and it is a controversial issue. Many therapists have heard clients discuss a seemingly insatiable appetite for pleasure, in whatever form; they do not know when to stop and simply feel gratitude for the pleasure they have experienced. In the beginning of most addictions, there is sufficient relief to encourage the further use of an acquired outlet, whether it be positive or negative at this time. Because addictive people have a strong sense of denial, they seem to be unable to envision the inevitably destructive phase of their choice for relief.

One question that arises regarding excessiveness is how to teach a person balance when American society in general does not know how to achieve this goal. The United States has been called a nation of overachievers for profit, success, and power. People are rewarded highly for these motives and are considered well-adjusted by their fellow citizens if they achieve them. A problem arises when one considers that addictive personalities are a mass of excessive desires to begin with. They lack impulse control, and there is a strong need to achieve self-validation any way they can.

A thirteen-year-old boy who is growing up in a city atmosphere finds that there is constant stimulation and temptation around him. A normal, healthy boy wishes to be accepted by those who are important to him, and he wishes to have fun. In a city, age-appropriate stimulation is vast, and inappropriate stimulation may easily be overpowering to a child who lacks impulse control, may have a low self-esteem, and probably has already found a way to self-medicate. Even to a thirteen-year-old child without addictive personality tendencies, city stimulation can be overpowering. Some researchers say that at age thirteen, life in general is overpowering and that the child needs strong but nurturing guidance. At this age, a child will look to society for guidance and approval; in his or her role models is the hope for the tools necessary to create a balance between what is available and what the child needs to function and mature.

The implications of the effect on society of negative addiction are far reaching. Each year there are more accidents being caused by people who are under the influence of alcohol or other drugs; there are more strokes and heart attacks caused by overwork, lack of sufficient exercise, and improper nutritional habits. More babies are being born addicted than ever before. On the other hand, there is the idea of a positive addiction, or compulsive behavior that actually enriches the individual and the society in which that person lives. (Even this behavior can get out of control when a person who has problems with setting healthy limits attempts to use it.)

Whether addictive behavior is learned for survival, genetically passed on, or an intricate combination of both, there appears to be a set of symptoms which can predispose a person toward addiction—or, at the least, can place a person in a high-risk group. If these symptoms can be identified early enough, the chance to teach potential addicts the path toward balance increases, and the compulsive life-style can be decreased or channeled in a healthy way. Yet it does seem that American society values addictive behavior in the form of overachievers and rewards them accordingly, therefore actually encouraging a form of addiction. As long as addictive behavior is encouraged in any form, there will be a part of the population that has trouble differentiating excess from balance.

## Context

Addictions and their victims have been studied and described at least since the beginning of written language, and probably since humanity first communicated by storytelling. A concentrated effort was made in Ohio in 1935 by Robert Smith and William Wilson to help the addictive personality through the organization of Alcoholics Anonymous (AA) a self-help group of alcoholics in various stages of recovery.

The success of Alcoholics Anonymous is world renowned, and it is considered by most professionals and nonprofessionals who have contact with it to be one of the more complete recovery programs in the world. The twelve-step program, an idea that AA started, transcends the boundaries of alcohol abuse and has been applied to many addictions. AA is run by recovering alcoholics who are nonprofessionals—simply individual humans helping others. Yet it was not until the early 1970's that addictive people gained national and international attention.

In 1971, the National Institute on Alcohol Abuse and Alcoholism conducted research that showed addiction to be threatening American society. A concentrated effort was made to study the addictive person and attempt to find symptoms that could predict high-risk individuals. The federally funded studies, it was hoped, would find ways to help prevent and reduce the tremendous health, social, and economic consequences of addiction in the United States. Assessing dependence potential and discovering vulnerability or high-risk factors through demographic characteristics, psychological status, and individual drug history became its focus. The funding of these studies has become a critical component in the fight to better understand the addictive personality. National programs were begun to attempt to show individuals and communities how to deal with the behavioral aftermath of addictive thinking.

David M. Murco, of the Psychiatric Research Center, University of Maryland School of Medicine, and Lawrence J. Hatterer, a psychiatrist at New York Hospital, Cornell Medical Center, both leaders in the area of addictive personalities, have obtained similar findings in their individual research. They conclude that neglect from parents, absence of family support, and inconsistent or permissive behavior on the parents' part can place children in the high-risk category. With the further sophistication of genetic studies, researchers are slowly compiling an addictive profile which may lend itself to early intervention and prevention.

Internationally, it has been surmised that advanced, technological societies seem to give rise to more kinds of dependency than do more slowly developing countries, a fact which could help researchers focus on some societal misconceptions of overall health. For example, in the United States and some other technologically advanced societies, there seems to be a belief pattern, propagated by the mass media, that supports instant gratification. If one is tense, one should take a pill; if one is lonely, one can call a certain number for conversation. If one is bored, have an alcoholic drink. If one wants to be part of the in-crowd, smoke; if one is unhappy, eat. People who are addicted to a negative anxiety releaser have been described as "committing suicide on the installment plan." Societies, governments, and researchers must unite in a desire to unveil all possible symptoms of addiction, to identify those at high risk toward them, and to employ successful recovery methods.

## Bibliography

Berger, Gilda. *Addiction: Its Causes, Problems, and Treatments.* New York: Franklin Watts, 1982. Berger, a former special education teacher, writes about the subject of addiction and its problems with sensitivity and depth. She fully explores the idea of compulsive dependency on pleasure-giving substances such as alcohol, illegal drugs, tobacco, caffeine, and food. She also provides insight into causes, treatments, and societal attitudes.

May, Rollo. *The Meaning of Anxiety.* New York: Ronald Press, 1950. This classic work by one of the masters of humanism is well-written, clear, and concise. It covers the subject of anxiety, an intricate component of most addictive behaviors, from modern interpretation to management of clinical analysis. Included are self-testing devices in the appendices, an extensive bibliography, and clear and informative notes.

Mule, S. Joseph, ed. *Behavior in Excess: An Examination of the Volitional Disorders.* New York: Free Press, 1981. This set of nineteen chapters is a must for the beginning student of addictive personalities and behavior. Explains the many drugs of choice available to the addictive person as well as the societal addictions of eating, work, gambling, sports, television, sex, and smoking. Explores the environmental influence on excessive behaviors and psychodynamic and behavioral treatments. An excellent group of writings.

Oxford, Jim. *Excessive Appetites: A Psychological View of Addictions.* New York: John Wiley & Sons, 1985. This internationally focused, easily read book begins by proclaiming that the author himself is an addict in recovery—a workaholic. It is well organized into two parts, one dealing with the topic of the excessive appetite and the other with psychological viewpoints on causes and treatments. The summary at the end draws most of the central themes together in an easily accessible format.

Wilson, Bill. *Alcoholics Anonymous.* 3d ed. New York: Alcoholics Anonymous World Services, 1976. In this compilation of stories, words of wisdom, and insights into the world of the addicted person, the cofounders of Alcoholics Anonymous have been the impetus for an inspiring group of writings. Together with one of their original associates, Sister Ignatia of St. Thomas Hospital in Akron, Ohio, and many others, they have put into words the heart and soul of an addictive person's behavior—physically, emotionally, and spiritually. An essential part of any student's reading in the field of compulsive behavior.

*Frederic Wynn*

## Cross-References

Alcoholism, 213; The Codependent Personality, 534; Coping: Social Support, 700; Hunger: Psychological Bases, 1223; Obesity, 1688; Motivation: Opponent Process Theory, 1611; Self-Esteem, 2188; Substance Abuse: An Overview, 2489.

# ADLERIAN PSYCHOTHERAPY

*Type of psychology:* Psychotherapy
*Fields of study:* Cognitive therapies; humanistic therapies; psychodynamic therapies

*Adlerian psychotherapy covers the assessment and therapeutic techniques developed by Alfred Adler and followers of his individual psychology school. This approach can be seen as a precursor of later forms of brief, humanistic, empathic, and cognitive psychotherapy.*

*Principal terms*
> EARLY RECOLLECTIONS: a projective technique in which the patient attempts to remember things that happened in the distant past; these provide clues to the patient's current use of private logic
> INDIVIDUAL PSYCHOLOGY: Adler's school of personality theory and therapy
> INFERIORITY: a complex or feeling from which all individuals suffer; most overcome it successfully
> ORGAN DIALECT: a situation in which a patient's private logic is reflected in his or her physical illnesses
> PRIVATE LOGIC: unconscious reasoning that the patient uses to explain away feelings of inferiority
> TRANSFERENCE: the transferring of emotions that a patient feels about other people onto the therapist treating the patient

## Overview

Alfred Adler's individual psychology, his approach to psychotherapy, starts with the assumption that all people suffer from a feeling of inferiority. Though most people outgrow this complex by developing healthy compensations through their career, family, and friends, many individuals turn inward and attempt to compensate with a private logic. This is a personal and unconscious "fictional" way of understanding self and reality in such a way as to assuage the feelings of inferiority. Reliance on private logic impairs the individual's ability to cope.

The concept of private logic underlies Adler's understanding of psychopathology. Each disorder represents a different approach to private logic. Schizophrenics cope with the inferiority complex by believing their own private logic so thoroughly that they separate from external reality and live in a delusional world in which they are intensely talented and important. The schizophrenic's neologisms (invented words) can be seen as evidence of creativity. On the other hand, the critical auditory hallucinations often experienced by schizophrenics can be understood as the schizophrenic's inability to master totally the internal world.

The obsessive-compulsive patient has focused attention exclusively on some private issue of no real objective importance; in the person's private logic, however, the issue has a great importance, perhaps conferring on the person some special status. The paranoid's private logic allows the person to believe that he or she is the most important person in the world—why else would the Mafia, CIA, or Martians persecute the person so?

Adler began his practice of medicine not as a psychiatrist but as a general practitioner. As such, he saw all sorts of patients, most of whom did not define their various diseases and problems as mental. Psychosomatic, hypochondriacal, and somatoform patients illustrate what Adler called organ dialect, in which their bodies' problems reflect their dysfunctional approaches to life. Such physical disorders (real or imagined) mitigate feelings of inferiority by serving as an excuse for failure and/or a plea for sympathy.

Depressed patients suffer from low self-esteem, which may include feelings of hopelessness, helplessness, and guilt. The private logic of such a patient may be inadequate to lift the patient out of the inferiority complex. Some depressed patients even seem to rely upon their own suffering as a sham sense of merit: "I suffer, therefore I am worthy." Personality disorders, delinquency, and crime may spring from the attempt to overcome feelings of inferiority through defiance and a façade of toughness rather than meaningful contributions to society. Prostitutes and chemically dependent individuals have an unresolved inferiority complex coupled with an ambivalent attitude toward dependency.

What unifies people with different kinds of mental disorders, according to Adler, is that their private logic gives them a mistaken understanding of themselves and the world. They persist in their dysfunctional behaviors and attitudes in order to preserve their sham sense of self-esteem, but at the price of effective coping. When Adler set out to diagnose a patient, he was less interested in labeling that patient with a specific disorder than reaching a deeper understanding of who that person was: It is not so important what disease the patient has, but what kind of person has the disease. Therefore, Adler's approach to diagnosis was more qualitative than quantitative, more tailored to the individual situation than systematic and structured. There were, however, about a half dozen techniques that Adler regularly employed.

His first diagnostic technique was to observe the patient's body language. This included not only the organ dialect of the presenting (physical) problem but also all sorts of nonverbal behaviors: how the patient walked into the room, how he or she wiggled or slouched in the seat, the kind of handshake, the degree of eye contact, and so on. Adler once said that one can learn more from patients in a minute of watching them as if they were mimes (and ignoring anything they say) than one can in an hour of listening to them.

A second approach was the use of direct and specific questions, not only about the manifest symptoms, but also about the patient's background. Since Adler was convinced that the formative stage of personality development is the first six years of life, he was most interested in asking about early childhood: relations with parents, siblings, teachers, and others, as well as a lifetime history of medical problems. Adler believed that people are purposive creatures and that mental disorders (and possibly physical disorders as well) are means to the end of assuaging feelings of inferiority; he would sometimes directly ask his patients: "If you were cured of this disorder, what would happen to you?" The answer could reveal what the patient most feared—sometimes that he or she would have higher expectations of his or her own performance in the areas of interpersonal relations and career.

During his ten-year association with Sigmund Freud, Adler learned to use dreams as a way of exploring the patient's unconscious. He believed that dreams were ways in which the patient rehearsed coping for waking life. The behavior of the dreamer reflects his or her real-life coping patterns and private logic.

One diagnostic technique that originated with Adler was the use of early recollections. These would be elicited by the question "What is the farthest back that your memory can go?" The patient would reintegrate a memory from early childhood. Adler realized that such recollections would be hazy on the facts, but they would provide excellent vehicles for expressing the patient's private logic. Such recollections, like the patient's dreams or works of art, could be seen as projective techniques, rich with the markings of the patient's personality. Additionally, the patient's current mood would color the mood of the recollection, and conflicts currently on the patient's mind would be projected into the story. As the patient improves in psychotherapy, the early recollections change to a more positive tone, reflecting more effective coping strategies.

Adler's own character is evident from the earliest recollection of his childhood. Young Alfred was lying in bed, very ill, and overheard the doctor out in the hall telling his father that Alfred would not make it through the night. Adler recalls that he resolved to live and prove the doctor wrong, and to become a doctor and fight death. The memory shows Adler's tremendous willpower as well as a desire to overcome suffering.

The first step in Adlerian psychotherapy was to use the previously mentioned diagnostic techniques to comprehend the patient's underlying private logic. The next step was to use empathy to develop the patient's trust. (This should not be allowed to evolve into a transference, which Adler regarded as a childish dependency that would lengthen therapy and delay progress.) Then, patients had to be led to the identification of their own guiding private logic and to an insight that it was truly dysfunctional. This may include direct confrontation of the patient's misfocusing, abstractness, closed-mindedness, or excessive self-expectations. The last stage of therapy was the cultivation of the patient's social interest and involved encouraging the patient to venture forth into interpersonal relations and the world of work—emerging from the protective shell of the private logic and into the normal world's challenges.

Unlike Freudian psychoanalysis, Adler's approach to psychotherapy was directive. In addition to direct confrontation, Adler sometimes attempted to shake up the patient's guarded structure of private logic by answering with the unexpected. When one patient called him at home at three o'clock in the morning to report some trivial symptom, she ended by apologizing for awakening him; Adler responded that he had been sitting by his telephone awaiting her call. She thus gained the insight that she was behaving like a pampered child. Another patient was obsessed with the idea that he had contracted syphilis, and he had compulsively sought the attention of many physicians around Vienna, all of whom had reported no evidence of the disease. Adler immediately agreed with the patient that he did, indeed, have the dreaded disease, thus pushing the patient to accept the validity of the previous diagnoses.

A variant of this technique was developed by one of Adler's protégés, Rudolf Dreikurs, who became one of the foremost apostles of individual psychology in America. Dreikurs used antisuggestion, urging patients who complained of an uncontrollable urge to give in to it and even practice it.

Unlike practitioners of classical psychoanalysis, Adler believed that therapy should be brief. Progress should be apparent in weeks, and termination should be possible in less than a year. Even after their sessions have ended, patients often continue to progress on their own. Unlike the humanistic and emotional therapies of the 1960's, Adlerian psychotherapy does not try to provoke abreaction (the expression of repressed emotions or thoughts), but to build the patient's capacity for self-control.

## Applications

Case studies of diagnosis and counseling with three very different patients can illustrate Adlerian techniques. Jay, age forty, had a psychophysiologic disorder (an ulcer) and was mildly depressed. He attributed his problems to organizational changes at the small firm by which he had been employed for a dozen years. An outstanding engineer with an earned doctorate and MBA and numerous patents, Jay was convinced that his own efforts had helped the company grow and survive. As vice president for research and development, Jay was now advocating several new projects to get the firm's sales moving again; however, the other major figures in the company largely ignored Jay's plans and lurched from one budget-cutting scheme to another. "I am working eighty-hour weeks and worrying about the company all the time, but I just can't get things moving."

Jay's body language included averting his gaze and slouching, which he attributed to Vietnam War wounds. Upon direct questioning, he said that he was an only child: His father, fifty-five when Jay was born, wanted no children and resented the "accident" of Jay's conception, while his mother wanted more children and had to be satisfied with one son. Jay found that his mother was extremely encouraging and loving, perhaps spoiling Jay somewhat, while his father tended to ignore him except when some major accomplishment got his father's attention. Jay's guiding private logic was: I must work hard and accomplish something great, then I will get attention. This drove Jay to earn his degrees, invent new products, and work hard at the company. His current frustration came from the fact that the old hard formula was not working in his changing corporate culture.

Jay was most angry at his company's chief executive officer and board of directors, whom he regarded as intellectually inferior to him. The CEO was an incredibly charming (and handsome) MBA from the sales division who rejected most of Jay's suggestions for new products but had few ideas of his own. Jay admitted feeling envious of the CEO's sustained popularity, "especially considering that he has been running the company into the ground for seven years."

The earliest childhood recollection that Jay produced was that he was watching his mother use the toilet, sitting down on the bowl with the seat up, and that Jay was telling her that it was dangerous to do it that way. When the therapist encouraged Jay to ask his parents what had really happened, Jay found out that he was toilet trained early, and because he would urinate on the floor (through the crack between the seat and the bowl), his mother encouraged him to sit down on the bowl. His mother recalled that Jay then developed a fear of falling backwards into the toilet. The interesting thing about Jay's recollection is that he inverted his role with his mother's: He was the one warning her of the danger. While a Freudian would say something about the Oedipus Complex or anal fixation here, Adlerians are more concerned with the power quality of the interpersonal relations. Jay saw himself as the one who points out the danger; he was also very frustrated when the parental figures (the CEO and members of the board of directors) failed to heed his warnings.

Jay's ulcer was a badge of merit, like his earned degrees or patents ("look at how much I have suffered for this company!"). Sacrifice and success have been Jay's strategy for winning the attention of his "parents," but now that strategy is not working, so he has become depressed.

An intelligent man, Jay rapidly gained insight into his private logic. After four sessions, he had the following dream: "I am going through one of my rental houses, and I discover a room that I did not remember before—a living room that looked so comfortable, I just wanted to sit and read for pleasure." Jay enjoyed the dream and agreed that it reflected his ongoing resolution of his problem. The dream represents new possibilities in Jay's life: a more mellow life-style in which he sees less need to push himself on the fast track in order to maintain his self-esteem.

Jay terminated after eight sessions, having made plans to seek a position with another firm. After two years in the new position, Jay reports that he makes almost as much money, has slightly less status, works half as many hours, but has twice as much enjoyment. His ulcer and depression have not recurred.

Dan was also a forty-year-old engineer when he began counseling. He met most, though not all, of the criteria for a narcissistic personality. Although a brilliant computer programmer, Dan had never obtained a college degree. He had never remained with one company for more than a year, and most of his work history had been with "job shops" or as an independent consultant. The presenting problem for Dan was that he had gotten his girlfriend pregnant, and he was ambivalent about getting married and becoming a father.

Direct questioning revealed that Dan was the third of four children. His grandfather had been a famous politician, his father was an attorney, and an older brother was an accomplished (and very wealthy) surgeon. Dan directly denied feeling inferior to these male family members, for he was convinced that he was smarter than any of them and had a broader range of knowledge. Dan's private logic worked something like this: "Everyone else needs to get a degree and work in one career line for twenty years in order to be a success; I don't have to, because I am more brilliant than anyone else. Finishing my education or sticking with one company would be an admission that I am not more brilliant."

During the first few sessions, Dan used big words and attempted to impress the therapist with his knowledge of psychology. While Dan claimed an inability to come up with an early recollection, he was able to remember a dream: "I am at a new restaurant, and I am given a table next to the kitchen; although the waiters go back and forth, they ignore me. Finally, I am given the check and realize that I do not have enough money." After much resistance and intellectualization, Dan agreed that the dream exposed his dissatisfaction with his life: the fear that the honors and accomplishments of the other males in his family will pass him by, and that he will be unable to achieve as much.

The cultivation of Dan's social interest took eight months, but it did progress. He accepted a position (which he initially thought to be beneath his talents) offering stable employment and advancement. He married his pregnant girlfriend and reports to be satisfied with his role of father, although he finds his wife to be a little too "naggy." He does not try so hard to impress people with his intelligence.

Alicia, a sixty-four-year-old widow of fifteen years, went into therapy complaining of depression and suicidal thoughts. Her inferiority feeling was expressed primarily as helplessness and ruminations of guilt. Direct questioning and discussion engendered by dreams indicated that she still blamed herself for her husband's fatal heart attack ("I cooked food that was too rich"), for her son's accidental death ("I encouraged him to follow his heart and become a pilot"), and her daughter's upcoming marriage to a former priest ("I did not instill enough religion in her"). The function of her depressive illness was that her daughter was talking about delaying her marriage until her mother got better.

Her earliest recollection was that her parents would punish her for wetting the bed by making her sit in a tub of cold water; one time when her parents were out of the house, she wet the bed. When her parents returned they found her sitting in a tub of cold water, telling herself "You sit there." This consolidated the identification of her private logic: "I am responsible for things that go wrong, and I must punish myself when things go wrong."

Alicia developed the insight that her private logic was dysfunctional and her own depression was a manipulative, though effective, way of reacting to her daughter's forthcoming marriage. The facilitation of social interest in this case focused on getting Alicia out of the enmeshed relationship with the daughter and more involved with activities outside the home, such as religion and charity work.

## Context

Most of Sigmund Freud's patients were "hysterical" women (with what would now be called somatoform or dissociative reactions) from the middle and upper classes of Viennese society. Most of Adler's patients were from the poor and working classes; they were not as articulate as Freud's, so Adler had to assume a more directive stance. Adler remained in general medical practice, treating all kinds of physical illnesses and injuries as well as mental problems. Although he probably saw more patients in any given month than Freud saw in his professional lifetime, the brevity of Adler's counseling may have given only a superficial understanding of their problems.

Adler, like Joseph Breur, Carl Jung, and Otto Rank, broke with Freud and came up with an alternative to psychoanalysis. He redefined Freud's use of dreams and interpretation of patient resistance (it is a reaction against the threat to the private logic which assuages inferiority feeling). Adler rejected transference as an artificial by-product of therapy and as a license for the patient to continue infantile behavior. He redefined the unconscious, not as a repository of sexual energy, but as the limitations of consciousness to understand one's own private logic.

Adler's emphasis on empathy and appreciating the uniqueness of each individual patient can be seen as a precursor to the humanistic approaches (such as that of Carl Rogers) that surfaced in the 1950's and 1960's. Adler's focus on the patient's private logic and coping strategies was echoed in the 1970's and 1980's growth of the cognitive approach (exemplified by Aaron Beck and Albert Ellis).

Some of Adler's ideas have been challenged by modern research. The correlation between birth order and personality, for example, is lower than Adler believed. Adler's notion that healthy people have no need to dream has been challenged by evidence from sleep laboratories that all people dream several times a night, though they might not remember their dreams. Nevertheless, Adler's specific techniques of diagnosis and therapy are useful tools that eclectic therapists often add to their collection.

## Bibliography

Adler, Alfred. *The Individual Psychology of Alfred Adler.* Edited by Heinz L. Ansbacher and Rowena R. Ansbacher. New York: Basic Books, 1956.

_____. *Superiority and Social Interest.* Edited by Heinz L. Ansbacher and Rowena R. Ansbacher. Evanston, Ill.: Northwestern University Press, 1964. There is no standard edition or comprehensive collection of Adler's writings; however, the above two edited works by the Ansbachers take representative excerpts from Adler's numerous books and, together with editorial comments, present a good picture of the techniques Adler developed for assessment and therapy.

Brink, Terry L. *Geriatric Psychotherapy.* New York: Human Sciences Press, 1979. A how-to manual for counselors who work with the aged. Adlerian theory is used to understand the psychodynamics of later life. Examples of Adlerian assessment techniques (early childhood recollections, dreams) are given, along with ways of cultivating social interest.

Dinkmeyer, Don C., and W. L. Pew. *Adlerian Counseling and Psychotherapy.* 2d ed. Columbus, Ohio: Charles E. Merrill, 1987. This is a good summary of different

Adlerian techniques for psychotherapy. It is written for the practitioner at all levels, from youth guidance counselor to psychiatrist.

Dreikurs, Rudolf. *Fundamentals of Adlerian Psychology.* New York: Greenberg, 1950. The author was an Adlerian disciple who became the leader of the Adlerian movement in the United States after World War II. His simple style and straightforward advice is very much in keeping with the style of Adler himself. Dreikurs' own expertise was in the area of child development.

Mosak, Harold H., ed. *Alfred Adler: His Influence on Psychology Today.* Park Ridge, N.Y.: Noyes Press, 1973. This edited volume contains a section on clinical applications in education and psychiatry.

Mosak, Harold H., and Birdie Mosak. *A Bibliography of Adlerian Psychology.* Washington, D.C.: Hemisphere, 1975. A very comprehensive bibliography covering individual psychology through the early 1970's; even small articles in newsletters are included. There are more than a hundred citations on psychotherapy alone.

*T. L. Brink*

## Cross-References

Abnormality: Cognitive Models, 46; Clinical Interviewing, Testing, and Observation, 527; Cognitive Therapy, 586; Dream Analysis, 830; Individual Psychology: Alfred Adler, 1275; Psychoanalysis: Classical versus Modern, 1898; Psychotherapeutic Goals and Techniques, 1996.

# ADOLESCENCE: COGNITIVE SKILLS

*Type of psychology:* Developmental psychology
*Fields of study:* Adolescence; cognitive development

*Adolescence brings the capacity for logical and theoretical reasoning, systematic problem solving, and acquisition of abstract concepts; adolescent cognitive skills are reflected in social and personality development as well as in learning and problem-solving behavior.*

*Principal terms*

CONCRETE OPERATIONS STAGE: the stage, according to Piaget's theory, between ages seven and twelve, during which children acquire basic logical rules and concrete concepts

EGOCENTRISM: the inability to see things from the perspective or point of view of another person

FORMAL OPERATIONS STAGE: the stage, according to Piaget's theory, corresponding to adolescence, during which children acquire sophisticated logic and abstract concepts

IMAGINARY AUDIENCE: the belief that the self is constantly being watched and critiqued by other people

INFORMATION-PROCESSING APPROACH: the study of how people perceive information, remember information, think, and solve problems

PERSONAL FABLE: the belief that one's own experiences are unique and different from anyone else's

PSEUDOSTUPIDITY: the appearance of stupidity resulting from seeing problems and situations as much more complicated than they really are

PSYCHOMETRIC APPROACH: the study of cognition through intelligence testing

## Overview

Psychologists approach the study of adolescent cognitive skills from three perspectives: the psychometric, the developmental, and the information-processing. The psychometric approach focuses on defining and measuring intellectual skills. Psychometric research typically involves studies of performance on intelligence tests. The developmental approach seeks to identify the types of cognitive skills which are unique to the adolescent years. This approach has been heavily influenced by the cognitive stage theory of Swiss psychologist Jean Piaget. The information-processing approach examines the characteristics of memory and problem solving. It views adolescent cognitive skills as parameters that determine how the brain stores and analyzes information.

In the psychometric view, adolescence is a period of cognitive stability. Intelligence test (IQ test) scores show little change during adolescence. Although IQ scores often fluctuate during early childhood, scores generally stabilize about age eight. It is not uncommon to find temporary periods of instability in IQ scores after age eight, such as at the onset of puberty or during other stressful times, but dramatic and long-term score changes are rare. According to this perspective, adolescence does not bring significant changes in cognitive skills.

This statement may be confusing. Clearly, sixteen-year-olds must "know more" than eight-year-olds, and adolescents have the capacity to learn school subjects beyond the grasp of elementary school children. The psychometric approach, however, is not designed to contrast the nature of cognitive skills at different ages. Intelligence tests are scored by comparing a specific person to other people of the same age. A score of 100 at age eight means that a person performs similarly to the average eight year old; a score of 100 at age eighteen means that a person performs similarly to the average eighteen-year-old. IQ score is expected to remain the same if the person matures at a relatively normal rate.

The developmental approach, centered around the work of Piaget, seeks to identify the cognitive skills of adolescence and to contrast them with the skills found at other ages. Two of Piaget's stages are of particular importance to the study of adolescence: the concrete operational stage (ages seven to twelve) and the formal operational stage (age twelve and up). During the concrete operational stage, children acquire basic logical concepts such as equivalence, seriation, and part-whole relations. Children also master reversibility, a skill allowing them mentally to restore a changed object or situation to its original state. With reversibility, children can recognize that a small glass of juice poured into a taller and thinner glass may look like more juice but is actually the same amount.

The formal operational stage supposedly begins at adolescence. During this stage, thinking becomes more logical, more abstract, more hypothetical, and more systematic. Unlike their concrete operational counterparts, formal thinkers can study ideologies, generate a variety of possible outcomes to an action, and systematically evaluate alternative approaches to a problem. Formal thinkers also are better able to adopt a new course of action when a particular strategy proves unsuccessful.

Research has called into question the link between adolescence and the stage of formal operational thought, however; most adolescents show some evidence of formal thinking but fail to demonstrate the consistency necessary for this stage to be aligned specifically with adolescence. Performance does not necessarily improve with age. Adults also show variability in formal thinking, implying that people may become only partially formal operational. Many psychologists are beginning to question whether formal operational thought is a coherent stage of cognitive development. In addition, research indicates that cultural background affects performance on problems requiring formal thinking. Perhaps experience determines the extent of formal operational thinking.

In spite of the controversy surrounding the stage of formal operations, there is evidence that cognitive skills change as children enter adolescence. The information-processing approach provides additional information about these child/adolescent contrasts. According to John Flavell, cognitive growth is the acquisition of increasingly sophisticated and efficient problem-solving skills. For example, adolescents can hold more information in memory than children, which enhances their ability to solve complex problems. Improvements in memory reflect more than changes in capacity. Adolescents are better able to develop associations between words and ideas, which in turn facilitates remembering them. Part of their improvement is a result of the fact that adolescents know more than children. Adolescents also are better able to think abstractly and develop hypotheses. These skills in part reflect improvements in generalization, identifying similarities between previous situations and new ones. Changes in thinking and hypothesizing also enable adolescents to generate a wider variety of problem-solving strategies, which also enhances their performance. Finally, adolescents know more about the nature of thought and memory. This metacognition, or ability to "think about thinking," increases the planfulness of their problem-solving behavior.

## Applications

The research on adolescent thinking has been applied to the study of learning, personality, and social behavior during adolescence. For example, research on adolescent cognition has influenced the development both of curricula and teaching methods at the middle-school and high-school levels. As individuals who are entering the stage of formal thinking, adolescents are better equipped to handle abstract topics such as geometry and physics. Their emerging ability to consider systematically the effects of several factors when solving a problem make adolescents good candidates for laboratory science courses.

Some applications of research on adolescent cognitive skills are the subject of much debate, however; ability tracking is a case in point. Psychometric research indicates that intellectual functioning becomes relatively stable in preadolescence. From this point onward, children continue to perform at the same level relative to their age-mates on standardized measures such as IQ tests. The stability of test performance has been used to support the creation and maintenance of ability tracks beginning in the middle-school years. Proponents of tracking maintain that ability grouping or tracking enables teachers to challenge more able students without frustrating less capable students. Opponents of tracking maintain that less able students benefit from both the academic challenges and the competent role models provided by superior students in ungrouped classrooms. In fact, critics of tracking charge that the level at which performance stabilizes actually results from subtle differences in how teachers interact with their students, differences often based on inaccurate assumptions about student potential. Perhaps students with low test scores, many of whom are poor or minority students, perform poorly because people expect them to be less capable.

David Elkind sees the emergence of features of formal thinking reflected in adolescent personality characteristics. According to Elkind, the ability to think abstractly and hypothetically enables adolescents to develop their own idealistic, theoretical views of the world. The ability to distinguish between reality and theory, however, can lead to disillusionment, and the recognition that adolescents' idols have "feet of clay." Elkind identifies three somewhat bizarre ways of thinking that result from cognitive growth in combination with a lack of experience. In personal fable, young adolescents see themselves as unique and special. Personal fable may lead adolescents to take unnecessary risks because they believe they are so different from others: "I can drink and drive." "Only other people get pregnant." Personal fable also makes adolescents believe that no one else can understand how they feel or offer any useful suggestions: "No one has ever had a problem like mine."

In imaginary audience, adolescents believe that "everyone" is watching them. Elkind sees this self-consciousness as an application of hypothetical thinking: "If my characteristics are so obvious to me, they must also be obvious to everyone else." In pseudostupidity, newly acquired cognitive skills prove difficult to control, causing adolescents literally to think too much and unnecessarily complicate the problems they face. As a result, they often appear "stupid" rather than mature.

Cognitive changes also affect social behavior by inducing changes in social cognitive development. Social cognition refers to an individual's understanding of people and of interactions between people. According to Piaget, changes in cognition are reflected in the way we think about ourselves and other people. The thinking of preadolescents (seven to eleven years) begins to focus less on the obvious features of objects, events, and people. They are better able to translate patterns of behavior into psychological characteristics, such as concluding that a particular person is "nice" or "rude." They are becoming less egocentric, better able to appreciate that people have different points of view. It is not surprising, then, that they are better able to see the world from the perspective of another person. As they enter formal operations (eleven or twelve years and older), adolescents are able to think in more logical and abstract ways. These changes are reflected in their ability to describe people in abstract terms, such as "cooperative" or "uncoordinated," and compare people along psychological dimensions.

Robert Selman has observed that changes in social cognition occur in stages that closely parallel Piaget's stages of cognitive development. According to Selman's research, most concrete operational preadolescents (ages ten to twelve) recognize the existence of different points of view. Many of them, however, have difficulty evaluating conflicting perspectives or understanding how perspectives relate to membership in different social groups. As adolescents become more fully formal operational (twelve to fifteen years and older), they become able to understand the relationship between another person's perspective and their membership in social systems. For example, the difference between two people's points of view may reflect their membership in different racial or ethnic groups. Progress through Selman's stages also is influenced by social experiences. In other words, it is possible for a person to mature intellectually and to become less egocentric without becoming skillful at role-taking.

## Context

Theory and research on cognitive skills began with the development of modern intelligence tests, such as Alfred Binet's 1916 test; however, the intelligence-testing, or psychometric, approach has contributed little to an understanding of adolescent cognitive skills. Intelligence tests are best suited to the study of individual differences, or how people compare to others of their age. It is difficult to use intelligence testing to compare and contrast cognitive skills at different ages.

Intelligence tests also are used to study the stability of intellectual level and the likelihood it will change in later years. Research indicates, however, that intelligence test scores in adolescence generally are similar to scores during childhood, although scores may fluctuate during childhood as a function of changes in factors such as diet, socioeconomic status, and education. Again, the psychometric approach seems poorly suited to the study of adolescent cognitive skills.

Psychometric (IQ score) research also contributes little to understanding the process of cognitive development. The developmental approach addresses both the qualities of thought and the process of change. In 1958, Piaget and his coworker, Barbel Inhelder, published *The Growth of Logical Thinking from Childhood Through Adolescence*, a detailed account of his four stages of cognitive development. In addition to proposing that specific cognitive skills emerge in each stage, Piaget proposes that the move from one stage to the next is largely maturational.

Piagetian theory has been notoriously difficult to evaluate. Research indicates that performance on Piagetian tasks depends on understanding the instructions, being able to attend to the relevant aspects of the problems, and being interested in the problems themselves. Adolescents who perform best on formal operational tasks are often those with interests in the natural sciences—an unlikely finding if cognitive change is largely maturational.

Although the popularity of Piagetian theory has declined, it remains one of the most influential theories in developmental psychology. In fact, it was Piagetian theory that led information-processing psychologists to become interested in cognitive development. Although disputing Piaget's proposals about cognitive stages, many of these psychologists noted parallels between Piaget's descriptions of cognitive skills and their own. Information-processing began to devote increasing attention to age-related changes in cognitive processes.

Information-processing research has helped explain some of the inconsistencies that appear in Piagetian research. According to Piagetian theory, people are located within particular cognitive stages and will reason at those levels of maturity in all problem-solving situations. Why, then, do most people show features of several stages, depending on the type of problem presented? According to information-processing research, variability in performance across different problem types is to be expected. The more one knows, the easier it is to use efficient cognitive processes. People will appear more cognitively mature performing tasks about which they are knowledgeable.

Understanding cognitive skills during adolescence requires some familiarity with all three perspectives, in spite of the weaknesses of the psychometric and Piagetian approaches. Each has made a unique historical contribution to current views of cognition.

## Bibliography

Bervonsky, M. "Formal Reasoning in Adolescence: An Alternate View." *Adolescence* 13 (1978): 280-290. A review of the research on formal thinking. Suggests that formal thinking typically emerges at eleven to fifteen years but that the ability to utilize this thinking varies among individuals.

Elkind, David. *The Child's Reality: Three Developmental Themes.* Hillsdale, N.J.: Lawrence Erlbaum, 1978. Discusses the ways in which adolescent cognitive skills are reflected in personality and in social behavior. Excellent presentations on egocentrism, ideologies, personal fable, imaginary audience, and pseudostupidity.

Flavell, John. *Cognitive Development.* Englewood Cliffs, N.J.: Prentice-Hall, 1985. Presents theory and research on cognitive development from an information-processing approach. Discusses relationship between information-processing and Piagetian theory. An excellent effort to compare and contrast these two perspectives.

Ginsburg, Herbert, and Sylvia Opper. *Piaget's Theory of Intellectual Development.* Englewood Cliffs, N.J.: Prentice-Hall, 1988. In its latest edition, this now classic work contains an updated presentation of Piaget's theory of cognitive development, including a detailed analysis of formal operational thinking.

Muuss, R. E. "Social Cognition: Robert Selman's Theory of Role Taking." *Adolescence* 17, no. 67 (1982): 499-525. Discusses the relationship between adolescent cognitive skills and the ability to adopt another person's point of view. Includes an overall summary of Robert Selman's model of social cognitive development.

*Lisa Friedenberg*

## Cross-References

124

# ADOLESCENCE: CROSS-CULTURAL PATTERNS

*Type of psychology:* Developmental psychology
*Field of study:* Adolescence

*Adolescence, generally considered to be the years between the ages of twelve and eighteen, is a time of rapid development and confusion, both physically and emotionally. Adolescence is viewed differently in different cultures; although certain characteristics seem to be widespread, they are not necessarily universal.*

*Principal terms*
FORMAL OPERATIONS: according to Piaget, the stage of cognitive development reached at adolescence, characterized by the ability to engage in abstract thinking
GENDER-ROLE ORIENTATION: the part that gender plays in one's family and social life
IDENTITY CRISIS: according to Erikson, the central developmental issue in adolescence; encompasses a struggle between identity and role confusion
KIBBUTZ: an Israeli collective settlement, particularly a collective farm
SELF-ESTEEM: the feelings one has about oneself, based on one's self-concept; it may be high or low

## Overview

Adolescence is a time of rapid and difficult changes unlike any other period in a human's life. Both physical development and cognitive development enter dramatic new stages. The physical changes of puberty signal the onset of sexuality; cognitive abilities progress to the sophistication needed for mathematics and complex word use. Social relationships outside the family become much more important than before. Adolescents frequently enter a stage of rebellion against parental authority. It is no wonder that this time is widely regarded as the most turbulent period of life and that adolescents restlessly seek their own identity (psychoanalyst Erik Erikson referred to the process as the "identity crisis" stage of development).

Both psychological and general Western cultural views of adolescence reflect the way this period is perceived in Western society. Two of the most widely discussed psychological models of adolescence—Jean Piaget's cognitive stage of "formal operations" and Erikson's view of the identity crisis—exemplify this Western orientation. Piaget's model of the stages of cognitive development (beginning in infancy), in particular, has been studied cross-culturally; that is, researchers have explored whether the stages apply equally well to various different cultures. It has been found that the stages do not universally occur in the order that Piaget suggested.

Historically, the idea of adolescence as a separate stage is a relatively new idea.

Before the mid-nineteenth century, in fact, a person was simply considered to pass from childhood to adulthood. Historically, and in different cultures, there have been various types of initiation rituals or rites of passage to mark this transition. In contemporary American society, one event that typically occurs in adolescence that could be considered such a rite of passage is learning to drive. This event embodies some of the complexities of modern society in that learning to drive symbolizes a new autonomy, yet the adolescent is nevertheless dependent on parents (or parent): The first car driven is usually theirs, they often pay the necessary insurance, and they set restrictions such as curfews.

Many tribal cultures have puberty rituals that reflect the way puberty is viewed in the culture. The Arapesh, a society in New Guinea, have a ceremony for girls at their first menstruation in which a menstrual hut is built for her; she is rubbed with stinging nettles by the older women, and she fasts for a number of days. Among the Mano of Liberia, boys participated in a pubertal ceremony in which they underwent a symbolic death, complete with chicken's blood to make it seem that they were punctured by a spear. The Pueblo Indians' traditional puberty ceremony for boys involves whipping, a largely ceremonial event in which no blood was drawn. During the initiation, children are supposed to be very frightened; they are not ashamed to cry aloud. Taking a psychoanalytical approach to studying male initiation ceremonies across cultures, John Whiting, Richard Kluckholm, and Albert Anthony noted that, in some cultures, mother and newborn infant share a bed exclusively for a year or more after childbirth. They concluded that such societies are more likely to have a ceremony of transition from boyhood to manhood, with the ritual helping to sever the boy's emotional bond with his mother. In various cultures, hazing, harsh endurance tests, and genital operations have all been performed in the name of initiation protocol.

Cultural attitudes and expectations of adolescence, as well as the behaviors and skills of adolescents, show both similarities and differences in different cultures. Much has been learned about this by studying the conflicts and difficulties experienced by adolescents of minorities and adolescents whose families have immigrated to the United States. These youths often have conflicting role models (or worse, no effective role models). The experiences of Asian-American youths from Southeast Asia have been discussed by J. F. Nidorf. Living in the United States, the youth feels that he or she must develop autonomy from parents in order to attain a personal identity and sense of worth. Yet the parents believe that the adolescent should remain "indefinitely in a position of mutual interdependence with family members" and that a sense of self-worth comes from subordinating one's own needs and assuming greater responsibility for the needs of other family members. In other words, the adolescent hears that one should "become a success in the United States, but find a way to do it without becoming an American." In another example, in traditional Chinese families, dating, as practiced in the United States, does (or did) not exist. As B. L. Sung puts it, in China, teenagers are kept "under wraps" until they are married; in the United States, they are "titillated."

## Applications

Among the cultures in which various aspects of childhood and adolescent development have been studied are Israel and Japan. The Israeli kibbutz is a collective settlement, either agricultural or industrial. The profits that are generated supply the members' basic needs as well as medical and social services. Approaches to child-rearing vary among kibbutzim; children are often reared as much by other supervising adults and by the community as a whole as by their biological parents. Traditionally, adults have their own living quarters, but children often live separately from their parents in special children's housing (this is by no means true of all kibbutzim). Cooking and dining are communal activities.

Psychoanalyst Edith Buxbaum practiced in Israel in 1965-1966 at Oranim, the child guidance clinic of the kibbutzim; she wrote of her experiences there in "Problems of Kibbutz Children" in *Troubled Children in a Troubled World* (1970). She noted that behavior considered to be delinquent was not usually reported as such, but that it occurred in connection with other symptoms. The peer group has a very strong influence on kibbutz adolescents (as on kibbutz children of all ages), in part because of the fact that the children are together so much of the time. The peer group is as much a consistent factor in a child's life as are the child's parents; the group is together from infancy until graduation from high school. The group is a primary source of security as well as of rules and demands. From about the age of ten, children are often given work to do on the adult farm, and shirking one's duty is looked upon very unfavorably by the peer group.

Although adolescence in most cultures is a time of belonging to groups, they are most frequently voluntary groups. This is not true of kibbutz adolescents, Buxbaum points out, and she compares the general attitude of loyalty and helpfulness among teenagers there to that among students at institutions such as boarding schools. In most adolescent groups, the voluntary aspect gives the group much of its character; it leads to a sense of assertion and rebelliousness. This rebellious quality is largely missing from the kibbutz adolescent group; here, individual rebellion must be directed against the group itself. In its extreme cases, rebellion may cause an adolescent or young adult to leave the kibbutz altogether—often for a different kibbutz.

Possibly the biggest rite of passage for a person reared on a kibbutz occurs at the end, not the beginning, of adolescence. At the age of eighteen, both men and women leave the kibbutz temporarily to perform Israel's compulsory military service. For some, this will be their first extensive experience with the "outside" world. Some who leave do not return, although leaving can involve challenges caused in part by a lack of preparedness for living outside the kibbutz. The purpose of kibbutz upbringing and education is primarily to help the child reach his or her potential while preparing the individual for life on the kibbutz. It is not necessarily designed to promote success in the wider society, since the kibbutz prefers that the young person return.

In Japan, it has only been since the 1950's that the concept of an adolescent, or teenager, in the Western sense, has become popular. Its arrival has largely been attributable to Western, especially American, influences, and to an increase in affluence. Historically, a young person passed from childhood to adulthood. There is no real Japanese-language equivalent for the word "teenager." High school students are commonly referred to as children (young people age seven or eight through fourteen are called *shonen*, and those fifteen to twenty-four are called *seinen*). The skepticism and questioning attitude toward society that has come to be associated with late adolescence also came to Japan relatively recently, and typical Japanese adolescent rebellions pale in comparison with Western proportions and standards.

Japanese adolescents associate mostly with same-sex friends, tending to associate with people their own age (as opposed to spending time with their elders) much more than previous generations have. The changes wrought by technological advances have increased the importance of the nuclear family structure in Japan, although adolescents spend most of their nonschool time with their friends. The family's primary demand on the adolescent is for academic achievement. Students spend several hours a day on homework. Values such as diligence, endurance, dedication, and the willingness and ability to choose a difficult task play important roles in education. Socialization is also very important in Japanese culture, generally much more so than in American society.

A 1984 study that looked at self-concept and sex-role development in Japan concluded that major inequalities exist between girls' and boys' levels of self-esteem, which proved to be considerably lower in girls. An even greater discrepancy was found in sex roles, self-concepts, and perceived sex-role norms. Girls are much more conditioned to conform to traditional sex-role expectations. Educational institutions demand, either explicitly or implicitly, that students—especially girls—conform to traditional sex-role stereotypes. In a 1989 study of Japanese and German students' own perceptions of socialization and gender, it was noted that the Japanese students reported significantly more parental acceptance and parental control than their German counterparts. Traditional gender-role orientations were also more apparent in Japanese students.

## Context

The study of behavior in different cultures has traditionally been the province of anthropology and sociology rather than psychology. A few psychological theorists in the 1960's, however, did begin to question psychology's nearly total reliance on Western cultural values for its models of normality and abnormality, noting, for example, the similarities between symptoms of "madness" and types of religious experiences such as shamanistic trances.

One of the first widely read works dealing with adolescence in a non-Western society was anthropologist Margaret Mead's *Coming of Age in Samoa* (1928). Causing something of a sensation when it first appeared, the book described puberty and adolescence in a simple Pacific island culture (her study focused only on girls). Mead's methodology and findings have since been reexamined and called into question by such researchers as Derek Freeman, who wrote a 1983 volume intended to "right the wrongs" committed by Mead and present a more accurate picture of traditional Samoan society. Nevertheless, her work, flawed though it may have been, was influential in focusing interest on other societies' approaches to life stages and to sexuality.

The study of adolescence in American society began in earnest in the 1950's, an era of postwar prosperity in which teenagers as a group had increasing visibility and mobility, attributable in part to the automobile. There was a growth of behavior labeled juvenile delinquency—illegal antisocial behavior, including gang activity—that caused concern among sociologists, law-enforcement agencies, and parents alike. The image of rebellious teenagers riding motorcycles and listening to rock 'n' roll caught the public imagination and became the fodder for many motion pictures.

In many cultures, adolescence is a time of strong peer-group attachments. Moreover, cognitive abilities reach new levels of sophistication (Piaget's "formal operations" stage). Therefore, as adolescents are being formally or informally initiated into the ways of adulthood, they are also able to question those ways; the types of questions asked, the satisfaction with traditional answers, and the levels of actual rebellion that occur vary from culture to culture and from time to time. Similarly, the skills and behaviors necessary for success in a society vary, depending on the society's complexity and stratification. In technological societies, such as exist in the United States and Japan, formal education becomes tremendously important. Whatever the needs of a particular society, however, the period of adolescence is a critical time for learning what the necessary skills are and discovering one's ability to acquire them.

## Bibliography

Barnouw, Victor. *Culture and Personality.* 4th ed. Belmont, Calif.: Wadsworth, 1985. Presents a historical view of various dimensions of culture as they relate to personality. Examines correlational studies, specifically cross-cultural surveys.

Bondy, Ruth. *The Israelis.* New York: Sabra Books, 1969. Offers a multifaceted look at the kibbutz in Israeli society in the 1960's. Contains considerable information on the Israeli people's behavior and past.

Buxbaum, Edith. *Troubled Children in a Troubled World.* New York: International Universities Press, 1970. Buxbaum takes a psychoanalytical approach to children's and adolescents' psychological problems. Two chapters, "The Group in Adolescence" and "Problems of Kibbutz Children," are especially relevant to adolescence. The latter looks at kibbutz children generally and at a few particular case studies.

Feldman, S. Shirley, and Glen R. Elliott, eds. *At the Threshold: The Developing Adolescent.* Cambridge, Mass.: Cambridge University Press, 1990. A comprehensive collection of essays on adolescence that presents the findings of a Carnegie Foundation study. Primarily concerned with American society, it does include interesting references to minority adolescents and other cultures as well as historical perspectives. Well-indexed and has an exhaustive list of references.

Freeman, Derek. *Margaret Mead and Samoa.* Cambridge, Mass.: Harvard University Press, 1983. Freeman's primary purpose is to "right the wrongs" that Mead committed in her *Coming of Age in Samoa.* He presents detailed empirical evidence to advance his arguments and remove readers' doubts about his point of view.

Schoenbrun, David. *The New Israelis.* New York: Atheneum, 1973. A thorough probe of Israel as a culture and a people. Explores issues of family expectations of children and the function of military service as they relate to the psychology of adolescence and adulthood.

White, Merry. *The Japanese Educational Challenge.* New York: Free Press, 1987. Clear and compelling investigation of the Japanese educational system. Explores the concept of a system that focuses on parental guidance and the development of strong human relationships outside the home.

*Denise S. St. Cyr*

## Cross-References

Adolescence: Cognitive Skills, 118; Adolescence: Sexuality, 130; Identity Crises: Erikson, 1255; Juvenile Delinquency, 1375; Teenage Suicide, 2527.

# ADOLESCENCE: SEXUALITY

*Type of psychology:* Developmental psychology
*Field of study:* Adolescence

*Adolescent sexuality examines the physical, psychological, and behavioral changes that occur as the individual leaves childhood, acquires sexual maturity, and incorporates the various aspects of sexuality into his or her identity. This emerging sexuality may cause adjustment problems, which can be severe.*

*Principal terms*
ADOLESCENCE: the period extending from the onset of puberty to early adulthood
ADOLESCENT GROWTH SPURT: a rapid increase in height and weight that begins at about eight or nine in girls and ten or eleven in boys
MENARCHE: the term for a female's first menstrual period
PRIMARY SEX CHARACTERISTICS: the physiological features of the sex organs
PUBERTY: the stage of development when the individual reaches sexual maturity and becomes capable of reproduction
SECONDARY SEX CHARACTERISTICS: physical features other than genitals that distinguish women and men
SEXUAL SCRIPT: a stereotypic pattern that defines how individuals should behave sexually

## Overview

Perhaps no single event during the adolescent years has as dramatic or widespread effects as the realization of sexuality. The lives of both males and females become wrapped in this new dimension. Adolescence is a time of sexual exploration and experimentation, of sexual fantasies and sexual realities, of incorporating sexuality into one's identity. It is not surprising, then, that the adolescent's emerging sexuality causes adjustment problems.

Adolescence is the life stage between childhood and adulthood. Its age limits are not clearly specified, but it extends roughly from age twelve to the late teens, when physical growth is nearly complete. Puberty, a term often confused with adolescence, occurs at the end of childhood and lasts from two to four years. It is the period of adolescence during which an individual reaches sexual maturity.

Human beings grow most rapidly at two times during their lives: before they are six months old and again during adolescence. The second period of accelerated growth is often referred to as the adolescent growth spurt. Adolescents grow both in height and weight, with the increase in height occurring first. As they gain weight, the amount and distribution of fat in their bodies change, and the proportion of bone and muscle tissue increases. In girls the adolescent growth spurt usually begins between the ages of nine and eleven and reaches a peak at an average of twelve-and-a-half years. Then growth slows and usually ceases completely between the ages of fifteen and eighteen. The growth spurt in boys generally begins about two years later than it does in girls and lasts for a longer time. It begins between the ages of eleven and fourteen, reaches a peak at about age fifteen, and slowly declines until the age of nineteen or twenty.

The teenager's body grows at differing rates, so that at times adolescents look a bit awkward. Big feet and long legs are the early signs of a changing body, but even these changes do not occur at the same time. First the hands and feet grow, then the arms and legs; only later do the shoulders and chest grow to fit the rest of the developing body. Changes in body proportion become obvious. The trunk widens in the hips and shoulders, and the waistline narrows. Boys tend to broaden mostly in the shoulders, girls in the hips.

Puberty is chiefly characterized by sexual development. Sexual development can be best understood by examining the maturation of primary and secondary sex characteristics. Primary sex characteristics are the physiological features of the sex organs. For males, these organs are the penis and the testes; for females, they are the ovaries, uterus, clitoris, and vagina. Secondary sex characteristics are not directly related to the sexual organs but nevertheless distinguish a mature male from a mature female. Examples of secondary sex characteristics are the male beard and the female breasts.

In girls, the onset of breast development is usually, but not always, the first signal that puberty has begun. This typically occurs between the ages of ten and eleven, but can occur as late as ages thirteen and fourteen. There is simultaneous development of the uterus and vagina, with enlargement of the labia and clitoris. Menarche (the first menstrual period), although perhaps the most dramatic and symbolic sign of a girl's changing status, occurs relatively late in puberty, after the growth spurt has reached its peak velocity. The first menstrual periods tend to be irregular, and ovulation (the release of a mature egg) does not usually begin until a year or so after menarche.

The first noticeable change in boys is usually growth of the testes and scrotum. The growth of the genitals begins, on average, about the age of twelve and is completed, on average, by about the age of fifteen. Boys generally become capable of ejaculation about a year after the penis begins to grow. These first emissions may occur as a result of nocturnal emissions, the ejaculation of semen during sleep. Nocturnal emissions are a normal phase of development and are frequently caused by sexual excitation in dreams or by some type of physical condition, such as a full bladder or even pressure from pajamas.

As adolescents' bodies become more adultlike, their interest in sexual behavior increases sharply. They must learn the necessary behavior to satisfy that interest, and they must face the issue of a mature gender identity. This includes the expression of sexual needs and feelings and the acceptance or rejection of sex roles. The onset of dating and the beginning of physical intimacies with the opposite sex can provoke frustration and anxiety. As this unfamiliar territory is explored, the adolescent is often very underinformed and overly self-conscious. Conflicting sexual values and messages are frequently encountered, accentuating the problem of integrating sexual drives with other aspects of the personality.

## Applications

Adolescents are acutely aware of the rapid changes taking place in their bodies. How they react to such changes greatly affects how they evaluate themselves; it is in this manner that physical and psychological development are related.

Physical changes may cause psychological discomfort. Adolescents are particularly concerned about whether they are the "right" shape or size and whether they measure up to the "ideal" adolescent. Rapid growth, awkwardness, acne, voice changes, menarche, and other developments may produce emotional distress. Therefore, it is not surprising that the timing of physical and sexual maturity may have an important influence on psychosocial adjustment. Adolescents are generally concerned about anything that sets them apart from their peers. Being either the first or last to go through puberty can cause considerable self-consciousness.

In general, boys who mature early have a distinct advantage over those who mature late. They tend to be more poised, easygoing, and good-natured. They are taller, heavier, and more muscular than other boys their age. They are also more likely to excel at sports, achieve greater popularity, and become school leaders. In contrast, late-maturing boys not only are smaller and less well developed than others in their age group, but they also are not as interested in dating. When they do become interested in girls, they often lack social skills; they are more likely to feel inadequate, anxious, and self-conscious. These personality characteristics tend to persist into early adulthood, although they become less marked and often disappear as time goes by.

For girls, early maturation appears to be a mixed blessing. Girls who mature early grow taller, develop breasts, and go through menarche as much as six years before some of their peers. Their larger size and more adult physique may make them feel conspicuous and awkward, while at the same time they may be popular with boys and experience more dating opportunities. They also may have to deal with parents and other caregivers who have reacted to their early sexual development by being overly restrictive. For these reasons, the late-maturing girl often finds adolescence a little easier than her early-maturing peer. As with boys, the consequences of early and late maturation decrease over time.

Sexual maturation has other psychological consequences as well. In particular, patterns of sexual behavior change tremendously with the arrival of sexual maturity. As adolescents' bodies become more adult, their interest in sexual behavior increases sharply; as they explore their sexual identities, they develop a sexual script, or a stereotyped pattern for how individuals should behave sexually.

The sexual script for boys is frequently different than the sexual script for girls. As a result, males and females generally think differently about sex. This discrepancy can cause problems and confusion for adolescents as they struggle with their sexual identities. For males, the focus of sexuality may be sexual conquest, to the point that young men who are nonexploitative or inexperienced may be labeled with negative terms such as "sissy." Males are more likely than females to see intercourse as a way of establishing their maturity and of achieving social status. As a consequence, boys are more likely to have sex with someone who is a relative stranger, to have more sexual partners, and to disassociate sex from love and emotional intimacy.

Adolescent girls are much more likely than adolescent males to link sexual intercourse with love. The quality of the relationship between the girl and her partner is a very important factor. Most females would agree that sexual intercourse is acceptable if the two people are in love and is not acceptable if the two people are not in a romantic relationship. Consequently, females are less likely than males to list pleasure, pleasing their partner, and relieving sexual tension as reasons for having sex.

Given their different sexual motives, boys generally expect sex sooner in a relationship than girls. Since girls usually want to wait until an emotional commitment and intimacy have developed, they may feel pressured into having sex before they are ready. Therefore, girls may be somewhat uncomfortable with a decision to engage in sexual intercourse.

During the past several decades, attitudes toward sexual activity have changed dramatically. Views regarding premarital sex, extramarital sex, and specific sexual acts are probably more open and permissive today than they have been at any time in recent history. Young people are exposed to sexual stimuli on television and in magazines and motion pictures to a greater extent than ever before. Effective methods of birth control have lessened the fear of pregnancy. All these changes have given the adolescent more freedom. These changes also produce more conflict, however, since guidelines for "appropriate behavior" are less clear-cut than they were in the past. In some families, the divergence between adolescent and parental standards of sexual morality is great.

## Context

Sexual behavior as a subject for scientific investigation has traditionally met with much resistance; historically, the majority of individuals in the fields of medicine and psychology have not considered sex to be an appropriate topic for investigation. As a result, knowledge regarding this important dimension of life has been slow to develop. Only since the 1940's have researchers been able to explore the physical and psychological aspects of human sexuality objectively.

Sigmund Freud, the father of psychodynamic theory, was one of the first scientists to demonstrate the influence of sexuality in human life. He clearly described the existence of sexuality in infants and children and developed a detailed theory of psychosexual development. Although his theory has been criticized, his rich observations and concepts have had a great impact on psychological thinking. At about the same time that Freud was developing his ideas, Havelock Ellis was publishing a seven-volume series called *Studies on the Psychology of Sex* (1897-1928). Ellis, an English physician, devoted much of his life to sexual research. He focused on the varied nature of human sexual behavior and challenged ideas commonly held at the time. For example, he did not agree that women were basically asexual, and he recognized the common occurrence of masturbation in both sexes.

Alfred Kinsey was another sexologist who has been instrumental in furthering understanding of human sexual behavior. Although severely criticized for his work, Kinsey paved the way for detailed, objective research. He and his colleagues conducted extensive face-to-face interviews with twelve thousand people from all segments of the population. This research produced a large amount of detailed data, resulting in the publication of two major works: *Sexual Behavior in the Human Male* (1948) and *Sexual Behavior in the Human Female* (1953).

The research of Kinsey and others focused on interviews and case histories. The goal was to discover how people behaved sexually, addressing such issues as how often and when they engaged in sexual activity as well as specific behaviors involved. It was not until the 1950's that William Masters and Virginia Johnson began to study what people actually did. Masters was trained as a gynecologist, and Johnson received her training in social work and psychology. Working as a team, they began to study sexual anatomy and physiology as well as psychological and sociological data. Under laboratory conditions, they observed and recorded the details of human sexual activity. In 1966, their findings were published in a report titled *Human Sexual Response*.

Research specifically directed toward the exploration of adolescent sexuality was not seriously undertaken until the 1950's and 1960's. Even then, the few studies that were conducted handled the topic delicately and focused on attitudes rather than behavior. When behavior was emphasized, age at first intercourse was generally selected as the major variable. Later studies have been more detailed and expansive; however, a paucity of research in this area still exists.

Jeanne Brooks-Gunn and Frank Furstenberg, in the book *Adolescent Behavior and Society* (4th ed., 1900, edited by Rolf E. Muuss), suggest that numerous issues have received little or no exploration. Included in their list of "research omissions" are the following: frequency of behaviors other than intercourse, pubertal education aimed at boys on topics such as ejaculation and condom use, the relation of sexual behavior to other adolescent behavior, the meaning of eroticism in adolescents' sex lives, and differences between younger and older adolescents.

Social concerns such as teenage pregnancy, sexually transmitted diseases, and sex education have focused attention on the need to understand clearly the dynamics of adolescent sexuality. This awareness should encourage broader perspectives for the study of teenage sexual behavior and produce detailed knowledge of sexuality as it occurs in the adolescent experience.

## Bibliography

Bell, Ruth, et al. *Changing Bodies, Changing Lives: A Book for Teens on Sex and Relationships.* New York: Random House, 1987. A comprehensive book that includes information on various aspects of adolescent sexuality. Written specifically for a teenage audience. Teens from around the United States were surveyed in order to determine the book's contents, and they share their unique perspectives on sexuality. This is perhaps one of the best resources available for teens.

Bowe-Gutman, Sonia. *Teen Pregnancy.* Minneapolis: Lerner, 1987. An excellent book which discusses values involving sexuality, health issues for adolescent mothers and their babies, contraception, parenting readiness, and the economics of raising a child. The book includes five case studies of pregnant teens, and offers advice for teens who think they may be pregnant.

Johnson, Eric W. *Love and Sex in Plain Language.* Philadelphia: J. B. Lippincott, 1985. This book was originally written in 1968; this fourth revision remains an excellent resource for the study of human sexuality. It is concise and comprehensive. The author discusses the development of male and female reproductive systems in an understandable manner. Illustrations, a glossary, and an index make the information readily accessible.

McCoy, Kathy, and Charles Wibbelsman. *The New Teenage Body Book.* Los Angeles: Body Press, 1987. An excellent resource, the book is concerned with the overall health of adolescents. Included is an excellent section on sexually transmitted diseases. Provides addresses of nationwide agencies that assist adolescents with health and sexual concerns. Comprehensive and readable, with illustrations and an index to complement the text.

Madaras, Lynda, with Area Madaras. *The What's Happening to My Body? Book for Girls: A Growing Up Guide for Parents and Daughters.* Rev. ed. New York: Newmarket, 1987. Written especially for adolescents and their parents. The author is a leading sex educator, and she is joined by her daughter. The primary focus is on female puberty; however, topics such as sexual feelings and sexual intercourse are also discussed. Well written, with illustrations that enhance the text.

Madaras, Lynda, with Dane Saavedra. *The What's Happening to My Body? Book for Boys: A Growing Up Guide for Parents and Sons.* 2d rev. ed. New York: Newmarket, 1987. Written by a leading sex educator with the assistance of an adolescent male. The book deals primarily with male puberty, but includes information about sexual feelings and sexual intercourse. A very useful and informative book, written in a conversational style which makes complicated information available to teens. Illustrations and an index are included.

*Doyle R. Goff*

## Cross-References

Adolescence: Cognitive Skills, 118; Homosexuality, 1182; Identity Crises: Erikson, 1255; Psychosexual Development, 1969; Sex Hormones and Motivation, 2234; Sexual Behavior Patterns, 2246; Sexual Variants and Paraphilias, 2259.

# THE ADRENAL GLAND

*Type of psychology:* Biological bases of behavior
*Field of study:* Endocrine system

*The paired adrenal glands situated above the kidneys are each divided into two portions, a cortex and a medulla. The cortex produces steroid hormones, involved in the control of metabolism, inflammation, and other important processes; the medulla produces the amino acid-derived catecholamines, which are thought to be important in brain behavior.*

*Principal terms*

AFFECTIVE DISORDERS: functional mental disorders associated with emotions or feelings; also called mood disorders

ENDOCRINE GLAND: a gland that produces one or more hormones and secretes them into the blood so that they can serve as intercellular messengers

HORMONE: a chemical messenger made by an endocrine gland that controls, in other organs, necessary biochemical processes

PROTEIN: amino acid polymers that have many biological functions, including acting as enzymes (biological catalysts) and hormone receptors

PSYCHOSIS: a severe mental disorder, with or without organic damage, characterized by deterioration of normal intellectual and social function and partial or complete withdrawal from reality

RECEPTOR: a protein that interacts with a specific hormone to enable it to carry out messenger functions in target organs

SCHIZOPHRENIA: any of a group of psychoses characterized by withdrawal from reality with accompanying affective, behavioral, and intellectual disturbances

STEROID HORMONE: a hormone that is a fatlike chemical derived from cholesterol

TARGET ORGAN: an organ that responds to a hormone by changes in its biological capabilities

## Overview

The adrenal glands are a pair of triangular endocrine glands, one lying on top of each of the kidneys. These glands secrete several hormones that are essential to life in that they regulate the body's metabolism of fats, carbohydrates, and proteins; help to maintain appropriate amounts of body fluids, thus participating in blood-pressure regulation; fight the effects of stress and injury on the body; participate in the immune response; and function in nerve-impulse transmission and brain function.

By definition, endocrine glands secrete their chemical products directly into the blood, rather than through ducts, as do the exocrine glands (such as the kidney, pancreas, or stomach). Hormones themselves are trace chemicals—present in tiny amounts—that act as extracellular messengers, controlling body processes in target organs far from the endocrine gland that produced them.

The adrenal gland is divided into an outer cortex and an inner medulla. The cortex produces about three dozen hormones, all fatlike steroids. These adrenal corticosteroids are divided into two main groups, glucocorticoids and mineralocorticoids; the adrenal cortex also produces steroid sex hormones. Glucocorticoids, whose production is controlled mostly by the pituitary gland (via the protein pituitary hormone adrenocorticotropin, or ACTH), mediate the ways in which the body breaks down and uses fats, carbohydrates, and proteins. The most abundant and potent of these hormones is cortisol (hydrocortisone). In times of stress (such as injury, extreme temperature change, illness, surgery, or ingestion of toxic chemicals), ACTH will stimulate production of glucocorticoids. The glucocorticoids also have tremendous ability as anti-inflammatory agents, fighting inflammation caused by arthritis and allergic reactions. For this reason, they are utilized medically to combat allergy, asthma, and arthritis. In some instances, overdosage of glucocorticoids can cause abnormal mental behavior.

The second major group of adrenal corticosteroids is the mineralocorticoids. These hormones control the body's salt levels (sodium and chloride ions), which are important to the maintenance of body water balance and to the cellular import and export of both nutrients and wastes. If too much sodium chloride is retained in blood and tissues, the total fluid volume in the blood vessels increases and produces high blood pressure. Mineralocorticoids also control potassium levels, important because this ion is essential to nerve-impulse transport. The main mineralocorticoid, aldosterone, interacts with a kidney protein (called renin) to maintain appropriate blood volume by controlling the rate of salt and water excretion. Diseases of underproduction or overproduction of adrenal steroids, including the sex hormones, can have serious consequences.

The adrenal steroids all act by forming complexes with special receptor proteins in target organs, transporting hormone-receptor complexes to cell nuclei, and stimulating the production of key cell proteins by interaction with the hereditary material (gene derepression) in cell nuclei.

The adrenal medulla—which arises from fetal nervous tissue—produces amino acid-derived hormones called catecholamines, stores them, and releases them on receiving an appropriate signal. The main catecholamines are epinephrine (adrenaline), norepinephrine (noradrenaline), and dopamine. These chemicals are linked with the nervous system in several ways. First, epinephrine and norepinephrine are hormones that control the "fight or flight" responses that enable the body to respond to emergencies (by anger or fear reactions). Such responses are partly attributable to linkage between the adrenal medulla and the sympathetic nervous system, which can produce the signals that cause release of catecholamines in times of stress.

Such release has many useful effects, including the dilation of eye pupils to allow better sight; elevation of the blood pressure and increasing of the heartbeat to allow better transport of energy-producing food; release of energy reserves of sugar from liver and muscle; and contraction of blood vessels near the skin, to minimize bleeding if wounds should occur. Epinephrine, norepinephrine, and dopamine also heighten the reactions of the central nervous system, acting as neurotransmitters in different parts of the brain and evoking responses needed for fight, flight, and normal brain function.

These actions of catecholamines can be harmful, as shown in a disease called pheochromocytoma, in which adrenal medullary hormones are overproduced because of tumors of the medulla or the sympathetic nervous system. Afflicted persons exhibit symptoms that include high blood pressure, heart palpitations, nervousness, anxiety, and neurotic symptoms. Abnormalities of catecholamine levels are implicated in a primary fashion in many psychological disorders. Catecholamine actions, like those of steroid hormones, involve specific receptors; however, catecholamine-related processes do not involve hormone-receptor interactions with the hereditary material. Rather, they utilize a "second messenger" mechanism in which already existing proteins are activated.

## Applications

Mental illness is frequently divided into two basic types: "organic" and "functional" disorders. Organic mental illness is a consequence of a known disease, such as diabetes or a tumor of the adrenal gland, that alters the structure of the brain or its ability to function correctly, or produces a malfunction of some other part of the nervous system. Cure of organic mental illness uses surgery or other methods that eradicate the causative disease. In contrast, the exact basis for functional mental illness has often evaded understanding and has long been viewed as being caused by operational flaws of mental function. Among the most widely publicized mental disorders are schizophrenia and manic-depressive psychosis (bipolar disorder).

Relatively clear understanding has begun to develop for bipolar disorder, wherein afflicted persons alternate rapidly between an excessively happy (manic) state and a severely depressed (depressive) state, thus being unable to cope with the world around them. This understanding begins with consideration of the function and malfunction of the human nervous system, composed of a central computer—the brain—and a network of neuron wires—nerves—that communicate with the rest of the body via nerve impulses. When nerve impulses pass through the nervous system correctly, they allow recognition and appropriate response to the world. Malfunction of nerve-impulse generation and passage through the nerves or brain is believed to produce some functional mental illness.

The terms "synaptic gap" and "neurotransmitter action" should be explained. Nerve cells (neurons) are separated from one another by minute synaptic gaps, and the passage of nerve impulses through a nerve requires the impulses to cross thousands of such gaps. Nerve-impulse transport across synaptic gaps is mediated by biochemicals called neurotransmitters. The best known of these is acetylcholine, which acts in "cholinergic" nerves. The dysfunction of cholinergic nerves, via disruption of acetylcholine action, is believed to be a major component of functional mental disease. This idea came partly from observation of impaired mental function in people exposed to nerve gases and insecticides that act by disrupting acetylcholine production and use.

Other neurotransmitters associated with mental disorders include catecholamines and chemicals called indoleamines. The main catecholamine neurotransmitters are the adrenal medulla hormones epinephrine and norepinephrine and their close cousin, dopamine (also made by the adrenal medulla). The catecholamines control nerve-impulse transmission by "adrenergic" portions of the nervous system. The indoleamines (especially serotonin) act in neurons related to sleep and sensory perception.

Some theories of depression and mania have arisen from the catecholamine (actually, norepinephrine) hypothesis of Joseph Schildkraut and others. The theory proposed that depression is attributable to suboptimum production or utilization of norepinephrine (decreased noradrenergic activity) and that mania arises from increased noradrenergic activity. Its acceptance led to the examination of norepinephrine levels in normal and mental disease states; use of observed levels of the neurotransmitter to explain how existing drugs, electric shock, and other psychiatric treatments affected functional mental illness; choice of new therapeutic drugs on the basis of their effects on norepinephrine levels; and study of effects of other catecholamines and related "biogenic amines."

These efforts soon showed that dopamine, a catecholamine cousin of norepinephrine, was implicated in central nervous system function. Then it was observed that several important tranquilizers (among them reserpine) decreased both norepinephrine and dopamine levels. Consequently, the catecholamine hypothesis was expanded to include dopamine. In fact, low levels of dopamine were shown to be more intimately involved in depression than are low epinephrine levels.

The biogenic indoleamine serotonin was next implicated in depression, because it is also depleted by tranquilizers such as reserpine. It was then shown that the action of therapeutic drugs called tricyclic antidepressants is also related mostly to alteration of serotonin levels. Because of this, an indoleamine (serotonin) corollary was added to the catecholamine hypothesis of affective disease.

In 1972, David Janowsky and coworkers, at Vanderbilt University's psychiatry department, proposed a new hypothesis of affective disease. Their hypothesis focused on the cholinergic neurotransmitter acetylcholine but expanded the conceptual basis for functional mental illness. Unlike preceding concepts, it recognized the importance of interaction between the various systems participating in nerve-impulse transmission and suggested that the affective state of any individual represents a balance between adrenergic and cholinergic activity. Furthermore, the hypothesis proposed depression as a disease of "relative cholinergic predominance," while mania was said to be attributable to "relative adrenergic predominance."

## Context

Until the advent of the catecholamine (and later indoleamine) hypothesis of affective mental disorder and the realization of the adrenal medullary involvement in psychiatric disorders, the primary treatments attempted for functional mental disease included procedures such as lobotomy, electroconvulsive (shock) therapy, and insulin coma. These procedures are now viewed as being imprecise at best, though some use of each has persisted, most often as part of mixed psychotherapy (that adds them to psychoanalysis and treatment with psychotherapeutic drugs) or therapy involving patients extremely difficult to treat.

Much of the basis for use of such drugs evolved from examination of therapeutic drugs for the ability to alter catecholamine and indoleamine levels. Among the first psychotherapeutic drugs were the tricyclic antidepressants, organic chemicals that affected catecholamine and serotonin levels. Another useful family of these drugs is a group of chemicals called monoamine oxidase (MAO) inhibitors. MAO inhibitors prevent biological modification of catecholamines by the enzyme monoamine oxidase, prolonging their presence in the body. In addition, the importance of lithium-containing chemicals in fighting functional mental illness is also believed to be attributable to a mechanism that includes alterations of catecholamine and indoleamine concentrations in the nervous system.

The developing understanding of the role of the adrenal medulla in both normal and pathological processes in the nervous system has led to a more complete understanding of the basis for the utility of major tranquilizers in treatment of the severely mentally ill. It has also enabled better differentiation of schizophrenia from affective disorders and led to explanations of the causes of (and some useful treatments for) the psychogenic manifestations of many illegal addictive drugs. Understanding of the adrenal gland has also led to the discovery of additional neurotransmitter chemicals that promise better understanding of the nervous system. Furthermore, examination of the steroid hormones of the adrenal cortex has shown that they can produce some psychopathology.

## Bibliography

Berkow, Robert. *The Merck Manual.* 15th ed. Rahway, N.J.: Merck Sharpe & Dohme Research Laboratories, 1987. Chapter 12 provides information on psychiatric disorders that includes explanation and differentiation of the various types of these disorders, description of their symptoms, and rationales behind therapeutic treatments. Covered are personality disorders, drug dependence, psychosexual problems, neuroses, mood disorders, schizophrenia, and suicidal behavior.

Janowsky, David S., M. Khaled El-Yousef, John M. Davis, and H. Joseph Sekerke. "A Cholinergic-Adrenergic Hypothesis of Mania and Depression." *The Lancet* 2 (September, 1972): 632-635. This landmark article recognizes the importance of the several systems of nerve-impulse transmission and proposes that the affective state represents balance between noradrenergic and cholinergic activity. Depression and mania are viewed as attributable to relative cholinergic and adrenergic predominance, respectively. Manic-depression is seen as overreaction by part of the nervous system.

Janowsky, David S., Robert N. Golden, Mark Rapaport, John Cain, and J. Christian Gillian. "Neurochemistry of Depression and Mania." In *Depression and Mania*, edited by Anastasios Georgotas and Robert Cancro. New York: Elsevier, 1988. Reviews development of modern concepts of the neurochemistry of these mental diseases, including norepinephrine and the catecholamine hypothesis; acetylcholine and the cholinergic-adrenergic hypothesis; and serotonin, dopamine, neuropeptides, and other neurotransmitters. Throughout, interaction of these systems is stressed. More than 160 references are included.

Lehninger, Albert L. *Principles of Biochemistry*. New York: Worth, 1982. Chapter 25 of this college textbook presents an introductory survey of the steroid hormones and related chemicals. Includes their structures, their biochemistry, their biological properties, and their interactions with receptors. Description is simple and scholarly, with several useful references included.

O'Malley, Bert W., and William T. Schrader. "The Receptors of Steroid Hormones." *Scientific American* 234, no. 20 (1976): 32-43. This succinct article describes many aspects of the hormone-receptor concept. These include some of its history, receptor interaction with target cells, molecular biology involvements in the process, and uses of the concept in medicine. Some nice graphics clarify many issues and several important references are provided.

Schildkraut, Joseph J. "The Catecholamine Hypothesis of Affective Disorders: A Review of Supporting Evidence." *American Journal of Psychiatry* 122, no. 5 (1965): 509-522. Schildkraut describes the clinical basis for the catecholamine (norepinephrine) hypothesis of affective disorders. It is pointed out that depression and elation are associated with "catecholamine" deficiency and excess, respectively, at crucial brain sites. Evidence for the hypothesis is cited.

Valenstein, Elliot S. *Great and Desperate Cures: The Rise and Decline of Psychosurgery and Other Radical Treatments for Mental Illness*. New York: Basic Books, 1986. Describes the basis for the development, rise, and decline of psychosurgery. Its coverage also includes other therapeutic methods used at the time, the theories of mentation that led to such techniques, and reasons for technique replacement or retention. Many useful illustrations and references are included.

*Sanford S. Singer*

## Cross-References

# AFFILIATION AND FRIENDSHIP

*Type of psychology:* Social psychology
*Fields of study:* Interpersonal relations; social motives

*Affiliation is the tendency to seek the company of others; people are motivated to affiliate for several reasons, and affiliation also meets many human needs. Friendship is an important close relationship based on affiliation, attraction, and intimacy.*

*Principal terms*
   AFFILIATION: the tendency to seek the company of others and to be with one's own kind
   ATTRACTION: the preference for contact with specific individuals
   COMMUNAL RELATIONSHIP: a long-term relationship based on common investments rather than balanced exchange
   COMPLEMENTARITY: the possession of qualities that complete or fulfill another's needs and abilities
   CONSENSUAL VALIDATION: the verification of subjective beliefs by obtaining a consensus among other people
   EXCHANGE RELATIONSHIP: a short-term relationship based on balance of benefits given and received
   PROPINQUITY: proximity or nearness to others
   PROSELYTIZE: to preach or convert with propaganda
   SOCIAL COMPARISON: the comparison of oneself to others to judge the appropriate way to behave

## Overview

Affiliation is the desire or tendency to be with others of one's own kind. Many animal species affiliate, collecting in groups, flocks, or schools to migrate or search for food. Human affiliation is not controlled by instinct, but is affected by specific motives. One motivation for affiliation is fear: People seek the company of others when they are anxious or frightened. The presence of others may have a calming or reassuring influence. Research in 1959 by social psychologist Stanley Schachter indicated that fear inducement leads to a preference for the company of others. Further work confirmed that frightened individuals prefer the company of others who are similarly frightened, rather than merely the companionship of strangers. This preference for similar others suggests that affiliation is a source of information as well as reassurance.

The value of obtaining information through affiliating with others is suggested by social comparison theory. Social comparison is the process of comparing oneself to others in determining how to behave. According to Leon Festinger, who developed social comparison theory in 1954, all people have beliefs, and it is important to them that their beliefs be correct. Some beliefs can be objectively verified by consulting a reference such as a dictionary or a standard such as a yardstick. Others are subjective beliefs and cannot be objectively verified. In such cases, people look for consensual validation—the agreement of others—to verify their beliefs. The less sure people are of the correctness of a belief, the more they rely on social comparison as a source of verification. The more people who agree with one's opinion about something, the more correct one feels in holding that opinion.

Beyond easing fear and satisfying the need for information or social comparison, mere affiliation with others is not usually a satisfactory form of interaction. Most people form specific attractions for other individuals, rather than being satisfied with belonging to a group. These attractions usually develop into friendship, love, and other forms of intimacy. Interpersonal attraction, the experience of preferring to interact with specific others, is influenced by several factors. An important situational or circumstantial factor in attraction is propinquity. Propinquity refers to the proximity or nearness of other persons. Research by Festinger and his colleagues has confirmed that people are more likely to form friendships with those who live nearby, especially if they have frequent accidental contact with them.

Further research by social psychologist Robert Zajonc indicated that propinquity increases attraction because it increases familiarity. Zajonc found that research subjects expressed greater liking for a variety of stimuli merely because they had been exposed to those stimuli more frequently than to others. The more familiar a person is, the more predictable that person seems to be. People are reassured by predictability and feel more strongly attracted to those who are familiar and reliable in this regard.

Another important factor in attraction and friendship is physical attractiveness. According to the physical attractiveness stereotype, most people believe that physically attractive people are also good and valuable in other ways. For example, physically attractive people are often assumed to be intelligent, competent, and socially successful. Attraction to physically attractive persons is somewhat modified by the fear of being rejected. Consequently, most people use a matching principle in choosing friends and partners: They select others who match their own levels of physical attractiveness and other qualities.

Matching implies the importance of similarity. Similarity of attitudes, values, and background is a powerful influence on interpersonal attraction. People are more likely to become friends if they have common interests, goals, and pastimes. Similar values and commitments are helpful in establishing trust between two people. Over time, they choose to spend more time together, and this strengthens their relationship.

Another factor in interpersonal attraction is complementarity. Research has failed to confirm that "opposites attract," since attraction appears to grow stronger with similarities, not differences, between two people. There is some evidence, however, that people with complementary traits and needs will form stronger relationships. For example, a person who enjoys talking will have a compatible relationship with a

friend or partner who enjoys listening. Their needs are different but not opposite—
they complete each other, hence the term "complementary."

Friendship begins as a relationship of social exchange. Exchange relationships
involve giving and returning favors and other resources, with a short-term emphasis
on maintaining fairness or equity. For example, early in a relationship, if one person
does a favor for a friend, the friend returns it in kind. Over time, close friendships
involve shifting away from an exchange basis to a communal basis. In a communal
relationship, partners see their friendship as a common investment and contribute to
it for their mutual benefit. For example, if one person gives a gift to a good friend,
he or she does not expect repayment in kind. The gift represents an investment in
their long-term friendship, rather than a short-term exchange.

Friendship also depends on intimate communication. Friends engage in self-
disclosure and reveal personal information to one another. In the early stages of
friendship, this is immediately reciprocated: One person's revelation or confidence
is exchanged for the other's. As friendship develops, immediate reciprocity is not
necessary; long-term relationships involve expectations of future responses. According to psychologist Robert Sternberg, friendship is characterized by two experiences:
intimacy and commitment. Friends confide in one another, trust one another, and
maintain their friendship through investment and effort.

## Applications

Theories of affiliation explain why the presence of others can be a source of comfort. In Stanley Schachter's classic 1959 research on fear and affiliation, university
women volunteered to participate in a psychological experiment. After they were
assembled, an experimenter in medical attire deceived them by explaining that their
participation would involve the administration of electrical shock. Half the subjects
were told to expect extremely painful shocks, while the others were assured that the
shocks would produce a painless, ticklish sensation. In both conditions, the subjects
were asked to indicate where they preferred to wait while the electrical equipment
was being set up. Each could indicate whether she preferred to wait alone in a
private room, in a large room with other subjects, or had no preference.

The cover story about electrical shock was a deception; no shocks were administered. The fear of painful shock, however, influenced the subjects' preferences:
Those who expected painful shocks preferred to wait with other subjects, while
those who expected painless shocks expressed no preference. Schachter concluded
that (as the saying goes) misery loves company. Further research gave subjects the
choice of waiting with other people who were not research subjects. In this study,
subjects who feared shock expressed specific preference for others who also feared
shock: Misery loves miserable company.

The social comparison theory of affiliation explains the appeal of group membership. People join groups such as clubs, organizations, and churches to support one
another in common beliefs and to provide one another with information. Groups can
also be a source of pressure to conform. One reason individuals feel pressured to

conform with group behavior is that they assume the group has better information than they have. This is termed informational influence. Cohesive groups—groups with strong member loyalty and commitment to membership—can also influence members to agree in the absence of information. When a member conforms with the group because he or she does not want to violate the group's standards or norms, he or she has been subjected to normative influence.

Studies of interpersonal attraction and friendship have documented the power of circumstances such as propinquity. In their 1950 book *Social Pressures in Informal Groups*, Leon Festinger, Stanley Schachter, and Kurt Back reported the friendship preferences of married students living in university housing. Festinger and his colleagues found that the students and their families were most likely to form friendships with others who lived nearby and with whom they had regular contact. Propinquity was a more powerful determinant of friendship than common background or academic major. Propinquity appears to act as an initial filter in social relationships: Nearness and contact determine the people an individual meets, after which other factors may affect interpersonal attraction.

The findings of Festinger and his colleagues can be applied by judiciously choosing living quarters and location. People who wish to be popular should choose to live where they will have the greatest amount of contact with others: on the ground floor of a high-rise building, near an exit or stairwell, or near common facilities such as a laundry room. Zajonc's research on the power of mere exposure confirms that merely having frequent contact with others is sufficient to predispose them to liking.

Mere exposure does not appear to sustain relationships over time. Once people have interacted, their likelihood of having future interactions depends on factors such as physical attractiveness and similarity to one another. Further, the quality of their communication must improve over time as they engage in greater self-disclosure. As friends move from a tit-for-tat exchange to a communal relationship in which they both invest time and resources, their friendship will develop more strongly and satisfactorily.

Research on love has identified a distinction between passionate love and companionate love. Passionate love involves intense, short-lived emotions and sexual attraction. In contrast, companionate love is calmer, more stable, and based on trust. Companionate love is strong friendship. Researchers argue that if passionate love lasts, it will eventually calm down and become transformed into companionate love.

Researcher Zick Rubin developed a scale to measure love and liking. He found that statements of love involved attachment, intimacy, and caring. Statements of liking involved positive regard, judgments of similarity, trust, respect, and affection. Liking or friendship is not simply a weaker form of love, but a distinctive combination of feelings, beliefs, and behaviors. Rubin found that most dating couples had strong feelings of both love and liking for each other; however, follow-up research confirmed that the best predictor of whether partners were still together later was how much they had liked—not loved—each other. Liking and friendship form a solid basis for love and other relationships that is not easily altered or forgotten.

## Context

Much early research on affiliation and friendship developed from an interest in social groups. After World War II, social scientists were interested in identifying the attitudes and processes that unify people and motivate their allegiances. Social comparison theory helps to explain a broad range of behavior, including friendship choices, group membership, and proselytizing. Festinger suggested that group membership is helpful when one's beliefs have been challenged or disproved. Like-minded fellow members will be equally motivated to rationalize the challenge. In their 1956 book *When Prophecy Fails*, Festinger, Henry Riecken, and Schachter document the experience of two groups of contemporary persons who had attested a belief that the world would end in a disastrous flood. One group was able to gather and meet to await the end, while the other individuals, mostly college students, were scattered and could not assemble. When the world did not end as predicted, only those in the group context were able to rationalize their predicament, and they proceeded to proselytize, spreading the word to "converts." Meanwhile, the scattered members, unable to rationalize their surprise, lost faith in the prophecy and left the larger group.

Research on propinquity combined with other studies of interpersonal attraction in the 1960's and 1970's. Friendship and love are challenging topics to study since they cannot be re-created in a laboratory setting. Studies of personal relationships are difficult to conduct in natural settings; if people know they are being observed while they talk or date, they behave differently or leave the scene. Natural or field studies are also less conclusive than laboratory research, since it is not always clear which factors have produced the feelings or actions that can be observed.

Friendship has not been as popular a topic in relationships research as romantic love, marriage, and sexual relationships. Some research has identified gender differences in friendship: Women communicate their feelings and experiences with other women, while men's friendships involve common or shared activities. Developmental psychologists have also identified some age differences: Children are less discriminating about friendship, identifying someone as a friend who is merely a playmate; adults have more complex ideas about friendship forms and standards.

As research on close relationships has gained acceptance, work in communication studies has contributed to the findings of social psychologists. Consequently, more is being learned about the development and maintenance of friendship as well as the initial attractions and bonds that encourage people's ties to others.

## Bibliography

Duck, Steve. *Friends, for Life: The Psychology of Close Relationships.* New York: St. Martin's Press, 1983. Duck, an influential theorist in the field of close relationships, explains the value of friends, the strategies by which friendships are developed, and the ways in which friendships can be assessed and strengthened. Readable and engaging.

Festinger, Leon, Stanley Schachter, and Kurt Back. *Social Pressures in Informal*

*Groups.* Stanford, Calif.: Stanford University Press, 1950. This classic work documents the authors' research on housing and friendship preferences and ties work on friendship to theories of group structure and function.

Hendrick, Clyde, and Susan Hendrick. *Liking, Loving, and Relating.* Monterey, Calif.: Brooks/Cole, 1983. The Hendricks provide a thorough review of the processes of affiliation and interpersonal attraction. They include a discussion of issues in contemporary relationships, such as separation and divorce, blended families, changing sex roles, and dual-career couples.

Huston, Ted L., ed. *Foundations of Interpersonal Attraction.* New York: Academic Press, 1974. This edited volume brings together chapters by major researchers in close relationships. Most chapters emphasize theory and are directed at the college student and graduate student.

Rubin, Lillian B. *Just Friends: The Role of Friendship in Our Lives.* New York: Harper & Row, 1985. A very accessible popular work examining a much-neglected topic. Considers gender differences in friendships and how friendships coexist with other close relationships in people's lives.

*Ann L. Weber*

## Cross-References

The Affiliation Motive, 148; Attraction Theories, 332; Cooperation, Competition, and Negotiation, 689; Group Decision Making, 1114; Groups: Nature and Function, 1125; Love, 1486; Self-Disclosure, 2182.

# THE AFFILIATION MOTIVE

*Type of psychology:* Motivation
*Fields of study:* Interpersonal relations; motivation theory; social motives

*The affiliation motive is the tendency for individuals within a society to form groups or associations that are recognized components of the society's cultures. Affiliation may be based on cooperation, friendship, mutual interests, age, sex, protection, acquisition of physical resources, and social pressures to conform; affiliations transcend the usual kinship organizational structures of most societies.*

*Principal terms*

AFFILIATION: the joining of an individual to a group of individuals, many of whom may be unrelated, based upon such things as cooperation, mutual interests, friendship, age, gender, and protection

AGGREGATION: a grouping of members of a species for mutual protection and acquisition of resources; an important social event that requires affiliative motives

ALTRUISM: a phenomenon in human and animal behaviors in which individuals unselfishly sacrifice their own genetic fitness in order to help other individuals in a group

ANTISOCIAL: behavior in which an individual or individuals do not adequately participate within the cultural norms of society, or a situation in which certain individuals are not accepted by society

ASSOCIATION: an accepted social organization into which individuals affiliate based upon common interests, friendship, age, and so on, for the attainment of the society's cultural goals

CASTE: a ranked grouping of certain members of society, found in many human cultures and in various social animal species, wherein the individuals who are members of the caste are assigned a particular level of dominance, power, and control of resources

DOMINANCE HIERARCHY: a pecking order; a behavioral organization of groups into ranked groupings containing dominant to progressively more subordinate individuals

DRIVE: the motivation or momentum of an individual to achieve certain goals, the successful completion of which require personal sacrifices and interactions with other individuals

INCENTIVE: a motivating force or system of rewards that is presented to an individual if he or she behaves or successfully performs specified tasks according to the norms of society

KINSHIP: the primary social organizing force in many human and animal societies, based upon the relatedness of individuals

# Overview

Social behavior is a characteristic of animals having highly developed nervous systems, in particular the vertebrates (mammals, birds, reptiles, amphibians, fish) and the invertebrate social insects (ants, termites). In all these species, there are behaviors that are exclusively instinctive (endogenous); however, in mammals and birds, the process of learning from environmental experiences (exogenous behaviors) becomes pronounced. In mammalian and bird species, complex social interactions have evolved in which individuals aggregate and work together for the benefit of the group as a whole.

Such highly social species form aggregations composed of both males and females. These aggregations usually are migratory, as the individuals of the aggregate search for food, or are territorial, in areas of abundant food supply. The social aggregation is designed to find food for the sustenance of the group, to reproduce, and to protect the group members from predators. Single individuals or very small groups generally have more difficulty in finding food and in defending themselves than do large groups. This easily can be seen in birds or cattle, which flock and herd, respectively, at the approach of a predator.

Within such aggregates or societies, male and female associations develop; both associations are based upon dominance hierarchies. A dominance hierarchy, or pecking order (as in chicken societies), is a precisely ranked ordering of individuals from most dominant to most subordinate. Dominance hierarchies are important features of practically all mammalian and avian (bird) societies. They are dynamic social structures which are constantly changing because of continual interactions, encounters, and conflicts between individuals and groups of individuals. Several less dominant males may cooperate to usurp the power of the dominant male, for example. Young males or females usually start at the bottom of a dominance hierarchy and gradually work their way up the scale of dominance. Older individuals generally fall down the dominance scale as they weaken from intergroup competition. The overall format of the dominance hierarchy guarantees the best territory, the most mates, the most and best food supply, and the best protection from predators for the most dominant individuals. The most subordinate individuals usually have the worst territory, few if any mates, poor nutrition, and great susceptibility to predation.

Such dominance hierarchies permeate human societies, although their presence is often subtle within the context of much more complex social and cultural systems. Human societies, whether primarily technological, agricultural, or hunting, consist of institutions, organizations, religions, clubs, and other groups with which individuals become affiliated, or involved. To some extent, many of these groups serve the same purposes as do groups in other animal societies: food assimilation, reproduction, and protection from predators, enemies, or other "undesirable" people. Human societies, however, employ unique rationales for individual affiliation. Humans may become affiliated with certain groups because of friendship, mutual interests, age, gender, or race.

The affiliation motive behind an individual's joining a particular group lies within all these factors. Nevertheless, lurking beneath these factors are some very basic sociobiological principles. It is the individual's advantage to affiliate with other individuals. Through interactions with others, one can assert one's position within the existing dominance hierarchy, in so doing gaining recognition for oneself not only in terms of dominance relationships but also in terms of meeting the society's views of acceptable behavior. Outcasts and other individuals who fail to affiliate within the accepted social institutions are frowned upon by their peers and are subject to prejudicial treatment. Antisocial behavior is strongly discouraged and is often punished in many societies.

The dominance hierarchy without question is a major evolutionary adaptation for the survival of social animal species. In every association of individuals, the dominance hierarchy is expressed in the power structure of the group as well as in the peer pressure aimed at forcing all societal members to conform. Conformity means affiliation with acceptable societal groups and submission to the dominance hierarchy.

An individual's drive, or motivation, to affiliate with other individuals may be attributable to common interests or characteristics, but often this drive is tempered by social pressures to conform to the stability of the existing dominance structure. In many instances, the motivation to affiliate is influenced by societal incentives. Affiliation with some groups may bring prestige, a better standard of living, and other benefits. Such affiliations usually are easier when kinship (relatedness) with group members exists. Otherwise, the individual may have to make certain sacrifices.

Human societal groups include organizations such as elitist country clubs and social clubs or special interest groups (gem clubs, astronomy clubs), professionally related organizations, women's clubs, men's clubs, teen groups, elderly groups, churches, volunteer rescue squads and fire departments, and sports teams. Even youth gangs, mobsters, and hate groups fall within such categories. Affiliation is a social behavior in which practically everyone participates in some way, either willingly or unwillingly.

One phenomenon of affiliation behavior that is prevalent in numerous groups is altruism, an unselfish contribution on the part of an individual for others even if they are not genetically related to the individual. Altruism occurs in numerous species, although it usually occurs between related individuals. Humans exhibit an unusual level of altruism even toward unrelated individuals. There is some philosophical debate over whether such behavior in humans is truly unselfish. A number of investigators seek other underlying motives in such behavior and dismiss the notion that people help others purely out of a sense of caring.

Affiliation motives, therefore, are based upon mutual interest and characteristics between people, altruistic behavior, and peer pressure associated with existing social dominance hierarchies. Affiliation is an important component of the stable structuring of society. It is of major concern in specific cases where individuals are barred from groups because of intelligence, family background, political affiliation, religious beliefs, race, or personal wealth.

## Applications

Affiliation is a major subject of study for psychologists, sociologists, and social-cultural anthropologists. A critical behavior in the formation of the complex societies which characterize mammalian and bird species, it is very pronounced in human societies. Psychologists and anthropologists study group associations in many different human societies, comparing the characteristics of these different groups to ascertain the importance of affiliation and other group interactions in the development of the individual, the development of culture, and the evolution of human civilization. Studies are also made of group behaviors in primates and other closely related species to arrive at the sequence of evolutionary events leading to group adaptations.

Affiliation motives and drives reveal the psychological background of various individuals and, as a result, enable the researcher to understand differences between people in achievement of goals. Such knowledge can be of great value in uncovering the psychological and physical blocks which prevent some people from reaching their maximum intellectual and physical potential. Dominance hierarchies, while representing a very central, structured component of practically all societies, are stumbling blocks to many people. Understanding of how they operate can be of great use in assisting the smooth, nonviolent interaction of differing peoples. It also can be of use in unraveling the roots of antisocial behavior.

Social and cultural anthropologists have studied the structure and organization of hundreds of different societies throughout the world. These societies exhibit many of the same social processes and patterns of organized behavior. They all exhibit dominance hierarchies, acceptable rules of individual and group behavior, and strong orderliness based upon kinship. Some such societies (Hindu, for example) relegate their members to separate castes, permanent divisions based upon genetic inheritance and particular trades maintained by descendants of specific castes. In advanced technological societies, large populations, fast-paced life-styles, and high regional mobility result in social structures based less upon kinship and more upon other factors, such as mutual interests, age, gender, and race.

The study of social groups and affiliation motives for such groups provides an informative analysis of human social evolution within the context of rapidly changing societies. The psychological impact of such changes upon the individual and upon the group as a whole can provide an understanding of societal problems such as crime, social inequality, and intergroup tensions. Underlying all these situations is the natural biological tendency for individuals to aggregate for the common good of all members, thereby reducing the chance of danger to individual members. Humans, like all animals, have a need to interact and associate with other members of their own species. The drive to affiliate is related to the need for acceptance and the subsequent goals of recognition, power, protection, and mating.

Societal pressures to conform and to affiliate are great. During the twentieth century, numerous psychologists have propounded theories describing the psychological bases behind an individual's motives to affiliate with other individuals. These theories are in agreement as to the goals of affiliation—objectives such as friendship, mutual interests, mating, acquiring food, and ensuring protection. These theories differ, however, in the psychological mechanisms behind the affiliation motive.

Among the most famous of these motivational theories comes from the work of the psychoanalytical pioneer Sigmund Freud. Freud proposed that all motivational drives within an individual center around two principal components of the individual psyche: the libido and the Eros instinct. The libido is an aspect of one's psychological makeup whose prime focus is sexual reproduction, whereas the Eros instinct is one's inner need to survive. Influenced by Darwinian evolutionary theory, Freud maintained that all motives, including the affiliation motive, are aimed at satisfying one's sexual and survival needs.

The analytical psychologists Kurt Goldstein and Abraham Maslow maintained that an individual's psyche organizes itself about a tiered arrangement of personal needs and goals. These tiers include basic bodily needs such as food, protection, the need to be loved, and "self-actualization." According to their theories, different individuals focus upon different aspects of these psychological needs. They further maintained that all one's psychological needs emerge from the need for self-actualization, the need to be recognized as an important member of society. Psychological disorders were believed to occur as a result of conflicts within these inner needs.

Other theories of social involvement and motivation include those of Carl Jung and Alfred Adler. Jung concentrates upon individuals as being introverts or extroverts. Adler concentrates upon inferior people overcompensating to become superior, with inferiority complexes arising when inferior individuals choose socially unacceptable means of becoming superior. All these theories and others employ many of the same basic concepts. They generally center around basic instinctive desires (sexuality, food acquisition, protection from danger) and the need for recognition (dominance, personal achievement). Consequently, they reflect the biological basis of behavior that has evolved in animals over the past few hundred million years.

The psychological theories of motivation and the cultural manifestations of association and affiliation fall within the domain of sociobiology, a branch of biological thought advanced by numerous behaviorists and analytical psychologists that has been considerably refined and compellingly presented by Harvard University entomologist Edward O. Wilson. The motive of individual affiliation in any animal society, including human society, is the achievement of personal and group needs, which essentially boil down to views of survival and reproduction similar to those expressed by Freud.

## Context

What motivates people to affiliate with others in associations? Psychology and animal behavior have isolated the basis of affiliation and of behavior in general: one's instinctive needs as a living organism. This rationale stems from the fact that humans are animals and are the products of at least 3.8 billion years of evolutionary change on Earth. The nature of all life is to survive and to reproduce. Therefore, the activities of all organisms are centered on the achievement of these goals. In sociobiology theory, animal behavior and animal societies are driving forces in the survival, reproduction, and evolution of any given animal species. This theory has produced much controversy and debate; however, there is considerable evidence supporting it.

Affiliation is one of the foci of social behavior. Animals have a need to associate with other individuals of their own species. In so doing, they ensure their own safety and enhance their own reproductive potential. An individual's behavior is directed toward these ends. Another sociobiological viewpoint is that of the "selfish gene," a concept developed by modern molecular biologists and advanced by Richard Dawkins in a book of that name. The selfish gene concept maintains that evolution occurs at the level of the gene and that individual organisms are the means by which genetic information is copied and transmitted to future generations. All aspects of the organism and populations of organisms are geared to this end. Biochemical changes within an individual's nervous and endocrine systems facilitate such motivations. The physiology of motivation is an object of intense study.

While such a view of life may seem belittling, it is a logical explanation of humankind's very existence. It explains much of the structure of human social groups, particularly in terms of individual affiliations and group politics. It also explains the sources of conflict and inequality in Western society. Individuals wish to belong to groups; therefore, they join organizations that advance their own mutual interests. If they are rejected by a group, they very well may join an opposing group to exact retaliation. American society supposedly is desegregated; however, evidence of racism and segregation is apparent in many institutions, ranging from social clubs to churches. Such segregation also exists in the structure of cities, where neighborhood-by-neighborhood sectioning separates the rich and the poor. In politics, Americans are expected to register to vote as Democrats or Republicans, two political parties that are nearly identical in philosophy; affiliation with other political parties is discouraged, as is evidenced by the "unaffiliated" registration and a population that votes for candidates without any real understanding of the issues involved.

The technological advance of *Homo sapiens* has greatly outpaced human psychological development. Humans have divided themselves into conflicting nations, religions, and cultures based upon mutual fear. A growing awareness of the fragility of the earth and the responsibility of humans to save the planet and the life that inhabits it has encouraged the idea that humans need to unaffiliate themselves. The affiliation motive for the twenty-first century ideally would be to save life on the earth, including human life, in a world that is becoming overpopulated and devastated by the effects of technology.

## Bibliography

Chagnon, Napoleon A. *Yanomamo: The Fierce People.* 2d ed. New York: Holt, Rinehart and Winston, 1977. Chagnon's anthropological study of the Amazonian Yanomamo people is a classic in the field of social and cultural anthropological research. He explores the intricacies of Yanomamo society and culture plus their interactions with other tribes. He devotes considerable attention to group behaviors and individual motives for affiliation. Chapter 3, "Social Organization," is an extensive analysis of Yanomamo kinship, marriage patterns, division of labor, status differences, and individual social life.

Chaplin, James Patrick, and T. S. Krawiec. *Systems and Theories of Psychology.* New York: Holt, Rinehart and Winston, 1960. Chaplin and Krawiec's survey of psychology, its history, major theories, and experimental research is an interesting, lively account of the subject. They discuss classical and contemporary approaches to psychological research and the principal contributions of leading psychologists of the twentieth century. They also address famous experiments in human and animal behavior. Chapter 9, "Motivation," is a thorough survey of theories and experiments in human behavioral drives.

Hall, Edward T. *The Hidden Dimension.* Garden City, N.Y.: Doubleday, 1966. Hall's insightful work is an anthropological and psychological analysis of human individual and group interactions, primarily in modern technological societies. Concentrates primarily on personal and private distance levels between individuals in individual-individual and group-group encounters. Chapter 10, "Distances in Man," describes such levels and their significance upon individual behavior. From these studies, Hall draws important conclusions and recommendations for improving human society.

Hammond, Peter B. *An Introduction to Cultural and Social Anthropology.* New York: Macmillan, 1978. Hammond's excellent introduction to anthropology for the beginning student and layperson is a comprehensive survey of relevant research and theory concerning the development and maintenance of human cultures throughout the world. Chapter 8, "Associations," compares social groups in various human societies and the motivations by which individuals enter these groups.

Manning, Aubrey. *An Introduction to Animal Behavior.* 3d ed. Reading, Mass.: Addison-Wesley, 1979. Manning's work is a concise, thorough survey of important animal behavior research. He cites numerous research studies on many different animal species, and he compares competing theories and models aimed at describing these behaviors. Chapter 4, "Motivation," is a detailed analysis of animal drives based upon biological principles, including group cohesiveness, aggressiveness, sexual and feeding needs of the individual, and hormonal influences. An extensive reference list is provided for further research.

Skinner, B. F. *Science and Human Behavior.* New York: Macmillan, 1953. This outstanding discussion of human behavior, written by one of the great psychologists/behavioral scientists of the twentieth century, thoroughly and clearly presents all principal aspects of human behavior to a general audience. Chapter fifteen, "Self-Control," is a study of the behavioral and physiological mechanisms by which an individual regulates conduct. Chapter 27, "Culture and Control," analyzes sociocultural restraints upon human impulses and drives.

Zimbardo, Philip G., ed. *The Cognitive Control of Motivation: The Consequences of Choice and Dissonance.* Glenview, Ill.: Scott, Foresman, 1969. This informative collection of research papers by leading psychologists and behavioral scientists focuses upon experiments with individuals to test various types of individual motivation and the factors which influence variations in motivation. Essay 10, "Dissonance and the Need to Avoid Failure," by A. R. Cohen and Zimbardo, discusses social pressures as individual motivators. Other essays by Zimbardo, his colleagues, and his students illustrate the principal human motivations and drives.

*David Wason Hollar, Jr.*

## Cross-References

Achievement Motivation, 96; Affiliation and Friendship, 142; The Aggression Motive, 174; Groups: Nature and Function, 1125; Motivation: Cognitive Theories, 1606; Self: Definition and Assessment, 2162; Social Identity Theory, 2297; Social Perception: Others, 2311.

# AGEISM

*Type of psychology:* Developmental psychology
*Fields of study:* Aging; prejudice and discrimination

*Ageism refers to prejudice and discrimination directed toward persons because they are elderly. These negative attitudes and perceptions affect the ways that individuals and society treat the elderly and may determine one's own reactions to growing older.*

### Principal terms

AGE IDENTIFICATION STUDIES: research efforts in which persons of various ages are asked to identify themselves as being young, middle-aged, or old

DISCRIMINATION: behaving unfairly or illegally toward a person or group of persons

GERONTOPHOBIA: an exaggerated fear of older persons or the aging process

PREJUDICE: attitudes toward a social group that are factually inaccurate or incorrect

STEREOTYPING: the attitude that a group of people, such as all elderly persons, are identical or very similar in their beliefs and behavior

## Overview

The term ageism was coined by Robert Butler, the first director of the National Institute on Aging. Like racism and sexism, ageism involves prejudice and discrimination directed toward a specific segment of the population. When someone claims that blacks are inferior to whites or that females are less intelligent than males, the listener usually realizes that racist and sexist attitudes are being presented. Many persons, however, will accept the notion that the aged are senile, asexual, inflexible, poverty-stricken, and incapable of learning without recognizing the prejudicial nature of such statements. In nearly all instances, the stereotypical elderly person is viewed negatively; the prevailing attitude in the United States is that young is good and old is inferior.

Surveys and other research indicate that ageist attitudes are widely held. Any attitude must be learned, and there are many sources available in American society. On television and in motion pictures, there are comparatively few older characters. The few older persons portrayed are typically depicted as either bumbling, forgetful souls who beget laughter and ridicule or saintly paragons of virtue who possess great wisdom. Neither portrayal is realistic. In actuality, these are stereotypes—what people believe old persons should be. Magazines and television present innumerable images of healthy, attractive young adults laughing, exercising, dancing, playing sports, and generally having a good time. It is not surprising that children begin to associate youth with goodness and old age with decrepitude.

The media also report cases of elderly persons who are found living in isolation, abandoned by relatives, and who are so poor that they resort to eating things such as cat food. Such cases are news precisely because of their rarity. There are destitute older persons; but reports produced by the federal government indicate that the percentage of aged persons (those above sixty-five years of age) below the official poverty line is actually less than the percentage in the general population. The elderly poor tend to be persons who have been impoverished for most of their lives. A minority of the elderly are actually lonely and deserted by relatives; surveys indicate that most older persons live within a thirty-minute drive of at least one child and have frequent contact with offspring. Also, less than 10 percent of those over the age of sixty-five report that they do not have enough friends. Only about 5 percent of the aged are in a nursing home at any one time.

Children and others hear many "jokes" told about the aged. Analysis indicates that these jokes are usually derogatory and concern topics such as sexual behavior, physical ailments, and cognitive deficits. As is the case with "ethnic" jokes, whether the jokes are funny depends on the listener. A person seldom laughs at jokes that ridicule his or her own social group; persons who are racist or ageist, however, will find these jokes amusing and perceive them as being accurate.

Another factor in the ubiquity of ageism is that there may be less contact with the elderly in modern life than in the past. Families are more mobile today, and the extended family, in which several generations live in the same dwelling, is much less common. Many youngsters grow up without interacting extensively with aged persons; those with such limited contact are very likely to believe the ageist notions presented by others or by the media. In contrast, persons who have close relationships with several older individuals usually realize that most aged individuals are healthy and productive.

Ageism is not restricted to young persons or the uneducated. Ageist attitudes are often maintained even into old age. Ironically, this means that an older person may be prejudiced against his or her own age group. Resolution of this dilemma often focuses on the person's refusal to label him- or herself as "old" or "elderly." Age identification studies typically find that the majority of persons over the age of sixty-five identify themselves as being "middle-aged." Even among subjects over eighty years of age, there is a considerable percentage (10 to 30 percent) who deny that they are "old." This denial allows the aging person to maintain ageist beliefs. Conversely, ageism may contribute to the denial. If one believes that old persons are all senile and so on, and one is obviously not that way oneself, then it follows that one must not be old.

Research suggests that ageist attitudes are prevalent even among physicians and other professionals. Geriatrics, the branch of medicine that deals with disorders and diseases of the aged, is not a popular specialty among doctors. In Robert Butler's *Why Survive? Being Old in America* (1975), data are presented to demonstrate that the elderly are given very low priority by physicians. For example, less thorough physical examinations are given to older patients. Psychiatrists and clinical psychologists report very little contact with aged clients and may be prone to believe that older persons cannot really suffer from the same mental disorders that younger clients do. Senility (an ambiguous term that is not a clinical diagnosis) is not a normal aspect of aging. Alzheimer's disease and other organic brain syndromes are diseases which afflict only a small proportion of the aged. Most cases of confusion and disorientation in the aged are produced by drug intoxication or poor blood circulation to the brain. Nevertheless, such patients may be viewed as suffering from irreversible disorders and given little professional attention other than further medication, which often exacerbates the symptoms.

## Applications

Ageism almost certainly affects social policy and laws dealing with the elderly. As mentioned previously, studies have found that the aged, as a group, are as well off financially as the general population. Nevertheless, most states and the federal government grant tax relief in various forms to all aged citizens, rich and poor. Many businesses such as pharmacies, restaurants, and hotels give discounts to elderly customers. Some banks offer higher interest rates on savings and free checking to "senior citizens." Despite the fact that such practices might seem discriminatory, there is little public protest. The general acceptance of these policies may be based on the mistaken belief that most aged persons are living in or near poverty.

Older persons often confront ageist attitudes when trying to obtain, or continue, employment. There are widely held perceptions that the aged cannot learn new skills ("You can't teach an old dog new tricks"), miss many work days because of illness, are prone to work-related accidents, and work significantly more slowly than younger workers. Each of these notions is inaccurate. Research involving a variety of occupations has determined that older persons are productive employees who actually have fewer accidents at work and miss fewer work days than younger workers. Although motor responses are slowed with age, most workers increase their productivity as a result of increased experience. Learning new skills does usually require slightly more time for older workers, but they can, and do, learn.

Despite these research findings, many employers have discriminated against older applicants and have refused to hire them because of their advanced age. In response, Congress passed the Age Discrimination in Employment Act (ADEA), which outlaws age discrimination in hiring practices and sets seventy years as the age of mandatory retirement for most occupations. Fortunately, many companies have begun to realize the efficacy of older workers and have encouraged them to become employees. The "McMasters Program," established by McDonald's, is one example of a business welcoming older applicants.

Gerontophobia is closely related to ageism. Believing that the aged are decrepit, lonely, and likely to be senile makes one fear growing older. Many companies produce products that play upon this fear; indeed, these businesses have a financial stake in perpetuating gerontophobia. Commercial advertisements bombard consumers with messages indicating that to be old is to be ugly, and Americans spend enormous sums of money trying to look younger through cosmetic surgery, dyeing hair, using "wrinkle removers," and so on. People are even encouraged by friends to try to look young. Many gerontologists, however, view these efforts as costly and futile attempts; these procedures can alter one's appearance, but they do not stop or retard the aging process.

Gerontophobia may also reflect the association often made between old age and death. In the past, many babies and young persons died of infectious and communicable diseases. Infant mortality is much lower today, and life expectancy has increased dramatically. Therefore, death in old age is typical, and this fact may well increase the fear of growing old that many persons experience.

Ironically, holding ageist views may adversely affect one's own aging. Indeed, many psychologists think that beliefs or expectations may be self-fulfilling. More simply put, an expectation may affect one's behavior so that eventually one acts in accordance with the expectation. A common example involves sexual behavior. An ageist view persists that older persons are no longer sexually viable. Males, especially, seem to accept this notion and to worry about their sexual performance. If, for example, a sixty-year-old man does experience an inability to achieve orgasm during intercourse, he may attribute this "failure" to aging; he may then be extremely anxious during his next sexual episode. This anxiety may cause further sexual problems and preclude orgasm. Believing that he is now too old for sex, this male may even terminate coital activity. In contrast, if he attributes his initial problem to stress or some other transitory variable, then his future sexual behavior may be unimpeded.

## Context

Varying beliefs and attitudes concerning the aging process have existed throughout the history of Western civilization. Indeed, in the Old Testament, longevity is granted to those who are faithful to God, and the elders are viewed as a source of great wisdom. Contemporary views toward aging, which typically are much more negative, have been influenced significantly by social policies. In an attempt to help end the Depression, the federal government initiated the Old Age and Survivors' Program ("Social Security") in 1935 to encourage retirement and reduce unemployment among younger workers. Medicare and Medicaid began in the mid-1960's. These measures served to identify older Americans as a homogeneous group of persons in need of special aid from the rest of society; old age thus became a distinct stage of development.

The late 1960's were years of tremendous political and social unrest, as numerous minority groups clamored for greater power and fairer treatment. The aged had been delineated as a special-interest group with distinct needs. As the aged began to be defined solely by their age, a group consciousness began to emerge. Older persons, as a group, are more interested in politics and more likely to vote than their younger counterparts. Politicians became aware of and became more sensitive to elderly issues. Out of this milieu, Robert Butler helped to make these concerns salient by inventing the term ageism.

Ageism has been heightened by medical advances, and the concomitant increased life expectancy enjoyed in technologically advanced societies has altered views about aging. As a higher percentage of people now live into old age, death has become increasingly associated with growing old. Without doubt, the fear of death causes some people to shun the elderly and to view them as being "different from us." To admit that one is old is tantamount to confronting one's own mortality squarely. Many gerontologists and sociologists argue that the United States is a death-denying society. Death is a taboo topic in most circles; the majority of deaths in the United States occur in institutions. The denial and fear of death may encourage ageist notions.

Ageism may decline in the near future, simply because the median age of Americans is increasing. The baby-boomers, a large and influential segment of society, are aging, and their impact is likely to be substantial. People in this age-group have dramatically changed society as they have developed. When they were children, more schools had to be built, and education was emphasized. Their adolescence produced a rebellious period in the late 1960's, and a lowering of the voting age. As young adults, they touched off a boom in construction, as many new houses were needed. As the baby-boomers become senior citizens, their sheer numbers may cause a shift toward more positive attitudes toward the elderly. Also, more aged persons are maintaining good health and active life-styles today than in the past. This trend will undoubtedly help counteract stereotypical ideas about the infirmities of the elderly.

On the other hand, the possibility of intergenerational conflict does exist, particularly in financial matters. Expenditures for Social Security and Medicare make up a substantial portion of the federal budget, and these payments will increase as the population continues to age. Younger workers may continually be asked to contribute more federal taxes and Social Security outlays to finance these programs. If this happens, then the aged may be perceived more and more as a burden and drain on society's well-being.

## Bibliography

Achenbaum, W. A. "Societal Perceptions of Aging and the Aged." In *Handbook of Aging and the Social Sciences*, edited by Robert H. Binstock and Ethel Shanas. 2d ed. New York: Van Nostrand Reinhold, 1985. Examines attitudes toward aging from a historical perspective and assesses the impact of modern innovations such as technology and bureaucratization upon these attitudes. An extensive reference list containing more than one hundred entries is provided.

Barrow, Georgia M. *Aging, the Individual, and Society.* 4th ed. St. Paul, Minn.: West, 1989. Written in clear, nontechnical language. Examines recent research concerning society's views of the aged. Pictures, graphs, and topical short articles from other sources are incorporated into the cogent writing.

Botwinick, Jack. *Aging and Behavior: A Comprehensive Integration of Research Findings.* New York: Springer, 1984. A well-written compilation of extant research concerning aging. The second chapter deals specifically with stereotyping of the elderly.

Butler, Robert N. *Why Survive? Being Old in America.* New York: Harper & Row, 1975. This Pulitzer Prize-winning book is written for lay readers and provides a comprehensive overview of the prejudices and other problems faced by older Americans. Strongly critical of the fashion in which physicians, nursing home operators, politicians, and others deal with the elderly.

Ferraro, Kenneth F. "The Gerontological Imagination." In *Gerontology: Perspectives and Issues.* New York: Springer, 1990. Provides an overview of seven themes within research on aging, pointing out that "aging frequently gets a bad name for things it did not cause." Describes a three-year project in which a young female disguises herself as an elderly woman in order to note the ageist reactions of others.

Macdonald, Barbara, and Cynthia Rich. *Look Me in the Eye: Old Women, Aging, and Ageism.* San Francisco: Spinsters Ink, 1983. Presents a series of compelling and thought-provoking essays concerning the special problems and issues faced by aging females. Argues that current societal trends may actually be increasing the financial, sexual, and familial difficulties of women.

Oberleder, Muriel. *Avoid the Aging Trap.* Washington, D.C.: Acropolis Books, 1982. Examines many of the myths concerning aging in the light of research. Offers practical suggestions to attenuate the actual effects of aging. Numerous exercises, such as a test to compute one's "Aging Quotient," maintain reader interest. Especially recommended for the middle-aged reader.

*Charles H. Evans*

## Cross-References

# AGGRESSION: DEFINITIONS AND THEORETICAL EXPLANATIONS

*Type of psychology:* Social psychology
*Field of study:* Aggression

*Aggression is conceptualized as a diverse category of behaviors that are intended to injure or harm another. Psychological theories of aggression seek to explain, and ultimately to control, people's hostile or antisocial behaviors. Generally, psychological theories address the relative influences of biological factors (such as aggressive instincts or physiological arousal) and situational factors associated with aggression in animals and humans.*

### Principal terms

CATHARSIS: a reduction of psychological tension and/or physiological arousal

DEFENSE MECHANISM: according to Sigmund Freud, a psychological strategy by which an unacceptable sexual or aggressive impulse may be kept from conscious thought or expressed in a disguised fashion

DISPLACEMENT: according to Freud, a defense mechanism by which a person redirects his or her aggressive impulse onto a target that may substitute for the target that originally aroused the person's aggression

FRUSTRATION: a psychological state of arousal that results when a person is prevented from attaining a goal

HOSTILE AGGRESSION: aggressive behavior that is associated with anger and is intended to harm another

INSTINCTIVE AGGRESSIVE BEHAVIOR: aggressive behavior that does not result from learning experiences; such behavior is expressed by each member of a species with little variation in its expression

INSTRUMENTAL AGGRESSION: aggressive behavior that is a by-product of another activity; instrumental aggression occurs only incidentally, as a means to another end

OBSERVATIONAL LEARNING: learning that results from observing other people's behavior and its consequences

SUBLIMATION: according to Freud, a defense mechanism by which a person may redirect aggressive impulses by engaging in a socially sanctioned activity

THANATOS: the instinctive aggressive instinct located in the human unconscious

## Overview

Aggression is any antisocial behavior that is harmful or injurious to another. This may include overt physical and verbal behaviors (for example, firing a gun or screaming at someone in anger) as well as nonverbal behaviors, such as the display of obscene gestures. Psychologists consider aggression to be a category of diverse behaviors under which two subordinate categories of behaviors can be subsumed. The first category, instrumental aggression, consists of aggressive behaviors that are simply a means to another end. Hence, the primary goal of instrumental aggression is not necessarily to injure another person; aggression is used to attain a desired outcome. For example, a soccer player might knock her teammate down as they both run to tackle a ball. The girl's aggressive behavior was not intended to harm her teammate; rather, her goal was to gain possession of the ball and to score. The second category, hostile aggression, is often the result of anger, and its sole purpose is to injure or harm its target. Hostile aggression includes cases of physical assault, verbal abuse, and other antisocial behaviors. Most of the theoretical perspectives and empirical studies of aggression in psychology are concerned with hostile aggression.

There are three major psychological perspectives on aggression. The first perspective adopts a strongly biological stance on the development and maintenance of aggression in the human species. The second perspective takes the position that aggression is a result of the buildup of psychological frustration. The third perspective argues that aggression is a learned social behavior.

The first theoretical perspective, instinct theories, adopts the position that human nature includes an inborn drive for aggression. The ethologist Konrad Lorenz studied the instinctive nature of aggression in animals and humans. According to his work, aggression is a species-specific impulse that builds within the body and is eventually released by specific stimuli that elicit aggression. For example, an aggressive impulse might be unleashed by the presence of one's enemy. In some cases, however, the expression of this instinct may be inhibited by certain stimuli (for example, a parent may become angered by a child's behavior but not strike the child). Ethologists argue that the "babyish" facial characteristics of infants and young children serve as stimuli that inhibit the expression of aggressive behavior by adults.

Another instinct theory, psychoanalytic theory, posits that the seeds of aggression lie in the human personality. According to Sigmund Freud, a significant portion of one's unconscious psychological processes are governed by Thanatos. Thanatos, or the death instinct, is a reservoir of aggressive, and often self-destructive, tendencies that Freud considered to be part of the human species' evolutionary heritage. The psychic energy dedicated to Thanatos is thought to build over time until it is released in aggressive behavior. Periodic discharge, or catharsis, of this psychic energy is necessary for psychological health. Catharsis can occur either directly through overt aggression or indirectly through a number of disguised avenues. Many of Freud's defense mechanisms allow for a safe outlet of a person's aggressive impulses. For example, a man might be angered by his abusive employer's demands. Instead of accosting his employer directly, however, he might drive to his health club and "blow off steam" by sparring with a boxing partner. His aggressive urge is thus reduced through displacement of his aggressive impulse. As another example, an angry and sarcastic young girl may become a prosecuting attorney upon reaching adulthood.

By aggressively prosecuting accused criminals and interrogating defense witnesses, a necessary part of her profession, this woman may be sublimating her aggressive tendencies.

The second theoretical perspective was introduced by John Dollard and his colleagues' early work investigating S-R (stimulus-response) theory. Their theory of aggression consisted of two simple propositions. First, aggression must always result from frustration. Second, frustration always leads to aggression. Thus, aggression was thought to be attributable to the thwarting of one's purpose or being prevented from attaining a valued goal. This theory, the frustration-aggression hypothesis, was later revised by Leonard Berkowitz, who argued that the frustration-aggression relationship was not quite so clear-cut. He posited that frustration simply makes a person ready to be aggressive. Aggression will result from frustration if, and only if, a cue for aggressive behavior is present. Aggressive cues are social stimuli, such as potential weapons, that have been associated with aggression in the past. Thus, the revised frustration-aggression hypothesis posits that aggressive tendencies will accumulate as a response to frustration. Catharsis is likely to occur when situational cues support an aggressive response.

The final perspective, social learning theory, emphasizes the role of social and situational factors in the learning and expression of aggressive behaviors. According to Albert Bandura, aggressive behaviors can be learned through two primary avenues, direct experience and observational learning. Learning by direct experience involves the actual enactment of aggressive behavior. If aggression is rewarded, then it is likely to recur. If aggression is punished, then it is likely to be suppressed, especially in the presence of the punishing agent. Observational learning, on the other hand, involves a process whereby people attend to the behaviors of people in their environment and the consequences of these behaviors. Bandura stated that people are most likely to attend to, and thus learn from, the behaviors of three salient model categories: families, subcultures, and the media. For example, a young boy may observe the aggressive behavior exhibited by the fellow members of his neighborhood gang. This modeling by other gang members not only may teach him novel behaviors but also may lower his inhibitions to be aggressive. Thus, when this boy becomes aroused by an aversive event, such as a taunt from a rival gang member, he will be likely to respond in an aggressive manner.

## Applications

Much of the psychological research investigating the nature of aggression has been focused on the control of aggression. Of particular interest to researchers is the notion that allowing limited expression of low levels of aggression (catharsis) might play an important role in controlling the expression of high levels of aggression and antisocial behavior. The concept of catharsis is a central component of both psychoanalytic theory and the frustration-aggression hypothesis. Further, the idea of catharsis is intuitively appealing to many people who feel that periodically "blowing off steam" is important to positive mental health.

Psychologists Russell Geen, David Stonner, and Gary Shope designed a laboratory study to define the role that catharsis plays in aggression. In this study, male college students were angered and then administered electric shock by a confederate of the experimenters. When these subjects were allowed to retaliate against the confederate, they experienced a drop in their blood pressure (defined by the experimenters as a cathartic release). At this point in the experiment, the role of catharsis in moderating physiological arousal was supported. The experimenters, however, also wanted to know the effect of catharsis on subjects' subsequent behavior, so they next provided subjects with an opportunity to administer shocks to the confederate. Geen and his colleagues found that the subjects who had experienced catharsis (reductions in blood pressure) actually delivered higher levels of shock to the confederate. Thus, while catharsis was reflected in decreased physiological arousal, it was associated with higher, not lower, levels of actual aggression. These researchers concluded that they were unable to find support for psychoanalytic theory or the frustration-aggression hypothesis, both of which would predict that catharsis would reduce subsequent aggression.

Laboratory studies have been subjected to a number of criticisms because they isolate people from their natural social environments and perhaps encourage the expression of artificial behavior. Laboratory studies of aggression are particularly vulnerable to such criticism, because they may provide subjects with a safe arena within which they may be encouraged to behave in an unnaturally aggressive manner. In response to these critics, many psychologists have studied the aggressive behavior of adults and children in typical social environments. Leonard Eron and his associates investigated the role that television might play in modeling aggressive behavior for a sample of elementary school children. First, the children's viewing habits were observed, to establish the nature of the programming they preferred and the amount of time they spent watching television. These children were followed up twenty-two years later to observe the effect their television viewing habits might have had on their behavior. Eron and his colleagues found that the amount of television these children had watched was significantly related to their level of aggressive behavior in young adulthood. The criminal records of certain children revealed that the more serious crimes were committed by the children who had been the heaviest consumers of violent television programming. The researchers interpreted these results to support social learning theory; that is, the media may be effective models of aggression, both immediate and long-term.

Proponents of handgun legislation point to studies such as these to argue for the control of privately owned firearms. They point to violent models in the media that may be related to the high rate of homicides in the United States. Additionally, they argue that the presence of a handgun itself may serve as a cue that elicits aggression and that the use of a handgun allows the aggressor to distance himself or herself physically from the victim. At firing range, the cues that elicit empathy and inhibit aggression are not so readily apparent. The influence of gun control on homicide rates was studied by a group of physicians led by John Henry Sloan. This team selected two cities for comparison. One city, Vancouver, British Columbia, had adopted restrictive handgun regulations. The comparison city, Seattle, Washington, was similar to Vancouver on a number of important demographic variables, but had no handgun control. The crime rates for both cities were compared for six years (1980 through 1986). Although the rates in both cities for burglary, robbery, and assault were not significantly different, the homicide rate was significantly higher in Seattle. They found that the citizens of Seattle had a 4.8 times higher risk of being killed with a handgun than did the citizens of Vancouver. These researchers concluded their report with the suggestion that handgun control legislation might reduce community homicide rates.

## Context

Early psychological theories of aggression were quite pessimistic in the inferences they made about human nature. Much of Sigmund Freud's writings about the nature of Thanatos and the expression of aggression in humans occurred against the backdrop of the two world wars that he experienced in Europe. Becoming increasingly pessimistic about human nature and civilization, he revised his theory of the libido to include not only the sexual instinct, Eros, but also the aggressive instinct, Thanatos. Other theorists of that time entertained similar views of aggression as an instinct. For example, social psychologist William McDougall included aggression in his taxonomy of innate human instincts.

During the 1930's, John Dollard and his colleagues at Yale attempted to reformulate psychoanalytic theory by use of S-R theory. These researchers were concerned with the mentalistic nature of Freud's theory, and they attempted to test his propositions by reconceptualizing libidinal impulses as biological drives. The frustration-aggression hypothesis grew out of this research program and generated a considerable amount of empirical research for a number of years. Interest in this concept then flagged, for the most part, until the 1960's, when Berkowitz published his revised frustration-aggression hypothesis that acknowledged the important role of social cues in the instigation of aggression.

Berkowitz's revision of the frustration-aggression hypothesis reflected the increased focus of American psychologists on social learning theory. Albert Bandura's classic studies of the social learning of aggressive responses, published in the early 1960's, were influential in two ways. First, they generated considerable empirical research. Second, they provided a theoretical framework and methodology by which the effects of a relatively new social phenomenon, television, could be studied. Since then, more than two thousand studies have looked at the role of television in the modeling and maintenance of aggression in adults and children.

That is not to say that the instinct theories have fallen into disfavor. Konrad Lorenz's influential book, *On Aggression*, published in 1966, again brought instinct theories into the public eye. His book captured the interest not only of the comparative psychologists who studied aggression in other species but of the general reading public as well.

## Bibliography

Bandura, Albert. *Aggression: A Social Learning Analysis.* Englewood Cliffs, N.J.: Prentice-Hall, 1973. Bandura presents a thorough overview of his social learning theory of aggression. He outlines the important antecedents of aggression and the critical factors in the instigation and maintenance of aggressive behavior. He also describes relevant social learning principles and applies these principles that are useful techniques for behavioral change. Accessible to the college-level reader.

Berkowitz, Leonard. *Aggression: A Social-Psychological Analysis.* New York: McGraw-Hill, 1962. This classic volume presents the frustration-aggression hypothesis. Contrasts the frustration-aggression hypothesis with instinct theories of aggression and discusses situational factors implicated in the expression and inhibition of aggression. The role of catharsis in aggression is also discussed.

_____. "Biological Roots: Are Humans Inherently Violent?" In *Psychological Dimensions of War*, edited by Betty Glad. Newbury Park, Calif.: Sage, 1990. This is an excellent, easy-to-read critique of instinct theories of aggression. Berkowitz presents the frustration-aggression hypothesis and applies this theory to an analysis of international conflict. The role of aggression in the human condition and international relations is thoroughly discussed.

Geen, Russell G. *Human Aggression.* Pacific Grove, Calif.: Brooks/Cole, 1990. The author, a prominent researcher in the field, provides a solid empirical and theoretical discussion of the concept of aggression. Individual differences in aggression are discussed as well as interpersonal and environmental factors that mediate the actual expression of aggressive behavior.

Groebel, Jo, and Robert A. Hinde, eds. *Aggression and War: Their Biological and Social Bases.* New York: Cambridge University Press, 1989. This edited volume presents a lively discussion of the biological, psychological, and cultural factors in human aggression. Physiological and individual differences in aggression are presented in addition to social and situational forces that are useful in the control of aggression and the encouragement of prosocial behaviors. Cultural and political issues relevant to aggression are discussed.

Lorenz, Konrad. *On Aggression.* New York: Methuen, 1966. This easy-to-read classic is a comparative study of aggression in a number of species. Lorenz documents the evolutionary significance of aggression and describes its expression in fish, animals, and humans. He argues that aggression plays an important social role in same-species interactions.

Luschen, Gunther. "Psychological Issues in Sports Aggression." In *Sports Violence*, edited by Jeffrey H. Goldstein. New York: Springer-Verlag, 1983. Describes the cathartic role of sports in both athletes' and spectators' aggressive behaviors. The author summarizes the central role that catharsis plays in several psychological and philosophical perspectives on aggression, then presents the results of empirical studies investigating the links between sports and aggression.

Segall, Marshall H. "Cultural Roots of Aggressive Behavior." In *The Cross-Cultural Challenge to Social Psychology*, edited by Michael Harris Bond. Newbury Park,

Calif.: Sage, 1988. Segall presents a summary and critique of important cross-cultural studies of aggression. His presentation focuses on the manner in which gender roles, biology, and cultural forces interact in the socialization of aggression across the globe. An intriguing and quite accessible article.

*Cheryl A. Rickabaugh*

## Cross-References

Aggression: Reduction and Control, 169; The Aggression Motive, 174; Crowd Behavior, 737; Ethology, 992; Hormones and Behavior, 1189; Psychoanalytic Psychology and Personality: Sigmund Freud, 1912; Social Learning: Albert Bandura, 2304; S-R Theory: Miller and Dollard, 2369; Violence and Sexuality in the Mass Media, 2603.

# AGGRESSION: REDUCTION AND CONTROL

*Type of psychology:* Social psychology
*Field of study:* Aggression

*Aggressive behavior has been a problem for humans since before the beginning of recorded history. Psychologists have developed many theories of aggression, and there are many different ideas as to how—or whether—aggression might be controlled.*

### Principal terms

BEHAVIORISM: a school of psychology which holds that learning, centering on a stimulus, a response, and reinforcement, is central to behavior

CATHARSIS: the idea that experiencing aggression or violence vicariously will relieve an individual's aggressive drives

FRUSTRATION-AGGRESSION HYPOTHESIS: a concept pioneered by John Dollard stating that aggressive behavior is born of frustration in attempting to reach a goal

SOCIAL LEARNING THEORY: a theory introduced by Albert Bandura stating that behavior is learned by observing others model that behavior

SOCIOBIOLOGY: a field of biology that views behavior as being extensively based on inherited characteristics

### Overview

Aggression has been humankind's steady companion throughout history—in life, literature, and art. Many hypotheses have been suggested by psychologists and other scientists concerning the nature of aggression; some have suggested that it is learned behavior, others that it is an innate, genetically inherited drive. The fields of ethology and sociology have mustered evidence to support the evolutionary (genetic) basis of aggression. Theories based on these viewpoints hold that at some point in humankind's past, aggressiveness was an adaptive trait—that is, aggression helped ensure the survival of the individual who possessed that quality, thereby enabling the aggressive trait to be passed on to future generations. Social psychologists, on the other hand, have studied the effects of modeling aggressive behavior. When children, for example, have been exposed to aggressive behavior modeled (acted out or demonstrated in some way) by others, they have shown an increase in aggressive behavior. In other words, the children observe and learn the behavior. Albert Bandura's social learning theory describes this concept of aggression.

The frustration-aggression hypothesis, as described by John Dollard, holds that both violence and aggression are the result of being frustrated in an attempt to reach a goal. When basic needs have been thwarted, aggression appears. As Leonard Berkowitz stated it in *Roots of Aggression* (1969), "If a person is aggressive, he has been frustrated. If a person is frustrated, he has become aggressive." Negative environmental factors are also believed by many to have a major impact on aggression. Studies have found links, for example, between a high number of violent crimes and high air temperature. Overcrowding and economic hard times are also associated with higher crime rates. These studies tend to support negative affect theory, which holds that exposure to stimuli that create discomfort leads to aggression.

The amount of hope one holds for the possibility of reducing or controlling aggression depends, to some extent, on the theory of aggression that one believes to be most accurate. If aggressive behavior is an integral part of the genetic makeup of the human species, the outlook is not nearly as promising as it is if aggression is primarily a behavior learned from others and reinforced by certain rewards. In the former case, aggressive actions can perhaps be controlled by societal strictures, but the aggressive instinct will always remain within. In the latter case, decreasing the modeling of aggression or increasing the modeling of and rewards for nonaggressive behavior could conceivably produce effective results. Different studies have produced different results concerning the effectiveness of various attempts to reduce aggressive behavior.

Another complication in understanding and controlling aggression is that different people will react very differently when in similar circumstances. When frustrated, some people will react aggressively, while others will become withdrawn and depressed. Depression itself can lead to aggression, however, and this type of delayed aggression can produce seemingly unpredictable acts of violence. Psychologists simply do not have all the answers to why some people react aggressively and others do not when faced with identical predicaments.

## Applications

Psychologists Matthew McKay, Martha Davis, and Patrick Fanning (1981) adapted Donald Meichenbaum's concept of stress inoculation training to produce one technique that allows an aggressive person to control his or her own aggressive behavior. McKay and his colleagues present simple, concise, step-by-step directions to deal with aggression. Since aggression is often fueled by emotional distress, they offer a technique of "covert assertion" through the development of two separate skills: thought interruption and thought substitution. When becoming angry or frustrated, the potential aggressor thinks of the word "stop" or some other interrupting device. The void suddenly created is then filled with a reserve of previously prepared positive, nonaggressive thoughts. This technique can be mastered, the authors maintain, if it is practiced conscientiously throughout the day for three days to a week.

The creation of an "aggression stimulants structure" gives the individual who is compelled to be negatively aggressive the opportunity to take a personal inventory of who (or what) the targets of his or her aggression are, what the feelings associated with those people are, and what would occur if a plan of "attack" against them were to be put into action. This type of analysis lends itself well to self-accountability; it allows the individual to "own" the problem and to believe that it can be controlled if he or she chooses to control it. It also allows, through its identification of specific targets and imaging of the act of aggression, a global perspective on what can otherwise seem a very fragmented problem.

Aggression in the work environment can be damaging and disruptive both for individuals and for organizations. In an article in the *Journal of Occupational Psychology*, Philip L. Storms and Paul E. Spector (1987) claimed that high frustration levels of organizational employees were positively related to interpersonal aggression, sabotage, and withdrawal. Suggestions for dealing with aggression in the workplace have included such strategies as training courses and the use of humor to defuse tensions. Diane Lamplugh notes that aggression in this arena can range from whispered innuendo to harassment to violence. She maintains that a training course that focuses on tension control, relaxation techniques, customer-relations orientation, assertiveness practice, aggression-centered discussions, and self-defense training can be helpful. She also states that support from management in identifying problem areas and formulating guidelines for staff support is crucial. William A. Kahn promotes humor as a means for organizational members to make statements about themselves, their groups, or their organization. Humor, he notes, is a non-threatening vehicle that allows people to say things that might otherwise insult or offend coworkers, thereby making them defensive and threatening working relationships.

Written or unwritten laws, rules, and codes of conduct are established in an attempt to curb unacceptably aggressive behavior. A company may terminate an employee who does not adhere to certain standards of behavior; athletes are benched for aggression or violence. Society as a whole formulates laws to control its members' aggressive behavior. When individuals act in ways that are damagingly aggressive to other people or to the property of others, law enforcement agencies step in to safeguard the population. Perpetrators are fined or sentenced to prison terms.

Studies disagree as to the most effective means of rehabilitating offenders, but many studies do suggest that rehabilitation is possible. One avenue that is frequently explored is the use of various techniques founded in behaviorism. In *Psychological Approaches to Crime and Its Correction* (1984, edited by Irving Jacks and Steven G. Cox), for example, Stanley V. Kruschwitz investigates the effectiveness of using a voluntary token reinforcement procedure to change the behavior of inmates who are difficult to manage. In the same volume, Albert F. Scheckenbach makes an argument for behavior modification as it relates to adult offenders. Modeling positive behaviors and holding group discussions have been found at least somewhat effective in rehabilitating juvenile delinquents, as has the development of behavioral contracts. John Lochman and his colleagues (1987), using what they called an "anger coping mechanism," explored cognitive behavioral techniques for reducing aggression in eleven-year-old boys. The boys treated with this procedure showed vast improvements—a reduction of disruptive classroom behavior and an increase in perceived social competence. Such techniques, used with young people, might reduce their high-risk status for later difficulties.

## Context

Acts of aggression have been central in human history, myth, literature, and even religion. In the biblical account, for example, humankind has barely come into existence when Cain kills his brother Abel. Almost as old are questions concerning the causes of aggression and the debate over how to control it.

Sigmund Freud saw aggression as the result of struggles within the psyche of the individual; the tension produced in the struggle between the life instinct and the death instinct creates outward aggression. Alfred Adler, another psychodynamic theorist, stated that aggression represents the most general human striving and is a necessity of life; its underlying principle is self-assertion. Humanistic theorist Rollo May notes that attention to aggression has nearly universally focused on its negative aspects. In *Power and Innocence* (1972), May wrote that "we have been terrified of aggression, and we assume—delusion though it is—that we can better control it if we center all our attention on its destructive aspects as though that's all there is."

It was first the behaviorist school, then social learning theorists (such as Albert Bandura), that explored ways to reduce and control aggression. The frustration-aggression hypothesis, for example, was developed in the 1930's. Behaviorists tended to approach aggressive behavior in terms of stimuli, responses, and reinforcement. In a general sense, any approaches that seek to punish unacceptably aggressive behavior or to reward positive behavior are related to the behavioral view. Bandura and other social learning theorists found that, in some situations, children would respond to viewing aggressive acts by performing aggressive acts themselves. The implications of this have been widely argued and debated; one aspect concerns the effects of viewing television and motion-picture violence. Viewing violence on television does seem to cause increased aggressive behavior, although because of the nature of the types of studies most often performed, it can be difficult to draw unarguable cause-and-effect relationships.

The debate over whether aggression is learned, innate, or both (and, if both, over the relative importance of the two aspects) is not likely to end soon. Debates over how to control aggression will also continue. As in many areas of psychology, bridging the gap between the theoretical and the practical is difficult. As only one example, negative affect theory suggests that noxious environmental stimuli can produce negative emotions and, therefore, aggression; however, it is virtually impossible to remove such stimuli, except on a very small scale. Yet another area that will be increasingly explored is the relationship between aggression and biochemical factors. Studies have found correlations, for example, between aggressiveness and high levels of norepinephrine and low levels of serotonin, two important neurotransmitters. The significance of such chemical findings remains to be ascertained.

## Bibliography

Bach, George R., and Herb Goldberg. *Creative Aggression*. New York: Avon Books, 1975. A guidebook for people who cannot confront conflict as well as for those who choose to seek conflict. Helps the reader to assess himself or herself honestly and to approach aggressiveness in new ways.

Berkowitz, Leonard, ed. *Roots of Aggression.* New York: Atherton Press, 1969. Revisits the frustration-aggression hypothesis. Examines such areas as catharsis, frustration, and conditions facilitating the occurrence of aggression.

Dworetzky, John P. *Psychology.* New York: West, 1982. This text has a strong research base and contains extensive detail to reinforce the material presented. Good discussion of aggression.

Jacks, Irving, and Steven G. Cox, eds. *Psychological Approaches to Crime and Its Correction.* Chicago: Nelson-Hall, 1984. Covers a wide range of topics related to aggression and positivistic points of view in the face of crime. Examines the modification of aggressive behavior.

May, Rollo. *Power and Innocence.* New York: W. W. Norton, 1972. Probes the sources of violence. Advances solutions for contemporary society, examining the concept of innocence and challenging traditional views of aggression.

*Denise S. St. Cyr*

**Cross-References**

Aggression: Definitions and Theoretical Explanations, 162; The Aggression Motive, 174; Emotion and Attribution Theory, 921; Instinct Theory, 1309; Psychoanalytic Psychology and Personality: Sigmund Freud, 1912; Violence and Sexuality in the Mass Media, 2603.

# THE AGGRESSION MOTIVE

*Type of psychology:* Motivation
*Fields of study:* Aggression; interpersonal relations; social motives

*A broad range of theories have addressed the motives that lead a person to harm another. These theories illuminate the biological, intrapsychic, and interpersonal bases for aggressive behavior.*

### Principal terms

AGGRESSION: behavior intended to harm or injure another person
ANGRY AGGRESSION: aggression carried out in the heat of the moment for the sole purpose of hurting someone
CATHARSIS: the reduction of aggressive drives resulting from engaging in or witnessing an aggressive act
DEATH INSTINCT: the unconscious desire to die in order to escape the tensions of living
DISPLACEMENT: aggressing against a substitute target because of inhibitions of aggressive urges toward the real source of frustration
FRUSTRATION-AGGRESSION HYPOTHESIS: the proposition that frustration is the source of all motives to aggress
INSTRUMENTAL AGGRESSION: aggression performed in order to benefit the aggressor
NEGATIVE AFFECT THEORY: the view that exposure to noxious stimuli is responsible for aggression
SOCIAL LEARNING THEORY: the view that behavior can be learned through observation of others and the consequences of their actions
SOCIOBIOLOGY: the application of the principles of evolutionary biology to the understanding of social behavior

## Overview

Human history is filled with examples of people harming, injuring, and even killing each other. To address the question of why people engage in aggressive behavior, social psychologists often make a distinction between instrumental aggression and angry aggression. Instrumental aggression is a means to an end, as when a mugger harms a victim to steal money. Instrumental aggression is motivated by a desire to attain some form of self-benefit, but aggression merely provides the means to attain that goal. In contrast, angry aggression is motivated by a desire to harm as an end in itself. Theories of aggression have generally assumed that most human aggression is of the self-oriented, instrumental type rather than of the angry type. These theories, however, differ greatly in their views of the form of self-benefit that motivates aggression and in their emphases on the biological, intrapsychic, and interpersonal bases of aggressive behavior.

Sociobiology is a theoretical view that explains social behavior by applying the principles of evolutionary biology. Sociobiologists suggest that acting aggressively was adaptive for humans at some point in evolutionary history, so more aggressive individuals were more likely to survive, reproduce, and pass on their genes, including the genes that produced aggressive behavior, to future generations. Acting aggressively may have been beneficial for individual survival as well as the survival of the human species.

Sigmund Freud also viewed aggression as having a biological basis, although he emphasized the intrapsychic process directly giving rise to aggression. Freud proposed that humans possess a strong life instinct that conflicts with and frustrates the typically weaker death instinct. The frustration of the death instinct prevents a person from taking his or her own life to avoid the pain of living; however, the tension produced by the death instinct must be released in some way. Freud proposed that the urge to aggress against the self is displaced onto others, allowing reduction of the tension.

The frustration-aggression hypothesis suggests an even more general role of frustration in producing aggression. According to this view, frustration of any desired goal will always lead to aggression, and all aggression ultimately results from some type of frustration. Displacement of aggressive urges occurs when the frustrated person is unable to aggress successfully against the frustrating agent. Aggression is seen as a drive much like hunger. Hunger is caused by deprivation of food; aggression is caused by frustration of desired goals. Specific acts of aggression, however, are learned responses to frustrating events.

Negative affect theory proposes that exposure to noxious stimuli that produce discomfort, even if no specific goal is frustrated, will result in aggression. This theory is useful for explaining the effects of a variety of unpleasant environmental conditions on aggression, such as the effects of crowding and high temperature. On a hot summer day, people may not necessarily feel frustrated by the weather; such weather may be expected. Nevertheless, tempers may rise as temperatures rise, leading to aggression.

Social learning theory provides an explanation for aggression in marked contrast to the theories described above. Social learning theory suggests that in addition to learning through direct experience, people learn by example from others. If a person observes a model who is rewarded for acting aggressively, the person may both learn how to act aggressively and be more likely to perform the aggressive act. Observation of models can both elicit direct imitation and reduce inhibitions against performing the modeled behavior. Frequent exposure to aggressive models may account for the prevalence of violence by people in certain cultures and nations.

Theories of aggression span a wide range of biological, intrapsychic, and interpersonal explanations. It is interesting, however, that these theories generally assume that most aggression is performed as an instrumental means to attain some form of self-benefit. According to the sociobiological explanation, aggression is instrumental for enhancing individual survival or the survival of the species. Freud's psychodynamic explanation views aggression as instrumental for reducing the tension produced by frustration of the death instinct. The frustration-aggression hypothesis views aggression as a means for satisfying aggressive drives produced by any form of frustration. According to negative affect theory, aggression is a response to discomfort produced by noxious environmental conditions. Social learning theory proposes that exposure to a model who is rewarded for aggressing will lead an observer to aggress in order to obtain the same rewards. These theories do not propose that aggression is performed for the sake of harming another as an end in itself. An important challenge for theories and research on aggression is to determine if angry aggression exists and, if so, why it occurs.

## Applications

The study of aggression has led to insights about the determinants of aggressive behavior and how such behavior can be controlled. Some theories are more optimistic about the prospect of controlling aggression than others. At one extreme, the sociobiological explanation of aggression would suggest that human aggression is perhaps inevitable because it is part of genetic heritage. Short of genetic engineering, human aggression may be impossible to control. At the other extreme, social learning theory suggests that human social behavior, including aggressive behavior, is largely a function of observation of models' behavior. Controlling aggression may require no more than ensuring that people are exposed only to nonaggressive models and not to aggressive models. Even among the theories that are more optimistic about the prospects of controlling human aggression, there are marked differences in the success of the techniques that are suggested for reducing aggression.

The frustration-aggression hypothesis suggests that aggressive urges can be displaced to substitute targets when aggressive acts against the source of the frustration are inhibited. A view adopted by both Freud and frustration-aggression theorists is that performing or witnessing nonharmful aggressive acts (such as making hostile jokes, cursing, or observing fictionalized violence) can reduce aggressive drives, a view captured by the concept of catharsis. Although intuitively appealing, applications of the concept of catharsis have not proved to be widely successful in the control of aggression.

There seem to be several reasons for the lack of effectiveness of cathartic release for reducing aggression. One reason is that although catharsis can reduce arousal caused by being provoked or frustrated, providing an opportunity to aggress against the source of the frustration often can more quickly and completely reduce the arousal. Another reason is that even though catharsis may reduce arousal, aggressive intent may still remain. Finally, engaging in or witnessing cathartic aggressive acts may sometimes increase subsequent aggression. As would be suggested by social learning theory, witnessing a model who is rewarded for acting aggressively can disinhibit aggression in the observer. In sum, although catharsis initially appeared to be a promising technique for controlling aggression, it has failed to live up to its promise.

A straightforward application of negative affect theory's explanation for aggression is that prevention of exposure to noxious stimuli should reduce aggression. This idea, unfortunately, is often difficult to put into practice. Many noxious environmental conditions, such as crowding and inclement weather, are difficult, if not impossible, to control. Negative affect theory, however, suggests an alternative method for reducing aggression. This method is based on the notion that if a person is led to experience sadness, humor, or some other emotion incompatible with aggression when exposed to noxious stimuli, the likelihood of aggression will be greatly reduced. Evoking incompatible emotional responses has proven successful in reducing aggression, but the technique has limits. For example, it may be impossible to lead a person to laugh about the unpleasantness of the weather if conditions are truly unbearable.

Social learning theory is extremely optimistic about the prospects of controlling human aggression, and considerable research has been devoted to testing whether application of its principles leads to success in reducing aggression. This research has supported the view that aggressive behavior enacted by models influences observers' own aggressiveness and has yielded important additional information about the effects of observing modeled behavior and its consequences. For example, exposure to aggressive models has been found to lead sometimes to even less aggression than exposure to nonaggressive models, but only if the models' aggression is met with swift, severe punishment.

Exposure to aggressive models who are punished, however, may have a long-term negative effect. The models' behavior may lead to the learning of specific aggressive acts that are performed only when the chances of meeting the same swift, severe punishment that the models received are slim. Therefore, exposure to aggressive models who are punished can lead to reduced aggression overall but, unfortunately, also to increased aggression when the person performing it stands to benefit and not be punished.

The effects of exposure to nonaggressive models who are rewarded for their actions is more uniformly positive. Exposure to such models teaches the important lesson that there are rewarding alternatives to the perhaps natural response to aggress when provoked. Such models also promote restraint, which allows arousal caused by being provoked to dissipate. In sum, exposure to models of nonaggression who are rewarded seems to provide a more effective way for reducing aggression than exposure to models of aggression who are punished.

Whether human aggression can ever be totally and successfully controlled may depend on whether humans are endowed with an innate capacity for violence and aggression, as is suggested by sociobiology. This capacity normally may be kept in check if individuals are not subjected to intense frustration or extremely noxious stimuli and have learned to be nonaggressive, but it may be released when individuals are strongly provoked. Theory and research on aggression need to explore whether strong provocation leads to angry aggression and, if so, the mechanisms leading to a desire to harm for its own sake.

## Context

Psychological theories of aggression have their roots in Charles Darwin's theorizing during the middle 1800's on evolutionary processes. Darwin's ideas on how environmental pressures influence the physical characteristics of organisms were well known, but less well known was Darwin's view that environmental pressures also influence the behavioral characteristics of species. He viewed the cooperative behavior of social insects such as ants, for example, as resulting from an instinctual, genetically based adaptation that promoted the survival of the species. The sociobiological explanation of human aggression is a direct extension of Darwin's view of the evolutionary basis for social behavior. Human aggression results from an instinctual, genetically based adaptation to a hostile environment over the course of human evolution.

Sigmund Freud often made use of the notion of instincts in the psychodynamic theories of behavior that he developed during the late 1800's and early 1900's. Perhaps nowhere in his theorizing is the instinctual basis for behavior more prominent than in his explanation for human aggression. Still, his account of the conflict between the life instincts and death instincts, which results in outward-directed aggression, is typical of his other theorizing in that intrapsychic conflict plays a more direct role than do instincts in influencing behavior.

The development of behaviorism as a major influence in psychology in the United States during the early 1900's saw a rejection of many of the principles of Freudian psychodynamic theories. The most prominent behaviorist explanation for aggression came in the form of the frustration-aggression hypothesis, developed by John Dollard and his colleagues in the late 1930's. Dollard was part of a movement by behaviorists to translate Freudian theories into behaviorist terms. In the case of the frustration-aggression hypothesis, Freud's influence is clear, even to the point of including the notions of displacement of aggressive urges and catharsis. The major innovation of the frustration-aggression hypothesis was replacement of the unobservable, instinctual basis for aggression suggested by Freud with observably frustrated goals.

Television became widely available shortly after World War II, and people soon became concerned with the impact of television programming on viewers' behavior. Social learning theory developed during the 1950's and was similarly concerned with the effects of exposure to models on observers' own behavior. Social learning theory prompted considerable research on the effects of viewing televised violence on aggression.

Behaviorism began to decline as an important influence in psychology during the 1960's and was replaced by a reawakening of interest in the effects of internal states on behavior. Negative affect theory was developed in the 1970's. It proposes that negative emotions such as anger are often produced by exposure to noxious environmental stimuli, but it also suggests that emotional responses incompatible with aggression can sometimes be elicited under aversive stimulation. Subjective emotional experience directly influences the aggressiveness of behavior.

## Bibliography

Bandura, Albert. *Aggression: A Social Learning Analysis.* Englewood Cliffs, N.J.: Prentice-Hall, 1973. Presents the social learning explanation for aggression and reveals the surprising complexity of the effects of observing models' behavior. The chapters on the prevention and control of aggression are especially interesting.

Baron, Robert A., and D. R. Richardson. *Human Aggression.* 2d ed. New York: Plenum Press, 1991. A comprehensive overview of theory and research on the biological, environmental, and interpersonal determinants of aggression. Uses negative affect theory to integrate a variety of diverse causes of aggression.

Dollard, John, Leonard W. Doob, Neal E. Miller, O. Hobart Mowrer, and Robert R. Sears. *Frustration and Aggression.* New Haven, Conn.: Yale University Press, 1939. A classic book detailing the role of frustration in producing aggression. It is historically very interesting, because it reveals how behaviorists attempted to recast Freudian notions into stimulus-response terms.

Freud, Sigmund. "Civilization and Its Discontents." In *The Standard Edition of the Complete Psychological Works of Sigmund Freud,* edited by James Strachey. Vol. 21. London: Hogarth Press, 1961. Expresses Freud's pessimism about the human condition, as seen in his later work. Includes Freud's notion of the death instinct and its role in aggression.

Groebel, Jo, and Robert A. Hinde, eds. *Aggression and War: Their Biological and Social Bases.* 2d ed. Cambridge, England: Cambridge University Press, 1991. Authors from diverse disciplines contribute to this volume dealing with the causes of aggression and conflict at the interpersonal, group, and societal levels. Illustrates that principles explaining conflict at one level may not be applicable at other levels.

Wilson, Edward O. *Sociobiology: The New Synthesis.* Cambridge, Mass.: Harvard University Press, 1975. The authoritative text explaining the principles of sociobiology and its account of the evolution of social behavior. Shows how evolutionary pressures can lead not only to antisocial, aggressive behavior, but also to prosocial, cooperative behavior.

*Jim Fultz*

## Cross-References

Aggression: Definitions and Theoretical Explanations, 162; Aggression: Reduction and Control, 169; Drive Theory, 843; Instinct Theory, 1309; Violence and Sexuality in the Mass Media, 2603.

# AGING: COGNITIVE CHANGES

*Type of psychology:* Developmental psychology
*Fields of study:* Aging; cognitive processes

*Psychologists study cognitive changes across the life span in order to assist individuals with the aging process and in order to comprehend the secrets of brain-behavior interrelationships and aging.*

*Principal terms*
COGNITIVE ABILITIES: psychological capabilities including attention, learning, intelligence, memory, language and speech, perception, concept formation, and problem solving
CRYSTALLIZED INTELLIGENCE: the form of intelligence that reflects knowledge acquired through education and everyday life experiences across time and maturity
FLUID INTELLIGENCE: the form of intelligence that reflects speed of information processing, reasoning, and memory capacity
INFORMATION PROCESSING: cognitive capabilities that involve processing memories
NEURON: a brain cell specialized for the transmission of information in the nervous system

## Overview

Behavioral scientists have become increasingly interested in studying the cognitive changes that occur in the elderly across time. These studies have been conducted in order to assist individuals in their adjustment to aging as well as to unlock the secrets of the aging process itself. Cognitive changes refer to those changes which occur in overall mental functions and operations. Cognition encompasses all mental operations and functions, including attention, intelligence, memory, language and speech, perception, learning, concept formation, thought, problem solving, spatial and time orientation, and motor/behavior control. Psychologists have worked hard to define and measure various areas of cognitive functioning, even though there has been no consensus about these areas. Understanding the progression of cognitive functioning requires an understanding of brain structure and those human functions emanating from the brain and its fullest human potentiality, the mind. There is considerable debate within the scientific community about what type of cognitive functions actually exist as well as the nature of the mental mechanisms that are necessary to understand cognitive functioning.

There is a common belief that cognitive abilities decline markedly in older individuals. More and more, however, this idea is being shown to be exaggerated. Studies have shown that the diminishment of cognitive skills with age may not be significant, especially before the age of about seventy-five. Aging has been found to have different effects on long-term and short-term memory processes. The capacity of short-term memory (which is quite limited in all age groups) remains essentially the same for older people. Long-term memory, however, does show a decline. This decline can be minimized by various strategies; the use of mnemonic devices is very effective, as is taking extra time in learning and remembering.

Both biological and environmental factors have been studied in regard to aging and cognition. An environment that induces apathy or depression has been found to have a lowering effect on cognitive abilities. Environments that provide stimuli to interest the individual can reduce cognitive decline. Moreover, at least one study has found that providing challenging stimuli can even reverse cognitive declines that have been observed. There is a tremendous range of aging effects from individual to individual, with some showing virtually no changes and others showing serious decay of functions. It should be noted that this discussion concerns cognition in healthy individuals; diseases, such as Alzheimer's disease and Parkinson's disease, and events such as strokes (cardiovascular accidents) have effects on memory that are considered separately from the normal effects of aging.

Contemporary research on cognitive changes caused by aging emphasizes the information-processing capabilities of individuals as reflected in memory capacities. Memory is a basic psychological function upon which higher-level psychological processes such as speech, learning, concept formation, and problem solving are based. Lester Sdorow describes the brain's information-processing capacities as the human being's active acquisition of information about the world. Sensory stimuli are transmitted to the brain, where replicas of the external world are stored briefly in the sensory registry (one second for visual stimuli and four seconds for auditory memory). Information is then transferred to short-term memory (STM) for about twenty seconds, unless it is actively rehearsed, then into long-term memory (LTM), where it is potentially retained for a lifetime.

Information processing is a view of cognitive development that is based on the premise that complex cognitive skills develop as the product of the integration of a heirarchy of more basic skills obtained through life experience and learning. According to this view, prerequisite skills are mastered and form the foundation for more and more complex skills.

Information-processing theories emerged as psychologists began to draw comparisons between the way computers operate and the way humans use logic and rules about the world as they develop. Humans use these rules for processing information. New rules may be added and old rules modified throughout childhood and adulthood as more information is obtained from interactions with the world. The cognitive changes that occur throughout adult life, as more useful and accurate rules are learned, are every bit as important as the cognitive advances that occurred during childhood, as long as the basic rules acquired in childhood were not distorted by aberrant experiences. Each advance refines the ability to process information. Elizabeth F. Loftus points out that the terms cognition and information processing have supplanted the term "thinking" among contemporary cognitive scientists. Similar efforts have been made to redefine other human abilities such as problem solving (by H. A. Simon) and intelligence (by Robert Sternberg) in order to describe greater specificity of function.

Researchers have spent much time and effort defining and redefining memory constructs, although theorists remain in the early stages of understanding memory. Much debate has focused on naturalistic versus laboratory methodologies, with few resolutions as to how the results of both can contribute to a permanent knowledge base of memory.

The mediation school of thought suggests theoretical mechanisms of encoding, retention, and retrieval to explain memory functioning. Consequently, concerted efforts have been made to attribute memory changes across the life span to the specific deterioration of such mechanisms. Researchers continue to debate the importance, even existence, of such constructs. Similarly, the dichotomy of long-term versus short-term memory continues to be debated. In order to test the empirical validity of such theories, constructs must be able to be disproved if false, and these metaphorical constructs have proved difficult or impossible to test because of their abstract nature.

The greatest controversy in memory research focuses on laboratory versus naturalistic experiments; some researchers, such as M. R. Banaji and R. G. Crowder, state that naturalistic experiments have yielded no new principles and no new methods of memory research and should be abandoned. Others, such as H. P. Bahrick, however, claim that the naturalistic approach has provided in ten years what the laboratory has not in a hundred years. Banaji and Crowder criticize naturalistic experiments for their lack of control and thus, their lack of generalizability. Yet confining a study to a specific population in a contrived laboratory setting does not seem to generalize any further. An exclusive reliance on either strategy is not parsimonious. S. J. Ceci and Urie Bronfenbrenner emphasize the need to focus on the process of understanding, whatever that process might be. As Endel Tulving notes, the polemics that have ensued from this debate are not going to advance the science of memory. He concludes that there is no reason to believe that there is only one correct way of studying memory.

## Applications

In examining cognitive changes in aging populations, aside from the theoretical debates, researchers have reported that cognitive processes progressively decline as chronological age advances. Studies have tended to describe the cognitive declines as gradual and general, rather than being attributable to discrete cognitive losses in specific areas of functioning.

Psychologists who have studied memory change identify diminished memory capacity in the elderly as attributable to a number of processes, such as slowed semantic access and a reduced ability to make categorical judgments. Other researchers concluded that older subjects were slower in mental operations but were not less accurate. Some researchers hypothesized that slower speed tied up processing functions, resulting in apparent memory impairment. Still others have hypothesized that older adults have more trouble with active memory tasks because of an increased competition for a share of memory processing resources, whereas others have linked the aged's poor performance on working memory tasks to an actual deficiency in processing resources. Finally, some researchers have concluded that older adults might simply have less mental energy to perform memory tasks. These studies accept gradual memory decline, or a slowing of processing, as a normal by-product of aging.

R. A. Hock, B. A. Futrell, and B. A. Grismer studied eighty-two elderly persons, from sixty to ninety-nine years of age, who were living independently in the community. These normal adults were tested on a battery of eight tasks that were selected to reflect cognitive functioning, particularly measuring primary and secondary memory, memory for nonverbal material, span of attention, the capacity to divide attention between competing sources of stimulation, and two motor tasks requiring psychomotor integrity. This study found a gradual, progressive decline in cognitive functioning but found that the decline did not reach statistically significant levels. The decline was general, suggesting that it may have been a function of reduced attention, rather than more discrete losses. This finding appears to be consistent with the notion that crystallized intellectual or abstract processes are well maintained across time. There were suggestions that speed of information processing is a sensitive measure of the aging process.

It is possible, however, that the tasks selected for this study did not discriminate between younger and older aging adults because the tasks may be more reliable for assessing brain injuries and psychologically impaired persons, which were not included in the population studied. Consequently, further studies on the same cognitive tasks with impaired aged adults would be necessary to see if the same relationships and conclusions would apply. Individuals with impaired cognitive functioning offer a unique opportunity to determine if the brain continues to show the same propensity to function as a unitary, global system as is observed with individuals who experience the normal aging process.

Although the brain does exhibit localization of functions, with specialization of certain brain cells for specific functions, its overall mode of operation is as a total unit. The brain has an exceptional capacity to compensate for the loss of some specific functions and continue the rest of its mental operations. This capacity or flexibility in brain function has been termed equipotentiation. Further studies of individuals with brain impairments will help to show how the brain attempts to carry out its overall functions when more specific impairments have been sustained. When cognitive disorders result in faulty information processing, actual observable changes may occur in a person's daily behavior. The previously neat person, for example, may neglect personal hygiene. The person who previously exhibited exceptional verbal abilities may speak in a socially inappropriate manner. The staid conservative businessperson may act impulsively or even make unreasonable decisions about personal finances, and may show impaired social judgment.

## Context

Studies of cognitive changes across the life span must distinguish between normal gradual change in the elderly and change that is associated with disordered functioning. Studies must also respect the complexity of the human brain. Morton Hunt notes that cognitive scientists have concluded that there may be 100 billion neurons in the interior of the brain. Each of these neurons may be interconnected to hundreds of others by anywhere from one thousand to ten thousand synapses or relay points. This may enable the average healthy person to accumulate five hundred times as much information as is contained in the entire *Encyclopædia Brittanica*, or 100 trillion bits ($10^{14}$) of information. The circuitry in one human brain is probably sixty times the complexity of the entire United States telephone system. Given this complexity, even the daily estimated loss of 100,000 brain cells from the aging process may leave human beings capable of sound cognitive functioning well into old age.

Paul Baltes notes that it used to be considered "common knowledge" that cognitive abilities decline with age, but today this view is highly debatable. When the effects of disease and injury are separated out in studies of the healthy elderly, no drastic decline in cognitive ability is found. This conclusion may be one reason that studies of cognition and aging have begun to make a distinction regarding intelligence. The distinction is between crystallized intelligence, involving the accumulation of facts and knowledge, which holds up with age, and fluid intelligence, which is the rapid processing of new information, a function that appears particularly associated with the young and vulnerable to the effects of age or disease. Studies of neurologically healthy aging adults have revealed no consistent evidence of a reduced ability to learn. Studies have further shown that very little practice may be required to improve substantially an elderly person's ability to perform some cognitive tasks, reflecting a motivational factor. Studies of mentally active persons in their eighties have concluded that loss of cognitive ability stemmed more from intellectual apathy or boredom than from actual physical deterioration.

John Darley and his colleagues concluded that on average, the decline of intellectual capability with age is slight and probably does not occur before age seventy-five. When declines do occur, they do not occur equally across cognitive functions. Vocabulary and verbal skills may actually improve with age, whereas skills involving spatial visualization and deductive reasoning are more likely to diminish. In general, verbal skills and accumulated knowledge are maintained with aging, while tasks that require quick responses are more susceptible to aging.

## Bibliography

Bahrick, H. P. "A Speedy Recovery from Bankruptcy for Ecological Memory Research." *American Psychologist* 46, no. 1 (1991): 76-77. This article addresses the controversy between those who favor naturalistic memory studies and those who favor strict experimental studies; Bahrick favors the naturalistic approach.

Banaji, Mahzarin R., and Robert G. Crowder. "The Bankruptcy of Everyday Memory." *American Psychologist* 44, no. 9 (1989): 1185-1193. This article addresses the controversy between naturalistic and experimental research; the authors favor more controlled experimental approaches.

Ceci, S. J., and Urie Bronfenbrenner. "On the Demise of Everyday Memory." *American Psychologist* 46, no. 1 (1991): 27-31. Addresses the naturalistic versus experimental memory study issue, offering a balanced perspective and inviting scientific inquiry regardless of the type of methodology.

Darley, John M., Samuel Glucksberg, and Ronald A. Kinchla. *Psychology.* 3d ed. Englewood Cliffs, N.J.: Prentice-Hall, 1986. This introductory text summarizes the findings of studies of cognitive change with aging adults.

Hunt, Morton M. *The Universe Within.* New York: Simon & Schuster, 1982. Hunt's book discusses the findings of the scientific specialty called cognitive science, arguing for a greater appreciation for the humanity of the human mind than detractors have allowed.

Loftus, Elizabeth F. *Memory: Surprising New Insights into How We Remember and Why We Forget.* Reading, Mass.: Addison-Wesley, 1988. Loftus discusses the development of the cognitive sciences in seeking greater specificity for human abilities such as thinking and memory.

Sternberg, Robert J. *Intelligence, Information Processing, and Analogical Reasoning: The Componential Analysis of Human Abilities.* Hillsdale, N.J.: Lawrence Erlbaum, 1977. Focuses on a redefinition of human abilities by redescribing intellectual processes in more accuracy than the historical view of intelligence as a static capacity to learn.

*Robert A. Hock*

## Cross-References

# AGING: INSTITUTIONAL CARE

*Type of psychology:* Developmental psychology
*Field of study:* Aging

*The elderly who are institutionalized in nursing homes, state hospitals, and prisons require care that is sensitive to their needs. The elderly are a heterogeneous population, and this fact underscores the significance of understanding why the elderly become institutionalized and of designing care that will best address the needs of the elderly in each type of institution.*

    *Principal terms*
        ALZHEIMER'S DISEASE: progressive and irreversible brain changes which are the most frequent cause of dementia; estimated to affect 5 percent of individuals over sixty-five
        DEMENTIA: globally impaired intellectual functioning in adults as a function of brain impairment; it does not mean "craziness" but a loss or impairment of mental power
        DEPRESSION IN THE ELDERLY: depression can range from mild to severe and can include sadness, discouragement, hopelessness, helplessness, memory loss, lack of appetite, and sleeplessness
        MEDICARE: a federally funded program that covers some medical costs for individuals over sixty-five and for some disabled individuals
        NEUROPSYCHOLOGICAL ASSESSMENT: the evaluation of brain functions by testing memory and attention, reasoning, coordination, writing comprehension, and verbal expression
        SKILLED NURSING HOME CARE: in contrast to facilities that provide primarily custodial care, skilled care requires direct rehabilitative services by licensed professionals
        SUPPORT GROUP: a group designed to assist family members in coping when a family member has a disease such as Alzheimer's disease

## Overview

The term "institution" refers to highly organized residential establishments such as prisons, hospitals, and nursing homes with long-stay populations. The goal of these facilities is care, treatment, or custody of residents ranging in age from the very young to the very old. The care of one segment of this population, the institutionalized elderly, is receiving increasing attention as health care providers emphasize the complexity of geriatric treatment needs. The elderly require special consideration as a result of numerous age-related biological and psychosocial changes.

The percentage of elderly inmates in prisons is expected to increase steadily for many years. Twenty-five percent of persons over age sixty-five will spend some time in nursing homes. Gary Moak points out that even though many elderly state hospital residents have been transferred to long-term-care facilities such as nursing homes, the elderly still constitute more than 20 percent of residents in state hospitals, and 5 percent of new admissions to state hospitals are elderly.

Elderly people are living longer, and, as the population of the United States continues to age, it is clear that society is not prepared to provide medical and psychological care, shelter, protection, and custody to all the elderly who will depend on institutions for care. Most traditional institutions, such as prisons and state hospitals, are not designed to provide for a large number of elderly residents. Nontraditional institutions, such as nursing homes, designed to fill the need for appropriate long-term care options for the elderly, are becoming custodial warehouses as well. Ideally, the characteristics of the elderly who reside in each institution should determine the type of medical, psychological, and social care that is provided.

The typical profile of the elderly inmate serving time in prison is that of a white, unmarried male lacking a high school education. According to Sol Chaneles, there are three types of elderly inmates who are serving time. First is the old-timer who has been sentenced to a long mandatory term that guarantees he will grow old in prison. Second is the career criminal, a continual recidivist, who probably will not be released until he is very old. Third is the old offender who is serving time for his first serious offense, often a violent crime such as murder.

In contrast, the typical profile of the elderly nursing-home resident is that of an eighty-six-year-old woman with poor or declining health and reduced mental functioning. The ratio of female to male in nursing homes is 2.5 to 1. Women have a longer life expectancy than men and therefore outnumber them among the oldest elderly.

The elderly institutionalized in nursing homes share such characteristics as multiple concurrent medical conditions and functional disabilities such as gait abnormalities, falls, dementia, incontinence, and other diminished levels of self-sufficiency. Elderly people who are unable to perform the activities of daily living such as preparing meals, getting dressed, maintaining personal hygiene, and moving to and from the toilet, bed, or chair are likely to enter nursing homes. Of all functionally impaired elderly persons, those most likely to be admitted to nursing homes lack sufficient caregiver support, have the lowest incomes, and are most socially isolated. Clinical conditions most likely to precipitate entering an institution are incontinence and dementia, each of which imposes especially stressful burdens on caregivers.

Although it may appear that institutionalizing the elderly in nursing homes is preferable to state hospital placement, there are times when state hospitals are valid options. There is no set profile of the elderly in state hospitals. Some elderly have grown old in state hospitals because they were not successfully deinstitutionalized and suffer from the combined effects of chronic mental illness, long-term institutionalization, and age-related functional decline. Often this type is an elderly individual suffering from schizophrenia.

Moak notes that elderly persons who are institutionalized for the first time are admitted for assaultiveness, inability to care for themselves, disruptive behavior, suicidal behavior, wandering, self-abusive behavior, and treatment refusal. Aggressive behavior and wandering rather than the need for custodial care are among the most common reasons for admission of elderly with Alzheimer's disease and other forms of dementia. The diagnosis of organic brain syndrome or senile dementia has been a convenient reason for the placement of many elderly persons in state hospitals.

In general, elderly persons referred to state hospitals can be divided into four groups, according to Paul Lerman. First are those suffering from a major psychiatric illness. Second are those suffering from cognitive impairment associated with the aging process, such as organic brain syndrome or some type of dementia. Third are those with primarily physical illnesses. Fourth are those in a satisfactory physical and mental state but who need financial assistance and shelter.

## Applications

Bob Knight and Peggy Carter, reporting on a study to reduce inpatient stays for older adults hospitalized for psychiatric reasons, pointed out that older patients tend to be overrepresented in inpatient services and take up a disproportionate amount of services. The authors speculated that the reason for the longer inpatient stays for these adults was stereotyping by staff caring for older patients. In other words, most staff tended to view older inpatients as "Alzheimer's cases" for whom not much could be done. In addition, the authors believed that staff was simply unfamiliar with services available for the aged on an outpatient basis and, in addition, was unprepared for the medical and psychiatric problems occurring together in the same patient.

Knight and Carter set up an intensive care management program whereby older patients were given concentrated attention by the health provider staff. They found that intensive care combined with thorough searching of placement facilities reduced the amount of time older patients needed to be in a psychiatric facility when compared to older patients in a unit that did not provide this type of intensive care. It was suggested that an intensive care program is one way of attempting to reduce inpatient stays for older adults.

Daniel Malcolm Spica and Norman Abeles have studied dilemmas in coping with aging, among them "late-life forgetting," which has also been called age-associated memory impairment. Everyone is aware that some older individuals are more forgetful and absent-minded. What is not known is whether this represents "normal" aging or the beginning of dementia or Alzheimer's disease. The term late-life forgetting is applied to individuals over the age of fifty who complain of memory problems in tasks of daily living and whose memory problems can be documented by existing psychological tests.

The study found that there are psychological tests which can differentiate with reasonable accuracy individuals who are "normal" elderly (with no significant memory impairments) from late-life forgetters (who have some memory loss but remain within the range of satisfactory functioning). Both these groups can clearly be differentiated from individuals who manifest dementia. Spica and Abeles noted that the classification system was 88 percent correct. None of the late-life forgetters or normal elderly was classified as demented, but some of the normal individuals were classified as late-life forgetters and vice versa. The overall aim of this kind of research is to prevent otherwise healthy elderly persons with isolated memory impairments from being mislabeled as having incurable dementia.

Samuel Perry, Allen Frances, and John Clarkin described a case that shows some pitfalls in assuming that an elderly person's problems with memory or functioning are attributable to dementia. In this case, the behavior of a seventy-nine-year-old woman changed markedly after her husband returned home following a short hospital stay. When he returned from a relatively minor procedure, she became noticeably irritable and began preparing for death. Her family, naturally concerned about this change in behavior, took her to a psychiatrist, who prescribed medications for her depression. Instead of getting better, however, she began experiencing severe memory problems, became disoriented, and was admitted to a psychiatric hospital, where she was treated with various medications. Psychologists noted that her ability to learn was impaired; it was assumed that her problems were organic in nature.

After some time in the hospital, she was discharged to her home. Later, after still another hospitalization for her condition, she was discharged, and medications were discontinued. She continued to be depressed, although her memory seemed to improve. In part because she seemed to have such great sensitivity to medications and because her memory had improved, doctors suggested that she receive psychotherapy for her concerns.

Clinicians noted that this patient had been very upset when her father died when she was eight years old, and her family's financial circumstances had deteriorated markedly. Furthermore, it was noted that the patient had often become depressed around the time of year of her father's death and had received psychiatric treatment for this when she was in her thirties. Her doctors wondered whether there might be a connection between the patient's depression and the brief hospitalization of her husband.

Perry, Frances, and Clarkin used this case to describe a condition known as pseudodementia. This condition is a false dementia, since it includes loss of memory and intellectual power as a consequence of depression. It is assumed that as the depression lifts, the intellectual and memory deficits also begin to disappear. Pseudodementia, as the authors point out, usually starts with a clearcut onset, and patients are aware of their memory losses. In contrast, dementia frequently does not have a specific onset, and memory complaints are denied. It is estimated that 10 to 20 percent of dementias are not diagnosed correctly and are pseudodementias.

## Context

In order to plan for the future, it is necessary to understand the history of institutionalism. In the past, most families took care of their sick elderly members, including the mentally ill; communities were responsible for those who had nobody to look after them. One of the results was the organization of institutional care in poorhouses or alms houses.

The early twentieth century was characterized by a great buildup of state mental hospitals. They were established as part of a great humanitarian movement to provide treatment for the mentally ill instead of merely depositing them in prisons or poorhouses. In the nineteenth century, advocates of "moral treatment" had worked to improve the quality of care in the state hospitals. Leslie Libow points out that the poorhouses of the nineteenth century also gave rise to the nursing home. The Social Security Act of 1935 precipitated the establishment of the boarding home, since the act denied payment to any individual who lived in an institutional setting such as a public poorhouse. Elderly people were forced to seek board in private homes, which hired nurses as their residents grew more infirm. Federal legislation later contributed to the creation of big-business nursing homes as Medicare and Medicaid payments became available.

Today, institutions are changing; changes in institutional placement, planning, and treatment have nevertheless largely ignored the institutionalized elderly. In many cases, elderly persons who make up the resident aging population in prisons, nursing homes, and state hospitals are socially isolated and depressed. They are likely to have medical illnesses that are not satisfactorily treated because of a lack of adequate resources to treat the physical concomitants of aging. Furthermore, those who are cognitively impaired are labeled demented and are forgotten.

The institutionalized elderly are seen as needing a highly controlled, restricted environment, but Robert Kahn has stated that the practice of merely providing custodial care has resulted in a message of hopelessness that undermines the successful care of the elderly in each type of institution. If society is to learn from the past, it is clear that changes in how society cares for the elderly who are institutionalized in nursing homes, prisons, and state hospitals are necessary and overdue.

## Bibliography

Binstock, R. "Health Care of the Aging: Trends, Dilemmas and Prospects for the Year 2000." In *Aging 2000: Our Health Care Destiny*, edited by Charles M. Gaitz. New York: Springer-Verlag, 1985. Binstock presents an overview of health care issues, including materials on the capacity of older persons to pay for health care and long-term care for the elderly. He also outlines long-term policy issues, including the prospect of rationing health care on the basis of old-age criteria.

Gelfand, Donald E. *The Aging Network.* 3d ed. New York: Springer, 1988. This four-part book first describes the status of older Americans, then moves on to income-maintenance programs. Most important, the last two sections focus on major programs of aging and service delivery for the elderly. Examines the status of nursing homes.

Kohut, Sylvester, Jr., Jeraldine J. Kohut, and Joseph J. Fleishman. *Reality Orientation for the Elderly.* Oradell, N.J.: Medical Economics, 1987. Written by an administrator, a nurse, and a clinical psychologist, this book discusses institutionalization of the elderly and treatment methods for older adults. The authors focus on bridging the gap between theory and practice by providing practical guidelines designed to improve the quality of life for older adults. It can be understood by high school and college students.

Mace, Nancy L., and Peter V. Rabins. *The Thirty-Six-Hour Day.* Baltimore: The Johns Hopkins University Press, 1981. A practical and detailed book which helps family members who are caretakers of individuals with memory problems and dementia. Uses a number of examples to demonstrate how impaired family members can be helped and answers practical questions. Can be understood by the general public.

Parmelee, P., and P. Lawton. "The Design of Special Environments for the Aged." In *Handbook of the Psychology of Aging*, edited by James E. Birren and K. Warner Schaie. 3d ed. San Diego: Academic Press, 1990. The authors emphasize older people's need for independence even as they move into special housing environments. They discuss security as a primary need for older adults and discuss various types of living arrangements, including continuing care retirement, residential care homes, and nursing homes. They urge more research on the topic of special environments for the aged. Accessible to college students.

*Norman Abeles*
*Barbara Clark*

## Cross-References

Ageism, 156; Aging: Cognitive Changes, 180; Aging: Physical Changes, 192; Theories of Aging, 198; Coping: Social Support, 700; Dementia, Alzheimer's Disease, and Parkinson's Disease, 783; Forgetting and Forgetfulness, 1049.

# AGING: PHYSICAL CHANGES

*Type of psychology:* Developmental psychology
*Fields of study:* Aging; stress and illness

*Physical aging is a process of change. Psychosocial factors such as the degree of autonomy in an older person's life can affect the degree to which health problems are present. In the wake of pioneering studies on gerontology beginning in the 1950's, the U.S. federal government began providing programs for the elderly in American society.*

Principal terms
AUTONOMY: the extent to which an individual is able to make decisions about his or her own life
GERONTOLOGY: the study of aging
IMMUNE SYSTEM: the body's mechanism for fighting disease
METABOLISM: the process by which a particular substance is utilized by the body
OSTEOPOROSIS: a condition in which the bones become dangerously thin and fragile

## Overview

Scientists agree that 115 to 120 years is probably the longest that people live. The scientists who study aging are called gerontologists; they do not know exactly what the aging process is or why it proceeds differently in different people. It is known that predictable changes occur in the body as it gets older. Some are easily noticed, such as hair turning gray, hair loss, and wrinkles. Other changes, such as a tendency toward rising blood pressure, are not visible.

In general, research on aging has emphasized losses. More recently, increased interest in the aging process has stimulated physiological, sociological, and psychological research on aging. Although many physiological variables show major losses with advancing age, it is important, when looking at the average, to note that there is substantial variability at all ages throughout life. Scientists are finding that some changes in blood pressure and cholesterol levels that had originally been interpreted as age specific are common in industrial societies but not in agricultural ones.

Advancing age is associated with progressive impairments in the capacity to metabolize glucose. Again, there is substantial variability of the results in successive age groups, with many older individuals metabolizing glucose as well as their younger counterparts. The carbohydrate intolerance of aging may carry substantial risk, even in the absence of disease. Attempts have been made to determine which components of the age-associated alterations in carbohydrate intolerance are related to aging itself and which components might be related to diet, exercise, or medications. It is thought that factors such as physical fitness may decrease the likelihood of carbohydrate intolerance with advancing age. Metabolism also begins to slow at around age twenty-five. For each decade thereafter, the number of calories required to maintain one's weight drops by at least 2 percent. Muscle mass gradually shrinks, so that people tend to have more body fat than they did when younger.

Aging is also associated with a decline in bone density in both males and females, but primarily females. About 24 million Americans develop osteoporosis, a condition in which the bones become dangerously thin and fragile. Osteoporosis is a major problem for the elderly. Bone mass reaches its peak in the thirties for both men and women, then begins to drop by about 1 percent per year. Brittle bones are the major cause of the fractures that cripple many of the elderly. It is estimated that by age sixty-five, one-third of women will have fractures of the vertebrae in the spinal column, and by age eighty-one, one-third of women and one-sixth of men will have suffered a hip fracture. A number of studies suggest that bone loss can be reduced in advanced age by adherence to moderate exercise programs, in addition to adequate calcium intake throughout life.

The sense organs of the elderly also go through changes. Taste diminishes as the nose loses its sense of smell. Odors account for most of the overall sensation of flavors, so taste is lost as a function of loss of smell. Loss of taste can lead to lack of appetite and to serious nutritional deficiencies. Hearing fades, particularly in the high-frequency range. Vision begins deteriorating at about forty. The lens hardens and becomes cloudy, letting less light into the eye. More than half of those sixty and older have some cataract formation.

Changes occur in the skin. The topmost layer, or epidermis, becomes dry, whereas the middle layer, or dermis, becomes thin and less elastic. Along with loss of fat from the underlying subcutaneous layer, these changes cause the skin to sag and become wrinkled.

There are other physiological changes that accompany aging. For example, the immune system starts to decline at around age thirty. The white blood cells that fight off invaders such as viruses and bacteria lose some of their effectiveness as a person gets older. The gradual weakening of the immune system makes it harder to keep from getting ill.

The respiratory system undergoes many changes with age. There is a reduction in breathing efficiency because the lungs no longer expand to take in as much air. In fact, lungs lose on the average 30 to 50 percent of their maximum breathing capacity between ages thirty and eighty. There is a diminished uptake of oxygen in the lungs, so less oxygen is carried by the blood, which has health ramifications since oxygen is necessary for the synthesis of amino acids and fatty acids, and for the production of energy.

Several theories attempt to explain the aging process. There are genetic theories, as well as nongenetic and physiological ones. The aging of cells is a complex process that scientists still do not completely understand. Genetic theories emphasize that changes occur at the subcellular level in deoxyribonucleic acid (DNA) and ribonucleic acid (RNA), resulting in an inability to form correctly the enzymes that are necessary for cells to function. The nongenetic theories are more concerned with the effects of waste products and free molecules on the cell's functioning. Finally, physiological theories describe the breakdown in system integration and function that occurs with age, explaining the effects of aging on the whole body rather than the cellular origins of aging.

## Applications

The number of elderly people in the United States has increased rapidly in recent years. Since 1950, the number of Americans sixty-five or older has more than doubled. Americans are living longer than ever before. The Bureau of the Census predicts that by 2030, the number of elderly Americans will grow to nearly 65 million and will make up more than 20 percent of the population. It is estimated that by 2050, one in twenty Americans will be older than eighty-five years of age.

National surveys by the Institute for Social Research and other organizations show that life generally seems less troublesome and freer to older people than it does to younger adults. In a review of what researchers have learned about subjective well-being, including happiness, life satisfaction, and positive emotions, psychologist Edward Diener reported that most studies show a slow rise in satisfaction with age. Whereas younger people appear to experience higher levels of joy, older people tend to think about their lives in more positive ways than younger people do. Money is often thought to be a key to a happy retirement, but psychologist Daniel Ogilvie has found another factor to be of major importance. His research shows that once people have a minimum amount of money, life satisfaction depends primarily on how much time they spend doing things they find meaningful. Ogilvie thinks retirement planning seminars should focus more on helping people decide how to use their skills and interests after retirement.

One popular misconception disputed by recent research is the idea that aging means inevitable physical and sexual failure. While some changes necessarily occur, many of the problems associated with old age fall into the category of secondary aging. Secondary aging means that the problems are not the result of age but of abuse and disuse, which often can be controlled by the individual. Researchers have found that people wear out faster from disuse than they wear out from overuse. This also applies to sexuality. Studies from the time of Alfred Kinsey's work in the 1940's and 1950's to the present show that sexual interest and activity decrease with age, but the drop varies greatly among individuals. Psychologist Marion Perlmutter reported that one of the best predictors of continued sexual intercourse is past sexual enjoyment and frequency. People who have never enjoyed sexuality much may consider age a good reason to give up sex.

Psychosocial factors have been studied, and they sometimes reveal how older men and women feel about the physical changes happening to their bodies. It is important that family members and members of the helping professions, along with the elderly themselves, come to understand that the physical changes that occur with passing time produce needs that are real, and that elderly people are not simply trying to make demands for attention. Elderly people must be helped to retain their dignity and allowed to remain as active and independent as possible. No one, whatever his or her age, likes to be helpless or to be perceived as a helpless person. As a result of helplessness, researchers find lowered self-esteem, health problems, depression, and sometimes death.

Considerable research has been done in the broad area of control or autonomy—that is, the extent to which individuals are able to make decisions regarding such things as choice of activity, method and manner of engagement, time, and pace. The research shows a remarkable convergence: Lack of control has adverse effects on emotional states, performance, subjective well-being, and physiological indicators. Older people commonly experience reductions in autonomy and control for many reasons, including physical impairments, reduced incomes, residential moves from separate households to institutional living arrangements, and so on. The extent to which autonomy and control are encouraged or denied may be a major determinant of whether aging is usual or successful on a number of physiological and behavioral dimensions. In 1976, E. J. Langer and Judith Rodin conducted an experiment in a nursing home in which residents on one floor were given a treatment that enhanced their personal control. The treatment consisted of a lecture from the nursing home administrator about decisions that residents could and should make for themselves. A comparison group, on another floor, heard a lecture that emphasized what the staff would do in taking care of such matters. During the first three weeks after the experimental treatment, people in the experimental group were happier and more active, according to their own reports. They spent more time in social activities, according to the nurses. The differences between groups continued to increase over the following eighteen-month period that they were studied.

Several lines of research on psychosocial factors and health focus on the idea of social support. Empirical research has found consistent relationships between social support and various indicators of health and well-being. Social networks and support are persistent conditions that affect the mortality of older people. Support-disrupting life events have specific negative effects on both mortality and morbidity. The positive effects of social support have been demonstrated by means of intervention studies. Most of the intervention has involved supportive behaviors by health care professionals. Positive effects include increased rate and completeness of recovery from injuries, a fewer number of heart attacks, decreased incidence of cancer, and fewer physical illnesses.

## Context

Important early studies of aging were performed in the 1950's, including the Human Aging Study, conducted by the National Institute of Mental Health; the Duke Longitudinal Studies, done by the Center for the Study of Aging and Human Development at Duke University; and the Baltimore Longitudinal Study of Aging. These pioneering studies and hundreds of others have benefited from growing federal support.

A nonprofit professional organization called the American Geriatrics Society

(AGS) was established in 1942 by physicians and scientists who realized that the area of aging was an important one in medicine and would become increasingly important as time passed. The membership of the society has grown considerably, promoting research in the field of aging. The AGS has established a journal called the *Journal of the American Geriatrics Society*, published monthly, and is responsible for the development and expansion of geriatric training centers in the United States and Canada.

The Association for Gerontology in Higher Education (AGHE), a nonprofit organization, was founded in 1974. Its membership includes hundreds of colleges and universities that provide education in the field of aging. The main goal is to provide a network that assists faculty and administrators in improving the quality of gerontology programs in higher education. The AGHE runs a clearinghouse from its national headquarters in Washington, D.C., as a source of technical information on gerontology programs and is politically active in the promotion of gerontological education.

The National Association of State Units on Aging (NASUA) was founded in 1964. Since then, federal agencies have also designed programs for the elderly. Many of the programs are a result of the Older Americans Act, which became law in 1965. The Older Americans Act required states to set up agencies for the reception of funds and the development of long-term aging plans. In 1973, Congress enacted amendments that called for the establishment of substate units, called Area Agencies on Aging (AAAs). Each AAA was to set up plans to show how the agency would pool the existing resources for the elderly within its boundaries.

In 1975, the National Association of Area Agencies on Aging (NAAAA) was incorporated, with the goal of providing direction to membership and acting as the central leader in the national network on aging. The NAAAA, together with the NASUA, maintains a national database on aging and provides information about services available to older Americans, along with details concerning state and local agencies on aging. The database is updated annually and contains statistics related to aging. Funds from the Older Americans Act help support state and local ombudsman programs, many of which are affiliated with the National Citizens' Coalition for Nursing Home Reform. As can be seen, people in the United States are becoming increasingly aware that a growing portion of the population is older than sixty-five and are trying to provide for the elderly by addressing their needs and concerns.

## Bibliography

Birren, James E., and K. Warner Schaie, eds. *Handbook of the Psychology of Aging.* 2d ed. New York: Van Nostrand Reinhold, 1985. Presents information on the psychology of adult development and aging in an edited handbook format. Provides the reader with chapters written by experts on a wide range of topics. An authoritative review, serving as a definitive reference source for students, researchers, and professionals.

Cox, Harold. *Later Life: The Realities of Aging.* 2d ed. Englewood Cliffs, N.J.: Prentice-

Hall, 1988. The writing style is clear and straightforward. The author has packed the book full of practical information about all aspects of later life, including husband-wife relations, biological and health correlates of aging, theoretical perspectives on aging, work and retirement patterns, and even death and dying.

Geist, Harold. *The Psychological Aspects of the Aging Process.* St. Louis: W. H. Green, 1968. Although this book is somewhat dated, it is easy to read and covers a variety of topics, such as a comparison of care of the aged in a variety of countries, sex differences in aging, biological and psychological aspects of aging, and social and cultural aspects of the aging process.

Kausler, Donald H. *Experimental Psychology and Human Aging.* New York: John Wiley & Sons, 1982. Presents a survey of psychological research on human aging. The book has a developmental psychology flavor, but it summarizes research on gerontology and emphasizes the process of conducting psychological experiments in order to study behavior of the elderly.

Kermis, Marguerite D. *The Psychology of Human Aging: Theory, Research, and Practice.* Boston: Allyn & Bacon, 1984. A textbook that presents a comprehensive picture of diverse topics in aging. Written for students who have no previous background in gerontology. Covers many areas that are not traditionally covered, such as health policies and preventive medicine. Contains numerous case studies of psychological aging as well as practical applications of the research.

*Deborah R. McDonald*

## Cross-References

Ageism, 156; Aging: Cognitive Changes, 180; Aging: Institutional Care, 186; Theories of Aging, 198; Death and Dying: Theoretical Perspectives, 763; Dementia, Alzheimer's Disease, and Parkinson's Disease, 783; Hearing Loss, 1157; Memory: Physiology, 1523; Stress: Physiological Responses, 2425; Stress-Related Diseases, 2464.

# THEORIES OF AGING

*Type of psychology:* Developmental psychology
*Fields of study:* Aging; endocrine system; stress and illness

*Aging is an entropic (energy-disorder) phenomenon that is exhibited by most multicellular organisms. Three major theories have been suggested to explain the mechanisms of aging: the free-radical theory, the genetic program theory, and the error catastrophe theory. While each theory emphasizes different aspects of the aging process, they almost certainly are interrelated.*

*Principal terms*

ANTIOXIDANT: an enzyme, such as catalase, or other molecule, such as vitamin C, that inactivates oxidizing free radical molecules that damage cellular molecules upon contact

CATALASE: an enzyme (protein) that is encoded by and found in the cells of many living organisms, both prokaryotes and eukaryotes, and that scavenges oxidizing free-radical molecules, thereby reducing the effects of these toxins

ENTROPY: disorder; a fundamental property of the universe in which any system loses energy because of inefficiency and breaks down, or dissipates, with the passage of time

ENZYME PATHWAY: a series of enzyme-mediated chemical reactions within a living cell that control the cell's metabolism and survival by linking many different aspects of the cell's mechanical or chemical makeup

FREE RADICAL: a molecule (for example, oxygen, superoxide, or hydrogen peroxide) that is highly reactive, often because of the presence of extra electrons, and that therefore reacts with other molecules, often irreparably altering their basic structures

GENE: any protein-encoding region of a chromosome (DNA); most living organisms contain tens of thousands of genes, exact copies of which are found in every cell of the organism

HORMONE: a molecule, usually composed of protein or steroids, that is produced in certain cells of an organism and that communicates information to the genes of other cells

MUTATION: a change in the nucleotide coding sequence of the DNA of a gene that alters the structure and function of the protein encoded by that gene, thereby affecting the living cell

OXIDANT: an oxidizer; a molecule that contains extra electrons and that is highly reactive with other molecules, often damaging those molecules upon contact

SUPEROXIDE DISMUTASE: an antioxidant enzyme that scavenges the free radical superoxide, a highly reactive derivative of oxygen, within the cells of many organisms, including animals, plants, and bacteria

## Overview

The aging process occurs in all living organisms, although it is most pronounced in vertebrate animals, animals having a cartilaginous, bony endoskeleton, an efficient heart, and a highly developed nervous system. It is part of the basic sequence of animal development from conception to reproductive maturity to death. It follows the second law of thermodynamics, a physical principle of the entire universe which maintains that the disorder (entropy) of the universe is constantly increasing because of the dissipation of energy and the gradual transfer of energy from system to system. Living organisms age because of the inefficiency of the chemical reactions within their cells, thereby creating disorder as is evidenced by breakdowns in physiological rhythms (for example, nerve cell functioning, blood pressure changes, and reduced kidney filtration) and physical structure (for example, bone deformations, muscle weakness, and hair loss). The second law of thermodynamics maintains that no machine is 100 percent efficient; therefore, energy will be lost continuously with accompanying decay of the system, or body.

In humans and other mammalian species, the process of aging follows a very predictable pattern. An individual is conceived by the union of genetic information from the mother via egg and the father via sperm, thereby producing a single-celled zygote. By the connected processes of mitosis (chromosome duplication followed by separation) and cytokinesis (cell division), the zygote divides into two cells, which later divide to make four cells, then eight cells, and so on until an individual composed of approximately 100 trillion cells is produced. Very early in development (for example, a few hundred cells), different cells in various locations begin to specialize, or differentiate, by hormonally initiated changes in gene expression within these cells, thereby giving rise to specialized structures such as nerves, muscle, skin, bone, eyes, and fingers.

After the individual organism is fully developed and can survive in the environment on its own, it will either exit the mother's body or hatch from a protective egg case, or shell. Subsequent juvenile development will include brain neuronal changes (plasticity) as a result of learning and social interactions, and physiological changes, leading to sexual maturity, or adulthood. Development up to adulthood does technically constitute aging, although there is little evidence of physiological decay. Various hormones, particularly steroid hormones, are prominent during an individual's sexual stage when the individual is capable of sexual reproduction. The individual is at his or her physical peak during the reproductive period. At the end of the critical reproductive period (menopause in females), the degenerative physical effects of true aging become very evident and accelerate with time as the individual becomes older. In a biological sense, the purpose of an organism is to reproduce and continue the transfer of genetic information. By menopause, the female individual should have achieved this objective. Consequently, the individual organism begins progressive deterioration after menopause toward death, thereby making room in the environment for its descendants. This is a harsh, but real, view of an organism's life. The key to understanding why deteriorative aging occurs lies in the hormones, chemicals, and cellular changes that are present in the organism just before menopause.

Among the physiological effects of aging that are evident very early are heart and respiratory changes. Upon birth, the average human newborn has a pulse of 120 heartbeats per minute, a breathing rate of 40-45 breaths per minute, and a blood pressure of 60 systolic/30 diastolic. These data indicate a very high metabolic rate in individuals during early development. As humans age, both pulse and breathing rates decrease, whereas blood pressure increases. The average healthy adult has a pulse of approximately 60-80 heartbeats per minute, a breathing rate of approximately 8-12 breaths per minute, and a blood pressure somewhere around 120 systolic/70 diastolic. Neuronal plasticity of the brain and, therefore, learning peak during the early reproductive years and decline after menopause, around the age of forty-five to fifty. Most physiological processes undergo a steady decline after menopause.

When an organism dies, the electrical activity of billions of brain neurons ceases along with cessation of heart and respiratory muscle contractions. In more than 80 percent of human deaths by "natural causes," however, the exact cause of death cannot be determined. While the physiological causes of aging and death remain poorly understood, three major theories have been proposed to explain the mechanisms of aging (senescence) in living organisms: the free-radical theory, the genetic/cellular programmed theory, and the error catastrophe theory. While the theories emphasize different aspects of cellular aging, they are complementary. All three may be correct in their combined interpretations.

The free-radical theory of aging maintains that the degenerative events which occur within the cell and the entire organism during aging are caused by the toxic effects of oxidizing free-radical molecules. Free radicals are molecules that have a free extra electron per molecule that can be donated to another molecule. As a result, free radicals are highly reactive with most substances that they encounter. Their chemical reaction with a recipient molecule may affect the structure and function of that molecule so that it does not function properly. In a living cell, such an event could have disastrous consequences. The deoxyribonucleic acid (DNA) nucleotide sequence of any gene could be mutated, or altered, by a free radical, thereby altering the structure or function of the protein encoded by that gene and affecting all cellular functions controlled by that specific protein. If the protein is essential for the cell's survival, the result could be cellular death or cellular transformation to the cancerous state. Free radicals such as superoxide, hydroxyl radical, and hydrogen peroxide are naturally produced as by-products of the cell's metabolic activities. The cells of most living organisms produce antioxidant enzymes such as catalase, glutathione peroxidase, and superoxide dismutase to scavenge and inactivate free radicals wherever they occur. No such capture operation is 100 percent efficient, however. Some free radicals react with cellular molecules; the accumulated effects of these reactions over time may be responsible for cellular aging.

The genetic/cellular programmed theory of aging maintains that the cells of all living organisms contain genes that encode signaling protein hormones. These hormones, when produced, elicit aging-related changes within the cells at specific times during the organism's development, including death. Another viewpoint within this theory is that the cells of various tissues within living organisms are programmed to die after undergoing a specified number of genetically encoded divisions.

The error catastrophe theory of aging, very similar to the free-radical theory in scope, maintains that the accumulation of mutations within cells of living organisms over time is responsible for cellular aging. These mutations are caused by ionizing radiation (for example, ultraviolet light and X rays) and mutagenic chemicals to which the human body is constantly being exposed. Some of the cells in a human's body do become cancerous every few minutes, although they usually are destroyed by an active immune system (which declines with age).

## Applications

Active research into the mechanisms of the aging process is currently being conducted in laboratories throughout the world. The problem is being tackled from many different perspectives, including biochemical, genetic, physiological, gerontological, psychological, and sociological approaches. The topic is of particular interest in countries such as the United States where the overall population is becoming progressively older. Whereas much of the research is devoted to medical care for the elderly, many scientists are exploring the biochemistry of aging with hopes of understanding the process and possibly slowing or reversing it.

The three principal theories of aging (senescence), when combined, provide a very good working model for attacking the aging problem. The free-radical theory of aging provides the cause, the error catastrophe theory provides the effects, and the genetic programmed theory provides an overall developmental view of the phenomenon. There can be no question that there are certain genes within all living cells that in a step-by-step manner control the sequential development of the entire organism. At the same time, free-radical molecules are constantly being produced within body cells and these same cells are being exposed to mutagenic (mutation-causing) radiation and chemicals. These substances will cause accumulated cellular damage over time, even with the body's combined defenses of antioxidant enzymes, immune system cells, and kidney filtration of impurities from blood. These defenses work extremely well up to the end of the individual's reproductive period; then, they decline rapidly, almost as if they were programmed to do so.

Biochemical and genetic analyses of the aging process involve the study of the chemical reactivity of oxidizing free radicals, the measurement of the enzymatic action of antioxidant enzymes, the identification of substances that can enhance antioxidant enzyme activity, the location of antioxidant protein-encoding genes on chromosomes, the study of the effects of antioxidant gene mutations on the organism, the study of the effects of accumulated mutations on living cells, and the identification of genes and hormones that control major events within the cell. The properties and chemical reactivities of natural free radicals such as superoxide, hydroxyl radical, and hydrogen peroxide have been extensively studied. The mechanisms of action of antioxidant enzymes such as superoxide dismutase (which scavenges superoxide), catalase (which scavenges hydrogen peroxide), and glutathione peroxidase are fairly well understood. The chromosomal locations of the genes that encode these enzymes have been determined in several different animal, plant, and bacterial species. Mutations in antioxidant protein-encoding genes such as superoxide dismutase have been generated, and the effects of these mutations on their host organisms have been studied; such organisms usually are very sickly and have a reduced life span. Vitamin C, vitamin E, and the element selenium are three substances that may assist antioxidant enzyme activity and that may help to prolong an individual's life span, although the only proven means of extending life span is to decrease the bulk size of an individual's diet by half. The hormonal and genetic mechanisms of cellular control represent an intense area of research that has yielded many important results but still has many more mysteries to resolve.

Among humans, several unusual pathologies exist that are of interest to scientists who research aging. Among these is the disease progeria, a condition in which the aging process is greatly accelerated. Individuals suffering from this apparently genetic disorder exhibit all of the symptoms of old age by the end of their first ten years. They die of old age usually before reaching their early teenage years. The mutated genes that contribute to this disorder have not been identified. Isolation of these genes would be of tremendous medical significance not only in terms of treating progeria but also in terms of extending the human life span. If a set of critical genes can be mutated to accelerate aging, as in progeria, then it would seem reasonable that the same genes could be modified to slow the aging process.

The aging process is also emphasized in acquired immune deficiency syndrome (AIDS) and the genetic disorder autoimmune deficiency syndrome. In both situations, an individual's entire immune system is rendered useless, thereby leaving the individual's body defenseless against the continuous onslaught of usually harmless bacteria, viruses, and mutations. In AIDS patients, the immune system is inoperative because of the destruction of essential T-lymphocytes by the human immunodeficiency virus (HIV). In autoimmune deficient patients, mutated genes have resulted in an inoperative immune system. In either case, aging is accelerated because of the removal of critical obstacles that routinely stop the action of free radicals and other error-generating substances. With a conservative estimate of ten million HIV-infected people worldwide, research in this area is intense and must continue to be so.

Another immune-related disease is cancer, a situation in which certain body cells become transformed and begin multiplying out of control, often resulting in death for the host individual. There are several dozen types of cancer, based upon the affected tissues, although the cause of these cancers can be traced to free radicals, chemical mutagens called carcinogens, ionizing radiation (for example, X rays and gamma radiation), and certain types of viruses (for example, hepatitis B). Certain cells in all individuals become cancerous every few minutes because of mutations caused by these substances. Normally, if an individual is healthy, the immune system destroys these cancerous cells before they have a chance to proliferate. If an individual is sick, stressed, or elderly, however, the immune system is not operating at optimal efficiency; consequently, the cancerous cells may proliferate and spread throughout the body so rapidly that identification and medical treatment are both too late. Cancer can affect people of any age; however, the incidence of cancer greatly increases with age, usually skyrocketing in individuals who have passed their reproductive years. Scientists are beginning to look at cancer not as a mysterious disease but as a symptom of the aging process. Aging is the problem; cancer is one manifestation of the aging process. As medical care extends the life span of individuals, the problem of cancer will continue to grow proportionally.

The process of aging can be understood and controlled to a certain extent. It is a phenomenon that all humans experience. Its basis, however, lies within fundamental physical principles and the evolution of gene regulation in living organisms. The discovery of the hormonally controlled mechanisms by which genes and cells are controlled will enable medical science to improve the quality of human life during advanced years and to extend the average human life span by many decades, perhaps even several hundred years, barring accidents and other catastrophes.

## Context

The process of aging occurs within all living organisms. Theories describing the mechanisms of aging are of relevance to psychology because the aging process is a developmental process that encompasses all bodily systems, including the brain and central nervous system. As conscious beings, humans are aware of their own aging. It is a fundamental focal point of consciousness, religious beliefs, and social structure. Humans are afraid of dying. As a result, aging is incorporated into human religions, behavior, and culture. Society stresses youthfulness, so humans go to great lengths and expense to reverse the effects of aging with skin creams, baldness cures or coverups, clothing, body-building, and the like.

Psychology is a phenomenon of intelligent living organisms, and living organisms are complex entities consisting of intricate chemical reactions. These biochemical reactions, which are responsible for all aspects of life, follow the fundamental physical and chemical properties of the universe. One of these physical processes is the second law of thermodynamics, which maintains that any system loses energy due to inefficiency and therefore becomes more disordered, or entropic. Therefore, aging is an entropic process for the entire universe. Living organisms do undergo a building process during early development that is antientropic; however, after a certain time, specifically the end of the reproductive period, entropy takes over and accelerates. All aspects of the living animal, including the brain, deteriorate.

The free-radical, genetic programmed, and error catastrophe theories of aging have provided scientists with greater insights into the mechanisms of the aging process. These three theories also give researchers ideas for attacking aging as a disease that can be treated. While the so-called fountain of youth represents wishful thinking, research on aging realistically can lead to the prolongation of human life and the definite improvement of the quality of human life. The latter benefit of aging research includes the elimination or treatment of maladies such as heart disease, Alzheimer's disease, cancer, and general aging-related declines in most bodily functions.

One factor that permeates human biology in terms of aging, disease, and abnormal psychological behavior is stress. Research has repeatedly linked stress with accelerated aging, increased susceptibility to many diseases (including cancer), decreased mental agility and memory, and insanity. The accelerating explosion of human population and technological growth during the twentieth century has been paralleled by a rapid increase in individual stress levels; stress-related diseases such as heart disease, stroke, and cancer; acts of violence, devastating wars, torture, exploitation, and destruction of human life; and the use of alcohol and illegal drugs to "relieve" stress. Reevaluation of the way that one treats fellow humans, a slowing of the fast-paced society, major social reforms, and medical advances in the treatment of stress all will be needed for decreasing stress, a major killer and contributor to the aging process.

All living organisms age because of constant exposure to radiation and mutagenic chemicals. Errors constantly are being introduced into the cells of the body. Some cells become cancerous, and the debilitating effects accumulate over time. The best that humans can do is to live their lives as healthfully and as meaningfully as possible. Advances in biochemical and genetic medical research probably will produce means for extending life within the next century. Whether or not human longevity is extended, aging will continue.

## Bibliography

Curtis, Helena. *Biology.* 3d ed. New York: Worth, 1979. An excellent introduction to biology for the beginning student. The text is clearly written with numerous illustrations and photographs. Provides an informative study of organismal development and aging that includes a discussion of Leonard Hayflick's experiments, demonstrating that human tissue cells have a definite life span based upon programmed cell divisions.

Goodenough, Ursula. *Genetics.* 2d ed. New York: Holt, Rinehart and Winston, 1978. A comprehensive presentation of genetics for individuals familiar with basic biology. Describes major concepts and mechanisms of genetics in great detail, including classic experiments, molecular genetics, and the role of genes in organismal development. Includes a discussion of the mechanisms by which mutations occur within genes, including aging effects such as those seen in Down syndrome, a condition whose incidence increases with maternal age.

Karp, Gerald. *Cell Biology.* New York: McGraw-Hill, 1979. An interesting discussion of the structure and biochemistry of the living cell. Describes how the parts of the cell function together, plus how cells function within the context of organismal physiology. Includes an excellent discussion of the causes of both cancer and senescence in living cells, including the role of free radicals and mutation, in chapter 19.

Lewin, Benjamin. *Genes.* 3d ed. New York: John Wiley & Sons. 1987. Describes in great detail the major concepts of molecular biology and genetics. Much of the book is devoted to cutting-edge research studies on the identification and isolation of critical developmental genes. Chapter 33 discusses the processes of mutation in genes and how the cellular machinery combats these errors.

Sang, James H. *Genetics and Development.* New York: Longman, 1984. Provides a summary of major research studies into DNA, genes, and the effects of gene regulation upon organismal development. Aimed at the advanced student. Includes a good discussion of major events in the tissue development of many species and discussions on specialized topics, such as lethal genes.

Shapiro, Bennett M. "The Control of Oxidant Stress at Fertilization." *Science* 252 (April 26, 1991): 533-536. A summary of cellular regulatory systems that prevent damage to eggs by oxidizing free radicals during fertilization by sperm. Uses sea urchin eggs as a species example, although work on other species by other researchers is cited. Clearly describes the intracellular effects of oxidizing free radicals such as hydrogen peroxide and the cellular antioxidant activities of specific enzymes.

Wilson, Edward O. *Sociobiology: The New Synthesis.* Cambridge, Mass.: The Belknap Press of Harvard University Press, 1975. A very strong presentation of the controversial theory of sociobiology, which maintains that animal behavior is a driving force in animal species evolution. Includes hundreds of supporting case studes. Discusses many different aspects of animal societies, including the role of aging in population structure and stability.

*David Wason Hollar, Jr.*

## Cross-References

Aging: Cognitive Changes, 180; Aging: Physical Changes, 192; Coping with Cancer, 711; Death and Dying: Theoretical Perspectives, 763; Dementia, Alzheimer's Disease, and Parkinson's Disease, 783; The Endocrine System, 966; Neuropsychology, 1667; Effects of Stress, 2417; Stress: Physiological Responses, 2425; Stress-Related Diseases, 2464.

# AGORAPHOBIA AND PANIC DISORDERS

*Type of psychology:* Psychopathology
*Fields of study:* Anxiety disorders; biology of stress; cognitive therapies

*Panic disorder with agoraphobia is a condition characterized by the presence of severe anxiety attacks coupled with avoidance of a wide range of situations. Considerable progress has been made toward understanding its cause and treatment.*

### Principal terms

DEPERSONALIZATION: a feeling of unreality regarding oneself or one's body
DEREALIZATION: a feeling of unreality regarding the external world
FEAR OF FEAR: a fear of one's anxiety, which has been hypothesized by some researchers as an important causal factor in panic disorder
FLOODING: prolonged and intense exposure to feared stimuli
HABITUATION: a process by which physiological or psychological responses decline in intensity with repeated stimulation
HYPERVENTILATION: overly rapid or deep breathing
MITRAL VALVE PROLAPSE SYNDROME: a condition in which the heart's mitral valve bulges into the atrium
PALPITATION: pronounced pounding of the heart
PARESTHESIA: numbness or tingling, particularly in the extremities
SOCIAL PHOBIA: a condition characterized by fear of the possible scrutiny or criticism of others

## Overview

Panic disorder is a condition characterized by frequent panic attacks—that is, intense surges of anxiety. These attacks of anxiety often occur unexpectedly or "out of the blue"; the individual frequently is unable to identify an external trigger for them. Between attacks, the panic-disorder patient often ruminates about the possibility of additional attacks.

Panic attacks tend to be accompanied by a number of physical symptoms. Hyperventilation—overly rapid or deep breathing—is common, as are choking and smothering sensations, dizziness, faintness, and paresthesias—sensations of numbness and tingling, particularly in the extremities. Other common symptoms during panic attacks are sweating, trembling, nausea, abdominal distress, hot or cold flashes, accelerated heart rate, chest pain, and palpitations (feeling one's heart pound). Not surprisingly, many individuals who are having a panic attack believe that they are experiencing a heart attack.

Panic attacks are also frequently characterized by a number of psychological symptoms. Depersonalization and derealization are among the most common of these symptoms. Depersonalization is marked by feelings of unreality regarding oneself or one's body—sensations of being "disconnected" from oneself or of "watching" oneself as would an outside observer are frequent. Derealization refers to feelings of unreality concerning the external world; objects or people may seem somehow "strange" or unfamiliar. Also common during panic attacks are fears of dying (for example, from a heart attack or stroke), losing one's mind, or performing embarrassing behaviors (such as screaming uncontrollably).

The difficulties of many patients with panic disorder do not end here, however; many, but not all, of these patients develop an often debilitating syndrome known as agoraphobia. Agoraphobia is a fear of situations in which escape is difficult, inconvenient, or potentially embarrassing, or in which assistance might not be readily available. Specifically, what appears to occur is that many panic patients, dreading the possibility of a future attack, begin to fear and (in many cases) avoid situations that might precipitate such an attack. The situations feared or avoided by agoraphobics are extremely varied, but they include public transportation, open spaces, shopping malls, supermarkets, large social gatherings, elevators, driving in heavy traffic, passing over bridges or through tunnels, standing in long lines, and sitting in crowded theaters or churches.

In mild cases, agoraphobics may experience moderate discomfort while traveling or shopping alone, and may avoid those situations in only certain cases. In severe cases, agoraphobics may be unwilling to leave their house unaccompanied. The fears of agoraphobics are generally alleviated by the presence of another individual, particularly one close to the patient. This is probably because this person would presumably be available to provide help in the event of an emergency, such as a heart attack.

The prevalence of panic disorder with agoraphobia in the general population of the United States has been estimated to be approximately 5 percent; an additional 2 percent have been estimated to have panic disorder without agoraphobia. Thus, panic disorder is relatively common and is perhaps the most frequent reason individuals seek outpatient psychiatric care. In addition, isolated panic attacks occur frequently among individuals in the general population. G. Ron Norton and his colleagues, for example, have found that approximately 34 percent of college students experience occasional panic attacks.

Panic disorder and agoraphobia have been reported to occur more frequently among females than males, although this difference is probably more marked for agoraphobia than for panic disorder. In addition, the prevalence of panic disorder appears to decline with age; its frequency has generally been reported to be highest among individuals under thirty and lowest among individuals over sixty-five. The course of panic disorder tends to be chronic but fluctuating. In other words, its symptoms often persist for many years, but they typically wax and wane depending upon the level of life stress and other factors.

In addition, panic disorder patients appear to have an elevated rate of several medical conditions. A subset of these patients, for example, has been reported to have mitral valve prolapse syndrome (MVPS), a condition in which the heart's mitral valve bulges into the atrium. Because MVPS results in physical symptoms such as palpitations and chest pain, it may be a risk factor for panic disorder in some individuals. In addition, a subset of panic patients appear to have disturbances of the vestibular system, an apparatus in the inner ear responsible for maintaining balance. As dizziness is a common symptom of panic attacks, vestibular dysfunction may be an important precipitant of some panic attacks.

A number of psychiatric conditions are commonly found among patients with panic disorder and agoraphobia. Depression is a particularly frequent complication of both syndromes; in many cases it probably results from the distress produced by panic attacks and the constriction of activities produced by agoraphobia. This depression may have tragic consequences; panic disorder patients have been reported to be at greatly increased risk for suicide compared with individuals in the general population. In addition, many panic disorder patients turn to alcohol or other substances to alleviate their anxiety. Also commonly associated with panic disorder is social phobia, a condition characterized by fears of the possible scrutiny or criticism of others. Like panic disorder patients, many social phobics experience panic attacks. Nevertheless, in social phobia these attacks are almost invariably triggered by situations in which the patient is the perceived focus of others' attention.

## Applications

A variety of models have been proposed for the causation of panic disorder and agoraphobia. Early explanations tended to focus largely or exclusively on physiological factors. In the 1960's, Donald Klein and his colleagues reported that panic disorder improved following administration of imipramine, a drug traditionally used to treat depression, whereas more sustained and long-lasting ("generalized") anxiety did not. Based upon this finding, Klein and his coworkers argued that panic is biologically distinct from other forms of anxiety. Although Klein's observation was important, it should be noted that making inferences about the nature of a disorder from the treatment of that disorder is logically flawed: A condition's treatment bears no necessary implications for its cause (for example, one would not be justified in concluding that headaches are caused by a lack of aspirin).

Nevertheless, it seems likely that physiological factors play an important role in panic disorder. Identical twins (who share all the same genes) with panic disorder are more likely than are fraternal twins (who share only half of their genes, on average) to have co-twins with panic disorder, suggesting that genetic factors play at least some role in this disorder. It is not known, however, whether these genetic factors predispose a person to panic disorder per se or to anxiety in general. In addition, there is evidence that the locus coeruleus, a structure in the pons (which is located at the back of the brain), is overactive during panic attacks. This is important because the locus coeruleus is a major center for norepinephrine, a chemical transmitter in the nervous system that appears to play a major role in the genesis of arousal and anxiety. Finally, it has been found that, in contrast to normals, many panic disorder patients develop panic attacks following infusion of certain substances, such as sodium lactate and caffeine. It is possible, however, that this is simply attributable to greater arousal on the part of panic disorder patients; the infusion of these substances may provoke attacks in these patients because they are already on the verge of panicking.

Many subsequent models of the causation of panic disorder have attempted to move beyond physiological abnormalities to examine how panic disorder patients react to and construe their environment. One of the most influential of these might be termed the "fear of fear" model. According to Dianne Chambless, Alan Goldstein, and other proponents of this model, individuals who are afraid of their own anxiety are particularly prone to the development of panic disorder. During frightening experiences, this "fear of fear" can spiral into a panic attack.

A more recent theory of panic disorder is the "cognitive model" of David Clark, Aaron Beck, and other researchers. According to this model, panic attacks result from the catastrophic misinterpretation of unusual or unexpected bodily sensations. In other words, panic attacks may occur when a physical symptom (such as rapid heartbeat or dizziness) is misinterpreted as presaging a disastrous outcome (heart attack or stroke). Interestingly, many of the physical symptoms of anxiety, such as a rapid heartbeat, can themselves be exacerbated by anxiety, as anyone who has felt his or her heart race uncontrollably while giving a speech can attest. Thus, the misinterpretation of certain physical sensations may set in motion a cycle in which these sensations progressively increase in intensity, giving rise to further misinterpretations and ultimately culminating in a panic attack. The cognitive model is also consistent with the evidence, mentioned earlier, that some panic patients have physiological abnormalities, such as MVPS and vestibular dysfunction. These abnormalities might be chronically misinterpreted by some individuals as indicative of serious consequences, and thereby provide a repeated trigger for panic attacks.

There is good evidence that many cases of panic disorder and agoraphobia are treatable by means of either medication or psychotherapy. Imipramine, as well as several other anti-depressant drugs, appears to ameliorate the symptoms of these syndromes. It is not clear, however, whether these drugs actually exert their impact upon panic or whether they instead work by alleviating the depressive symptoms so common to these patients. Alleviating depressive symptoms may then provide agoraphobics with the energy and confidence needed to confront previously avoided situations.

Panic disorder and agoraphobia also are amenable to interventions involving confrontation with feared situations. For example, many panic patients improve following flooding, a technique involving prolonged and intense exposure to feared stimuli. In the case of panic disorder, the patient is typically exposed, in graduated fashion, to increasingly anxiety-producing situations. The patient is typically encouraged to remain in the situation until his or her anxiety subsides.

The efficacy of flooding and related treatments for panic disorder and agoraphobia can be explained in at least two ways. One possibility is that flooding works by a process known as "habituation." Habituation is a process in which physiological or psychological responses decline in intensity with repeated stimulation. For example, many parachute jumpers find that their anxiety reactions gradually decrease with each succeeding jump; habituation may be the basis of this phenomenon. A second possibility is that flooding works by means of the cognitive model. That is, prolonged exposure to feared stimuli may demonstrate to patients that these stimuli are not as dangerous as they had believed.

## Context

The term "panic" derives from the Greek god Pan, who let out a terrifying scream whenever he was awakened by passersby. Most of the earliest accounts of panic attacks emphasized their physiological nature. In 1871, Jacob DaCosta described a syndrome he termed "irritable heart," which was characterized by palpitations, shortness of breath, dizziness, and other symptoms now recognized as typical of panic disorder. DaCosta observed this condition both in Civil War soldiers and in individuals not involved in military combat. Irritable heart syndrome became a frequent diagnosis among anxiety-stricken soldiers in the Franco-Prussian and Boer wars. Other early terms for this syndrome were "effort syndrome" and "neurocirculatory asthenia"; again, both of these terms emphasized overexertion of the heart and circulatory system as the principal causes of panic symptoms.

At approximately the same time, Sigmund Freud was describing a syndrome he called "anxiety neurosis." Freud noted that this neurosis could occur in a diffuse, long-lasting form (what would today be called generalized anxiety) or in sudden, discrete attacks marked by symptoms such as excessive heartbeat and respiration (what would today be called panic disorder). In contrast to DaCosta and other writers of this period, Freud emphasized unconscious psychological factors as the primary determinants of panic disorder. According to Freud, anxiety attacks resulted from a massive damming up ("repression") of sexual impulses. In his later writings, Freud revised his position to assert that anxiety served as a signal to the individual that sexual impulses needed to be repressed. According to this later view, anxiety (including panic) is a cause, rather than a result, of the repression of sexual urges. Although many psychologists did not concur with Freud's conjectures, by World War II there was increasing appreciation that many of the panic reactions seen among soldiers were largely of psychogenic origin.

The term "agoraphobia" stems from the Greek *agora*, meaning marketplace. As noted earlier, however, although agoraphobics fear marketplaces and similar situations, their fears tend to be extremely varied. "Agoraphobia" was coined by Alexander Westphal in 1871, who observed that many patients experienced anxiety while walking across open spaces or deserted streets. Interestingly, Moritz Benedikt had observed a similar syndrome in 1870; he labeled it *Platzschwindel* (dizziness in public places), a term that presaged findings of vestibular dysfunction in some of these patients.

For many years, panic disorder and agoraphobia were believed to be two quite different, although often overlapping, conditions. In the third edition of the American-can Psychiatric Association's *Diagnostic and Statistical Manual of Mental Disorders* (DSM-III, 1980), for example, panic disorder and agoraphobia were listed as separate disorders. Nevertheless, research has increasingly indicated that agoraphobia is, in most cases, a consequence of panic attacks. Therefore, in the 1987 revision of DSM-III, a new diagnosis called "panic disorder with agoraphobia" was christened, thereby explicitly acknowledging a causal association between what were previously viewed as distinct conditions.

## Bibliography

Barlow, David H. *Anxiety and Its Disorders: The Nature and Treatment of Anxiety and Panic.* New York: Guilford Press, 1988. In this comprehensive and well-written volume, Barlow surveys the major theoretical issues relevant to anxiety (such as the relation of anxiety to other emotions, the biological origins of anxiety, and the classification of anxiety disorders) and discusses the literature on each anxiety disorder. This is one of the finest and most complete sources on anxiety disorders.

Chambless, Dianne L., and Alan J. Goldstein, eds. *Agoraphobia: Multiple Perspectives on Theory and Treatment.* New York: John Wiley & Sons, 1982. Contains several chapters on more specialized topics than are found in other texts on agoraphobia, such as agoraphobia and the marital relationship, and the association between agoraphobia and obsessions. Chambless' chapter, which summarizes the typical characteristics of agoraphobics, and Goldstein's chapter, which includes several detailed case histories, are especially useful.

Goodwin, Donald W., and Samuel B. Guze. "Panic Disorder (Anxiety Neurosis)." In *Psychiatric Diagnosis.* New York: Oxford University Press, 1989. A brief but excellent introduction to the most important psychiatric research on panic disorder. The reader will find a clear discussion of topics such as diagnosis, family studies, and differentiating panic disorder from other conditions. The reference section is a good resource for readers wishing to pursue research on panic disorder in greater depth.

Mathews, Andrew M., Michael G. Gelder, and Derek W. Johnston. *Agoraphobia: Nature and Treatment.* New York: Guilford Press, 1981. The authors review the literature on the symptomatology, assessment, and pharmacological treatment of agoraphobia, and discuss the behavioral treatment of this syndrome in depth. The appendices, which include a detailed self-help manual for agoraphobics and a brief package of assessment materials, will be of particular interest to many readers.

Walker, John R., G. Ron Norton, and Colin A. Ross, eds. *Panic Disorder and Agoraphobia: A Comprehensive Guide for the Practitioner.* Pacific Grove, Calif.: Brooks/Cole, 1991. This edited volume provides a thorough overview of the literature on the diagnosis, causation, and treatment of panic disorder and agoraphobia. The coverage of material on assessment and on psychotherapeutic and pharmacological interventions is especially complete. Although intended for the clinician, this volume is also a good reference for the layperson.

*Scott O. Lilienfeld*

## Cross-References

# ALCOHOLISM

*Type of psychology:* Psychopathology
*Field of study:* Substance abuse

*Alcoholism, the compulsive chronic or periodic drinking of alcoholic beverages, is a widespread substance-abuse problem that can lead to irreversible brain damage, other tissue damage, and death. It also causes crime and many fatal traffic accidents. The causes of alcoholism are not clearly understood; it can be arrested but not cured.*

*Principal terms*

CEREBRAL CORTEX: the outer layer of the cerebral hemispheres of the brain; it is largely responsible for higher nervous functions

CIRRHOSIS: a chronic liver disease symptomized by destruction of liver cells and their replacement by nonfunctional tissue; it ultimately causes blocked blood circulation, liver failure, and death

DELIRIUM TREMENS: a severe alcohol withdrawal syndrome that includes anxiety attacks, confusion, depression, delirium, and terrifying hallucinations; as it worsens, tremors can develop

KORSAKOFF SYNDROME: alcohol-induced brain damage that causes disorientation, impaired long-term memory, and production of false memories to fill memory gaps

MANIC-DEPRESSIVE DISORDER: a psychiatric condition involving rapidly alternating manic elation and melancholic depression

NEURITIS: an inflammation of a nerve that causes pain, loss of reflexes, and muscular atrophy

PSYCHOSIS: any severe mental disorder characterized by deterioration of normal intellectual and social function and partial or complete withdrawal from reality

SUBSTANCE ABUSE: excessive use of any controlled substance—such as alcohol—that leads to physical dependence and psychological abnormalities

## Overview

Pure ethyl alcohol is a colorless, mild-smelling liquid that boils at 79 degrees centigrade and evaporates quickly at room temperature. It is made either by fermentation of grain mashed and suspended in water or fruit juice, followed by the distillation (boiling) of the beer or wine that is produced, or by chemical synthesis from the petrochemical ethylene. Ethyl alcohol—usually simply called alcohol—has many uses, including the sterilization of surgical instruments and inclusion in the fuel gasohol; it is the liquid in which many medicines are dissolved, serves as the main component of perfumes and colognes, and is used in the manufacture of many useful chemicals. The best-known use of alcohol, however, is in alcoholic beverages, viewed by many as recreational beverages because of the mood-altering properties of the alcohol they contain.

It is believed that alcoholic beverages have been made since prehistoric times. The oldest records of widespread brewing of beer and production of wine have been found in what were ancient Babylon and Egypt, respectively. According to historians, the main reasons for the preparation of alcoholic beverages by early civilizations were that their antimicrobial properties kept grape juice and other food sources from which they were prepared from spoiling, and the fact that drinking sparing amounts of fermented beverages were a preventive of many illnesses that people contracted from contaminated drinking water or from other unfermented beverages.

The abuse of alcoholic beverages has certainly occurred since their discovery; however, it became widespread during the Middle Ages, when the art of distillation became more universal, producing hard liquors (containing five to ten times the alcohol of beer and wine) that made it much easier to attain alcoholic euphoria and stupor. It has been estimated that nearly 70 percent of Americans use alcoholic beverages and that more than ten million of these people are involved in severe abuse of alcohol. These last people are called alcoholics; their compulsive alcohol abuse makes it difficult for them to retain a job, obtain an education, or perform responsible societal roles. Ultimately, alcoholics damage their brains and other body tissues irreversibly, often dying of the affliction or by suicide.

Unlike with nonalcoholics, once an alcoholic takes a drink, self-control is lost and a drinking spree begins that ends only in stupor, when intoxication is complete. Continued alcoholism over a long time period affects many body organs. Among them is the brain, where related mental disorders include delirium tremens (the DTs), acute alcoholic hallucinations, and Korsakoff syndrome. Both the DTs—characterized by hallucinations and other psychotic symptoms—and Korsakoff syndrome may be accompanied by physical debility that can require hospitalization.

Alcoholic neuritis will develop when alcohol is the sole food eaten. In addition, alcoholism damages the liver (causing cirrhosis that can be lethal), the kidneys, the heart, and the pancreas. In fact, a large percentage of diseases of these organs stems from alcohol abuse. Furthermore, evidence suggests that severe alcoholism, combined with excessive cigarette smoking, greatly enhances the incidence of cancer of the mouth and throat.

There is no clear physical explanation for the development of alcoholism. Rather, it is most often proposed that alcoholism develops as the result of social problems and psychological stress. Much support is given to the high likelihood of alcoholism arising in the socioeconomic groups where consumption of alcoholic beverages is equated with manliness or sophistication. Other major bases proposed for the development of alcoholism include domineering parents, adolescent peer pressure, personal feelings of inadequacy, loneliness, job pressures, and marital discord.

There is no known cure for alcoholism. A thorough review of the literature led Diane M. Riley and coworkers to the conclusion that "treatments for alcohol problems with demonstrated enduring effectiveness do not exist, regardless of treatment orientations or treatment goals." It is a disease that can be handled only by total abstinence from alcoholic beverages, medications that contain alcohol, and any other potential sources of alcohol in the diet. A single contact with alcohol from any source frequently leads to a relapse. Its recognition as a medical problem has led to many alcohol-rehabilitation treatment centers, where psychiatric treatment, medication, and physical therapy—in various combinations—provide valuable treatments. Furthermore, many experts believe that Alcoholics Anonymous (AA) programs are effective deterrents to a return to alcohol abuse.

## Applications

As pointed out by Andrew M. Mecca, before 1935 the main opinion on alcoholism was that it was criminal behavior that merited punishment. Around 1935, the identification of the problem as a disease began. Crucial to the successful treatment of alcoholism was the advent of Alcoholics Anonymous, founded in that year. This organization operates on the premise that abstinence is the best course of treatment for alcoholism—an incurable disease that can be arrested by cessation of all alcohol intake. The goal of the organization is sobriety: the permanent stoppage of a person's drinking.

The methodology of Alcoholics Anonymous is psychosocial. It brings alcoholics to the realization that they cannot use alcoholic beverages without succumbing to alcoholism. It identifies the need for help from a higher power, and it develops a support group of people with the same condition. As stated by Mecca, "Alcoholics Anonymous never pronounces the disease cured. . . . [I]t is arrested." Estimates of the membership of the organization are between 1.5 and 3 million, meaning that up to a third of American alcoholics are affected by its tenets. These people achieve results ranging from periods of sobriety (usually lasting longer and longer as membership in the organization continues) to lifelong sobriety. A deficit of sole utilization of Alcoholics Anonymous for treatment—according to many experts—is a lack of medical, psychiatric, and trained sociological counseling.

As to medical treatment aiming at abstinence via therapeutic drugs, two well-known drugs for enforcing sobriety are disulfiram (Antabuse) and citrated calcium carbonate (Abstem). These drugs may be given to alcoholics who wish to avoid using any alcoholic beverages and who require a deterrent to help them stop drinking. Neither drug should ever be given in secret by well-meaning family or friends because of the serious danger they cause in the presence of alcoholic beverages.

These dangers are attributable to the biochemistry of alcohol utilization via the enzymes (biological protein catalysts) alcohol dehydrogenase and aldehyde dehydrogenase. Normally, alcohol dehydrogenase converts alcohol to the toxic chemical acetaldehyde, then aldehyde dehydrogenase quickly converts acetaldehyde to acetic acid, the main biological fuel of the body. Abstem or Antabuse turns off aldehyde dehydrogenase. This causes acetaldehyde buildup in the body, when alcohol is consumed, and quickly leads to violent headache, flushing, nausea, dizziness, heart palpitation, and vertigo. Consumption of alcohol in several drinks (or even in cough medicines) in the presence of either drug can be fatal. An interesting sidelight is the view of some researchers, such as Cleamond D. Eskelson, that abstinence from alcohol may be genetically related to the presence of too much alcohol dehydrogenase and/or too little aldehyde dehydrogenase in the body, producing enough acetaldehyde to cause aversion to alcohol consumption.

Other therapeutic drugs that have been utilized to treat alcoholics include lithium (more often given to manic-depressive psychiatric patients), and tranquilizers. Their usual function is to soften the severe discomfort of alcohol withdrawal on the alcoholic patient. Lithium treatment, which must be done with great care because it can become toxic, appears to be effective only in a subset of alcoholics who drink because of depression or manic-depressive psychosis.

The use of tranquilizers (and related sedative hypnotics) must also be done with great care, under the close supervision of a physician. There are two main reasons for this: many of these drugs can be addicting, and their abuse can simply substitute another drug dependence for alcoholism; and alcohol and some of these drugs have additive effects that can be fatal if an alcoholic backslides during therapy.

The great value of the psychiatrist in alcoholism therapy has been identified by various sources. David H. Knott, in his book *Alcohol Problems: Diagnosis and Treatment* (1986), points out that while a psychotherapist cannot perform miracles, psychotherapy can be very valuable in helping the alcoholic patient by identifying factors leading to "destructive use of alcohol"; exploring and helping to rectify problems associated with alcohol abstinence; providing emotional support that helps many patients to rebuild their lives; and interfacing in referring patients to Alcoholics Anonymous and other long-term support efforts. The psychotherapist also has irreplaceable experience with psychoactive therapeutic drugs, behavioral modification techniques, and identifying whether a given individual requires institutionalization.

Knott also points out the importance of behavioral modification as a cornerstone of alcohol psychotherapy and makes it clear that a wide variety of choices are available to alcoholics desiring psychosocial help. An interesting point made by A. E. Bennet, in *Alcoholism and the Brain* (1977), is that autopsy and a variety of sophisticated medical techniques, including computerized axial tomography (CAT) scans, identify atrophy of the cerebral cortex of the brain in many alcoholics. This damage is viewed as a factor in the inability of alcoholics to stop drinking, as well as in loss of motor skills and eventual development of serious conditions such as Korsakoff syndrome.

## Context

The excessive use of alcoholic beverages, with resultant alcoholism, has occurred for many centuries. In recent years, however, the problem of alcoholism has assumed epidemic proportions; it affects more than ten million Americans. Two societal observations that are particularly disturbing are the estimates that 10 to 25 percent of American high school students get drunk once a week and the observation that alcoholism appears to be self-perpetuating: More than 50 percent of alcoholics are the offspring of alcoholic parents.

Modern efforts to deal with alcoholism are often considered to have begun in the early twentieth century, with the activities of the American temperance movement that culminated with "Prohibition" upon the passage of the 1919 Volstead Act by the U.S. Congress. The idea behind the Volstead Act was that making liquor "impossible to get" would force sobriety on the nation. Prohibition turned out to be self-defeating, however, and several sources point out that it actually increased the incidence of alcoholism in the potential problem drinker. It was repealed in 1933.

The next, and much more useful, effort to combat alcoholism was the psychosocial approach of Alcoholics Anonymous, started in 1935 and still operating well. Yet that organization does not reach the majority of alcoholics, so other efforts needed to evolve as treatment methodologies. Among these have been the wide use of psychiatric counseling, alcohol rehabilitation centers, family counseling, and alcohol management programs in the workplace.

These options—alone or in various combinations—have had considerable success in reaching alcoholics, and combined alcoholism therapy seems to work best; however, it has not yet been possible to stem the tide of increasing alcoholism or to cure the disease. Instead, these techniques—like those of Alcoholics Anonymous—can only arrest it. Part of the reason for this is the fact that the basis for alcoholism is not clearly understood by those attempting to eradicate it.

One hope for curing alcoholism is ongoing basic research into the biochemistry, pharmacology, and physiology of alcoholism. A number of aspects of such efforts are discussed in Ronald Ross Watson's *Diagnosis of Alcohol Abuse* (1989). While the information and answers so far obtained are not yet clear-cut or applicable, it is hoped that the continuation of such efforts will help to provide better insight and solutions to the problem.

## Bibliography

Becker, Charles E. "Pharmacotherapy in the Treatment of Alcoholism." In *The Diagnosis and Treatment of Alcoholism*, edited by Jack H. Mendelson and Nancy K. Mello. New York: McGraw-Hill, 1979. This article, with sixty-five references, in a very useful book aimed at effective treatment of alcoholism, describes the uses and pitfalls of the therapeutic drugs utilized. Topics include management of intoxication and alcohol withdrawal syndrome, postwithdrawal assistance, chronic assistance, and alcoholism and depression.

Bennett, Abram Elting. *Alcoholism and the Brain*. New York: Stratton Intercontinental Medical Book, 1977. Deals with relationships between brain function and alcoholism as a brain disease. Coverage includes the concept of alcoholism as a disease, alcohol actions in the brain, testing for alcoholic brain disease, constructive relationships between psychiatry and other aspects of alcoholism treatment, and rehabilitation methodology.

Cox, W. Miles, ed. *The Treatment and Prevention of Alcohol Problems: A Resource Manual.* Orlando, Fla.: Academic Press, 1987. This edited work contains much information on many of the psychiatric, psychological, and behavioral aspects of alcohol. It is also widely useful in many other related alcoholism issues, including Alcoholics Anonymous, marital therapy, family therapy, and alcoholism prevention.

Eskelson, Cleamond D. "Hereditary Predisposition for Alcoholism." In *Diagnosis of Alcohol Abuse,* edited by Ronald Ross Watson. Boca Raton, Fla.: CRC Press, 1989. This article, in a book full of state-of-the-art information, gives considerable useful data on the hereditary aspects of alcoholism, concentrating on alcohol metabolism, animal and human studies, genetic aspects, and genetic markers for the disease. Sixty-five related references are included.

Knott, David H. *Alcohol Problems: Diagnosis and Treatment.* New York: Pergamon Press, 1986. Provides physicians with useful information on diagnosis and treatment of alcoholism. Topics include alcohol use and alcoholism; biochemical factors in alcohol use and abuse; epidemiology, diagnosis, and treatment of the disease; information on special populations affected by alcoholism; and perspectives on its control and prevention.

Mecca, Andrew M. *Alcoholism in America: A Modern Perspective.* Belvedere, Calif.: California Health Research Foundation, 1980. This interesting book is useful, entertaining reading, with a wide factual base. It covers the history of alcoholic beverages, the nature of alcoholism, effects of alcoholism on the body, its treatment, community alcoholism prevention, and future perspectives. Included are numerous sources of additional information and a useful glossary.

Riley, Diane M., et al. "Behavioral Treatment of Alcohol Problems: A Review and a Comparison of Behavioral and Nonbehavioral Studies." In *The Treatment and Prevention of Alcohol Problems: A Resource Manual,* edited by W. Miles Cox. Orlando, Fla.: Academic Press, 1987. Evaluates behavioral treatment of alcoholism and the efficiency of various treatment methods. Included are sections on behavioral treatment, relaxation training, skills training, marital-family training, contingency management, self-management, comparison with nonbehavioral treatment, future prospects, and conclusions. More than two hundred references are provided.

Rix, Keith J. B., and Elizabeth M. Lumsden Rix. *Alcohol Problems: A Guide for Nurses and Other Health Professionals.* Bristol, England: Wright, 1983. The purpose of this book (with more than two hundred references) is to "provide nurses with information that will contribute to . . . improved education." Contains information on causes of alcoholism, its epidemiology, characteristics of alcohol intoxication and withdrawal, medical treatments, psychosocial aspects, and intervention models and methods.

Watson, Ronald Ross, ed. *Diagnosis of Alcohol Abuse.* Boca Raton, Fla.: CRC Press, 1989. This edited work contains fifteen chapters on various aspects of current alcoholism research. They include basic science issues in biochemistry, genetics enzymology, and nutrition. Other topics covered include diagnosis of alcoholic liver disease, identification of problem drinkers, alcohol testing, and alcoholism screening efforts.

*Sanford S. Singer*

## Cross-References

Addictive Personality and Behaviors, 102; The Cerebral Cortex, 500; The Codependent Personality, 534; Coping: Social Support, 700; Hunger: Psychological Bases, 1223; Motivation: Opponent Process Theory, 1611; Self-Esteem, 2188; Substance Abuse: An Overview, 2489.

# ALTERED STATES OF CONSCIOUSNESS

*Type of psychology:* Consciousness
*Field of study:* Cognitive processes

*The investigation of altered states of consciousness began in psychology with the recognition that consciousness is not a fixed, unvarying state, but is in a continual state of flux. Consciousness can be altered by many chemical and nonchemical means, and there is some evidence to indicate that certain altered states are necessary for normal psychological functioning.*

  *Principal terms*
      BIOFEEDBACK: a process that allows one to monitor an automatic
          function in the body, such as blood pressure, skin temperature, or
          heart rate, for the purpose of eventually becoming able to regulate
          that function consciously
      CIRCADIAN RHYTHM: a bodily cycle that repeats about once every twenty-
          four hours
      ELECTROENCEPHALOGRAM (EEG): the graphic recording of the electrical
          activity of the brain (brain waves)
      HYPNAGOGIC AND HYPNOPOMPIC STATES: the transition states,
          characterized by vivid dreamlike imagery, that occur as one goes
          into and comes out of sleep
      HYPNOSIS: an altered state of consciousness brought on by special
          induction techniques (usually progressive relaxation instructions) and
          characterized by varying degrees of responsiveness to suggestions
      LUCID DREAMING: a dream state in which one is aware of the dreaming
          while it is happening
      MEDITATION: a set of techniques designed to create an altered state of
          consciousness characterized by inner peace and tranquillity and,
          eventually, by a state of union with one's "higher self"
      PSYCHOACTIVE DRUGS: chemical substances that act on the brain to create
          psychological effects; usually classified as depressants, stimulants,
          narcotics (opiates), hallucinogens, or antipsychotics
      RESTRICTED ENVIRONMENTAL STIMULATION (RES): also called sensory
          deprivation, RES refers to the alteration of consciousness by
          significantly reducing sensory stimulation, usually by means of an
          isolation chamber

## Overview

The great psychologist William James, in his 1890 textbook *The Principles of Psychology*, made the following now-famous observation regarding states of consciousness:

Our normal waking consciousness, rational consciousness as we call it, is but one special type of consciousness, whilst all about it, parted from it by the filmiest of screens, there lie potential forms of consciousness entirely different.

James went on to say that the understanding of human psychological functioning would never be complete until these alternate states were addressed. Most psychologists would now acknowledge that a person's normal waking consciousness is readily subject to changes. These changes are referred to as altered states of consciousness. What constitutes a genuine altered state and how many such states may exist are both subjects of some controversy.

Physiological psychologist Karl Pribram lists the following states of consciousness: states of ordinary perceptual awareness; states of self-consciousness; dream states; hypnagogic and hypnopompic states; ecstatic states (such as the orgiastic experience); socially induced trance or trancelike states; drug-induced states; social-role states; linguistic states (for example, a multilingual person thinking in one, rather than another, language); translational states (as when one linguistic universe is being recorded or translated in another); ordinary transcendental states (such as those experienced by an author in the throes of creative composition); extraordinary transcendental states that are achieved by special techniques; other extraordinary states (such as those that allow "extrasensory awareness"); meditational states; dissociated states, as in the case of pathological multiple personality; and psychomotor states manifest in temporal-lobe epilepsies. To that list could be added the following additional states: sleep; the hyperalert state, characterized by increased vigilance while one is awake; the lethargic state, characterized by dulled, sluggish mental activity; states of hysteria, with intense feeling and overpowering emotion; regressive states, such as senility; daydreaming with rapidly occurring thoughts that bear little relation to the external environment; coma; sleep deprivation; sensory overload or deprivation; and prolonged strenuous exercise. This list is by no means exhaustive.

Some of the above-mentioned states clearly represent greater degrees of alteration from "normal" consciousness than others. There is, however, no universal agreement on what constitutes the normal state of consciousness. Charles Tart and other authors have suggested that what is usually called "normal" consciousness is not a natural, given state, but a construction based mainly on cultural values and inputs. In any case, some altered states of consciousness are experienced on a daily basis by everyone, while others are much more rare and may require great effort or special circumstances to achieve.

Some alterations in conscious functions are induced by daily changes in biological rhythms. Bodily events that occur in roughly a twenty-four-hour cycle are referred to as circadian rhythms, from the Latin *circa* ("about") and *dies* ("day"). It is thought that these cycles are created by natural events, such as the light-dark cycle, and by other cues in the daily routine, such as mealtimes. The sleeping-waking cycle is the major circadian rhythm, but there are others, such as fluctuations in body temperature. This daily body-temperature cycle appears to be directly related to levels of mental activity. When all external cues are removed, circadian rhythms extend to about twenty-five hours. As a result of prolonged isolation, the cycle can become completely distorted, with periods of up to forty hours of waking followed by periods of up to twenty-two hours of sleep. When the change is gradual in this way, the individual has a distorted sense of time and believes that he or she is experiencing normal periods of sleep and waking. Abrupt changes in circadian rhythms, as when one crosses several time zones, are what lead to that sleepy, uncomfortable feeling known as jet lag.

In addition to biological rhythms, there are other regular daily variations in consciousness. On the way to sleep each night, people enter a kind of "twilight" period known as the hypnagogic state. The state of consciousness that is entered immediately before waking is called the hypnopompic state. In both these states, one is partially asleep and partially continuing to process environmental stimuli. Both are characterized by vivid imagery, and many people have reported creative insight during these periods.

Sleep itself is not a unified state, but consists of five distinct stages: one stage of rapid eye movement (REM) sleep and four stages of nonrapid eye movement (NREM) sleep. During a typical night's sleep, one moves in and out of these stages four or five times. REM sleep is primarily associated with periods of dreaming. Sleeping subjects awakened during a period of REM sleep report having just experienced a dream about 80 percent of the time, compared with less than 10 percent when NREM sleep is interrupted. Psychologists are still unclear on exactly why humans need to sleep, but the need for periods of REM sleep might be part of the reason. When sleeping subjects are deprived of REM sleep (and their NREM sleep is undisturbed), they often show many of the symptoms of not having slept at all. Also, when later given the opportunity for uninterrupted sleep, they spend a greater percentage of time in the REM stage, as if they were trying to make up for the lost REM sleep (this is referred to as the REM-rebound effect). The REM-rebound effect is lessened if the individual is encouraged to engage in an increased amount of daydreaming, which indicates a possible connection between day and night dreams.

The use of psychoactive drugs is a common method for altering consciousness. Several drugs, such as nicotine, caffeine, and alcohol, are so much a part of the lifestyle in modern society that users may not even think of them as drugs. The use of many psychoactive drugs can lead to physical and/or psychological dependence, or addiction, as the body/mind develops a physiological/psychological need for the drug. The body can also build up a tolerance for a drug, which means that higher and higher doses are necessary to produce the same effects. Once addiction has been established, discontinuing the use of the drug can lead to withdrawal symptoms, such as nausea, fever, convulsions, and hallucinations, among others, which can sometimes be fatal.

The type of altered state produced by a psychoactive drug depends on the class to which the drug belongs. Depressants, such as alcohol, barbiturates, and tranquilizers, depress central nervous system functioning and usually produce relaxation, anxiety reduction, and—eventually—sleep. Narcotics (opiates), such as heroin, morphine, and codeine, depress activity in some areas of the cortex but create excitation in others, producing feelings of euphoria and providing relief from pain. Stimulants, such as amphetamines, cocaine, caffeine, and nicotine, stimulate central nervous system activity, producing feelings of alertness and euphoria and lack of appetite. Hallucinogens, such as lysergic acid diethylamide (LSD), mescaline, and psilocybin, can produce hallucinations, delusions, exhilaration, and, in some cases, quasi-mystical experiences.

Two popular nonchemical techniques for altering consciousness are hypnosis and meditation. Hypnosis was first discovered in the eighteenth century by Franz Mesmer, and its history has been full of controversy ever since. An altered state is induced in hypnosis by the suggestive instructions of the hypnotist, usually involving progressive relaxation. The hypnotized subject often appears to be asleep but remains alert inside, exhibiting varying degrees of responsiveness to the suggestions of the hypnotist. Only about 10 percent of the population can enter the deepest hypnotic state, while another 10 percent cannot be hypnotized at all. The rest of the population can achieve some degree of hypnotic induction. Psychologists argue about whether hypnosis is a genuine altered state or simply a form of role playing.

There is less controversy regarding meditation as a true altered state. Since the mid-1960's, there has been extensive research on the physiological changes that occur during meditation. Some of the findings include a decrease in oxygen consumption of 16 percent during meditation (compared with an 8 percent drop during the deepest stage of sleep), a cardiac output decrease of 25 percent, and an average slowing of the heart rate by five beats per minute. During meditation, electroencephalogram (EEG) patterns are dominated by the alpha rhythm, which has been associated with relaxation. Researchers R. K. Wallace and Herbert Benson believed that there was sufficient physiological evidence to justify calling the meditative state a "fourth major state of consciousness" (along with waking, dreaming, and sleeping), which they termed a "wakeful, hypometabolic [reduced metabolic activity] state." Beginning meditators usually report feelings of relaxation and "ordinary thoughts," while advanced practitioners sometimes report transcendental experiences of "consciousness without content."

## Applications

Research on altered states of consciousness has led to many benefits. The analgesic properties of hypnosis were verified in research conducted by Ernest Hilgard at Stanford University. He found that hypnotic suggestion could be used to reduce or eliminate experimentally induced pain. Even though subjects were not consciously aware of the pain, Hilgard found that, with the right questions, he could uncover a "hidden observer," a dissociated aspect of the subject's conscious awareness that did monitor the feelings of pain. Hilgard reports that hypnotic relief from pain has been reported for the chronic pain of arthritis, nerve damage, migraine headaches, and cancer. For individuals who are unable to be anesthetized because of allergic reactions or fear of needles, hypnosis is often used as an effective substitute for the control of pain. It has been effectively applied in cases involving dental work, childbirth, burns, abdominal surgery, and spinal taps. Hypnotic suggestion has also been effective in reducing the nausea associated with cancer chemotherapy.

The use of hypnosis to recover forgotten memories is much more controversial. One dramatic phenomenon displayed with certain hypnotic subjects is age regression, in which the individual not only is able to recall vividly childhood memories but also seems to reenact behaviors from childhood, including body postures, voice, and handwriting characteristics of a given age. There is no way of knowing, however, whether this represents true recall or is simply a type of fantasy and role playing. Hypnosis has also been used to enhance the memories of crime witnesses in court proceedings. There is evidence, however, that actual recall does not become more accurate and that the witness may be unintentionally influenced by the suggestions of the hypnotist, which could lead to inaccuracies and distortions in the "remembered" events. For this reason, courts in many states automatically disqualify testimony obtained by means of hypnosis.

Research on the physiological effects of meditation led to the application of meditative techniques as a treatment to combat stress-related illnesses. Meditators have often experienced significant decreases in such problems as general anxiety, high blood pressure, alcoholism, drug addiction, insomnia, and other stress-related problems. Researchers have also found that the scores of meditators on various psychological tests have indicated general mental health, self-esteem, and social openness. Many psychologists argue, however, that these effects are not unique to meditation and can be produced by means of other relaxation techniques. Meditation researcher Robert Ornstein has suggested that the long-term practice of meditation may induce a relative shift in hemispheric dominance in the brain from the left hemisphere, which is associated with such linear processes as language and logical reasoning, to the right hemisphere, which is associated with nonlinear processes such as music perception and spatial reasoning. Consistent with this idea are findings that meditators are better on certain right-hemispheric tasks such as remembering musical tones but worse on verbal problem-solving tasks that involve the left hemisphere.

Early research on advanced meditators in India indicated that they could exhibit control over what are normally autonomic processes in the body—for example, speeding up or slowing down the heart rate at will, stopping the heart for up to seventeen seconds, controlling blood flow to different areas of the body, and controlling brainwave patterns at will. At first, these results were met with skepticism, but it is now known that humans and animals can learn to control previously involuntary processes by using a technique known as biofeedback. Through biofeedback training, an individual who is connected to a special measuring device can monitor autonomic events such as blood pressure, skin temperature, and muscle tension. Having this information can allow the individual gradually to gain control over these autonomic processes. Biofeedback techniques have been applied to an enormous variety of clinical problems. EEG biofeedback, for example, has been used to train epileptics to emit brainwave patterns that are incompatible with those that occur during brain seizures. Other disorders that have been successfully treated by means of biofeedback include cardiac disorders, high blood pressure, tension headaches, anxiety, and neuromuscular disorders such as cerebral palsy.

Other applications have grown out of research on altered states of consciousness produced by restricting sensory stimulation from the environment. Researchers in the 1950's completed extensive studies on the effects of prolonged sensory deprivation. Subjects placed in soundproof isolation chambers with translucent goggles to eliminate vision and padded arm tubes to minimize touch sensation often experienced negative psychological effects after about a day. Most subjects suffered from extreme boredom, slowed reaction time, and impaired problem-solving ability. Some subjects reacted to sensory deprivation by creating their own internally generated sights and sounds in the form of hallucinations. These results led to the institution of special procedures to help reduce the effects of sensory deprivation in certain occupations; for example, airline pilots on long night flights, astronauts living for prolonged periods in tiny space capsules, and individuals working in isolated weather stations. A controlled form of sensory deprivation known as restricted environmental stimulation therapy (REST) has been used to reduce the effects of overarousal and hyperactivity. REST sessions usually involve floating in heavily salted warm water in a dark, soundproof tank. Most subjects find this floating sensation very pleasant, and there have been many reports of long-term reductions in high blood pressure and other stress-related problems.

## Context

States of consciousness have always been central to the attempt to understand human nature. For example, every society of which any record exists has possessed both chemical and nonchemical means of altering consciousness.

From a historical point of view, Sigmund Freud may have done more than any other theorist to stimulate interest in states of consciousness. Freud's psychoanalytic theory of personality held that there were three primary levels of consciousness: consciousness, preconsciousness, and unconsciousness. The conscious level includes mental activities of which one is unaware. The preconscious level consists of mental material of which one is currently unaware but that can be voluntarily recalled—roughly equivalent to memory. The unconscious level, which held the greatest interest for Freud, contains thoughts, feelings, memories, and drives that are blocked from awareness because they are unpleasant or arouse anxiety. In addition to his interest in these three levels of consciousness, Freud's interest in altered states at various points in his career was manifested in investigations of cocaine, hypnosis, and the analysis and interpretation of dreams.

In the early twentieth century, with the growth of behaviorism, which insisted that in order to be a science psychology should confine itself to investigating only objective, observable behavior, the study of altered states of consciousness fell out of favor. Events in the larger culture during the 1960's and 1970's, however, helped stimulate interest in altered states within psychology. During this period, efforts to expand consciousness by means of drugs, meditation, Eastern religious practice, and new ways of relating to oneself and others led to the active study of altered states of consciousness. The attempts of psychologists to study altered states of experience will perhaps be viewed in the future as a landmark in the development of psychology as a science. The willingness of psychology to explore the novel realms that altered states represent may help to expand the understanding of both consciousness and reality.

Although traditional scientific methods are poorly suited to the study of consciousness, many beneficial tools that can be used to measure the physiological correlation of altered states, such as the electroencephalograph, have been developed as an outgrowth of the study of states of consciousness.

Psychologist Charles Tart has suggested the creation of state-specific sciences. In reaching this conclusion, he argues that any particular state of consciousness (including ordinary waking) is a semiarbitrary construction—a specialized tool that is useful for some things but not for others and that contains large numbers of structures shaped by a particular culture's value judgments. Thus, science is observation and conceptualization carried out within the highly selective framework provided by a culturally determined ordinary state of consciousness. Tart suggests that, since altered states of consciousness often represent radically different ways of organizing observations and reworking conceptualizations of the universe (including oneself), if the scientific method were applied to developing sciences within various states of consciousness, there would be sciences based on radically different perceptions, logics, and communications, and thus science as a whole would gain new perspectives that would complement the existing one.

Regardless of whether this suggestion is taken seriously, it is clear that the study of states of consciousness has achieved legitimacy in scientific psychology. The investigation so far has revealed that human consciousness is much more diverse and varied than many psychologists had previously believed.

## Bibliography

Borbely, Alexander. *Secrets of Sleep.* New York: Basic Books, 1986. An excellent book for the student or general reader that thoroughly covers such topics as sleep, sleep deprivation, why sleep is necessary, and sleep as a biological rhythm.

Hilgard, Ernest Ropiequet. *Divided Consciousness: Multiple Controls in Human Thought and Action.* New York: Wiley-Interscience, 1977. A discussion of consciousness by one of the most respected experimental psychologists. Included are discussions on the hidden observer phenomenon in hypnosis and on other dissociation phenomena such as multiple personality, amnesia, and fugue states.

Ornstein, Robert Evan, ed. *The Nature of Human Consciousness.* San Francisco: W. H. Freeman, 1973. This anthology contains essays by many of the pioneers in the psychological study of altered states of consciousness, including Carl Jung,

Roberto Assagioli, Arthur Deikman, and many others. Topics include meditative states, psychosynthesis, Sufism, and synchronicity.

——————————. *The Psychology of Consciousness.* 2d rev. ed. New York: Penguin Books, 1986. This is considered a classic text on altered states of consciousness. It provides in-depth discussions of the psychology of meditation and the relationship of altered states to hemispheric differences in the brain.

Tart, Charles T. *States of Consciousness.* El Cerrito, Calif.: Psychological Processes, 1983. Tart presents his proposals for "state specific" sciences and develops what he calls the systems approach to the study of states of consciousness. Parts of this book are somewhat technical, but most of it is accessible to the general reader.

Wolman, Benjamin B., and Montague Ullman, ed. *Handbook of States of Consciousness.* New York: Van Nostrand Reinhold, 1986. This is an excellent sourcebook on psychological theory and research on altered states of consciousness. Discusses, in addition to the topics covered in this article, trance states, lucid dreams, ultradian rhythms, and many other things.

*Oliver W. Hill, Jr.*

## Cross-References

Circadian Rhythms, 514; Levels of Consciousness, 663; Dreams, 836; Hypnosis, 1241; Meditation and Relaxation, 1499; Sleep: Stages and Functions, 2277; Substance Abuse: An Overview, 2489.

# ALTRUISM, COOPERATION, AND EMPATHY

*Type of psychology:* Social psychology
*Fields of study:* Interpersonal relations; prosocial behavior

*Altruism and cooperation are types of prosocial behavior. Empathy involves identification with another, and it leads to increased prosocial behavior.*

### Principal terms

ALTRUISM: an unselfish regard for another's welfare
COOPERATION: mutually beneficial behavior in which individuals work together to achieve a common goal
EGOISM: a selfish concern for one's own welfare
EMPATHY: an identification with another; produced by similarity or attachment to another
PROSOCIAL BEHAVIOR: behavior intended to benefit another; can be motivated by either egoistic or altruistic concern

## Overview

Social psychologists, like other social scientists and social philosophers, have long been intrigued by what is called the altruism paradox. The altruism paradox arises from the fact that individuals sometimes engage in self-sacrificial acts that benefit another. This contradicts the assumption of most theories of motivation that individuals only engage in behavior that is beneficial to themselves. There are two basic ways to resolve the altruism paradox. One way is to try to identify the perhaps subtle self-benefits from helping that motivate seemingly altruistic prosocial behavior. The second way is to assert that individuals do engage in behavior that benefits others, irrespective of any benefit to the self. Theories and research on prosocial behavior make use of both ways of resolving the altruism paradox.

Theories of egoistic motivation for helping assume that some form of self-benefit motivates individuals to act prosocially. The self-benefits from helping are most easily recognizable in the case of cooperation. Cooperation is a type of prosocial behavior in which the self-benefit is the same as the benefit to the person helped: Individuals mutually benefit by achieving a common goal. An individual's self-interest is often best served by cooperating with others because, without cooperation, the individual may be unable to achieve a desirable goal. Selfishness, then, may prompt cooperation; if it does so, the motivation to act prosocially is egoistic, not altruistic. The benefit to the other is a by-product of acting prosocially in order to benefit the self.

Theories of egoistic motivation for helping point out that cooperation is not the only type of prosocial behavior that can be mutually beneficial for both the persons giving and receiving help. The self-benefit for the person giving help also can be different from the benefit for the person receiving help. This principle forms the basis of the arousal-reduction explanation for helping developed by Jane Piliavin and her colleagues. Their theory proposes that individuals experience aversive physiological arousal when they encounter another person in need. One way to reduce this aversive arousal is to help the person in need, because alleviating the other's need terminates the stimulus causing the bystander's own distress. Thus, the theory proposes that bystanders will help as a way to reduce their own aversive arousal. The persons giving and receiving help benefit in different ways, but it is important to recognize that the egoistic desire to reduce aversive arousal motivates the bystander's helping, not unselfish regard for the other's welfare.

Other theories of egoistic motivation for helping propose that prosocial behavior can be based on factors different from the arousal caused by witnessing another's suffering. For example, the "negative state relief" explanation for helping developed by Robert Cialdini and his colleagues in the 1970's proposes that temporary depression or sorrow can motivate helping as way to dispel the negative mood state. This negative state, it is reasoned, produces helping because people learn through socialization that feelings of personal satisfaction accompany the performance of good deeds. Helping, therefore, occurs as a way to lift the spirits of the temporarily depressed individual. An important implication of this theory is that even affective states that are not caused by witnessing another's suffering can produce helping. A personal failure, thinking about a sad event, or watching a sad motion picture all can produce helping as a way to relieve the negative mood state. Benefiting a person in need occurs as a way to benefit the self by dispelling a negative mood.

Additional theories of egoistic motivation for helping propose that many forms of selfishness can lead to helping. For example, motives to maintain a positive mood state, avoid guilt for failing to help, and gain social approval have been suggested to promote prosocial behavior. In general, theories of egoistic motivation for helping resolve the altruism paradox by proposing some form of self-benefit that motivates seemingly self-sacrificial behavior. In contrast, theories of altruistic motivation for helping propose that individuals do engage in behavior that benefits another, irrespective of any benefit to themselves. Such theories generally concur in assuming that empathy is an important source of altruistic motivation, if it exists.

Conceptions of empathy, however, vary greatly. Although all assume that empathy involves identification with another, different approaches emphasize the cognitive, affective, or behavioral components of empathy, or some combination of each. In the study of the possibility of genuine human altruism, empathy is typically conceived as an emotional response to another's suffering that is characterized by feelings of sympathy, compassion, tenderness, and the like. The suggestion that this emotional response leads to prosocial behavior motivated by unselfish concern for the other's welfare has come to be called the empathy-altruism hypothesis.

The research efforts of C. Daniel Batson and his colleagues beginning in the 1980's are largely responsible for the advancement of the empathy-altruism hypothesis from a theoretical possibility to a plausible explanation for some, but certainly not all, prosocial behavior. Through their efforts, empathy has been shown to be an emotional response to another's suffering that is distinct from aversive arousal or temporary depression and that leads to motivation to help that is different from egoistic motivation to reduce aversive arousal or to relieve negative mood. A major challenge is to determine whether empathy leads to motivation to help that is different from all possible egoistic motives for acting prosocially.

## Applications

The study of prosocial behavior has led to important insights into the determinants of the amount and the type of help that an individual provides to another when given the opportunity. Individuals often act apathetically or even antisocially toward one another because they lack sufficient incentives for acting prosocially. Competitive relationships involve situations in which one individual's gain is incurred at another individual's expense, so self-interest is best served by exploiting the other. Competitive relationships therefore often lead to antagonism and antisocial behavior. If it is possible to change the reward structure, however, this behavior can be changed. Instituting a superordinate goal, defined as a shared goal that can be achieved only through cooperation among individuals, reduces the antisocial behavior and increases the prosocial behavior of individuals in formerly competitive relationships. Prosocial behavior can be increased simply by making it more rewarding for individuals to act positively toward one another and less rewarding for them to act negatively toward one another.

Prosocial behavior can be increased by a variety of explicit material rewards (for example, money) or social rewards (for example, praise), but it also can occur in the absence of explicit rewards. For example, a bystander is often likely to intervene in an emergency when the emergency is unambiguous and there are no other potential helpers present. Research on the bystander effect, the phenomenon in which the presence of others decreases helping, has revealed several factors that contribute to the lack of responsiveness of large groups of bystanders. These factors include increased uncertainty about the need for help, potential embarrassment about offering help, and diffusion of the responsibility for helping. The absence of these factors, however, is insufficient for explaining the responsive behavior of a single witness to an emergency. If there are no material or social rewards for helping, and no punishments for not helping, why would an anonymous witness to an emergency stop to help?

One way to explain bystander intervention in the absence of explicit rewards for helping is to acknowledge that a victim's current state can affect the bystander's own state. Interestingly, the capacity to be affected by another's current state appears to be inborn. Even newborn babies respond emotionally to signs of distress in others. They often cry when they hear other babies cry. Adults also become more physiologically and emotionally aroused when exposed to another in need. The theory that arousal reduction serves as motivation for helping builds on the fact that people do respond emotionally to another's need. As the theory would predict, there is considerable evidence that people help rapidly and more vigorously the greater the arousal they experience in emergency situations.

There may be innate sources of motivation to help in emergencies, but much pro-social behavior occurs in nonemergency situations. The motivation to help in non-emergency situations is often assumed to result from socialization. In general, children become more helpful as they grow older. Developmental theories of prosocial motivations suggest that children's helpfulness is first encouraged by material rewards, later by social rewards, and finally by self-rewards produced by the internalization of social norms advocating helpfulness. The ability to reward oneself for helping leads the socialized individual to act prosocially even in the absence of explicit material or social rewards, because helping is accompanied by the positive feelings that become associated with doing good deeds during socialization. Helping thus acquires reinforcing properties and becomes particularly likely to occur when individuals are in need of reinforcement. It is well known that people self-indulge when they are saddened or depressed. People often treat themselves to a favorite dessert, a shopping trip, or a television show when they are sad, because self-indulgence relieves depression. Developmental theories of prosocial motivation would suggest that socialized individuals also use acting helpfully as a form of self-indulgence. Consistent with this suggestion, and with the prediction of the negative state relief explanation for helping, adults often act more prosocially when they are temporarily saddened than when they are in a neutral mood.

Given that there are both innate and socialized sources of motivation to help, it may seem curious that people do not always act prosocially. Egoistic theories of motivation to help, however, point out an important exception to the rule that people will help others in order to benefit themselves: Helping will occur only if it is a relatively uncostly, gratifying way to benefit the self. Thus, if helping is a more costly behavior than putting the victim's suffering out of sight and out of mind by leaving the scene, helping should not occur. Similarly, temporarily saddened individuals facing the prospects of large costs and small rewards for helping would not be expected to help because it would not be perceived as gratifying overall. Helping would be expected to occur only when the self-benefits of helping outweigh the costs. Egoistic theories of motivation for helping therefore provide a way to explain not only why people do help but also why they do not.

A problem for egoistic theories of motivation for helping is to explain the effects of feeling empathy (sympathy, compassion) on helping a person in need. Heightened empathy leads to increased prosocial behavior across a wide variety of both emergency and nonemergency situations. Furthermore, research testing the empathy-altruism hypothesis suggests that empathy does not lead to any of the more common types of egoistic motivation for helping. If the empathy-altruism hypothesis is valid, unselfish motives, as well as selfish ones, must be included in theories of why people act prosocially.

## Context

Social psychology emerged as a distinct field of psychology after World War II, during the years in which behaviorism was the dominant theoretical perspective in psychology. Initially, social psychologists devoted little attention to the study of prosocial behavior, perhaps because it was assumed that the general determinants of individual behavior would also apply to interpersonal behavior, as behaviorist theory would dictate. During the 1950's, some research on prosocial behavior was initiated. This research tended to focus on cooperation, however, to the exclusion of other forms of prosocial behavior. Behaviorist principles were often applied to determine, for example, if rewarding cooperation made it more likely to occur and competition less likely to occur.

In 1964, a troubling murder captured the attention of social psychologists and spurred interest in studying emergency intervention and other forms of prosocial behavior. In March of that year, a young woman named Kitty Genovese was attacked on the street near her home late at night. The attack continued for more than an hour, and her screams woke many of her neighbors, but none of them left their homes to help her. Interest in the behavior of the unresponsive bystanders during this attack prompted social psychologists to investigate factors that lead people not to intervene in emergencies. This research led to demonstration of the bystander effect and revealed a number of factors that contribute to the unresponsiveness of groups of bystanders who witness an emergency.

Research on bystander intervention also revealed that certain circumstances make it quite likely for a bystander to offer help. The decline of behaviorism by the early 1970's provided a climate in which researchers could explore the effects of internal motives as well as external reinforcers on helping. Several influential egoistic theories of motivation for helping were developed during the 1970's. By the end of the decade, these theories clearly displaced earlier behaviorist theories as prominent explanations for prosocial behavior.

Another trend to develop in the 1970's was the study of the effects of empathy on helping. By the 1980's, several theorists were proposing that empathy for a person in need leads to genuinely altruistic motivation for helping. Research during the 1980's quite consistently showed that empathy leads to helping even in situations in which egoistic motivation would not be expected to lead to help. Demonstrating that humans are capable of transcending selfishness and acting out of concern for another's welfare would have profound implications for psychological theories of motivation and views of human nature. It would be necessary to acknowledge that human behavior can be influenced by unselfish motives as well as by selfish ones.

## Bibliography

Batson, C. D. "Prosocial Motivation: Is It Ever Truly Altruistic?" In *Advances in Experimental Social Psychology*, edited by Leonard Berkowitz. Vol. 20. San Diego: Academic Press, 1987. A thorough and detailed chapter outlining the empathy-altruism hypothesis and its implications. Reviews the breakthrough research on the effects of empathy on helping, and discusses strategies for determining the nature of the motivation for helping.

Cialdini, Robert B., D. J. Baumann, and D. T. Kenrick. "Insights from Sadness: A Three-Step Model of the Development of Altruism as Hedonism." *Developmental Review* 1 (September, 1981): 207-223. A readable account of the development of the ability to self-reward for helping. Describes research showing how helping progresses from being externally determined to being internally motivated. Includes discussion of the negative state relief explanation for helping.

Eisenberg, Nancy, and Janet Strayer, eds. *Empathy and Its Development.* Cambridge, England: Cambridge University Press, 1987. Contributions by developmental, clinical, and social psychologists illustrate the multiplicity of approaches to the study of empathy. Many chapters review research on the effects of empathy on helping. Well referenced; an excellent source for those interested in pursuing research on empathy.

Hinde, Robert A., and Jo Groebel, eds. *Cooperation, Prosocial Behaviour, Trust, and Commitment.* Cambridge, England: Cambridge University Press, 1991. Authors from diverse disciplines contribute to this volume, bringing together knowledge about human prosocial activity at the individual, group, and international levels. Chapters are well integrated, relatively free from technical terms, and thought provoking.

Piliavin, Jane Allyn. *Emergency Intervention.* New York: Academic Press, 1981. A comprehensive treatment of research relevant to the arousal-reduction explanation for helping. Details the development of the arousal/cost model of helping into a comprehensive theory of human prosocial behavior. Discusses implications for structuring a more prosocial society.

*Jim Fultz*

## Cross-References

Affiliation and Friendship, 142; Attraction Theories, 332; Cooperation, Competition, and Negotiation, 689; Helping: Bystander Intervention, 1163; Helping: Theoretical Perspectives, 1169; Love, 1486.

# AMNESIA, FUGUE, AND MULTIPLE PERSONALITY

*Type of psychology:* Psychopathology
*Fields of study:* Anxiety disorders; models of abnormality; organic disorders

*Amnesia, fugue, and multiple personality form a group of mental disorders that are typically referred to as the dissociative disorders; they are called dissociative because some area of memory is split off, or dissociated, from conscious awareness.*

### Principal terms

AMNESIA: total or partial memory loss, which is often acute and follows an emotional or physical trauma

BIOGENIC DISORDER: an illness that is attributable primarily to some type of physiological trauma or sickness

DIAGNOSIS: the classification or labeling of a patient's problem within one of a set of recognized categories of abnormal behavior

DISSOCIATIVE DISORDERS: disorders that occur when some psychological function, such as memory, is split off from the rest of the conscious mind

FUGUE STATE: a flight from reality in which the individual leaves his or her present situation, travels to a new location, and establishes a new identity

MULTIPLE PERSONALITY: a rare mental disorder characterized by the development and existence of two or more relatively unique and independent personalities in the same individual

PSYCHOGENIC DISORDER: an illness that is attributable primarily to some psychological conflict or to emotional stress

## Overview

Amnesia, fugue, and multiple personality are considered by most mental health professionals to be the three major types of dissociative disorders—disorders in which some important area of memory is split off (dissociated) from the individual's conscious awareness.

Like all the dissociative disorders, amnesia has long fascinated both mental health professionals and the general public. Most professionals define amnesia as the sudden inability to recall important personal information, such as one's name, occupation, or family. Amnesia victims, or amnesiacs, suddenly wonder who they are and why they are in their present circumstances.

In some cases, amnesia is caused by biological factors. A variety of physical traumas, such as a blow to the head, gunshot wound to the brain, stroke, or history of chronic alcoholism, can cause an individual to suffer from impaired memory. When amnesia is caused by such physical problems, the amnesia is said to be biogenic. A person who suffers from biogenic amnesia will typically experience the loss of both personal and general knowledge. For example, a concert pianist with biogenic amnesia not only will lose personal information such as name and family history but also will lose such general information as knowledge of music and the ability to play the piano. If physicians are able to treat the physical causes of biologically based amnesia in a successful manner, the afflicted individual's memory often tends to return slowly—over a period of weeks, months, or even years.

When amnesia is caused by emotional factors, the individual's situation is somewhat different. In these cases, the person is said to have psychogenic amnesia. This person will typically suffer the loss of personal, but not general, information. For example, the concert pianist with psychogenic amnesia may forget such personal information as his or her name and address but will still be able to play difficult pieces of music and recall the complexities of music theory. Such a case of psychogenic amnesia will typically occur when a person is suffering from numerous emotional stressors, such as marital, financial, or career problems, or when the person receives a severe emotional shock, such as the unexpected death of a loved one. The amnesia may thus help the person escape such unpleasant circumstances. Many theorists believe that psychogenic amnesia victims forget in order to avoid the unbearable anxiety that is associated with their problems or traumatic experiences.

A few cases of psychogenic amnesia have continued for the rest of the victim's life. In most cases, however, the afflicted individual will regain his or her memory anywhere from a day to several years after the syndrome's onset; no one knows why many amnesiacs are suddenly able to regain their memory. Psychogenic amnesia will often come and go in a rapid manner.

Like amnesia, a fugue syndrome tends to begin and end abruptly. Fugue (also known as psychogenic fugue) occurs when the afflicted individual takes an unexpected trip or excursion, forgets his or her identity, and assumes a new identity. The term fugue is derived from the Latin word *fuga*, meaning flight. This is an appropriate name, since the fugue victim is usually in a state of flight, fleeing some intolerable situation. While amnesiacs may wander about in a confused manner, fugue patients tend to travel in a way that appears both purposeful and deliberate. Fugue patients also tend, unlike amnesiacs, to manufacture a new identity. This new identity allows these individuals greater freedom and an escape from their troubles.

The length of fugue states varies considerably. In most cases, the person travels for little more than a day or two and goes no farther than the next town. A small group of fugue patients, however, will travel hundreds of miles, create new identities, and pursue their new lives for months or even years. During the fugue state, the patient will appear normal to other people. When the person finally "wakes up," he or she will have no memory of what took place during the fugue state. Like amnesia, fugue states seem to occur when a person has numerous troubles or has experienced an unbearable psychological trauma. For this reason fugue states, which are normally quite rare, are more common in wartime or after natural disasters.

While fugue patients travel to a new place to be someone else, individuals with multiple personality disorder stay in one place as they experience the existence of two or more separate personalities. Each personality will have a unique set of habits, tastes, and learned behaviors. Only one personality will dominate the person's thoughts and consciousness at a given time, and the shifts from one personality to the next will be quite abrupt and dramatic. While cases of multiple personality are very rare, this disorder has received considerable attention from the popular media because of its bizarre and fascinating nature.

Most individuals with multiple personality disorder have one primary personality, as well as one or more secondary personalities. The primary personality is the individual who is known to most people. This personality is often quiet, meek, and obedient, while the secondary personalities tend to be more aggressive, irresponsible, and pleasure-seeking.

Though it is not entirely clear how an individual comes to have more than one personality, many professionals now believe that this disorder stems from a history of extreme emotional, physical, or sexual abuse during one's childhood. If a small child is severely beaten or molested, he or she may attempt to cope by pretending that the abuse is happening to someone else. The child may even give a name to this "other" person. As the child comes to rely repeatedly on this other person to cope with the abuse, the secondary personality eventually takes on a life of its own.

## Applications

Like all psychiatric diagnoses, the dissociative disorders are useful when they help mental health professionals understand the experience of a disturbed individual. If it is known that someone suffers from a particular syndrome, such as amnesia, the knowledge may facilitate the individual's treatment. Diagnostic categories also enable psychologists to place individuals in groups, so that their problems and potential treatment can be studied by research scientists. One way to understand how knowledge of dissociative disorders can help professionals make sense of an individual's problems is to review some of the well-known case studies in this field.

In 1967, Henry Laughlin published the story of a patient named Robert who joined the Army and served for a year during a fugue state. Laughlin reports that Robert was a fifteen-year-old boy who was attending high school in a small New Jersey town. At the onset of his fugue state, Robert was beset by numerous problems. He was unusually large for his age and was frequently teased by peers. He was also engaging in a number of quarrels with his parents and was making poor grades at school. Robert was apparently quite upset by these problems, and he had begun to believe that his current situation was hopeless. One afternoon Robert came home and, with a sense of utter despair, threw his school books on the front porch.

Robert then remembered nothing more until approximately one year later. At that time, Robert, who was successfully serving under another name in the Army, suddenly recalled his life as a high school student. The last thing he remembered was throwing his books on the front porch. Robert had no idea why he was on an Army base, and he could remember nothing of his military career. His family was eventually contacted, and he was discharged for being underage.

Robert's fugue state was typical in that he had been experiencing considerable stress before the onset of his illness. Like most fugue patients, he temporarily escaped his troubles by creating a new identity in a new locale. Robert was also like most fugue patients in that he regained his memory rapidly and was then unable to recall what had transpired during his travels and military career. Although Robert's fugue state did last for an unusually long time, his case is in many ways a classic example of psychogenic fugue.

A case that is perhaps even more sensational than Robert's is the story of Eve White, a multiple personality patient described by Corbett Thigpen and Hervey Cleckley. Thigpen and Cleckley indicate that Eve White was a young woman who sought medical assistance because of severe headaches and occasional blackouts. This woman was described as "demure, retiring, in some respects almost saintly." Eve White was a devoted mother who worked extremely hard to support and rear a young daughter. Friends and coworkers found Eve White to be quiet, sensitive, and at times a little too serious.

One day as Eve White was describing her problems to her therapist, she was seized by a sudden headache and put both hands to her head. Thigpen and Cleckley report that "after a tense moment of silence, her hands dropped. There was a quick, reckless smile and, in a bright voice that sparkled, she said, 'Hi there, Doc!'" The patient began to talk about Eve White in a casual and carefree manner; she referred to Eve White as "her" and "she." When asked her name, the patient stated "Oh, I'm Eve Black." As time went on, the therapist began to discover that Eve Black was "a party girl, shrewd, childishly vain, and egocentric." While Eve White was suffering from blackouts, Eve Black would attend parties, flirt with men in bars, and engage in wild spending sprees. Eve Black would then retreat and force Eve White to deal with the consequences of her reckless behavior. Eve White had no awareness of Eve Black. Eve Black was, however, typically conscious of Eve White and her troubles. Eve Black was also able to remember a number of painful childhood memories that Eve White was completely unable to recall. For example, as treatment progressed, it was Eve Black who was able to tell the therapist how Eve White was severely beaten by her parents as a child.

Eventually a third personality emerged from this young woman. This personality, named Jane, was aware of both Eve White and Eve Black. Jane was described as more mature, thoughtful, and balanced than either Eve White or Eve Black. The emergence of Jane may thus have represented an attempt on the part of this patient to integrate the disparate aspects of Eve White and Eve Black into one cohesive personality.

As the three personalities became better known, Thigpen and Cleckley eventually published a popular account of them in a book entitled *The Three Faces of Eve* (1957). Eve's case history serves as a clear example of how an individual can develop multiple personalities, each of which can take on a life of his or her own.

## Context

Mental health professionals have known about the existence of dissociative disorders for many years. Sigmund Freud and his followers began to study psychogenic amnesia around the beginning of the twentieth century, and the first widely publicized case of multiple personality was reported by Morton Prince in 1905. Since the time of this early work, both professionals and the general public have been fascinated with the dissociative disorders.

Despite the widespread interest in psychogenic amnesia, psychogenic fugue, and multiple personality, these disorders are actually quite rare. Many experienced psychiatrists and clinical psychologists have never encountered a patient with one of these dissociative disorders in their practice. Because of the extreme rarity of these conditions, the dissociative disorders are not a major mental health problem in the United States.

Many social scientists, however, continue to believe that these disorders merit further study. It is difficult to conduct large-scale research projects on the dissociative disorders, simply because it is so hard to obtain an adequate number of subjects. Carefully conducted case studies, however, will continue to further understanding of the disorders. These case histories may be able to teach some important lessons about human nature. Although most individuals do not experience the dramatic memory problems of amnesia or multiple personality patients, the dissociative experience should not be seen as completely foreign to the ordinary person. Expressions that suggest dissociative reactions are commonly used to describe ordinary individuals. One might say that someone is "running away from his problems," is "not quite herself today," or "has become a different person." All these expressions suggest that the person has somehow disavowed a part of his or her conscious experience or personality style. It is possible that the dissociative disorders of psychogenic amnesia, psychogenic fugue, and multiple personality may thus be nothing more than a very extreme and dramatic exaggeration of a common human experience.

## Bibliography

Bliss, Eugene L. "Multiple Personalities: A Report of Fourteen Cases with Implications for Schizophrenia and Hysteria." *Archives of General Psychiatry* 37 (December, 1980): 1388-1397. This journal article is written by a leading scholar in the field of multiple personality. In clear language, the author describes his controversial theory, which suggests that multiple personality disorders develop when children use self-hypnosis as a coping mechanism. Recommended for the reader who is interested in the causes and diagnosis of multiple personality.

Bootzin, Richard R., and Joan Ross Acocella. *Abnormal Psychology: Current Perspectives.* 5th ed. New York: Random House, 1988. This textbook contains an excellent chapter on the dissociative disorders that describes relevant case studies and explains how different psychological theorists view the dissociative diagnoses. The author's discussion of psychogenic amnesia and psychogenic fugue is particularly informative. Clear, easy to read, and understandable by the high school or college student.

Davison, Gerald C., and John M. Neale. *Abnormal Psychology.* New York: John

Wiley & Sons, 1990. Contains a very readable chapter on somatoform and dissociative disorders. The authors give a well-organized overview of the topic and enhance their discussion with a number of lively examples. Recommended for the high school student, college student, or casual reader.

Greaves, G. B. "Multiple Personality: 165 Years After Mary Reynolds." *Journal of Nervous and Mental Disease* 168 (1980): 577-596. This article provides the reader with a solid understanding of the ways in which a history of sexual or physical abuse during one's childhood can lead to the development of multiple personality disorder. Recommended for college students who wish to know more about the causes of multiple personality.

Keyes, Daniel. *The Minds of Billy Milligan.* New York: Random House, 1981. A journalistic account of a young man's illness with multiple personality disorder. Especially helpful to readers who are interested in the relationship between mental illness and the criminal justice system, since the story's protagonist was convicted of raping several women. An interesting discussion of the insanity defense is included.

Sackheim, H., and W. Vingiano. "Dissociative Disorders." In *Adult Psychopathology and Diagnosis,* edited by Samuel M. Turner and Michel Hersen. New York: John Wiley & Sons, 1984. Provides the reader with a scholarly overview of the dissociative disorders. Relevant diagnostic issues are discussed, in conjunction with a thorough review of the major research studies that have been conducted on amnesia, fugue, and multiple personality. Ideal for the student who seeks a detailed and challenging discussion of the dissociative disorders.

Schreiber, Flora Rheta. *Sybil.* New York: Warner Books, 1974. This popular account of a young woman's struggle with multiple personality disorder reads like a well-written novel. The author provides a fascinating description of both the development and treatment of multiple personality. This book will be especially helpful to individuals who are interested in the psychotherapy process.

*Steven C. Abell*

## Cross-References

Abnormality: Psychodynamic Models, 74; Abnormality Defined, 89; Anxiety Disorders: Theoretical Explanations, 272; Dementia, Alzheimer's Disease, and Parkinson's Disease, 783; Emotion and Stress, 941; Forgetting and Forgetfulness, 1049.

# ANALYTICAL PSYCHOLOGY: CARL G. JUNG

*Type of psychology:* Personality
*Field of study:* Psychodynamic and neoanalytic models

*Analytical psychology is one of the most complex theories of personality. It attempts to improve on Sigmund Freud's work by deemphasizing sexual instincts and the abnormal side of human nature. Three of its more significant contributions are the notions of psychological types, the concept of the collective unconscious, and the depiction of the unconscious self as the most critical structure within the psyche.*

*Principal terms*

ANIMA and ANIMUS: major archetypes that represent the feminine aspects of males (anima) and the masculine aspects of females (animus)

ARCHETYPES: structures contained within the collective unconscious that determine behaviors and ways of interpreting the environment

COLLECTIVE UNCONSCIOUS: memory traces that have been passed down to all humankind as a function of evolutionary development; includes inherited tendencies to behave in certain ways

CONSCIOUS EGO: the conscious mind; it represents one's identity from a conscious perspective and is therefore at the center of consciousness

ENTROPY: a concept maintaining that aspects of a person's psychic energy that are not in balance will tend to seek a state of equilibrium

EQUIVALENCE: a principle stating that an increase in energy or value in one aspect of the psyche is accompanied by a decrease in another area

PERSONA: a major archetype representing one's public personality; it is the mask that one wears in order to be acceptable to society at large

PERSONAL UNCONSCIOUS: items removed from the consciousness of the individual; this can occur through forgetting or unconscious repression, and the items may be remembered at a later time

SELF: the most important psychic structure in Jung's theory; it is the archetype which provides the whole psyche with a sense of unity and stability

SHADOW: the archetype indicative of the animal side of human nature; the shadow represents unsocial thoughts that are typically not overtly expressed by the person

## Overview

Analytical psychology is perhaps the most complex major theory of personality. It includes the presentation and analysis of concepts and principles based on numerous disciplines within the arts and sciences. Because this complexity is combined with

Carl Gustav Jung's often awkward writing, the task of mastering his theory is a challenge even for experts in the field of personality.

Jung's theory can best be understood by examining the key structures he proposes and the dynamics of personality. Jung divides the personality or psyche into three levels of consciousness. At the conscious level, there is the conscious ego. The conscious ego lies at the center of consciousness. In essence, it is the conscious mind— one's identity from a conscious perspective. It is particularly important to the person whose unconscious self is not yet fully developed. As the unconscious self begins to develop, the importance of the conscious ego will diminish.

Beneath the conscious ego (in terms of consciousness) is the personal unconscious. This involves material that has been removed from the consciousness of the person. This information may leave consciousness through forgetting or repression. Because the personal unconscious is close to the surface which is consciousness, items in it may be recalled at a later date. This is similar to Sigmund Freud's notion of the preconscious. Material within the personal unconscious is grouped into clusters called complexes. Each complex contains a person's thoughts, feelings, perceptions, and memories concerning particular concepts. For example, the mother complex contains all personal and ancestral experiences with the concept of mother. These experiences can be both good and bad.

The deepest level within the unconscious is called the collective unconscious. This contains the memory traces that have been passed down to all humankind as a function of evolutionary development. It includes tendencies to behave in specific ways, such as living in groups or using spoken language. While people have their own personal unconscious, they all share the same collective unconscious. The key structures within the collective unconscious that determine how people behave and respond to their environment are labeled archetypes. Each archetype enables people to express their unique status as human beings.

Archetypes are divided into major and minor archetypes. The major archetypes include the persona, animus, anima, shadow, and self. The persona is one's public personality, which one displays in order to be accepted by society. One's goal is to balance the needs of the persona with the desire to express one's true self. In contrast to the persona, the shadow represents the dark side of the psyche. It includes thoughts and feelings which the person typically does not express because they are not social. These cognitions can be held back on either a conscious or an unconscious level. The anima represents the feminine aspects of males, while the animus represents the masculine aspects of females. These archetypes have come about as a function of centuries of interactions between males and females. They have the potential to improve communication and understanding between males and females. Finally, the self is the most important archetype. It provides the psyche with a sense of unity, harmony, and stability. The major goal of each person's life is to optimize the development of the self.

In an effort to optimize the development of the self, each person develops his or her own psychological type. Each type (Jung conceived of eight types) consists of a combination of a person's basic attitude and basic function. Jung's two attitudes are extroversion and introversion. These terms follow societal stereotypes, with the extrovert being outgoing and confident and the introvert being hesitant and reflective. These attitudes are combined with four basic functions, or ways of relating to the world. These functions are thinking, feeling, sensing, and intuiting, which are consistent with a general societal view of these terms. Jung used the possible combination of the attitudes and functions to form the eight possible psychological types. Each person is thought to have dominance within one of the available types.

In addition to providing key psychic structures, Jung provides personality dynamics. He claimed that each person is endowed with psychic or libidinal energy. Unlike Freud, however, Jung did not view this energy as strictly sexual. Rather, he perceived it as life-process energy encompassing all aspects of the psyche. According to Jung, this energy operates according to two principles of energy flow: equivalence and entropy. The principle of equivalence states that an increase in energy within one aspect of the psyche must be accompanied by a decrease in another area. For example, if psychic energy is increasing in the unconscious self, it must decrease elsewhere, such as in the conscious ego. The principle of entropy states that when psychic energy is unbalanced, it will seek a state of equilibrium. For example, it would not be desirable to have the majority of one's psychic energy located in the conscious ego. The energy needs of the other levels of consciousness must also be met.

Jung's psychic structures, along with his views on the dynamics of personality, have provided psychologists with a wealth of information to consider, many complexities to address, and numerous possible ways to apply his ideas to human development and personality assessment.

## Applications

Carl Jung made significant contributions to knowledge of areas such as human development and personality assessment. In terms of human development, Jung emphasized that personality development occurs throughout the life of the person. This was critical in that Freud's theory, the dominant theory at that time, emphasized the first five years of life in examining personality development. The overall goal of the person in Jung's approach to development is the realization of the self, which is a long and difficult process. Unlike Freud, Jung was particularly interested in development during the adulthood years. He emphasized the changes that occur beginning at the age of thirty-five or forty. He believed that this was often a time of crisis in the life of the person. This notion of a midlife crisis (which Jung experienced himself) has continued to be the source of significant theoretical and empirical claims.

Jung believed that the concept of a crisis during middle age was necessary and beneficial. Often, a person has achieved a certain level of material success and needs to find new meaning in life. This meaning can be realized by shifting from the material and physical concerns of youth to a more spiritual and philosophical view of life. The person seeks gradually to abandon the emphasis on the conscious ego which is dominant in youth. A greater balance between the unconscious and conscious is pursued. If this is successfully achieved, the person can reach a state of positive psychological health that Jung labels individuation. Perhaps the key to the midlife years in Jung's theory is that these are the years in which the person is attempting to discover the true meaning of life. Finally, Jung stated that religion can play an important role in life during the midlife and old-age years. During the midlife years, a sense of spirituality rather than materialism is important in personality development; looking at the possibility of life after death can be positive for the older adult.

Jung made use of several interesting assessment techniques in addressing the problems of his patients. Like Freud, Jung was an advocate of the case-study method. He believed that much could be learned through an in-depth analysis of the problems of his patients. In his cases, Jung made extensive use of dream analysis. Jung maintained that dreams serve many purposes. They can be used to address and resolve current conflicts or to facilitate the development of the self. Dreams can therefore be oriented toward the future. While Freud focused his analysis on individual dreams, Jung would examine a group of dreams in order to uncover the problems of the patient. This examination of multiple dreams was viewed by Jung as a superior approach to gaining access to the deeper meanings of dreams, which could often be found in the collective unconscious.

Another important assessment device used by Jung which continues to have applications today is the word-association test. In this test, a person responds to a stimulus word with whatever comes to mind. Jung originally worked with a group of one hundred stimulus words and would focus on issues such as the response word given by the patient, the length of time it took the patient to respond, the provision of multiple responses, the repetition of the stimulus word, and the absence of a response. These and other factors could be used to establish the existence of an underlying neurosis as well as specific conflicts and complexes.

Applications of Jung's theory are too numerous to mention. In many ways, his key contribution was taking the study of psychology beyond the claims made by Freud. Jung's emphasis on adult development and personality types and his willingness to break with strict Freudian teachings were major contributions within the history of psychology in general and personality in particular.

## Context

The development of Carl Jung's analytical psychology can be traced to the development of his relationship with Sigmund Freud and the subsequent split that occurred between the two theorists. In 1906, Jung published a book which concerned the psychoanalytic treatment of schizophrenia. He sent a copy of this book to Freud, who was thoroughly impressed by Jung's work. Jung became one of the strongest Freudian advocates from 1907 to 1912. During this time he collaborated with Freud and was viewed by many within psychoanalytic circles as the heir apparent to Freud. Jung had in fact been elected president of the prestigious International Psychoanalytic Association. In 1913 and 1914, however, he abandoned Freud and his psychoanalytic theory. Three basic problems led to this split. The first was Freud's emphasis on sexuality. Jung believed that while sexual instincts did exist, they should not be emphasized at the expense of other relevant aspects of the psyche. Second, Jung believed that Freud overemphasized abnormality. He maintained that Freud appeared to have little to say about the normal aspects of human nature. Finally, unlike Freud, Jung wished to emphasize the biology of the species rather than the biology of the individual.

The split between Freud and Jung was important for practical as well as theoretical reasons. Jung was rejected for a period of time by other analytically oriented thinkers because of his split with Freud. In addition, the break with Freud led Jung to experience a mental crisis which lasted for several years. This combination of factors eventually led Jung to conclude that he must develop his own view of the psyche, along with appropriate treatment techniques.

While the challenges encountered by Jung in his life were difficult to overcome, they clearly played a major role in his ability to develop the most complex theory of personality ever formulated. His key concepts and psychic structures, including the collective unconscious, personal unconscious, archetypes, self, and personality typology, continue to be among the most interesting theoretical contributions in the history of personality psychology.

## Bibliography

Brome, Vincent. *Jung: Man and Myth.* New York: Atheneum, 1981. This is a sound biography of Jung and discussion of his work. Perhaps its main advantage is that it provides an analysis which is fair to both Jung and his critics.

Hannah, Barbara. *Jung: His Life and Work.* New York: Putnam, 1976. This positive biographical view of Jung is provided by a Jungian analyst who was a friend and colleague of Jung for three decades. While it may not be as objectively written as other accounts, it has the advantage of being written by a scholar who had firsthand knowledge of many of Jung's ideas.

Jung, Carl Gustav. *Memories, Dreams, Reflections.* New York: Pantheon Books, 1963. Jung's autobiography. It thoroughly portrays the evolution of Jung's thinking, including all those factors that were critical to his theoretical conceptions. Essential reading for anyone interested in gaining further insights into Jung and his work. It should be remembered, however, that Jung's writing is often difficult to follow.

_____. *Psychological Types.* Translated by Richard and Clara Winston. New York: Harcourt Brace, 1923. Provides both an overview of the basic principles of Jung's theory and an analysis of the derivation of the attitudes and functions that yield his psychological types. Particularly important to those who are interested in the derivation of Jung's view of typology.

McGuire, William, ed. *The Freud/Jung Letters.* Princeton, N.J.: Princeton University Press, 1974. Provides a unique analysis of the development of the relationship between Freud and Jung. Accurately portrays the promise of unity and collaboration within the relationship in its early years, beginning around 1907, and exposes the problems that eventually led to the Freud/Jung split, which was complete by 1914. Provides a context for examining the remainder of Jung's work and the personal problems that he was to encounter following his split with Freud.

*Lawrence A. Fehr*

## Cross-References

Abnormality: Psychodynamic Models, 74; Analytical Psychotherapy, 246; Archetypes: Origins and Nature, 286; The Collective Unconscious, 592; Dream Analysis, 830; Midlife Crises, 1575; Personality Theory: Major Issues, 1804; Projective Personality Traits, 1885; Psychoanalytic Psychology: An Overview, 1905.

# ANALYTICAL PSYCHOTHERAPY

*Type of psychology:* Psychotherapy
*Field of study:* Psychodynamic therapies

*Analytical psychotherapy is associated with the theory and techniques of Carl Gustav Jung. Similar to other psychodynamic therapies, it stresses the importance of discovering unconscious material. Unique to this approach is the emphasis on rec- onciling opposite personality traits that are hidden in the personal and collective unconsciouses.*

### Principal terms

COLLECTIVE UNCONSCIOUS: memories and emotions of which people are usually unaware but which are shared by all humanity

COMPENSATORY FUNCTION: displaying denied aspects of one's personality; a characteristic of dreams

CONFESSION: the first stage of Jungian psychotherapy, in which the patient relates conflicts in an emotional fashion

EDUCATION: the third stage of Jungian psychotherapy, in which the therapist communicates the danger of one-sided personality development

ELUCIDATION: the second stage of Jungian psychotherapy, in which the patient acts toward the therapist as toward some significant person from the patient's past

METHOD OF ACTIVE IMAGINATION: the process of discovering unconscious material from the patient's artistic productions

METHOD OF AMPLIFICATION: a Jungian technique for dream analysis in which the patient makes multiple associations to the contents of the dream

PERSONAL UNCONSCIOUS: a structure of personality that contains thoughts and emotions that are too anxiety-provoking for conscious awareness

TRANSFERENCE: acting toward the therapist in a similar way as to some significant person from the patient's past

TRANSFORMATION: the fourth stage of Jungian psychotherapy, in which the patient seeks self-discovery through reconciling opposite personality traits

## Overview

Analytical psychotherapy is an approach to psychological treatment pioneered by Carl Gustav Jung (1875-1961), a Swiss psychoanalyst. A follower of Sigmund Freud, Jung was trained in the psychoanalytic approach, with its emphasis on the dark, inaccessible material contained in the unconscious mind. Freud was fond of Jung and believed that he was to be the heir to the legacy he had begun. Jung began to disagree with certain aspects of Freud's theory, however, and he and Freud parted ways bitterly in 1914.

Jung's concept of the structure of personality, on which he based his ideas of psychotherapy, was obviously influenced by Freud and the psychoanalytic tradition, but he added his own personal and mystical touches to its concepts. Jung believed that the personality consists of the ego, which is one's conscious mind. It contains the thoughts, feelings, and perceptions of which one is normally aware. Jung also proposed a personal unconscious that contains events and emotions of which people remain unaware because of their anxiety-provoking nature. Memories of traumatic childhood events and conflicts may reside in the personal unconscious. Jung's unique contribution to personality theory is the idea of a collective unconscious. This consists of memories and emotions that are shared by all humanity. Jung believed that certain events and feelings are universal and exert a similar effect on all individuals. An example would be his universal symbol of a shadow, or the evil, primitive nature that resides within everyone. Jung believed that although people are aware of the workings of the conscious ego, it is the unavailable material contained in the personal unconscious and collective unconscious that has the greatest influence on one's behavior.

Jung believed that emotional problems originate from a one-sided development of personality. He believed that this is a natural process and that people must constantly seek a balance of their traits. An example might be a person who becomes overly logical and rational in her behavior and decision making while ignoring her emotional and spontaneous side. Jung believed this one-sided development eventually would lead to emotional difficulty and that one must access the complementary personality forces that reside in the unconscious. Even psychotherapists must be aware that along with their desire to help others, they have complementary darker desires that are destructive to others. Jung believed that emotional problems are a signal that one is becoming unbalanced in one's personality and that this should motivate one to develop more neutral traits.

The process of analytical psychotherapy, as in most psychodynamic approaches, is to make the patient conscious or aware of the material in his or her unconscious mind. Jung believed that if the conscious mind were overly logical and rational, the unconscious mind, to balance it, would be filled with equally illogical and emotional material. To access this material, Jung advocated a free and equal exchange of ideas and information between the analyst and the patient. Jung did not focus on specific techniques as did Freud, but he did believe that the unconscious material would become evident in the context of a strong, trusting therapeutic relationship. Although the patient and analyst have equal status, the analyst serves as a model of an individual who has faced her or his unconscious demons.

Analytic psychotherapy proceeds in four stages. The first stage is that of confession. Jung believed that it is necessary for the patient to tell of his or her conflicts and that this is usually accompanied by an emotional release. Jung did not believe that confession is sufficient to provide a cure for one's ills, however, nor did he believe (unlike Freud) that an intellectual understanding of one's difficulties is adequate. The patient must find a more neutral ground in terms of personality functioning, and this can only be accomplished by facing one's unconscious material.

The second stage of psychotherapy is called elucidation, and it involves becoming aware of one's unconscious transferences. Transference is a process in which a patient transfers emotions about someone else in his or her life onto the therapist; the patient will behave toward the therapist as he or she would toward that other person. It is similar to meeting someone who reminds one of a past relationship; for no apparent reason, one might begin to act toward the new person the same way one did to the previous person. Jung believed that these transferences to the analyst give a clue about unconscious material. A gentle, passive patient might evidence hostile transferences to the therapist, thus giving evidence of considerable rage that is being contained in the unconscious.

The third stage of analytic psychotherapy consists of education. The patient is instructed about the dangers of unequal personality development and is supported in his or her attempts to change. The overly logical business executive may be encouraged to go on a spontaneous vacation with his family with few plans and no fixed destinations. The shy student may be cajoled into joining a debate on emotional campus issues. Jung believed in the value of experiencing the messages of one's unconscious.

The final stage of psychotherapy, and one that is not always necessary, is that of transformation. This goes beyond the superficial encouragements of the previous stages and attempts to get the patient to delve deeply into the unconscious and thereby understand who he or she is. This process of understanding and reconciling one's opposites takes considerable courage and exploration into one's personal and cultural past. It is a quest for one's identity and purpose in life that requires diligent work between the analyst and patient; the result is superior wisdom and a transcendent calm when coping with life's struggles.

### Applications

Jung developed several techniques aimed at uncovering material hidden in the unconscious. Like Freud, Jung believed that the content of dreams is indicative of unconscious attitudes. He believed that dreams have a compensatory function; that is, they are reflections of the side of personality that is not displayed during one's conscious, everyday state. The sophisticated librarian may have dreams of being an exotic dancer, according to Jung, as a way of expressing the ignored aspects of personality.

Jung gives an example of the compensatory aspects of dreams when describing the recollections of a dutiful son. The son dreamed that he and his father were leaving home and his father was driving a new automobile. The father began to drive in an erratic fashion. He swerved the car all over the road until he finally succeeded in crashing the car and damaging it very badly. The son was frightened, then became angry and chastised his father for his behavior. Rather than respond, however, his father began to laugh until it became apparent that he was very intoxicated, a condition the son had not previously noticed. Jung interpreted the dream in the context of the son's relationship with his father. The son overly idealized the father while refusing to recognize apparent faults. The dream represented the son's latent anger at his father and his attempt to reduce him in status. Jung indicated to the young man that the dream was a cue from his unconscious that he should evaluate his relationship with his father with a more balanced outlook.

Jung employed the method of amplification for interpreting dreams. This technique involved focusing repeatedly on the contents of the dream and giving multiple associations to them. Jung believed that the dream often is basically what it appears to be. This differs dramatically from Freudian interpretation, which requires the patient to associate dream elements with childhood conflicts.

The amplification method can be applied to a dream reported by a graduate student in clinical psychology. While preparing to defend his dissertation, the final and most anxiety-provoking aspect of receiving the doctorate, the student had a dream about his oral defense. Before presenting the project to his dissertation committee that was to evaluate its worth (and seemingly his own), the student dreamed that he was in the bathroom gathering his resources. He noticed he was wearing a three-piece brown suit; however, none of the pieces matched. They were different shades of brown. Fortunately, the pieces were reversible, so the student attempted to change them so they would all be the same shade. After repeated attempts he was unable to get all three pieces of the suit to be the same shade of brown. He finally gave up in despair and did not appear for his defense. With a little knowledge about the student, an analytical therapist would have an easy time with the meaning of this dream. This was obviously a stressful time in the young man's life, and the dream reflected his denied anxiety. In addition, the student did not like brown suits; one that does not match is even more hideous. It is apparent that he was unhappy and, despite his best attempts to portray confidence, the budding clinician was afraid that he was going to "look stupid." Jung would have encouraged him to face these fears of failure that were hidden in his unconscious.

A final application of analytical psychotherapy stems from Jung's method of active imagination. Jung believed that unconscious messages could come not only from dreams but also from one's artistic productions. He encouraged his patients to produce spontaneous, artistic material. Some patients sketched, while others painted, wrote poetry, or sang songs. He was interested in the symbols that were given during these periods, and he asked his clients to comment on them. Jung believed that considerable material in the unconscious could be discovered during these encounters. He also talked with his patients about the universal meanings of these symbols (as in his idea of the collective unconscious), and they would attempt to relate this material to the patients' cultural pasts.

Many modern therapies, such as art, music, and dance therapy, draw heavily from this idea that one can become aware of unconscious and emotional material through association involving one's artistic productions. These therapists believe, as did Jung, that patients are less defensive during these times of spontaneous work and, therefore, are more likely to discover unconscious material.

## Context

Jung's analytical psychotherapy was a pioneering approach during the very early era of psychological treatment. He conformed to the beliefs of other psychodynamic therapists, such as Sigmund Freud and Alfred Adler, in the importance of discovering unconscious material. The psychoanalysts would be followed by the behavioral school's emphasis on environmental events and the cognitive school's focus on thoughts and perceptions. Psychoanalysis brought a prominence to psychology it had not known previously.

Jung expanded on Freud's beliefs about the unconscious. Rather than focus on instinctual forces, Jung chose to focus on the human being's spiritual side through his idea of the collective unconscious. His mystical beliefs about humankind's spirituality were new to the growing field of psychotherapy and have not been equalled since. Jung also took into account a person's cultural past. He proposed the idea of a universal human relatedness with his idea of common cultural symbols; however, it would be many years before this idea was fully developed.

Analytical psychotherapy is not considered a mainstream approach to psychotherapy, but it does have a small group of devoted followers. Some of Jung's techniques have been adapted into other, more common approaches. Many therapists agree with Jung's deemphasis on specific techniques in favor of a focus on the establishment of a supportive therapy relationship. Jung moved away from the stereotypical analyst's couch in favor of face-to-face communication between doctor and patient. Many psychotherapists endorse Jung's belief that the analyst and patient should have relatively equal status and input. Jung also reduced the frequency of meeting with his patients to weekly, which is the norm today.

Jung's analytical approach changed the focus of psychotherapy from symptom relief to self-discovery. He was interested not only in patients with major problems but also in those who were dissatisfied with their mundane existences. These people were usually bright, articulate, and occupationally successful.

Jung's most lasting contributions probably have been his insights into the polarity of personality traits. The Myers-Briggs Type Indicator, based on Jungian personality descriptions, is one of the most widely used personality tests in business and industry. Jung also believed that personality changes throughout one's life, and he encouraged a continual evaluation of oneself. The idea of a "mid-life crisis," a period when one reevaluates personal and occupational goals, is a product of Jung's theory. He believed that individuals continually should strive to achieve a balance in their personality and behavior.

## Bibliography

Campbell, Joseph. *The Hero with a Thousand Faces.* New York: Pantheon Books, 1949. Campbell was a contemporary theorist who developed Jung's ideas of universal symbols and the power of myth. This book discusses Jung's idea of the hero, and Campbell relates this idea to spiritual leaders such as Moses, Jesus, and Muhammad.

Engler, Barbara. *Personality Theories: An Introduction.* 3d ed. Boston: Houghton Mifflin, 1991. Engler's chapter on Jung and his psychotherapy is easy to read and contains a good balance between theory and practical application.

Hall, Calvin Springer, and Gardner Lindzey. *Theories of Personality.* 3d ed. New York: John Wiley & Sons, 1978. This is a classic text in personality theory and application, and it gives a detailed description of Jung's theory. Recommended for the serious student of Jung.

Hall, Calvin Springer, and Vernon J. Nordby. *A Primer of Jungian Psychology.* New York: New American Library, 1973. This paperback attempts to provide a comprehensive treatment of Jung's ideas. It is intended for the beginning student of Jung.

Hannah, Barbara. *Jung: His Life and Work.* New York: Putnam, 1976. This is an interesting biographical account of Jung by a psychoanalyst who was his friend for more than thirty years. Gives an insight into how his personal beliefs and experiences shaped his theory.

Wehr, Gerhard. *Portrait of Jung: An Illustrated Biography.* New York: Herder and Herder, 1971. This is an interesting biography of Jung as well as a good introduction to his theory and therapy. Contains numerous fascinating pictures that give insight to the man and his ideas.

*Brett L. Beck*

## Cross-References

Abnormality: Psychodynamic Models, 74; Analytical Psychology: Carl G. Jung, 240; Archetypes: Origins and Nature, 286; The Collective Unconscious, 592; Dream Analysis, 830; Midlife Crisis, 1575; Psychoanalytic Psychology: An Overview, 1905.

# ANIMAL EXPERIMENTATION

*Type of psychology:* Psychological methodologies
*Fields of study:* Experimental methodologies; methodological issues

*Psychologists study animals and animal behavior as well as humans; sometimes the goal is to understand the animal itself, and sometimes it is to try to learn more about humans. Since there are many biological and psychological similarities between humans and other animals, the use of animal models can be extremely valuable, although it is sometimes controversial.*

*Principal terms*

ANALOGY: behavioral similarity between two species based on similarity of their environments and life-styles; often used in contrast to "homology"

APPLIED RESEARCH: research intended to solve existing problems, as opposed to "basic research," which seeks knowledge for its own sake

HOMOLOGY: behavioral similarity between two species based on genetic relatedness; often used in contrast to "analogy"

INSTITUTIONAL ANIMAL CARE AND USE COMMITTEES: local committees which, by federal law, are mandated to oversee animal research to ensure humane treatment

INVASIVE PROCEDURES: experimental techniques that involve direct bodily intervention, such as surgery, force-feeding, or the administration of drugs

**Overview**

Research psychologists are the fourth-largest group of scientists in the United States to use animals as experimental subjects, accounting for approximately 10 percent of the 25 to 35 million animals used per year. Psychologists who study animals can be roughly categorized into three groups. Biopsychologists, or physiological psychologists, study the genetic, neural, and hormonal controls of behavior, for example, eating behavior, sleep, sexual behavior, perception, emotion, memory, and the effects of drugs. Learning theorists study the learned and environmental controls of behavior, for example, stress, stimulus-response patterns, motivation, and the effects of reward and punishment. Ethologists and sociobiologists concentrate on animal behavior in nature, for example, predator-prey interactions, mating and parenting, migration, communication, aggression, and territoriality.

Psychologists study animals for a variety of reasons. Sometimes they study the behavior of a particular animal in order to solve a specific problem. They may study dogs, for example, to learn how best to train them as watchdogs; or study chickens to learn how to prevent them from fighting one another in hen houses; or study wildlife to learn how to regulate populations in parks, refuges, or urban areas. These are all examples of what is called "applied research."

Most psychologists, though, are more interested in human behavior but study animals for practical reasons. A developmental psychologist, for example, may study an animal which has a much shorter life span than humans so that each study takes a much shorter time and more studies can be done. Animals may also be studied when an experiment requires strict controls; researchers can control the food, housing, and even social environment of laboratory animals but cannot control such variables in the lives of human subjects. Experimenters can even control the genetics of animals by breeding them in the laboratory; rats and mice have been bred for so many generations that researchers can special-order from hundreds of strains and breeds and can even get animals that are as genetically identical as identical twins.

Another reason psychologists sometimes study animals is that there are fewer ethical considerations as compared to research with human subjects. Physiological psychologists and neuropsychologists, in particular, may utilize invasive procedures (such as brain surgery or hormone manipulation) that would be unethical to perform on humans. Without animal experimentation, these scientists would have to do all their research on human victims of accident or disease, a situation which would reduce the number of research subjects dramatically as well as raise additional ethical considerations.

There are drawbacks to using animals as experimental subjects. Most important are the clear biological and psychological differences between humans and nonhuman animals; results one gets in a study using nonhuman animals simply may not apply to humans. In addition, animal subjects cannot communicate directly with the researchers; they are unable to express their feelings, motivations, thoughts, and reasons for their behavior. If a psychologist must use an animal instead of a human subject for ethical or practical reasons, the scientist will want to choose an animal which is similar to humans in the particular behavior being studied. Three factors can create similarity between animal and human behavior; each of these three must be considered.

The first factor is homology. Animals that are closely related to humans are likely to have similar physiology and behavior because they share the same genetic blueprint. Monkeys and chimpanzees are the animals most closely related to humans and thus are homologically most similar. Monkeys and chimpanzees make the best subjects for psychological studies of complex behaviors and emotions, but because they are expensive and difficult to keep, and because there are serious ethical considerations when using them, they are not used when another animal would be equally suitable.

The second factor is analogy. Animals that have a similar life-style to humans are likely to have some of the same behaviors. Rats, for example, are social animals, as are humans; cats are not. Rats also show similarity to humans in their eating behavior (which is one reason rats commonly live around human habitation and garbage dumps); thus, they can be a good model for studies of hunger, food preference, and obesity. Rats, however, do not have a similar stress response to that of humans;

for studies of exercise and stress, the pig is a better animal to study.

The third factor is situational similarity. Some animals, particularly domesticated animals such as dogs, cats, domestic rabbits, and some birds, adapt easily to experimental situations such as living in a cage and being handled by humans. Wild animals, even if reared from infancy, may not behave normally in experimental situations. The behavior of a chimpanzee that has been kept alone in a cage, for example, may tell something about the behavior of a human kept in solitary confinement, but it will not necessarily be relevant to understanding the behavior of most people in typical situations.

By far the most common laboratory animal used in psychology is *Rattus norvegicus*, the Norway rat. Originally, the choice of the rat was something of a historical accident. Since the rat has been studied so thoroughly over the past century, it is now often the animal of choice so that comparisons can be made from study to study. Fortunately, the rat shares many analogous features with humans. Other animals frequently used in psychological research include pigeons, mice, hamsters, gerbils, cats, monkeys, and chimpanzees.

## Applications

One of the most important topics for which psychologists use animal experimentation is the study of interactive effects of genes and the environment on the development of the brain and subsequent behavior. These studies can only be done using animals as subjects because they require individuals with a relatively short life span that develop quickly, invasive procedures to measure cell and brain activity, or the manipulation of major social and environmental variables in the life of the subject.

In the 1920's, E. C. Tolman and Robert Tryon began a study of the inheritance of intelligence using rats. They trained rats to run a complex maze and then, over many generations, bred the fastest learners with one another and the slowest learners with one another. From the beginning, offspring of the "bright" rats were substantially faster than offspring of the "dull" rats. After only seven generations, there was no overlap between the two sets, showing that "intelligence" is at least partly genetic and can be bred into or out of animals just as size, coat color, or milk yield can be.

Subsequent work with selectively bred bright versus dull rats, however, found that the bright rats would only outperform the dull rats when tested on the original maze used with their parents and grandparents; if given a different task to measure their intelligence, the bright rats were no brighter than the dull rats. These studies were the first to suggest that intelligence may not be a single attribute that one either has much or little of; there may instead be many kinds of intelligence.

Traditionally, intelligence (IQ) tests measure two kinds of intelligence: one related to verbal skills and one related to spatial skills. Newer theories and tests, however, attempt to address the possibility that there are dozens of different kinds of intelligence. The newer tests may help to identify special talents that may otherwise go unrecognized, undeveloped, and unrewarded in people who are not especially good at tasks measured by the more traditional tests. The new theories of multiple intelligences are also being used in the field of artificial intelligence to develop computer and robotic systems which utilize less sequential processing and more parallel systems or netlike processing, more like the human brain.

Another series of experiments that illustrate the role of animal models in the study of brain and behavior is that developed by David Hubel and Torsten Wiesel, who study visual perception (mostly using cats). Hubel and Wiesel were able to study the activity of individual cells in the living brain. By inserting a microelectrode into a brain cell of an immobilized animal and flashing visual stimuli in the animal's visual field, they could record when the cell responded to a stimulus and when it did not.

Over the years, scientists have used this method to map the activities of cells in several layers of the visual cortex, the part of the brain that processes visual information. They have also studied the development of cells and the cell connections, showing how early experience can have a permanent effect on the development of the visual cortex. Subsequent research has demonstrated that the environment has major effects on the development of other areas of the brain as well. The phrase "use it or lose it" has some accuracy when it comes to development and maintenance of brain connections and mental abilities.

Perhaps the most famous psychological experiments on animals were those by Harry Harlow in the 1950's. Harlow was studying rhesus monkeys and breeding them in his own laboratory. Initially, he would separate infant monkeys from their mothers. Later, however, he discovered that, in spite of receiving adequate medical care and nutrition, these infants exhibited severe behavioral symptoms: They would sit in a corner and rock, mutilate themselves, and scream in fright at the approach of an experimenter, a mechanical toy, or another monkey. As adolescents, they were antisocial. As adults, they were psychologically ill-equipped to deal with social interactions: Male monkeys were sexually aggressive, and females appeared to have no emotional attachment to their own babies. Harlow decided to study this phenomenon (labeled "maternal deprivation syndrome") because he thought it might help to explain the stunted growth, low life expectancy, and behavioral symptoms of institutionalized infants which had been documented earlier by René Spitz.

Results of the Harlow experiments profoundly changed the way psychologists think about love, parenting, and mental health. Harlow and his colleagues found that the so-called mothering instinct is not very instinctive at all but rather is learned through social interactions during infancy and adolescence. They also found that an infant's attachment to its mother is based not on its dependency for food but rather on its need for "contact comfort." Babies raised with both a mechanical "mother" that provided milk and a soft, cloth "mother" that gave no milk preferred the cloth mother for clinging and comfort in times of stress.

Through these experiments, psychologists came to learn how important social stimulation is, even for infants, and how profoundly lack of such stimulation can affect mental health development. These findings played an important role in the development of staffing and activity requirements for foundling homes, foster care, daycare, and institutions for the aged, disabled, mentally ill, and mentally retarded. They have also influenced social policies which promote parent education and early intervention for children at risk.

## Context

Prior to the general acceptance of Charles Darwin's evolutionary theory in the late nineteenth century, animals were considered to be soulless machines with no thoughts or emotions. Humans, on the other hand, were assumed to be qualitatively different from other animals because of their abilities to speak, reason, and exercise free will. This assumption made it unreasonable to try to learn about the mind by studying animals.

After Darwin, however, people began to see that, even though each species is unique, the chain of life is continuous, and there are similarities as well as differences between species. Since animal brains and human brains are made of the same kinds of cells and have similar structures and connections, it was reasoned, the mental processes of animals must be similar to the mental processes of humans. This new insight led to the introduction of animals as psychological research subjects around the year 1900. Since then, animal experimentation has taught much about the brain and the mind, especially in the fields of learning, memory, motivation, and sensation.

For the same reasons that animals are useful in studying psychological processes, however, people have questioned the moral justification for such use. Since it is now realized that vertebrate animals can feel physical pain, and that many of them have thoughts and emotions as well, animal experimentation has become politically controversial.

In response to such concerns, Congress amended the Animal Welfare Act in 1985 so that it would cover laboratory animals as well as pets. (Rats, mice, birds, and farm animals are specifically excluded.) Although the new regulations do not state specifically what experimental procedures may or may not be done on laboratory animals, they do set standards for humane housing, feeding, and transportation, and they require that all research on warm-blooded animals (except those listed above) be approved by a committee before it can be carried out. Each committee (they are called Institutional Animal Care and Use Committees, or IACUCs) is composed of at least five members that must include an animal researcher; a veterinarian; someone with an area of expertise in a nonresearch area, such as a teacher, lawyer, or clergyman; and someone who is unaffiliated with the institution where the experimentation is being done who can speak for the local community. In this way, those scientists who do animal experiments are held accountable for justifying the appropriateness of their use of animals as research subjects.

Alternatives to animal experimentation are becoming more widespread as technology progresses. Computer modeling and bioassays (tests using biological materials such as cell cultures) will never replace animal experimentation in the field of psychology, however, because computers and cell cultures will never exhibit all the properties of mind that psychologists want to study. At the same time, the use of animals as psychological research subjects will never end the need for study of human subjects. While other animals may age, mate, fight, and learn much as humans do, they will never speak, compose symphonies, or run for office. Animal experimentation will always have an important, though limited, role in psychological research.

## Bibliography

Committee on the Use of Animals in Research Staff of the National Academy of Sciences and the Institute of Medicine Staff. *Science, Medicine, and Animals.* Washington, D.C.: National Academy Press, 1991. This thirty-page pamphlet answers commonly asked questions about the use of animals in biomedical research. Although not focusing specifically on psychology, it does address research in psychomedical areas such as brain research and drug addiction.

Fox, Michael Allen. *The Case for Animal Experimentation.* Berkeley: University of California Press, 1986. Although the author is philosophically in favor of most animal experimentation, he gives a clear and thorough discussion of the entire context of animal experimentation from both sides. Includes sections on animal rights, similarities and differences between human and nonhuman subjects, the role of methodological considerations and replicability in scientific progress, and alternatives to animal testing. The author specifically addresses some of the uglier behavioral studies on animals, including some by Harry Harlow.

Gross, Charles G., and H. Philip Zeigler, eds. *Motivation.* Vol. 2 in *Readings in Physiological Psychology.* New York: Harper & Row, 1969. Although there are dozens of newer collections of articles in the area of physiological psychology, this one does a particularly good job of covering the broad diversity of topics in the field. In addition, all the work represented in this particular collection came from animal studies. This or a similar collection can be consulted for illustration of many specific methodologies utilized in research with animals.

Miller, Neal E. "The Value of Behavioral Research on Animals." *American Psychologist* 40 (April, 1985): 423-440. Good discussion of advances in the behavioral sciences that came from animal studies, including studies on effects of early experience on the brain and behavior, drug effects, eating disorders, and diseases of aging. Also includes some discussion of applied studies which benefit nonhuman species.

Rowan, Andrew N. *Of Mice, Models, and Men: A Critical Evaluation of Animal Research.* Albany, N.Y.: State University of New York Press, 1984. The author is in fact a supporter of the use of animals in scientific research; he addresses the history of animal research and the controversies surrounding it. In addition to psychological research, he covers the use of animals in medical and industrial testing.

U.S. Congress Office of Technology Assessment. *Alternatives to Animal Use in Research, Testing, and Education.* Washington, D.C.: Author, 1986. This 441-page document provides much more than its title indicates. In addition to alternative methodologies, the report discusses government use of animals, economic and ethical considerations, statistics and patterns of animal use, and federal policy.

*Linda Mealey*

## Cross-References

Conditioning: Pavlovian versus Instrumental, 649; Emotion in Primates, 947; Ethology, 992; Hunger: Biological Bases, 1217; Imprinting and Learning, 1262; Instinct Theory, 1309; Instrumental Conditioning: Acquisition and Extinction, 1315; Memory: Animal Research, 1505; Pavlovian Conditioning: Acquisition, Extinction, and Inhibition, 1757; Sexual Behavior Patterns, 2246; Visual Neural Processing, 2629.

# ANOREXIA NERVOSA AND BULIMIA NERVOSA

*Type of psychology:* Psychopathology
*Field of study:* Childhood and adolescent disorders

*Anorexia and bulimia nervosa are disorders characterized by a distorted body image, an intense fear of becoming obese, and a desperate attempt to lose weight; these disorders most frequently occur in female adolescents, and they present serious health risks.*

*Principal terms*

BEHAVIORAL THERAPY: a treatment that emphasizes the utilization of learning principles—the use of positive reinforcers and negative consequences—in order to change maladaptive behavior

BINGING: a period of excessive eating in which as many as 15,000 calories may be consumed in a few hours

COGNITIVE BEHAVIOR THERAPY: a therapy approach which, in addition to behavioral techniques, uses cognitive methods such as modifying maladaptive personal beliefs and expectations

DISTORTED BODY IMAGE: misperception of one's body size or shape such that one sees oneself as "fat" even though one may be underweight

HYPOTHALAMUS: a brain structure that regulates bodily functions such as hunger, hormonal balance, temperature, and sexual interest

NEUROTRANSMITTERS: the chemical messengers within the brain that transmit nerve impulses between nerve cells

PSYCHOANALYTIC THERAPY: a therapy approach based on Sigmund Freud's theory of personality that traces maladaptive behavior to disturbances in early development and unconscious conflicts

PURGING: a method of weight reduction that most commonly involves the emptying of one's digestive organs either through self-induced vomiting or the use of laxatives

WEIGHT PHOBIA: an intense fear of gaining weight accompanied by an avoidance of eating that increases as weight loss progresses

## Overview

Anorexia nervosa and bulimia nervosa are two of several types of eating disorders—ways of managing food and/or weight that are unhealthy. "Anorexia" literally means a "severe loss of appetite," while "nervosa" means "nervousness." Actually, the word "anorexia" is somewhat of a misnomer, given that most people with anorexia nervosa have not lost their appetites. The syndrome of anorexia nervosa consists of four prominent symptoms, according to the American Psychiatric Association. The first symptom is a failure to maintain a normal weight for one's age and height such that one's weight is less than 85 percent of what is considered normal.

The weight of most anorectics (persons with anorexia nervosa) is usually much less than 85 percent of their normal weight. For example, a review of treatment studies for anorexia nervosa found that the average anorectic weighed 37 kilograms (82 pounds), 69 percent of normal weight (R. C. Qualls and J. S. Berman, 1988).

The second symptom of anorexia nervosa is an intense fear of gaining weight that increases even as the anorectic continues to lose weight. This second symptom has been labeled weight phobia by some researchers because of the anorectic's anxiety toward food and the desperate attempts she (most documented anorectics have been girls or women) makes to avoid food. The third major symptom of the syndrome is distorted body image. Distorted body image involves the anorectic seeing herself as obese when in reality she is extremely underweight. For example, when an anorectic is asked to view her body in a mirror, she is likely to comment on how fat she looks. The final symptom for women with anorexia nervosa is the absence of at least three menstrual cycles, which is caused by their being severely underweight.

Bulimia nervosa refers to the recurring cycle of binging, a period of excessive over-eating, followed by purging, engaging in drastic efforts to lose the weight gained by binging. For the bulimic, binge episodes may consist of consuming up to 15,000 calories, more than five times the recommended daily number, within a few hours. Purging may be accomplished through several means including vomiting (done either by gagging oneself or through the consumption of certain drugs), the use of laxatives, strict dieting, or stringent exercising. In order to meet this first criterion of bulimia, one must engage in the binge-purge cycle at least two times per week for three months.

In addition to the recurrent binging and purging, other symptoms of bulimia nervosa include the feeling that one has no control over one's eating binges and constant concern regarding one's body shape or weight. In contrast to anorectics, who are grossly underweight, bulimics may be normal weight or even slightly obese. That is, the weight-loss effects of a bulimic's purging are often negated by the weight gained during her binging.

There are numerous potential health problems that may occur as a result of anorexia or bulimia. The health problems of anorectics include an abnormally low body temperature and blood pressure, irregular heart functioning, and bone thinning. Of those diagnosed with anorexia, approximately 4 percent die. The health complications of bulimia include the erosion of tooth enamel; sudden mineral depletions, particularly potassium reduction; irregular heart functioning; and a variety of disorders affecting digestive organs. A significantly lower number of people are thought to die from bulimia as compared to anorexia.

When compared to the most common eating disorder, obesity, anorexia and bulimia are rare. Approximately 30 percent of all Americans are reported to be obese. In contrast to the thirty out of one hundred who are obese, about one out of every one thousand Americans will have anorexia during his or her life (L. N. Robins et al., 1984). The incidence of anorexia among adolescent females, however, is about ten times higher than in the general population. In comparison, bulimia is estimated to occur in approximately three out of every one hundred Americans. Again, the incidence of bulimia among adolescent females is believed to be significantly higher.

The proposed causes of anorexia and bulimia can be grouped into the following four categories: biological, sociocultural, familial, and psychological. The notion of biological causes of anorexia and bulimia involves the idea that anorectics and bulimics have specific brain or biochemical disturbances that lead to their inability to maintain a normal weight and/or eating pattern. The most popular biological explanation for the occurrence of anorexia and bulimia is the existence of an abnormal amount of certain neurotransmitters. Neurotransmitters are chemical messengers within the brain that transmit nerve impulses between nerve cells. Potential abnormal levels of the neurotransmitters norepinephrine and serotonin have received the most investigation as causes of anorexia and bulimia.

In contrast to biological explanations, sociocultural causes are factors that are thought to exist within a society that lead certain individuals to develop anorexia or bulimia. Joan Brumberg, a historian of anorexia, has outlined the sociocultural forces of the late nineteenth and twentieth centuries that many believe promoted the increased incidence of eating disorders among women (1988). These societal forces included an emphasis on weight reduction, aesthetic self-control, and the regarding of women as sexual objects. The most prominent of these suggested cultural factors is the heightened (some would say obsessive) importance placed on being thin.

Some researchers believe that particular family types cause certain of their members to develop anorexia and bulimia. For example, family investigators believe that a family whose members are too emotionally close to one another may lead one or more family members to strive for independence by refusing to eat, according to Salvador Minuchin, Bernice Rosman, and Lester Baker. Other researchers believe that families whose members are controlling and express an excessive amount of hostility toward one another promote the occurrence of bulimia.

Psychological features make up the final category of causes for anorexia and bulimia. The most prominent of the suggested psychological causes for anorexia and bulimia are those expressed by researchers who take psychoanalytic or cognitive behavioral perspectives. For example, cognitive behavioral theorists emphasize the role of distorted beliefs in the development and continuation of anorexia and bulimia. These distorted beliefs include, "I am only attractive when I weigh _____ pounds [a number well below normal weight]," or "If I eat certain types of food [for example, carbohydrate-rich foods], I will become fat."

## Applications

In general, the initial treatment for anorexia occurs within the hospital setting, given the risk of death associated with this disorder. Follow-up therapy for anorexia, as well as the typical treatment for bulimia, takes place on an outpatient basis. Numerous treatments have been used for individuals afflicted by these disorders. These treatments can be broadly grouped into the categories of medical and psychological therapies.

Prior to the 1960's, medical therapies for anorexia included such radical approaches as lobotomies and electroconvulsive therapy (ECT). The performing of a lobotomy involves the surgical removal of prefrontal portions of the brain. Electroconvulsive therapy, commonly known as "shock treatment," involves the introduction of an electrical current into a patient's body through electrodes placed on the patient's head. These treatments were shown to be of no benefit for anorectics. Although a controversial treatment, various types of tube feeding continue to be used when a patient's malnutrition from anorexia poses an imminent risk of death. Tube feeding can be accomplished either intravenously or by inserting a tube via a patient's nasal cavity into the patient's stomach.

Since the 1960's, medications are used more often as the medical treatments of choice for anorexia and bulimia. These medications include such categories of drugs as antidepressants and major tranquilizers. For anorexia, these drugs are thought to increase eating behavior and promote weight gain by correcting imbalances in an individual's neurotransmitters. For bulimia, certain medications are thought to reduce carbohydrate cravings that precede the binge-purge cycle. In addition, antidepressant medication may be prescribed for bulimia because of the depression that often accompanies binging and purging.

Different psychological interventions also have been attempted for anorexia and bulimia. These psychological treatments include individual, family, and group interventions. One type of individual therapy for anorexia is behavioral therapy. In behavioral therapy, weight gain is promoted through the use of positive reinforcers for increases in weight and negative consequences for weight decreases or the absence of weight gain. These positive reinforcers include such things as access to telephone and visitation privileges. Negative consequences for remaining the same weight or weight loss include confinement to bed and denial of all unit privileges. Besides behavioral treatment, other types of individual therapy include cognitive behavioral, Gestalt, hypnosis, and psychoanalytic interventions.

Another common treatment for both anorexia and bulimia is family therapy. The family treatment of an anorectic patient involves the therapist seeking to change the interactions among family members that serve to maintain the self-starvation of the patient. In attempting to correct faulty family interactions, the family therapist might address the overprotectiveness of the patient by her parents or the way that family members manipulate one another's behavior. For the bulimic patient, the family therapist would seek to lower the amount of family conflict or to redirect conflict between the parents away from the bulimic.

Another frequently employed method of treatment for bulimia is group therapy. Group treatment initially involves educating bulimics about their disorder, including its negative health consequences. The group experience provides members with the opportunity to share with fellow bulimics regarding their eating problems and to find support from one another in overcoming bulimia. In addition, the therapist or therapists initiate discussions regarding healthy eating and exercise habits as well as specific ways to curb the binge-purge cycle.

A final issue involved in surveying the different interventions for anorexia and bulimia is the effectiveness of these treatments. The effectiveness of treatments for anorexia was addressed by Christopher Qualls and Jeffrey Berman in a 1988 study that grouped treatments reported in one hundred studies according to their type and then analyzed the effectiveness of each. The results of their study indicated that the average anorectic gains approximately 8 kilograms (18 pounds) during the initial phase of treatment and another 5 kilograms (11 pounds) by the time of a follow-up evaluation about four years later. There were only small differences between the various types of treatment for the amount of weight produced during therapy, although behavioral treatments appeared to work faster. Less research has been conducted investigating the effectiveness of different therapies for bulimia. No one therapy for bulimia, however, whether medical or psychological, has shown clear superiority in its effectiveness as compared to other interventions.

## Context

Anorexia is a disorder that can be traced as far back as seven hundred years ago. The disorder was specifically written about in 1874, when Sir William Gull published an article giving the disorder its present name. Bulimia nervosa, as a disorder separate from anorexia, has received meaningful attention only since the late 1970's. There is evidence to suggest that the incidence of both disorders has increased in the last two decades. As previously discussed, the increased emphasis being placed on thinness within current Western societies represents a likely explanation for the increase in eating disorders such as anorexia and bulimia.

Another area within the study of anorexia and bulimia that has begun to receive attention is the prevention of eating disorders. In discussing the prevention of eating disorders, Catherine Shisslak and colleagues have suggested that preventive efforts should be targeted at adolescent females, given that they are at increased risk for developing an eating disorder. These efforts should focus on issues such as the physical as well as emotional and social changes that occur in maturation. Also, information regarding diet and exercise should be provided, and the connection between emotions and eating should be discussed, as should ways to resist the pressure to conform to peers' and societal expectations for one's appearance. It should also be recognized that there are those who oppose preventive efforts, including segments of the media, fashion, and exercise industries.

With evidence of the increasing prevalence of anorexia and bulimia, it is important to learn more regarding the causes and effective treatment methods of these disorders. In these areas, some of the questions that remain to be definitively answered are: Why do certain groups of people have a greater likelihood of developing anorexia and bulimia (notably, white adolescent females) as compared to other groups? Are the underlying causes of anorexia different from those of bulimia? Can a treatment with superior effectiveness be developed for those suffering with anorexia and bulimia? Anorexia and bulimia nervosa remain elusive syndromes for professionals and patients alike. It is hoped that present and future endeavors will answer these and other remaining questions regarding these disorders.

## Bibliography

Boskind-White, Marlene, and William C. White, Jr. *Bulimarexia: The Binge/Purge Cycle.* New York: W. W. Norton, 1983. A comprehensible overview of bulimarexia (more commonly referred to as bulimia). Takes a nonpathologizing, empathetic approach in addressing the problems of individuals with bulimia. Filled with illustrative patient histories.

Bruch, Hilde. *The Golden Cage: The Enigma of Anorexia Nervosa.* Cambridge, Mass.: Harvard University Press, 1978. A classic work by a pioneer in the field of eating disorders. Portrays the development of anorexia nervosa as an attempt by a young woman to attain a sense of control and identity. Discusses the etiology and treatment of anorexia from a modified psychoanalytic perspective.

Brumberg, Joan J. *Fasting Girls: The History of Anorexia Nervosa.* Cambridge, Mass.: Harvard University Press, 1988. Outlines the history of anorexia nervosa. Examines the syndrome from multiple perspectives while leaning toward a cultural and feministic perspective. A well-researched and very readable work.

Minuchin, Salvador, Bernice L. Rosman, and Lester Baker. *Psychosomatic Families: Anorexia Nervosa in Context.* Cambridge, Mass.: Harvard University Press, 1978. A classic work which outlines the development and treatment of anorexia nervosa from a family systems perspective. Includes a complete description of Salvador Minuchin's famed "family lunch session," in which Minuchin conducts a family assessment and begins treatment of an anorectic patient while eating lunch with the patient and her family.

Mitchell, J. E., and E. D. Eckert. "Scope and Significance of Eating Disorders." *Journal of Consulting and Clinical Psychology* 55 (1987): 37-43. Summarizes relevant research regarding the prevalence, etiology, and treatment of both anorexia and bulimia. The authors' overview of the suggested causes of anorexia and bulimia highlights potential biologial factors. Very readable for a scientific piece.

Shisslak, C. M., Marjorie Crago, M. E. Neal, and B. Swain. "Primary Prevention of Eating Disorders." *Journal of Consulting and Clinical Psychology* 55 (1987): 44-51. Washington, D.C.: American Psychological Association, 1987. Discusses the need for preventive efforts in addressing the rising rate of anorexia and bulimia. Outlines specific prevention strategies that would be appropriate for different age groups. A very readable journal article.

*R. Christopher Qualls*

## Cross-References

# ANTISOCIAL PERSONALITY

*Type of psychology:* Psychopathology
*Fields of study:* Aggression; personality disorders; personality theory

*Antisocial personality is a personality disorder characterized by chronic criminal and otherwise irresponsible behaviors. Although extensively researched, it is one of the most controversial diagnostic categories, and its causes and treatment remain largely an enigma.*

*Principal terms*

AROUSAL MODIFICATION: the technique of increasing arousal in order to decrease the motivation for antisocial behavior

CONDUCT DISORDER: a disorder, beginning in childhood, in which the rights of others and age-appropriate social norms or rules are repeatedly violated

DYSSOCIAL PSYCHOPATHY: a syndrome in which antisocial behavior results from allegiance to a culturally deviant subgroup

NEUROTIC PSYCHOPATHY: a syndrome in which antisocial behavior is a consequence of psychological conflict and turmoil

PERSONALITY DISORDER: a disorder in which personality traits are rigid and maladaptive, and produce considerable impairment or distress for the individual

PSYCHOPATHIC PERSONALITY: a personality disorder characterized by traits such as guiltlessness, dishonesty, charm, fearlessness, callousness, and egocentricity

SOMATIZATION DISORDER: a condition characterized by multiple physical symptoms lacking any demonstrated medical basis

SUCCESSFUL PSYCHOPATHY: a category consisting of psychopathic personalities who are functioning highly

YERKES-DODSON LAW: the principle that moderate levels of arousal tend to yield optimal performance

## Overview

By personality disorder, psychologists mean a disorder in which personality traits are rigid and maladaptive, and produce considerable impairment and distress for the individual. In the case of antisocial personality, these traits are thought to be manifested in criminal and otherwise irresponsible behaviors, which create problems for the individual and, more important, for society—hence the term "antisocial."

Antisocial personalities have a childhood history of conduct disorder—a pattern in which both the rights of others and age-appropriate social norms or rules are repeatedly violated—and continue to exhibit criminal and other irresponsible behaviors in adulthood. The major symptoms of antisocial personality include theft, school truancy, fire setting, vandalism, physical cruelty toward animals and people, financial irresponsibility, repeated lying, reckless driving, sexual promiscuity, and poor parenting. Not surprisingly, a large percentage of incarcerated criminals fulfill the criteria for this disorder.

Many of the symptoms of antisocial personality were identified by the sociologist Lee Robins in her influential work *Deviant Children Grown Up* (1966). Robins found that between 20 and 30 percent of children with conduct disorder develop antisocial personality in adulthood. There is also evidence that a subset of children with hyperactivity (attention-deficit hyperactivity disorder) develop antisocial personality in adulthood. Nevertheless, because many of these same children have conduct disorder, it may be conduct disorder, rather than hyperactivity, that is the major determinant of antisocial personality.

In addition to the behaviors mentioned above, antisocial personalities have a number of other psychological and interpersonal difficulties. For example, they have high rates of alcohol and drug abuse, divorce, venereal disease, out-of-wedlock pregnancies, and depression. In addition, individuals with this disorder are more likely than those in the general population to die prematurely from violent crimes and accidents. Antisocial personality is also associated with criminal recidivism: Individuals with this disorder who are released from prison are at high risk for subsequent incarceration.

In the United States, about 3 percent of males and 1 percent of females have antisocial personalities. The reason for this sex difference is unknown; some authors have speculated that females who are predisposed to antisocial personality may be likely to develop somatization disorder, a condition characterized by multiple physical complaints lacking any demonstrated medical basis. Indeed, somatization disorder is found among many of the female relatives of antisocial personalities. Thus, somatization disorder may be an alternative manifestation of antisocial personality that is found primarily among females, although considerably more research will be needed to corroborate this hypothesis. Antisocial personality is also associated with low social class, although the causes of this relationship are unknown.

What happens to antisocial personalities over time? There is evidence that many such individuals "burn out" in middle age: Their antisocial behaviors decrease in frequency and severity in later adulthood. The reasons for this burnout phenomenon are unclear, but it may be a consequence of the decline in activity level and energy seen in most individuals with age.

Little is known about the treatment of antisocial personality, except that no clearly effective treatment has been found. A number of therapies have been attempted, including psychoanalysis, behavior therapy, group therapy, and medication, but there is little evidence that any of them have been especially successful. As the symptoms of antisocial personality begin early in life and are easily identifiable, it may be prevention, rather than treatment, that holds the greatest promise for reducing the prevalence of this disorder.

Many antisocial personalities possess a constellation of personality traits known as the psychopathic personality. In his classic book *The Mask of Sanity* (1941), psychiatrist Hervey Cleckley provided a detailed description of this syndrome. According to Cleckley, psychopathic personalities (or, as they are sometimes called, psychopaths) tend to be superficially charming individuals who are relatively free of anxiety and seem possessed of excellent reason. Nevertheless, they also tend to be guiltless, callous, dishonest, and self-centered persons who rarely learn from their mistakes or take responsibility for their behavior.

Some psychologists believe that psychopathic personality is a more valid category than antisocial personality. According to these researchers, many antisocial personalities lack the traits characteristic of psychopathic personality, and instead exhibit antisocial behavior for a variety of other reasons. For example, some antisocial personalities may fall into a category known as dyssocial psychopathy, a syndrome in which antisocial behavior results from allegiance to a culturally deviant subgroup. Many gang delinquents or members of organized crime could probably be classified in this group. The behavior of still other antisocial personalities may result from neurotic psychopathy, a syndrome in which antisocial behavior is a consequence of internal psychological conflict and turmoil. Many neurotic psychopaths are probably socially anxious individuals who inhibit their anger for long periods of time and then erupt intermittently but violently.

Conversely, some critics of the antisocial personality diagnosis have argued that many psychopaths do not fulfill the criteria for antisocial personality. Indeed, some psychopaths may function highly in society, and would thus not be detected by the antisocial personality criteria in many cases. Cathy Spatz Widom has found that many persons who possess the traits described by Cleckley can be found outside prisons, and in some cases have socially valued occupations (for example, corporate executive). Further study of these "successful" psychopaths may shed light on factors that allow individuals at risk for antisocial personality to avoid legal and interpersonal problems.

## Applications

One of the most active areas of research on antisocial personality concerns possible causes of the disorder. Psychologist David Lykken, for example, has theorized that the behavior of many antisocial personalities, particularly those who are psychopaths, can be traced to fearlessness.

Lykken has found that, compared with other individuals with antisocial behavior and with "normals," psychopaths tend to exhibit less sweating of the palms prior to a buzzer that has been repeatedly paired with a painful electric shock. Robert Hare has similarly shown that psychopaths tend to show relatively little palmar sweating during the countdown period prior to a painful electric shock or jarring blast of white noise. Because palmar sweating is often indicative of fear or arousal, the findings of Lykken and Hare can be interpreted to mean that psychopaths are not frightened or aroused by signals of impending punishment. This, in turn, might explain why many psychopaths engage in repeated antisocial behavior: The warning signs that would deter most people from performing such acts have little impact upon the psychopath. The average child or adult is prevented from committing antisocial acts largely by signals that punishment or danger is imminent: a parent or teacher saying "No" as a child reaches for a forbidden piece of candy, the watchful eye of a museum guard as one passes by a valuable painting, a light turning yellow as one approaches a busy intersection. If such signals arouse little or no fear in a person, however, his or her threshold for committing antisocial acts will surely be lowered.

Lykken also constructed a "mental maze" task, in which subjects were required to learn a complex series of lever presses. On each trial, some errors were punished with painful shock, whereas others were not. Lykken found that, compared with other subjects, psychopaths did not make more errors overall, indicating that they can learn certain tasks as well as other individuals. Nevertheless, Lykken found that psychopaths made more punished errors than other individuals, suggesting that they have difficulty learning from punishment. Again, this finding is consistent with the fearlessness hypothesis, because the capacity to benefit from punishment is largely dependent upon the capacity to become frightened of this punishment. Moreover, this finding has important implications; the psychopath's failure to learn from punishment in the laboratory may be a useful model for the antisocial personality's recidivism in the real world.

An alternative hypothesis for the behavior of antisocial personalities is that these individuals have unusually low levels of arousal. According to the Yerkes-Dodson law, moderate levels of arousal are optimal for performance and psychological functioning. Thus, as Herbert Quay and other psychologists have argued, many of the thrill-seeking and dangerous behaviors of antisocial personalities may represent attempts to bring their arousal to higher and thus more optimal levels. George Skrzypek has found that psychopathic delinquents, compared with other delinquents, have a greater preference for complex and novel stimuli. This is consistent with Quay's hypothesis, because such stimuli would be expected to increase arousal. Skrzypek also found that after both groups were placed in sensory isolation, psychopaths' preference for complex and novel stimuli increased more compared with nonpsychopaths.

One implication of these findings is that at least some antisocial personalities might benefit from treatments that boost their arousal levels. For example, antisocial personalities could be encouraged to find occupations (for example, combat soldier) or avocations (for example, skydiving) that might provide outlets for their risk-taking tendencies. Similarly, some researchers have explored the possibility that some antisocial personalities might be helped by stimulant medication. Stanley Schachter and Bibb Latané found that when psychopaths were asked to perform Lykken's mental-maze task while taking adrenaline, a stimulant drug, they were as successful as were nonpsychopaths at learning to avoid punishment. Nevertheless, as these "arousal modification" approaches have not been adequately researched, their potential as treatments for antisocial personality remains speculative.

There is considerable evidence that antisocial personality is influenced by genetic factors. Identical twins (who share all their genes) with antisocial personality are much more likely than are fraternal twins (who share only half their genes on average) to have co-twins with the disorder. Nevertheless, many of the co-twins of identical twins with antisocial personality do not have the disorder, which indicates that environmental factors play an important role in the development of antisocial personality. In addition, adopted children whose natural parents had antisocial personality are more likely to develop the disorder than are adopted children whose natural parents did not. Again, this is consistent with a genetic influence upon antisocial personality.

Nevertheless, several important questions concerning the genetics of antisocial personality remain. First, it is not known what factors are being genetically transmitted. Second, it is not known whether this genetic influence applies to all, or only some, individuals with antisocial personality. For example, this genetic influence might only play a role in individuals with psychopathic personality. Third, it is not known how environmental factors combine or interact with genetic factors to produce antisocial personality. These three questions are likely to occupy researchers for a number of years to come.

## Context

Although the term "antisocial personality" did not enjoy widespread currency until the latter half of the twentieth century, individuals with chronic antisocial symptoms have been described by a variety of labels over the years. In 1809, Phillipe Pinel discussed a syndrome called *manie sans délire:* mania without delusion. Such individuals, according to Pinel, are driven by strong instinctual forces but maintain good contact with reality. In 1835, James Pritchard coined the term "moral insanity" to refer to a condition characterized by severe deficits in ethical behavior.

In 1891, German psychiatrist August Koch referred to a group of conditions called "psychopathic inferiorities." In doing so, Koch broadened the concept of the disorder to include a diverse spectrum of abnormalities, not all of which were characterized by moral depravity. Koch's tradition was followed by the great German classifier Kurt Schneider, who in 1923 described a wide variety of psychopathic personalities, each of which was considered to be an exaggeration of a normal personality style. Thus, the German conceptualization was generally more inclusive than that of Morel and Pritchard, and viewed psychopathic personality as a set of conditions that created problems for the individual, society, or both.

It was authors such as Cleckley and Benjamin Karpman who were largely responsible for shaping contemporary notions of psychopathic personality. These authors emphasized personality traits as the key features of the disorder, and they de-emphasized antisocial and criminal behaviors. This view was reflected in the second edition of the American Psychiatric Association's *Diagnostic and Statistical Manual of Mental Disorders* (DSM-II) in 1968, which focused upon personality traits such as guiltlessness and selfishness as the primary criteria for the disorder.

This personality-based approach, however, came under attack in the 1970's and

1980's for its subjectivity. After all, what one diagnostician might view as a pathological absence of guilt might be viewed by another as a healthy absence of self-criticism. Thus, in 1980, the third edition of the *Diagnostic and Statistical Manual of Mental Disorders* (DSM-III) introduced "antisocial personality disorder," a new diagnosis in which explicit references to personality traits were all but expunged. Instead, the emphasis in DSM-III (as well as in its 1987 revision, DSM-III-R) was upon easily agreed-upon transgressions against society. The advantage of this new approach was its objectivity: Clinicians could easily agree upon whether an individual had committed a robbery or driven while intoxicated.

Although advocates of this behavior-based approach contend that their diagnosis identifies a homogeneous group of individuals, many researchers remain convinced that lumping together virtually all chronically antisocial individuals under a single rubric is bound to fail. Nevertheless, advocates of these two approaches agree upon one thing: Their disagreement is more than semantic. Is the smooth confidence artist who bilks others without remorse fundamentally different from the loyal gang member who sacrifices his or her livelihood for the good of the group? The answer to this and related questions will almost certainly have profound implications for psychologists' conceptualizations of antisocial personality, as well as for their approaches to understanding and treating it.

## Bibliography

Cleckley, Hervey. *The Mask of Sanity.* St. Louis: C. V. Mosby, 1941. In this classic work, Cleckley delineates the primary features of psychopathic personality in considerable detail, and provides a wealth of case history material that vividly illustrates the symptomatology of this disorder. Although many of Cleckley's speculations concerning the causation of this disorder are somewhat outdated, his clinical descriptions remain unparalleled in their depth and richness.

Hare, Robert D. *Psychopathy: Theory and Research.* New York: John Wiley & Sons, 1970. Perhaps the best overview of early research on the psychopathic personality. Reviews the evidence for a number of models of the causation of this disorder, and describes the research literature clearly, thoughtfully, and critically. An excellent primer for the layperson who wishes to learn more about psychopathic and antisocial personalities.

Hare, Robert D., and Daisy Schalling, eds. *Psychopathic Behaviour: Approaches to Research.* New York: John Wiley & Sons, 1978. Contains perhaps the finest collection of chapters on research issues relevant to psychopathic and antisocial personalities. Coverage of research on biological models is particularly impressive. Chapters on the history of the psychopathic personality concept and on assessment issues are also highly recommended.

Reid, William H., ed. *The Psychopath: A Comprehensive Study of Antisocial Disorders and Behaviors.* New York: Brunner/Mazel, 1978. Another edited volume that contains a number of informative chapters on topics such as the neurological bases of antisocial behavior, psychophysiological findings in psychopaths, and the relation between antisocial personality and substance abuse. Nevertheless, the quality of the book is rather uneven; several chapters are marred by unbridled speculation regarding the psychodynamics of the disorder.

Robins, Lee. *Deviant Children Grown Up.* Baltimore: Williams & Wilkins, 1966. Describes Robins' classic study of the long-term outcome of conduct disordered children, and provides a remarkably detailed examination of early risk factors for antisocial personality. Should be required reading for all individuals interested in the development of antisocial and criminal behavior.

*Scott O. Lilienfeld*

## Cross-References

Addictive Personality and Behaviors, 102; Alcoholism, 213; Borderline, Histrionic, and Narcissistic Personalities, 441; Hyperactivity, 1235; Juvenile Delinquency, 1375; Psychological Diagnosis and Classification: DSM-III-R, 1925; Substance Abuse: An Overview, 2489.

# ANXIETY DISORDERS: THEORETICAL EXPLANATIONS

*Type of psychology:* Psychopathology
*Fields of study:* Anxiety disorders; behavioral and cognitive models; psychodynamic and neoanalytic models

*Anxiety is a central concept in many different schools of psychology, and there are many widely varying theories concerning it; theories of anxiety often have spawned approaches to treating anxiety disorders.*

*Principal terms*

EGO: in psychoanalytic theory, the mostly conscious part of the mind that deals with reality

LIBIDO: in psychoanalytic theory, the psychological aspect of sexual energy or drive

OPERANT CONDITIONING: learning in which a behavior increases or decreases depending on whether the behavior is followed by reward or punishment

PAVLOVIAN CONDITIONING: learning in which two stimuli are presented one after the other, and the response to the first changes because of the response automatically elicited by the second stimulus

PHOBIA: an anxiety disorder involving an intense fear of a particular thing (such as horses) or situation (such as heights)

PREPAREDNESS: the theory that animals and human beings are prepared by evolution to learn certain things—for example, that snakes are dangerous

REPRESSION: in psychoanalytic theory, a defense mechanism that keeps unacceptable thoughts and impulses from becoming conscious

THREE-SYSTEMS APPROACH: an important concept in behavioral formulations of anxiety, stating that anxiety has behavioral, physiological, and verbal components and that they do not necessarily provide the same information

TWO-FACTOR THEORY: a behavioral theory of anxiety that states that fear is caused by Pavlovian conditioning and that avoidance of the feared object is maintained by operant conditioning

VICARIOUS LEARNING: learning (for example, learning to fear something) without direct experience, either by observing or by receiving verbal information

## Overview

Anxiety is an important concept in many schools of psychology; thus, there are many different theories about the nature and origin of anxiety disorders. The two most important and influential viewpoints on anxiety are the Freudian and the behavioral viewpoints. Although these theories attempt to explain many anxiety disorders, an examination of how they apply to phobias presents a good indication of how they work.

Sigmund Freud, who said that understanding anxiety "would be bound to throw a flood of light on our whole mental existence," had two theories of anxiety, an early (1917) and a later (1926) theory. In the early theory, libido (mental energy, often equated with sexual drive) builds up until it is discharged by some pleasurable activity. Sometimes the energy cannot be discharged, for example, when the sexual object is not attainable or is morally unacceptable. This undischarged energy is anxiety, and remains even when its original, unacceptable object is repressed, or eliminated from conscious awareness. This anxiety may attach itself to an otherwise harmless object, resulting in a phobia. This theory is best illustrated in one of Freud's most famous cases, that of "Little Hans," a five-year-old who developed a phobia of horses. Freud believed that Hans had a sexual desire for his mother and wanted his father dead so that he could have his mother to himself. This desire for his mother and hatred of his father were unacceptable impulses, and so were repressed from consciousness, resulting in anxiety. This anxiety attached itself to horses, Freud thought, because the black blinders and muzzle of the horse symbolized his father's glasses and mustache.

In Freud's first theory, repression causes anxiety. In the later theory, the relationship between them has changed: Anxiety causes repression. In this theory, anxiety acts as a signal to the ego (in Freud's theory, the rational, conscious part of the mind) that a forbidden impulse (such as Little Hans's desire for his mother) is trying to force its way into consciousness. This signal alerts the ego to try to repress the unwanted impulse. If the ego cannot successfully repress the forbidden impulse, it may try to transfer the forbidden impulse to an irrelevant object (horses, in Little Hans's case). This object can arouse all the emotions associated with the forbidden impulse, including the signal anxiety. In this way, it becomes a phobic object.

One influential behavioral approach to anxiety is O. Hobart Mowrer's two-factor theory. It uses the principles of Pavlovian and operant conditioning to explain fear and phobic avoidance, respectively. Fear is acquired through Pavlovian conditioning when a neutral object or situation is paired with something painful or punishing. For example, having an automobile accident can result in a fear of driving. At this point, operant learning principles take over to explain phobic avoidance. In operant learning, any action that leads to a reward is likely to be repeated. The person who is anxious about driving might avoid driving. Because this avoidance is rewarded by reduced anxiety, the person is more likely to avoid driving in the future. Continued avoidance makes it harder to get back behind the wheel again.

Many problems were found with two-factor theory, and many modifications have been made to it. Two problems will be discussed here to illustrate these changes. First, the theory predicts that people will be likely to fear things that are most often associated with pain. There are very few people in modern society, however, who are phobic of electrical sockets and end tables, even though almost everyone has received a shock from the former and stubbed a toe on the latter. On the other hand, many people are afraid of snakes and spiders, even if they have never been bitten by one. This has been explained through the concept of preparedness: Our evolutionary history has prepared us to learn that some things—such as reptiles, insects, heights, darkness, and closed spaces—are dangerous. These things are "easy" to learn to fear, and they account for a large proportion of phobias. On the other hand, our evolutionary ancestors had no experience with electric sockets or guns, so we are not prepared to become phobic of these objects even though they cause much more pain in modern society than do snakes or spiders.

Two-factor theory states that in order for something to cause fear, it must be paired with a painful or punishing experience. Yet people sometimes become phobic of objects or situations with which they have never had a bad experience. Indeed, many people who have never seen a live snake are afraid of them. Thus, there must be other ways in which fear is acquired. One of these is through vicarious transmission: Seeing someone act afraid of something can lead to acquiring that fear. For example, whether an infant becomes afraid of being in a high place depends on whether its mother is smiling or has an expression of fear on her face. In an ingenious set of experiments, Susan Mineka and her colleagues showed that vicarious transmission of fear is influenced by preparedness. She showed that rhesus monkeys who watched a videotape of other monkeys acting afraid of a snake became afraid of the snakes themselves. Monkeys that watched other monkeys act afraid of rabbits, however, did not become afraid of rabbits because they were not evolutionarily prepared to fear rabbits. Human beings also can acquire fear by being told that something is dangerous. A child can come to avoid running in front of oncoming cars by being told not to do this by his or her parents; luckily, he or she does not have to be hit by a car or watch someone get hit in order to acquire this information.

## Applications

All theories of anxiety disorders attempt to explain and organize what is known about fear and anxiety. Some of the theories, including the ones described here, also have been applied in developing treatments for anxiety disorders. As might be expected, clinical psychologists with very different ideas about the cause of anxiety will recommend very different treatments to eliminate it.

In the case of Little Hans, Freud thought that his anxiety about horses was caused by repressed sexual impulses toward his mother and hatred of his father. From this, it follows that these repressed impulses would need to be brought out into the open and resolved before his anxiety about horses would diminish. This was the basic goal of the psychoanalytic therapy Freud recommended for Hans.

On the other hand, if Little Hans's parents had taken him to a behaviorally oriented therapist, the therapist would have assumed that the child's fear stemmed from a fright he suffered in the presence of a horse. In fact, Freud stated that the phobia began when Hans saw a horse fall while pulling a bus. Further, the therapist would assume that now Hans was rewarded for avoiding horses by anxiety reduction and by getting extra attention from his parents. Treatment would involve having the boy gradually think about, look at, and even pet horses, and it would include being rewarded for approaching (rather than avoiding) horses.

Presented with these vastly different theories and treatments, the question arises: Which is right? The theoretical issues are still debated, but it is clear that treatments based on a behavioral model of anxiety are much more successful in reducing fear than are treatments based on the theories of Freud or his followers.

Cognitive theories of anxiety also illustrate how theory is applied to develop a treatment. There are many different cognitive models of anxiety, but all are similar in that they assume that there is a cognitive cause of the fear state. This cognitive step is sometimes called an irrational belief. A cognitive theorist might explain Little Hans's fear in the following way: Hans is afraid of horses because he has some irrational belief that horses are dangerous. The specific belief might be "The horse will bite me" or "The horse might get spooked and run into me" or even "Horses have germs, and if I go near one, I'll catch its germs and get sick." The theory assumes that anxiety will stop when the irrational belief is eliminated. Thus, a cognitive therapist would first carefully question Hans to find out the specific irrational belief causing his fear. Once that is determined, the therapist would use persuasion, logical reasoning, and evidence to try to change the belief. (Little Hans was used here only to continue with the same example. A therapist probably would not try to reason with a five-year-old, and a different treatment would be used. Cognitive therapies are more commonly used with adults.)

Physiological theories of anxiety are increasing in importance. As with behavioral, psychodynamic, and cognitive theories, there are many physiological theories. They differ with respect to the brain areas, pathways, or chemicals implicated in anxiety. It is likely that many physiological theories contain an element of truth. Anxiety is a complex state, involving multiple interacting parts of the nervous system, and it will take much additional research to develop a complete model of the brain's role in anxiety.

One physiological variable that has been integrated into many theories of anxiety is the panic attack. This is a sudden and usually short-lived attack that includes trouble with breathing, heart palpitations, dizziness, sweating, and fear of dying or going crazy. These attacks appear purely physiological in that they seem to come "out of the blue" at first; however, psychological factors determine whether they progress into a full-blown disorder. People can become anxious about having panic attacks, and this added anxiety leads to more attacks, producing panic disorder. Some people become afraid of having an attack in a place where they will be unable to cope or receive help. These people may progressively avoid more and more places. This is known as agoraphobia, which at its worst can result in people who are afraid to leave their homes.

The development of physiological theories also illustrates an important point in the relationship between theory and therapy. Thus far, it has been stressed that theories of anxiety help determine treatment. This relationship also works in reverse:

Success or failure of treatments adds information used in theory development. This is most clear in physiological theories. For example, the physiological mechanisms of different types of anxiety-reducing tranquilizers have been investigated to provide clues as to how the brain is involved in anxiety.

## Context

The concept of anxiety is one of the most often-used and loosely defined concepts in psychology. It can be used to describe a temporary state ("You seem anxious today") or an enduring personality trait ("He is an anxious person"). It is used to assign cause ("He stumbled over the words in his speech because he was anxious") and to describe an effect ("Having to give a speech sure makes me anxious"). It is seen as the result of discrete objects or situations such as snakes or heights, or as evolving from basic existential problems such as the trauma of birth or the fear of death. All major theories in psychology in some way confront anxiety.

Just as most theories in psychology have a view of anxiety, anxiety is an important concept in many areas of psychology. Obviously, anxiety is very important in the fields of psychopathology and psychotherapy. It also has been very important in learning theory; experiments with conditioned fear have advanced knowledge about Pavlovian and operant conditioning. Anxiety is also an important trait in theories of personality, and it figures in theories of motivation. It might be said that anxiety is everywhere in psychology.

Theoretical developments in anxiety have also been incorporated into other areas of psychology. For example, in the early 1960's, Peter Lang described fear and anxiety as being composed of three systems—that is, there are three systems in which fear is expressed: verbal (saying "I'm anxious"), behavioral (avoiding or running away from a feared object), and physiological (experiencing an increase in heart rate or sweating). An important point in understanding the three systems of fear is that the systems do not always run along parallel tracks. A person may speak of being anxious about the condition of the world environment without any physiological arousal. Alternatively, a boy's heart might pound at the sight of a snake in the woods, but he reports no fear and does not run away in the presence of his friends. Describing fear in a three-systems framework presents an important challenge to any theory of anxiety. An adequate theory must explain why the three systems sometimes give the same information and sometimes do not. The three-systems approach not only has been very influential in anxiety theory and research, but also has been applied to many other areas of psychology, such as studying emotion, stress, and pain.

Another major challenge for theories of anxiety is to begin to integrate different positions. The present theories are not all mutually exclusive. The fact that a behavioral theory of anxiety has some validity does not mean that cognitive approaches are wrong. Also, psychological theories need to be integrated with physiological theories that describe brain activity during anxiety. Although theory and research in anxiety has a long and fruitful history, there is much work to be done, and many important developments lie ahead.

## Bibliography

Barlow, David H. *Anxiety and Its Disorders.* New York: Guilford Press, 1988. The author, one of the leaders in the field of anxiety research, presents his integrative theory of anxiety. The book also describes assessment and treatment of anxiety, and includes a separate chapter on each recognized anxiety disorder. The book's intended audience is graduate students and professionals in psychology, but it is very well written and worth the effort for anyone interested in an up-to-date and comprehensive presentation of anxiety disorders.

Delprato, D. J., and F. D. McGlynn. "Behavioral Theories of Anxiety Disorders." In *Behavioral Theories and Treatment of Anxiety*, edited by Samuel M. Turner. New York: Plenum Press, 1984. Behaviorally oriented psychologists have been extremely active in testing and revising theories of anxiety. This chapter of nearly fifty pages describes the obvious and the subtle differences between various behavioral theories. It also compares behavioral to cognitive theories of anxiety.

Freud, Sigmund. "Analysis of a Phobia in a Five-Year-Old Boy." In *The Standard Edition of the Complete Psychological Works of Sigmund Freud*, edited by James Strachey. Vol. 10. London: Hogarth Press, 1955. Originally published in 1909, this is Freud's description of the case of Little Hans, the most famous patient in the history of anxiety disorders. Freud is an excellent writer, and he presents many vivid details in this case history, making it interesting to read. One could also look up Joseph Wolpe and Stanley Rachman's behavioral interpretation of Little Hans's phobia, "Psychoanalytic 'Evidence': A Critique Based on Freud's Little Hans," in *Journal of Nervous and Mental Disease* 131, no. 2 (1960): 135-148.

_____. "Inhibition, Symptoms, and Anxiety." In *The Standard Edition of the Complete Psychological Works of Sigmund Freud*, edited by James Strachey. Vol. 20. London: Hogarth Press, 1959. In this paper, originally published in German in 1926, Freud describes his revised theory of anxiety. The paper covers a wide range of topics (including a redescription of Little Hans) and is not as readable as the initial presentation of the case. It is, however, an interesting illustration of the change in Freud's thinking about anxiety.

Marks, Isaac Meyer. *Living with Fear: Understanding and Coping with Anxiety.* New York: McGraw-Hill, 1978. This is a work written for the general public by Britain's foremost authority on fear and anxiety. It is accessible and provides a good introduction to theory and treatment of anxiety.

Tuma, A. Hussain, and Jack D. Maser, eds. *Anxiety and the Anxiety Disorders.* New York: Lawrence Erlbaum, 1985. This thousand-page book contains forty-three chapters of high quality, with most of the leaders in the field of anxiety represented. Every important theoretical approach to anxiety is covered. There are two hundred pages of references, an author index, and a subject index, making it easy to find information on specific topics.

*Scott R. Vrana*

## Cross-References

Abnormality: Behavioral Models, 33; Abnormality: Cognitive Models, 46; Abnormality: Psychodynamic Models, 74; Agoraphobia and Panic Disorders, 206; Amnesia, Fugue, and Multiple Personality, 234; Instrumental Conditioning: Acquisition and Extinction, 1315; Observational Learning, 1694; Obsessions and Compulsions, 1707; Pavlovian Conditioning: Acquisition, Extinction, and Inhibition, 1757; Phobias, 1816; Preparedness and Learning, 1866.

# APHASIAS

*Type of psychology:* Language
*Field of study:* Cognitive processes

*Aphasias include a variety of conditions in which a partial or total loss of the ability to understand or produce language-based material occurs; the deficits can be in speech, reading, or writing. Knowledge of aphasias can aid in the localization of brain injuries. An understanding of aphasias is also important because they cause communication problems that require treatment.*

*Principal terms*

CEREBRAL VASCULAR DISORDERS: cerebral ischemia, migraine stroke, cerebral hemorrhage, and aneurysm, conditions that may result in aphasia; cerebral vascular accident (CVA) is used synonymously with stroke

EQUIPOTENTIALITY: a theory of cerebral functioning that holds that, although sensory input may be localized, perception involves the whole brain

EXPRESSIVE APHASIA: severe impairment of previously intact language-production abilities as a result of brain injury or cerebral dysfunction

GLOBAL APHASIA: substantial impairments in both language production and language comprehension

INTERACTIONIST THEORY: the idea that perception and behavioral output are based on interactions between basic components; although component processes are localized, there is redundancy in regard to function

LOCALIZATIONIST THEORY: the idea that specific sensory, perceptual, and behavioral processes are controlled by particular cerebral structures and/or areas of the brain

NEUROPSYCHOLOGY: the study and application of information concerning central nervous system functioning to the diagnosis and treatment of mental and physical disorders

ORGANIC ETIOLOGY: dysfunction resulting from trauma, chemical imbalances, or disease processes that directly affect the brain

PARAPHASIA: impairment in which articulation is intact but unintended sounds are substituted for others (phonemic paraphasia) or words are substituted (semantic paraphasia)

RECEPTIVE APHASIA: severe impairment of previously intact language-comprehension abilities as a result of brain injury or other cerebral dysfunction

## Overview

Nearly all definitions of aphasia agree on the following four points: Aphasia refers to a condition in which a person suffers a loss in the ability to understand or produce language-referenced material; the deficits can be in speech, reading, and/or writing; the impairment is assumed to be caused by cerebral rather than peripheral impairments; and aphasias represent a devastation of a previously manifested ability rather than a developmental failure.

A fifth point, included or implied in most descriptions of aphasias, is that they occur as a result of structural damage or disease processes that directly affect the brain—an organic etiology. This view is taken because functional mental disorders that produce aphasic-like symptoms are best understood in the context of the psychological and environmental events that produce them. Aphasias, however, are best comprehended in relationship to the physical injuries and structural changes that cause their appearance. Furthermore, interventions that would be effective for the treatment of aphasias would have little or no relevance for the amelioration of aphasic-like symptoms that result from functional causes.

Vascular disorders, particularly strokes, are the most frequent cause of aphasia. Other conditions likely to lead to aphasia include traumatic head injuries, brain tumors, infections, toxins, and dementia.

It is left-hemisphere damage that is most commonly associated with aphasia. For most persons, language abilities are localized in the left hemisphere of the brain. Damage to the right side of the brain seldom results in any noticeable effect on language skills. The fact that left-handers sometimes show speech impairments following injury to the right side of the brain has often been taken as evidence that left-handers are right-brain dominant in regard to language. Research has failed to support this contention. Most left-handers show bilateral or left-hemisphere dominance for language, with no more than 15 percent showing primary control of speech via the right hemisphere.

Aphasias can be divided into three general categories: expressive aphasias, receptive aphasias, and mixed or global aphasias. Most persons with aphasia show a mixture of expressive and receptive symptoms.

Expressive aphasia is often referred to as Broca's aphasia, motor aphasia, nonfluent aphasia, executive aphasia, or verbal aphasia. Expressive aphasia can be considered to subsume subfluent aphasia, anarthric aphasia, expressive dysprosody, kinetic (efferent) motor aphasia, speech apraxia, subcortical motor aphasia (pure word-dumbness), transcortical motor aphasia (dynamic aphasia), conduction (central) aphasia, anomic (amnestic or nominal) aphasia, and agraphia.

Expressive aphasia describes a condition in which language comprehension remains intact but speech—and quite often the ability to write—is impaired. People who suffer from expressive aphasia understand what is being asked of them, and their ability to read is unaffected; they have difficulty, however, communicating their understanding.

When expressive aphasia is extreme, the affected person may be totally unable to speak (aphonia) or may be able to speak only in so distorted a way that he or she becomes incomprehensible. Still, as is the case with all other forms of aphasia, singing and swearing are generally preserved.

Paraphasias are a common form of expressive aphasia. Paraphasia differs from articulation problems, which are also quite prominent. When a person with expressive aphasia has difficulties with articulation, he or she has trouble making recognizable speech sounds. Paraphasia, on the other hand, refers to a condition in which articulation is intact but unintended syllables, words, or phrases are inserted. For example, one patient, in referring to his wife, always said "my dog."

Telegraphic speech, in which speech is reduced to its most elemental aspects, is frequently encountered in expressive aphasia. In telegraphic speech, the meaning is often clear; however, communications are reduced to the bare minimum and consist of simple noun-verb phrases.

Verbal fluency, the capacity to produce uninterrupted phrases and sentences, is typically adversely affected in expressive aphasias. As a result of word-finding difficulties, speech may take on a halting and labored character.

Receptive aphasia is often referred to as Wernicke's aphasia, sensory aphasia, fluent aphasia, or agnosia. Receptive aphasia can be considered to subsume semantic aphasia, jargon aphasia, visual aphasia (pure word-blindness), transcortical sensory aphasia (isolation syndrome), syntactical aphasia, and alexia. In receptive aphasia, speech is generally fluent, with few, if any, articulatory problems; however, deficits in language comprehension are always present.

While fluent, the speech of a person with receptive aphasia is seldom normal. People who have receptive aphasia may insert nonwords—neologisms—into their communications, and in severe cases their communications may contain nothing but jargon speech. For example, one patient, when asked what he had for breakfast, responded, "Eating and food. Got no more heavy come to there. No come good, very good, in morning."

Unlike people who have expressive aphasia, who generally show great distress in regard to their disorder, people who have receptive aphasia may appear oblivious to their disorder. They may produce lengthy nonsensical utterances and then look at the listener as if confused by the listener's lack of comprehension.

Global aphasia describes a condition in which there is a mixture of receptive and expressive deficits. Global aphasia is typically associated with less focalized brain injury. Although comprehension is generally less impaired than production in global aphasia, this disorder does not fit neatly into either the expressive or the receptive category. The prognosis is generally much poorer for persons with global aphasia than for those with purely receptive or expressive deficits.

## Applications

An appreciation for the nature and extent of aphasias is important because such knowledge can facilitate the identification of disease processes that may be affecting cerebral functioning, can assist in the localization of brain injuries, and can provide information that must be considered in making post-discharge placements. Finally, and perhaps most important, knowledge of aphasias is needed because they cause significant communication deficits that require treatment.

There are a variety of conditions that can lead to aphasic-like symptoms: functional mental disorders, peripheral nervous system damage, peripheral motor impairments, congenital disorders, degenerative disease processes of the brain, cerebral vascular injury, central nervous system toxins, epilepsy, migraine, brain tumors, central nervous system infections, and cerebral trauma. Being able to discriminate between true aphasias (those caused by cerebral complications) and aphasic-like symptoms brought on by other causes can enable the selection of the most effective treatment and improve prognostic prediction. For example, depression, Parkinson's disease, and certain focal lesions can cause persons to appear emotionally unreactive (flat affect) and speak in a manner that lacks expressive intensity and intonation (dysprosody). The treatments of choice for these disorders are substantially different, and some interventions that would be recommended for one disorder would be contraindicated for another. Similarly, knowing that cerebral hemorrhage is most often associated with global aphasia and diffuse tissue damage—whereas cerebral embolisms typically damage areas served by the left middle cerebral artery, resulting in more specific aphasias—has implications in regard to patient monitoring, treatment, and prognosis.

The interrelationships between aphasias and localized brain injuries have important ramifications. Among other implications, knowing the neural basis for language production and processing can facilitate the identification of the best candidate sites for surgical intervention and can provide clues regarding whether a disease process has been arrested or continues to spread. For example, an aphasia that begins with clear articulation and no identifiable deficits in language production would be consistent with conduction aphasia, and it might be assumed that damage to the arcuate fasciculus had occurred. If, over the course of time, the person began to manifest increasing difficulty with speech comprehension but articulation continued to appear intact, it could be inferred that damage was spreading downward and affecting a broader region of the temporal lobe. Such information would have important treatment and prognostic ramifications.

Given the importance of language and the ability to communicate in managing daily affairs, it can be seen that having information concerning the nature and the extent of aphasia is an important consideration that must be taken into account when making post-discharge plans. On the one hand, if the person's deficits are purely expressive in nature, it can be assumed that he or she will more likely be able to manage his or her daily affairs and will be more capable of managing independent placement. On the other hand, persons with receptive aphasia, despite wishes to the contrary, may have to be referred to a more restrictive environment. Not being able to understand the communications of others and perhaps manifesting deficits in safety and judgment require that the person with receptive aphasia be carefully assessed to ascertain the degree to which he or she is competent to manage his or her affairs.

Aphasias cause significant communication problems that require treatment and amelioration. While there is no doubt that considerable spontaneous recovery takes place in regard to aphasia, research shows that treatment can have a facilitating effect. Furthermore, the earlier treatment is initiated, the more profound its effects.

Under most circumstances, therapy for aphasia is one element of a more comprehensive treatment process. Aphasia seldom occurs in isolation, and, depending on the type of damage, one is likely to see paresis, memory deficits, apraxias, agnosias, and various difficulties related to information processing occurring in conjunction with the aphasia. As a result, the person with aphasia is likely to be treated by an interdisciplinary team. The team will typically consist of one or more physicians, nurses, nursing support personnel, physical therapists, occupational therapists, speech therapists, a rehabilitation psychologist or neuropsychologist, a clinical psychologist, and one or more social workers. Each team member is expected to have an area of expertise and specialization, but the team approach requires that team members work together and, individually and collectively, support each discipline's treatment goals.

The most common treatments for the aphasic person are systematic stimulation, behavioral teaching programs, deblocking, and compensation therapy. Systematic stimulation involves the use of everyday objects and everyday situations to stimulate language production and to facilitate language comprehension. Behavioral teaching programs are similar to systematic stimulation but are more organized, are designed more precisely to take into account known structural damage, and frequently employ behavior modification techniques. Deblocking, a less frequently used therapy, consists of stimulating intact language functions as a vehicle for encouraging rehabilitation of damaged processes. Compensation therapy includes teaching the person alternative communication strategies and utilizing intact abilities to circumvent the functional limitations that result from her or his aphasia.

## Context

The study of aphasias dates back more than four thousand years. An Egyptian papyrus dated between 3000 and 2500 B.C. provides a case example of language deficits following traumatic head injury.

The Greeks variously subscribed to hypotheses that mental processes were located in the brain or the heart. Not until the time of the physician Galen (A.D. 130 to 201) did the brain hypothesis gain full sway. Galen based his arguments on dissection and clinical experience—he spent five years as a physician to the gladiators of the Roman circus, where he was exposed to multiple cases of traumatic head injury.

Over the next thirteen hundred years, little progress was made in relation to an appreciation of cerebral anatomy or physiology. With the anatomical observations of Andreas Vesalius (1514-1564) and the philosophical speculations of René Descartes (1596-1650), however, the stage was set for a new understanding of cerebral functioning.

In the early nineteenth century, phrenology, which postulated that specific areas of the brain controlled particular intellectual and psychological processes, became influential. Although it was subsequently discredited, phrenology provided the foundation for the localizationist position in neuropsychology.

Paul Broca (1824-1880) can be credited with raising the study of cerebral localization of speech to a scientific level. Broca's first case study was "Tan," a patient with apparently intact receptive abilities whose expressive skills had been reduced to uttering the word "tan" and a few colorful oaths. According to Broca, "Tan" was shown in an autopsy to have a lesion of the left anterior lobe of his brain, which caused his speech problems. Subsequently, the syndrome he described became known as Broca's aphasia. Furthermore, the posterior third of the left third frontal convolution of the left hemisphere of the brain became known as Broca's area.

Carl Wernicke (1848-1905) was the next person to make major contributions to the understanding of cerebral organization and language functioning. Wernicke proposed a sequential processing model that held that several areas of the brain affected language development, production, and expression. Following his work, the left first temporal gyrus was named Wernicke's area, and the particular type of receptive aphasia that resulted from damage to this area became known as Wernicke's aphasia.

Over the ensuing years, arguments raged regarding whether the localizationist position was tenable. As a general rule, researchers supporting equipotentiality (sensory input may be localized, but perception involves the whole brain) held sway. By the 1950's, interactionist theory had gained the ascendancy. Interactionist theory holds that basic functions are localized; however, there is redundancy in regard to function. Therefore, damage to a specific area of the brain may or may not cause a deficit in higher-order behaviors, since the damaged functions may be assumed by redundant or parallel backup components.

Recent years have seen notable advances in the understanding and treatment of aphasias. Psychometric instruments founded on modern principles of test construction have become available. Experimental techniques that take into account known aspects of cerebral functioning have been developed. Furthermore, advances in brain imaging have done much to aid in understanding cortical function and the effects of injury as they relate to the development of aphasias.

## Bibliography

Broida, Helen. *Coping with Stroke: Communication Breakdown of Brain Injured Adults.* San Diego: College-Hill Press, 1979. Broida provides a nontechnical introduction to stroke and aphasia. Answers many questions regarding functional deficits, treatment, and prognosis.

Brubaker, Susan Howell. *Sourcebook for Aphasia: A Guide to Family Activities and Community Resources.* Detroit: Wayne State University Press, 1982. Brubaker describes activities that relatives of aphasia patients can use to enhance the recovery process. The absence of an introduction to aphasia and minimal guidance regarding which exercises are appropriate for particular symptom presentations are limiting factors in this text.

Collins, Michael. *Diagnosis and Treatment of Global Aphasia.* San Diego: College-Hill Press, 1986. Collins focuses on the practical implications of what is known about global aphasia. The text is somewhat technical, but it is valuable for persons who want to learn more about this disorder.

Ewing, Susan Adair, and Beth Pfalzgraf. *Pathways: Moving Beyond Stroke and Aphasia.* Detroit: Wayne State University Press, 1990. The authors summarize the experiences of six families that attempt to cope with the aftermath of a stroke. Practical and emotional problems that must be confronted by the patient and the family are discussed.

Fitch, James L. *Clinical Applications of Microcomputers in Communication Disorders.* Orlando, Fla.: Academic Press, 1986. Fitch provides an entry-level introduction to the use of computers in audiology and speech pathology. The text lacks an adequate discussion of the use of computers as adaptive devices, but many potential applications are discussed.

Murdoch, B. E. *Acquired Speech and Language Disorders: A Neuroanatomical and Functional Neurological Approach.* London: Chapman and Hall, 1990. Murdoch provides a comprehensive description of the various types of aphasia and dysarthria. Additionally, the author supplies an extended discussion of agnosia and apraxia. Furthermore, the author elucidates how neurological damage and disease processes affect language production and comprehension.

Sarno, Martha Taylor, ed. *Acquired Aphasia.* 2d ed. San Diego: Academic Press, 1991. Contributions to this volume tend to be technical, but the book contains valuable information concerning neurological and linguistic factors associated with aphasia. The chapters on intelligence, artistry, and social sequelae are unique offerings.

*Bruce E. Bailey*

## Cross-References

Brain Injuries: Concussions, Contusions, and Strokes, 448; Brain Specialization, 455; Dementia, Alzheimer's Disease, and Parkinson's Disease, 783; Dyslexia, 849; Language and Cognition, 1401; Neuropsychology, 1667; Speech Disorders, 2342; Speech Perception, 2348.

# ARCHETYPES: ORIGINS AND NATURE

*Type of psychology:* Personality
*Field of study:* Classic analytic themes and issues

*According to Carl Jung, archetypes govern the instinctual patterns of human be-
havior which originate in the deepest layers of the unconscious mind. Archetypes
defy a rigorously scientific, empirical definition and thus form a bridge between
psychology and philosophy, religion, mythology, and anthropology.*

*Principal terms*
> ANIMA and ANIMUS: the archetype which is the feminine part of the
> male psyche (anima) and the masculine part of the female psyche
> (animus)
> ARCHETYPES: universal, inherited themes that exercise an influence on
> virtually all human beings, such as the motifs of the self, hero, and
> shadow
> COLLECTIVE UNCONSCIOUS: the transpersonal or universal and deepest
> layer of the unconscious mind, which is shared by all humankind and
> contains the archetypes
> HERO: the archetype which guides the individual to fight evil, slay the
> dragon, or sacrifice self for others
> INDIVIDUATION: the process by which a person becomes whole and
> unique, involving integration of opposites
> PERSONA: the archetypal social front that a person presents to others
> PERSONAL UNCONSCIOUS: the associated web of memories and emotions
> repressed from consciousness, explicable in terms of the individual's
> life history (not universal or inherited)
> PSYCHE: the total inner world, composed of both conscious and
> unconscious elements
> SELF: the archetype of deity, the master archetype that governs the
> individuation process; for example, the symbol of Christ or Buddha
> SHADOW: the archetype of evil, opposite the conscious ideal of self; for
> example, the devil or villain
> SYMBOL: an image or representation, embodying an archetype, which
> can release or transform psychic energy, for example, the Cross of
> Jesus

## Overview

Most newborn infants readily become very attached to their mothers. When slightly
older, many individuals readily develop a fear of snakes or spiders. Many individuals
also readily accept belief in a supreme being or creator of the universe. If one examines the history, mythology, and experience of people from other times and cultures,

these same tendencies are evident. Carl Jung (1875-1961), a Swiss psychiatrist and contemporary of Sigmund Freud, was deeply puzzled by these cross-cultural and recurrent patterns of behavior. In addition to observing similar recurrent patterns and symbols in the dreams and symptoms of his psychiatric patients, Jung discovered further evidence of "archetypal" patterns in the subject matter of philosophy, religion, art, history, and anthropology. He believed these patterns to be evidence of underlying archetypes in what he termed the collective unconscious.

Jung's investigations led him to postulate two additional parts of the psyche beyond the traditional Freudian model: the archetypes and the collective unconscious. It is impossible to understand the archetypes without some grasp of the personal and collective unconscious. Like Freud, Jung acknowledged a personal unconscious which consists of complexes, or painful ideas and emotions that are repressed and inaccessible to the individual's conscious ego. These repressed ideas and emotions are simply a result of the individual's own personal history. Here, however, is where Jung breaks radically with Freud. Beneath this personal unconscious, Jung postulated a deeper layer of the unconscious which is composed of the archetypes. This collective layer of the unconscious is inferred, based on the idea that the eternal, recurrent themes of mythology, folklore, and art cannot simply be a product of a given individual's particular history. Jung believed that the cross-cultural similarities in myth and symbol between cultures that developed independently was strong evidence for this underlying substratum of the psyche called the collective or transpersonal unconscious.

The collective unconscious consists of primordial images, or archetypes, inherited from primitive man. Archetypes are the fundamental forces operating deep in the collective unconscious and manifested in certain behavior patterns, myths, dreams, and rituals. Jung pointed out that humankind is not unique in displaying patterns of behavior. Beavers display a propensity for dam building, while honeybees display a propensity for honey collection. These behaviors are inherently unconscious. Each species has its own unique patterns of behavior. Despite the fact that these behavior patterns appear to be unconscious, they are purposeful. The behavior of the nest-building robin follows a purpose, of which the robin is hardly conscious. Similarly, the family that decorates a Christmas tree every December may be quite unconscious of creating a death-rebirth archetypal symbol.

Archetypes are not to be confused with animal instincts. Instincts only provide the drive or energy, while archetypes channel the instincts along their appropriate path. The archetypal image expresses the essence or meaning of the instincts in humans. The archetypes represent time-honored solutions through which humans have come to terms with their external world. Archetypes are the inherited predisposition to react to events repeatedly experienced by human ancestors. For example, human ancestors repeatedly came into contact with various poisonous reptiles; consequently, humans have developed an almost biological aversion to reptilian creatures. Note that reptiles often symbolize evil, further suggesting a universal negative reaction to reptiles; Jung suggests that an archetype is at work.

Jung devoted most of the last forty years of his life to investigating and writing about archetypes. Myths, dreams, rituals, creative imagination, and psychotic symptoms are the best source of data for investigating archetypes; however, humankind has moved away from these data sources, while increasingly relying upon scientific and physical explanations of human behavior, to the detriment of an adequate understanding of the psyche. Jung's recognition of the deeper levels of the psyche and the archetypes restores the "soul" to the science of psychology. This restoration of the soul requires that psychology redefine itself to include the data contained in that rich hinterland of the psyche containing the archetypes.

The number of archetypes is equal to the number of typical situations in life. Among the many archetypes that Jung cataloged are the self, shadow, trickster, wise old man, hero, divine child, persona, and anima/animus. Some of these archetypes are of such magnitude that they function as relatively autonomous subsystems in the total personality. These are the hero, persona, shadow, anima/animus, and the self. Several examples of how these specific archetypes can be applied to certain human phenomena will make them more readily understood.

## Applications

The idea of archetypes has been applied primarily in the areas of psychotherapy, mythology, and religion. Jung's analysis of the plight of contemporary humankind provides an excellent example of how the psychology of archetypes may be applied. Jung held that the modern individual is at a distinct disadvantage in establishing an adaptive relationship with the self, the world, and significant others. This disadvantage is a result of the repression of archetypes. Specifically, the archetypes of spirit, shadow, and anima/animus have generally been repressed by materialistic culture. In their obsession with controlling external reality, people have abandoned the inner world of the archetypes. Although this obsession has led to an increase in physical science's understanding and control of the natural world, it has ultimately alienated people from the natural and social worlds. Modern humankind is especially vulnerable to developing psychological disorders as a result of this alienation, Jung would argue; people have banished their gods in exchange for a consumers' paradise. The extroverted success of scientific materialism has occurred at the expense of the total psyche, especially the archetypes and collective unconscious. For this particular form of mass madness, the reintegration of the archetypes may provide a solution. The depth and charisma of the archetypes might compensate for the extroverted superficiality of the modern worldview. Through regaining access to the archetypes, people may regain the inner connections to their own souls. According to Jungian theory, optimal human functioning depends on the courage and inspiration that myth, mediated by the archetypes, alone can provide.

In his popular work *Modern Man in Search of a Soul* (1933), Jung points out that neurotic suffering entails a loss of meaning. This loss has been caused by modern humanity's loss of soul. People no longer have a myth by which to live. Jung thought that the traditional archetypal symbols of Western religion were probably obsolete, similar to polytheism at the time of Jesus. A modern person looks up at the familiar moon and no longer sees a romantic orb, but so much mass surrounded by cold, airless space. This experience of emptiness can be healed by the emergence of archetypes. For countless ages, the individual had beheld a somber moon beneath an infinite sky and cried for meaning. After that cry, through the ages, countless individuals have heard the reply of the Creator of the universe. In other words, they have had an encounter with the archetype of "spirit," which has served to guide, heal, and encourage the individual. Jung believed that the exact form this new myth or embodiment that the God archetype would assume for modern humankind was yet unclear; however, he proposed that the archetype of self contained the answer.

Hence, the Jungian therapist would look for the archetype of self in a patient. Unlike a psychoanalyst or a materialistically minded psychologist, the Jungian would not dismiss the experience of spirit as an infantile wish for a cosmic father figure to protect a neurotic ego. Rather, the experience of spirit would be viewed as a healing possibility for the psyche. The archetype of self functions as a master archetype which guides the individual into the next stage of personality development.

In the Western world, the image of the newborn Jesus often carries the archetype of self or divine child. Thus, in therapy, the Jungian analyst will work with a patient's thoughts and dreams of a newborn child as a symbol that provides a possible solution to the patient's dilemma. It should be noted that although a Jungian conceptualizes religious experience in archetypal terms, this does not in any way invalidate or reduce the experience to a strictly psychological event. For Jung, the archetypal images arise from a level of the psyche which is undifferentiated from the cosmic basis of all life, and consequently a valid expression of ultimate reality.

Jung believed that many neuroses are caused by an improper relationship between the individual's conscious ego and the archetypes. For example, when the archetype of deity is not properly integrated into the psyche, the person may suffer ego inflation. Since the inflated ego knows no god, it may become its own god. The inflated ego insatiably pursues the narrowly defined objectives of prestige, power, and control. The failure to subordinate the conscious ego to the greater reality of the total psyche may lead to addictions, compulsions, and self-destruction. Here the Jungian analyst might help the patient pop the illusory bubble of being the master of his or her own fate by detailed exploration of the unconscious forces which toss the conscious ego about like a small boat on the ocean and demand surrender to a greater reality.

Jung contended that Western society, in its idolatry of achievement-oriented goals, has lost touch with the archetypal world. Consequently, people tend to project their archetypes onto external screens. This is especially true of the shadow archetype. The shadow is the part of one's psyche that is the opposite of all one consciously would like to be. Hence, a religious leader might develop a shadow that is lascivious, unforgiving, and sadistic. Conversely, a prison inmate might have a shadow that is gentle and compassionate, unlike the "tough regular" image that he strives to present to guards and other inmates. Moreover, since the shadow is unconscious in early stages of therapy, a patient is likely to project it onto others. Thus, the patient's own besetting character flaws will only be seen in those around him or her. One of the therapist's goals is to help the patient consciously assimilate the unconscious shadow material rather than project it onto a neighbor. Projecting the shadow can lead to anything from interpersonal mischief to international war.

For example, a religiously self-righteous man might bring a dream to his therapist in which his wife is unfaithful to him. Although the Jungian analyst respects the wisdom of dreams, he or she would be slow to support the idea that the patient's wife has actually been unfaithful to him. Rather, the therapist would carefully explore the patient's inner relationship to the archetypes—in this case, especially the shadow and anima. This exploration of the patient's unconscious shadow material would be done while looking for the patient's own promiscuous sexual wishes that he is projecting onto his wife. The patient's relationship to his own inner feminine side (anima) would also require consideration. Thus, the patient's relationship to his inner world of archetypes would be targeted as being where the real problem resides.

The anima/animus is a prominent archetype. The anima refers to the largely unconscious feminine side of the male psyche, which tends to compensate for consciously male attitudes. The animus is the masculine part of the female psyche, which serves to give assertiveness, logic, and strength to compensate for conscious female qualities. Consider the hypothetical case of "Margaret," who has a recurrent dream in which she tries to lock a strange man out of her home, but he eventually breaks in and physically batters her. The Jungian analyst might consider the message of this dream to be an objective statement about how in the real world, Margaret allows others to push her around. More important, though, if this dream revealed an animus figure trying to enter Margaret's conscious attitudes, the therapist might encourage her to embrace the intruder—that is, to integrate her own inner masculinity. This could be done by cultivating more traditionally male qualities in her everyday behavior—by taking up karate, or by painting the intruder's picture, depending on her interests.

The application of Jung's theory of archetypes has gone beyond the domains of psychotherapy and religion to include alchemy, art, literature, cinema, philosophy, and even the observation of unidentified flying objects (UFOs), or flying saucers, which Jung thought represent a projected archetype of self. An exhaustive account of the range of applications which Jung's theory of the archetypes has found would require volumes. In fact, Jung's collected works span nineteen volumes, which is only a partial compendium of his entire publications and the areas to which he applied his revolutionary ideas.

## Context

Archetypal theory arose in the context of Freudian and behavioristic psychology. Both these approaches to psychology attempted to reduce human behavior, either to biological drives or to environmental determinism. Freud claimed that all behavior is a result of the unconscious interplay of sexual and aggressive drives. The American behaviorism that was present in Jung's time favored environmental learning as the primary determinant of behavior. Jung's theory of archetypes posited causal factors in human behavior not included in the reductionistic theories of his contemporaries. Jung's ideas were both nonreductionistic and more optimistic than those of his peers. His approach to psychology presaged the development of humanistic and transpersonal psychology in the latter part of the twentieth century.

Jung's personal family background sheds some light on his development of a theory which contained possibilities of religious experience. His father was a clergyman from whom Jung appeared to "inherit" religious concerns, if not preoccupations. In Jung's autobiography, *Memories, Dreams, Reflections* (1963), he describes a dream in which a large mass of feces falls from the sky, destroying a church. He interpreted that dream as meaning that orthodox religious beliefs were no longer viable. The cry of the philosopher Friedrich Nietzsche from the nineteenth century, that "God is dead," was heard by Jung in this dream. The theory of archetypes was in part a response to the spiritual crisis Jung underwent. Jung did not think that the institutionalized form of organized religion was necessarily the answer. The solution was for the individual to have an inner, personal experience mediated through the archetypes. Jung seemed to suggest that the archetype of self had replaced the role of the traditional Western God in the modern psyche. Many twentieth century intellectuals have held that Jung was essentially correct in his diagnosis of the ills of modernity.

Jung's place in the history of ideas will probably be outside the realm of academic psychology departments. In fact, the only idea of Jung's to gain much currency in academic psychology has been his distinction between extroversion and introversion. Although Jung is passingly mentioned in most theories-of-personality classes, it is in the departments of religion or English that one occasionally finds an entire course offered on him.

The theory of archetypes in one form or another is likely to endure for centuries to come. It has already been in existence since the time of Plato, in the doctrine of the "forms." The most recent development in the field of psychology is the transpersonal paradigm of psychology, which has heralded Jung as an inspiring forerunner. The theory of archetypes enables a psychologist to conceptualize religious or transpersonal experience in a manner that does not reduce it to a neurotic illusion. In the last decade of the twentieth century, it seems to have occurred to many people that human progress may not best be made by discovering cheaper energy sources or by colonizing Mars. True human progress lies in exploring the frontier of inner space, where Jung's archetypal psychology has already charted some of the most prominent features.

## Bibliography

Campbell, Joseph. *The Hero with a Thousand Faces.* New York: Meridian, 1956. Reviews the many faces of the hero archetype. Considered by many to be a classic in archetypal themes. Folklore, myth, and various rituals are used to explain how the archetypes further individuation. A framework for understanding one's own journey of individuation is provided. Clear, interesting, and written for the general reader.

Jung, Carl Gustav. *The Archetypes and the Collective Unconscious.* 2d ed. Princeton, N.J.: Princeton University Press, 1968. This is volume 9, part 1 of the prestigious Bollingen Series, and Jung's definitive work on the nature and origin of archetypes. Covers the relationship of the archetypes to the collective unconscious. The archetypes of anima, mother, rebirth, child, and individuation are dealt with in considerable depth, with illustrations and clinical examples. For the very serious student of Jung who has already read the basic introductory works.

_____. *Man and His Symbols.* Garden City, N.Y.: Doubleday, 1964. The inspiration for this book came to Jung in a dream which depicted the masses gaining knowledge of his theory. Jung consequently set out to write a book that would popularize his ideas without vulgarizing them. Luxuriously illustrated, this volume is available in an oversize edition that maximizes the effect of the many color images that exemplify Jungian archetypes and symbols. The most accessible account of Jung's thought.

_____. *Modern Man in Search of a Soul.* New York: Harcourt Brace, 1933. This short work covers the basis of Jungian psychology and is recommended by most Jungians as a primer. Jung's approach to psychotherapy, dreams, literature, religion, and the modern crisis are included. Jung puts his ideas into the context of what he sees as the twentieth century bias and its dangers.

_____. *Two Essays on Analytical Psychology.* New York: Meridian, 1956. A solid introduction to the bulk of Jung's theories. Covers the core of Jung's personality theory. If read in combination with Jung's *On the Nature of the Psyche*, gives any interested reader an in-depth and comprehensive introduction to Jung's work. Recommended for the serious scholar.

*Paul August Rentz*

### Cross-References

Analytical Psychology: Carl G. Jung, 240; Analytical Psychotherapy, 246; The Collective Unconscious, 592; Dream Analysis, 830; Humanism: An Overview, 1203; Psychoanalytic Psychology: An Overview, 1905.

# ARCHIVAL DATA

*Type of psychology:* Psychological methodologies
*Fields of study:* Descriptive methodologies; experimental methodologies;
methodological issues

*Archival data, or information already on record, offer several real advantages to resourceful researchers: the saving of time, access to very large quantities of information, and the avoidances of some ethical issues, to list a few. At the same time, use of such data carries with it several real risks, the worst of which is potential inaccuracy.*

*Principal terms*

ARCHIVAL DATA: information collected at an earlier time by someone other than the present researcher, often for purposes very different from those of the present research

EXPERIMENTATION: a research technique in which a scientist changes one aspect of a situation to assess the impact on another aspect

OBSERVATION: a research technique in which a scientist systematically watches for and records occurrences of the phenomena under study without actively influencing them

RELIABILITY: pertaining to data, the degree of consistency of measurements; high reliability is needed to achieve validity

SELF-REPORT MEASURES: techniques such as interviews and questionnaires in which people themselves provide data requested by a researcher

VALIDITY: the extent to which data actually represent what the researcher claims

## Overview

A major part of any research enterprise is the gathering of data—the information from which conclusions will be drawn and judgments made. This gathering can be accomplished in many ways, each with its advantages and drawbacks. Often, by using a combination of methods, a skilled researcher can let the strengths of one method compensate for the weaknesses of another. Which method, or combination of methods, is most appropriate depends on several factors. If research is intended to be only descriptive, the scientist may find observation adequate; if the research is intended to establish cause-and-effect relationships clearly, experimentation is all but essential.

The methods mentioned—observation and experimentation—actively involve the scientist in the gathering of data to be used. This involvement allows considerable control over possible sources of error, but it also limits what can be accomplished. For example, a scientist cannot step back into the past, cannot observe (or experiment with) more than a fairly small number of subjects during most research, and cannot avoid the possibility that the subjects' knowledge that they are involved in research will distort the answers most people give or the behaviors they display. When they can be located and used, archival data eliminate many of these problems for descriptive research and may, because they extend across time, give hints of cause-and-effect relationships typically revealed only by experimentation.

The term "archival data" may first suggest only information shelved in public archives such as courthouse records. Indeed, such a location may hold much useful information, but it is only one of dozens of possibilities. Similarly, data may first suggest only collections of numbers; here again, however, many other possibilities exist. For example, almost sixteen hundred years ago, Aurelius Augustinus, better known as Saint Augustine, wrote his autobiography, *Confessions*, well aware that its contents would fascinate his own and later generations. It seems likely that he also realized that he was presenting more than information about himself to his readers. Personal documents may also be used by contemporary researchers in ways unlikely to have been anticipated by their source. Comparing many autobiographies written over the centuries, a developmental psychologist might today examine how earlier generations behaved during the period now known as "adolescence." A career counselor might examine how people who changed their original occupations in midlife managed to do so.

In recent years, with worldwide distribution of printed material, films, and electronic media, mass communications have been able to serve well as archival data pertaining to hundreds of topics. One problem, however, may be the presence of so much information that a sampling procedure must be devised to decide what to use. A caution regarding the use of mass media as sources can also apply to personal documents and statistical data, to be discussed below. Researchers who today want to extract data from, for example, United States newspaper reports of 1945 must consider the reliability of what they find. If they plan to use the reports as indicators of national public opinion, they must select several newspapers published across the nation. A single newspaper might serve to suggest what its own editor and readers believed, but dozens might be required to suggest national beliefs, and even dozens might not provide what researchers originally sought. If different papers carried very different accounts of an event, or divergent editorials regarding it, researchers might have to focus on differences, rather than unanimity of belief.

In his *Confessions*, Saint Augustine discussed the possibilities that writers might not know something about themselves or might deceitfully state something they know to be untrue. This validity issue also applies to the electronic media and, like differences of opinion across several newspapers, must be dealt with by consulting several independent sources, if they can be located.

Statistical data—measurements or observations converted to numerical form—can be the most immediately useful, yet possibly the most dangerous, archival data for a researcher to use. Most typically in psychological research, information is converted to numbers, the numbers are processed in some manner, and conclusions are drawn. When researchers gather data themselves, they know where the numbers came from, whether they should be considered approximations or precise indicators, and a host of other facts essential to their interpretation. When researchers process archival data—information gathered by others for their own purposes—such information essential to their interpretation is often unknown and must be sought as part of the research.

For example, a psychologist seeking information about the education levels of employees in a company might find it directly available on application blanks on file. If those blanks recorded the applicants' *stated* education levels, however, and there was no evidence that those statements had been verified as a condition of hiring, it would be risky to consider them highly accurate data. Most archival data need to be verified in some manner; how fully this is done should depend upon the degree of certainty needed in the research.

## Applications

Sociologist Émile Durkheim's use of archival data in his classic work *Le Suicide* (1897; *Suicide*, 1951) illustrates how much a master researcher can learn from already available material. Hypothesizing that social factors are key bases for suicide, he first gathered years of suicide records from European countries where they were available, then examined these statistics in the light of additional archival data to evaluate several alternative hypotheses.

Noting that suicide rates increased from January to June, then fell off, he considered the possibility that suicide is influenced by temperature. Finding, again from records, that suicides did not vary directly with temperature increases and decreases, he was drawn back to his favored hypothesis that social factors were of key importance. To elaborate on such factors, he considered religion, family, and political atmosphere, again through archival data.

The advantages that Durkheim gained over limiting himself to data personally gathered were enormous. For example, had he personally interviewed families and friends of suicide victims, far fewer cases would have been available to him, probably ones restricted to a fairly limited geographic area. He also would have been limited by time factors: It seems unlikely that interviewing years after the event would have been possible for most of the cases. Unavoidably, he ran risks in accepting available records as accurate, but he judiciously chose records likely to have been carefully assembled and unlikely to have contained willful distortions. As the world has changed remarkably since Durkheim's day, so have the opportunities to apply archival data to research questions. Part of the change results from there now being more numerous and more varied archives; additionally, there are almost incredible new methods of searching them.

For Durkheim, information that existed in print or still photographs, or could be told to him from someone's memory, was all that was available. For today's researcher, those possibilities remain, and the addition of new, mainly electronic, media since the beginning of the twentieth century has dramatically changed both the form and the amount of archival data in existence. Silent motion pictures, phono-graph records, radio (with transcription discs), sound motion pictures, audio record-ing wire and then tape, television (with video recording tape), and, most recently and most important, computer storage have increased available information almost immeasurably. They have also created the possibilities for finding obscure fragments of data not before available.

Researchers studying attitudes leading to war, for example, have for centuries been able to work with written sources—documents, books, and newspapers. From the early 1900's on, social psychologists could add to those archival sources newsreel footage of political leaders' participation in war-related events, as well as a few phonograph records of their speeches. From the late 1920's on, they could add tran-scriptions (disc recordings) of radio broadcasts and sound motion-picture coverage. From the late 1940's on, they could add films, then television broadcasts and video-tapes of them.

Beginning in the mid-1980's, a new sort of archive emerged, one that allows enor-mous amounts of information to be saved, distributed worldwide, and searched elec-tronically for desired information. Computer storage of data has created a change in the handling of information comparable to the change created centuries ago by the invention of the printing press. Pulling information from storage media ranging from magnetic tape to CD-ROM (compact disc read-only memory) storage, researchers can gain access to libraries of information—from indexes to research literature to archival data—and can sort through it with speed and accuracy never before known.

For example, a researcher with a personal computer equipped with a CD-ROM drive can scan the entire works of William Shakespeare, encyclopedias, atlases, *Bart-lett's Familiar Quotations*, world almanacs, and more, in a fashion that can be consid-ered a modern version of looking for "a needle in a haystack." The old phrase suggests looking for something that exists but is so hidden that chances of finding it are nil. Computer searching is the equivalent of searching the haystack with a power-ful metal detector and electromagnet to pull the needle from the depths of the stack.

Studying attitudes toward old age, for example, a scientist could direct searches for many key words and phrases (old age, elderly, retiree, senile, respected, and so on), some only very remotely related to the topic. The speed and accuracy of digital technology make feasible "needle-in-haystack" searches that were impractical to consider by earlier methods. A world atlas might contain very few age-related refer-ences, but with a search at lightning-speed possible, the one or two references to "retirement" might be worth seeking.

## Context

Although scientific psychology has always taught its students how to generate data through their own research, in no way has it denied them the right to use data al-ready available if the data meet their needs. Like other data, archival data must meet reasonable standards of consistency (reliability) and accuracy (validity), standards not always easy to assess when several sources, perhaps over an extended span of time, have generated the data.

Researchers who use other researchers' data probably have the fewest worries. Since the 1920's, published research standards have been uniform enough that today's readers can clearly understand what was done to produce data, and from that understanding can judge their quality. Researchers who work from personal documents have a more difficult task in determining data quality. What the writers stated might be distorted for a variety of reasons, ranging from intentional deception through the writers themselves not understanding what they reported. If the new researcher is working to assess the personality of an author, for example, checking the internal consistency of the document may be a useful, if not definitive, way of evaluating data quality. If the new researcher is studying some historical event, comparing the diary of one observer with those of others could help validate data obtained.

Researchers who work from mass media, which may carry carelessly assembled or intentionally slanted information, or those who work from public records that might, a century or more ago, have ignored minority populations—or even those who work from a state-of-the-art CD-ROM disc that contains only works written in the English language—have special problems of data accuracy, and each must devise ways of discovering and working around them.

As compensation for the special problems that archival data present, they possess an advantage that all but eliminates worry about "invasion of privacy," often a major ethical issue. By very definition, archival data are already public information, and rarely does new analysis by researchers produce sensitive conclusions. In the rare case where it does, the researcher can simply decide not to report a particular conclusion, and no one has been hurt. By contrast, in certain experimental research, when subjects reveal something that they prefer had remained unknown (perhaps that they would cheat to succeed at some task), the ethical harm is already done if the subjects realize that the experimenter knows of their failing. Not publishing the results cannot remove their discomfort.

## Bibliography

Freud, Sigmund, and William C. Bullitt. *Thomas Woodrow Wilson, Twenty-eighth President of the United States: A Psychological Study.* Boston: Houghton Mifflin, 1967. Written between 1919 and 1932, then revised to the authors' greater satisfaction in 1939, this book was not published until after the death of the late president's wife. To have a "new" book by Freud almost thirty years after his death guaranteed that it would be noticed; not all notice was favorable. As archival research by a major scholar, however, it is unequaled.

Hilgard, Ernest Ropiequet. *Psychology in America: A Historical Survey.* San Diego: Harcourt Brace Jovanovich, 1987. Although "archival data" is not found within Hilgard's index, chapter 15, "Developmental Psychology," discusses infant biographies and other archival sources of developmental data, and chapter 16, "Social Psychology," discusses topics for which archival data are often used. This encyclopedic text can serve to place the topic within the many other research methods available to psychologists.

Langer, Walter Charles. *The Mind of Adolf Hitler.* New York: Basic Books, 1972. A fascinating account of a World War II archival research project that attempted to generate a psychiatric profile of the German leader. (Writing "psychohistory," as this approach has come to be called, is a controversial activity, often condemned by psychologists and historians alike.)

Selltiz, Claire, Marie Johoda, Morton Deutsch, and S. Cook. *Research Methods in Social Relations.* New York: Holt, 1959. Still a rich source of information related to research, this book's ninth chapter, "The Use of Available Data as Source Material," offers excellent detail on the use of archival data. Three other chapters describe in detail other research methods, and one chapter discusses problems of data accuracy. The book should be available in most college and university libraries.

Sherman, Chris, ed. *The CD-ROM Handbook.* New York: McGraw-Hill, 1988. In addition to an explanation of the CD-ROM format and many details of its potential, this handbook includes a thirty-seven-page discography by Steve Holder of about 150 CDs available as of the date of publication. Titles range from the honored *Reader's Guide to Periodical Literature* to such unexpected ones as *Ship Population Disc*, which gives "population and housing characteristics from the 1980 census for all states, regions, metro areas, counties and congressional districts; population estimates for counties annually. . . . estimates by age, race, and sex," as well as population projections "through the year 2000."

*Harry A. Tiemann, Jr.*

### Cross-References

Case-Study Methodologies, 481; Developmental Methodologies, 817; Field Experimentation, 1031; Observational Methods in Psychology, 1700; The Scientific Method in Psychology, 2148.

# ARTIFICIAL INTELLIGENCE

*Type of psychology:* Cognition
*Fields of study:* Cognitive processes; thought

*The development of the digital computer provided a new metaphor for understanding human cognitive processes and a new method for testing psychological theories. Attempts to construct artificially intelligent machines provide insights into human cognitive processes, and psychological data and theories provide insight into the possible production of artificially intelligent machines.*

*Principal terms*

ARTIFICIAL INTELLIGENCE (AI): the endeavor to develop mechanical formal systems capable of producing output that, if produced by a human, would be judged intelligent

COMPUTATION: a process in which one symbol (or set of symbols) is mapped onto another symbol (or set of symbols)

EXPERT SYSTEM: an AI system consisting of a large data base and rules of inference designed to simulate the reasoning and decision making of an expert

MENTAL REPRESENTATION: the form of information during processing or storage by the human cognitive system; information may be represented at several different levels, and the information at each level systematically maps onto prior and subsequent levels

PARALLEL DISTRIBUTED PROCESSING (PDP): a neurally inspired model in which information is processed in a massively parallel and interactive network; the course of processing is determined by the connection strengths between units of the network

SCRIPT: a knowledge structure that contains information about the typical sequence of events, actions, actors, and props involved in a type of event

SYMBOL: an object, sign, pattern, or other type of representation that stands for something else; symbols are usually arbitrary and do not resemble that which they represent

VERBAL PROTOCOL: a transcription of what subjects say as they "think out loud" while attempting to solve a problem

## Overview

For most of recorded history, humans have been the only cognitive, sentient entities of which humans themselves were aware. Beginning in the 1940's, some theorists began to speculate that computers might be capable of humanlike thought. This view was philosophically defensible; for example, seventeenth century philosopher

René Descartes had suggested that the test of intelligence, of sentience, was the ability to calculate. Given that computers are calculating machines par excellence, questions arise whether computers may be useful in understanding human intelligence and whether computers possess "intelligence" in their own right. Although these questions are relevant throughout the cognitive sciences, the field of artificial intelligence (AI) is a key discipline in their investigation.

Computers input information, make decisions based on the input, store some or all of the input, create new expressions, and output the result. Computers are not mere "number crunchers"; rather, they manipulate symbols (including, but not limited to, numerical symbols), arbitrary representations that stand for something else. Spoken and written languages are excellent examples of symbol systems; for example, the letters *c*, *h*, *a*, *i*, and *r*, or the vibrations created in the air when those letters are pronounced, do not resemble something to be sat upon (the symbol is arbitrary), but those symbols are nevertheless understood by one who speaks English as denoting something upon which a person may sit. Similarly, people take in information, remember and transform it, make decisions, and translate these internal states into outward behavior. In fact, Ulric Neisser defined cognitive psychology as the study of how sensory input is "transformed, reduced, elaborated, stored, recovered, and used." By analogy, the symbols 2, +, and 2, can be inputted into a computer, and the computer will respond by producing the symbol 4. Thus, with computers, scientists had machines that seemed to behave as humans do, but because computers are machines, they could take them apart, change their programs, and do many things they could not do with humans. If researchers understood how computers computed, some theorists suggested, perhaps that would provide insight into how humans compute.

Considering humans as "computing" various functions and human cognition as "computational" has important implications. For example, how computers compute some tasks (such as statistical analyses or determining moves in chess) is usually explained at the software, or program, level ("it wants to get its queen out early"), not at the hardware level (circuits and silicon chips, "a given gate open or closed"). By analogy, an understanding of how a human "computes" some mental task could be specified at the software level (mental and cognitive processes) rather than at the hardware level (neurons and cell bodies). A focus on cognitive or computational processes (that is, on mental processes inside the organism) is diametrically opposed to behaviorism, which focuses on external factors, and reductionism, which emphasizes a lower level of description.

Some programmers have attempted to produce programs capable of engaging in meaningful dialogue with humans and have suggested that if a computer responds as a human would, this would be sufficient to establish that the computer itself, with the appropriate program, is intelligent. The Turing test (named for Alan Turing, a British mathematician during the 1930's) involves placing two people and a computer in three different rooms. These three participants are allowed to communicate via keyboards and printers. One human asks questions of the other two participants and must determine, based solely on the answers, which participant is the computer and which is the other human. If the questioner cannot distinguish between the computer and the other human, then the computer has passed the Turing test. In such a case, if one attributes intelligent thought, cognitive processes, understanding, and so forth to the human, then one should also attribute these qualities to the computer. Thus, a human and a computer could conceivably run equivalent programs, resulting in equivalent information processing, or "thoughts." The goal of psychology, under this approach, becomes to determine the programs governing human action, and intelligence becomes a function of the execution of a given program—and not of the mechanism that executes that program. Such an approach is referred to as functionalism; the contemporary use of this term differs from that during the early history of psychology.

Within contemporary AI, there are two primary approaches: general all-purpose programs that simulate intelligent behavior in a large number of areas, and expert systems, which perform like human experts in some very limited domain. In general, expert systems differ from general cognitive programs in two ways. Expert systems contain very large data bases (based on the assumption that experts have considerable knowledge about their field), and expert systems do not necessarily attempt to emulate the way human beings appear to solve a problem. While many of the general all-purpose programs are psychologically based and attempt to model the processes of human cognition, many expert systems do not have psychological modeling as a goal.

## Applications

A number of expert systems in different areas have been developed. One early program, DENDRAL, identifies organic compounds based on mass spectrographic analysis. Another early expert system, MYSIN, diagnoses bacterial infections and recommends treatments. An expert system used in legal reasoning, HYPO (for "hypothetical") generates hypothetical cases and aids legal experts in evaluating cases, arguments, and consequences. A final example involves AM, which models mathematical discovery and includes a rich base of data and explicit rules for discovery. As expert systems, these are not necessarily concerned with psychological processes.

Allan Newell and Herbert Simon have developed general programs explicitly based on psychological data and theory. With Cliff Shaw, Newell and Simon gave the first evidence that intelligent procedures could be implemented in computers with their 1956 program Logic Theorist (LT). LT devised proofs for many basic theorems of mathematics and, in one case, produced a proof more elegant than one previously proposed by Alfred North Whitehead and Bertrand Russell. LT worked by procedures that were, according to Newell and his coworkers, modeled after those of human problem solvers.

After the success of LT, Newell and Simon sought a program to solve not only logical proofs but also problems from a variety of domains. Human subjects were asked to "think out loud" as they solved various types of problems and puzzles, and transcripts of what subjects said (referred to as verbal protocols) provided information used in constructing a program that would purportedly solve problems in the same way that these humans had. This program, the General Problem Solver (GPS), ultimately utilized means-ends analysis—that is, it solved smaller subgoals en route to reaching its larger primary goal. If the main goal is not immediately attainable, GPS determines what is obstructing attainment of the goal and what must be done to remove the obstruction, then sets as a subgoal the removal of the obstruction. GPS was implemented using "production systems," or "if-then" pairs in which the "then" actions would be executed if the "if" conditions were satisfied.

While Newell, Simon, and their colleagues were developing GPS, other researchers were focusing on programs dealing with more specific domains. One program, PARRY, written by Kenneth Colby, models personality disorders. A similar program, ELIZA, was written by Joseph Weizenbaum and models a Rogerian therapist. Both PARRY and ELIZA scan the input for certain key words or phrases (such as "father" or "I"). If a key is found, the input is transformed or a stock reply is given (if "father" is in the input, the computer responds, WHAT ELSE COMES TO MIND ABOUT YOUR FATHER?). If no key is found, then the computer gives a "content-free" response such as TELL ME MORE or WHY DO YOU THINK THAT?).

In the late 1970's, a different approach to understanding linguistic material came from researchers developing programs capable of understanding narrative text. Roger Schank and Robert Abelson introduced the idea of a script—a set of events, objects, and actors that one can expect in a given setting, such as visiting a restaurant or a doctor's office—and suggested that scripts could be useful in both understanding human intelligence and developing artificial intelligence programs. For example, when people visit a restaurant, they have expectations regarding the order of events and what they and others are supposed to do. A restaurant script containing this information could be input into a computer, and the computer could then be given the following information: "John went to a restaurant. He sat down. He got mad. He left." The computer will then produce the following paraphrase:

> John was hungry. He decided to go to a restaurant. He went to one. He sat down in a chair. A waiter did not go to the table. John became upset. He decided he was going to leave the restaurant. He left it.

The program makes a number of inferences concerning information not explicitly stated in the input, such as "A waiter did not go to the table." Humans make the same types of inferences; in fact, a script is a type of memory schema.

An important early effort in artificial vision, SHRDLU, was published by Terry Winograd in 1972. SHRDLU's world was a limited domain of blocks of various sizes, shapes, and colors that could be moved, stacked, and piled in various ways. SHRDLU could reply to questions about its world, execute commands on its world, and report the results of its actions. Unlike previous vision programs, SHRDLU was provided with a rudimentary "understanding" of its world and was able to draw on this knowledge in responding to questions and manipulating objects. For example,

SHRDLU asks for clarification when given ambiguous input, learns new structural forms (such as steeple), and properly interprets and keeps track of pronoun references. Other examples of visual AI programs include Adolfo Guzman's SEE, which identifies objects and regions belonging to various objects by examination of vertices and angles at which vertices intersect, and David Marr's programs on stereo matching—comparing inputs from the two "eyes," noting the differences, and using this information to compute distances of the objects from the observer.

During the 1980's, many AI programs shifted from a serial approach to a more parallel approach. In parallel approaches, the information relevant to a given concept is not stored with that concept but is distributed across an entire network; this approach is often referred to as "parallel distributed processing" (PDP, also referred to as "neural nets"). PDP programs specify a network of units which are typically layered to reflect different levels of organization. For example, in James McClelland and Jeffrey Elman's 1986 TRACE model of speech perception, the model is organized into three levels of perceptual units (features, phonemes, and words), and the connections between units at different levels and units within the same level are the critical parameters. Input to the program involves activation, or stimulation, of units at the lowest (typically feature) level, and activation then spreads through excitatory and inhibitory connections throughout the network. Similar structures are found in a variety of other programs, such as David Rumelhart's HEARSAY model of reading (feature, letter, word, syntactic, semantic), James McClelland's PABLO model of reading (letter, word, central letter, central word), and Jamshed Bharucha's MUSACT model of harmony (tone, chord, and key).

## Context

Since the time of Descartes, mind and body have been considered separate. The stuff of thought has not been considered in the same kind of rigorous or theoretical terms that described biological or physical substances. The "mind-body problem" was solved (or, rather, ignored) during the behaviorist era by reducing mind to brain or denying the existence of mind entirely. Computer science and AI provided an alternative approach—mental representations could be represented by symbols and cognitive processes as manipulations of those symbols. Psychology could then construct rigorous theoretical statements for hypothetical mental processes, and mental activities could be described in terms as concrete and quantifiable as the atoms and molecules of physical chemistry.

Contemporary cognitive psychology draws much inspiration from computer science; for example, the fields share a common vocabulary, including terms such as memory registers, buffers, and information processing. The computer became a new metaphor in psychology, and psychological theories are increasingly simulated on computers and evaluated, in part, by the way they perform on these simulations. There are, however, caveats when considering whether human cognition is equivalent to or can be simulated by computer processing. First, computers are still primarily digital, high-speed serial processing devices, whereas significant portions of the human brain and central nervous system operate in parallel. Second, aspects of cognition that are not computational or do not work in a computational fashion might be ignored by computational approaches; for example, verbal protocols access only information available in a verbal form, so nonverbal forms of representation, (such as imagery), might not be adequately represented in computational models based on verbal protocols. Third, studies of human problem solving and reasoning show that humans use a variety of heuristics and are influenced by contextual factors that should not influence purely logical systems. The defense can certainly be made, however, that these difficulties are only temporary and that better engineering will overcome these differences. The issues remain open.

The value of AI programs in providing psychological theories has been questioned from both inside and outside AI. From inside AI, David Marr has suggested that an adequate psychology should include explanations at three levels: computational, algorithmic, and hardware. The computational level provides an abstract formulation of the task (in vision, for example, mapping the two-dimensional retinal image onto a three-dimensional cognitive model), the algorithmic level concerns how that task is realized (the program), and the hardware level concerns the physical instantiation of the other levels (such as the neuron or silicon chip). Marr regarded the computational level as fundamental because it determines questions asked by the other levels, but he suggested that much work in AI has proceeded in the absence of a computational theory and is thus relatively useless. According to Marr, without a computational-level formulation, AI is irrelevant to psychology and psychology itself is a mere assortment of unrelated facts. From outside AI, philosopher John Searle has forcefully argued that while computers can execute the proper commands in manipulating symbols (syntax), they have no understanding of what those symbols mean (semantics).

Some theorists (among them Newell and Simon, Schank and Abelson) claim that a computer running the appropriate program understands in the same way a human understands and has cognitive states, such as beliefs, in the same way a human has cognitive states; other theorists (Colby, Searle, and Weizenbaum) disagree. Even if computers that appear intelligent can be developed, however, they need not achieve their intelligence through procedures similar to those of humans or experience all the concomitants of human intelligence. Metaphors have a way of changing, and as technology has changed and improved, the metaphors of mind have included hydraulic systems, telephone switchboards, and digital computers. While the computer metaphor has certainly been useful, there is no consensus that it should be taken more literally than a metaphor. Indeed, the computer may not be the final metaphor for the mind, as it is quite conceivable that future theory, science, and technology might provide better (or at least different) metaphors. For the moment, however, computer science and AI do promise insight into the human mind.

## Bibliography

Boden, Margaret A. *Artificial Intelligence and Natural Man.* 2d ed. New York: Basic

Books, 1987. An excellent introduction to early attempts at artificial intelligence, including detailed discussions of "neurotic" programs, SHRDLU, SEE, learning programs, and the psychological, philosophical, and social implications of artificial intelligence.

——————. *Computer Models of Mind.* New York: Cambridge University Press, 1988. Examines attempts to simulate human cognition on computers and to use humans as models for building intelligent machines. Boden examines computer models in a wide range of areas, including vision, language, and reasoning.

Born, Rainer, ed. *Artificial Intelligence: The Case Against.* New York: St. Martin's Press, 1987. This collection of essays presents the views of a variety of philosophers, psychologists, and computer scientists on the nature and future of artificial intelligence.

Haugeland, John. *Artificial Intelligence: The Very Idea.* Cambridge, Mass.: MIT Press, 1985. A very readable accounting of the nature of formal systems and some of the central issues and definitions of artificial intelligence.

McClelland, J. L., and D. E. Rumelhart, eds. *Parallel Distributed Processing: Explorations in the Microstructure of Cognition.* Vol. 2. Cambridge, Mass.: MIT Press, 1986. Provides examples of PDP models of schemata, speech perception, and reading, and discusses other potential applications of the PDP approach. The chapters are long and detailed, and readers may find the text daunting.

Marr, David. *Vision.* New York: W. H. Freeman, 1982. Presents Marr's philosophical approach to AI and discusses his programs for the perception of surfaces. The book is well illustrated, but once Marr finishes his discussion of the philosophical approach, some readers may get lost in the mathematics and technicalities of his ideas.

Pylyshyn, Z. W. *Computation and Cognition.* Cambridge, Mass.: MIT Press, 1984. Pylyshyn presents the case that cognition is a form of computation and that human mental representations can be encoded in the same way that computer representations are encoded. Explains how a computational view can provide a foundation and framework for both cognitive psychology and artificial intelligence.

Searle, John R. *Minds, Brains, and Science.* Cambridge, Mass.: Harvard University Press, 1984. In a very readable style, Searle summarizes his argument that computers do not possess an understanding of semantics, addresses the larger mind-body problem, and discusses the implications of his views for the social and cognitive sciences.

Weizenbaum, Joseph. *Computer Power and Human Reason.* New York: W. H. Freeman, 1976. The creator of the ELIZA program argues that some aspects of the human mind cannot be understood in information-processing (computational) terms. Weizenbaum also claims there are many tasks in which computers should not be used, particularly those requiring human reason, wisdom, or morality. Written in an easy and engaging style.

*Timothy L. Hubbard*

## Cross-References

# ATTACHMENT AND BONDING IN INFANCY AND CHILDHOOD

*Type of psychology:* Developmental psychology
*Fields of study:* Infancy and childhood; interpersonal relations

*Bonding and attachment are two theoretical constructs that psychologists have used to describe and explain the intense emotional tie that develops between a caregiver and child. Research has helped psychologists to explain the development of several common social behaviors in infancy and to use individual differences in infant behavior to predict aspects of later development.*

### Principal terms

APPROACH BEHAVIORS: infant behaviors that bring the infant closer to the mother, such as clinging, non-nutritional sucking, and following

ATTACHMENT BEHAVIORS: a general term used to describe any infant behavior that serves to bring the caregiver and infant into closer contact

AVOIDANCE: an infant response to the return of a caregiver following a brief period of separation; involves ignoring the mother and showing no sign of positive or negative affect

FELT SECURITY: an infant's sense of security in the availability and predictability of the caregiver; the ultimate goal of the infant's developing attachment to the caregiver

RESISTANCE: an infant response to the return of a caregiver following a brief period of separation; includes signs of ambivalence about seeking and maintaining contact with the caregiver and evidence of anger

SEPARATION PROTEST: an infant's negative response to the departure of a caregiver, most often evidenced in fussing, crying, and clinging

SIGNALLING BEHAVIORS: infant behaviors that bring the mother closer to the child, such as crying, babbling, and clinging

"STRANGE SITUATION": an experimental technique designed to measure the quality of the mother-infant attachment relationship

STRANGER ANXIETY: the negative reaction of an infant to an approaching stranger, most often expressed as fussing or crying

## Overview

Bonding refers to the development of an emotional tie of the mother to the infant. This biologically based process is believed to occur in mothers shortly after the birth of an infant, a time period during which the mother's intense emotional response is triggered by contact with her newborn. The existence of such a bond is then evidenced in the mother's behavior. Attachment, on the other hand, refers to a relation-ship between the caregiver and infant that develops over the infant's first year of life; the quality of the attachment is apparent in the behavior of the infant.

Evidence for the biologically based bonding process has been inconsistent. In contrast, there exists considerable scientific evidence to support the notion of attach-ment. Thus, the remainder of this discussion will focus on the development of the attachment relationship.

The work of British psychiatrist John Bowlby played an important role in the acceptance and understanding of the notion of mother-infant attachment. Bowlby argued that the behaviors of infants are not random and that, in fact, some of the behaviors exhibited most commonly by infants actually serve a single goal. Specifi-cally, he argued that the infant behaviors of crying, babbling, smiling, clinging, non-nutritional sucking, and following all play an important role in bringing the infant into close contact with the caregiver. He believed that, for the infant, seeking and maintaining proximity to the caregiver are essential for survival because the infant is dependent upon the caregiver for food, shelter, and protection. Thus, the infant's behavior is organized and goal-directed. During early infancy, however, this goal is neither understood nor learned by the infant. Rather, humans are born with a biolog-ical predisposition to engage in certain behaviors that aid in the maintenance of proximity to the caregiver. Thus, the goal of maintaining proximity is built into the human infant, as are some initial behaviors that serve the function of achieving that goal. With further development, the infant becomes more aware of the goal, and therefore his or her behaviors become more intentional.

The infant's emotional state is also believed to play an important role in attempts to seek and maintain proximity to the caregiver. That is, the infant's behavior is dependent upon his or her sense of emotional security. For example, as long as a child is in the immediate presence of the attachment figure, or within easy reach, the child feels secure and may then attend to important developmental tasks such as exploration of the environment, using the mother as a secure base from which to explore. Upon the threat of loss of the attachment figure, however, the infant may lose that sense of security and may exhibit attachment behaviors designed to in-crease the proximity of the attachment figure. Thus, the infant's attempts to seek or maintain proximity to the caregiver are determined by how secure he or she feels with the caregiver in a specific environment.

The attachment relationship and the infant's sense of security develop over the period of infancy. Bowlby has described four phases in the development of the at-tachment to the caregiver. In phase one, the newborn shows limited discrimination of people and therefore exhibits no preferential or differential behaviors, thus behaving in a friendly manner toward all people. In phase two, the eight- to twelve-week-old infant shows the ability to discriminate the caregiver from others but exhibits no preferential behavior toward the caregiver. In phase three, which generally appears at approximately seven or eight months of age, the infant clearly discriminates the care-giver from other people and begins to show preferential treatment toward him or her.

For example, the infant begins to follow a departing mother, greets mother upon her return, and uses her as a base from which to explore an unfamiliar environment. Furthermore, during phase three, the infant begins to treat strangers with caution and may withdraw from a stranger. In phase four, the child maintains a "goal-directed partnership" with the caregiver, a more complex relationship in which the child is acquiring some insight into the caregiver's own feelings and motives, and thus interacts with the caregiver as a partner. This final phase is not apparent in most children until after age two.

## Applications

During the second half of the first year of life (after about eight months of age), infants begin to show very clear attempts at exploration when their mothers are present. In fact, research reported by Mary Ainsworth in the mid-1970's suggests that once an infant is able to crawl, he or she does not always remain close to the mother. Instead, the child begins to move away from the mother, more carefully exploring objects and people. From time to time he or she returns to her, as if to check her whereabouts or to check in with her. If the mother moves away, however, or if the infant is frightened by some event, he or she will either approach the mother or will signal to bring the mother in closer proximity. For example, the infant often fusses, cries, and clings to the caregiver at the first sign of the caregiver's possible departure, a response known as separation protest. At about the same time, infants begin to express stranger anxiety or stranger wariness by fussing and crying when an unfamiliar person enters the room or approaches.

Ainsworth designed a special laboratory technique, known as the "strange situation," that allows direct observation of the interactions between the behaviors associated with exploration, attachment, separation protest, and stranger anxiety. This situation places an infant in an unfamiliar setting with a stranger, both in the presence and in the absence of the mother. The procedure consists of a series of three-minute episodes (the process lasts a total of about twenty minutes) in which the child is exposed to an unfamiliar playroom containing a set of age-appropriate toys. During the initial episodes, the mother remains in the playroom with the infant. Mother and infant are then joined in the playroom by a female stranger, who first talks to the mother, then approaches the baby. Next, the mother leaves the room, and the baby and stranger are left alone together. Mother then returns and the stranger leaves, so that the baby is reunited with the mother. Following this episode, the baby is left alone in the room, then joined by the stranger; finally, the mother again returns and the stranger leaves.

This strange situation, therefore, exposes a child to three potentially upsetting experiences: separation from the caregiver, contact with a stranger, and unfamiliar surroundings. The episodes are arranged in such a way that they present a series of stressful experiences to the infant and thus present an opportunity to observe not only the infant's immediate response to a stranger and to separation from the mother, but also his or her ability to derive comfort from the mother and to use her as a secure base for exploration.

Ainsworth has reported that, while there are many similarities in infant responses to this strange situation, there are also important individual differences. In her initial study of twelve-month-old infants and their mothers, Ainsworth reported three distinct patterns of responding to the events of the strange situation, and the validity of these behavior patterns has been demonstrated by much additional research.

A majority of the infants exhibited active exploration of the new environment and the available toys when their mothers were present. Some of these infants showed distress during the first separation from mother, and by the second separation, the majority of these infants expressed distress. Upon reunion with their mother, they actively sought contact with her and were easily comforted by her, showing considerable signs of positive emotion but very little, if any, signs of negative emotion. Furthermore, these infants frequently returned to play and exploration after a period of contact with their mother. In general, then, these infants used their mothers as a secure base from which to explore the novel environment, exhibited appropriate attachment behaviors following her departure, and were easily comforted by the mother upon her return. Ainsworth suggested that this pattern of behavior reflects a secure attachment relationship.

A second group of infants showed a very different pattern of behavior. This minority group showed no evidence of distress during separation. They did sometimes show distress when left alone in the playroom but were easily comforted by the returning stranger. Furthermore, this group actually avoided or ignored their mothers when they returned. In essence, the mothers were treated very much as were the strangers. These infants showed virtually no signs of separation protest or stranger anxiety and exhibited very few attachment behaviors. Ainsworth suggested that this pattern of behavior reflects an insecure, avoidant attachment relationship.

Finally, a third group of children were extremely distressed upon separation yet, despite their obvious separation and stranger anxiety, resisted comfort from their mothers. Their behavior suggested an angry ambivalence—they objected to being left alone, but they refused to be consoled when reunited with their mothers. This group of infants often exhibited distress upon first entering the unfamiliar room with their mothers, and they rarely left her side to explore the toys or the environment, either before or after separation, suggesting a lack of a sense of security. Ainsworth suggested that this behavior pattern reflects an insecure, resistant, or ambivalent attachment relationship.

The development of these distinct patterns of attachment is believed to be the result of the history of interaction between the caregiver and infant. Specifically, attachment theory suggests that responsive and consistent caregiving results in a secure mother-infant attachment, unresponsive caregiving results in an avoidant attachment, and inconsistent caregiving results in a resistant/ambivalent attachment. The "avoidant" mother has been described as cold and disliking physical contact with the infant, who responds by acting aloof and avoiding social interaction. The "resistant" mother, on the other hand, has been described as unpredictable, sometimes responding but sometimes not, and the infant often responds with anger and ambivalence.

As the infant matures, the specific behaviors that indicate the existence of the attachment relationship may change. The research evidence strongly suggests, however, that such individual differences in the quality of the mother-infant attachment relationship are predictive of later behavior. For example, infants who exhibit secure attachment patterns at one year of age have been found to be more cooperative with adults, to show greater enthusiasm for learning, to be more independent, and to be more popular with their peers during the preschool years. Thus, the quality of the mother-infant attachment relationship may have long-range effects. This does not mean that the child's future is determined solely by the quality of the attachment relationship. The evidence indicates that certain negative consequences of an insecure attachment relationship may be overcome by changes in the nature of the child's important relationships.

## Context

The existence of a mother-infant attachment relationship has been recognized for many years. For most of those years, however, psychologists explained the development of this attachment by way of traditional learning theory. That is, behaviorists argued that the infant-mother attachment develops because mothers are associated with the powerful, reinforcing event of being fed. In this way, the mother becomes a conditioned reinforcer. This reinforcement theory of attachment, however, came into question as a result of the work of Harry and Margaret Harlow in the early 1960's.

The Harlows' work was not with human infants but with infant rhesus monkeys. They removed newborn monkeys from their mothers at birth and raised them in the laboratory with two types of artificial or surrogate mothers. One surrogate mother was made of terrycloth and could provide "contact comfort." The other surrogate mother was made of wire. A feeding bottle was attached to one of the substitute mothers for each of the monkeys. Half of the monkeys were fed by the wire mother; the other half were fed by the cloth mother. This allowed the Harlows to compare the importance of feeding to the importance of contact comfort for the monkeys.

In order to elicit attachment behaviors, the Harlows introduced some frightening event, such as a strange toy, into the cages of the young monkeys. They expected that if feeding were the key to attachment, then the frightened monkeys should have run to the surrogate mother that fed them. This was not the case, however: All the young monkeys ran to their cloth mothers and clung to them, even if they were not fed by them. Only the cloth mothers were able to provide security for the frightened monkeys. The Harlows concluded that a simple reinforcement explanation of attachment was inaccurate and that the contact comfort, not the food, provided by a mother plays a critical role in the development of attachment.

This research provided the impetus for the development of Bowlby's ethological account of attachment. Since that time, research by Mary Ainsworth and Alan Sroufe, as well as many others, has provided important information for the continuing development of understanding of the complex relationship between caregivers and infants.

# Bibliography

Ainsworth, Mary D. Salter, Mary C. Blehar, Everett Waters, and S. Wall. *Patterns of Attachment*. Hillsdale, N.J.: Lawrence Erlbaum, 1978. Outlines, in general terms, the development of Bowlby's attachment theory. Describes in detail the procedures and scoring techniques for the strange situation and describes the patterns of behavior associated with the secure, avoidant, and resistant attachments. Discusses the research that addresses the antecedents of individual differences in the attachment relationship.

Bowlby, John. *Attachment and Loss*. 2d ed. New York: Basic Books, 1982. Examines the theoretical foundation of the attachment construct and discusses attachment behavior. Outlines the development, maintenance, and function of attachment in both humans and animals.

Crockenberg, S. B. "Infant Irritability, Mother Responsiveness, and Social Support Influences on the Security of Infant-Mother Attachment." In *Contemporary Readings in Child Psychology*. 3d ed., compiled by E. Mavis Hetherington and Ross D. Parke. New York: McGraw-Hill, 1988. Describes a research project that shows that infant characteristics, such as infant temperament, as well as maternal responsiveness, can influence the development of the mother-infant attachment relationship. Also shows that the availability of social support to the mother can influence the development of attachment.

Damon, William. *Social and Personality Development*. New York: W. W. Norton, 1983. This textbook is an introduction to the social development of the child. Contains an excellent discussion of attachment theory and presents many clear, concise examples of infant and child attachment behaviors. Relates the development of attachment behavior to other important developments in infancy and early childhood.

Dunn, Judy. *Distress and Comfort*. Cambridge, Mass.: Harvard University Press, 1977. Addresses questions commonly asked by parents about infant and child distress. Outlines the development of separation protest and stranger anxiety and discusses the importance of parental behavior in the continuing emotional development of the child.

Lamb, Michael E., and Joseph J. Campos. *Development in Infancy*. New York: Random House, 1982. A comprehensive textbook on infant development that presents a variety of theories of infant emotional development.

*Loretta A. Reiser-Danner*

# Cross-References

# ATTENTION

*Type of psychology:* Consciousness
*Field of study:* Cognitive processes

*Humans are not able to be fully conscious of everything around them simultaneously; attention refers to a person's selection of only some of a number of things of which a person could be conscious. Studies have provided information on what things enter consciousness and how a person selects those things.*

*Principal terms*
BOTTOM-UP: a term describing attentional capture that starts with small units (features)
DICHOTIC LISTENING: a technique in which two different messages are simultaneously played through earphones, with a different message to each ear
EARLY SELECTION: attentional selection that occurs immediately following sensory registration, before the meaning of an input can be determined
FEATURE INTEGRATION THEORY: a theory in which focused attention is described as the "glue" that binds separate features into a unitary object
FILTERING: attending to a single source of information on the basis of its sensory properties
FOCUSED ATTENTION: attention directed toward only a single source of information or a single perceptual task
ILLUSORY CONJUNCTION: an inappropriate combination of features, according to feature integration theory
LATE SELECTION: attentional selection that occurs after the meaning of the input is determined
SHADOWING: the technique of asking listeners to repeat the verbal input they are receiving, usually in a particular ear
TOP-DOWN: a term describing voluntary attentional capture that starts with higher-level information such as expectations or context

## Overview

Attention usually refers to concentrating upon a particular aspect of the external environment, although it is possible to attend to one's own thoughts and other internal states. The flavor of the typical use of the term is captured in a statement by nineteenth century German physiologist Hermann von Helmholtz, who noted that an observer may be steadily gazing at a fixation mark, yet at the same time can concentrate attention upon any given part of the visual field. The point in space to which one is directing one's eyes and the point to which one is attending thus are not necessarily the same, and one does not have to move the eyes to shift visual attention.

Attention has long been considered an important topic in psychology. William James devoted a chapter to attention in his *The Principles of Psychology* (1890). He noted that attention can be involuntary and effortless, or else voluntary and effortful. According to James, attention allows people to perceive, conceive, distinguish, and remember better than they otherwise could. Edward Titchener, in his *Lectures on the Elementary Psychology of Feeling and Attention* (1908), reinforced this point by stating that attention determines what people are conscious of as well as the clarity of their conscious experience.

Attention can be drawn automatically (involuntarily and effortlessly) by certain characteristics of stimuli in the environment. These include abrupt brightness changes or vivid colors at particular locations; both intensity and clarity are important. Auditory attention is automatically drawn by changes in pitch or location. Such automatic attentional capture is often termed "bottom-up" or "data-driven." A person readily attends to familiar stimuli, although these more often invoke voluntary and effortful processing—that which is "top-down" or "internally driven." A person can voluntarily attend to any aspect of the environment the person chooses.

How does a person select the things to which he or she will attend? This question leads to a consideration of "early" (before meaning is analyzed) versus "late" selection. Donald Broadbent, in 1958, championed the view that selection is made early through a process analogous to filtering incoming information according to its sensory properties. For example, after a brief glimpse, a person can report the identity of items in the environment accurately if a cue indicating which items to report refers to their spatial location, but much less accurately if it refers to semantic properties (for example, asks for only the letters from a display of several letters and digits intermixed).

Other researchers, such as J. Anthony Deutsch and Diana Deutsch, have argued that people unconsciously analyze all incoming information for its meaning, although selection cannot be made on this basis as easily as on a sensory basis. Support for late selection is forthcoming in tasks such as naming the ink colors of printed letters. J. Ridley Stroop found that if the letters form a word that is the name of a color different from the ink color (for example, the word "blue" written in red ink), it takes much longer to name the ink color than if the combination of letters is meaningless (in the example, a row of red $X$'s). People cannot avoid reading the word, no matter how hard they try. Thus, word meaning appears to be activated automatically, and people cannot selectively attend to the color. Nevertheless, if the color to be named appears as a patch, separated in space from the inconsistent color word, color naming is not slowed. Selection of what to attend to thus can be made easily on the basis of location, color, or brightness, but not on the basis of meaning.

Attention is necessary because people do not have the capacity to be conscious of all aspects of their environment at once. Questions arise concerning the extent to which people can be conscious of more than one aspect simultaneously, and if so, of what aspects they can be simultaneously conscious. Because what is to be attended to can so easily be selected on the basis of its location, these questions often have been posed in relation to whether people can attend to nonadjacent areas simultaneously.

It is important first to point out that the observations of von Helmholtz, James, and Titchener have been verified in sensitive laboratory experiments. Subjects gazing at the center of a computer screen were first given information about the spatial location on the screen of a target that would later appear away from fixation. The correct location usually was indicated, but sometimes an incorrect location was indicated. In comparison with instances when no location information was shown, detection of the target was aided by valid information but harmed by invalid information. If the target did not appear in the indicated location, however, detection was better when it appeared near the indicated location than when it appeared farther away. The edges of the attended area thus are vaguely rather than sharply defined. Yet can attention be split between nonadjacent locations? Most research has shown that this is not possible; people cannot attend to two separate areas simultaneously, although a few studies have indicated that they can attend to ringlike areas with attention devoted to the ring but not the surrounding area nor the center.

In contrast to splitting visual attention between two separate locations, dividing attention between two different senses is possible. People can, for example, listen (attend) to a conversation while watching (attending to) the road when driving. Nevertheless, unless one of the tasks is very easy or highly practiced, performance still suffers in comparison to when attention is dedicated to one sense.

Directing attention on the basis of spatial location appears to be very important. Ulric Neisser described the visual determination of what is present as occurring rapidly in two stages. The first he called "preattentive" because it involves only a rough, global analysis of information in the entire visual field, before attention is directed to any one location. People can detect simple visual features such as color, brightness, and the direction in which a straight line points on the basis of preattentive analysis. More precise determination of combinations of these simple features requires what is called "focal attention," in which attention is focused on particular spatial locations containing the preattentively detected simple features. For example, seeing that a line in a particular orientation is of a certain color requires focal attention. Without it, a person could tell that the color is present somewhere, and that a line of that orientation is present somewhere, but not that the line is of that color. Focal attention therefore is required to combine simple features.

This feature integration theory has received experimental confirmation in the work of Anne Treisman and her colleagues. They found that when focal attention is diverted or cannot be applied because of an interfering task, simple features are often matched incorrectly to produce what they termed "illusory conjunctions." For example, when a red horizontal line and a green vertical one are shown, in the absence of focal attention, a subject is likely to be conscious of the horizontal line as green and the vertical line as red.

A person can direct attention on bases other than a spatial one. That is, even overlapping shapes can be selectively attended. Neisser has described a study in which a basketball game and a hand slapping game were shown simultaneously in outline form in the same location on a television screen. Observers could attend to only one game and indicate each occurrence of some event (for example, a throw of the ball from one player to another) as well when both games were shown as when only the relevant one was shown alone. Further, observers were largely unaware of events occurring in the unattended game. People can attend to only one game when both are being shown on the basis of expectations inherent in the way they understand and mentally represent the game. These mental representations are called "schemata." Through them, attention has its effects as an alerting and sustaining process whereby receptivity to certain information can be maintained over the short or long term. Finally, consistent with results on tasks involving attempts to split attention spatially, observers were unable to attend to both games at once (and thereby indicate when a point had been scored in either one).

One additional phenomenon involves what Colin Cherry referred to as the "cocktail-party problem." The setting is a cocktail party or any gathering where people are engaged simultaneously in different conversations. A person can listen selectively to one conversation and apparently not be conscious of others. Auditory attention therefore seems fully focused on only one conversation; however, the listener might hear his or her name mentioned in any one of a number of other conversations and immediately shift attention to it. How can people attend fully to one source of information, yet simultaneously be sensitive to important information from other sources? Can their attention be focused and yet divided among a number of possible sources of information at the same time? The answer lies in the fact that stimuli outside the focus of attention are sometimes processed to the level of meaning, especially if they correspond to active and important schemata such as one's name.

## Applications

Understanding how attention operates makes possible the design of environments that make it easier for people to attend to important characteristics. For example, hunters often are cautioned to wear a piece of clothing colored "blaze orange." A bright color is a simple feature that draws attention automatically. Another hunter's attention will be drawn to the blaze orange, and focusing attention on the color will allow it to be conjoined with other simple features, such as shape. The second hunter thus will almost immediately be conscious of the hunter wearing the blaze orange as a hunter and will be unlikely to misperceive this hunter as game (in addition, the color of game is never blaze orange). The same principle is applied when emergency vehicles such as fire trucks are painted bright red or yellow.

Principles stemming from basic research on attention have been applied in the development of what is known as "heads-up" displays in aircraft such as helicopters. Typically, a pilot faces a windscreen through which the environment can be seen, with a cluster of instruments designating altitude, speed, and so on nearby.

With this configuration, the pilot must look away from the windscreen and at the instruments to check them. As helicopters are capable of traveling at a high rate of speed and often are flown close to the earth and to objects into which they might crash, it is important that looking away from the windscreen be minimized. In a heads-up display, the instruments are placed at an angle below the windscreen so that they reflect onto it. The pilot thus can check the instruments without having to divert his eyes from the windscreen.

Can the pilot attend to the instruments and the environment outside the windscreen simultaneously? They spatially overlap and thus are visible at the same time, yet studies of attention indicate that the pilot cannot attend to them both at once. The experiment described by Neisser in which two games were superimposed on a screen is relevant here. An observer could attend to one game or the other but not to both at the same time. This does not mean that heads-up displays are without value. Attention can be directed from the instruments to the environment or vice versa without the pilot's moving the head or eyes; and either type of physical movement is much more time-consuming than a relatively rapid shift of attention.

One popular laboratory task is to have listeners "shadow" material presented to them. In shadowing, the listener hears a series of words spoken at a normal conversational rate and tries to repeat aloud each word as it is heard. The task is difficult, and subjects must devote considerable attention to the shadowing. Often a listener is asked to shadow material played with a tape recorder to one ear while different material is played by another tape recorder to the other ear (earphones are used). Certain characteristics of the material not being shadowed can be varied. After the task, the listener can be asked a number of questions regarding that of which he or she was conscious in the unshadowed message.

Consistent with Cherry's cocktail-party phenomenon, listeners are conscious of the presence of the unshadowed message and of whether there is an abrupt change of pitch (as in a change of voice from a man's to a woman's, or the introduction of a whistle). These global physical characteristics of the unshadowed message can be determined preattentively. Listeners are not conscious, however, of the contents or language of the unshadowed message, of whether the language changed during the message, or even of whether speech or nonsense sounds were presented, unless a change of pitch had occurred. Many variations of this experiment have been performed, and all have produced the same results: Consciousness of the unshadowed material is limited to that which could be detected preattentively. There is no consciousness of the meaning of the unshadowed message, except that listeners sometimes are conscious of their own name if it appears as a result of powerful schemata for something as important as one's own name. The results are exactly what would be expected from what has been shown to be true of attention thus far and from the original description of the cocktail-party problem.

## Context

Attention has been of interest for a very long time. Hermann von Helmholtz wrote of attention in 1850, in a book on physiological optics. William James, a pioneer in the study of psychology, devoted much space to attention in his book published in 1890. He described its variety, its nature, and its effects. Other leading figures from the early history of psychology, such as Wilhelm Wundt and Edward Titchener, agreed with James that the issue of attention was of great importance. Titchener believed that attention determined both the quality and content of conscious experience, and regarded its prominence as one of the major achievements of experimental psychology. Interest was maintained through the period following World War I. Karl Dallenbach noted in the late 1920's that more studies had been reported on attention in the preceding three years than in any comparable period in history. After World War II the study of attention received an even greater boost with the increasing concern over human-machine interactions, especially in the military.

The first complete theory of attention was not proposed until 1958, when Donald Broadbent introduced his concept of attention as a filter that admitted only certain information, selected on the basis of sensory characteristics, into the limited-capacity system. This marked the continuation of interest in attention by researchers in England, beginning with Colin Cherry in 1953. In 1963, J. Anthony Deutsch and Diana Deutsch of Oxford, England, proposed that all incoming information is analyzed to the level of meaning.

Many of the fundamental issues in attention, raised decades ago, have been recast somewhat, in the information-processing mode, beginning in the late 1960's. For example, attention is described in terms of "selection," "resources," "features," "input," and so on. Whereas the emphasis had been on hearing, visual attention began to receive more emphasis. Many of the findings were like those on hearing, although factors such as color and brightness were considered.

Attention remains central to the study of consciousness and cognitive psychology. As Michael Posner noted in 1975, "Attention is not a single concept, but the name of a complex field of study." Accordingly, questions about early versus late selection, automatic processing, and other issues in the control of attention have not yet been fully answered.

## Bibliography

Boff, Kenneth R., Lloyd Kaufman, and James P. Thomas, eds. *Handbook of Perception and Human Performance.* 2 vols. New York: John Wiley & Sons, 1986. Includes three chapters relevant to attention: chapter 2, on information processing; chapter 26, on auditory information processing; and chapter 43, on vigilance.

Johnston, William A., and Veronica J. Dark. "Selective Attention." In *Annual Review of Psychology* 37. Stanford, Calif.: Annual Reviews, 1989. Provides a very thorough and well-organized review of the research on selective attention. Outlines eleven phenomena associated with attention, and the degree to which each of a number of theories accounts for these phenomena.

Parasuraman, R., and D. R. Davies, eds. *Varieties of Attention.* Orlando, Fla.: Academic Press, 1984. Includes articles by a variety of contributors. Many topics are covered, such as search, vigilance, levels of processing, and applications to industrial settings.

Posner, Michael I., and O. S. M. Marin, eds. *Attention and Performance XI.* Hillsdale, N.J.: Lawrence Erlbaum, 1985. A collection of thirty-five chapters from a conference on attention, covering topics such as the biological aspects of attention, covert attention, and divided attention.

Treisman, Anne. "Features and Objects in Visual Processing." *Scientific American* 225 (November, 1971): 114B-125. Treisman provides a clear summary of feature integration theory and includes figures producing readily observable attention effects.

*Garvin Chastain*

## Cross-References

Automaticity, 356; Cognitive Psychology: An Overview, 572; Functions of Consciousness, 656; Levels of Consciousness, 663; Memory: Sensory, 1531; Pattern Recognition as a Cognitive Process, 1747.

# ATTITUDE-BEHAVIOR CONSISTENCY

*Type of psychology:* Social psychology
*Field of study:* Attitudes and behavior

*Research on attitude-behavior consistency examines the extent to which self-reported attitudes predict and guide behavior. It has outlined the conditions under which attitudes can and cannot be expected to be consistent with behavior, and has provided an understanding of the process by which attitudes may influence behavior.*

### Principal terms
ATTITUDE: a positive or negative evaluation of a person, place, or thing
ATTITUDE ACCESSIBILITY: the ease with which an attitude can be remembered
HIGH SELF-MONITORS: people who strive to display behavior that is appropriate for whatever situation in which they find themselves
LOW SELF-MONITORS: people who tend to rely on their own attitudes and feelings to guide behavior
SUBJECTIVE NORM: a person's beliefs about how the important people in his or her life think he or she should behave

### Overview

Most people would answer the following questions—Why does John go to see films often? Why will Sue not eat broccoli? Why does Mark read mystery novels? Why does Mary usually wear green?—by referring to the attitudes of the person in question. An attitude is defined as a positive or negative evaluation of a person, place, or thing. John goes to films because he likes them; Sue will not eat broccoli because she does not care for broccoli; Mark reads mystery novels because he enjoys them; Mary wears green because it is her favorite color.

Social psychologists have found that most people routinely explain other people's behavior, and their own, in terms of underlying attitudes. People tend to believe that attitudes influence and are predictive of most behaviors. Despite these intuitive notions, however, research has suggested that attitudes in general are actually very limited predictors of behavior. That is, there is generally not a high degree of consistency between people's attitudes and their behaviors. In fact, the extent to which attitudes predict and are consistent with behavior appears to depend on a number of variables, including what type of behavior is to be predicted, how the attitude was formed, what kind of personality the person has, and how easily the attitude can be recalled.

Imagine that a researcher wanted to predict whether people regularly attend religious services. He or she might reasonably ask them about their attitudes toward organized religion, expecting that those with more favorable attitudes toward organized religion would be more likely to attend services regularly than those with less favorable attitudes. If the researcher did this, however, he or she would not be likely to find much correspondence at all between attitudes and behaviors.

The reason for this is that the researcher is asking about a very general attitude and very specific behavior. For attitudes to predict behavior, both must be measured at the same level of specificity. If the researcher wants to predict a specific behavior, he or she needs to ask about an attitude specific to that behavior. In this example, he or she should not ask about general attitudes toward religion, but rather about attitudes toward attending religious services. These latter attitudes will be much more predictive of behavior. Attitudes that best predict behavior are attitudes about that specific behavior.

Sometimes, however, even specific attitudes will not correspond to specific behaviors. Icek Ajzen and Martin Fishbein, in their theory of reasoned action, propose that attitudes toward a behavior are only one influence on behavior. A second factor to consider, they suggest, is the subjective norm, which refers to individuals' beliefs about what important others (for example, parents, teachers, peers) think they should do. For some behaviors, the subjective norm is more important than attitude in predicting behavior. Even though someone might have a positive attitude toward attending religious services, he or she still might not go because of a belief that important others do not think that he or she should go.

Even in the case of behaviors for which attitude is the more important influence, however, there are other factors that determine the extent to which that attitude will predict behavior. One factor concerns how the attitude was formed, which generally is in one of two ways. Attitudes may be based on direct, personal experience with the object or person in question. A person may dislike religious services because he or she attended a few and had a number of unpleasant experiences. Alternatively, attitudes may be based on indirect, secondhand experiences. A person may dislike services because of what he or she has read and heard about them. In general, attitudes based on direct experience are much more predictive of behavior than are attitudes based on indirect experience.

A second concern is the type of person someone is. According to psychologist Mark Snyder, when deciding how to behave in a social situation, some people look to the environment and try to be the type of person called for by the situation; they are known as high self-monitors. If the situation calls for a quiet, introverted person, they will be quiet and introverted. If the situation calls for a loud, extroverted person, they will be loud and extroverted. In contrast, low self-monitors look inside themselves and ask, "How do I feel right now?" They base their behavior on their feelings regardless of what is called for in the situation. If they feel like being introverted, they will be introverted; if they feel like being extroverted, they will be extroverted. As might be expected, low self-monitors display a higher degree of attitude-behavior consistency than do high self-monitors.

A last, but perhaps most important, consideration is the ease with which an attitude can be recalled from memory, known as the degree of attitude accessibility. Simply put, the more accessible the attitude, the more likely it is that the attitude will predict behavior. Interestingly, attitudes based on direct experience tend to be more accessible than attitudes based on indirect experience, and low self-monitors tend to have more accessible attitudes than do high self-monitors. In general, any factor that increases attitude accessibility increases the extent to which that attitude will guide future behavior.

## Applications

One arena in which attitude-behavior consistency is an important concern is politics. Millions of dollars are spent on advertising during a political campaign. These funds are spent in an effort to influence attitudes, in the hope that attitudes will then influence behavior. The question arises as to whether these dollars are well spent—whether attitudes toward political candidates predict voting behavior.

To investigate this question, psychologists Russell Fazio and Carol Williams examined the relations between attitudes toward the two major-party candidates in the 1984 United States presidential election, Ronald Reagan and Walter Mondale, and various behaviors, such as perceptions of the televised presidential debates and voting. They assessed individuals' attitudes toward the candidates in June and July of the election year. The presidential debates were held in October, the election in November. As it turns out, overall, attitudes were indeed very predictive of behaviors. Attitudes toward the candidates predicted reactions to the presidential debates, with Reagan supporters believing he was more impressive than Mondale and Mondale supporters believing the opposite. Attitudes also generally predicted voting behavior very well. Those supporting Reagan tended to vote for him, and those supporting Mondale tended to vote for Mondale. Although it is impressive that attitudes assessed in the summer months predicted behaviors three and four months later, so far the results may not be very surprising.

Fazio and Williams did not, however, simply examine the relations between attitudes and behaviors. When they assessed individuals' attitudes during the summer months, they also measured the accessibility of those attitudes—that is, how easily the subjects could call the attitudes to mind. To do this, they asked participants in their study to agree or disagree with different tape-recorded statements (for example, "A good president for the next four years would be Ronald Reagan") as quickly as possible by pressing one of five buttons on a computer; one button represented "strongly agree," one "agree," one "neutral," one "disagree," and one "strongly disagree." The computer then recorded how long it took the participants to respond after they heard the statements. Fazio and Williams reasoned that the more quickly people could respond, the more accessible their attitudes were.

Based on the results, Fazio and Williams classified some people as having highly accessible attitudes and others as having less accessible attitudes. When they then reexamined reactions to the presidential debates and voting behavior, they found that attitude-behavior consistency was much higher for those with highly accessible attitudes than for those with less accessible attitudes. That is, those with highly accessible attitudes were much more likely to act in a way consistent with their attitudes than were those with less accessible attitudes. For example, not everyone who agreed in June or July that Reagan would be a good president for the next four years voted for him in November. Those for whom this attitude could easily be brought to mind were much more likely to act on this attitude and vote for him than were those who had the same attitude but could not bring it to mind as quickly. It appears that, for attitudes to guide behavior successfully, they must be easily retrieved from memory.

Two of the factors that influence the ease with which attitudes can be recalled have already been discussed: how the attitude was formed, and whether one is a high or low self-monitor. An additional factor seems to be the number of times the attitude is expressed. In one study, students watched a videotape of five different puzzles and then expressed their interest in each of the puzzles. Some students were asked to express their attitudes once, while others were asked to express them three different times (on three different forms). When they were later asked to rate the puzzles along different dimensions as quickly as they could on a computer (just as in the voting study discussed above), those who had initially expressed their attitudes three times had quicker reaction times than those who had initially expressed their attitudes once, suggesting that repeated attitude expression makes attitudes more accessible. In a follow-up study, after students had seen the videotape of the puzzles and had expressed their attitudes toward the puzzles either one or three times, the researchers allowed the students actually to play with any or all of the puzzles. Attitudes toward the puzzles predicted playing behavior much better for those who had initially expressed their attitudes three times than for those who had initially expressed their attitudes once. The more often an attitude is expressed, the more accessible it becomes and the more likely it is to influence behavior.

## Context

The extent to which attitudes predict and influence behavior is at the heart of social psychology. At its inception, social psychology was defined as the study of attitudes, and although the importance of attitudes has waxed and waned as the field has matured, most social psychologists would still consider attitudes to be a central concept. In fact, at least half the articles in any given scholarly journal in the field generally discuss some aspect of attitudes.

In this context, one can imagine the shock that the social psychological community felt when, in 1969, A. W. Wicker published a review of numerous studies examining the relations between attitudes and behaviors which concluded that attitudes generally bear little relation to overt behavior and do not predict behavior well at all. Historically, it is interesting to note that, about this same time, a personality psychologist named Walter Mischel was making similar conclusions about personality traits. In the research he reviewed, there did not seem to be much relationship between people's personality traits and their behavior.

The reaction to Wicker's review was mixed. Some called for social psychology to abandon attitudes as a focal point of research. After all, they argued, if attitudes cannot predict behavior, and since the goal of any field of psychology is to predict behavior, it would be foolish to spend more time and effort studying attitudes.

Although this type of reaction had many supporters, others took a more optimistic approach to addressing what became known as the attitude-behavior problem. Wicker's review, they suggested, concluded that on average attitudes do not seem to predict behavior; yet in some of the studies he reviewed, attitudes did predict behavior quite well. The question for these researchers, then, was not whether attitudes predict behavior—because in some cases, they clearly do—but rather, when and under what circumstances attitudes predict behavior. As a result, in the 1970's and 1980's, considerable research was directed at identifying those factors that seemed to increase or decrease the degree of attitude-behavior consistency. It was these efforts that shed light on the role of direct experience and self-monitoring.

In the 1970's and 1980's, social psychologists became convinced that, under certain circumstances, attitudes do predict and influence behavior. The next area to be explored is the process by which attitudes influence behavior. The pioneering work of Fazio has pointed out a direction in which to travel to answer this question, but much more research is needed before this remaining section of the attitude-behavior consistency puzzle can be solved.

## Bibliography

Ajzen, Icek, and Martin Fishbein. *Understanding Attitudes and Predicting Social Behavior.* Englewood Cliffs, N.J.: Prentice-Hall, 1980. A very readable introduction to the authors' theory of reasoned action. Applied implications of the theory for specific areas such as political, consumer, and dieting behavior are also discussed, and more general implications for attitude change and persuasion are addressed.

Fazio, Russell. "How Do Attitudes Guide Behavior?" In *Handbook of Motivation and Cognition*, edited by Richard M. Sorrentino and E. Tory Higgins. New York: Guilford Press, 1986. An excellent introduction to Fazio's initial work on the role of attitude accessibility. Also provides a brief history of the attitude-behavior consistency controversy and attempts to show how issues of attitude accessibility may help resolve parts of the controversy.

Fazio, Russell, and Mark P. Zanna. "Direct Experience and Attitude-Behavior Consistency." In *Advances in Experimental Social Psychology*, edited by Leonard Berkowitz. Vol. 14. New York: Academic Press, 1981. A thorough review of the research and theory on the role that attitude formation plays in the attitude-behavior relationship. Offers examples of both field research and laboratory research. Ideas presented here lay the foundation for Fazio's later work on attitude accessibility.

Snyder, Mark. *Public Appearances/Private Realities: The Psychology of Self-Monitoring.* New York: W. H. Freeman, 1987. Very readable review of research and theory about the self-monitoring personality variable. Several chapters devoted exclusively to explaining how self-monitoring relates to issues of attitude-behavior consistency.

Zanna, Mark P., E. Tory Higgins, and C. Peter Herman, eds. *Consistency in Social Behavior: The Ontario Symposium.* Vol. 2. Hillsdale, N.J.: Lawrence Erlbaum,

1982. Perhaps the most important single volume on attitude-behavior relations. The twelve chapters, written by the leading authorities on the topic, raise and discuss all the important issues about not only attitude-behavior relations but personality trait-behavior relations as well. Important for anyone who wishes to understand attitude-behavior relations thoroughly.

*Kenneth G. DeBono*

## Cross-References

Attitude Formation and Change, 326; Causal Attribution, 487; Cognitive Dissonance Theory, 560; Crowd Behavior, 737; Personality Theory: Major Issues, 1804; Self-Concept Origins, 2175; Self-Perception Theory, 2193; Violence and Sexuality in the Mass Media, 2603.

# ATTITUDE FORMATION AND CHANGE

*Type of psychology:* Social psychology
*Field of study:* Attitudes and behavior

*Research has suggested six theories of attitude change; these theories have led to the development of numerous persuasion tactics and principles that find use in a variety of settings ranging from the mass media to consumer sales to organizational negotiations.*

### Principal terms

ATTITUDE: a person's evaluation of an object or thought
COGNITIVE DISSONANCE THEORY: an approach which holds that persuasion occurs as a result of an attempt to resolve the inconsistency between two discrepant cognitions
COGNITIVE RESPONSE ANALYSIS: posits that persuasion is dependent on the evaluative and elaborative nature of the thoughts running through recipients' heads as they process a message
FUNCTIONAL THEORIES: theories in which attitudes serve psychological functions such as helping to make sense of the world and oneself
LEARNING THEORY OF PERSUASION: a theory which holds that attitude change occurs when a person is rewarded for processing and accepting the conclusions of a message
SELF-PERCEPTION THEORY: holds that attitudes are inferred from behavior
SOCIAL JUDGMENT THEORY: sees attitude judgments as influenced by the context of the object to be judged

## Overview

An attitude is a person's evaluation of an object or thought; examples include "I support gun control," "I dislike brand X," and "I love the person next door." Much research finds that attitudes can influence a broad range of cognitive processes such as social inference, reasoning, perception, and interpretation, and can thereby influence behavior. In general, people favor, approach, praise, and cherish those things they like, and disfavor, avoid, blame, and harm those things they dislike. Given that attitudes can have pervasive effects on social behavior, it is important to understand how attitudes are formed and changed.

Attitudes and beliefs can be formed through a number of sources including the mass media, parental influence, socializing agents such as schools and religious organizations, important reference groups, total institutions such as prisons and cults, and observation of one's own behavior and direct experience with the attitude object. William McGuire notes that attitudes are one of the most extensively studied topics in social psychology. Much of this research has centered on the question, Who says what to whom, with what effects?

For example, research has varied the source (or "who") of a message and found that people tend to be most persuaded by credible, trustworthy, attractive, and similar communicators. Research on message characteristics (or "what") has shown that fear appeals increase persuasion if accompanied by specific recommendations for how to avoid the fear; that there is a tendency for arguments presented first to have more impact, especially after a delay; and that messages which present only one side of an issue are most effective when the recipient lacks the skills or motivation to process the information. In general, research shows that an audience (or "whom") is less persuaded if the message is wildly discrepant from original beliefs; such research also finds that an audience is less persuaded if it has been forewarned about the persuasion attempt and takes steps to prepare a counterargument. The effects of social influence are usually described in terms of compliance (attitude change, often short-lived, as a result of wanting to obtain rewards or avoid punishment), identification (change as a result of seeking to be similar to the source of a message), and internalization (change as a result of accepting a position on the basis of its merits).

Social psychologists have developed six major theories for explaining attitude formation and change: the learning model, the cognitive response approach, consistency theories, functional analysis, social judgment theory, and self-perception theory.

Perhaps social psychology's first theory of persuasion, the learning model is based on the research of Carl Hovland and his colleagues at Yale University in the 1950's. According to this model, a message is persuasive when it rewards the recipient at each of the following stages of psychological processing of a message: attention, comprehension, message learning, and yielding. For example, a highly credible source is persuasive because it is rewarding to attend to and comprehend what he or she says, and then to act on it.

One problem with the learning model of persuasion is that subsequent research in the 1960's found that persuasion could occur even if the message was only minimally comprehended and the message's content was forgotten or never learned. To account for these results, the cognitive response approach posited that the key determinant of persuasion was not message learning, but the thoughts running through a person's head as he or she received a communication. Effective communications are ones that direct and channel thoughts so that the target thinks in a manner agreeable to the communicator's point of view.

Although cognitive responses can vary on a number of dimensions, two of the most important ones are evaluation and elaboration. Most cognitive responses to a message are either positive (support arguments) or negative (support counterarguments) toward the message's conclusion. Studies that disrupt these cognitive responses using a mild distraction (for example, background noises or difficult-to-read print) have found that a distraction results in more persuasion when the recipient's natural tendency is to make arguments against the message, and less persuasion when the recipient normally would have supported the message. Elaboration refers to how much thought a recipient gives to a message. Richard Petty and John Cacioppo have suggested there are two routes to persuasion. In the peripheral route, recipients give little thought to a message, perhaps because they have little motivation to think about it or lack the necessary skills, and persuasion is based on simple persuasion cues such as the credibility of the source and the number of other people who agree with the message. In the central route, recipients carefully scrutinize a message, and persuasion is determined by the quality and cogency of the arguments.

The remaining four theories can be seen as addressing the question, What determines people's cognitive responses? According to consistency theories such as cognitive dissonance theory, people attempt to rationalize their behavior and to avoid a state of dissonance, or simultaneously holding two inconsistent cognitions (ideas, beliefs, or opinions). Persuasion occurs as a result of resolving this dissonance. For example, fraternity and sorority pledges often must perform embarrassing behavior to gain admission to the organization. The thoughts "I just ate a plate of grasshoppers as an initiation rite" and "It is stupid to eat grasshoppers" are dissonant with a positive view of oneself. One way to reduce this dissonance is to reevaluate the fraternity or sorority more positively: "I ate those grasshoppers because I wanted to join a great club."

Functional theories of attitude change assume that people hold attitudes to perform psychological functions such as making sense of the world and oneself. Attitude formation and change result from modifying these underlying functions or motivations. For example, consider someone who is prejudiced against an ethnic group. This negative attitude helps the person interpret, often incorrectly, social reality ("Members of the ethnic group can do no good and often are the cause of problems") and can help the person maintain a positive view of self ("I am better than they are"). Advertisers make use of functional theories when they market products to appeal to self-images; in such cases, a product is liked and used to obtain a desired image, such as appearing to be sophisticated, macho, a modern woman, and so on.

According to social judgment theory, objects are evaluated in the context of other objects. Attitude change can occur when the context for making judgments is changed. For example, in one study, males rated photographs of females as much less attractive after viewing the television show *Charlie's Angels*. In other words, the very attractive female stars of *Charlie's Angels* provided a highly positive context in which to rate the photographs, and thus made women of average attractiveness appear much less attractive.

Self-perception theory states that attitudes are based on observing one's own behavior and then attributing the behavior to underlying beliefs. For example, suppose a man is at a dinner party and is served brown bread, which he then eats. When asked, "Do you like brown bread?" he observes his eating behavior and concludes that he does (unless there is some other plausible reason, such as force or politeness). The self-perception theory reverses the causal sequence of the learning model from one of "attitudes cause behavior" to "behavior causes attitudes."

## Applications

Research and theorizing on attitude change have led to the development of numerous tactics and principles of persuasion. These principles are useful for interpreting persuasion effects such as those that occur in mass media and interpersonal or organizational settings, and for directing persuasion attempts. Three of the more popular tactics will be discussed here.

One of the simplest and most surefire ways to ensure positive cognitive responses is to induce the target to argue for the message conclusion, a tactic known as self-generated persuasion. For example, in one study during World War II, women were asked to "help" a researcher by coming up with reasons why other women should serve organ and intestinal meats (brains, kidneys, and so on) to their families as part of the war effort. These women were eleven times as likely to serve such meats as those who were merely lectured to do so. In another study, consumers were asked to imagine the benefits of subscribing to cable television versus being told about those benefits. Those who imagined subscribing were two-and-a-half times as likely to subscribe as those who were merely told about the benefits.

The "foot-in-the-door" technique makes use of cognitive dissonance theory. In this tactic, the communicator secures compliance to a big request by first putting his or her "foot in the door" by asking for a small favor that almost everyone will typically do. For example, in one study, residents were asked to place a large ugly sign in their yard that read DRIVE CAREFULLY. Few residents complied unless they had been "softened up" the week before by an experimenter who got them to sign a petition favoring safe driving. For those residents, putting the ugly sign in their yard helped avoid cognitive dissonance: "Last week I supported safe driving. This week I will be a hypocrite if I don't put this ugly sign in my yard."

Another effective tactic is to add a decoy, or a worthless item that no one would normally want, to a person's set of choices. For example, a real estate agent may show customers overpriced, run-down homes, or a car dealer may place an old clunker of a used car on his or her lot. Consistent with social judgment theory, such decoys create a context for judging the other "real" alternatives and make them appear more attractive. An unsuspecting consumer is more likely to select and buy these "more attractive" items.

## Context

As early as 1935, Gordon Allport declared that attitude is social psychology's "most indispensable construct." Research on attitudes began in the 1920's in the United States as a response to changing social conditions. The period was marked by the rise of new mass media such as radio and mass-circulated magazines, the development of large-scale consumer markets, and the changing nature of political activity. Such developments required that the attitudes and opinions of citizens toward a variety of issues be measured and tracked. Academic researchers responded by developing techniques of attitude scaling and measurement, and by laying the foundation for survey methodology. The first empirical research on attitudes sought to address questions such as "How are movies changing Americans' attitudes and values?" and "Has modern life changed traditional cultural attitudes?"

World War II changed the focus of attitude research from an interest in measurement to an interest in understanding attitude change and persuasion. Many of the post-World War II attitude researchers either had fled Nazi Germany or had worked for the Allies in an attempt either to defuse Nazi propaganda or to bolster their fellow citizens' attitudes toward the war effort. After the war, in the 1950's, many researchers attempted to explain the propaganda and attitude-change tactics used during the war and now increasingly employed in the mass media. This research resulted in the development of learning, functional, social judgment, and cognitive consistency theories of persuasion.

Attitude research since the 1960's has sought to test and develop the major theories of attitude change, to refine the principles of persuasion, and to apply these principles to an ever-expanding list of targets. For example, research on the relationship between attitude change and memory of a communication led to the development of a cognitive response analysis of persuasion in the late 1960's. Many of the compliance techniques described by Robert Cialdini, and by Anthony Pratkanis and Elliot Aronson, were first elaborated in this period. As knowledge of persuasion improves, the principles of persuasion are increasingly applied to solve social problems. Prosocial goals to which theories of persuasion have been applied include decreasing energy consumption and increasing waste recycling, slowing the spread of acquired immune deficiency syndrome (AIDS) by changing attitudes toward safe sex practices, lowering the automobile death toll by increasing seat belt use, improving health by promoting practices such as good dental hygiene and regular medical checkups, improving worker morale and worker relationships, and reducing intergroup prejudice.

## Bibliography

Allport, Gordon W. "Attitudes." In *Handbook of Social Psychology*, edited by Carl Allanmore Murchison. Worchester, Mass.: Clark University Press, 1935. The first review of the attitude concept. Provides a useful introduction to the historical origins of attitude research.

Cialdini, Robert B. *Influence: How and Why People Agree to Things.* New York: William Morrow, 1984. This highly readable account provides a fascinating discussion of six of the most frequently used compliance tactics.

Hovland, Carl Iver, Irving L. Janis, and Harold H. Kelley. *Communication and Persuasion.* New Haven, Conn.: Yale University Press, 1953. This first research monograph on persuasion covers issues such as source credibility, fear appeals, and personality and persuasion.

McGuire, W. J. "Attitudes and Attitude Change." In *Handbook of Social Psychology*, edited by Gardner Lindzey and Elliot Aronson. 3d ed. New York: Random House, 1985. One of the most comprehensive reviews of the topic. Covers issues such as the history of persuasion research, the definition of an attitude, and how attitudes are formed, and provides a critical analysis of attitude change theories and a detailed summary of attitude research.

Petty, Richard E., and John T. Cacioppo. *Attitudes and Persuasion: Classic and Contemporary Approaches.* Dubuque, Iowa: Wm. C. Brown, 1981. An excellent textbook that provides a description of major theories of persuasion and supporting research.

──────────. *Communication and Persuasion: Central and Peripheral Routes to Attitude Change.* New York: Springer-Verlag, 1986. Provides a detailed description of the role of elaboration in persuasion and provides a useful summary of recent research in persuasion.

Pratkanis, Anthony R., and Elliot Aronson. *The Age of Propaganda: The Everyday Use and Abuse of Persuasion.* New York: W. H. Freeman, 1992. A popular treatment of the role of persuasion in society. Describes numerous persuasion tactics and provides the reader with an in-depth analysis of how they work and what can be done to prevent unwanted propaganda.

Pratkanis, Anthony R., Steven J. Breckler, and Anthony G. Greenwald, eds. *Attitude Structure and Function.* Hillsdale, N.J.: Lawrence Erlbaum, 1989. The papers in this volume summarize how attitudes influence social processes such as cognition and behavior, and update functional theories of attitude.

Zimbardo, Philip G., and Michael R. Leippe. *The Psychology of Attitude Change and Social Influence.* Philadelphia: Temple University Press, 1991. This textbook presents an engaging review of attitude-change techniques and analyzes their use in various social settings.

*Anthony R. Pratkanis*
*Marlene E. Turner*

## Cross-References

Attitude-Behavior Consistency, 320; Cognitive Dissonance Theory, 560; Consumer Psychology: Decisions, 669; Decision Making as a Cognitive Process, 769; Self-Perception Theory, 2193; Survey Research: Questionnaires and Interviews, 2507.

# ATTRACTION THEORIES

*Type of psychology:* Social psychology
*Field of study:* Interpersonal relations

*Theories of interpersonal attraction attempt to specify the conditions that lead people to like, and in some cases love, each other. Attraction is a two-way process, involving not only the person who is attracted but also the attractor.*

### Principal terms

EQUITY THEORY: a theory suggesting that attraction tends to occur when two people both believe that their relationship is fair

MATCHING PHENOMENON: the tendency for people to choose romantic partners whose level of attractiveness is close to their own

MERE EXPOSURE: a psychological phenomenon in which liking tends to increase as a person sees more of something or someone

PHYSICAL ATTRACTIVENESS STEREOTYPE: the tendency to attribute other positive characteristics to a physically attractive person

PROXIMITY: physical closeness; a determinant of attraction

RECIPROCITY: a principle of attraction that suggests that people tend to like others who like them back

REINFORCEMENT MODEL: a general model of interpersonal attraction that suggests that attraction is determined by the rewards provided by the relationship

SOCIAL EXCHANGE THEORY: a theory that suggests that attraction is determined by weighing the benefits of a relationship against the costs involved

## Overview

Relationships are central to human social existence. Personal accounts by people who have been forced to endure long periods of isolation serve as reminders of people's dependence on others, and research suggests that close relationships are the most vital ingredient in a happy and meaningful life. In short, questions dealing with attraction are among the most fundamental in social psychology.

The major theories addressing interpersonal attraction have a common theme: reinforcement. The principle of reinforcement is one of the most basic notions in all of psychology. Put simply, it states that behaviors that are followed by desirable consequences (often these take the form of rewards) tend to be repeated. Applied to interpersonal relations, this principle suggests that when one person finds something rewarding in an interaction with another person (or if that person anticipates some reward in a relationship that has not yet been established), then the person should desire further interaction with that other individual. In behavioral terms, this is what is meant by the term "interpersonal attraction," which emerges in everyday language in such terms as "liking" or, in the case of deep romantic involvement, "loving." Appropriately, these theories based on the notion that individuals are drawn to relationships that are rewarding and avoid those that are not are known as reinforcement or reward models of interpersonal attraction.

The first and most basic theory of this type was proposed in the early 1970's by Donn Byrne and Gerald Clore. Known as the reinforcement-affect model of attraction ("affect" means "feeling" or "emotion"), this theory proposes that people will be attracted not only to other people who reward them but also to those people whom they associate with rewards. In other words, a person can learn to like others through their connections to experiences that are positive for that individual. It is important to recognize that a major implication here is that it is possible to like someone not so much because of that person himself or herself, but rather as a consequence of that person's merely being part of a rewarding situation; positive feelings toward the experience itself get transferred to that other person. (It also follows that a person associated with something unpleasant will tend to be disliked.)

For example, in one experiment done during the summer, people who evaluated new acquaintances in a cool and comfortable room liked them better than when in a hot and uncomfortable room. In another, similar, study subjects rating photographs of strangers gave more favorable evaluations when in a nicely furnished room than when they were in a dirty room with shabby furniture. These findings provide some insight into why married couples may find that their relationship benefits from a weekend trip away from the children or a romantic dinner at a favorite restaurant; the pleasant event enhances their feelings for each other.

There are other models of interpersonal attraction that involve the notion of rewards but consider the degree to which they are offset by the costs associated with a relationship. Social exchange theory suggests that people tend to evaluate social situations; in the context of a relationship, a person will compare the costs and benefits of beginning or continuing that relationship. Imagine, for example, that Karen is considering a date with Dave, who is kind, attractive, and financially stable but fifteen years older. Karen may decide that this relationship is not worth pursuing because of the disapproval of her mother and father, who believe strongly that their daughter should be dating a man her own age. Karen's decision will be influenced by how much she values the approval of her parents and by whether she has other dating alternatives available.

A third model of attraction, equity theory, extends social exchange theory. This approach suggests that it is essential to take into account how both parties involved in a relationship assess the costs and benefits. When each person believes that his or her own ratio of costs to benefits is fair (or equitable), then attraction between the two tends to be promoted. On the other hand, a relationship may be placed in jeopardy if one person thinks that the time, effort, and other resources being invested are justified, while the other person does not feel that way.

Considering the rewards involved in the process of interpersonal attraction provides a useful model, but one that is rather general. To understand attraction fully, one must look more specifically at what people find rewarding in relationships. Social psychological research has established some definite principles governing attraction that can be applied nicely within the reward framework.

## Applications

The first determinant of attraction, reciprocity, is probably fairly obvious, since it most directly reflects the reinforcement process; nevertheless, it is a powerful force: People tend to like others who like them back. There are few things more rewarding than genuine affection, support, concern, and other indicators that one is liked by another person.

The second principle, proximity, suggests that simple physical closeness tends to promote attraction. Research has confirmed what many people probably already know: People are most likely to become friends (or romantic partners) with others with whom they have worked, grown up, or gone to school. Other studies have shown that people living in dormitories or apartments tend to become friends with the neighbors who live closest to them. Simply being around people gives an individual a chance to interact with them, which in turn provides the opportunity to learn who is capable of providing the rewards sought in a relationship.

It seems, however, that there is yet another force at work, a very basic psychological process known as the mere exposure phenomenon. Research has demonstrated consistently that repeated exposure to something new tends to increase one's liking for it, and examples of the process are quite common in everyday life. It is not uncommon, for example, for a person to buy a new tape or compact disc by a favorite musical artist without actually having heard the new material, only to be disappointed upon listening to it. The listener soon discovers, however, that the album "grows" on him or her and finds himself or herself liking it quite a bit after hearing it a few times. Such occurrences probably involve the mere exposure phenomenon. In short, familiarity breeds liking, and physical closeness makes it possible for that familiarity to develop.

Generally speaking, the same factors that promote the development of friendships also foster romantic attraction. The third principle of attraction, physical attractiveness, is somewhat of an exception, however, since it is more powerful in the romantic context.

In a classic study published by Elaine (Hatfield) Walster and her associates in 1966, University of Minnesota freshmen males and females were randomly paired for dates to a dance. Prior to the date, these students had provided considerable information about themselves, some of it through personality tests. During the evening, each person individually completed a questionnaire that focused primarily on how much the person liked his or her date, and the participants were contacted for follow-up six months later. Despite the opportunity to discover complex facts about attraction, such as what kinds of personality traits link up within a couple to promote it, the only important factor in this study was physical appearance. For both sexes, the better-looking the partner, the more the person liked his or her date, the stronger was the desire to date the person again, and the more likely the individual was actually to do so during the next six months.

The potent effect of physical attractiveness in this study sparked much interest in this variable on the part of researchers over the next decade or so. The earliest studies determined rather quickly that both men and women, given the opportunity to select a date from a group of several members of the opposite sex representing a range of attractiveness levels, almost invariably would select the most attractive one. Dating in real life, however, is seldom without the chance that the person asking another out might be turned down. When later experiments began building the possibility of rejection into their procedures, an interesting effect emerged, one that has been termed the "matching phenomenon." People tend to select romantic partners whose degree of attractiveness is very similar to their own.

Other research revealed that physically attractive people are often judged favorably on qualities other than their appearance. Even when nothing is known but what the person looks like, the physically attractive individual is thought to be happier, more intelligent, and more successful than someone who is less attractive. This finding is referred to as the "physical attractiveness stereotype," and it has implications that extend the role of appearance well beyond the matter of dating. Studies have shown, for example, that work (such as a writing sample) will be assessed more favorably when produced by an attractive person than when by someone less attractive, and that a cute child who misbehaves will be treated more leniently than a homely one. What is beautiful is also good, so to speak. Finally, one may note that physical attractiveness fits well with the reward model: It is pleasant and reinforcing both to look at an attractive person and to be seen with him or her, particularly if that person is one's date.

The last principle of attraction, similarity, is the most important one in long-term relationships, regardless of whether they are friendships or romances. An extremely large body of research has demonstrated consistently that the more similar two people are, especially attitudinally, the more they will like each other. It turns out that the old adage, "opposites attract," is simply false. (Note that the matching phenomenon also reflects similarity.) A friend or spouse who holds attitudes similar to one's own will provide rewards by confirming that one's own feelings and beliefs are correct; it is indeed reinforcing when someone else agrees.

## Context

Much of the work on the social psychology of interpersonal attraction represents at least relatively recent developments in the field. Proximity was really the first factor to be investigated; its role in promoting attraction was established by the late 1950's. Much of the research on similarity was conducted in the 1960's, and its importance was well understood by the end of that decade. Still, it seems that interest in the psychology of attraction did not fully blossom until physical attractiveness emerged as a major research topic.

Curiously, although it would seem to be of obvious importance, physical appearance as a determinant of romantic attraction was simply neglected by researchers until the mid-1960's. Perhaps they mistakenly assumed the widespread existence of an old ideal that one should judge someone on the basis of his or her intrinsic worth, not on the basis of a superficial characteristic. Nevertheless, when the Minnesota study discussed earlier produced a physical attractiveness effect so strong as to eliminate or at least obscure any other factors related to attraction in the context of dating, social psychologists took notice. In any science, surprising or otherwise remarkable findings usually tend to stimulate additional research, and such a pattern definitely describes the course of events in this area of inquiry.

By around 1980, social psychology had achieved a rather solid understanding of the determinants of attraction to strangers, and the field began turning more of its attention to the nature of continuing relationships. Social psychologist Zick Rubin had first proposed a theory of love in 1970, and research on that topic flourished in the 1980's as investigators examined such topics as the components of love, different types of love, the nature of love in different kinds of relationships, and the characteristics of interaction in successful long-term relationships. Still other lines of research explored how people end relationships or attempt to repair those that are in trouble.

People view relationships with family, friends, and lovers as central to their happiness—a research finding that is totally consistent with common experience. One need only look at the content of motion pictures, television programs, musical lyrics, novels, and poetry—where relationships, particularly romantic ones, are so commonly a theme—to find evidence for that point. Yet nearly half of all marriages end in divorce, and the lack of love in the relationship is usually a precipitating factor. Whatever social psychology can teach people about what determines and maintains attraction can help improve the human condition.

## Bibliography

Berscheid, Ellen, and Elaine Hatfield Walster. *Interpersonal Attraction.* 2d ed. Reading, Mass.: Addison-Wesley, 1978. Presents a solid overview of the psychology of attraction. Directed toward the reader with no background in social psychology, the book is quite readable; nevertheless, it is highly regarded and frequently cited within the field. Clever illustrations feature many cartoons.

_____. "Physical Attractiveness." In *Advances in Experimental Social Psychology*, edited by Leonard Berkowitz. New York: Academic Press, 1974. A very thorough review of the research examining the role of physical attractiveness in interpersonal attraction. This is a frequently cited and extensively documented chapter that includes interesting discussions of how people judge attractiveness and how attractiveness affects the individual.

Duck, Steve. *Relating to Others.* Chicago: Dorsey Press, 1988. Duck deals briefly with the traditional work on interpersonal attraction, but this book is most notable for being devoted primarily to reviewing the research on personal relationships, which became important in the 1980's. It covers thoroughly such topics as developing and maintaining relationships, exclusivity in relationships, and repairing and ending them. A good reference for taking the reader beyond the principal focus of the present article.

Hatfield, Elaine, and Susan Sprecher. *Mirror, Mirror: The Importance of Looks in Everyday Life.* Albany: State University of New York Press, 1986. An extremely thorough and very readable review of all the different affects of personal appearance—not only on the attraction process but also on the person himself or herself. Explores how judgments of attractiveness are made and addresses the effects of beauty across the entire life span. Nicely supported with effective photographs and illustrations.

Myers, David G. *Social Psychology.* 3d ed. New York: McGraw-Hill, 1990. This very popular social psychology textbook features an unusually good chapter on interpersonal attraction. Offers a solid survey of the research relating to the principles of attraction and provides particularly good coverage of work on love. The author's engaging writing style makes this an excellent starting point for further exploration of the topic.

*Steve A. Nida*

## Cross-References

Affiliation and Friendship, 142; The Contact Hypothesis, 675; Theories of Intergroup Relations, 1356; Love, 1486; Reduction of Prejudice, 1855; Self-Presentation, 2200; Social Perception: Others, 2311.

# ATTRIBUTIONAL BIASES

*Type of psychology:* Social psychology
*Field of study:* Social perception and cognition

*Attributions about the causes of one's own behavior and the behavior of others play an important role in self-perception and the perception of others. Attributional biases are systematic errors that distort perceptions and attributions; the study of these provides insight into stereotyping, the blaming of victims, faulty decision-making, conflict, and depression.*

### Principal terms

ACTOR-OBSERVER BIAS: the tendency to attribute one's own behavior to situational factors and the behavior of others to personality traits

ATTRIBUTION: the process by which one gathers information and interprets it to determine the cause of an event or behavior

ATTRIBUTIONAL BIAS: an error in the attribution process that is not random; a tendency that is shared among people to use information in illogical or unwarranted ways

DEFENSIVE ATTRIBUTION: attributing more responsibility to victims similar to oneself than to dissimilar ones, or to victims who are more severely harmed than those who are less harmed

DEPRESSION: a psychological disorder characterized by feelings of sadness, hopelessness, or personal unworthiness, loss of energy, withdrawal, and either lack of sleep or excessive sleep

EXPECTANCY CONFIRMATION BIAS: interpreting ambiguous information as being supportive of expectations; mistakenly "seeing" what is expected

FUNDAMENTAL ATTRIBUTION ERROR: underestimating the influence of situations and overestimating the influence of personality traits in causing behavior

GENERALIZATION FALLACY: the underuse of reliable statistical or numerical data and overuse of less reliable data, such as anecdotes

SELF-SERVING BIAS: the tendency to attribute success to internal, personal factors and failure to external, situational factors

STEREOTYPE: a set of characteristics or traits associated with membership in a category or group; the assumption without proof that all *Y* people have *X* trait

## Overview

When trying to make sense of human behavior, one must be able to perceive behavior accurately and understand its causes. Theories that describe ways in which one can make these judgments about the causes of behavior are called attribution theories. Most attribution theories propose models that describe how people collect information and how attributions are formed from that information. Many specific attributions are possible, but generally these attributions can be grouped into two categories: personal and situational. If a situational attribution is made, the behavior is attributed to external forces or circumstances; for example, someone who trips may attribute his or her behavior to a slippery floor rather than to clumsiness. In a personal attribution, an internal cause, such as the person's personality, or an internal force, such as ability or effort, is seen as being the cause of the behavior. For example, if David observes Lois making a donation to charity, he may attribute her behavior to her generous personality rather than to some external circumstance. Attribution theories predict and explain the circumstances under which a personal or a situational attribution will be made.

Attribution theories provide logical models of how people gather and use information to form attributions, but people do not always seem to follow a logical process. Researchers have discovered that people frequently fall prey to attributional biases. These systematic errors teach much about human social cognition.

One attributional bias is so pervasive that it has earned the right to be called the fundamental attribution error. Social psychologist Lee Ross discovered that people tend to overestimate the role of personal, internal factors and underestimate the influence of situational factors; therefore, people make unwarranted personal attributions. In research demonstrating this bias, subjects were given essays supporting a particular position on an issue (in favor of abortion, for example). Despite the fact that the subjects were told that the authors had no choice but to take the stated position, the subjects rated the authors' attitudes as being in agreement with the essay.

Two explanations have been proposed for the fundamental attribution error. In 1958, Fritz Heider proposed that people are more aware of persons than situations because persons are the obvious, attention-getting figures, whereas situations are the more easily ignored background. Daniel Gilbert, in 1989, proposed that, contrary to what most attribution models propose, people do not initially use information to decide between personal and situational attributions; instead, they initially assume a personal attribution and then revise that attribution to include situational forces only if information that is inconsistent with a personal attribution forces them to do so. Supporting this hypothesis, he has found that if he keeps subjects too busy to use incoming information to revise their attributions, they are more likely to make personal attributions than are subjects who are allowed time to think about the information they are given.

The fundamental attribution error is related to the actor-observer bias. Research has shown that the fundamental attribution error pattern is often reversed when people are attributing their own actions; actors tend to overestimate situational factors and underestimate personal ones. This bias leads to situations in which people attribute their own actions to circumstances and others' often identical actions to personal factors, as in "I am late because of traffic, but you are late because you do not care about being punctual." This bias has been demonstrated in numerous studies; in one, researchers examined letters to "Ann Landers" and "Dear Abby" and found that the letter writers were more likely to attribute their own actions to situational factors and others' behavior to personal factors.

Perceivers are often motivated to make a particular attribution. One motivation that may affect attribution is the motive to be correct, which may lead the person making the attribution to interpret ambiguous information as being supportive of an initial expectation or attribution. This bias often takes the form of "seeing" a trait that one associates with another trait. For example, if Glenda has made the attribution that Jennie's astute decisions are the result of her intelligence, she may also assume that Jennie is exceptionally outgoing, not because she actually observed that trait, but because Glenda associates being intelligent with being outgoing. This expectancy confirmation bias is robust; unless the target person behaves in a way that is inconsistent with the assumption, the perceiver is unlikely to test the assumption.

One well-documented motivated attribution bias is the self-serving bias in attributing success and failure. When a person succeeds, he or she tends to attribute that success to personal, internal factors such as ability and effort; however, when that person fails, he or she is likely to attribute the failure to situational, external factors such as having a difficult task or bad luck. As its name implies, the self-serving bias is thought to be motivated by a desire to preserve or enhance self-esteem by taking credit for success and denying failure.

Another motivated bias is the tendency for observers to blame victims for their situations. This is called defensive attribution, because it has been found to be more likely to occur when the observer is similar to the victim than when the observer is dissimilar, and when the victim's harm is severe rather than mild. Kelly Shaver, the social psychologist who first discussed this bias, believes that it is motivated by fear. If observers blame the victims rather than their situations, the observers can also believe that they themselves are unlikely to be harmed. This is related to what Melvin Lerner calls the belief in a just world. People are motivated to believe that there is justice in the world and that people get what they deserve. This is comforting, because it leads to the conclusion that if one is good, one will get good outcomes; however, the belief in a just world also leads one to assume that victims deserve their outcomes.

Finally, people may fall prey to a group of biases that are collectively called the generalization fallacy. This fallacy is seen when people overgeneralize information from individual cases and personal experience and ignore more reliable information. One example of this bias is that many people believe that air travel is more dangerous than auto travel; in fact, the opposite is true. Because accidents involving airplanes are given greater attention than those involving automobiles, they are more vivid and therefore more memorable than the dangers associated with automobiles. As Heider suggested, vivid figures may be more salient than dull, statistical background information.

## Applications

Because accurate attributions help perceivers negotiate complex social environments, attributional biases can interfere with that process. Therefore, it is not surprising that examples of attributional bias are found in situations in which there is conflict. One situation in which the fundamental attribution error and the actor-observer bias are often involved is in arguments. If both parties believe that their own behavior is caused by circumstances but their partner's behavior is caused by his or her personality, they are likely to experience conflict. This can even be seen between nations; for example, each may attribute the other's cache of weapons to an aggressive personality but their own to necessity.

Another area of conflict that may involve attributional bias is stereotyping. Because stereotyping involves assuming the presence of other traits based on membership in some group, the expectancy confirmation bias has been used as a model for stereotyping. Further, if people act on stereotypes in ways that encourage the targets to behave in certain ways, they may behaviorally confirm the stereotype. For example, if a perceiver believes that all dark-haired men are hostile, she may act in ways that prompt hostility from them, thereby confirming her stereotype. The belief in a just world and defensive attribution may also play a part in stereotyping. In general, stereotypes of minority or less powerful groups are negative. The belief in a just world may lead people to reason that the targets of their stereotypes deserve their poorer outcomes because they have these negative traits. Defensive attributions may add to this by motivating perceivers to overestimate differences between themselves and the target group out of the fear that if they are similar, they may receive similar outcomes.

Researchers who investigate the generalization fallacy are often concerned that falling victim to it may lead to poor decisions. In one study, subjects who were given both reliable statistical information from a large group of car owners and the testimonial of one person tended to weigh the testimonial more heavily than the statistical information. Logically, a testimonial based on one car owned by one person is poorer data than information based on many cars owned by many people. Overreliance on unreliable but vivid data can lead to poor decisions.

Some psychologists believe that the absence of an attributional bias may be involved in depression. People who are depressed do not show the usual self-serving bias in attributing their successes and failures; severely depressed people can even show a reversal of the usual pattern, attributing failure to internal causes such as lack of ability, and success to external factors such as luck. In working with these patients, psychotherapists may help them learn to attribute their outcomes in ways that enhance their self-esteem.

## Context

In the late 1800's, psychology was defined as the science of the mind, and human cognition was at the forefront of early psychologists' interests. Wilhelm Wundt and his followers relied on introspection for their data; they observed their own cognitive processes and reported on them. Hermann Ebbinghaus taught himself lists of words and tested his knowledge after varying time periods to investigate human memory. Beginning in 1913, however, this early cognitive research was largely ignored in America, as John B. Watson redefined psychology as the science of behavior. The main proposition of behaviorism, as this school of psychology is known, is that psychology should use scientific methods of observation and data collection. Behaviorists argue that since cognitive processes are not observable and behaviors are, behaviors are the only proper subject for psychological study. Behaviorism ruled psychology almost exclusively until approximately 1960; although it is still an important force in psychology, it is no longer the dominant force it once was.

As behaviorism's influence has lessened, cognition has become once again a topic of interest to psychologists. Behaviorism left its mark on cognition in the form of more rigorous experimental methods; introspection has been replaced by objective data collection using groups of subjects. As research methods in cognitive psychology continue to become more sophisticated, theories that might have been untestable in earlier years have become the subject of research. One indication of the strength of cognition in the academic world as a whole is that many universities have introduced interdisciplinary departments of cognitive science in which psychologists, neuroscientists, philosophers, linguists, and experts in artificial intelligence study different aspects of cognition.

Attribution played a significant part in the cognitive revolution; Fritz Heider's *The Psychology of Interpersonal Relations* (1958) was an important early work in social cognition. Attribution is one of the most researched topics in social psychology; in fact, some would argue that—especially since it has been found to be useful in applied areas such as health psychology, cognitive psychology, and clinical psychology, as well as social psychology—it is one of the most influential concepts in the field. One of the characteristics of the cognitive revolution is an interest in such topics as ambiguity, uncertainty, and the effects of emotion on cognition. This emphasis provides an interesting context for the study of attributional bias and should open new avenues of inquiry for theorists and researchers. Because of this and the applied areas that have adopted and adapted attributional bias, it has become an area of interest in its own right as well as being important for the refinement of attribution theories.

## Bibliography

Brehm, Sharon S., and Saul M. Kassim. "Perceiving Persons." In *Social Psychology*. Boston: Houghton Mifflin, 1990. This chapter in a social psychology textbook provides an excellent overview of social perception and attribution, including a very complete discussion of attributional biases. Theory and research are presented clearly enough for a beginner to understand, yet in enough detail to be useful to the reader.

Fischoff, Baruch, and Ruth Beyth-Marom. "Hypothesis Evaluation from a Bayesian Perspective." *Psychological Review* 90 (July, 1983): 239-260. The authors of this article propose that social psychologists may be overestimating the occurrence of bias by ignoring the possibility that perceivers are using non-Bayesian logic. Their arguments are complex, although this article is clear and follows an orderly sequence of ideas; appropriate for more advanced students of the field.

Harvey, J. H., and G. Weary. "Current Issues in Attribution Theory and Research." In *Annual Review of Psychology* 35. Stanford, Calif.: Annual Reviews, 1984. Reviews attribution theory and research from 1978 to 1983, a particularly fertile period in the area. Includes a section on the effects of motivation on attribution. Well organized and clear.

Hayes, Brett, and Beryl Hesketh. "Attribution Theory, Judgmental Biases, and Cognitive Behavior Modification: Prospects and Problems." *Cognitive Therapy and Research* 13 (June, 1989): 211-230. Discusses the use of attributional concepts in therapy. Techniques to reduce biases are presented, along with a discussion of the limits of these attributional retraining or debiasing techniques. For a journal article aimed primarily at professionals, this piece is quite accessible.

Ross, M., and G. J. O. Fletcher. "Attribution and Social Perception." In *Handbook of Social Psychology*, edited by Gardner Lindzey and Elliot Aronson. 3d ed. New York: Random House, 1985. This chapter, a comprehensive overview of attribution theory, is clear, engaging, and suitable for readers of all levels. Much of the chapter is devoted to research and the implications of that research on theory; despite this work's status as a review article in a book intended for both academicians and nonspecialists, the authors of this article manage to take a critical stance and ask intriguing questions.

Schneider, D. J. "Social Cognition." In *Annual Review of Psychology* 42. Stanford, Calif.: Annual Reviews, 1991. Reviews social cognition theories and research with an emphasis on categorization and the formation of trait attributions from behaviorial information. Bias is discussed, including a section titled "In Defense of Accuracy." An insightful presentation of research and ideas, this article is an excellent resource for advanced readers.

Shaver, Kelly G. *An Introduction to Attribution Processes.* Cambridge, Mass.: Winthrop, 1975. Presents attribution theory in detail and with vivid, clear examples. There is some discussion of bias, but since this book was written in the heyday of attribution theory model-building, it is incomplete. This slim paperback is a classic—an excellent in-depth resource for beginners to the field.

*Brynda Holton*

## Cross-References

Causal Attribution, 487; Decision Making as a Cognitive Process, 769; Depression: Theoretical Explanations, 789; Emotion and Attribution Theory, 921; Theories of Intergroup Relations, 1356; Motivation: Cognitive Theories, 1606; Self-Perception Theory, 2193; Social Perception: Others, 2311.

# THE AUDITORY SYSTEM

*Type of psychology:* Sensation and perception
*Field of study:* Auditory, chemical, cutaneous, and body senses

*The auditory system is the sensory system that enables people to hear sounds and to learn spoken language well. Malfunction or lack of function of the auditory system makes it difficult to understand spoken language, and the resultant sensory deprivation can lead to psychological problems.*

*Principal terms*
ADVENTITIOUS DEAFNESS: deafness acquired after birth, through accident or disease
CARTILAGE: a tough white fibrous tissue, attached to articular surfaces of bones
LABYRINTH: an intricate biological structure composed of interconnecting anatomical cavities
MUCOUS MEMBRANE: the membrane lining body cavities that are in contact with the air (such as the respiratory and digestive systems), the glands of which secrete mucus
MUCUS: a thick mixture of cells, carbohydrate, water, and other chemicals that serves as a protective lubricant coating for mucous membranes
NEUROSIS: any functional disorder of the mind or the emotions, occurring without obvious brain damage and involving anxiety, phobic responses, or other abnormal behavior symptoms
OSCILLOSCOPE: an electronic instrument that produces a visual display of electron motion on the screen of a cathode ray tube
PSYCHOSIS: a severe mental disorder, with or without brain damage, characterized by deterioration of normal intellectual and social functioning and withdrawal from reality
TEMPORAL BONE: either of two complex bones that form the sides and base of the skull

## Overview

Communicating and understanding the world are essential to humans. One very important aspect of both these processes is the utilization of sounds, perceived by the auditory system. These include spoken language and the sounds produced by inanimate objects (such as wind, thunder, or music). The auditory system is composed of the ear and the auditory nerve (the eighth cranial nerve), which carries all perceived sounds to the brain for interpretation.

The ear is usually divided into three parts, for purposes of description: an outer ear, a middle ear, and an inner ear. The outer ear contains two important portions. First, a fleshy auricle (which people see and think of as the ear) is attached to the side of the head. The auricle—composed of cartilage, skin, and fat—catches sounds and conveys them into a short tube that enters the head.

This skin-covered, 3-centimeter-long tube, the external auditory canal (auditory meatus), is the second important part of the outer ear. The first third of the canal is lined with fine hairs and with tiny glands that produce ear wax. The hairs and wax keep dust and other foreign particles from injuring the rest of the canal. When too much wax forms in an ear canal, it should be removed by a physician, because the wax can shut off the canal and press against the eardrum, producing pain and/or decreasing the ability to hear.

The end of the external auditory canal, the eardrum, lies against one end of the middle ear (the tympanic cavity), a small space in the temporal bone of the skull. When a sound enters the ear, it passes through the external ear canal and causes the eardrum to vibrate. Then, three small, attached bones—the hammer (malleus), anvil (incus) and stirrup (stapes)—in the middle ear also vibrate. These bones span the middle ear and transmit sounds across it. The transmission begins when the malleus, attached to the eardrum, vibrates. The vibration is next transmitted to the incus, and finally to the stapes. The stapes fits into an interior opening of the cavity, the so-called oval window, and when sound waves cause it to vibrate, the vibrations ultimately stimulate the auditory nerve.

Some hearing is retained even when a large hole is made in the eardrum or when one bone of the inner ear is missing. This residual hearing is attributable to several things. First, a secondary eardrum that can vibrate and carry sound is located in a hole—the round window—just below the oval window, and its vibration can also stimulate the auditory nerve. Second, sound can be carried through the bones of the skull—bone conduction—to the auditory nerve. Bone conduction and secondary eardrum action are not nearly as effective as sound transmission via an intact eardrum and functional malleus, incus, and stapes bones.

The air-filled tympanic cavity is connected to the throat by the eustachian tube, which equalizes the air pressure on both sides of the eardrum, preventing unequal pressure from bursting the eardrum. Pressure equalization occurs when yawns or swallowing open the tube, which is usually closed; such opening can spread throat infections to the mucous membrane of the middle ear.

The 2-centimeter-long inner ear, or bony labyrinth, connects the middle ear to the auditory nerve. This labyrinth begins with a chamber, or vestibule, that leads into three semicircular canals involved in balance and a bony cochlea, involved in hearing; the cochlea looks somewhat like a snail shell. The soft, interior contents of the bony labyrinth are the vehicle for connection to the auditory nerve. This tissue is surrounded by a fluid called perilymph and filled with a fluid called endolymph. The outermost portion of the membranous labyrinth contains the connections to the auditory nerve.

Within the vestibule, a saclike portion of the membranous labyrinth (the saccule) is connected to the middle ear and to the cochlea. The cochlea itself is divided by membranes into vestibular, tympanic, and cochlear canals, which run its entire length.

Vestibular and tympanic canals, filled with perilymph, receive vibrations (sound waves) from the stapes (stirrup bone) and the secondary eardrum, respectively.

The cochlear canal contains the organ of Corti, filled with thousands of fibers (or hairs) of differing lengths. These fibers are relatively short at the beginning of the cochlea but increase in length as they approach its end. When sound waves move through the perilymph of the inner ear, they make the fibers vibrate. Low-pitched sounds make long fibers vibrate, and high-pitched sounds make short fibers vibrate. Because of the variation of lengths of the fibers, the average human ear can distinguish sounds that exhibit nearly sixteen hundred differences in pitch. The cochlea is only 0.5 centimeter long.

Sounds arise from sound waves, which range from low-pitched ones that vibrate fifteen times a second to very high-pitched ones that vibrate twenty thousand times a second. The vibration of the organ of Corti fibers stimulates the auditory nerve and carries a complex sound message to the brain, where it is translated. Loud sounds are loud because they stimulate the vibration of many more fibers than soft sounds do.

The ear is easily damaged by disease and by accidents. For example, it is easily reached by mouth and throat infections, which produce ear infections. Inadequate treatment can damage the ear and lessen the ability to hear, causing partial hearing loss or deafness, the complete inability to hear. Sounds that are excessively loud can also damage the ear and hearing.

Furthermore, some careless actions meant in fun, or done in ignorance, can produce ear and hearing damage. Two common occurrences of this kind are "boxing" a person's ear and attempting to remove ear wax from one's own ear. The first action, a blow to the ear with an open palm that completely covers the ear, can push air into the ear forcefully enough to rupture an eardrum and cause deafness. Attempts to clear ear wax from an ear with cotton swabs or sharp objects are also potentially dangerous because they can rupture the eardrum and may push the wax further into the ear, where it can cause damage that will decrease hearing. For these reasons, physicians often advise people to keep all objects "smaller than an elbow" out of their ears.

## Applications

An understanding of the anatomy and mechanistics of the auditory system allows examination of the basis for hearing. It can be shown with electrodes inserted into the ear, for example, that the cochlea transduces all audible sounds into electrical impulses, acting much like a microphone. The action of this auditory microphone can be amplified and recorded on an oscilliscope and can be converted into sounds by use of a loudspeaker. In addition, when the different areas of the cochlea are tested in this way, it can be shown that low tones are picked up by fibers at its apex and high tones are picked up by those at its base. It is believed that the auditory microphone then stimulates the auditory nerve and carries the sound to the brain for interpretation.

Three classical theories of the mechanism of hearing are a resonance theory, which bases differentiation of sounds on the place at which stimulation of the cochlear system occurs; a frequency (telephone) theory, supposing that the frequency of individual sound waves is translated directly to nerve impulses; and a combined theory, which is more current. The telephone theory was proposed in 1886. Its main shortcoming is the fact that nerve fibers cannot transmit impulses at high enough rates to allow detection of all the sounds that humans can hear.

The resonance theory was proposed by Hermann von Helmholtz in the middle of the nineteenth century. It views the cochlear apparatus as a vibrational analyzer that responds, at specific places, to individual sound frequencies, activating specific nerve sites. Helmholtz viewed such nerve activation as causing subsequent activation of the brain at a specific point—depending on the original sound—to produce the perception of a particular pitch. Among the observations that led researchers to question the complete validity of this theory is the fact that cochlear nerve fibers are not organized appropriately to allow resonance recognition to happen precisely.

More recently, a "resonance-volley" theory has become accepted as a compromise that explains the observations of contemporary research. The theory proposes that within certain limits, several nerve fibers can act together—in a volley—to allow the perception of sounds that exceed the upper limit of a single fiber. Above a permissible range, it is presumed that a frequency mechanism takes over. Therefore, the perception of low-pitched sounds is believed to depend on the telephone theory, while that of higher-pitched ones is presumed to depend upon the position of nerve stimulation.

Although many deaf people are born lacking hearing (congenital deafness), adventitious deafness can develop at almost any time in life. Both congenital and adventitious deafness can be divided into conductive, sensorineural, and central types. These problems arise, respectively, from impaired sound conduction to the inner ear, abnormalities of the inner ear or the auditory nerve, or dysfunction of the central nervous system.

Deafness can result from a wide variety of causes; already mentioned are buildup of ear wax, accidents such as breaking an eardrum by boxing an ear, and ear infection. Middle ear infection—otitis media—is a common cause of conductive deafness. Such infections often begin when upper respiratory infection or allergy causes nasal secretions to back up the eustachean tube, block the middle ear, and cause pressure inequalities. These inequalities can restrict eardrum action or even rupture the eardrum.

Many genetic problems cause deafness, including oterosclerosis, in which decalcification of the bone is followed by the production of abnormal bone that prevents the movement of the stirrup bone (stapes) and greatly decreases the amount of sound that reaches the inner ear. Certain chemicals, loud noises, loss of sensory cells in old age, and central nervous system damage are only a few of the other causes of deafness.

Deafness at birth is a serious disability, because the acquisition of spoken language through hearing pervades all aspects of life. People with congenital deafness have diminished communication capacities. Their educational achievement, intellectual function, personality and vocational development, and overall quality of life can all be affected. The presumption that other senses "sharpen" to compensate for a lack of hearing is not true, according to experts such as Brian Bolton. Studies have shown deaf people to be more introverted than individuals with unimpaired hearing; depression has also been linked to deafness.

## Context

The primary problem associated with the auditory system is deafness. Handling deafness in the young is particularly important. Better understanding of the auditory system has led to more effective methods for the prevention, the diagnosis, and the treatment of some of the problems related to deafness. For example, it is presently realized that immunization against viral disease, careful attention to upper respiratory bacterial infections (accompanied by quick antibiotic therapy), and removal of the tonsils and/or adenoids helps to prevent many potential hearing problems that lead to deafness. Successful use of such methodologies have somewhat decreased the incidence of deafness.

As to diagnostic techniques, the use of professional audiologists has become more common, which both allows early identification of the symptoms that indicate developing hearing impairment and shows how best to treat the problem. Such diagnosis and treatment are currently available in hospitals, in schools, and in hearing clinics.

Once hearing impairment or deafness is identified, treatment methods available include antibiotic therapy and various types of surgery. One example of surgical treatment is stapedectomy, where the oterosclerotic patient can be rescued by repairing the junction between the oval window of the inner ear and the stapes (stirrup) bone. The immobile stapes and oval window are removed and replaced by a tissue graft coupled to an artificial stapes that is connected appropriately with the incus (anvil) bone of the middle ear. Other surgical techniques available include repair of perforated eardrums (myringoplasty) and cochlear implants that can help to restore hearing by allowing direct electrical stimulation of the auditory nerve.

Nonmedical treatments of hearing impairments include use of electroacoustic hearing aids and special education techniques that teach deaf people to communicate by nonaural methods, including sign language. In addition, social counseling and the efforts of psychologists and psychiatrists have become quite useful for treatment of neuroses and psychoses that may stem from sensory deprivation and other problems that accompany deafness.

The best approaches to deafness are still cautious conservation of hearing by avoiding loud noise and other environmental occurrences that can produce deafness; obtaining quick, effective treatment for diseases that can cause hearing impairment; and early identification of impairment, followed by its cure before deafness results. It is hoped that continuing research will increase the avenues for prevention of deafness by surgical, medical, and psychological methods and will identify methods for preventing congenital deafness.

## Bibliography

Ballantyne, John Chalmers, and J. A. M. Martin. *Deafness.* 4th ed. Edinburgh: Churchill Livingstone, 1984. This expert book attempts "a general account couched in simple terms, of the disability of deafness and its relief." Coverage includes description of the auditory system, diagnosis of deafness and explanation of its causes, description of hearing aids, exploration of psychological aspects, and rehabilitation of the deaf.

Bess, Fred H., and Larry E. Humes. *Audiology: The Fundamentals.* Baltimore: Williams & Wilkins, 1990. This introductory book is designed for students of audiology. Its clear, simple language, abundant vignettes, and many literature references make it useful. Topics of interest include the nature of sound, auditory system structure and function, assessment of auditory function, and management strategies for the hearing impaired.

Bolton, Brian, ed. *Psychology of Deafness for Rehabilitation Counselors.* Baltimore: University Park Press, 1976. Provides useful information on problems associated with deafness and their treatment. A good counterpoint to the aspects of the normal auditory system. Included are aspects of intellectual and vocational development, academic achievement, psychiatry of deafness, and intervention and rehabilitation programs.

Daniloff, Raymond, Gordon Schuckers, and Lawrence Feth. *The Physiology of Speech and Hearing: An Introduction.* Englewood Cliffs, N.J.: Prentice-Hall, 1980. This introductory book does a thorough job, using clear, simple language. The chapter entitled "Audition: The Sense of Hearing" is important. In addition, chapters providing overviews of speech and hearing, basic neuroscience, and acoustics are quite useful.

Keidel, Wolf Dieter, S. Kallert, and M. Korth. *The Physiological Basis of Hearing.* New York: Thieme-Stratton, 1983. This expert, technical text comprehensively reviews the physiology and operation of the auditory system. Well worth examining, it includes excellent descriptions of the anatomy, physiology, and operation of the auditory system, as well as theories of its operation, with experimental and theoretical explanations. Almost thirteen hundred references are included.

*Sanford S. Singer*

## Cross-References

Hearing: Loudness, Pitch, and Frequency, 1146; Hearing and Sound Waves, 1151; Hearing Loss, 1157; Kinesthesis and Vestibular Sensitivity, 1381; Signal Detection Theory, 2271; Sound Localization, 2335; Speech Perception, 2348.

# AUTISM

*Type of psychology:* Psychopathology
*Field of study:* Childhood and adolescent disorders

*Autism, a poorly understood, nonschizophrenic psychosocial problem, includes great social unresponsiveness, speech and language impairment, ritualistic play activity, and resistance to change. It causes the parents of autists great grief and disrupts the life of the entire family, although the autist is oblivious to the familial trauma.*

*Principal terms*
AFFECTIVE: behavior resulting from emotions or feelings, rather than from thought
APHASIC: one who has lost the ability to articulate ideas because of brain damage
AUTIST: an autistic person
COGNITIVE: relating to the mental process or faculty by which humans acquire knowledge
ECHOLALIA: an involuntary and parrotlike repetition of words or phrases spoken by others
ELECTROENCEPHALOGRAM (EEG): a graphic record of the brain's electrical activity, used diagnostically to identify brain damage and psychiatric problems
EPILEPTIC SEIZURE: an attack of epilepsy, characterized by convulsion, motor, sensory, and psychic malfunction
SCHIZOPHRENIA: any of a group of psychotic reactions characterized by withdrawal from reality, with accompanying affective, behavioral, and intellectual disturbances
SEROTONIN: a neurotransmitter produced from the amino acid tryptophan; implicated in a number of psychological disorders
TARDIVE DYSKINESIA: slow, involuntary motor movements, especially of the mouth and tongue, which can become permanent and untreatable

## Overview
The modern term "autism" was originated by Leo Kanner in the 1940's. In "Autistic Disturbances of Affective Contact" (1943), he described a group of these children; he viewed them as much more similar to one another than to the schizophrenics, with whom they generally had been associated. Until that time, the classical definition for autism (still seen in some dictionaries) was "a form of childhood schizophrenia characterized by acting out and withdrawal from reality." Kanner believed that these children represented an entirely different clinical psychiatric disorder. He noted four main symptoms associated with the disease: social withdrawal or

"extreme autistic aloneness"; either muteness or failure to use spoken language "to convey meaning to others"; an "obsessive desire for maintenance of sameness"; and preoccupation with highly repetitive play habits, producing "severe limitation of spontaneous activity." Kanner also noted that autism—unlike other types of childhood psychoses—began in or near infancy.

Over the years, several attempts have been made to establish precise diagnostic criteria for autism. The criteria that were given in the American Psychiatric Association's *Diagnostic and Statistical Manual of Mental Disorders* (3d ed.; 1980, DSM-III) are onset prior to thirty months of age; pervasive lack of responsiveness to other people; gross deficits in language development; if speech is present, peculiar patterns (such as delayed echolalia and pronoun reversals); bizarre reaction to environmental aspects (resistance to change); and the absence of any symptoms of schizophrenia. These criteria are largely a restatement of Kanner's viewpoint.

Although the basic cause of autism is still in dispute, it is believed to be attributable to a fundamental cognitive deficit. The prevalence of autism is generally estimated at between 0.1 and 0.4 percent of the population of the world. Study of the sex distribution shows that it is 2.5 to 4 times as common in males as in females.

Largely because of Kanner's original sample (now known to have been atypical), many people believe that autistic children come from professional families and have the capacity for quite normal intellectual function. Subsequent studies have indicated that this is not so. Rather, autistic children come from families within a wide socioeconomic range, and more than 70 percent of them are mentally retarded, exhibiting quite stable intelligence quotient (IQ) scores over a wide age range.

The behavior that characterizes the autistic personality strongly suggests that the disorder is related to other types of neurologic dysfunction. Identified neurological correlations include soft neurologic signs (such as poor coordination), seizure disorders (such as phenylketonuria), abnormal electroencephalograms, and unusual sleep patterns. This emphasis on neurologic—or organic—explanations for autism is relatively new; autism was previously thought to be an entirely emotional disorder.

The difficulties that autistic children show in social relationships are exhibited in many ways. Most apparent is a child's failure to form social bonds. For example, such youngsters rarely initiate any interactions with other children. Moreover, unlike nonautistic children, they do not seek parental company or run to parents for solace when distressed. Many sources even point to frequent parental statements that an autistic child is not as "cuddly" as normal babies and that autists do not respond to their mothers or to affectionate actions. Autistic children avoid direct eye contact and tend to look through or past other people. In addition, autistic children rarely indulge in any cooperative play activities or strike up close friendships with peers.

Sometimes speech does not develop at all. When speech development does occur, it is very slow and may even disappear again. Another prominent speech pathology in autism is either immediate or delayed repetition of something heard but simply parroted back (such as a television commercial), phenomena called immediate and delayed echolalia, respectively. Yet another problem seen is lack of true language comprehension, shown by the fact that an autistic child's ability to follow instructions is often dependent on situational cues. For example, such a child may understand the request to come and eat dinner only when a parent is eating or sitting at the dinner table.

Behavior denoting resistance to change is often best exemplified by rigid and repetitive play patterns, the interruption of which results in tantrums and even self-injury. Some autistic children also develop very ritualistic preoccupations with an object or a schedule. For example, they may become extremely distressed with events as minor as the rearrangement of furniture in a particular room at home.

## Applications

Autistic children can be very frustrating to both parents and siblings, disrupting their lives greatly. Often, autists also cause grief and guilt feelings in parents and may diminish their social standing. According to Mary Van Bourgondien, Gary Mesibov, and Geraldine Dawson, in "Pervasive Developmental Disorders: Autism" (1987), this can be ameliorated by psychodynamic, biological, or behavioral techniques. These authors point out that all psychodynamic therapy views autism as an emotional problem, recommending extensive psychotherapy for the autist and the rest of the family. In contrast, biological methodology applies psychoactive drugs and vitamins. Finally, behavioral therapy uses the axioms of experimental psychology, along with special education techniques that teach and reinforce appropriate behavior.

Some interesting aspects of behavioral techniques are described in *Effective Teaching Methods for Autistic Children* (1974), by Rosalind Oppenheim. For example, it is pointed out that many autists have the speech problems associated with aphasic children and the odd body movements of children with perceptual problems. A suggested technique used successfully by Oppenheim is teaching an autistic child to write and then asking "why" questions, to be answered in writing. This technique is reported to be quite successful at enhancing the "inner intellectual development" of some autists.

One autistic child cited by these authors was a teenager designated as Bill. Initially, Bill was uncommunicative, failed to look at his teacher or school work, and persisted in being uncooperative. Within about five months he was reported as having made substantial improvement in a number of academic areas and in speech. The regimen utilized to cause the improvement was a combination of the use of multiple-choice questions and longer written answers to questions.

A wide discussion of the use of biological intervention can be found in *The Biology of the Autistic Syndrome* (1985), by Mary Coleman and Christopher Gillberg, and in *Autism: Nature, Diagnosis, and Treatment* (1989), edited by Geraldine Dawson. As these authors and others point out, the therapeutic drugs of most frequent choice are anticonvulsants, amphetamines, phenothiazines, Haldol, and megavitamins. Anticonvulsants are utilized to control epileptic seizures because of frequent occurrence of this problem in up to 40 percent of autists. The medications of widest use are those that do not cause hyperactivity, another problem often observed in autistic children. Also used to combat hyperactivity are amphetamines; concurrent with their calming effect, these drugs may make autists more teachable.

Phenothiazines and Haldol are used mostly to reduce the occurrence of aggression and self-injury seen in some autists. It is necessary to use carefully monitored doses of these drugs to prevent the occurrence of epileptic seizures and tardive dyskinesia. Along these lines, the use of large amounts of standard vitamins (megavitamins) has also been attempted, with varying effects.

A major aspect of many drug treatments concerns efforts to alter the serotonin levels in autists, as this neurotransmitter (associated with other psychiatric disorders and elevated in some autists) is thought by many to be related to autism. Such conceptualization has also led to utilization of a drug called fenfluramine, a diet drug that lowers serotonin levels in the general population. Neither consistent results nor clear interrelationships between serotonin level alteration and easing of autistic symptoms have been obtained, however; in some cases, biological intervention has had good results, but successes have been low overall.

Similarly, the psychodynamic approach has had varied success. Regrettably, no widepread and predictable results have been achieved in treating autism with any of the methods tested by the 1980's; the treatment of autistic children remains highly individualized. It has been proposed that this is partly the result of an insufficiency of facilities that provide for special learning and other needs of autists.

## Context

It is widely reported that autistic children, as defined by Kanner in the 1940's, were at first perceived as victims of an affective disorder brought on by their emotionally cold, very intellectual, and compulsive parents. The personality traits of these parents, it was theorized, encouraged such children to withdraw from social contact with them, and then with all other people. This conceptualization fit not only with the data available but also with the highly behavioristic bent of psychiatry and psychology at the time.

In the years that have followed, additional data—as well as conceptual changes in medicine and psychology—have led to the belief that autism, which may actually be a constellation of disorders that exhibit similar symptoms, has a biological basis that may reside in subtle brain and hormone abnormalities. These concepts have been investigated and are leading to definitive changes in the therapy used to treat individual autistic children. Although no general treatment or unifying concept of autism has developed, promising leads include modalities that utilize drugs which alter levels of serotonin and other neurotransmitters, as well as examination of patients by nuclear magnetic resonance and other new techniques useful for studying the brain and the nervous system.

The evolution of educational methodology aimed at helping autists has also been useful, aided by legislation aimed at bringing severely developmentally disabled children into the mainstream. Some cities and states have developed widespread programs for educating autistic people of all ages. Instrumental here has been the development of the National Society for Autistic Children, which has focused some of its efforts on dealing with autistic adolescents and adults.

The fruits of all these efforts are the fact that combined therapy, biological intervention, and educational techniques have helped autistic persons and their families to cope; have decreased behavior problems in autists; have enhanced the scholastic function of a number of these people; and have produced hope for autistic adults, once nearly all institutionalized.

## Bibliography

American Psychiatric Association. *Diagnostic and Statistical Manual of Mental Disorders.* 3d ed. Washington, D.C.: Author, 1980. This manual (often called DSM-III-R) contains diagnostic criteria and many other useful facts about a wide variety of mental disorders. It provides information useful to the categorization of autism and its comparison with other mental diseases with similar symptoms.

Coleman, Mary, and Christopher Gillberg. *The Biology of the Autistic Syndrome.* New York: Praeger, 1985. Goes into considerable detail at a professional, but readable, level on many aspects of autism. Includes clinical considerations; a review of pertinent literature, disease entities, and treatments within the autistic disorder; and hypotheses concerning its basis. Hundreds of references are included.

Dawson, Geraldine, ed. *Autism: Nature, Diagnosis, and Treatment.* New York: Guilford Press, 1989. Contains a wealth of useful information and many useful references. Seventeen chapters cover a broad range of topics, under the general headings perspectives on the nature of autism, neurobiological issues in autism, and new directions in autism diagnosis and treatment.

Kanner, Leo. "Autistic Disturbances of Affective Contact." *Nervous Child* 2 (1943): 217-250. This landmark article began the modern conceptualization of autism. It describes autistic behavior and differentiates autism from "childhood schizophrenia," as others had previously labeled the disorder. Kanner also identifies the good cognitive potential of autistic children, a belief no longer held.

Oppenheim, Rosalind C. *Effective Teaching Methods for Autistic Children.* Foreword by Bernard Rimland. Springfield, Ill.: Charles C Thomas, 1974. This useful book describes educational techniques that Oppenheim, the mother of an autistic son, developed for teaching autistic children. Identifies child-management methods for overcoming autistic children's behavioral difficulties. Includes information on the use of questions and written answers to aid in developing language abilities.

Powers, Michael D., and Jan S. Handleman. "Nature and Needs of Severely Developmentally Disabled Clients." In *Behavioral Assessment of Severe Developmental Disabilities.* Rockville, Md.: Aspen Systems, 1984. This succinct chapter includes useful introductory material, a historical perspective, diagnostic techniques, diagnostic criteria—including comparison of those from DSM-III and from the National Society of Autistic Children—and aspects of patient needs. Contains more than two hundred references.

Schopler, Eric, and Gary B. Mesibov, eds. *Autism in Adolescents and Adults.* New

York: Plenum Press, 1983. This edited work distills material presented at a conference attended by national experts in the area. It covers aspects of adult and adolescent autism including perspectives and issues; linguistics; educational, recreational and vocational issues; medical requirements; and familial coping. Covers many issues that are not often described.

Van Bourgondien, Mary E., Gary B. Mesibov, and Geraldine Dawson. "Pervasive Developmental Disorders: Autism." In *The Practical Assessment and Management of Children with Disorders of Development and Learning*, edited by Mark L. Wolraich. Chicago: Year Book Medical Publishers, 1987. Succinctly and clearly describes autism, including its definition, incidence, etiologies and pathophysiologies, assessment and findings, and management. Also included are 133 useful references. Technically written, the article is nevertheless very useful to the beginning reader.

*Sanford S. Singer*

### Cross-References

Abnormality: Behavioral Models, 33; Abnormality: Biomedical Models, 39; Abnormality: Family Models, 53; Attention, 313; Brain Injuries: Concussions, Contusions, and Strokes, 448; Language and Cognition, 1401; Schizophrenia: Background, Types, and Symptoms, 2129; Schizophrenia: Theoretical Explanations, 2141.

# AUTOMATICITY

*Type of psychology:* Consciousness
*Field of study:* Cognitive processes

*Automaticity refers to the ability to perform certain types of mental and motor skills with very little attention; skills become automatic when they are highly practiced under consistent conditions. The development of automaticity can improve human performance in many ways, but it can also lead to errors in responding when conditions change rapidly.*

### Principal terms

AUTOMATIC PROCESS: a mental skill or motor act that can be performed with little attention but that is difficult to change

CONSISTENT MAPPING: a situation in which a particular stimulus always calls for the same response

CONTROLLED PROCESS: a mental skill or motor act that requires considerable attention but that is relatively easy to modify

DUAL-TASK METHODOLOGY: the use of two tasks that a subject tries to perform simultaneously in order to assess the difficulty of one of the tasks

REACTION TIME: the time needed for a subject to make a response to a stimulus

VARIED MAPPING: a situation in which a stimulus should sometimes be responded to and sometimes ignored

## Overview

Psychologists have found it useful to classify many aspects of human mental and motor performance as either "automatic" or "controlled." Automatic processes are those that are carried out with ease, often requiring little or no attention. They can usually also be performed simultaneously with other tasks. Controlled processes, on the other hand, are more difficult and typically require a person's full attention. Because they require so much attention, it is difficult to do anything else at the same time. Research on automaticity has outlined the conditions under which each type of processing can develop, as well as the conditions under which each works best.

To illustrate automaticity and its development, consider the task of driving an automobile. (Driving really involves many tasks, such as steering, looking out for traffic and pedestrians, checking for traffic lights and signs, changing speed—and starting and stopping—as traffic changes, and perhaps even discussing directions with a passenger.) When first learning to drive, most people have difficulty doing all these things at once. When they see a stop sign, for example, they may have to decide consciously and deliberately which pedal to push to stop the car. For novice drivers, holding a conversation while driving is also difficult—if they pay attention to their driving, they will not hear what their passenger says, but if they listen and respond to their passenger, they may be endangering themselves and others. After some experience, however, the same person (now a relatively expert driver) will stop at a stop sign, check for oncoming traffic, and proceed safely, all while holding up his or her end of a conversation.

What has changed that makes the response to a stop sign so much easier? Psychologists describe this phenomenon by saying that for the novice driver the act of stopping at a stop sign was controlled, but, through practice, has become automatic. Another example of this change is reading, which is initially very difficult. With practice, however, a skilled reader no longer has to think about reading as a deliberate act. Instead, when one points one's eyes at a printed page, words are recognized automatically.

Walter Schneider and Richard Shiffrin have been active in working out the details of how (and under what conditions) a process changes from controlled to automatic. The change from controlled to automatic processing is a gradual one. Put another way, automaticity is a matter of degree. From the examples above, it is clear that practice is a key ingredient in automaticity. Their research has highlighted the relevance of the kind, as well as the degree, of practice. They have described two kinds of practice: practice with consistent mapping, which promotes automaticity, and practice with varied mapping, which does not. The term "mapping" here refers to the relationship between stimulus and response, or which response is "mapped" onto each stimulus.

To pursue the example of driving, the difference between consistent and varied mapping can be likened to the difference between a stop sign and a yield sign. A stop sign involves consistent mapping, because the only response one should ever make to a stop sign is to stop. The sign never calls for any other response. In addition, a stop sign always calls for the response of stopping. These are the hallmarks of consistent mapping: a particular response is always (consistently) mapped to a particular stimulus. That is the only response to make to the stimulus, and the stimulus never appears under circumstances when it should be ignored. As a result of always stopping at stop signs, that response becomes automatic and can be executed without a pause in a conversation between the driver and a passenger. A yield sign, on the other hand, is an example of varied mapping. When a yield sign is seen, it sometimes means that one should continue without stopping (if no traffic is coming). If there is other traffic coming, however, it means that one should stop. A driver sometimes has to respond to a yield sign by stopping but at other times only needs to check quickly for other traffic.

To promote automatic processing, large amounts of practice with consistent mapping are needed. The mental or motor act thus practiced becomes automatic: It is now easy to perform and can easily be shared with other activities, but it is very difficult to change, in part because it calls so little attention to itself. There are costs to as well as benefits from automaticity. One cost is the large amount of practice required for the development of automaticity. The inflexibility of automatic processes can also lead to inappropriate responses if the situation changes. As an example, imagine the difficulties faced by drivers in Sweden when, in the 1960's, the nation switched from driving on the left side of the road (as in the United Kingdom) to driving on the right. Drivers setting off to work on the morning after the change might well have found themselves driving on the (now) wrong side of the road. That is an extreme example, but any time that flexibility of response is required, controlled processes, though somewhat slower, may be better. Where flexibility is not a problem and quick response is needed, automaticity should be encouraged.

## Applications

Much of the research conducted on the development of automaticity has involved a letter search task, in which a subject is seated before a computer monitor. Subjects are told to look for a letter (or several different letters). They start the task and begin seeing a series of letters on the screen. Whenever one of the items they are looking for appears, they are to press a key on the computer keyboard. Usually they do many such trials, divided into two types. On some series of trials, they always search for the same letters, such as $P$ and $C$. This is consistent mapping, because any time they see a $P$ or a $C$ they are to press the key. On another series of trials, however, the letters for which they are to search change every few trials; a letter for which subjects searched a moment before may now appear on the screen but no longer be a target. This is varied mapping. Note that if the letters $P$ and $C$ were used for the consistently mapped condition they never appear as distractors (nontargets) in the varied mapping condition. The only time the subject sees them is when they are targets.

To test for the development of automaticity, a common approach is to employ a dual-task methodology. After considerable training at the task described above (typically twenty to thirty hours), a second task is added, which is to be performed at the same time. One task that has often been used is a category search task, in which the subject (in addition to searching for certain letters) also sees words displayed on the screen and must decide whether the word fits into a certain category (for example, "pieces of furniture"). The typical finding is that subjects who are searching for the consistently mapped letters ($P$ and $C$, in this example) will show little change in reaction time, or the time from when they see the letter to when they respond to it. They will continue to make rapid, accurate responses to the letter search task while also doing well at the category search task. On the other hand, subjects who are looking for target letters that were practiced with varied mapping will suddenly become slower and less accurate, and they will do poorly on the category search task. Just as the novice driver has to think about what to do when approaching a stop sign and will pause in a conversation, so the subject searching for varied targets will find sharing two tasks difficult.

One interesting example of the degree to which a task may become automatic was given by the concert pianist Charles Rosen. When practicing for a performance of a piano concerto that he knew well, he found that he became bored, so he began to read light novels while practicing. Reading is a relatively automatic task, which he could apparently combine easily with the (at least partially) automatic task of playing a well-practiced piece of music.

In examining many skills, it becomes evident that at least some aspects of them are (and probably must be) automatic. Driving is composed of many component skills, some automatic (such as steering and braking at stop signs) and some controlled (such as choosing at which corner to turn). The same is true in other areas as well. One reason for drill in practicing sports is to increase automaticity so that responses are quick and reliable. In baseball, a base runner who has to stop to plan how to slide into base would have a short career. In education, one must be able to recall the multiplication tables quickly and accurately in order to use them easily at each step in multiplying two three-digit numbers.

One practical issue raised by research on automaticity is the degree to which drill is necessary in educational practice. At one time, educational practice relied heavily on large amounts of drill. More recently, drill has been seen as boring and "irrelevant" to education. It is now clear, however, that drill, or repetitive practice, is absolutely essential to gaining many of the component skills necessary for success at larger skills. Without enough drill in algebra, for example, students find that their first course in calculus is mostly spent trying to figure out the algebra of the equations, with an accompanying reduction in understanding of the new material. Further research will provide more information about the optimum amount of drill: not enough to discourage people through boredom, but enough so that the skill being practiced can be easily integrated into more complex tasks.

## Context

In *The Principles of Psychology* (1890), William James, who was a principal founder of American psychology, described the fact that some mental acts are so easy that one hardly notices them, while others require careful thought and attention. It is exactly this distinction that finds modern expression in the distinction between automatic and controlled processes. It was not until the 1970's that experimental psychologists, including Schneider and Shiffrin, developed ways to study automatic processes, and especially the acquisition of these processes.

The development of cognitive psychology, beginning in the 1950's, has shown the benefit to psychology of studying complex psychological processes by trying to identify and study their various components. By focusing on one part of the overall task at a time, more adequate experimental control can be gained, and each component skill can more easily be studied. By knowing the conditions under which automaticity develops, and by having approaches such as dual-task methodology to help measure automaticity, those parts of a complex task that are best performed automatically can be isolated. That isolation can lead to improvements in learning, because aspects of a complex skill that can be performed automatically can be subject to drill. It also can lead to improved understanding of complex mental processes (such as reading), which can result in the discovery of ways to help new learners understand what is required for mastery.

The study of automaticity has added to the general study of phenomena of attention. Fully automatic processes, such as well-trained letter searches in a Schneider and Shiffrin experiment or braking at a stop sign, seem to require almost no attention at all. A popular view of attention is the "resource" approach, suggested by Daniel Kahneman, which treats attention as a limited resource that can be assigned fairly flexibly. When a task to which one is paying attention is fairly easy (that is, uses few attentional resources), it can often be performed at the same time as another task. If a task requires considerable attentional resources, however, one is unable to perform another task at the same time. To use the example of driving again, think of driving in a thunderstorm or on icy roads. Suddenly, holding a conversation becomes too much trouble, and the driver will probably not even respond if a passenger tries to start a conversation. In this case, the driver must attend and respond in a controlled manner to many aspects of driving that are usually automatic. Thus, the concepts of automatic and controlled processes fit well with one of the major approaches to the study of attention.

## Bibliography

Kahneman, Daniel. *Attention and Effort.* Englewood Cliffs, N.J.: Prentice-Hall, 1973. This book first made the resource notion of attention widely popular among psychologists. It details many experiments that lend support to that view. Although written for an audience of psychologists, it is readable by a wider audience and provides the contextual background in which the ideas of automaticity were developed.

Schneider, Walter. "Training High-Performance Skills: Fallacies and Guidelines." *Human Factors* 27 (1985): 285-300. This paper provides an excellent overview of what is known about the practical application of knowledge concerning automaticity to the training of high-level skills. The emphasis is on practice, rather than theory; the discussion is aimed at correcting some common errors made in training skilled personnel, including a tendency to ignore drill even when it is essential to learning.

Smyth, Mary M., et al. *Cognition in Action.* Hillsdale, N.J.: Lawrence Erlbaum, 1987. This very readable presentation of modern cognitive psychology includes a discussion of how automaticity comes about through training and how automaticity is demonstrated experimentally. A number of interesting experiments on dual-task performance are discussed. One of the more readable accounts of automaticity.

Solso, Robert L. *Cognitive Psychology.* 2d ed. Boston: Allyn & Bacon, 1988. Discusses automaticity within the context of resource models of attention. Solso includes several interesting descriptions of automaticity acting in everyday life.

Wickens, Christopher D. *Engineering Psychology and Human Performance.* Columbus, Ohio: Charles E. Merrill, 1984. Wickens provides a general survey of engineering psychology, or the application of knowledge from experimental psychology to engineering objects and systems for human use. Treats attention at length, as well as issues of automatic and controlled processing and their implications for the design of systems for human use.

*James D. St. James*

## Cross-References

Attention, 313; Cognitive Maps, 566; Functions of Consciousness, 656; Pattern Recognition as a Cognitive Process, 1747; Reflexes, 2066.

# THE AUTONOMIC NERVOUS SYSTEM

*Type of psychology:* Biological bases of behavior
*Field of study:* Nervous system

*The sympathetic and parasympathetic divisions of the nervous system are responsible for the maintenance of homeostasis in vertebrates. These two systems make constant physiological adjustments to compensate for changes that are occurring in the internal and external environment of the animal. In doing so, they influence the behavior of animals in many ways.*

*Principal terms*

ADRENAL GLAND: one of the endocrine glands associated with the autonomic nervous system

AUTONOMIC NERVOUS SYSTEM: the portion of the peripheral nervous system responsible for the maintenance of homeostasis

EPINEPHRINE: the neurotransmitter released from the adrenal gland as a result of innervation of the autonomic nervous system

HOMEOSTASIS: the maintenance of the internal environment of living organisms within narrow parameters that provide the optimum chance for survival

INNERVATION: the nervous stimulation of a muscle cell or another nerve

NEUROTRANSMITTERS: chemical messengers released from neurons that can conduct nerve impulses to other neurons or can stimulate the contraction of muscle cells

NOREPINEPHRINE: the neurotransmitter released from neurons and the adrenal gland when the autonomic nervous system is stimulated

## Overview

The nervous system of humans is categorized according to function into two discrete units, the somatic and the autonomic nervous systems. These systems not only have different functions but also operate through different parts of the brain and different nerves. The somatic system deals with those activities of the brain and spinal cord which stimulate the contraction of the skeletal muscle and thus control posture and movement. All these activities are under voluntary control, which means that the maintenance of posture and movements are dependent upon the will of the animal.

The autonomic nervous system is responsible for the maintenance of homeostasis, often referred to as the internal environment of the animal. The internal environment includes such things as heart rate, rate of respiration, and blood pressure. The activities of the autonomic nervous system are called the visceral responses and are generally considered to be involuntary. The animal is unaware of most of these activities, even though they are essential to life. The autonomic nervous system operates by stimulating smooth muscle, cardiac muscle, or glands.

The autonomic nervous system is further divided into two divisions, the sympathetic and the parasympathetic. Just as the somatic and autonomic systems use different nerves and have different functions, so the sympathetic and parasympathetic divisions of the nervous system are independent of each other and have different functions.

The sympathetic branch is responsive when a person is very active physically or is placed in a stressful situation. It not only involves the nervous system but also stimulates the medullary portion of the adrenal gland. During the sympathetic activity, epinephrine or norepinephrine (also called adrenaline and noradrenaline) are released by the nervous system, which in turn stimulates release of more neurotransmitter from the adrenal medulla. This has often been called the fight-or-flight reaction. The term is derived from the sympathetic responses of animals who are often subject to attack by predators. The fight-or-flight reaction suggests that the animal has been frightened or attacked by a predator and must either attempt an escape or prepare to remain and fight the predator. During this reaction there is an increase in heart rate and in the strength of contraction of the heart; there is also an elevation of blood pressure. Blood flow is directed to the skeletal muscle and to the brain, the pupils of the eyes are dilated, and the airways to the lungs are opened to allow more air to enter. Sweating becomes more common and, particularly in some animals, the hair stands on end. The body must also be concerned with supplying food to the muscles. In order to accomplish this, the liver breaks glycogen down to glucose, the adipose tissue of the body releases fatty acids into the bloodstream as a secondary source of food, and metabolic rate increases. All these responses are consistent with an increase in mental alertness and strenuous physical activity.

The parasympathetic system stimulates many of the same organs or glands as the sympathetic system; however, the response is not the same. The parasympathetic system directs the body's activities to a more vegetative state. When the parasympathetic system is active, the person is more relaxed and sedate. During the parasympathetic response, there is a decreased heart rate and blood pressure, respiration is slowed, and blood flow is directed to the digestive system for the absorption of food. The liver stores excess glucose as glycogen, and fatty acids in circulation are sequestered and stored in the adipose tissue. In addition, both the sympathetic and parasympathetic systems play an important role in reproduction. The parasympathetic system is responsible for erection in the penis of the male, and the sympathetic system is responsible for ejaculation.

During much of the day, a person is in a condition in which the state of the autonomic nervous system is a balance between the sympathetic and parasympathetic systems. The person is neither preparing for a stressful situation nor involved in digestion of food. The body can quickly switch from one state to another, and the response, though very rapid, may last for several minutes or even hours. This is possible because the response is directed by both the autonomic nervous system and the endocrine system. The nervous system generally has a very rapid response, which is local and is relatively short-lived because of the rapid metabolism or uptake of the neuro-transmitters. The endocrine system is slower to respond but has a much more general response, involving tissues in all parts of the body. The endocrine hormones remain in circulation far longer than the neurotransmitters, because they are much more slowly metabolized.

## Applications

The parasympathetic system is designed to ensure that, after eating, the body has the time, energy, and resources to metabolize food. All of its activities contribute to this activity. The classic example, often used, of a person whose body is being inner-vated by the parasympathetic system is the post-Thanksgiving dinner repose. The feeling is one of complete relaxation, associated with a sense of heavy limbs. It seems to be difficult to move, let alone to accomplish any chores.

Internally, the blood flow would be directed to the digestive system, where it would be absorbing nutrients to be distributed to the various parts of the body. The salivary glands would be producing large quantities of saliva, and other accessory glands of the digestive system would be producing their respective products that aid in digestion. Also in the digestive system, the muscles of the stomach and small intestine would be very active in an effort to move the food through the stomach at the appropriate rate.

In a parasympathetic mode, the heart rate would be slowed and, as a result, little blood would be circulated to the brain. Because of the decreased blood supply to the brain, it is difficult to concentrate and most persons would have little difficulty fall-ing asleep. Since the brain is not very alert, there is little need for light to enter the eye; the pupils are constricted. For most people, this is not the best time to study or to do any work that is mentally or physically demanding. The body is not at its peak for this type of activity during the parasympathetic response.

Innervation of the sympathetic system leads to physiological responses that are compatible with physical activity. During the sympathetic response, the body is pre-pared for action. Blood flow is directed away from the digestive system to the skeletal muscle and the brain. Increased blood flow increases the mental alertness and phys-iological activity of the brain. In addition, the eyes respond by dilating, allowing more light to penetrate, thereby improving visual acuity. A person who is experiencing a sympathetic response is prepared for enhanced concentration: These are ideal times to study and to perform challenging mental tasks. In public speakers, performers, or athletes, the sympathetic response may enhance performance and sharpen skills. In some cases, however, when the response is more extreme, the effect may interfere with performance. For example, when the parasympathetic response is turned off in favor of the sympathetic response, one of the effects is a decrease in saliva, which results in a very dry mouth—so dry as to make speaking difficult.

In humans, the sympathetic response can also be caused by a variety of other factors, such as job-related stress. In lower animals, the sympathetic response is relatively short-lived. The animal encounters the predator, then flees the site or fights the predator. In either case, the experience lasts only a short time; if it is lucky, the animal is free to go about the daily activities that ensure its survival. In humans who encounter job stress, the response may last for the entire day or, in some cases, continue even after leaving the workplace. The consequences are strain on the heart, elevated blood pressure, and the agitation induced by epinephrine or norepinephrine.

The sympathetic response in humans can also be experienced with strenuous physical activity such as jogging, weight training, or swimming. In this case, however, the duration of the response continues only as long as the exercise and is followed physiologically by a period of relaxation. All parts of the human body need to be used to be efficient. Regular exercise accomplishes this goal, and the activity of the heart and the circulatory response to the exercise followed by relaxation is beneficial to a healthy body.

In some cases, the body is suddenly changed from one state (sympathetic) to another (parasympathetic). The result may be discomfort or more serious consequences. One such example is the person who performs strenuous activity too quickly after having eaten a large meal. The parasympathetic system should be digesting food, but because of the strenuous activity, the blood is directed to skeletal muscle. This is likely to leave the person with nausea or stomach cramps.

The sympathetic system is also helpful in regulation of body temperature. Many of the activities of the system, such as muscular contraction and increased metabolism, increase body temperature. If the body experiences a decrease in body temperature of any consequence, there is likely to be a rapid sympathetic response. It is usually adequate to reverse slight changes in temperature. Temperature decreases that are long-term generally will be corrected by release of other hormones.

## Context

It was recognized in the seventeenth and eighteenth centuries that the body is equipped with an involuntary nervous system. Ganglia scattered throughout the body were presumed to be little brains, each with its own portion of the body to control. They were all believed to be working in concert to coordinate the body.

Claude Bernard was the first to propose the concept of the internal environment and regulatory mechanisms that keep it constant. It was during the nineteenth century that scientists came to understand the structure and function of the autonomic nervous system. J. N. Langley was the first to describe how the system operates and note the importance of the autonomic nervous system to the health body. He demonstrated the sympathetic and parasympathetic systems as antagonistic and coined the term "autonomic."

The autonomic nervous system is well understood, compared to some other aspects of the nervous system. The anatomy has been described, and it releases only three neurotransmitters: acetylcholine, epinephrine, and norepinephrine. Only recently have scientists begun to realize that the system is not as clear-cut and simple as once believed.

Since its discovery, it has been described as the involuntary nervous system. Now, however, investigators have come to realize that people do have voluntary control of some of the organs controlled by the autonomic nervous system. For example, adult humans can consciously control the emptying of the urinary bladder even though the brain receives a signal that it is full and that it is time for the parasympathetic system to empty the bladder. This skill must be learned.

It is also obvious that, with training, certain other parameters of the body once thought to be involuntary can be controlled by the will. This is the basis of biofeedback. In biofeedback, individuals can be taught to control their heart rate, blood pressure, distribution of blood, respiration rate, and other physiologic conditions. Some persons become very adept at controlling these functions. It does, however, take a long time to develop the skills necessary to achieve control of involuntary physiologic activities.

The extent to which a person can successfully achieve control of these functions is not yet clear; much work is being done in this area. This research, and the potential to control human behavior and disease through the use of biofeedback, has revitalized interest in the autonomic nervous system.

## Bibliography

Campbell, Neil A. *Biology.* Menlo Park, Calif.: Benjamin/Cummings, 1987. A biology textbook written for college students that is easily understood even by those with less scientific background. Background information describes the general concepts of the nervous system, chemical messengers, and the autonomic nervous system.

Durham, Ross M. *Human Physiology: Functions of the Human Body.* Dubuque, Iowa: Wm. C. Brown, 1989. An easily read textbook of general physiology that is illustrated with clear diagrams and colorful pictures. Understandable even by the novice with little background information.

Gordon, Malcolm S., George A. Bartholomew, et al. *Animal Physiology: Principles and Adaptations.* 4th ed. New York: Macmillan, 1982. The physiology of various types of animals is examined. The role of the endocrine system in lower vertebrates is included in this easily readable text. This book is well written and covers a broader scope than most books.

*The Nervous System: Circuits of Communication.* New York: Torstar Books, 1985. An informative and well-illustrated book for the layperson. It clearly describes the autonomic nervous system and its role in behavior. Anyone should be able to read it and understand the information. Includes a history of the subject and supportive information relevant to the topic.

Vander, Arthur J., James H. Sherman, and Dorothy S. Luciano. *Human Physiology: The Mechanisms of Body Function.* 5th ed. New York: McGraw-Hill, 1990. This general physiology text for the college student can be easily read by the high school student. The chapter on homeostatic mechanisms, which includes a section on receptors, will shed much light on the study of the autonomic nervous system.

Well illustrated and contains a wealth of knowledge in an easy-to-understand format. References are provided for further reading.

*Annette O'Connor*

## Cross-References

Brain-Stem Structures, 461; The Central and Peripheral Nervous Systems, 494; Emotion: Neurophysiology and Neuroanatomy, 914; Forebrain Structures, 1043; Hindbrain Structures, 1175; Neural and Hormonal Interaction, 1648; Neurotransmitters, 1673; Stress: Physiological Responses, 2425; Stress and the Nervous System, 2452.

# AVERSION, IMPLOSION, AND SYSTEMATIC DESENSITIZATION THERAPIES

*Type of psychology:* Psychotherapy
*Field of study:* Behavioral therapies

*Aversion, implosion, and systematic desensitization therapies are effective therapy techniques based on the principles of Pavlovian conditioning. The latter two are most effective in treating fear and anxiety; aversion therapy is most often used in treating habit disorders such as cigarette smoking or drug abuse.*

*Principal terms*

AVERSION THERAPY: a therapy that involves pairing something negative (such as electric shock) with an undesired behavior (such as drinking alcohol or smoking cigarettes)

COVERT SENSITIZATION: aversion therapy using imagination or "imagery"; for example, having an alcoholic imagine vomiting or becoming sick after sipping a favorite drink

DESENSITIZATION HIERARCHY: a list of feared situations, ordered from the least fear-producing to the most fear-producing, for use in systematic desensitization

EXPOSURE THERAPIES: therapies in which real or imagined exposure to a fear-inducing situation reduces the fear response—for example, systematic desensitization, flooding, and implosion

FLOODING: a therapy in which a phobic person imagines his or her most-feared situation until fear decreases; differs from implosion in that it includes only the elements of the situation of which the patient is afraid

IMPLOSION THERAPY: a therapy in which the patient imagines his or her feared situation (plus elements from psychodynamic theory that the therapist thinks are related to the fear) until fear decreases

PAVLOVIAN CONDITIONING: learning in which two stimuli are presented one after the other, and the response to the first changes because of the response to the second stimulus

PHOBIA: an intense fear of a particular thing (such as dogs) or situation (such as heights) that can be treated by exposure therapy

SYSTEMATIC DESENSITIZATION: an exposure therapy in which the phobic person is gradually presented with a feared object or situation

## Overview

Systematic desensitization, implosion, and aversion therapy are all behavior therapy techniques that are based on Pavlovian conditioning. In Pavlovian conditioning, when one stimulus is paired with another, the response to the second stimulus can affect the response to the first. For example, if the presence of a dog is followed by a painful bite, the pain and fear that result from the bite can produce a conditioned response of fear toward dogs. An important process in Pavlovian conditioning is extinction: When the first stimulus is presented a number of times without the second stimulus, the response that became conditioned because of the pairing becomes extinguished. If, after having been bitten by a dog, a person spends time around dogs without being bitten, his or her fear of dogs will gradually disappear. Both systematic desensitization and implosion therapy use extinction to eliminate fear of an object or situation. Aversion therapy uses conditioning to attach a negative response to something pleasant but undesirable (such as cigarettes or alcohol) in order to eliminate a bad habit.

Systematic desensitization, developed and described by Joseph Wolpe in the 1950's, is one of the most well-accepted and effective psychological treatments. It is most successful when used to eliminate phobias, which are fears of specific objects or situations. The goal of systematic desensitization is to put the patient into a relaxed state and gradually present him or her with the feared situation, so that very little anxiety is actually experienced during treatment. The therapist usually presents the feared situation to the patient by having the patient vividly imagine being in the situation. Systematic desensitization starts out with the patient briefly imagining a situation that provokes very little anxiety. This is repeated until no anxiety is produced by the image; then the patient moves on to a slightly more anxiety-provoking image. This continues until the person can imagine his or her most-feared situation with little or no anxiety.

Implosion is similar to systematic desensitization in that a person repeatedly imagines a feared situation until the fear dissipates; however, if systematic desensitization is like lowering inch by inch into a cold pool, implosion is like diving headfirst into the deep end. Unlike systematic desensitization, which proceeds gradually and evokes little discomfort, implosion plunges the patient right into imagining his or her most intensely feared situation. Whereas systematic desensitization uses short image periods, implosion requires a person to keep imagining the feared situation for as long as it takes until the fear begins to decrease. Implosion works best with long sessions of imagining, sometimes two hours or more. As might be expected, flooding works faster than systematic desensitization but is more uncomfortable and is more likely to cause people not to want to try the treatment.

As originally described by Thomas Stampfl, implosion was a mixture of extinction and psychodynamic theory. In addition to imagining the situation that the patient presented as anxiety-provoking, the patient would imagine things the therapist thought were psychodynamic elements related to the anxiety, such as childhood fears or conflict. For example, the therapist might instruct the patient to imagine being rejected by his or her parents. Flooding is very similar to implosion, except that the image is restricted to the specific situations the client describes as fearful and does not include elements the therapist introduces from psychodynamic theory. Flooding is now a more commonly used therapy than implosion.

Both systematic desensitization and flooding can be done through exposure to the actual situation, as well as through imagining it. For example, a person with a phobia of dogs could approach a real dog rather than merely imagine it. Research has shown that confronting the actual fear situation is more effective than imagining it; however, sometimes there are practical constraints. It would be too expensive, for example, for a person who is afraid of flying to buy an airplane ticket every week to become desensitized to the situation; imagining an airplane trip costs nothing. In practice, treatment usually involves a combination of imagery and actual exposure. The flight phobic might imagine being on an airplane during therapy sessions and between sessions have a homework assignment to drive to an airport and watch planes take off.

Whereas systematic desensitization and flooding try to extinguish a fear response, the goal of aversion therapy is to attach a new, aversive response to a currently positive stimulus. This is usually done to eliminate a bad habit like drinking alcohol, smoking, or overeating. During treatment, the sight, smell, or taste of alcohol, cigarettes, or a favorite food might be followed by electric shock or a nausea-inducing drug. After experiencing a number of these pairings, the person begins to develop a negative response to the previously valued stimulus. Like flooding and systematic desensitization, aversion therapy can be performed either in actuality or through the use of imagery. The use of imagery in this case is called covert sensitization; an example would be an alcoholic who imagines becoming violently ill after sipping his favorite drink.

There are a number of concerns with using aversion therapy. First, there are always ethical concerns about any treatment that involves punishment or severe discomfort. Aversive procedures are preferred only when other effective treatments are not available or if other treatments have failed. A second concern with aversion therapy is its effectiveness. The alcoholic may avoid drinking when he is hooked up to the electric shock or has taken the nausea-producing drug, but aversion therapy may not be effective in stopping him from drinking after treatment, when no punishment will be suffered.

## Applications

Systematic desensitization is most useful, as noted earlier, when applied to reduce fear. The application of systematic desensitization is straightforward. The first step in systematic desensitization is to establish a list of ten to fifteen feared situations (called a desensitization hierarchy), ordered from least to most anxiety-provoking. For example, the hierarchy for a person afraid to fly might start out with making an airplane reservation a month before a scheduled trip and end with actually being in a plane while it is taking off. Creating the desensitization hierarchy is one of the most important parts of treatment and involves finding out what is most important to the phobia: It might be fear of heights, fear of crashing, or fear of being in a closed space with no escape. Two people with the same phobia may have completely different desensitization hierarchies.

When the hierarchy is complete, desensitization can begin. The therapist first gets the patient or client to relax deeply, usually by teaching a specific muscle relaxation technique the patient can practice at home. While the patient is relaxed, the therapist instructs him or her to imagine vividly the item on the hierarchy that provokes the least anxiety. This image is held for only a few seconds, so very little anxiety is felt; then the patient returns to relaxing. This is repeated until no anxiety is felt while imagining the scene; then the person imagines the next situation on the hierarchy. Over the course of a number of sessions, the patient progresses up the hierarchy until he or she can imagine the highest, most fear-provoking scene without feeling any fear. As noted earlier, treatment usually includes between-session homework assignments that involve confronting the fear situation.

Flooding is used in the treatment of similar problems. In this case, the client is immediately immersed in the most fearful situation he can imagine. The person with a fear of flying might be asked immediately to imagine being on a flight over the ocean while the plane is being jostled by severe turbulence. The phobic would continue to imagine this (sometimes for hours) until the anxiety reduces. One interesting and successful application of flooding has been in treating people with compulsive washing rituals. People with obsessive-compulsive disorder will often wash their hands until they are raw or bleeding, or will wash their clothes or clean house many hours a day, fearing unseen contamination and germs. Because of the time and energy this takes, the disorder can severely interfere with a person's life. Treatment involves having the person get his hands dirty by touching garbage or some other feared material (or put on dirty clothes), then not allowing the person to wash. This treatment is technically known as "exposure with response prevention." Because invisible germs are often what is most feared, the treatment also involves having the person imagine germs covering and infecting his skin. In severe cases, the person may need to be prevented from washing for days or even weeks before the anxiety goes away. This is obviously a very uncomfortable treatment for both patient and therapist, but it is one of the few long-lasting treatments for this disorder.

Aversion therapy is used much less frequently than systematic desensitization or flooding, and it is not used when other effective therapies are available. One relatively common application of aversion therapy is rapid smoking. In this technique a cigarette smoker will smoke one cigarette after another in a small, enclosed room until it causes a feeling of nausea. After a few sessions of this, the person begins to anticipate the nausea at the first cigarette, reducing the desire to smoke. Rapid smoking can be effective when used as one component of a treatment program and when there are no medical reasons for the person to avoid this technique.

Although aversion therapy is not used as often as systematic desensitization or flooding, an especially creative application of it, reported by Peter Lang and Barbara Melamed in 1969, illustrates its importance in certain situations. The case involved a nine-month-old infant who was failing to gain weight because he vomited his food ten minutes after every meal. No physical reason for this was found, despite three hospitalizations, many medical tests, and surgery. Several treatments were tried without success prior to beginning aversion therapy. When aversion therapy was begun, the child was in critical condition and was being fed through a nasogastric tube. Therapy involved giving an electric shock to the leg whenever the child was vomiting. Within three days, shocks no longer had to be given. His weight had increased 26 percent by the time he was discharged from the hospital thirteen days after treatment began. One year later, he was still progressing normally. This dramatic case shows that there is a place for aversion therapy in psychology.

## Context

Systematic desensitization, implosion, and aversion therapy were among the first psychotherapies that were developed from principles discovered in the experimental psychology laboratory. During the 1960's, they also were the first therapies to have their effectiveness confirmed in controlled experimental studies. In the 1950's, a patient seeking treatment for a phobia might have received a course of psychoanalysis, potentially stretching hundreds of sessions over several years with questionable effectiveness. By the 1970's, a patient going to a psychologist for the same problem would probably receive systematic desensitization or flooding, treatments with proven effectiveness and lasting only a handful of sessions.

On a broader level, these therapies and the research done on them ushered in a new era of scientific standards for clinical psychology. They led to the behavior therapy movement, which continued to develop therapy techniques from research done in experimental psychology and to test the effectiveness of these therapies. This led to an expectation that all therapies should have proven effectiveness. These therapies, then, represent a large step forward for the importance of scientific principles in all areas of clinical psychology and psychiatry.

Although systematic desensitization and flooding are standard and effective treatments, they are not 100 percent effective. Research continues to improve their effectiveness and to reach the percentage of people who do not seem to improve with these therapies. A particularly important area of research is to figure out how best to combine these therapies with drug therapies for fear and anxiety. Regardless of where this research leads, however, systematic desensitization and flooding will remain important therapy techniques in clinical psychology.

Aversion therapy also is important as one of the original scientifically derived and tested treatments, but it has more of a checkered history. One of its initial uses in the 1960's was to "treat" homosexual males by pairing pictures of attractive men with electric shock. It should be noted that this was in an era when society had a much different attitude toward homosexuality, and gay males voluntarily approached psychologists for this treatment. Nevertheless, aversion therapy contributed to an early popular view of behavior therapy as dehumanizing behavior control that took away free will and reduced individual rights. When used thoughtfully and ethically by competent psychologists, aversion therapy has an important role in psychological treatment; however, psychologists will surely continue to debate the ethics and effectiveness of aversion therapy.

## Bibliography

Bellack, Alan S., and Michel Hersen. *Behavior Modification: An Introductory Text-book.* Baltimore: Williams & Wilkins, 1977. This book, by two of the leaders in the field of behavior therapy, contains extensive chapters describing research and treatment using systematic desensitization, flooding, implosion, and aversion therapy. Since it is a textbook, it places these treatments in the context of other behavior therapy techniques.

Foa, Edna B., G. S. Steketee, and L. M. Ascher. "Systematic Desensitization." In *Handbook of Behavioral Interventions: A Clinical Guide,* edited by Alan Goldstein and Edna B. Foa. New York: John Wiley & Sons, 1980. This book was written as a "how-to" guide for the psychotherapist; however, the beginner will also find it readable and engaging. It is very well written and is filled with interesting case material and direct transcripts from therapy sessions. This is the best place to experience what systematic desensitization is actually like for the client and the therapist.

Levis, D. J. "Implementing the Techniques of Implosive Therapy." In *Handbook of Behavioral Interventions: A Clinical Guide,* edited by Alan Goldstein and Edna B. Foa. New York: John Wiley & Sons, 1980. This is another chapter from the book described above, and the positive comments above apply to this chapter as well. This book also contains an interesting chapter by Joseph Wolpe on how to gather information to plan treatment and chapters on how to apply exposure therapy to specific disorders such as agoraphobia and obsessive-compulsive disorder.

Paul, Gordon L. *Insight vs. Desensitization in Psychotherapy.* Stanford, Calif.: Stanford University Press, 1966. This short book is a classic. It describes an early and very influential study that showed systematic desensitization to be superior to insight-oriented psychotherapy for treating public speaking anxiety. It was one of the first studies to evaluate therapy effectiveness and is a good illustration of how research to test the effect of therapy is done.

Wolpe, Joseph. *The Practice of Behavior Therapy.* 3d ed. New York: Pergamon Press, 1982. This book describes the practice of behavior therapy in detail, especially systematic desensitization. It includes chapters on aversion therapy and flooding as well as other therapy techniques, and illustrates how these techniques can be extended to treat problems other than fear and anxiety.

——————. *Psychotherapy by Reciprocal Inhibition.* Stanford, Calif.: Stanford University Press, 1958. The classic book in which Wolpe introduces and advocates systematic desensitization as an alternative to psychoanalytic treatment developed by Sigmund Freud. Describes the basic principles and practice of systematic desensitization for psychiatrists of the late 1950's, who generally had no knowledge of these techniques.

*Scott R. Vrana*

## Cross-References

Abnormality: Behavioral Models, 33; Avoidance Learning, 375; Obsessions and Compulsions, 1707; Operant Conditioning Therapies, 1714; Pavlovian Conditioning: Acquisition, Extinction, and Inhibition, 1757; Phobias, 1816.

# AVOIDANCE LEARNING

*Type of psychology:* Learning
*Fields of study:* Aversive conditioning; instrumental conditioning; Pavlovian conditioning

*Studies of avoidance learning have provided important information about the ways in which organisms respond to aversive stimuli. Although much of the work has been done in animal laboratories, the findings have resulted in broad application to the clinical treatment of anxiety disorders in humans.*

### Principal terms

ACTIVE AVOIDANCE: an avoidance task that requires some specific response to avert the presentation of an aversive stimulus

AVOIDANCE RESPONSE: a response occurring during a signal that averts the presentation of an aversive stimulus

CONDITIONED STIMULUS (CS): a neutral stimulus that predicts the occurrence of a biologically important stimulus

ESCAPE RESPONSE: a response that terminates an aversive stimulus

FREE OPERANT AVOIDANCE: an avoidance task in which the unconditioned response is predicted by the passage of time rather than by an explicit conditioned response

PASSIVE AVOIDANCE: an avoidance task in which the aversive stimulus can be avoided by simply not performing some response

SHUTTLE BOX: a two-compartment chamber that is used in the study of avoidance learning

TWO-FACTOR THEORY: a theory which holds that avoidance learning involves both Pavlovian and instrumental conditioning

UNCONDITIONED STIMULUS (US): a biologically important stimulus

## Overview

Avoidance learning is behavior that reduces or prevents exposure to aversive situations. In a typical laboratory experiment, a rat is placed into one end of a rectangular box that has a metal bar floor. A bell begins to ring; after five seconds, the grid floor is electrified, and the rat experiences an electrical shock. During the next few seconds, the rat tries various behaviors until, finally, it jumps over a small barrier to safety in the other end of the box. The rat is returned to the first chamber, and the process is repeated. After a few such trials, the rat quickly moves to safety when the shock begins. Later, the rat moves to safety as soon as the bell rings, avoiding the shock altogether.

The terminology used to describe avoidance learning is as follows: The aversive event is called the unconditioned stimulus (US). The event that signals the forthcoming US is called the conditioned stimulus (CS). The period of CS presentation before the US begins is the CS-US interval. Once the US begins, the response that leads to safety is the escape response. A response that occurs during the CS-US interval and negates exposure to the aversive event is an avoidance response. There are several categories of avoidance learning.

In passive avoidance, the US can be avoided by passively not engaging in some behavior. For example, if a child touches a hot radiator, future exposures can be avoided simply by not going into that corner of the room.

Shuttle-box avoidance is one of the most common forms of avoidance learning. The apparatus is a two-compartment chamber in which the subject avoids the US by "shuttling" from one side to the other, as described above. In one-way avoidance, each trial begins by placing the rat into the same side of the apparatus, with avoidance (or escape) responses all being in the same direction. In two-way avoidance, the shuttle box is symmetrical, such that the CS and US can be presented in either chamber. After the first presentation of the CS followed by the US, the subject has reached safety by shuttling in one direction into the other chamber. After an appropriate period of time, the next trial begins by presenting the CS and US in the "safe" chamber, and the rat shuttles back in the opposite direction, and so on.

On the surface, these two procedures appear to be essentially identical. In practice, one-way avoidance tends to be easily mastered, whereas two-way avoidance learning is extremely difficult. These differences offer insights into the nature of avoidance learning. The subject does not learn a surgically precise response to the CS. In one-way avoidance, the subject also learns that one location is dangerous and another is safe. Most subjects will perform the response after a few trials even if the CS is not presented. In two-way avoidance, however, there is no safe location. On each trial, the CS is presented and the subject is being asked to return to the same (dangerous) location from which it just escaped. In other words, this task involves a passive avoidance component that interferes with the active avoidance by creating a conflict.

Free operant avoidance (sometimes called Sidman avoidance) does not use an explicit CS; the passage of time is the CS. In a typical setting, the subject is placed into an operant chamber that has a lever. After a few seconds, brief pulses of electric shock are delivered through the grid floor at specified intervals (typically about five seconds apart). These shocks will continue until the lever is pressed, which delays the occurrence of the next shock for some longer period of time (typically about twenty seconds). The free operant procedure is defined by the S-S interval (time between shocks) and the R-S interval (time between a response and the next shock). Subjects can avoid the US by pressing the lever at least once each twenty seconds, but typical subjects respond two to three times faster than the rate required by the R-S interval.

Avoidance learning seems straightforward enough but presents the question of how subjects, especially simple organisms such as rats or earthworms, can base their behavior on some event that is going to take place in the future. Learning theorists solved the problem of ongoing motivation by developing the two-factor theory of avoidance learning. The two factors are classical conditioning of fear and instrumental learning of responses that reduce the fear. Initially, the subject has no way of knowing the requirements of the task. The CS is followed by the US, and the subject responds in various ways until it successfully escapes. Buried within this experience, however, are the elements of classical conditioning. Each pairing of the CS and US gives the CS the ability to elicit fear. After a few pairings, the subject does not have to look into the future for some reason to behave: The CS is itself aversive. Responses that terminate the CS are rewarding because they reduce fear, in the same way that responses that terminate the US are rewarding because they reduce discomfort. According to this theory, avoidance learning is, in some sense, learning to perform escape responses to reduce a learned fear.

## Applications

Avoidance learning is interesting in its own right, but it also contributes to a better understanding of the human condition. Aversive situations—hot stoves, small places, big places, big dogs, elevators, reprimands, snakes, failing grades, and unrequited love, to name a few—are a fact of life. As a result, much of human behavior is directed toward the escape from or avoidance of aversive consequences. Normally, this is an efficient process. In some cases, however, the individual dedicates more and more energy to avoidance behavior, and it begins to interfere with other activities.

Phobias are irrational fears of everyday objects or situations (for example, elevators or examinations). Phobic individuals avoid contact with the feared object, sometimes so successfully that the problem goes unrecognized by other people, or even by the affected individual. Some everyday situations, however, are impossible to avoid, and the individual suffers intense distress from both actual exposure and fear of exposure. The initial cause of the fear may remain a mystery. Some aversive consequence (perhaps a loud noise or a menacing individual) may have occurred in the presence of an everyday object, which then becomes a CS that predicts aversive consequences. The seed of fear has been planted, and avoidance behavior conserves that fear while imagined consequences nurture it.

Fortunately, it is not necessary for one to know the initial cause of the phobia to treat it. The most successful treatment, called systematic desensitization, uses the laws of classical conditioning to reverse the fear. Consider, for example, a person who fears elevators. The therapist first trains the individual to relax in a quiet setting. Then, the subject is asked to think about some remote example of the feared object, perhaps looking down the street at a tall building. If relaxation continues, the subject is asked to imagine standing in front of the building. The therapist works carefully and progressively to guide the subject through imagery that is closer and closer to the feared object, all the while maintaining relaxation. After a few sessions, the individual may be able to stand in the hallway by an elevator while maintaining relaxation. After a few more sessions, the individual may be able to ride the elevator, and the irrational fear dissolves.

The most common problem involving learned fear is termed vague anxiety. The individual cannot identify a specific fear, but a disturbing sense of foreboding permeates the day's activities. The cause of this vague anxiety may be some specific fear of an aversive consequence in the workplace or the home that has not been fully recognized by the individual. While it may seem odd that a source of debilitating fear might not be recognized, it must be kept in mind that one effective avoidance response is to avoid thinking about the disturbing problem. Vague anxieties may also involve the misinterpretation of bodily symptoms of fear. For example, muscle tension caused by poor posture at a work station may be misinterpreted as anxiety. In treating these cases, the therapist trains the individual to recognize the early stages of anxiety and to engage in relaxation techniques to counter these feelings.

A particularly debilitating form of vague anxiety is agoraphobia, which literally means "fear of the marketplace." This condition may begin as a specific phobia (for example, fear of elevators). This fear generalizes to buildings that may contain elevators, streets that may go near these buildings, neighborhoods that these streets lie within, and so on. This gradually restricts the range of activities until the individual may be too fearful even to leave the home. This disorder is more difficult to treat than simple phobias but still responds to many of the same treatment strategies. Unfortunately, the nature of the disorder makes it unlikely that the individual will seek help, because therapists are more likely to be found in the "marketplace" than in one's home.

To summarize, avoidance learning can be viewed in the much larger context of the response of humans to adversity. In the normal course of events, a person comes into contact with a wide range of aversive stimuli, ranging from the purely physical to complex social interactions. An individual learns to fear these stimuli and to fear the stimuli with which they are associated. In some cases, these associated stimuli are everyday objects or situations, and the fear is deemed by others to be irrational.

The all-too-common response to irrational fears is to treat them as inappropriate behaviors. Children may taunt individuals who have such fears, employers may suspect them, casual acquaintances may evade them, and family members may punish them. All these approaches heighten the fears and anxieties to make a bad situation worse.

The study of avoidance learning has provided a deeper understanding of the nature of these disorders. Most fears are established through classical conditioning. Specific responses that reduce these fears are acquired and strengthened as avoidance responses; however, the fears may be reduced in ways that do nothing to alleviate the actual problem. Furthermore, successful avoidance responses may interfere with other behaviors.

The foundation for the successful treatment of these disorders is the application of the laws of avoidance learning. Therapists use counter-conditioning techniques to replace fears with more positive feelings. They replace ineffective avoidance responses that conserve fear with responses that actually reduce the aversive situation. In most cases, the application of this knowledge can eliminate the fears and return the individual to more comfortable and productive activities.

## Context

Psychologists began to study avoidance learning in the early 1900's as part of a more general effort to define the laws of learning. Ivan Pavlov, a Russian physiologist, had already described many of the laws of association that are now known as Pavlovian, or classical, conditioning. The important distinction of classical conditioning is that the subject has no ability to control the stimuli, but simply learns the association between the stimuli. American psychologists, under the guidance of Edward L. Thorndike, took a more interactive approach and concentrated most of their efforts on Thorndikian, or instrumental, conditioning. In instrumental conditioning, the subject can learn to manipulate and control certain aspects of the environment. Studies of the aversive control of behavior progressed naturally from escape learning to avoidance learning.

Some learning theorists had difficulty with avoidance behavior, especially in simple organisms, because there was an implication that the behavior was based on purely cognitive events such as expectancies. This dilemma was solved by O. Hobart Mowrer, who introduced the two-factor theory of avoidance learning in 1939. According to this theory, avoidance responses were reinforced directly by the reduction of classically conditioned fear. In the 1960's, Richard Solomon and his students provided direct support for this theory by showing that classically conditioned stimuli could directly influence an instrumental avoidance response. In particular, a stimulus that had been used as a Pavlovian CS to predict shock increased the rate of a free operant avoidance response. By contrast, a stimulus that had been explicitly unpaired with shock—a safety signal—reduced the rate of avoidance responding. Neither of these stimuli had ever been experienced during the free operant task, so the clear interpretation was that the changes in behavior were the result of conditioned fear and conditioned safety, respectively.

Studies of avoidance learning and, especially, the two-factor theory caused a tremendous increase in the interest of American psychologists in Pavlovian conditioning. The notion that fears can be learned through direct association of stimuli in the environment and that these fears can then influence a person's interactions with the environment has become the cornerstone for understanding many forms of clinical disorders. As experimental psychologists described the laws that apply to aversively controlled behavior, clinicians began to find that the application of these principles improved their ability to treat patients suffering from phobias, anxiety disorders, and even depression.

## Bibliography

Flaherty, Charles F. *Animal Learning and Cognition.* New York: Alfred A. Knopf, 1985. Provides a thorough, clearly written review of the experimental and theoretical foundations of learning theory. Contains references to and discussions of all major contributions to the study of avoidance learning.

Hamilton, Leonard W., and C. Robin Timmons. *Principles of Behavioral Pharmacology.* Englewood Cliffs, N.J.: Prentice-Hall, 1990. Although the emphasis of this textbook is on pharmacology, three chapters are devoted to the effects of aversive control of behavior. Topics include anxiety, fear, pain, and depression.

Pavlov, Ivan P. *Conditioned Reflexes.* London: Oxford University Press, 1927. This translation of Pavlov's work has become a classic in psychology. Early chapters clearly outline the principles of classical conditioning; later chapters go into considerable detail.

Seligman, Martin E. P. *Helplessness: On Depression, Development, and Death.* San Francisco: W. H. Freeman, 1975. An easy-to-read account of the role of aversive conditioning in the cause and treatment of clinical disorders in humans.

Solomon, Richard L. "The Opponent-Process Theory of Acquired Motivation: The Costs of Pleasure and the Benefits of Pain." *American Psychologist* 35 (1980): 691-712. Provides an excellent summary of opponent-process theory, which is a modern extension of the two-process theory of avoidance learning. Includes speculation on a variety of disorders, including addictive behaviors.

*Leonard W. Hamilton*

## Cross-References

# BED-WETTING

*Type of psychology:* Psychopathology
*Field of study:* Childhood and adolescent disorders

*Bed-wetting, technically known as enuresis, is a disorder characterized by the frequent failure to maintain urinary control by a certain age. It most frequently occurs in young children, although it may continue through adulthood.*

### Principal terms

ANTIDIURETIC HORMONE (ADH): a naturally occurring hormone within the body, produced by the pituitary gland, that controls urine production

DIURNAL ENURESIS: the presence of enuretic episodes when the individual is awake

NOCTURNAL ENURESIS: the failure to maintain urinary control during sleep

ORGANIC ENURESIS: a type of enuresis caused by identifiable physical problems, such as diabetes

OVERLEARNING: a behavioral principle that involves the enuretic practicing the ability to maintain urinary control under more difficult circumstances than are typically present

PRIMARY ENURESIS: the presence of enuresis in an individual who has never maintained adequate urinary control

SECONDARY ENURESIS: the recurrence of enuresis in an individual who previously has maintained urinary control

URINE ALARM: a device designed to awaken enuretics when they begin to void their urine

## Overview

Enuresis is a disorder characterized by an individual's repeated inability to maintain urinary control after having reached an adequate age. Although enuresis may continue into adulthood, it most frequently occurs in young children. For example, at age five, approximately 15 percent of all children are enuretic at night on a once-a-week basis. By age eighteen, however, only about 1 percent of adolescents are enuretic. Among children under the age of eleven, boys are more likely to be enuretic than girls. After age eleven, however, boys and girls have equal rates of enuresis, according to Arthur C. Houts and Hillel Abramson. It should be noted that bed-wetting by children under five years of age and occasional bed-wetting by older children are common and usually not cause for concern.

Because of the many different types of enuresis, there are several distinctions that should be made in discussing the disorder. The first distinction involves the cause of the disorder. If enuresis is the result of obvious physical causes, such as a urinary tract infection or diabetes, it is referred to as organic enuresis. Although estimates vary, fewer than 5 percent of enuretic cases are thought to be the result of physical causes. The majority of the cases of enuresis are referred to as functional enuresis because no physical cause can be identified. Even though most cases of enuresis are functional types, a medical examination always should be conducted in order to make certain that the enuresis is not the result of a physical problem.

Another important distinction to make in discussing enuresis involves the time at which it occurs. Nocturnal enuresis, bed-wetting, refers to the loss of urinary control when an individual is sleeping. Diurnal enuresis refers to the loss of urinary control during an individual's waking hours. Nocturnal enuresis occurs much more frequently than diurnal enuresis. Diurnal enuresis is more often the result of physiological causes, such as urinary tract infections.

A final useful distinction is that between primary and secondary enuresis. Primary enuretics are individuals who have never demonstrated proper bladder control. Secondary enuretics are individuals who, after a substantial period of urinary control (six months to a year), become enuretic again. Approximately 80 percent of all nocturnal enuretics have never gained proper urinary control. Although professional differences of opinion exist, most researchers believe that the causes of primary and secondary enuresis are usually the same and that children with both types respond equally well to treatment. In order to avoid possible confusion, the remainder of this section will focus on the most common type of enuresis in children: functional primary nocturnal enuresis.

Over the years, numerous explanations have been given for the occurrence of nocturnal enuresis. These various explanations can be grouped into one of three areas: emotional, biological, or learning. An emotional explanation for the occurrence of enuresis involves the idea that the enuretic is suffering from an emotional disorder that causes him or her to lose urinary control. Examples of these proposed emotional disturbances include anxiety disorders, poor impulse control, and passive-aggressive tendencies. Recent research indicates, however, that few enuretic children have emotional problems that cause their enuresis. In fact, among enuretic individuals who do have emotional disturbance, it may be that their enuresis actually causes their emotional problems. In this regard, it is widely accepted that the occurrence of enuresis lowers children's self-esteem as well as increases family conflict.

Biological deficiencies are a second suggested cause of enuresis. Approximately 50 percent of enuretic children have a parent or close family member who has had the disorder. The tendency for enuresis to occur within certain families increases the likelihood that enuresis has a biological cause. There are various biological maladies that have been proposed to cause enuresis, including sleep disorders, small bladder capacity, and a deficiency of antidiuretic hormone.

Danish researcher J. P. Norgaard and his associates have investigated the potential physical causes of enuresis. At one time, it was believed by many professionals that enuretics engaged in deeper sleep than nonenuretics. For this reason, they were unable to awaken in response to the sensation of a full bladder. Norgaard's precise measurement of the time that enuretic and nonenuretic individuals spend in different levels of sleep, ranging from light to deep sleep, failed to demonstrate consistent differences between the sleep patterns of these two groups.

The second suggested biological cause, small bladder capacity, has received limited support. The best evidence suggests that while enuretics tend to have small bladder capacities, this factor alone is insufficient to account for their enuresis.

The third suggested biological cause appears to have the most scientific support. This explanation involves the failure of enuretic children to release a sufficient amount of antidiuretic hormone during their sleeping cycle. Antidiuretic hormone (ADH) is secreted by the pituitary gland and is responsible for the control of urine production. Because enuretics do not produce adequate amounts of ADH during sleep, they produce more urine, leading to a greater risk of bedwetting.

The improper learning of bladder control is the final category of proposed causes of enuresis. This proposition rests on the notion that bladder control is a learned response and that enuretic children have not properly mastered this response. Some support for this proposition comes from the fact that mentally retarded children take longer to control their elimination functions, such as urination and defecation, than intellectually normal children. Enuresis researcher Arthur Houts has proposed that nonenuretic children may be better able to inhibit the contractions of the muscles responsible for urination; that is, while enuretic children may not have impaired muscle reflexes, they may have greater difficulty voluntarily inhibiting these muscles as compared to nonenuretic children.

## Applications

Consistent with the large number of suggested causes of enuresis, or bed-wetting, numerous treatments have been attempted. Early "treatments" for enuresis, dating back some three thousand years, included such things as giving the child juniper berries, cypress, and beer, or having the child consume ground hedgehog. Currently, drug and behavioral therapies are the two treatments that have been utilized and studied to the greatest extent.

Among the drug therapies, Imipramine was the first drug widely used in the treatment of enuresis. Imipramine has been widely prescribed in the treatment of depression for more than thirty years. In addition to its antidepressant qualities, it was observed early in its usage to stop previously enuretic patients from bed-wetting. Imipramine appears to stop bed-wetting by causing the contraction of the muscles responsible for the release of urine. Based on a review of the scientific literature, Houts and Abramson have concluded that Imipramine is effective in treating about half of the children with whom it is used. Unfortunately, once the medication is withdrawn, almost all the successfully treated children return to wetting their beds.

A more recent medication that has shown promise in the treatment of enuresis is desmopressin (DDAVP). DDAVP is a drug administered internasally that is hypothesized to prevent enuresis by causing the kidneys to concentrate urine, thus preventing its passage into the bladder during sleep. DDAVP is completely effective in about 40 percent of the children for whom it is prescribed; however, the removal of this medication also results in a very high recurrence of bed-wetting.

The second category of enuresis treatment to be discussed is behavioral therapy. Variations of behavioral therapy have been used with enuretics since the early 1900's. The "urine alarm" is at the center of the behavioral treatment approach; it is a device that typically is attached to the underwear of enuretics prior to their going to bed. When urine comes in contact with the sensors of the device, a loud noise is emitted by the alarm attached to the undershirts or pajama tops of the children. The alarm's sound is utilized in order to awaken the children and the parents at the first emission of urine. It is necessary for parents to be awakened by the alarm because initially the children may have difficulty rousing themselves when the alarm sounds. In order for the children to be sufficiently awakened, it is often necessary to have them wash their faces as a way of increasing alertness. Once the children are awake, they are instructed to void the remainder of their urine. After voiding, the children return to their bedrooms, where they check the dampness of the bedding and, if it is sufficiently wet, change the bedding. At this point, the children put on dry under-wear, reattach the sensors, and return to bed.

During the treatment process, the child and the parents record the child's progress through the use of a chart on which stars are placed when the child has a dry bed. The accumulation of a certain number of stars usually results in the child's earning a reward of his or her choice. The treatment goal is for the enuretic not to wet the bed for fourteen consecutive nights. It typically takes ten to twelve weeks before this goal is met. It is best to instruct all members of the family regarding the purpose and the exact workings of the treatment in order to avoid misunderstandings and potential frustrations during the process. The lack of parental compliance with the treatment procedures is the most frequent reason for therapy failure.

Additional components often are added to the basic behavioral treatment in order to improve therapy effectiveness. Overlearning is one of these additional compo-nents; it begins once the previously enuretic child has been dry for fourteen consec-utive nights. Based on the child's age, he or she is instructed to drink a certain amount of fluid prior to going to bed. The amount of fluid is gradually increased as the child demonstrates the ability to remain dry during the night. Once the child is able to remain dry after the intake of a maximum amount of fluid (2 ounces plus 1 ounce for every year of the child's age), the procedure is stopped. Overlearning typically reduces the recurrence of bed-wetting by 50 percent as compared to the use of the standard treatment alone.

Urine retention exercises are often another procedure added to the standard be-havioral treatment. These exercises involve the child drinking a certain amount of water (for example, 8 ounces) during the daytime and then telling the parents when he or she first feels the need to urinate. At this point, the child is instructed to hold the urine for a specific period of time. Upon successful completion of urine reten-tion, the child is allowed to urinate. Over a period of days, the amount of time the child is asked to wait before urination is increased from three minutes to a maxi-mum of forty-five minutes. The effectiveness of this procedure is based on its ability to increase the child's bladder capacity and to strengthen the muscles responsible for urine release.

Compared to drug therapy, behavior therapy is viewed by the majority of professionals as the most effective treatment for enuresis. In a review study conducted by Houts and Abramson, approximately three out of every four children treated with a behavioral treatment stopped bed-wetting after ten to twelve weeks. In contrast to the high relapse rates of drug treatments, the percentage of children who return to bed-wetting after a behavioral treatment is relatively small. As previously mentioned, this 40 percent relapse can be substantially reduced by the addition of auxiliary treatment components.

## Context

Enuresis is a disorder that has probably existed since the beginning of humankind. In spite of the fact that since the 1960's considerable scientific research has been conducted examining enuresis, many misconceptions continue to exist. For example, many believe that children's bed-wetting is a result of their "laziness" and not wanting to take the time to use the bathroom. This is not the case; most enuretic children desperately want to stop their bed-wetting.

Another misconception is that children will "outgrow" their bed-wetting. In fact, the yearly spontaneous remission rate for enuretic children, a measure of how many children stop wetting their beds without treatment during a year's time, is only about 15 percent. According to Houts and Abramson, on average, it takes more than three years for enuretic children to stop wetting the bed on their own. During this time, the enuretic child may develop poor self-esteem and feelings of failure and isolation.

Misconceptions also continue regarding the effectiveness of different treatments for enuresis. For example, many parents believe if they sufficiently shame or punish their child for bed-wetting that it will cease. This is not an effective approach, and it exerts a negative influence on a child's self-concept. A more humane but also ineffective treatment technique is the restriction of fluids given to the child prior to bedtime. Restricting fluids prior to bedtime is ineffective because the bladder will continue to empty even when fluids are withheld for long periods of time.

One of the reasons for these continued fallacies is the secrecy that often accompanies the disorder. The parents of enuretic children are often unwilling, because of embarrassment, to ask others, including professionals, for assistance in dealing with an enuretic child. When the parents of an enuretic child do seek guidance, they are often given advice that is ineffective in treating the problem. For this reason, better efforts are needed to educate parents and professionals who work with enuretics. In this regard, the basic message that should be delivered to parents is that enuresis is a treatable problem and that they should not be reluctant to take their child to a qualified professional for evaluation and treatment.

## Bibliography
Azrin, Nathan H., and Victoria A. Besalel. *A Parent's Guide to Bedwetting Control.*

New York: Simon & Schuster, 1979. A self-help book written for parents with enuretic children in which Nathan Azrin's "dry-bed training" is described. Azrin's treatment is based on behavioral principles; the specific procedures are discussed in terms that most nonprofessionals will understand.

Houts, Arthur C., and Hillel Abramson. "Assessment and Treatment for Functional Childhood Enuresis and Encopresis: Toward a Partnership Between Health Psychologists and Physicians." In *Child and Adolescent Disorders*, edited by Sam B. Morgan and Theresa M. Okwumabua. Hillsdale, N.J.: Lawrence Erlbaum, 1990. Summarizes work in the field of enuresis and encopresis, an elimination disorder involving involuntary soiling. Chapter sections include the assessment, causes, and treatment of enuresis. Reviews types and effectiveness of both behavioral and medical treatments.

Houts, Arthur C., and Richard M. Liebert. *Bedwetting: A Guide for Parents and Children*. Springfield, Ill.: Charles C Thomas, 1984. Another self-help book intended for parents that outlines a treatment package for enuresis called the "full spectrum home training" system. This effective treatment approach is described in understandable terms, although the authors advise that the treatment is best conducted under professional supervision.

Mills, Joyce C., and Richard J. Crowley. *Sammy the Elephant and Mr. Camel*. New York: Magination Press, 1988. An illustrated book for children that presents a metaphorical story regarding enuresis. Designed to promote the self-esteem of enuretic children and to provide a useful way of discussing bed-wetting with children in a nonthreatening way.

Schaefer, Charles E. *Childhood Encopresis and Enuresis: Causes and Therapy*. New York: Van Nostrand Reinhold, 1979. Provides an overview of the suggested causes and treatment of enuresis and encopresis. Outlines the physiology of bowel and bladder functioning, examines changes in the suggested causes and treatments of the disorder across time, and reviews present treatment procedures. Useful features include diagrams of important material and a glossary of technical terms.

Walker, C. Eugene, Mary Kenning, and Jan Faust-Campanile. "Enuresis and Encopresis." In *Treatment of Childhood Disorders*, edited by Eric J. Mash and Russell A. Barkley. New York: Guilford Press, 1989. Provides an overview of enuresis and encopresis. Presents a case study examining the assessment and treatment of an enuretic child, and provides the addresses of different companies that manufacture urine alarms. Largely written for a professional audience.

*R. Christopher Qualls*

## Cross-References

Instrumental Conditioning: Acquisition and Extinction, 1315; Motor Development, 1623; Operant Conditioning Therapies, 1714; Reinforcement Schedules, 2077; Reinforcers and Reinforcement, 2084; Sleep: Stages and Functions, 2277.

# BEHAVIORAL ASSESSMENT AND PERSONALITY RATING SCALES

*Type of psychology:* Personality
*Field of study:* Personality assessment

*Behavioral assessment and personality rating scales are two methods of examining personality. Both use reports by the person or others of observable behavior rather than making inferences from more subjective sources to determine personality. Both approaches are much more direct than other personality assessment methods.*

*Principal terms*
DISCRIMINATIVE STIMULUS: an event that serves as a cue or a prompt for a response
LEARNING HISTORY: a person's accumulated life experiences, which result in a unique pattern of responding to new situations
RELIABILITY: the extent to which test results are repeatable across different testing sessions
TARGET BEHAVIOR: the specific behavior that is the object of the assessment or intervention
VALIDITY: the extent to which a test actually measures what it is supposed to measure

## Overview

Among the various ways of assessing human behavior are behavioral assessment and personality rating scales. These approaches to assessment arose from behavioral research, which offered explanations of human behavior that differed from traditional theories. For example, early behaviorists believed that a person's behavior was the appropriate focus for understanding the person, while other psychologists believed that behavior is only a symbolic representation of an unconscious conflict. Rating scales were developed by psychologists interested in behavioral assessment and in determining the intensity of a behavior experienced by a person. Behavioral assessment and rating scales differ from traditional assessment primarily in the philosophical underpinnings of each.

Traditional assessment approaches describe a person as having a particular trait or characteristic. For example, a person might be described as having an authority conflict or an anxious personality. In contrast, behavioral assessment describes the person's behavior in specific situations. For example, the behavioral assessment might say, "When the person is given an order by a superior, the person argues and makes sarcastic remarks." The behavioral assessment would go on to describe the consequences of arguing and talking back, which could be anything from the superior withdrawing the order to the superior punishing the person who argues.

Contemporary behavioral assessment is concerned with both internal and external events. Marvin Goldfried describes a model of behavioral assessment that includes a systematic analysis of internal and external events. Four classes of variables are assessed in this model: stimulus antecedents, organismic variables, response variables, and consequent variables. Stimulus antecedents refer to the environmental events that precede the occurrence of the target behavior. These are sometimes called discriminative stimuli, and they may be either external or internal. An example of an external event that serves as a stimulus antecedent is drinking a cup of coffee, which serves as a discriminative stimulus for lighting a cigarette. An internal event that might serve as a prompt for an emotional response is thinking about taking a test, which results in a feeling of anxiety. Both internal and external stimulus antecedents can produce behaviors that are experienced as either external (observable) or internal (unobservable).

This model of behavioral assessment includes a thorough description of organismic variables. These variables include anything that is personally relevant and could influence the response to the stimulus antecedents. Both acute and chronic medical conditions which may affect the perception of and/or response to the discriminative stimuli are noted. The influence of the person's genetic makeup is assessed when it seems relevant to the target behavior. Finally, the person's learning history is considered important in understanding the response to the antecedent stimuli. Organismic variables serve as mediators or filters between the stimulus antecedents and the responses.

Response variables are the person's behaviors in response to the stimulus antecedents and filtered through the organismic variables. The response variables are considered to be part of the triple-response system. The triple-response system requires the assessment of behavior in each of three domains: motor, physiological, and cognitive/emotional. Motor behavior refers to the observable actions of the person. Examples of motor behavior include lighting a cigarette, leaving a room, and throwing a temper tantrum. Physiological responses are unobservable behaviors that can be made observable by using specialized instruments. Heart rate is an unobservable physiological response until the person is placed on an instrument that detects and displays it. Cognitive and emotional responses are also unobservable events. The behavioral assessment of these responses requires the person to report his or her own thoughts and feelings in the presence of the stimulus antecedents.

The triple-response system is important from the perspectives of both assessment and treatment. While behaviorists have historically focused on motor behavior, it is well known that people experience physiological changes and cognitive/emotional changes concurrently with the motor behavior in the presence of the stimulus antecedents. As behavioral assessment has become more sophisticated, it has become apparent that the relative importance of the components of the triple-response system varies in different people. Thus, treatment may focus on cognition in one person because it is the most important behavior, and on physiological responses in another.

The final component of this model of behavioral assessment requires a consideration of consequent variables. The events that follow a response are the consequent variables. These variables are important in determining whether the response will be continued or discontinued. The consequences of a response also determine the strength of the response. Any consequence that leads to a reward for the person will strengthen the response it follows. Rewards may include getting something one wants (for example, studying results in a good grade on a test) or ending something that is unpleasant (for example, leaving a situation results in reduced anxiety). Consequences that do not reward the person lead to a weakening of the behavior he or she follows.

The goal of the behavioral assessment is to describe fully the problem behavior and the events that surround it. While earlier approaches tried to limit the assessment to one or two behaviors identified as problems, more recent approaches apply the assessment methodology to clusters of behaviors that may form syndromes or diagnostic categories.

A variety of approaches are used to gather the information that constitutes a behavioral assessment. Naturalistic observation is used to observe the person's behavior in the settings most germane to the behaviors of interest. These settings may include home, school, work, hospital, and others. In self-monitoring, the person observes and records each instance of the behavior of interest. Researchers use role playing and controlled observations to study the behaviors of interest while maintaining more control over the environment than is possible with naturalistic observation. Rating scales are also used to determine the intensity of the behavior under study.

"Personality" is a general term that summarizes the group of behaviors associated with a person's tendency to respond in certain ways. Most behaviorists think that personality is too general a term and that it does not provide much usable information. Nevertheless, personality is assessed in a variety of ways. One approach is to use rating scales. Rating scales assess the intensity of a particular behavior or feeling. The rating may be done by the person being rated (self-rating), by peers, by professionals, or by anyone in a position to observe the behaviors of interest.

Jerry Wiggins describes one rating scale that provides a multidimensional approach to assessing personality. The semantic differential asks respondents to describe the meaning of a word on each of three scales using dichotomous adjectives to measure the dimensions of evaluation (good versus bad), potency (powerful versus weak), and activity (active versus passive). This particular approach provides information about the intensity and meaning of emotionally laden words or concepts. Other rating scales focus on the intensity to which the concept being rated is experienced.

## Applications

Behavioral assessment and personality rating scales have many uses in psychology. There are three major ways of interpreting the data obtained from these assessment procedures. Client-referenced interpretation compares one performance on a task to another performance by the same person on the same task. The simplest example of this is a comparison of pretreatment and post-treatment performance on a task to see if the person improved after the intervention. There is no consideration of how other people do on the task. Criterion-referenced interpretation compares the person's performance to a previously established level of acceptable performance. Finally, norm-referenced interpretations compare an individual's performance to normative data; thus, it is possible to learn how a person compares to all others for whom norms are available. The comparison could be with everyone who has completed the task or taken the test in the normative sample, or with specific age or ethnic groups, genders, or occupational groups. Norm-referenced interpretations can be used to compare an individual to any group for which norms are available. It is up to the psychologist to ensure that the normative group used for comparison is one that is appropriate for the person being evaluated.

Behavioral assessment has been used in industrial and organizational settings. Robert P. Bush and others (1990) describe a procedure for developing a scale to assess the performance of people working in retail sales. They point out the shortage of good information about the performance of people in retail sales and the need for more research in this area. Their article describes the important role the sales force has in the success of the business and the need to measure the behavior of the sales representatives. Richard Reilly and others (1990) describe the use of a behavioral assessment procedure within the context of an assessment center. Assessment centers are established by businesses in order to simulate the tasks associated with different positions. It is assumed that superior performance in the assessment center will translate into superior performance on the job. Reilly and others demonstrated that by incorporating behavioral assessment procedures—checklists—into the assessment center procedures, the validity of the assessment center results was improved.

The clinical use of behavioral assessment procedures is quite extensive and includes both children and adults. Thomas Ollendick and Greta Francis have reviewed the use of behavioral assessment techniques in the assessment and treatment of children with phobias. These authors provide examples of how to obtain information about fears and phobias from children by asking them questions in both direct and indirect ways. A variety of rating scales are reviewed, including the Fear Survey Schedule for Children and the Children's Manifest Anxiety Scale. The Fear Survey Schedule for Children consists of eighty items pertaining to childhood fears, which the child rates on a scale ranging from "none" to "a lot." Normative data are available for children between the ages of seven and sixteen years. It is possible to obtain information about fear of failure, fear of the unknown, fear of danger and death, and so on. The Children's Manifest Anxiety Scale measures the extent of anxiety the child feels. This scale assesses the child's anxiety in the domains of physiological responsiveness, worry/oversensitivity, and concentration. It is appropriate for children between the ages of six and eighteen years.

Other scales for children, reviewed by Larry D. Evans and Sharon Bradley-Johnson, assess adaptive behavior. Adaptive behavior is the degree to which a child is able to cope effectively with the environment based upon the child's age. Deficits in adaptive behavior are an important part of the definition of mental retardation. These authors review several measures of adaptive behavior that are completed by teachers, care givers, or psychologists. Comparisons are made to existing scales assessing adaptive behavior. Rating scales are used to measure various behaviors in adolescents and children. In addition to the behaviors mentioned above, there are rating scales for attention and distractibility, autism, and various psychiatric syndromes.

Randall Morrison describes a variety of rating scales that assess adult psychopathology. These include scales of schizophrenic symptoms that are completed by the psychologist interviewing and observing the person suspected of having schizophrenia. A scale of global adjustment is also reviewed by Morrison. This scale is a 100-point rating scale that is useful with a wide variety of psychiatric patients. It focuses on the extent to which the person has coped effectively with environmental events during the past year. According to Morrison, it has some value in predicting how well a person will cope after treatment, as well as in assessing the effectiveness of the treatment.

There are many rating scales for children, adolescents, and adults. They assess a wide range of behaviors and vary in the degree to which they have been constructed with attention to the standards for test development and the compilation of appropriate norms.

## Context

The history of psychological assessment is replete with examples of attempts to measure the characteristics and traits of people. These traits and characteristics are defined as underlying psychological processes that are pervasive aspects of personality. In fact, they define the personality for many psychologists. Traditional approaches to psychotherapy try to identify the traits in order to develop a therapeutic strategy that will reveal the unconscious conflicts.

Unlike traditional approaches to psychological assessment and psychotherapy, behavioral assessment arose from the need of behavior therapists to describe more completely the events surrounding the problem behavior. The history of behavior therapy is one of defining a target behavior and designing a program to change the behavior. As behavior therapy developed and became more sophisticated, it became apparent that more information was needed to identify the antecedent stimuli, the organismic filters that were operating, which aspect of the triple-response system was relevant, and what the consequences of the target behavior were. In response to that need, behavioral assessment was developed. Initially, behavioral assessment was rather straightforward and did not bother much with the procedures of psychological test construction since the process itself was one of observing behavior rather than making inferences about behavior from test responses. As behavioral assessment has matured, it has become more concerned with meeting the standards of test construction applied to other assessment methods and has become more sophisticated and complex.

Behavioral assessment is used to measure clusters of behaviors and syndromes rather than merely isolated problem behaviors. More attention is paid to the extent to which standards of validity and reliability are met. Psychologists are putting behavioral assessment to the test of demonstrating its worth as an assessment procedure: It must add something to the understanding of the person being assessed in order to justify its use. The challenge is being met, and behavioral assessment continues to provide valuable information about the person being assessed. Information obtained is useful in determining the extent to which certain behaviors are problems. Other information is used in determining the personality of the individual, with all the attendant traits and characteristics.

## Bibliography

Barrios, B. A. "On the Changing Nature of Behavioral Assessment." In *Behavioral Assessment: A Practical Handbook*, edited by Alan S. Bellack and Michel Hersen. 3d ed. New York: Pergamon Press, 1988. This chapter is a good review of the principles associated with behavioral assessment, which are put in both historical and methodological contexts. The book is a thorough description of behavioral assessment and how it is used in various settings.

Bush, Robert P., Alan J. Bush, David J. Ortinau, and Joseph F. Hair, Jr. "Developing a Behavior-Based Scale to Assess Retail Salesperson Performance." *Journal of Retailing* 66, no. 1 (1990): 119-136. A good article describing the development of a rating scale of salesperson performance. An example of the scale content is provided.

Evans, Larry D., and Sharon Bradley-Johnson. "A Review of Recently Developed Measures of Adaptive Behavior." *Psychology in the Schools* 25, no. 3 (1988): 276-287. A thorough review of six rating scales of adaptive behavior. These are compared to older scales that have been in use for a number of years.

Goldfried, Marvin R. "Behavioral Assessment: An Overview." In *International Handbook of Behavior Modification and Therapy*, edited by Alan S. Bellack, Michel Hersen, and Alan E. Kazdin. New York: Plenum Press, 1982. This chapter provides a good introduction to behavioral assessment. It is part of a book that includes many examples of assessment and therapy.

Kanfer, Frederick H., and W. Robert Nay. "Behavioral Assessment." In *Contemporary Behavior Therapy: Conceptual and Empirical Foundations*, edited by G. Terence Wilson and Cyril M. Franks. New York: Guilford Press, 1982. A well-written chapter that provides a detailed description of the procedure of behavioral assessment. A fairly advanced description in the context of a presentation of behavior therapy.

Morrison, Randall L. "Structured Interviews and Rating Scales." In *Behavioral Assessment: A Practical Handbook*, edited by Alan S. Bellack and Michel Hersen. 3d ed. New York: Pergamon Press, 1988. This chapter is about equally split between describing the use of interviews and the use of rating scales in assessing personality. Clearly written; includes examples of both interviews and rating scales, with references.

Ollendick, Thomas H., and Greta Francis. "Behavioral Assessment and Treatment of Childhood Phobias." *Behavior Modification* 12, no. 2 (1988): 165-204. A very informative review of the normal aspects of fear and the problems associated with abnormal fear. Children's fears and assessment devices for children are the focus of this article.

Phares, E. Jerry. *Clinical Psychology.* 4th ed. Pacific Grove, Calif.: Brooks/Cole, 1991. Includes a chapter on behavioral assessment within the context of a more comprehensive description of the duties of clinical psychologists.

Reilly, Richard R., Sarah Henry, and James W. Smither. "An Examination of the Effects of Using Behavior Checklists on the Construct Validity of Assessment Center Dimensions." *Personnel Psychology* 43, no. 1 (1990): 71-84. A technical description of a study testing the value of a behavioral assessment procedure in the assessment center.

Wiggins, Jerry S. *Personality and Prediction: Principles of Personality Assessment.* Reading, Mass.: Addison-Wesley, 1973. A classic book that is a highly technical description of how to use personality assessment instruments correctly. Despite the technicality of the material, this is a very worthwhile book for the serious student of personality assessment.

*James T. Trent*

## Cross-References

Abnormality: Behavioral Models, 33; Behaviorism: An Overview, 401; Clinical Interviewing, Testing, and Observation, 527; Emotion: Cognitive and Physiological Interaction, 881; Observational Methods in Psychology, 1700; Personality: Psychophysiological Measures, 1790.

# BEHAVIORAL FAMILY THERAPY

*Type of psychology:* Psychotherapy
*Field of study:* Group and family therapies

*Behavioral family therapy is a type of psychotherapy that applies the principles of learning theory to the treatment of family problems. It is most frequently used to treat parent-child problems, with the parents being taught to apply behavioral techniques in order to correct their children's misbehavior.*

### Principal terms

CIRCULAR CAUSALITY: the concept that behavior occurs as the result of many factors and circumstances, not as the product of a simple, cause-and-effect relationship

CLASSICAL CONDITIONING: the process by which new behavior becomes more likely to recur because it has been paired with old behavior that has been positively reinforced

CONTINGENCY MANAGEMENT: the providing and removing of positive rewards in accordance with whether the individual being treated engages in the expected behavior

LEARNING THEORY: a set of principles derived from extensive laboratory experimentation that explain the production and modification of behavior

LINEAR CAUSALITY: the concept that a specific action happens as the direct result of the occurrence of another action (simple cause and effect)

OPERANT CONDITIONING: the process by which behavior is made to occur at a faster rate because a specific action is followed by positive reinforcement

OPERATIONALIZATION: the practice of describing treatment goals in such a way that the behavior necessary for the fulfillment of the goals is easily observable and measurable

POSITIVE REINFORCEMENT: the rewarding consequences that follow a behavior, which increase the rate at which the behavior will recur

RESPONSE COST: negative consequences that follow the commission of an undesired behavior, decreasing the rate at which the misbehavior will recur

## Overview

Behavioral family therapy is a type of psychotherapy that is used to treat families in which one or more family members are exhibiting behavior problems. Behavioral therapy was employed originally in the treatment of individual disorders such as phobias (irrational fears). Behavioral family therapy represents an extension of the use of behavioral techniques from the treatment of individual problems to the treatment of family problems. The most common problems treated by behavioral family therapy are parent-child conflicts; however, the principles of this type of therapy have been used to treat other familial difficulties, including marital and sexual problems.

The principles of learning theory underlie the theory and practice of behavioral family therapy. Learning theory was developed through laboratory experimentation largely begun by Ivan Pavlov and Edward L. Thorndike during the early 1900's. Pavlov was a Russian physiologist interested in the digestive processes of dogs. In the process of his experimentation, he discovered several properties regarding the production of behavior which have become embodied in the theory of classical conditioning. Pavlov observed that his dogs began to salivate when he entered their pens because they associated his presence (new behavior) with their being fed (previously reinforced old behavior). From this observation and additional experimentation, Pavlov concluded that a new behavior which is regularly paired with an old behavior acquires the same rewarding or punishing qualities that the old behavior had. That is, new actions become conditioned to produce the same responses as the previously reinforced or punished actions.

Another component of learning theory was discovered by Thorndike. Thorndike observed that actions followed closely by rewards were more likely to recur than those not followed by rewards. Similarly, he observed that actions followed closely by punishment were less likely to recur. Thorndike explained these observations on the basis of the law of effect. The law of effect holds that behavior closely followed by a response will be more or less likely to recur depending on whether the response is reinforcing (rewarding) or punishing. Building on the observations of Thorndike, B. F. Skinner developed the theory of operant conditioning in the 1930's. Operant conditioning is the process by which behavior is made to occur at a faster rate when a specific behavior is followed by positive reinforcement. An example that Skinner used in demonstrating operant conditioning involved placing a rat in a box with different levers. When the rat accidentally pushed a predesignated lever, it was given a food pellet. As predicted by operant conditioning, the rat subsequently increased its pushing of the lever which provided it with food.

The principles of classical and operant conditioning serve to form the foundation of learning theory. Although initially derived from animal experiments, learning theory also was applied to humans. Psychologists who advocated learning theory began to demonstrate that all behavior, whether socially appropriate or inappropriate, occurred because it was either classically or operantly conditioned. John B. Watson, a psychologist of the early twentieth century, illustrated this by producing a fear of rats in an infant named Albert by repeatedly making a loud noise when a rat was presented to Albert. After a number of pairings of the loud noise with the rat, Albert began to show fear when the rat was presented.

In addition to demonstrating how inappropriate behavior was caused, behavioral psychologists began to show how learning theory could be used to treat people with psychological disorders. Joseph Wolpe, a pioneer in the use of behavioral treatment during the 1950's, showed how phobias could be alleviated by using learning principles in a procedure termed systematic desensitization. Systematic desensitization involves three basic steps: teaching the phobic individual how to relax; having the client create a list of images of the feared object (for example, snakes), from least to most feared; and repeatedly exposing the client to the feared object in graduated degrees, from least to most feared images, while the individual is in a relaxed state. This procedure has been shown to be very effective in the treatment of phobias.

Behavioral family therapy makes the same assumptions regarding the causes of both individual and family problems. For example, consider the fictional case of the Williams family, who came to treatment because their seven-year-old son, John, refused to sleep in his own bed at night. In attempting to explain John's behavior, a behaviorally oriented psychologist would seek to find out what positive reinforcement John was receiving in response to his refusal to stay in his own bed. It may be that when John was younger his parents allowed him to sleep with them, thus reinforcing his behavior by giving him the attention he desired. Now that John is seven, however, his parents believe that he needs to sleep in his own bed, but John continues to want to sleep with his parents because he has been reinforced by being allowed to sleep with them for many years. This case provides a clinical example of operant conditioning in that John's behavior, because it was repeatedly followed by positive reinforcement, was resistant to change.

## Applications

Behavioral family therapy is a treatment approach that includes the following four steps: problem assessment, family (parent) education, specific treatment design, and treatment goal evaluation. It begins with a thorough assessment of the presenting family problem. This assessment process involves gathering the following information from the family: what circumstances immediately precede the problem behavior; how family members react to the exhibition of the client's problem behavior; how frequently the misbehavior occurs; and how intense the misbehavior is. Behavioral family therapy differs from individual behavior therapy in that all family members are typically involved in the assessment process. As a part of the assessment process, the behavioral family therapist often observes the way in which the family handles the presenting problem. This observation is conducted in order to obtain firsthand information regarding ways the family may be unknowingly reinforcing the problem or otherwise poorly handling the client's misbehavior.

Following the assessment, the behavioral family therapist, with input from family members, establishes treatment goals. These treatment goals should be operationalized; that is, they should be specifically stated in order that they may be easily observed and measured. In the example of John, the boy who refused to sleep in his own bed, an operationalized treatment goal would be as follows: "John will be able to sleep from 9:00 P.M. to 6:00 A.M. in his own bed without interrupting his parents during the night."

Once treatment goals have been operationalized, the next stage involves designing an intervention to correct the behavioral problem. The treatment procedure follows from the basic learning principles previously discussed. In cases involving parent-child problems, the behavioral family therapist educates the parents in learning theory principles as they apply to the treatment of behavioral problems. There are three basic learning principles that are explained to the child's parents. First, positive reinforcement should be withdrawn from the unwanted behavior. For example, a parent who meets the demands of a screaming preschooler who throws a temper tantrum in the checkout line of the grocery store because he or she wants a piece of candy is unwittingly reinforcing the child's screaming behavior. "Time-out" is one procedure used to remove the undesired reinforcement from a child's misbehavior. Utilizing time-out involves making a child sit in a corner or other nonreinforcing place for a specified period of time (typically, one minute for each year of the child's age).

Second, appropriate behavior that is incompatible with the undesired behavior should be positively reinforced. In the case of the screaming preschooler, this would involve rewarding him or her for acting correctly. An appropriate reinforcer in this case would be giving the child his or her choice of a candy bar if the child were quiet and cooperative during grocery shopping: behavior inconsistent with a temper tantrum. In order for positive reinforcement to have its maximum benefit, the child should be informed about what is expected of him or her and what reward he or she will receive for fulfilling these responsibilities prior to the beginning of the specific activity (for example, grocery shopping). This process is called contingency management because the promised reward is made contingent upon the child's acting in a prescribed manner. In addition, the positive reinforcement should be given as close to the completion of the appropriate behavior as possible.

Third, aversive consequences should be applied when the problem behavior recurs. That is, when the child engages in the misbehavior, he or she should consistently experience negative costs. In this regard, response cost is a useful technique because it involves taking something away or making the child do something he or she finds unrewarding as a way of making misbehavior cost him or her. For example, the preschooler who has a temper tantrum in the checkout line may have a favorite dessert, which he or she had previously selected while in the store, taken away as the cost for throwing a temper tantrum. As with positive reinforcement, response cost should be applied as quickly as possible following the misbehavior in order for it to produce its maximum effect.

Once the parents receive instruction regarding the principles of behavior therapy, they are actively involved in the process of designing a specific intervention to address their child's behavior problems. The behavioral family therapist relates to the parents as cotherapists with the hope that this approach will increase the parents' involvement in the treatment process. In relating to Mr. and Mrs. Williams as cotherapists, for example, the behavioral family therapist would have the couple design a treatment intervention to correct John's misbehavior. Following the previously described principles, the Williamses might arrive at the following approach: the couple would refuse to give in to John's demands to sleep with them; John would receive a token for each night he slept in his own bed (after earning a certain number of tokens, he could exchange them for toys); and John would be required to go to bed fifteen minutes earlier the following night for each time he asked to sleep with his parents.

Once the intervention has been implemented, the therapist, together with the parents, monitor the results of the treatment. This monitoring process involves assessing the degree to which the established treatment goals are being met. For example, in the Williamses' case, the treatment goal was to reduce the number of times that John attempted to get into bed with his parents. Therapy progress, therefore, would be measured by counting the number of times that John attempted to get into bed with his parents. Careful assessment of an intervention's results is essential in order to determine whether the intervention is accomplishing its goal.

## Context

The development of behavioral family therapy occurred in several stages, starting with the discovery of the principles of learning theory in the animal laboratories of Pavlov and Thorndike. These discoveries were refined by Watson and Skinner before being applied to the treatment of individual problems, most notably by Wolpe. Gerald Patterson and Richard Stuart, beginning in the late 1960's, were among the first clinicians to apply behavioral techniques, previously utilized with individuals, to the treatment of family problems. While Patterson worked primarily with parent-child problems, Stuart extended behavioral family therapy to the treatment of marital problems.

Given the increasing prevalence of family problems, as seen by the rise in the number of divorces and cases of child abuse, the advent of behavioral family therapy has been welcomed by many therapists who treat families. The findings of a study by William Quinn and Bernard Davidson (1984) revealed the increasing use of this therapy, with more than half of all family therapists reporting the use of behavioral techniques in their family therapy. In spite of its popularity, this type of therapy has not been without its critics. For example, behavioral family therapy's explanations regarding the causes of family problems differ from those given by the advocates of other family therapies. One major difference is that behavioral family therapists are accused of taking a linear (as compared to a circular) view of causality. From a linear perspective, misbehavior occurs because A causes B and B causes C. Those who endorse a circular view of causality, however, assert that this simplistic perspective is inadequate in explaining why misbehavior occurs. Taking a circular perspective involves identifying multiple factors that may be operating at the same time in order to determine the reason for a particular misbehavior. For example, consider John's refusal to sleep in his own bed. From a linear view of causality, John's misbehavior is seen as the result of being reinforced for sleeping with his parents. According to a circular perspective, however, John's behavior may be the result of many factors, all possibly occurring together, such as his parents' marital problems or his genetic predisposition toward insecurity.

Partially in response to this criticism, attempts have been made to integrate behavioral family therapy with other types of family therapy. Another major purpose of integrative efforts is to address the resistance often encountered from families during treatment. Therapeutic resistance is a family's continued attempt to handle the presenting problem in a maladaptive manner in spite of having learned better ways. In the past, behavioral family therapists gave limited attention to dealing with family resistance; however, behavioral family therapy has attempted to improve its ability to handle resistance by incorporating some of the techniques used by other types of family therapy.

In conclusion, numerous research studies have demonstrated that behavioral family therapy is an effective treatment of family problems. One of the major strengths of BFT is its willingness to assess objectively its effectiveness in treating family problems. Because of its emphasis on experimentation, behavioral family therapy continues to adapt by modifying its techniques to address the problems of the modern family.

## Bibliography

Clark, Lynn. *The Time-Out Solution.* Chicago: Contemporary Books, 1989. Provides the general reader with an excellent overview of the major techniques used in behavioral family therapy. A good resource for parents or others interested in correcting children's misbehaviors through the use of well-tested methods.

Dangel, Richard F., and Richard A. Polster. *Teaching Child Management Skills.* New York: Pergamon Press, 1988. Although child mental health professionals were the intended audience, this book is written in such a way that most nonprofessionals will readily understand it. Chapters 2 and 3 are the most useful because they outline and well illustrate the basic behavioral techniques used in behavioral family therapy.

Falloon, Ian R. H., ed. *Handbook of Behavioral Family Therapy.* New York: Guilford Press, 1988. Provides a thorough review of the applications of behavioral family therapy; written primarily for persons familiar with behavioral therapy. Six chapters are devoted to general issues in behavioral family therapy; twelve chapters illustrate the use of its principles with families whose members have specific clinical problems.

Gordon, Thomas. *Parent Effectiveness Training.* New York: P. H. Wyden, 1970. Written primarily for parents interested in successfully handling parent-child interactions. Contains sixteen easily understood chapters that address various topics which primarily relate to improving communication between parents and children as well as handling children's misbehavior.

Nichols, Michael P. "Behavioral Family Therapy." In *Family Therapy: Concepts and Methods.* New York: Gardner Press, 1984. A very readable, well synthesized chapter. Provides information regarding the leading characters, definitions of important terms, beliefs regarding causes of abnormal behavior, and techniques involved in behavioral family therapy. An excellent piece for the person interested in reading only an article about the topic.

Robin, Arthur L., and Sharon L. Foster. *Negotiating Parent-Adolescent Conflict: A Behavioral Family Systems Approach.* New York: Guilford Press, 1989. Illustrates the integration of behavioral family therapy with other types of family therapy. Fifteen chapters are nicely divided between assessment and treatment issues. For the person already familiar with the subject.

*R. Christopher Qualls*

## Cross-References

Abnormality: Behavioral Models, 33; Cognitive Behavior Therapy, 546; Conditioning: Pavlovian versus Instrumental, 649; Instrumental Conditioning: Acquisition and Extinction, 1315; Misbehavior and Learning, 1581; Operant Conditioning Therapies, 1714; Psychotherapy with Children, 2009; Strategic Family Therapy, 2382.

# BEHAVIORISM: AN OVERVIEW

*Type of psychology:* Origin and definition of psychology
*Fields of study:* Experimental methodologies; instrumental conditioning

*Behaviorism rejects the idea that psychology should be the study of conscious experience or mental processes, proposing instead that its proper subject matter is the objective and observable behavior of human and animal life. Behaviorists believe that the behavior of an organism is determined by its interactions with observable forces in its environment.*

### Principal terms

BEHAVIOROLOGY: the science that treats the study of behavior from a strict selectionist philosophy, or what is called radical behaviorism
CONTINGENCY: a relationship between a response and its consequence or between two stimuli; sometimes considered a dependency
ENVIRONMENT: the context or conditions in which behaviors take place
OPERANT: a behavior whose frequency can be altered by changing its consequences; usually, a striated-muscle response controlled by the "voluntary" nervous system
PSYCHOLOGICAL SYSTEM: a particular approach that states what psychology should be and how it should explain psychological issues
PUNISHMENT: a procedure that leads to a reduction in the frequency of a behavior
REINFORCER: a stimulus or event that, when delivered contingently upon a response, will increase the probability of the recurrence of that response
RESPONDENT: a behavior that is elicited by an antecedent stimulus; usually, a smooth-muscle or glandular response controlled by the "involuntary" nervous system

## Overview

Behaviorism is a philosophical point of view concerning the scientific study of human and other animal behavior. It is not the science of behavior but the philosophical underpinnings of that science. Behaviorism arose as a purely American system in reaction to other, primarily German, approaches to the study of psychological phenomena. Behaviorism begins with the assumption that the objective and observable behavior of all animal life is the proper subject matter of psychology. Behaviorists resist the idea that psychology should be the study of conscious experience or mental processes. They argue that the factors that establish and control behavior are found in the environment, not inside the organism. Thus, behavior is considered a product of the biological organism's interaction with events in the environment that literally select and "shape" individual behavior.

According to behaviorists, the way to study behavior is to manipulate objects and events in the environment and systematically observe changes in behavior in order to establish functional relationships. The explanation, or understanding, of observed behavior is simply a statement of those functional relations that exist between behavior and the manipulated environmental factors. That is, behavior is not regarded as caused by some unseen forces that allegedly exist in the mind but, rather, is viewed as a result of environment-behavior interaction. At its inception, this concept was a dramatic reconsideration of what psychologists should study. The philosophy of behaviorism has changed from the days of its origin, and it can no longer be treated as a single system. This essay broadly defines behaviorism with a bias toward the discipline known as the experimental analysis of behavior. This particular behavioral approach has had the most influence on psychology in general.

Behaviorists say that day-to-day behavior depends on its consequences, meaning that the consequences of an occurrence of a behavior will have profound effects on the subsequent probability of that behavior. For example, if a person touches a hot stove, the painful consequences of that action will reduce that person's "stove-touching behavior" in the future. The probability of the person's future stove-touching behavior has been influenced by the consequences of his or her experience. Conversely, a person who receives a perfect score on a test after studying is more likely to study before a test in the future. This may appear to be common sense. Good things following a behavior increase the future likelihood of that behavior, and bad things following a behavior reduce the future likelihood of that behavior.

Behaviorism is only one discipline within psychology; psychologists treat the source and control of behavior by means of many different systems and schools of thought. For example, the branch of psychology known as cognitive psychology is characterized not by a particular philosophy or set of principles but by a willingness to attempt to explain behavior by reference to unobserved mental processes. Behaviorism, in contrast, considers such an approach simply an appeal to "explanatory fiction" and rejects the entire idea. Behaviorists assume that behavior is lawful, determined, predictable, and objectively analyzable. Further, they believe that objective—not interpretive or speculative—behavior analysis will eventually explain behavior in terms of the functional relationships that exist between behavior and the environment. No intervening hypothetical variables such as a mind, a will, expectations, thoughts, or personalities are considered necessary. Behavior, for behaviorists, can be predicted and controlled, and therefore explained, by manipulation of and reference to environmental events. Explanations at other levels of analysis or speculation are considered unnecessary, diversionary, and wrong.

It does not really help a teacher or a parent, for example, to be told that a child has a poor "self-concept" or a "bad attitude." Behaviorists consider these terms as mere labels for certain observed behaviors, not explanations for those behaviors. The teacher and parent need to know which events (variables) in the environment can be manipulated so that the child becomes skillful and competent and obtains many positive consequences for behaving appropriately. Teachers and parents cannot read "minds" or deal with internal "attitudes," but they can attend to overt behaviors and the consequences that follow those behaviors. A behaviorist attributes inappropriate behavior to the individual's being reinforced for the wrong kinds of activities and not sufficiently reinforced for the right kinds. For example, a child may "act out" in school not because of a bad attitude but because other students praise or in some other way positively reinforce the acting out. In addition, the teacher may not positively reinforce good behavior often enough. The point is that the explanation for the behavior, according to the behaviorist, does not lie inside the child but in events in the environment.

Behaviorists advocate an experimental approach to behavior in the sense that objective data are carefully gathered, manipulations of response consequences are made, and subsequent changes in the behavior are again carefully observed. When such a series of events actually takes place, the behavior is said to be caused by, and under the control of, the contingencies in the environment that were manipulated, rather than by some hypothetical inner process or imagined internal thing such as an attitude. For example, a child asking for water does not ask because of thirst and an expectation that water will follow, but because asking has been followed by water on earlier occasions. Thus, it is the history of reinforcement that actually controls the asking response, not something unseen and only supposed to exist inside the child's mind—not even thirst.

A behavioral procedure is replicable in that if the conditions are stable it will result in the same behavioral outcome every time. Such controlled repeatability does not happen when interpretations or intuitions are made regarding the basic causes of behavior. A behavioral approach is based upon the fact that behavior is adaptive as a product of altering the consequences of the behavior.

Very few behaviors of much interest to behaviorists are "hard-wired" into the organism to such an extent that they cannot be altered by changing their consequences. Most physiological activity and behaviors called instincts are left for others (physiologists and ethologists) to understand. It is the systematic study of the relationship between antecedent and consequent environmental events *and* behavior that is the professional activity of interest to behaviorists. The genetics and neurochemistry of the organism are for other disciplines to study. Behaviorists consider behavior, by itself, an adequate problem for focused research. Nonbehavioral psychologists may observe behavior, but they are prone to attribute what they see to something they cannot see, such as cognition; behaviorists attribute what they see to things they can see—events in the environment.

## Applications

Behaviorism, as a systematic and coherent approach to studying and modifying behavior, is not very old. The manipulation of consequences to alter human behavior, however, is probably as old as humankind. Certainly any grandmother knows that when she gives a child a cookie for saying "please," the child is much more likely to say "please" the next time. She also knows that a child who was harmed by some action avoids that behavior in the future. Her grandparents knew it as well.

The use of rewards, or reinforcers, to increase the probability of the behavior's occurrence is well known. Dogs that become more obedient after being petted for coming when called have been reinforced by the petting. Children who are praised for doing good are more likely to do good in the future. Employees who receive fair pay and appreciation for a job well done will probably remain at that job and continue to do it well. If, however, a person is cursed, fined, spanked, or shocked for doing something, that person will probably do that thing much less often. Behavior is therefore a function of its consequences.

The behavioral consequence of an action cannot be accurately labeled as a reinforcer or a punisher until the behavioral effects of the consequating event are observed. One might think that some action is aversive or pleasant and will be suitable punishment or reinforcement, but that does not mean that everyone else will agree. Only after the change in behavior frequency is observed can the consequence be correctly labeled. A cow that receives a strong electric shock upon touching a wire with her nose does not often do that again. Such treatment is called punishment because of its effects on behavior, not because of the use of the electric shock. Punishment is the procedure of reducing the probability of a behavior by using contingent consequences. One cannot always predict beforehand what will be a reinforcer and what will be a punisher. For example, if an electric shock of a certain type and intensity is delivered directly to a particular area of the brain in humans, and many other animals as well, the individual human reports a pleasant sensation, and the animals will work to receive further shocks. The point is that the behavior-changing effects are what is important, not the stimulus. Thus, electric shock can either decrease behaviors and act as punishment or increase behaviors and act as reinforcement.

The principles of behavior analysis developed by behaviorists have been applied in almost all areas of human activity. Such applications have included individual therapy, training in business and industry, educational programming, experimental psychopharmacology, parenting, developmental disabilities, behavioral medicine, and pain management, to name only a few. Every activity involving the behavior of organisms can be approached by behavioral means. This is one of the features of behaviorism that sets it apart from most other schools of psychology. It is a practical and useful approach that has generated an extremely helpful technology of behavior management. Even such private events as thinking, feeling, perceiving, and reasoning have been, when these activities have been behaviorally defined, subjected to behavioral analysis and manipulation. They are not considered causes of behavior but instead are treated as, and considered to be, concomitants to operant and respondent behavior and are therefore subject to analysis.

Certain fundamental laws of learning that govern behavior are common to many different species of animals. In particular, the principles of reinforcement and punishment, stimulus control, and shaping, as well as many others, apply to human beings, rats, dogs, fish, birds, and many other creatures. These laws, having been worked out primarily by behaviorists in laboratories, apply to the prediction and control of behavior regardless of the species of the behaving organism. Some animals, such as humans, exhibit much more complicated behavior than others. All animals, however, share many basic mechanisms of selective adaptation.

Behavioral principles are often worked out in the laboratory with nonhuman species as subjects and then tested and used with humans in "real-world" situations. This approach of simplifying things in the laboratory first and then making applications to complex situations is a characteristic of the scientific method. Because behavior is the subject matter of behavioral investigation, the behaving animal species is not critical. A comparable situation is employed in other sciences, in which models or simple devices are used in controlled tests of predictions or theories.

## Context

Behaviorism as a way of considering psychological problems began as an alternative to the prominent German schools of structuralism and Gestalt psychology and to Sigmund Freud's psychoanalysis. It was developed as a school of psychology in the early years of this century by John B. Watson. In 1903, Watson received the first doctorate in psychology, awarded by the University of Chicago. In 1913, he wrote the behaviorists' manifesto, "Psychology as the Behaviorist Views It." It appeared to Watson that, if psychology were ever to become a "real" science, there needed to be some systematic application of the scientific method to behavior. Watson set out to develop an appropriate basic philosophy and an appropriate methodology. He began by saying that overt, objectively defined behavior was the subject matter of psychological inquiry and that the method of psychological analysis was to be objective observation. In other words, a behavioral scientist should report only what was actually observed and should not make inferences, or guesses, about the possibility of other events occurring at other levels. For example, most psychologists were (and many still are) interested in behavior only as evidence of some underlying process, often called the "mind." Such mentalism was to play no part in Watson's behaviorism.

Watson's behaviorism was of the stimulus-response type originally developed in Russia by Ivan Pavlov. Watson believed that the concept of the reflex (a stimulus eliciting a response) was the basis of all psychological phenomena; the reflex was his behavioral unit. Subsequent behaviorists, especially B. F. Skinner, viewed action on a larger scale, not merely the reflex, as the correct subject matter of psychology. Skinner separated behavior into two categories: operants, defined as skeletal muscle actions that operate upon the environment; and respondents, which are smooth-muscle or glandular responses elicited by some prior stimulus. Operants, which are controlled by the consequences they generate, are measured in terms of instances per unit time—that is, rate. Respondents, or reflexes, as Pavlov showed with salivating dogs, are elicited by a stimulus and measured in terms of latency and magnitude. Each of these two categories of behavior has its own set of experimental procedures and findings.

From the 1930's through the 1950's, behaviorism was the prevailing system of psychology. Among the major proponents of the behavioral approach, after Watson, were Edward Tolman, Edwin Guthrie, Clark Hull, and Skinner. Skinner became the most creative, active, and eloquent spokesperson for a behavioristic psychology that he called the experimental analysis of behavior. His philosophical position, known as radical behaviorism, held that the best way to study and understand behavior is to stop making inferences about possible inner causes (the mind) and to concentrate on the environment as the source of behavioral selection. For example, instead of attributing an instance of behavior to something called a "self-concept," Skinner argues that it is infinitely better to investigate which environmental variables could be involved in the production and management of such behavior. If "self-concept" behavior can be modified by environmental events, the supposition of an internal self-concept as a driving force is unnecessary. The behavior is the self-concept; it is not the manifestation of an internal nonbehavioral thing. The label for a behavior that anyone could observe is not to be taken as the cause of the behavior. Psychologists, it has been argued, will give a name to a behavior and then try to explain the behavior simply by referring to the name. (They say that a person exhibits autistic behavior and then say that the person acts that way because he has autism.)

As an objective orientation toward psychology and psychological issues, behaviorism has lost much of its standing in professional psychology. The division (number 25) of the American Psychological Association (APA) devoted to a behavioristic approach is a minority of the membership. It sometimes seems that psychology and behaviorology are two different disciplines and that they are not compatible in their philosophies, objectives, or methods. Nevertheless, the application of behavioral principles, research from a behavioral standpoint, commitment to a behavioral philosophy, and the promotion of behavioral organizations outside the APA are growing.

Psychology as an important field of study evolved from many sources, including theology, biology, and philosophy. The different orientations of these fields have affected, even confused, the development and maturation of psychology as a science. As a result, there are fads and cycles, and there has always been disagreement among psychologists regarding what the subject matter and methodology of psychology should be. Psychology has the complicated task of understanding behavior and devising ways of predicting, explaining, and controlling it. As a result of this complex assignment and psychology's divergent roots, there have been many suggestions about what psychology should do and how it should do it. Behaviorism is one of those suggestions.

## Bibliography

Boakes, Robert A. *From Darwin to Behaviorism*. New York: Cambridge University Press, 1984. The evolution of the scientific consideration of the minds of animals, including man, is described, along with a look at the people involved.

Chance, Paul. *Learning and Behavior*. 2d ed. Belmont, Calif.: Wadsworth, 1988. Chance defines and explains the basic principles of an experimental analysis of behavior in a very understandable way.

Ishaq, Waris, ed. *Human Behavior in Today's World.* New York: Praeger, 1991. Chapters written by different behaviorists indicate how a behavioral analysis is generated, what some basic principles are, and how they can be applied to cultural and social, as well as individual, actions.

Lee, Vicki L. *Beyond Behaviorism.* Hillsdale, N.J.: Lawrence Earlbaum, 1988. This book describes the differences between the positions of Watson and other "behaviorists," as well as the radical behaviorism of B. F. Skinner.

Rachlin, Howard. *Introduction to Modern Behaviorism.* 2d ed. San Francisco: W. H. Freeman, 1976. This dated but excellent text reviews the development of behavioral thinking and reviews how behaviorism is translated into action.

Skinner, B. F. *About Behaviorism.* New York: Alfred A. Knopf, 1974. This book is Skinner's attempt to explain his philosophy of behaviorism in terms of questions and behavioral answers.

——————————. *Science and Human Behavior.* New York: Macmillan, 1953. This early work sets forth the basics of radical behaviorism and discusses its application to many kinds of behavioral questions.

Watson, John Broadus. *Behaviorism.* New York: W. W. Norton, 1925. This is the ultimate statement of behaviorism as intended and presented by the father of this approach to psychology.

*Carl D. Cheney*

## Cross-References

# BILINGUALISM: ACQUISITION, STORAGE, AND PROCESSING

*Type of psychology:* Language
*Fields of study:* Cognitive development; cognitive processes

*Bilingualism refers to the use of two or more languages by either an individual or a community. The psychological study of bilingualism has contributed to an understanding of language acquisition, brain organization, methods of educating language-minority children, and the relationship between language and cognition.*

### Principal terms

ADDITIVE BILINGUALISM: the type of bilingualism that results when members of a majority culture learn a second language in addition to the language used by the mainstream society

BALANCED BILINGUAL: a bilingual person who has approximately the same degree of competence in both languages

BILINGUAL: a person who has enough control of two languages to function well with both languages in a number of different contexts

CODE-SWITCHING: a speech style used by many bilinguals that is characterized by rapid shifts back and forth between two languages within a single conversation or sentence

PARTIAL BILINGUAL: a bilingual person who has much more control over one of his or her languages

SEQUENTIAL BILINGUAL: a bilingual person who learned a second language after having acquired his or her mother tongue

SIMULTANEOUS BILINGUAL: a bilingual person who acquired both languages at the same time during early childhood

SUBTRACTIVE BILINGUALISM: the type of bilingualism that results when the acquisition of a majority language results in the weakening and eventual loss of a minority group's native language

## Overview

Bilingualism refers to the use of two languages, by either an individual or a community. It is estimated that more than half of the world's population is bilingual, and there are sizable numbers of bilinguals in every country. Psychologists have long been interested in understanding the process of learning two languages, as well as the social, psychological, and intellectual consequences of being bilingual. Areas of inquiry have included how the mind of a bilingual differs from that of a monolingual and whether people learn a second language in the same way they acquire their first language. The cognitive advantages and disadvantages of being bilingual have been investigated. One important question concerns what type of educational system is best for children who are exposed to more than one language.

At the community level, one can make a distinction between additive and subtractive bilingualism. Additive bilingualism generally occurs when members of a majority culture choose to learn a second language in addition to speaking the language used by the mainstream society. Both languages learned and used by bilinguals are viewed positively and supported by the society. Subtractive bilingualism, on the other hand, occurs when the acquisition of the majority language results in the weakening and possible loss of a minority group's native language, caused in part by the low status assigned to minority languages by the mainstream culture. Subtractive bilingualism is characteristic of many language-minority groups in the United States.

There is little agreement even among experts in the field as to how competent an individual has to be in a second language in order to be considered bilingual. Some believe that a minimal level of competence, such as being able to form a few grammatical sentences in a second language, is enough for a person to be called bilingual. Others believe that both nativelike fluency and functional literacy skills are necessary to be truly bilingual. Most people, however, would agree that bilingual individuals are those who have enough competence in a second language to function well with that language in a number of different contexts. Bilingualism is probably best thought of, then, as representing a range of second-language skills.

In contrast to first-language acquisition, there is considerable variation in how, when, and in what setting people learn a second language. Simultaneous bilingualism refers to the situation in which a child grows up learning two languages from the beginning (this is also known as early childhood bilingualism). Sequential or consecutive bilingualism describes individuals who acquire their second language after they have for the most part mastered their primary language. A balanced bilingual has approximately equal facility in both languages, while a partial or dominant bilingual is much stronger in one language.

Children who grow up learning two languages at the same time do not show any significant delays in language development compared to monolingual children, and indeed, they may even have advantages. For example, infants exposed to two languages are able to make more types of speech sounds than their monolingual counterparts. A common but unfounded fear is that language development will suffer as children become confused between the two languages. Before the age of two, children reared in bilingual environments do seem to treat both languages as if they were one system. That is, they mix the two languages and use words in one language for certain things and words in the other language for other distinct things. In an effort to help the child keep the languages separate, many two-parent families wishing to rear a child bilingually use a one-parent/one-language method. That is, each parent speaks to the child exclusively in one language. This strategy, however, does not seem to be necessary, because children, regardless of the type of early bilingual language input, are able to differentiate between the two systems of language quite well by about the age of two. By age three, in addition to being able to differentiate between the languages and use them appropriately in different contexts, simultaneous bilinguals become aware of their two languages and begin spontaneously to translate from one to the other.

There is much more variation in the development of a second language in the case of consecutive bilingualism. The ease and speed with which people learn a second language depends on the context as well as on the learner's attitude, motivation, and language-learning aptitude. As a group, consecutive bilinguals tend to take longer in learning a second language than do simultaneous bilinguals, and their progress in a second language is more influenced by their first language. The amount and type of this "interference" depends upon the characteristics of the particular languages involved.

There is some evidence that a "sensitive period" exists for second-language acquisition; that is, because language specialization in the brain is basically completed by puberty, it is easier for a person to learn a second language as a child than as an adult. Although this is probably the case for some language skills, such as pronunciation, it is important to note that the context in which adults learn a second language is often quite different from that of children. Adults and older children, in a supportive context, with the right motivation and much exposure to the target language, can certainly learn a second language as well as young children.

Different types of bilinguals may have different types of brain organization for language and memory. For the most part, the brains of simultaneous bilinguals are thought to be structured in a compound organization, whereas consecutive bilinguals have a coordinate organization. Compound organization means that both languages are stored in roughly the same place in the brain and that a person has a single memory store for concepts in both languages. Coordinate organization means that the two languages and the two sets of concepts are stored separately in the brain. Brain-lesion studies have found that after specific damage to the brain, certain bilinguals lose both of their languages while other bilinguals lose only one language. Despite the speculation about differing brain structures, it is thought that all bilinguals must have at least some overlapping common store in their brains; it would seem to be required in order for them to do the rapid processing, the switching back and forth, and the translating that is characteristic of bilinguals.

Bilingual individuals also seem to have a different brain organization for language from that of monolinguals. For most monolinguals, language information is stored and processed primarily by the left hemisphere of the brain. Bilinguals who learn their two languages at different times appear to use more of the right hemisphere and tend to have a bilateral (both-sided) organization for both languages. This does not seem to be the case for early-childhood bilinguals, who actually show faster and more left hemisphere lateralization than monolinguals do. A number of factors affect the degree to which bilinguals will either use the right hemisphere more or use both hemispheres in the processing of language. These include the type of languages learned (some languages naturally require more right-hemisphere processing), the setting in which the languages are learned (natural settings encourage right-hemisphere processing, whereas classrooms encourage the left hemisphere), the amount of time using the second language (the right hemisphere is favored at early stages of bilingualism, the left at later stages), the age at which the second language is learned (older learners use more right hemisphere), and the handedness and gender of the learner (left-handed people and females generally use more of both hemispheres for language processing).

Being able to speak more than one language has an effect on the way one can process cognitive information. Because of their access to two different systems of language, bilingual individuals are able to process different types of information, employ different types of strategies, and do so more flexibly than their monolingual counterparts. Bilinguals can think in two languages and switch back and forth as needed for a particular problem-solving situation. During speech, the switching back and forth between two languages within a single conversation or sentence is called "code-switching." Although at one time it was thought to be a sign that the person was confusing the two languages, code-switching is now understood to be a complex and mostly deliberate social, cognitive, and linguistic process, and it is one which many balanced bilinguals use frequently.

The use of code-switching follows both grammatical rules and linguistic constraints, and it serves a variety of important functions for both the speaker and listener. These include signaling cultural identity and intimacy, placing emotional emphasis, conveying a more subtle or connotatively correct meaning, and role playing. Translating spontaneously from one language to another also demands a special type of simultaneous information-processing skill which monolinguals do not develop. Even very young bilingual children, especially those from language-minority groups, translate both extensively and proficiently. Because translating and code-switching are skills that require both language-processing systems to be operating simultaneously, it appears that both languages can be active at the same time in the mind of the bilingual. Most of the time, however, the bilingual individual thinks and processes information in only one language.

## Applications

Psychologists who study bilingualism have made contributions in several areas. First, by applying their knowledge of second-language acquisition, psychologists have made helpful suggestions as to how to rear a child bilingually and how best to teach a foreign language. For example, works by François Grosjean and by Lenore Arnberg (listed in the bibliography) are excellent resources for interested parents and teachers. Another area in which the study of bilingualism has made an impact is in the understanding of, and behavior toward, language-minority groups in the United States. Because of an earlier lack of knowledge about bilingualism, minority children from homes where a language other than English was spoken have been misunderstood and treated as if they were somehow mentally handicapped. Now, however, it is becoming clear that knowing multiple languages is a valuable cognitive and cultural resource and that there is nothing about bilingualism, per se, that is detrimental to an individual.

Probably the most widespread application of the study of bilingualism has been in informing the planning and implementation of bilingual education programs for language-minority students. In the United States, the question of how best to educate students who do not speak English as a first language is a controversial, political, and emotional issue. As the number of immigrants living in the United States continues to rise (in the year 1990, one in every four children in the state of California spoke a language other than English in the home), questions about whether schools should teach children in their native language, and if so, how much and for how long, will become more and more critical. Psychologists who study bilingualism have been called upon to help answer many questions concerning bilingual education.

Because there are so many different types of bilingual education programs, it is difficult to talk about them as a single group in order to answer the question, "Is bilingual education effective?" Bilingual programs vary in how much time they spend giving instruction in the native language. While some programs use the minority language for the entire school day, most programs use some combination of the two languages, and some programs use exclusively English even though they are labeled "bilingual education" (presumably because of their high enrollment of minority children). Some classrooms use different languages for different subjects, while others alternate between both languages for all subjects. Most bilingual education programs are considered "transitional"—that is, their goal is to get children sufficiently proficient in English that they can enter all-English classes as soon as possible. Because these programs usually do not value the children's native language, the result is often subtractive bilingualism, or the eventual loss of the child's native language. Other programs are more "maintenance-oriented" in that, in addition to promoting English skills, they value and attempt to maintain the students' first language.

Overall, good bilingual education appears to have positive consequences for language-minority children. Children who receive instruction in a language other than English have no long-term delays in the development of academic skills compared to children in regular classes, and often they seem to do better academically than those who had been in all-English classes. Children who learn a concept in one language have no problem transferring it to the other language when needed. Bilingual education seems especially beneficial for those language-minority children who are particularly at risk of doing poorly in regular classrooms.

## Context

The first known systematic attempts to study the development of bilingualism took place in Europe during the early 1900's. Two scholars, German linguist Werner Leopold and French psychologist Jules Ronjat, published extensive diaries on the language development of their own infants who were being reared in a bilingual (German-English and French-German, respectively) environment. Both painted a positive picture of early-childhood bilingualism and concluded that young children have no problem growing up with two languages.

A different view of bilingualism, however, was forming in the United States at the same time. Coinciding both with the country's newly found fascination with intelligence quotient (IQ) tests and with its keen desire to limit immigration at that time, researchers in the 1920's in the United States were demonstrating that "bilinguals" (immigrant minorities) had lower IQs and were mentally and linguistically handicapped, confused, and racially inferior. A series of poorly controlled studies was done in which researchers typically gave IQ tests (in English) to children of recent immigrants who were poor and spoke little English, then compared their results to the IQ scores of white middle-class children. It is not surprising that under these poor testing conditions, without measuring whether the immigrant children were actually bilingual and without controlling for differences in socioeconomic status, researchers found significantly lower test scores for the language-minority children. Unfortunately, the negative views of bilingualism that were advanced by these early studies have persisted.

In the 1960's, a new wave of interest in the psychological study of bilingualism began, and psychologists have been steadily conducting research on the topic ever since. The study often credited for rekindling this interest was conducted by Elizabeth Peal and Wallace Lambert in 1962. Peal and Lambert compared balanced bilinguals to monolinguals who were from the same school system and socioeconomic background on a number of psychological tests, including IQ tests. They found that bilingual children performed better than their monolingual counterparts on nearly all the tasks, and they concluded that bilingualism is indeed positively associated with intelligence and cognitive skill. Since then, numerous investigations have examined in more detail the cognitive advantages of bilingualism. Studies suggest that, compared to monolingual children, bilingual children are more aware of and have more control over the subtle aspects of language, use more flexible problem-solving strategies, are better able to detect ambiguities and errors in language, are more original and creative, and are more sensitive to linguistic and social cues.

## Bibliography

Albert, Martin L., and Loraine K. Obler. *The Bilingual Brain: Neuropsychological and Neurolinguistic Aspects of Bilingualism.* New York: Academic Press, 1978. An excellent, accessible, but somewhat dated account of the theory and research on the structure of bilingual individuals' brains and how they differ from those of monolinguals. Written from both a linguistic and psychological perspective. Available either through the publisher or from most university libraries. Good bibliography.

Arnberg, Lenore. *Raising Children Bilingually: The Pre-School Years.* Philadelphia: Multilingual Matters, 1987. An excellent resource for parents interested in rearing bilingual children. Based on the author's experience with her own children in Sweden, this book discusses the issues involved in all types of childhood bilingualism. Should be easily available from either a public or university library.

Cummins, Jim. *Bilingualism and Special Education: Issues in Assessment and Ped-*

*agogy.* Clevedon, Avon, England: Multilingual Matters, 1984. Written by a leading expert in the field of bilingual education, this small book provides a thorough review of bilingual education programs and their corresponding theories. The author's popular perspective on the education of language-minority children is discussed. Accessible through either a public or university library, and possibly from teacher resource rooms.

Diaz, R. M. "Thought and Two Languages: The Impact of Bilingualism on Cognitive Development." In *Review of Research in Education*, edited by E. W. Gordon. Vol. 10. Washington, D.C.: American Educational Research Association, 1983. An excellent and well-written review of the history and status of the study of bilingualism and intelligence. Discusses problems with research designs and suggests a partial theory for understanding the relationship between intelligence and bilingualism. Should be available at any university library.

Grosjean, François. *Life with Two Languages: An Introduction to Bilingualism.* Cambridge, Mass.: Harvard University Press, 1982. A very readable and nontechnical book about bilingualism. Using many examples, it provides a comprehensive and enjoyable review of the topic. This book, along with the next book by Kenji Hakuta, might be more accessible to high school students than the others listed here. Good bibliography.

Hakuta, Kenji. *Mirror of Language: The Debate on Bilingualism.* New York: Basic Books, 1986. A pleasant, inexpensive, and easy-to-read book that discusses many important topics in the study of bilingualism. Excellent historical account of bilingualism as a field of study. Other topics covered include bilingualism and intelligence, second language acquisition in adults and children, the bilingual mind, and bilingual education. Good bibliography. Accessible through most public libraries.

Hamers, Josiane F., and Michel H. A. Blanc. *Bilinguality and Bilingualism.* Rev. ed. New York: Cambridge University Press, 1989. A comprehensive but somewhat technical volume on bilingualism. Good coverage of social, psychological, and cognitive aspects.

Padilla, Amado M., H. H. Fairchild, and C. M. Valadez, eds. *Bilingual Education: Issues and Strategies.* Newbury Park, Calif.: Sage, 1990. An excellent collection of articles about theories and types of bilingual education. Good discussion of the history of bilingual education in the United States from both a researcher's and teacher's perspective. Examples of model programs are given.

Peal, Elizabeth, and Wallace E. Lambert. "The Relation of Bilingualism to Intelligence." *Psychological Monographs* 76 (1962): 1-23. This is the classic research study that transformed many scholars' and laypersons' negative views of bilingualism into positive ones. An excellent account of the relationship between bilingualism and intelligence.

Romaine, Suzanne. *Bilingualism.* Oxford, England: Basil Blackwell, 1989. A textbooklike but readable account of the social and linguistic aspects of bilingualism from a community perspective. Topics covered include the bilingual community, the bilingual brain, types of childhood bilinguals, bilingual education, and attitudes toward bilingualism. Available from any university library and some public libraries. Extensive bibliography.

*Adam Winsler*

## Cross-References

Ability Tests: Uses and Misuses, 27; Language: The Developmental Sequence, 1387; Language Acquisition Theories, 1394; Language and Cognition, 1401; Neural Anatomy and Cognition, 1640; Psycholinguistics, 1918; Race and Intelligence, 2031; Racism, 2037; Thought Structures, 2565.

# BIOFEEDBACK AND RELAXATION

*Type of psychology:* Stress
*Fields of study:* Behavioral therapies; coping; stress and illness

*Responses to stress by the body have traditionally been thought to be made up of involuntary reactions which are beyond the control of the individual. Some of these responses become maladaptive, and may now be brought under control by using various relaxation techniques and biofeedback.*

### Principal terms

AUTOGENIC PHRASES: phrases used by the therapist to help the client while relaxing and performing biofeedback (for example, "Your hands feel heavy and warm")

CHEATING: a term coined by Neal E. Miller which implies that an autonomic response was not affected directly, but rather was influenced by a skeletal nervous system response

CLASSICAL CONDITIONING: learning that occurs by contiguously pairing two stimuli, whereby the second stimulus comes to yield a response similar to the first; traditionally thought to be successful with involuntary responses mediated by the autonomic nervous system

ELECTROENCEPHALOGRAPHY: measurement of the electrical output of the brain, which may be brought under voluntary control by biofeedback and relaxation

ELECTROMYOGRAPHY: measurement of the electrical output of muscles, which may be brought under voluntary control by biofeedback and relaxation

GALVANIC SKIN RESPONSE (GSR): a measurement of the electrical conductivity of the skin; an operational measure of anxiety which may be brought under voluntary control by biofeedback and relaxation

INSTRUMENTAL CONDITIONING: learning that occurs from reinforcing a response; traditionally thought to be successful with voluntary responses mediated by the skeletal nervous system

PROGRESSIVE MUSCLE RELAXATION: a relaxation technique that systematically works through all the major muscle groups of the body by first tensing, then relaxing, each group, and paying attention to the changes

THERMAL RESPONSE: a measurement of the amount of blood flow to various areas of the body recorded by heat sensors; may be brought under voluntary control by biofeedback and relaxation

## Overview

From the day people are born, and even before that, they are subjected to a variety of stressors from the environment around them. Each one of these exacts a certain toll on their bodies. Some stressors seem to affect individuals differently, while others seem to have a universal effect; in any case, both the mind and the body must mobilize to deal effectively with these factors. The individual is usually able to handle these problems by using various coping strategies to help alleviate the stress. The problem arises when too many stressors are present at one time or when these stressors last too long. The individual must adapt or change his or her coping strategies to return to a normal equilibrium. A coping strategy is a process which takes effort and is learned; the individual must acquire this coping skill as one acquires any skill. It must be practiced.

If the stressors are not dealt with adequately, fatigue and illness may result. In the most serious circumstances, the organism can die. Hans Selye reported on what he termed the general adaptation syndrome (GAS). As stressors affect an organism, a series of neurological and biological responses occur to protect the body. If these responses are prolonged and go unchecked, however, the body will begin to break itself down. In the first phase, the alarm phase, the body mobilizes itself. The adrenal glands enlarge, and release epinephrine (adrenaline) and steroids to cope. After a while, the body adapts and seems to be normal; this is the resistance stage. In fact, the body is not normal. It is very vulnerable to further stress, and, if subjected to additional stressors, it will enter the third stage, exhaustion. The organism can then become extremely sick or die.

It becomes essential for the individual to adopt a successful coping strategy in order to avert this progression of events. Two such techniques will be discussed here. Biofeedback is a procedure whereby the individual is given information about how a variety of body responses are reacting in various circumstances. The individual is generally unaware of these reactions, but biofeedback technology allows the individual to monitor them and eventually bring them under control. Autonomic, visceral responses to stress have traditionally been thought to be involuntary and automatic. Biofeedback is a technique aimed at gaining control over these reactions. Voluntary responses can affect these visceral responses, and this fact complicates the ultimate effectiveness of biofeedback.

Neal E. Miller was one of the early pioneers in the field. His work has been applied to the control of a wide variety of stress-related problems through the use of biofeedback. The control of what have been termed psychosomatic problems has been accomplished using Miller's assumptions. Individuals have learned to control blood pressure, heart rate, muscle spasms, headaches, and myriad other ailments through biofeedback techniques.

Miller believed that these responses to stress can be changed through the use of instrumental conditioning and reinforcement. When a machine makes this information available to a person, the responses can be reinforced (or they can reinforce themselves) when a therapeutic change occurs. The same principle is at work when an experimental rat learns to press a bar for food.

Another coping strategy which can be used to deal with stressors is the adoption of one of a variety of relaxation procedures. As odd as it may sound to some, people must learn to relax in many situations, and this takes practice. Relaxation techniques are often used in conjunction with biofeedback, which sometimes makes it difficult to determine which of the two procedures is responsible for the changes that occur and to what degree they are acting in relationship to each other.

There are several relaxation techniques, and different techniques are successful for different individuals. One of the most widely used techniques is progressive muscle relaxation, proposed by Edmund Jacobson. The individual is instructed to tense a particular muscle group and hold it for several seconds, paying attention to the feelings associated with this state. Then the individual is told to relax the muscle group and is asked to concentrate on the different feelings while the muscle is relaxed. The major muscle groups of the body are put through this procedure. Ultimately, the individual is able to reproduce the relaxed sensations when he or she feels tense.

Rhythmic breathing techniques are also used for relaxation in order to combat stress. The person learns to inhale through the nose to the count of three and exhale through the mouth to the count of five. Between each breath is a count of two. The breathing should be with the stomach as much as possible, as opposed to the chest. Meditation, another relaxation technique that often incorporates rhythmic breathing, may require that the person either visualize an object or repeat a word or phrase with each breath. This prevents the person's mind from wandering to the anxiety-provoking stimuli.

### Applications

One of the experiments that pioneered the use of biofeedback in a clinical setting was conducted by Neal Miller using white rats. Miller wanted to demonstrate that the animal was able to learn to increase the blood flow to one ear by dilating the capillaries in the ear. He needed to ensure that the animal was not using a skeletal response ("cheating") to influence this response. For example, a human can accomplish this task by covering the ear with the palm of the hand for a period of time. The question Miller was asking was, Could this be done without a skeletal response? Miller administered the drug curare to the rat to incapacitate the skeletal nervous system and kept the animal alive by using an artificial respirator. He attached a sensitive thermometer, which was able to detect slight changes in temperature caused by differential blood flow, to the animal's ear. When a slight increase in temperature was detected, the message was sent to a computer, which delivered an electrical reinforcement to the brain of the subject. This represents the same mechanism which establishes the bar-pressing response in a white rat: operant conditioning. The experiment was successful.

One of the first applications of this experiment to humans came when a woman who had suffered paralysis in an automobile accident was unable even to remain in a sitting position without her blood pressure dropping to dangerous levels. Miller and his staff assembled a biofeedback device which allowed the woman to determine the nature of her blood pressure from moment to moment. No external reinforcement (such as food) was necessary in this case; knowing that the response was therapeutic was reinforcement enough. The woman was able to learn how to raise and lower her blood pressure at will through the use of the biofeedback device. By learning to control her blood pressure (and eventually wean herself off the biofeedback machine), she was able to become more productive and do some tasks on her own.

The concept of biofeedback, then, can be generalized to learning to control any of the visceral responses to accomplish clinically a healthier state. As society's stressors increase, many of the visceral responses can cause clinical problems. Among the most common are headache symptoms: muscular (tension) and vascular (migraine). By using electromyography (EMG) biofeedback, a person can monitor the muscle tension in the forehead and learn to decrease the tension by obtaining constant auditory feedback. By the same token, thermal biofeedback machines can monitor blood flow to the cranial arteries and can teach a person how to reduce the volume of blood to this area and redirect it to the periphery of the body. This often helps other problems associated with migraines such as Raynaud disease, in which the extremities are cold because of lack of blood flow.

The galvanic skin response (GSR) is one of the most common responses used to measure the degree of anxiety and stress. In fact, it is one of the measures in a lie detector, which assumes that when one lies, anxiety increases automatically. The GSR can be brought under control using biofeedback methods. For example, if a pregnant woman is anxious about the upcoming birth, she can receive constant feedback from a GSR biofeedback apparatus and learn to lower the GSR by attending to the machine. As she learns to accomplish this, she can apply these skills on her own and eventually use them during the birth process.

Yet another application of biofeedback in coping with stress has been the use of the technique in controlling brain waves through electroencephalography (EEG) biofeedback. It is thought that the brain's alpha wave (eight to thirteen cycles per second) represents the resting brain. By placing electrodes on the scalp and having a machine monitor the amount of alpha activity from moment to moment, a person can learn to increase alpha production and reduce stress by doing so.

Prior to and during biofeedback training, various relaxation techniques are employed to help with the procedure. This actually leads to an academic problem: Which technique is working and to what degree? The use of Jacobson's progressive muscle relaxation with asthmatic children and adults helped to reduce the frequency and severity of the incidents. One of the common problems that arise from increased stress is insomnia. The use of Jacobson's technique has proved useful in combating this problem in several documented cases. Autogenic phrases are often employed with biofeedback, as well. For muscular disorders, phrases such as "My leg is heavy" can be used. For cardiac problems, a common phrase is "My heartbeat is calm and regular."

Meditation has been shown to produce an increase in alpha-wave activity, as has biofeedback. Practitioners of yoga focus on a phrase or word (a mantra) and exclude everything else. The nervous system shows evidence of reduced stress and arousal.

A variety of businesses have used meditation programs for their employees and have realized improved health and productivity from them.

## Context

The ability to gain voluntary control over the autonomic nervous system responses in order to help cope with stressors is a valuable skill. The area of biofeedback has important implications for both the theoretical and clinical sides of the field of psychology. First, it is traditionally thought that classical conditioning deals with the "involuntary" nervous system responses, while instrumental conditioning mediates the "voluntary" skeletal responses. Since biofeedback deals with visceral autonomic nervous system reactions and is basically a form of instrumental conditioning, this traditional dichotomy must be brought into question. Biofeedback, a phenomenon of the second half of the twentieth century, is still in its infancy. Biofeedback techniques ultimately aim at bringing unconscious, previously uncontrolled body responses into conscious awareness in order to bring them under control therapeutically. It is a wonderful example of the interaction of the mind and body and the complicated dilemma of how and when they interact.

Biofeedback therapy invariably uses other therapies, such as relaxation and meditation, along with it in the clinical setting. This naturally raises the question of whether, and to what degree, biofeedback, relaxation, meditation, and their interactions are responsible for changes in the condition of the client. Many experiments are being conducted to determine the answers to these questions and the results are equivocal. It is also important to know what type of feedback, what type of feedback schedule, and what additional therapies are indicated for various problems.

The control of stress-related disorders without drugs or surgery is obviously a desirable goal, and biofeedback, relaxation, and meditation seem to hold some promise in this field for certain types of cases. The applications seem extensive. Hypertension, insomnia, sexual dysfunction, cardiac arrhythmias, asthma, and gastrointestinal disorders are but a few of the problems which have been tackled so far, with varying degrees of success. The jury is still out concerning the degree of success of biofeedback and relaxation as coping strategies for dealing with stress. The results so far, however, are promising and are spawning much research.

## Bibliography

Birbaumer, Niels, and H. D. Kimmel, eds. *Biofeedback and Self-Regulation.* Hillsdale, N.J.: Lawrence Erlbaum, 1979. Reviews the theoretical and clinical issues surrounding biofeedback in particular, as well as relaxation techniques. Clinical examples of headache control, heart rate control, and brain wave control are among the many cases described. Complete indexes, tables, and graphs are included in this excellent book.

Jacobson, Edmund. *Modern Treatment of Tense Patients.* Springfield, Ill.: Charles C Thomas, 1970. A complete book on the theory and practice of progressive muscle relaxation, including the step-by-step method, instructions, and case studies. Illustrations of each step are included at the end of the book.

——————————. *Tension in Medicine.* Springfield, Ill.: Charles C Thomas, 1967. A wonderful description of progressive muscle relaxation, with a variety of case studies illustrating its application and success. Reports from a number of clinicians are included, with clear graphs illustrating the results.

Marcus, Jay B. *TM and Business.* New York: McGraw-Hill, 1977. Relatively light reading on the applications and benefits of meditation and relaxation skills in the workplace. Descriptions of specific programs in various companies are presented. A bit overstated at points, but a good introduction to a specific application of meditation.

Olton, David S., and Aaron R. Noonberg. *Biofeedback: Clinical Application in Behavioral Medicine.* Englewood Cliffs, N.J.: Prentice-Hall, 1980. An excellent review of the theory behind biofeedback and relaxation, along with numerous chapters on clinical applications of coping with stress-related problems. Precise tables and illustrations are provided.

*Jonathan Kahane*

## Cross-References

The Adrenal Gland, 136; Cognitive Behavior Therapy, 546; Coping Strategies: An Overview, 706; Emotion: Cognitive and Physiological Interaction, 881; General Adaptation Syndrome, 1068; Meditation and Relaxation, 1499; Operant Conditioning Therapies, 1714; Pain Management, 1734; Psychosomatic Disorders, 1975; Stress and the Endocrine System, 2445; Stress and the Nervous System, 2452; Stress-Related Diseases, 2464.

# BIPOLAR DISORDER

*Type of psychology:* Psychopathology
*Field of study:* Depression

*Knowledge about bipolar disorder, a cyclical mood disorder that includes shifts from mania to depression and back to normal mood, has grown extensively. Advanced neurobiological research and assessment techniques have shown the biochemical origins and the genetic element of this disorder; stress also may play a role in precipitating recurrence of episodes. The main treatment interventions include lithium and psychotherapy.*

### Principal terms

BREAKTHROUGH EPISODE: a relapse of either hypomania, mania, or depression in a client with bipolar disorder who has been relatively symptom-free

CYCLOTHYMIA: a milder version of a cyclical mood disorder in which mood swings can occur but are not as intense as in bipolar disorder

DEXAMETHASONE SUPPRESSION TEST (DST): a test of cortisol hypersecretion that diagnoses depression in many individuals

GENETIC MARKER: a particular gene or set of genes that investigators are attempting to locate which might account for the inheritance of a predisposition to bipolar illness

LITHIUM CARBONATE: an alkaline compound that modulates the intensity of mood swings and is particularly effective in the dampening of symptoms of manic excitability

MANIA: a phase of bipolar disorder in which the mood is one of elation, euphoria, or irritability; a disorder in which manic symptoms occur and then are followed by a return to normal mood state

MELATONIN: a hormone produced in the brain that increases in the dark winter months; people with this condition are diagnosed as having seasonal affective disorder (SAD), a form of cyclical depression

SEASONAL AFFECTIVE DISORDER (SAD): a form of bipolar illness that is associated with darkness and melatonin excess

TOXICITY: potential poisonous effects of medication, such as lithium on the kidneys, necessitating the monitoring of medication levels in the blood

## Overview

Bipolar affective disorder, or bipolar disorder (also called manic-depressive disorder), has been identified as a major psychiatric disorder that is characterized by dramatic mood and behavior changes. These changes, ranging from episodes of high euphoric moods to deep depressions, with accompanying behavioral and personality changes, are devastating to the victims of the disorder and perplexing to the loved ones of those affected. Clinical psychiatry has been effective in providing biochemical intervention in the form of lithium carbonate to stabilize or modulate the ups and downs of this illness; however, lithium treatment has only been effective for approximately 70 percent of those administered the compound. One medication, Depocate, is showing promise in helping some people with the disorder who were formerly referred to as lithium nonresponders. Psychotherapy, either for the individual or in the form of support groups such as the Manic Depressive Association, is seen by most practitioners as a necessary adjunct or in some cases a primary part of treatment.

Bipolar disorder has four subcategories. They are "bipolar, depressed," in which the moods cycle from normal to depressed; "bipolar, manic," in which moods cycle from normal to manic but there has been at least one episode of depression; "bipolar, mixed," in which the mood fluctuations cover all three phases (depressed, normal, and manic); and "seasonal affective disorder" (SAD), in which mood changes are thought to be triggered by a lack of sunlight and an increase in the hormone melatonin. Two associated categories are related to bipolar disorder. The first one is "cyclothymia," in which the mood swings and characteristic symptoms are less intense than in the full bipolar condition. In addition, there is a category called "bipolar disorder, not otherwise specified," which means that the symptom presentation differs from any of the other described categories but the cyclical nature of the mood changes is present. Bipolar disorder usually first manifests itself in early adulthood and is more common in single and divorced people. Bipolar disorder is also believed to be more prevalent in the homeless population than in the general population. The factor of increased stress in the environment of the homeless is no doubt a critical component in the reported higher rates.

The initial episode of bipolar disorder is typically one of mania or elation, although in some people a depressive episode may signal the beginning of the disorder. Episodes of bipolar disorder can recur rapidly—within hours or days—or may have a much slower recurrence rate, even of years. The duration of each episode, whether it is depression or mania, varies widely across individuals but normally remains fairly consistent for each individual. Manic episodes often have a shorter duration than the depressive episodes. Bipolar disorder must be differentiated from depressive disorders, which include major depression (unipolar depression) and dysthymia, a milder but chronic form of depression. It is also differentiated from mania, a mood disorder in which manic episodes are interspersed between normal mood functioning.

Biological scientists have attempted to locate genetic markers for the disorder. Their effort has been based on the observation that the disorder often affects several members of a given family. This was the goal when Janice Egeland published the findings of her study of the Old Order Amish sect of Lancaster County, Pennsylvania, in 1983. The Old Order Amish provided a relatively intact bloodline and were considered an ideal homogeneous population for the investigation of the potential genetic key to bipolar disorder. The Amish, a simple people, do not use electricity, do not use drugs or alcohol, and do not condone war or crime. Therefore, the generations of the original forebears had been largely preserved. The Amish were familiar with mood disorder (and with suicide associated with it) that appeared to affect only certain families and their offspring. As a result, they were eager to have Egeland help them find out about the disease they said "is in the blood."

Although Egeland had thought she could eventually locate a gene for bipolar disorder on the short arm of chromosome 11, subsequent analyses of the data indicated that the answer may be more complex. Some molecular biologists believe that more than one gene is responsible for transmission of the illness, and others believe the answer to be far more complicated. A diathesis-stress model has been proposed for some psychosomatic disorders such as hypertension and ulcers; this interactive model may also explain why some people develop bipolar disorder in early adulthood and others do not. In this model, a genetic or biochemical predisposition toward the disorder (the bipolar diathesis) may lie dormant until stress from puberty, adulthood, or physical or psychological trauma triggers the emergence of the illness.

A number of mediating factors, such as social support, coping skills, and regular sleep, exercise, and nutritional habits, may serve as buffers to protect a person against development of the disorder. Much more work is needed to prove or disprove these theories, although they offer clues for treatment. Prevalence rates of bipolar disorder run at about 1 percent (0.4 to 1.2) of the American population. The disorder is divided fairly equally along the gender dimension. As many as 15 percent of those with the illness have committed suicide. This frightening reality makes early intervention, relapse prevention, and treatment of the disorder necessary to prevent such a tragic outcome.

Many brilliant and successful people have reportedly suffered from bipolar disorder and have been able to function successfully with competent and responsible treatment. The book *The Key to Genius: Manic-Depression and the Creative Life* (1988), written by D. J. Hershman and Julian Lieb, provides an overview of the creativity and productivity of some people with the disorder. Some people who have taken lithium for bipolar disorder, in fact, have complained that it robs them of their energy and creativity and said that they actually miss the energy associated with manic phases of the illness. This perceived loss, some of it realistic, can be a factor in relapse associated with lithium noncompliance.

Local mental health associations are able to recommend psychiatric treatment by board-certified psychiatrists and licensed psychologists who specialize in the treatment of mood disorders. Often, temporary hospitalization is necessary for complete diagnostic assessment, initial mood stabilization and intensive treatment, medication adjustment, or monitoring an individual who feels suicidal.

## Applications

The heritability of the cyclical mood disorders has led to the search for biochemical or genetic markers. Modern brain imaging techniques such as the positron emission tomography (PET) scan have been utilized to help solve the biochemical under-pinnings of the disorder. Electroencephalograms (EEGs), used to study brain-wave functioning, have been instrumental in tracking the sleep disturbance and insomnia that often precede an episode of the disorder. John Hanley, in 1989, wrote that the EEG has been grossly underutilized as a potential tool for solving some of the mysteries of major psychiatric disorders, including bipolar disorder and schizophrenia.

Medications and diagnostic techniques have been developed to aid in correcting the biochemical imbalance thought to be part of the illness. Lithium carbonate is usually effective for about 70 percent of those who take it. Depocate, a newer medication, is under trial to help those whom lithium is unable to help. A diagnostic test called the dexamethasone suppression test (DST) was developed to determine which individuals suffer from "biological" depression in both unipolar depression and bipolar depression. The DST is a diagnostic test measuring cortisol hypersecretion that is thought to be diagnostic of depression in many individuals. Authors Frederick Goodwin and Kay Jamison wrote extensively about the DST and its pattern of results in individuals with bipolar disorder in their 1990 book *Manic-Depressive Illness.* They report that results of this test have been studied extensively in individuals with bipolar mood disorder.

There is apparently a wide range of abnormal DST results in clients with bipolar disorder during depressed phases; between 25 and 60 percent show abnormal DST results. Goodwin and Jamison summarize findings of those investigators who have found that the abnormal DST findings return to normal during manic or hypomanic episodes. They mention that several confounding variables can interfere with the results of the test.

One of the most intriguing treatments of a major mood disorder involves the use of "light therapy" for the treatment of one of the subcategories of bipolar disorder, seasonal affective disorder (SAD). Exposure to increased full-spectrum light, for two to three hours a day, is thought to aid the brain's metabolism of the hormone melatonin and thus prevent or alleviate episodes of depression associated with melatonin excess. SAD is thought to be more prevalent in females and in populations residing in high-latitude countries where there is a longer period of darkness in winter months.

Many individuals well known to the public have suffered from bipolar disorder; among them is actress Patty Duke, who wrote a book about her experiences with the illness in a book entitled *Call Me Anna: The Autobiography of Patty Duke* (1987). Political activist Abbie Hoffman, who died in 1989, also suffered from the disorder. Hoffman had been a "Yippie" and was one of the so-called Chicago Seven, a group of radical activists who attempted to disrupt the Democratic National Convention in 1968. He had been familiar with discrimination as a Jewish youth reared in a New York suburb; as a result, he made it his cause to fight against discrimination and racial oppression. This cause took him into the realm of political activism. Hoffman experienced legal problems associated with drug possession and use, however, and chose to go into hiding for an extended period of his life. He was eventually diagnosed with bipolar disorder, late in his life, and was treated with lithium. He reportedly wrote to his relatives of the exhaustion caused by the disorder shortly before he committed suicide from a Phenobarbital overdose. Although Hoffman had long been under stress from financial problems, his suicide was a shock to a public that had known him as a fighter. Even some of those people closest to him could not believe that he had chosen to take his own life. This example clearly shows the devastating toll the disorder can impose on those afflicted with it. Some believe that the illness puts people on an "emotional roller coaster" in which their ups and downs are so severe that resulting behavior can have its own disastrous consequences. For example, people suffering from episodes of mania sometimes use drugs, alcohol, money, or sex to excess, then later have to deal with an additional set of problems and trauma brought about by their behavioral excess and impulsivity.

Support groups such as the Manic Depressive Association have provided a way for people to share the pain as well as triumph over the illness. Many people have found comfort in knowing that there are others who have suffered from the mood shifts, and they can draw strength from one another. Family members and friends can be the strongest supporters and advocates for those who have bipolar disorder or other mood disorders. Many patients have credited their families' constant, uncritical support, in addition to competent treatment including psychotherapy and lithium, with pulling them through the devastating effects of the illness.

## Context

The characteristic pattern of cyclical mood swings and resultant shifts in personality and behavior caused by bipolar disorder (manic-depressive disorder) have been written about for more than two thousand years. Emil Kraepelin is credited with providing the world with one of the first clinical descriptions of the disorder in a 1921 monograph that included "manic depressive insanity."

Goodwin and Jamison cover what they term the "evolution of the bipolar-unipolar concept" in a thorough chapter in their *Manic-Depressive Illness.* The focus of the early Greeks on the biological imbalance presumed to underlie bipolar disorder is remarkably in tune with theoretical models of today. French scientists are credited with recognizing that mania and depression can be two sides of the same disorder; the "circular disorder" was discussed by French scientists in the nineteenth century. The distinction between unipolar and bipolar disorder has become more convincing over time, especially when one reviews clinical case histories that differentiate the two disorders. Goodwin and Jamison summarize the importance of the classification of unipolar and bipolar disorder as separate illnesses. They argue that this classification, in the *Diagnostic and Statistical Manual of Mental Disorders* (rev. 3d ed., 1987, DSM-III-R, the diagnostic manual of the American Psychiatric Association), has led to important research that helped uncover key information regarding genetic, biochemical, clinical, and medical (pharmaceutical) components of the major mood disorders.

Various differences in incidence (or rate of occurrence) of bipolar disorder has been noted for some time. In the early 1900's, Kraepelin reported higher rates of manic and depressive illness in people from Java and Singapore when compared to people of European descent. In a study by B. E. Jones et al., published in 1983, the authors reported that poor Hispanics in the city of New York had a prevalence rate of bipolar disorder that was more than three times that of the overall United States population. An earlier (1981) study by the same authors that investigated the prevalence rate of the disorder in poor urban blacks included findings that their rate was 15 percent. Research is needed that can separate the potential influence of poverty, stress, substance abuse, and urban environment from racial factors related to predisposition for the disorder. Chinese researchers report a prevalance of 2 to 3 percent for mood disorders; 1.2 percent had been diagnosed as having bipolar disorder. This figure corresponds to the 0.4 to 1.2 percent prevalence rate for the illness in the United States cited in DSM-III-R.

Cross-cultural studies of bipolar disorder are relatively rare, however, as most research on the disorder has been carried out in modernized, Western countries. Therefore, it becomes difficult to understand clearly the impact of cultural variables as they interact with individual genetic or psychological predispositions to bipolar disorder. Clearly, more research into these variables and into the complex picture of genetic markers and predisposition for bipolar disorder is desperately needed if scientists are to understand the complexity of interactive forces associated with the illness.

## Bibliography

Fieve, Ronald R. *Moodswing: The Third Revolution in Psychiatry.* New York: William Morrow, 1975. This popular book written for the general public offers helpful, informative insight into the many facets of bipolar disorder (manic depression). Accounts of famous people who had the disorder and yet were successful in their lives give hope to those afflicted.

Goodwin, Frederick K., and Kay Redfield Jamison. *Manic-Depressive Illness.* New York: Oxford University Press, 1990. A comprehensive book on bipolar disorder. Historical events, from diagnosis to treatment, are covered in depth. Issues of treatment and theory are also examined in great detail.

Hershman, D. Jablow, and Julian Lieb. *The Key to Genius: Manic-Depression and the Creative Life.* Buffalo, N.Y.: Prometheus Books, 1988. A publication for the general reader. This intriguing book covers some of the phenomena long written about, including facts of great men and women who may have suffered from bipolar illness.

Heston, Leonard L. *Mending Minds: A Guide to the New Psychiatry of Depression, Anxiety, and Other Serious Mental Disorders.* New York: W. H. Freeman, 1992. This leading-edge book, written for the layperson yet useful for the professional, covers many disorders—depression, bipolar disorder, and anxiety, to name a few. The types of treatments available, both biological and psychological, are explained from the viewpoint of the potential consumer of these specialized services. Includes a guide to support groups, more readings, and other resources.

Jefferson, James W., and John H. Greist. *Primer of Lithium Therapy.* Baltimore: Williams & Wilkins, 1977. Described as being for the layperson, but contains important information about the usefulness and special precautions of lithium therapy and prophylaxis.

*Karen Wolford*

## Cross-References

Clinical Depression, 521; Depression: Theoretical Explanations, 789; Psychoactive Drug Therapy, 1891; Psychotherapeutic Effectiveness, 1989; Seasonal Affective Disorder, 2155; Suicide, 2501.

# BIRTH: EFFECTS ON PHYSICAL DEVELOPMENT

*Type of psychology:* Developmental psychology
*Field of study:* Infancy and childhood

*Among the many areas of developmental psychology is the examination of the short-term and long-term physical and psychological effects of the birth process on the newborn and their impact on the mother-infant relationship.*

### Principal terms

ATTACHMENT: an emotional bond between infant and caregiver based on reciprocal interaction patterns

CRITICAL PERIOD: a time period during which a factor can exert its greatest influence on development

LAMAZE METHOD: a form of natural or prepared childbirth that utilizes an active coping strategy in order to reduce fear and pain; incorporates a "coach" for support

NATURAL/PREPARED CHILDBIRTH: a psychological means of coping with childbirth without medication, based on childbirth education, relaxation methods, and breathing techniques

PARADIGM: a model representing a school of thought of a prevailing era

TERATOGEN: a substance or factor that has the potential to cause birth defects

## Overview

Expectant parents face many choices surrounding pregnancy and birth—choices that may have a significant influence on their baby, their experience of the birth process, and the quality of their early relationships with their infant. Contemporary women are taking a much more active role in their pregnancies and deliveries, and modern society, in response to public demand for information, is changing to promote informed decision making. Technological and medical advances have had a strong impact on childbirth and have created confusion for many parents in their childbirth planning.

Birth may be defined as the passage from prenatal to postnatal existence. A baby's development may be influenced by factors present from conception through birth. At the end of nine months' gestation (pregnancy), birth will proceed through three stages of labor. In stage one, contractions widen the cervix (the opening between the uterus and vagina) to accommodate the passage of the fetus' head through the birth canal. Stage two is the fetus' journey through the vagina, which ends in birth. The last stage delivers the placenta, or "afterbirth."

If a woman fails to dilate completely, labor may be induced with drugs; however, induced labors are reported to be more painful, and consequently medication is often used to ease pain. Although birth complications sometimes necessitate medication, there are potential negative effects of obstetric medications on infant behavior and early maternal caregiving. Babies of medicated deliveries, compared to nonmedicated deliveries, may show depressive effects, such as lower arousal and responsiveness, decreased motor activity, irritability, and feeding difficulties; coupled with depressive drug effects on the mother, this can result in decreased mother-infant interaction. These effects may last for weeks, but whether there are any long-term effects is a matter of controversy.

Most deliveries are vaginal. A cesarean section (C-section) is a surgical procedure to remove the baby from the mother's abdomen under general or local anesthesia. Certain situations necessitate delivery by cesarean section—for example, breech (buttocks first) or crosswise positions or unduly long labors in which there is a danger of anoxia (a lack of oxygen that can lead to brain damage in the baby). Disadvantages of cesarean sections include risk of infection to the mother, longer recovery periods, and the physiological and psychological stress of surgery; however, no long-term effects of C-sections on mothers or babies have been reported.

Low birth weight is a high-risk factor for long-term developmental problems, such as intellectual deficits and school problems. Low-birth-weight infants are either preterm (those born several weeks early) or small for the date (full-term infants weighing less than 5.5 pounds). Mortality rates for babies with low birth weight are much lower than they once were because of medical advances, such as keeping environments temperature controlled and free from infection; however, such infants show lessened alertness, responsiveness, and motor activity; irregular sleep patterns; feeding difficulties; and hypersensitivity to sound. Their under-responsiveness and delayed development render interactions with parents less rewarding, and the primary caregiver may feel dissatisfied and even rejected by her baby. This may adversely affect the attachment process, since the primary emotional bond depends on reciprocal positive interactions. Research shows that parents of preterm infants tend to hold, touch, and talk to them less than parents of normal infants, especially if parents experience difficulty coping with the demands of a low-birth-weight baby. Many factors that influence fetal development may lead to low birth weight: for example, poor nutrition or maternal health, the mother's reproductive condition, alcohol and drug use, and smoking.

Parental age is another factor related to child development. The incidence of Down syndrome has been shown to increase with advancing maternal, and possibly paternal, age. This disorder, caused by an extra twenty-first chromosome, typically is characterized by distinct physical features, retardation, heart defects, and a greater susceptibility to infection. The risk is approximately one in fifteen hundred for women under thirty, rising to one out of one hundred by age forty.

In an effort to circumvent the drawbacks of medicated deliveries, attention has focused on non-Western cultural practices of easing the pain of childbirth. Research demonstrates the positive effects of music on reducing pain responses and facilitating relaxation. Tentative evidence suggests that upright birthing postures also may relieve discomfort. In Western society, the typical alternative to medicated delivery is natural childbirth. The Lamaze method is one active psychological strategy of coping with childbirth. The goal is to reduce fear by creating realistic expectations through childbirth education, to ease pain by relaxation methods and breathing techniques coordinated with contractions, and to provide a "coach," usually the father, for support through labor and delivery. The beneficial effects of Lamaze breathing techniques in reducing perception and endurance of pain are well documented; research findings show no medical advantages, however, regarding length of labor, birth complications, birth weight, or newborn health.

Frederick Leboyer's "gentle birthing" is designed to soothe the infant's emergence into the world. Babies are born in a softly lit room and placed on the mother's abdomen until independent breathing is established before the umbilical cord is cut. The infant then is bathed in warm water and gently massaged. Research has failed to substantiate Leboyer's claim of lasting physical and psychological benefits from this method.

The type of birthing practice used may affect the child's development. In general, any method that enhances the quality of the birthing experience for the mother may influence her early interaction with her newborn; a more positive experience fosters a highly desirable beginning for attachment.

## Applications

One of the most important applications of the study of birth and prenatal development involves the short-term and long-term effects of various procedures and substances on the newborn infant and the child the baby becomes. A substance that has the potential to harm the fetus, causing birth defects, is termed a teratogen. The teratogenic effects of many environmental agents depend in part on the timing of their exposure during prenatal development. The first trimester (twelve weeks) of gestation is considered to be a "critical period" in development: During this time, various bodily organs and structures are developing and are most vulnerable to teratogens. For example, if the eyes are being formed when a fetus encounters a harmful agent, the eyes are the most likely organ to be affected. Since some organs take longer to develop fully (for example, the brain continues to develop throughout the entire prenatal period), that organ may be affected beyond the first trimester. Maternal rubella (German measles) clearly illustrates the critical-period principle. If a mother contracts rubella during the first trimester, deafness and heart defects are likely outcomes, whereas the risk drops significantly by week sixteen and thereafter disappears. Some effects of teratogens appear immediately upon birth—for example, as gross anatomical deformities. Others are subtler, such as lowered responsiveness and alertness of infants because of medications used during the birth process. Still others may result in delayed effects, such as learning disabilities that go undetected until the child is in school. The tragic cases of babies born to mothers who took diethylstilbestrol (DES) in the 1950's and 1960's to prevent miscarriage illustrate effects that did not appear until adolescence, when some daughters developed vaginal cancer and some sons became sterile.

Most of what is known about birth defects comes from data that show a relationship between certain factors and subsequent damage. While these data cannot demonstrate a direct causal link between the factor and later birth defects, strong associations lead researchers to suspect that a particular outcome may be attributable to the factor in question. For example, researchers noted dramatically increased rates of mental retardation in the offspring of pregnant women who were exposed to radiation from the atomic bomb blast in Hiroshima during World War II.

Documentation on the negative effects of drug use during pregnancy is vast. Almost any drug in the mother's bloodstream can cross the placenta and affect the developing fetus. The mild tranquilizer thalidomide, given to pregnant women in the late 1950's and early 1960's, which resulted in gross limb deformities or absent limbs, provides a classic example of the teratogenic influence of drugs. Nicotine and alcohol affect both behavior and physical development. The clearest finding regarding maternal smoking is low birth weight. Newborns also show decreased responsiveness to their environment and may be at risk for developing sudden infant death syndrome (SIDS), which results in the sudden death of an apparently healthy infant. Long-term attentional problems and hyperactivity also have been reported.

A group of abnormalities associated with maternal alcohol consumption, known as fetal alcohol syndrome (FAS), includes mental and motor retardation, long-term behavioral problems such as hyperactivity and attentional deficits, and a constellation of facial features: widely spaced eyes, short eyelid openings, drooping eyelids, short upturned nose, thin upper lip, and small chin. Even "social drinking" may increase the risk of miscarriage, stillbirths, low birth weight, low arousal, motor difficulties, and learning disabilities. Since there is no known safe level of alcohol use during pregnancy, abstinence is advocated by many doctors.

Maternal cocaine use has been associated with an increased risk of miscarriage and with neurological problems (evidenced in a lessened interaction with and response to the environment). Babies born to heroin-addicted mothers are born addicted, typically preterm, and are at greater risk for infant mortality. Irritability and lessened alertness and responsivity are reported through early childhood. The effects of teratogens are additive. For example, if a mother smokes and drinks during pregnancy, the risks for low birth weight are greater than if she only smoked or only drank.

Prescription drugs administered during labor also affect the newborn; the seriousness of the effects of these drugs is still a subject of debate. Obstetric drugs, used to decrease pain and/or regulate the course of labor, fall into two broad classes, anesthetics and analgesics. General anesthesia results in a lack of consciousness, whereas local anesthesia blocks the sensation of pain. Analgesics are pain reducers. Medicated deliveries in general have negative effects on newborns—effects not found in natural deliveries. Effects of obstetric medications may include possible toxicity, behavioral abnormalities (such as short attention span), low responsiveness to external stimuli, and impairment in motor coordination. The dosage, type of drug, timing, duration, and route of administration (intravenous or intramuscular) all are factors that may influence the extent of these effects. In general, local anesthetics have fewer effects than general anesthetics. Preterm infants generally are more sensitive to the effects of obstetric drugs. Controversy exists over the duration of these drug effects, with some researchers reporting only short-term effects and others maintaining that effects may last throughout infancy. Advance discussion with her obstetrician about the various types of medications will enable the expectant mother to make an informed choice should birth complications mandate a cesarean delivery, necessitating use of some type of medication. The examples presented here have focused on particular types of drugs, but one should be aware that many other factors—for example, antibiotics, X rays, illnesses, and even vitamins—have been associated with birth defects.

## Context

Birthing practices vary cross-culturally. They evolve from predominant cultural and sociopolitical views on the birth process, which change as times change within a given society and culture. Recent birthing trends reflect both a return to an earlier, more natural view of the birth process itself and a greater awareness of scientific information than ever before. Historically, births took place at home, assisted by midwives. With the advent of organized medicine in the nineteenth century, midwifery fell out of favor and birthing sites shifted from the home environment to sterile hospital settings. In the 1950's, anesthetized deliveries were common. Fathers sat in waiting rooms while women gave birth in an unconscious state with no memory of the births of their babies. Babies were separated from mothers, and bottle feeding was advocated.

Two important events served as catalysts for change: Heightened public and professional consciousness of the negative effects of medications during pregnancy led to a decline in anesthetized deliveries, and increasing awareness of the psychological advantage of early contact between parents and their baby led to a revamping of hospital practices to allow parents more time with their newborns. The great sociopolitical changes of the 1960's helped spur the humanistic movement in psychology. This movement focused attention on the individual as a unique person capable of making healthy, rational choices. Expectant parents were demanding more facts, and they began to want to be awake and aware, and actively involved in making decisions for their pregnancies and deliveries.

Since the 1960's, natural childbirth methods have become a very popular alternative to the medicated deliveries of the preceding decades. Fathers' presence in delivery rooms and the use of birthing centers or hospital birthing rooms represent attempts to rekindle the familial experience of birthing. At the same time, scientific advances have contributed to the birthing experience. Prenatal diagnostic testing allows early detection of fetal problems that previously could not be detected before birth. Yet the rising rate of cesarean sections from 5 percent in 1968 to 10 to 15 percent in 1985 raises some questions; some see this as unnecessary surgery as well as a turning away from the naturalness of childbirth.

The shift in attitudes of many contemporary women parallels changes in psychological thought. The previous emphasis on unconscious processes eliminated free will and choice. In contrast, the Lamaze method is based on the psychological principles of classical conditioning, which belong to the psychological school of behaviorism. New breathing and muscular responses to the sensations of muscular contractions are substituted for old responses of fear and pain. Behaviorists emphasized behavior as the focus of study in psychology. Thus, both the behaviorist and humanistic paradigms have contributed much to the childbirth reform movement—behaviorists to the basis of Lamaze, and humanists to emphasizing choice in the birthing process.

## Bibliography

Broome, Marion E., and Charlotte Koehler. "Childbirth Education: A Review of Effects on the Woman and Her Family." *Family and Community Health* 9, no. 1 (1986): 33-44. Describes natural childbirth techniques in birthing. Comparison of effects on parents who participated in prepared childbirth classes versus nonprepared couples are explored as they relate to relationships with newborns. Very easy reading and easily comprehensible. Provides interesting and informative knowledge about prepared childbirth.

Fogel, Alan. *Infancy: Infant, Family, and Society.* New York: West, 1991. Provides a detailed account of physical, intellectual, and emotional aspects of development, beginning with the prenatal period and proceeding through the first thirty-six months of life. A very comprehensive work that includes cross-cultural information, an extensive bibliography, subject and author indexes, and appendices charting physical growth.

Hanser, Suzanne B., Sharon C. Larson, and Audree S. O'Connell. "The Effect of Music on Relaxation of Expectant Mothers During Labor." *Journal of Music Therapy* 20, no. 2 (1983): 50-58. An experimental investigation of music and its effect on pain responses and relaxation during childbirth. The small number of participants renders findings tentative, but the creative use of music coordinated with Lamaze breathing techniques provides interesting reading. Can be understood by the high school student.

Livingston, Martha. "Choice in Childbirth: Power and the Impact of the Modern Childbirth Reform Movement." *Women and Therapy* 6, nos. 1-2 (1987): 239-261. Livingston presents a historical overview of the evolution of birthing practices. Compares the midwife model to modern obstetrics and emphasizes birth as a social and psychological as well as a physiological event. The need for informed choice is emphasized. Very interesting reading and comprehensive coverage of birthing trends.

Oakley, Ann. "Social Consequences of Obstetric Technology: The Importance of Measuring Soft Outcomes." *Birth: Issues in Perinatal Care and Education* 10, no. 2 (1983): 99-108. Examines the responses of mothers to modern technological advances in obstetrics as they relate to Oakley's own experience of birthing. Social and psychological consequences of obstetric interventions for both parents and their relationship with their child are explored. Fluently written in simple, straightforward language.

Steinberg, Laurence D., Jay Belsky, and Roberta B. Meyer. *Infancy, Childhood, and Adolescence: Development in Context.* New York: McGraw-Hill, 1991. An introductory child development textbook that presents well-rounded chronological coverage of physical, intellectual, and emotional development from conception through adolescence. Acquaints the reader with basic terminology; includes an extensive bibliography, glossary, and name and subject indexes. Diagrams and charts.

*Arlene Confalone Lacombe*

## Cross-References

Attachment and Bonding in Infancy and Childhood, 307; Infant Perceptual Systems, 1290; Motor Development, 1623; Physical Development: Environmental versus Genetic Determinants, 1823; Prenatal Physical Development, 1861; Reflexes in Newborns, 2072; Sudden Infant Death Syndrome, 2495.

# BIRTH ORDER AND PERSONALITY

*Type of psychology:* Developmental psychology
*Fields of study:* Infancy and childhood; personality theory

*Although there is debate over the effects of birth order on personality, with some researchers claiming there is no effect, studies have found subtle differences between firstborn and later-born children; the order of children's births has also been found to influence how the parents treat them.*

> *Principal terms*
> ANXIETY: a great fear, usually in a person's mind and not objectively real
> CREATIVITY: a capability often said to consist of originality plus usefulness
> ONLY CHILD: a child without any siblings (brothers or sisters)
> SCIENTIFIC METHOD: a particular technique for gaining knowledge; it includes the testing of hypotheses in ways that can be verified .
> SELF-IMAGE: the self as one pictures or imagines it

## Overview

The child's order of birth into the family may influence how the parents treat the child. This treatment, in turn, produces personality differences. Most research has focused on comparing the firstborn child with later-born children. Thus, most of what is known about birth order has to do with ways in which firstborns and later-borns are different.

Parents tend to be overly anxious with regard to their first child. The birth of their first child is a major event in their lives, and it is a somewhat threatening event. They have never been parents before, and they do not know what they should do in many instances. Thus, parents tend to be overly restrictive with their first child, having many fears of the terrible things which will happen if they do not monitor and care for their child constantly. This anxiety influences the personality of the child. Firstborns often grow up to be more anxious than later-born children. By the time the parents have a second, third, or fourth child, they are more comfortable caring for children and know that they do not have to be overly concerned with protecting their child from every imaginable harm. Thus, they relax and allow the later-born children more freedom. Their treatment of the firstborn child results in someone who grows up with more than the average amount of anxiety; firstborns tend to be more anxious than later-borns.

It should be made clear that this does not mean that every firstborn child is more anxious than every later-born child. This only means that there is a tendency, greater than could be expected by chance, for firstborns to be more anxious than later-borns. There will be many exceptions, instances where a firstborn is not anxious or where a later-born is.

When the firstborn child is growing up, until the birth of a sibling, the child has the parents all to himself or herself. This probably accounts for another personality difference of firstborns relative to later-borns. Firstborns tend to score higher on intellectual measures. When the later-born children come, the parents will probably spend less time with them than they did with the first child; the later-born child will have as models the other children in the family. The first child had adults as models, and thus may acquire a more adultlike interest in things—and therefore score higher on intellectual measures. This may account, in part, for the fact that firstborns achieve at a greater rate than later-borns. For example, there are more famous firstborn scientists (for their proportion in the population) than would be expected by chance.

Another difference in personality has to do with the kinds of risks firstborns or later-borns will take. Firstborns will take risks if they believe they can handle the situation safely but will be less likely to engage in behavior that exposes them to potential injury. Thus, firstborns are less likely than later-borns to be college football players. Football is a violent sport, and injury is unavoidable no matter how skilled one is. On the other hand, firstborns are overrepresented among astronauts and aquanauts. These would seem to be potentially dangerous occupations, but firstborns probably believe that they can avoid harm via good training and high-quality skills. Thus, the issue may be perceived harm: Firstborns may believe that they can avoid harm as astronauts or aquanauts, while it is impossible to believe this about an inherently violent sport such as football.

Differences in creativity have been found between firstborns and later-borns, but to understand them one must consider sex differences as well. It is only by looking at both birth order and gender that the creativity results become clear. Firstborn males tend to score higher on creativity measures than do later-born males. Creativity can be defined as the combination of originality and usefulness, and there are tests developed to measure it. When testing females, however, the results are the opposite: Later-born females score higher on creativity than firstborn females. This could be explained by the ways parents treat their firstborn child as well as how parents treat their female children. The firstborn female child has a "double whammy." Not only are the parents anxious and restrictive because she is a firstborn, but the parents are also likely to restrict female children more so than they do their male children. Thus, the firstborn female would be the most restricted of all the birth order/sex groupings. Other researchers have found that the firstborn female tends to grow up with traditional values. Traditional beliefs may be fine in many instances, but they would tend to restrict creativity, which often needs a challenging of society's views in order to occur. That is, the creative person is often something of a rebel, at least as far as thoughts about traditional, accepted beliefs are concerned.

## Applications

Knowledge of the effects that birth order can have may be applied to attempts to promote greater self-understanding in those people who are most affected. For example, suppose a firstborn male sees his friends trying out for the football team. He knows that he does not wish to do so, but he feels like a "chicken." His self-image makes him feel inadequate because he is not like his friends. If he knew the research findings concerning firstborns, however, he would realize that he might be quite courageous and risk-taking in other pursuits, but probably will not be when there is clear-cut physical danger. This attitude was established long ago, as he grew up the firstborn child in his family. Thus, he would see the causes of his personality and be more self-accepting.

When people are anxious, they tend to talk. This talking may be an attempt to relieve their anxiety. This fact and the findings about birth order could be used in group situations to foster good discussions. Thus, a teacher or a group therapist could make sure that the group was composed of a combination of firstborns and later-borns, which should ensure a good group discussion. The anxious firstborns will be likely to speak up, and discussion will be facilitated. If the group were all firstborns, there might be too many people talking at once, while if the group were all later-borns, there might be too little discussion. Thus, a mixture of firstborns and later-borns may produce the best group discussion.

Another application might be in changing people from their typical tendencies. Thus, if we know that firstborn females tend not to be creative because of an over-dose of traditional beliefs, one could educate the firstborn female about different ways of thinking. Perhaps education could focus on challenging some of the traditional beliefs by offering alternative, more questioning attitudes for the firstborn female to consider. This might increase the chances that the firstborn female would come up with creative solutions and ideas.

The previously discussed birth order/sex difference findings can serve as a basis for making interventions to help people in all the different birth order/sex combinations. The major recipient of help might be the firstborn female, since she has probably received an overly restrictive upbringing. Teachers or therapists, if aware of the tendency of some firstborn females to be inhibited in their challenging of society's conventional beliefs, might help that person to think more critically. Later-born males may also, to a lesser extent, be inclined toward this inhibited thinking, if generalizations from the research are correct. They, too, could benefit from training or assistance in greater critical thinking which challenges the conventional beliefs they have learned. It should be emphasized that conventional beliefs are not necessarily wrong; one should, however, learn to think for oneself and not automatically accept everything one is told.

Although firstborn males and later-born females did the best on the creativity measures, they are by no means immune to society's teachings, which in some cases will lead to an inhibition of creativity. Firstborn males seem to have a high need for social approval, which at times may inhibit creativity and lead to conformity. When this conformity is undesirable or restrictive of creativity, it needs to be overcome. Later-born females, although scoring more creatively than firstborn females, still have the burden of being female in a society which places many inhibitions upon females. The point is that everyone can use help to think more critically, to be more challenging toward what they have been taught, and in this way to increase the likelihood of creative thinking and of production of creative products.

## Context

Alfred Adler was a psychoanalyst who was a follower of Sigmund Freud, the inventor of psychoanalysis. Adler, like several of Freud's early followers, believed that Freud neglected the social context of things, and he broke away to establish his own school of psychology, individual psychology. Among the many concepts which formed the basis of his approach was Adler's belief that birth order is worthy of study. He speculated in detail about how the ordinal position of the child affected the child's personality.

For many years, research psychologists did not study birth order to any extent. Part of the problem is that birth order is an actuarial variable, like age, gender, or social class, and psychologists did not see it as worth studying in and of itself. In 1959, however, Stanley Schachter published his book *The Psychology of Affiliation*, in which he showed that birth order is an important variable. Many other researchers started looking at birth order in their studies. Sometimes they had little understanding of what birth order should mean, but it was easy enough to ask subjects to list their birth order to see if any patterns became apparent. One problem was that the early researchers included only children (children with no siblings) as firstborns. It is now known that while they are sometimes similar, as in having the same adult orientation as firstborns, in other ways they are different. It is best to include only children as a separate category. Unfortunately, there are so few only children in the population that researchers usually do not study them. For example, if one were to ask a class of fifty to give their birth order, one might end up with only one or two only child subjects, which is not enough for statistical testing. Researchers often simply drop the only children from their analysis. As a greater understanding of birth order has been gained, it has become possible to do research based on what is known rather than treat birth order as simply one more variable.

## Bibliography

Adler, Alfred. *What Life Should Mean to You.* Edited by Alan Porter. New York: Capricorn Books, 1958. Alfred Adler, one of the most important people in establishing birth order as an idea worthy of study, spells out his original views on birth order in this book, originally published in 1931. He believed that the place of the child in the family influences how the parents treat the child, which in turn creates personality differences among the various birth orders. Not all his speculation is necessarily correct, but psychology is grateful to him for saying that birth order is an important concept.

Blake, Judith. *Family Size and Achievement.* Berkeley: University of California Press, 1989. Discusses the effects of family size on achievement. The author found that only children and children from small families are more able intellectually and gain more education than children who are not the only child or who are from large families.

Eisenman, Russell. *From Crime to Creativity: Psychological and Social Factors in Deviance.* Dubuque, Iowa: Kendall/Hunt, 1991. In addition to detailed discussions of creativity, this book deals with birth order and shows how it can relate to other things. For example, the book discusses birth order and projection, which is the tendency to see things in others that are really in oneself. Firstborns scored higher in the projection of sex and aggression when viewing ambiguous figures.

Hann, Della M., and Howard J. Osofsky. "Psychosocial Factors in the Transition to Parenthood." In *New Perspectives on Prenatal Care*, edited by Irwin R. Merkatz and Joyce E. Thompson. New York: Elsevier, 1990. Hann and Osofsky discuss the problems of being a parent for the first time and give examples of how things can go wrong for first-time parents. They also suggest interventions which can be made to help people be better parents. They cite research showing that depressed parents make their children depressed.

Schachter, Stanley. *The Psychology of Affiliation.* Stanford, Calif.: Stanford University Press, 1959. This book caused other researchers to begin birth-order studies. Schachter used female subjects and told them they were going to experience painful electric shocks. Firstborns preferred to wait for the alleged shocks with others who were also waiting to receive shocks. Thus, birth order was established as something which made a difference and could be studied.

*Russell Eisenman*

## Cross-References

Achievement Motivation, 96; Adolescence: Cognitive Skills, 118; Creativity and Intelligence, 731; Development: Theoretical Issues, 804; Parenting Styles, 1740.

# BORDERLINE, HISTRIONIC, AND NARCISSISTIC PERSONALITIES

*Type of psychology:* Psychopathology
*Fields of study:* Personality assessment; personality disorders; personality theory

*Borderline, histrionic, and narcissistic personalities are three of the major personality disorders in the diagnostic system. The diagnosis of these disorders is highly controversial, and their causes are largely unknown.*

*Principal terms*

ANTISOCIAL PERSONALITY: a personality disorder characterized by a history of chronic criminal and otherwise irresponsible behavior

EGO-SYNTONIC: perceived as acceptable to the person and as consistent with one's self-image

ENTITLEMENT: the expectation of special or unusually favorable treatment by others, which is commonly seen among narcissistic personalities

HETEROGENEITY: differences among individuals given the same diagnosis

OBJECT RELATIONS THEORY: a personality theory that focuses upon the relations among internalized persons and objects and their implications for personality development

PERSONALITY DISORDER: a disorder in which personality traits are rigid and maladaptive and produce considerable impairment or distress for the individual

RELIABILITY: the consistency of a psychological measure, which can be assessed by means of stability over repeated administrations or agreement among different observers

SCHIZOPHRENIA: a condition characterized by severe abnormalities in thinking processes

SOMATIZATION DISORDER: a condition characterized by multiple physical symptoms lacking any demonstrated medical basis

VALIDITY: the extent to which a psychological test measures what it is intended to measure

## Overview

Of all psychiatric disorders, the group of conditions that psychologists call personality disorders is perhaps the most puzzling and controversial. According to most researchers, personality disorders can be viewed as conditions in which personality traits are rigid and maladaptive and cause considerable impairment or distress for the individual. Some of these disorders are notable for the psychological pain that they cause the person afflicted with them. Others, however, are more notable for the psychological pain that they cause others. Borderline, histrionic, and narcissistic personality disorders fall primarily into this latter group. This is not to imply that individuals with these disorders do not suffer: Many such persons experience chronic feelings of depression, emptiness, and anger. Nevertheless, what distinguishes people with these disorders from the majority of other psychiatric patients is the distress that they inflict upon others, especially those close to them.

These three disorders share at least two important features. First, individuals with these disorders tend to view their problems as ego-syntonic—that is, as acceptable and as consistent with their self-image. As a result, such individuals tend to view their difficulties in life as stemming primarily from others' actions, rather than from their own. Second, the behavior of individuals with these disorders tends to be impulsive, unpredictable, and dramatic. Given the similarities among these three disorders, perhaps it is not surprising that they overlap substantially within individuals; a person with one of these disorders is likely to have features of one or both of the other two. Nevertheless, despite their commonalities, these disorders possess a number of important characteristics that differentiate them from one another; these are outlined below.

Individuals with borderline personality share one major feature: instability. More specifically, borderline personality, which is generally found among women, is characterized by instability in sense of self, relationships with others, and mood. In fact, borderline personalities have been described as possessing a kind of "stable instability"—their instability seems an ingrained part of their personality structure.

One of the central features of borderline personality is confusion with regard to identity. Borderline personalities often express concerns such as "I don't really know who I am," and they may be uncertain regarding what types of friends to have, values to hold, or career aspirations to pursue. In many cases, borderline personalities appear to rely heavily upon others to define their identity. Perhaps as a consequence, they often go to great lengths to avoid abandonment and frequently feel "empty" or bored, especially when alone.

Borderline personalities tend to be impulsive individuals who may excessively eat, drink alcohol, spend money, or have sex. In addition, they often explode angrily in response to minor provocations. Suicide attempts, threats, and gestures are common, as is self-mutilatory behavior such as wrist-slashing. The relationships of borderline personalities frequently alternate between the extremes of overidealization and devaluation: Friends or lovers are initially worshiped or "placed on a pedestal" but abruptly fall from grace when they are perceived as having erred. Borderline personalities also tend to be moody individuals whose emotions shift radically with little or no warning.

Histrionic personalities who, like borderline personalities, tend be to female, are characterized by excessive emotionality and attention-seeking. Such persons tend to be extremely dramatic and often seem to be playing the part of an actor or actress—hence the term "histrionic." They frequently express their emotions with great intensity; for example, they may cry uncontrollably after a mild rebuff or passionately hug individuals they have just met.

Histrionic personalities tend to enjoy "being in the spotlight" greatly and are often uncomfortable when they are not being showered with adoration or praise. Moreover, they are often sexually seductive individuals who behave flirtatiously and are overconcerned with their dress and appearance. Histrionic personalities are often vain and self-centered individuals who have difficulty postponing gratification. Finally, many histrionic personalities have been described as possessing a style of speech that is vague and impressionistic: For example, they may make frequent use of hyperbolic statements such as "Oh, it was just terrible," or "She is absolutely wonderful."

Finally, narcissistic personalities are characterized by egocentricity, lack of empathy, and oversensitivity to negative evaluation by others. (In contrast to borderline and histrionic personalities, little is known about the sex ratio of this disorder.) Narcissistic personalities often have an inordinate sense of self-importance and may be surprised or indignant when others fail to appreciate their "unique" qualities. In addition, they are often consumed with fantasies of greatness, power, or meeting the perfect romantic partner.

Such individuals commonly possess "entitlements," that is, expectations of unusually favorable treatment by others. For example, they may believe that certain rules or norms, such as having to wait one's turn in line or having to pay taxes, should not apply to them. Narcissistic personalities often appear to have little empathy; for example, they may become enraged when a friend who is very ill cancels a date. In addition, they often seem quite willing to "step on others' toes" to accomplish their goals. Finally, narcissistic personalities often tend to be very envious of other peoples' successes or accomplishments.

## Applications

Unfortunately, there has been relatively little research done on these three disorders. In part, this lack is probably a result of the fact that these disorders, especially borderline and narcissistic personality disorders, are relatively new additions to the diagnostic nomenclature. In addition, many of the symptoms of these disorders (for example, identity disturbance) are latent constructs that are difficult to measure with adequate reliability—that is, with consistency. Typically, the reliability of a psychiatric diagnosis is indexed by agreement among different observers. By this standard, the reliability of these disorders, as well as that of most personality disorders, is among the lowest of all psychiatric conditions: Two clinicians interviewing the same patient will often disagree on whether that patient has one of these disorders. This is important because reliability sets an upper limit upon validity—the extent to which a measure (in this case, a diagnosis) measures what it is intended to measure. As cited below, the validity of these disorders has been a major bone of contention among researchers.

Of the three disorders, borderline personality has been probably the most extensively researched. One question that has occupied many researchers is whether borderline personality is a single disorder or a group of disorders. Psychologist Harrison

Pope and his colleagues found that borderline personality seems to identify a rather heterogeneous group of patients—that is, there appear to be a number of important differences among individuals given a borderline diagnosis. Specifically, Pope found that some patients with borderline personality suffer from depression, whereas others suffer from a variety of personality disorders. Moreover, Pope reported that borderline personalities were difficult to distinguish from other personality-disordered patients with respect to variables such as outcome and family history of psychiatric illness. Similarly, Hagop Akiskal has found that borderline personality overlaps substantially with a variety of psychiatric conditions, especially depression and antisocial personality, and personality disorder characterized by a history of chronic criminal and otherwise irresponsible behavior. Akiskal also reported that a subset of borderline patients appear to suffer from a mild form of schizophrenia, a condition characterized by severe abnormalities in thinking processes.

What are the implications of these findings? Although more research is necessary, it appears that patients given a borderline personality diagnosis do not all suffer from the same major underlying problem. Instead, these patients seem to have a variety of underlying pathologies that are superficially similar to one another. A major challenge for future researchers will be to isolate subgroups of borderline patients who are relatively homogeneous in terms of factors such as family history, outcome, and response to treatment.

If the nature of borderline personality is unclear, the picture is perhaps even fuzzier for histrionic and narcissistic personalities. There has been relatively little research on histrionic personality, although several investigators have found that, like borderline personality, it overlaps substantially with antisocial personality. In addition, there is good evidence that histrionic personalities are at substantially increased risk for somatization disorder, a condition characterized by multiple physical symptoms lacking any demonstrated medical basis. The reasons for this association, however, are unknown.

Similarly, little is known about narcissistic personalities, although it has been reported that such individuals are prone to episodes of depressed mood, especially in middle age. These episodes may occur when these individuals perceive that others no longer admire or idolize them. Some authors, including Christopher Lasch, have argued that narcissistic personality may be increasing in prevalence in Western culture, perhaps as a result of social changes such as an increased emphasis upon individualism, success, and hedonism. Nevertheless, systematic research is not yet available to corroborate this conjecture.

Although the causes of these three disorders are largely unknown, it seems likely that genetic factors play at least some role. Auke Tellegen and his colleagues have found that genetic factors strongly influence traits such as impulsivity, risk-taking, and the propensity to experience negative emotions, all of which are commonly found among individuals with these three disorders. Nevertheless, it also seems clear that environmental factors play an important role. For example, there is some evidence that borderline patients have an elevated rate of physical and sexual abuse in childhood. Although genetic factors cannot be excluded as a mediator of this association, it seems plausible that such abuse might lead predisposed individuals to develop problems such as identity disturbance, chronic anger, and other symptoms common to borderline personalities.

Almost nothing is known about the treatment of these disorders. There is evidence, however, that a subset of borderline personalities may benefit from medications used to treat depression. This is consistent with the possibility that at least some of these patients have an underlying form of depression. Surprisingly, there have been virtually no systematic studies of the effectiveness of psychotherapy for any of these three conditions, although many individuals with these disorders have undergone psychotherapy for decades.

As noted earlier, these three conditions overlap substantially within individuals. A number of researchers have argued that this overlap calls into question the validity of these conditions, because psychiatric disorders have traditionally been viewed as fairly distinct categories that do not blend into one another extensively. Thus, perhaps the primary challenge for researchers in this area will be to determine whether these three diagnoses actually represent three different conditions or instead represent variants of one underlying disorder.

## Context

The term "borderline personality" has a long and rather checkered history. Initially, this term referred to a condition "on the border" between neurosis and psychosis. Later, however, the term increasingly came to refer to a disorder that is qualitatively distinct from these two broad classes of conditions. In 1968, Roy Grinker and his colleagues delineated several features that they believed distinguished borderlines from other patients, including chronic anger and identity problems.

Another influential approach to borderline (as well as narcissistic) personality has been object relations theory. This theory focuses upon the relations among internalized persons and objects and the implications of these relations for personality development. Otto Kernberg, for example, discusses the "borderline personality organization," a character structure that he believes results from disturbances in the child's psychological internalization of parental images. According to Kernberg, borderline individuals never learn to incorporate good and bad representations of themselves or others simultaneously; consequently, they lack the capacity to view themselves and others as possessing both good and bad attributes.

Unfortunately, the overlap among these different conceptualizations is not as great as might be hoped; in 1978, J. Christopher Perry and Gerald Klerman reported that four commonly used criteria sets for borderline personality differ substantially in the symptoms they assess. The third edition of the *Diagnostic and Statistical Manual of Mental Disorders* (1980, DSM-III), which first provided researchers with a standard set of criteria to assess the disorder, may result in increased comparability in the borderline personality concept.

Although the term "histrionic personality" did not formally appear until the advent of DSM-III, the "hysterical personality" has a lengthy history in psychiatry. Indeed, the concept of "hysteria" (literally, "wandering womb") dates back at least four thousand years to Egypt, where it was believed that the disorder was attributable to a displaced uterus. In the late nineteenth century, French neurologist Jean Charcot and, later, his student Sigmund Freud attempted to treat hysterics, many of whom probably had what would today be called histrionic personality, by means of hypnosis. In 1958, psychiatrists Paul Chodoff and Henry Lyons outlined the major features of hysterical personality, including vanity, dramatic behavior, and coquetry. Their conceptualization had a major influence upon subsequent criteria for histrionic personality.

Freud was one of the first major authors to discuss narcissism as a pathological character trait. According to Freud, narcissism resulted from a failure of the child to develop beyond the stage in which sexual impulses are focused upon the self. Thus, according to Freud, narcissistic individuals are psychologically "stuck" at a primitive stage of development characterized by an inability to direct sexual urges toward other individuals. More recently, object relations theorists, such as Heinz Kohut, have argued that narcissistic personality results from profound failures in parental empathy. As a result of these failures, according to Kohut, such individuals remain "stuck" at an early stage of development characterized by self-centeredness, resulting in a never-ending search for the love and admiration they never received.

## Bibliography

Cooper, Arnold M., Allen J. Frances, and Michael H. Sacks, eds. *The Personality Disorders and Neuroses.* New York: Basic Books, 1986. This edited volume contains chapters on each major personality disorder as well as a discussion of general theoretical and treatment models for the personality disorders and neuroses. Michael H. Stone's chapter on borderline personality, which contains a good overview of different uses of the term, and Otto Kernberg's chapters on narcissistic and histrionic personalities are particularly recommended.

Goldstein, Eda G. *Borderline Disorders: Clinical Models and Techniques.* New York: Guilford Press, 1990. Goldstein lucidly outlines the major clinical features of borderline personality, discusses its development from a variety of theoretical perspectives, and contrasts the major contemporary psychotherapeutic approaches to the disorder. Appropriate for the reader with some background in psychoanalytic theory.

Lasch, Christopher. *The Culture of Narcissism.* New York: Warner Books, 1979. Lasch outlines the characteristics of "the narcissistic personality of our time," discusses large-scale social changes that he believes are responsible for the increase in narcissism in Western culture, and provides compelling critiques of the awareness movement and other contemporary fads. Although Lasch's tone at times verges on the polemical, his observations are thought-provoking and perceptive.

Roy, Alec, ed. *Hysteria.* New York: John Wiley & Sons, 1982. Contains chapters dealing with a number of important issues relevant to histrionic personality, somatization disorder, and related conditions. The coverage of historical issues and genetic and biological factors is especially thorough. The chapters on multiple personality and the relation of hysteria to hypnosis may also be of interest.

Vallaint, George E., and J. Christopher Perry. "Personality Disorders." In *Comprehensive Textbook of Psychiatry*, edited by H. I. Kaplan and B. J. Sadock. Baltimore: Williams & Wilkins, 1985. Provides an overview of key conceptual issues relevant to personality disorders (for example, classification models, genetic and environmental factors, treatment approaches) and clearly discusses the clinical features of each disorder. Although this chapter may prove somewhat difficult for readers with little background in psychopathology, it provides one of the most succinct summaries of the personality disorders literature.

*Scott O. Lilienfeld*

### Cross-References

Antisocial Personality, 265; Clinical Depression, 521; Clinical Interviewing, Testing, and Observation, 527; Psychoactive Drug Therapy, 1891; Psychoanalytic Psychology and Personality: Sigmund Freud, 1912; Psychological Diagnosis and Classification: DSM-III-R, 1925; Psychosexual Development, 1969.

# BRAIN INJURIES: CONCUSSIONS, CONTUSIONS, AND STROKES

*Type of psychology:* Biological bases of behavior
*Field of study:* Nervous system

*Traumatic brain injury refers to the sudden impairment of brain function caused by mechanical forces (concussions and contusions) or vascular accidents (strokes). A primary characteristic of traumatic brain injury is its instantaneous onset, but the consequences of the injury vary. Appropriate treatment and rehabilitation strategies, as well as the prospects for recovery, depend upon an understanding of the specific consequences of the injury on the individual.*

*Principal terms*
   BRAIN STEM: the lower part of the brain, between the brain and spinal cord, which activates the cortex and makes perception and consciousness possible
   CONCUSSION: a transient loss of consciousness resulting from injury to the brain stem
   CONTUSION: bruising of the brain as a result of mechanical or other forces
   CORTEX: the surface (or outer layer) of the brain; it receives sensory input, interprets it, and relates behavior to external stimuli
   DIENCEPHALON: the middle part of the brain; it transfers information to more permanent memory (memory consolidation)
   NEUROPSYCHOLOGY: the study of brain-behavior relationships usually by using behavioral tests and correlating results with brain areas
   STROKE: a vascular accident resulting from either the rupture of a vessel or the blocking of blood flow in an artery

## Overview

The brain is composed of three separate but interconnected systems: the brain stem, the diencephalon, and the cortical system. The brain stem and related structures at the base of the brain receive input from sensory systems and relay this information through the thalamus to activate the cortex. This activation is essential for the cortex to function; without it, perception is not possible. In addition, the brain stem governs an individual's level of consciousness and ability to attend to incoming stimulation. Normal variations in the brain stem's level of activity are reflected by a person's being highly alert, moderately attentive, or asleep. When the brain stem is damaged, however, the higher systems cannot perceive stimuli; as a result, an individual is unresponsive. The person is in a coma.

Along with other structures, the diencephalon makes up the middle part of the brain, and its basic function is to monitor input to the body and determine which stimuli have significance or high survival value. Stimuli that cause pain directly influence this system, and conditions are established to move the individual away from the painful stimuli. In a similar manner, the diencephalon is involved in moving a person toward stimuli that are important (for example, things which the person desires or which are necessary for survival). This system, therefore, plays an important role in emotion and motivation. It is also essential for converting memories from temporary to long-term storage (memory consolidation). While memory consolidation may appear to be quite different from emotion and motivation, it fits into the same process because it is important for a person to remember things that are essential for survival. The degree of memory consolidation varies according to the importance of the stimuli. People tend to remember very important or unusual things (whether they are positive or negative) and not to remember more neutral things. Damage to the diencephalon, therefore, may alter emotion, motivation, and memory consolidation.

The third system includes the cortex and its associated components. This system, which makes up the outer portion of the brain, is the most complex and most specialized in its function. It is concerned with information processing; that is, it receives sensory information from the receptors and processes the information through various stages of complexity. The dominant hemisphere of the brain (usually the left hemisphere) is concerned with language processing, and the nondominant hemisphere deals with nonlanguage or spatial processing. Damage to this system directly affects cognitive processing by making perception difficult, disrupting the individual's ability to interpret new information, and increasing processing time. In addition, the most anterior region (the prefrontal cortex) is concerned with planning, problem solving, initiation of activity, sustained attention, and emotional control. Damage to this portion of the brain impairs these and other related abilities.

Although contusions, concussions, and strokes all result in damage to the brain, they differ in the degree and type of damage. A contusion (bruise) is usually focal, and it may or may not result in unconsciousness.

A concussion involves a brief or extended loss of consciousness (coma), and it usually results from different mechanical forces that occur while the head is mobile. According to research done by Ayub Ommaya and T. A. Gennarelli (1974), the head is usually thrown forward at impact, but the brain tends to lag behind because of inertia. The effect is that the skull suddenly moves and the brain resists, resulting in tearing (or shearing) of brain tissue. These shear forces are maximum at the surface of the brain (the cortex); therefore, even a mild injury (in which there is no loss of consciousness) can result in some damage to the cortex and lead to problems in cognitive functioning for a time after the accident. When the forces are greater, the shearing radiates down into the middle part of the brain (the diencephalon); the result is impaired memory consolidation, affecting the storage of new memories. The brain stem is usually the least affected since it is closest to the pivot point and moves the least distance; however, if the shear forces are great enough, they radiate down into the brain stem. Damage to this region results in unconsciousness or, if it is severe enough, death.

A stroke, on the other hand, is a vascular accident that is caused either by the rupture of a blood vessel or by the occlusion of a vessel (by a blood clot, air, or other material). Strokes are usually lateralized, resulting in a loss of function on the contralateral side of the body. Left-hemisphere strokes may result in loss of sensory and motor functions on the right side as well as impaired language functions. Right-hemisphere strokes cause loss on the left side, with problems in visuospatial perception and, sometimes, neglect of the left side.

In contrast to strokes, concussions usually involve more generalized impairment of the brain. Since the primary forces are shear forces as a result of rapid acceleration or deceleration of the skull, the damage is greater at the surface but extends to involve the brain stem (producing loss of consciousness). Contusions are more focal, usually result from a direct blow to the head, and may be greatest at the site of the impact and on the side opposite the impact.

Traumatic brain injury and strokes are similar in that they involve damage to the brain that is instantaneous. They differ in that traumatic brain injury occurs most frequently in the young. In fact, brain injury is the leading cause of death between the ages of four and forty-four. In contrast, strokes usually occur in individuals who are older than fifty-five years of age and result from some preexisting problem (such as diabetes, high blood pressure, high serum cholesterol, smoking cigarettes, and/or genetic tendencies).

Neuropsychological assessment provides an important source of information, regardless of the type of brain injury sustained. Since neuropsychology focuses on the relationship between the brain and behavior, such an assessment can provide important information as to the functional consequences of such an injury. Unlike computerized axial tomography (a CAT scan) and magnetic resonance imaging (MRI), which evaluate the structural integrity of the brain, the neuropsychological assessment investigates the effect that such damage has on the behavior of the individual. The type of behavior assessed by the neuropsychologist consists of cognitive functions (such as thinking, reasoning, and judgment), but it also includes the individual's emotional adjustment and ability to function at work and at home.

## Applications

The effects of brain injury extend far beyond the specific changes to the brain itself. Instead, because brain and behavior are closely related, structural damage to the brain influences almost all aspects of an individual's life. For example, the sudden change in cognitive functioning results in impaired perception, attention, memory, and motor responding. Often, these effects are subtle and more apparent to the brain-damaged individual than to others. Everyday tasks require more time and energy than they did previously. There is difficulty dealing with distractions, and, as a result, the person becomes easily confused, disoriented, and sidetracked. In addition, there may be problems with poor judgment, emotional control, appropriate behavior, and so on. Awareness of cognitive deficits and inability to function at the pre-injury level may also result in extreme depression and other emotional-adjustment problems.

If the above cognitive and emotional changes are not anticipated or understood, head-injured individuals may experience significant problems with friends, family, and employers. Because a brain injury is not an outwardly visible deficit, such individuals may not look sick or have other obvious impairments. As a result, they are expected to react and perform as they did prior to the injury—even though they are unable to do so. This often results in additional stress and frustration and puts additional strain on interpersonal relationships.

An example of the disruptive effects of brain injury is the experience of a twenty-year-old college student who was involved in an accident, remained unconscious for several days, and had a memory loss for about one month. Prior to his injury, he had maintained a B average while taking a full load of classes and working thirty hours per week. After being released from the hospital and resting for several months, he attempted to resume his preaccident work load. When he was seen by a neuropsychologist several months later, he was failing all of his courses and was unable to do his job. In addition, he complained of headaches, dizziness, fatigue, irritability, memory problems, and other postconcussion symptoms. Neuropsychological assessment revealed that he was functioning at about 30 percent below his estimated preinjury level. Based on these test findings, his strengths and weaknesses were outlined, and he was advised to take fewer classes and to drop one of these if he still had difficulty keeping up with the work. In addition, he was advised to quit his after-school job. He did this and earned a B in one course and C's in the other two (since he chose not to drop any classes). By the following year, he was able to take twelve hours of classes and perform satisfactorily. It should also be mentioned that the postconcussion symptoms he was experiencing were caused in part by his injury and in part by the stress of trying to function as he once did. Once adjustments were made in both his expectations and his schedule, these symptoms gradually subsided.

The important point of this illustration is that brain damage results in impaired cognitive functioning, which prevents individuals from functioning as they once did. Unless they understand this, they will be continually frustrated by their decreased level of performance. If they can be helped to understand the changes in their cognitive functioning, they can be aided in making adjustments that allow them time to recover their best level and not suffer significant emotional or situational problems.

Another example is that of a forty-four-year-old man who had a stroke in a small blood vessel in the left hemisphere involving the angular gyrus (the area important for reading). He initially encountered problems with all language tasks and with motor functions with his right hand. These were caused by the direct damage resulting from the ruptured vessel as well as secondary damage resulting from pressure effects from the blood and edema (swelling). After several months of recovery, he had a neuropsychological assessment which revealed that his remaining deficit related to an inability to read words or recognize letters. Suggested rehabilitation involved making flash cards, first with letters, then with simple words, and finally with more complex words. He progressed rather quickly, but a weakness in word recognition persisted. For this reason, when he returned to work, his job was modified so that he made notes by tape recorder instead of by writing.

As the foregoing examples illustrate, neuropsychological assessment clarifies the individual's strengths and weaknesses so that an effective plan of intervention can be developed. Perhaps the most important benefit from the assessment and intervention was expressed by the latter patient: He reported that, prior to the assessment, he felt that no one understood his problem and he was becoming depressed. The explanation and intervention helped him to understand his symptoms better, develop more realistic expectations, and feel that something constructive was being done about his problem. Although continuing to have some weaknesses, he was able to function on his job and avoid the development of significant emotional problems.

## Context

For a number of years, the medical treatment of brain injuries was undertaken from a totally neurological perspective. Surgeries and appropriate medications were the chosen interventions for severe or life-threatening brain injuries. Physical therapies were used to help recover impaired motor functions. Milder head injuries were normally treated by spontaneous recovery; that is, time and rest were regarded as nature's healers, and no medical interventions were thought to be of benefit. This approach implied that the only effects of brain injury were those specifically related to the area of damage; physical, emotional, and behavioral deficits were expected to be limited to those associated with the damaged portion of the individual's brain.

The problem with this approach is that the brain injury happens to a human being with a unique past history, personality, and cognitive capabilities. Each of these factors influences the degree of impairment, personal reaction to the resulting deficits, and potential outcome. In addition to the psychological and emotional stresses related to a reduced level of physical and/or cognitive functioning, the individual is affected by a host of other adjustments: changed family relationships, temporary or permanent job loss, financial pressures related to lost income and heavy medical expenses, and so on.

For these and associated reasons, traumatic brain injury has become the primary field of study in neuropsychology. According to this approach, in order to evaluate and treat brain-injured individuals, it is necessary to have some knowledge of both brain functions and the behavioral consequences of such damage. Patients who have sustained brain damage are not regarded as a diagnostic problem; rather, the focus is the extent to which neurological damage affects their behavior. In the case of accidents that cause contusion or concussion, neurological damage is often diffuse and the consequences are not revealed by MRI or CAT scans. Neuropsychological assessments are especially important in such cases.

Neuropsychologists, therefore, work closely with physicians, evaluating the strengths and weaknesses of the brain-injured patient's cognitive functioning and relating such findings to potential problems in day-to-day functioning. More severely injured patients may be referred to comprehensive rehabilitation facilities, whereas less severely impaired individuals are referred to day treatment or outpatient treatment programs. Perhaps the most important contribution of neuropsychology is that it allows psychologists to interact with and assist physicians with what were once thought to be solely medical problems (assessing the nature and degree of impairment, planning rehabilitation, and incorporating cognitive and emotional treatment as needed).

During the past decades, the medical profession has made great strides in focusing on the more comprehensive aspects of brain injury and illness. Physicians are now much more aware that, in cases of central nervous system involvement, the effects of structural damage greatly alter the individual's cognitive behavior, that cognitive changes may directly affect emotional adjustment, and that both may alter the individual's ability to function at work or at home. It is also now known that brain injury patients need cognitive training and that stroke patients need psychotherapy in the form of relaxation training and biofeedback.

Clearly, the future holds great promise in this area. While evaluation and treatment have significantly improved outcome following traumatic brain injury, much more needs to be accomplished. More careful investigations of the relationship between test findings and day-to-day functioning need to be conducted. In addition, the relationship between specific weaknesses and specific rehabilitation strategies will most likely be the primary area of future research. With such developments, treatments will become less the focus of a single specialty and more the efforts of a team of professionals focusing on a general problem.

## Bibliography

Levin, Harvey S., Jordan Grafman, and Howard M. Eisenberg. *Neurobehavioral Recovery from Head Injury.* New York: Oxford University Press, 1987. Reviews findings related to neuropsychological assessment, neurobehavioral outcome, and memory and attention deficits. Also presents information about common psychiatric sequelae experienced by brain-injured individuals.

Ommaya, A. K., and T. A. Gennarelli. "Cerebral Concussion and Traumatic Unconsciousness." *Brain* 97, no. 4 (1974): 633-654. A classic article dealing with the physical aspects of brain injury and subsequent recovery. Presents technical material at a level that can be understood by the general reader.

Parker, Rolland S. *Traumatic Brain Injury and Neuropsychological Impairment.* New York: Springer-Verlag, 1990. Deals with the sensorimotor, cognitive, and emotional adjustment problems experienced by both adults and children with traumatic brain injuries.

Prigatano, George P. *Neuropsychological Rehabilitation After Brain Injury.* Baltimore: The Johns Hopkins University Press, 1986. Presents information about cognitive deficits related to head injury and about common emotional and psychosocial adjustment problems. Also deals with rehabilitation issues and the type of brain-injured patients likely to benefit from psychotherapy.

Ylvisaker, Mark, and Eva Marie R. Gobble, eds. *Community Re-entry for Head Injured Adults.* Boston: Little, Brown, 1987. A practical reference presenting valuable information about cognitive and physical rehabilitation issues, family issues, personality changes, neuropsychological deficits, and outcome.

*Charles J. Long*
*Linda Collins*

## Cross-References

Brain Specialization, 455; Brain-Stem Structures, 461; The Central and Peripheral Nervous Systems, 494; The Cerebral Cortex, 500; Forebrain Structures, 1043; Hindbrain Structures, 1175; Neural Damage and Plasticity, 1655; Reticular Formation, 2103.

# BRAIN SPECIALIZATION

*Type of psychology:* Biological bases of behavior
*Field of study:* Nervous system

*Brain specialization involves the relationships between different physical parts of the brain and abilities, behaviors, and types of thinking; the seemingly inseparable whole of the self is the product of blended inputs from a diverse collection of structures. Right and left brain hemispheres are capable of independent thought and have specialized abilities.*

### Principal terms

BILATERAL: being present on two sides; areas found in both brain hemispheres are bilaterally represented

CEREBRAL CORTEX: the outer layer of the cerebrum and the most recently evolved part of the vertebrate brain; the most recent part of the cortex is the neocortex, which has six layers of cells

CEREBRUM: the large, almost bilaterally symmetrical brain structure that lies on top of the mammalian brain; it has several lobes with different functions and has nerve cell functions

LATERALITY: specialization by sides of almost symmetrical structures; speech is lateralized in human brains because it is mainly controlled by the left hemispheres of almost all right-handed people

LIMBIC SYSTEM: primitive parts of the cerebrum having fewer than six layers of cell; it has mainly emotion-related functions

MOSAIC THEORY: the idea that each part of the brain has its own discrete function, much as each tile in a pattern is a distinct entity

NEURON: the basic active cell of the nervous system, which consists of a cell body and processes

SUBCORTICAL: refers to parts of the brain that are not the cerebral cortex; they have functions related to motives, emotions, reflexes, and life-support systems

### Overview

In the 1800's, practitioners of a pseudoscience called phrenology claimed that they could predict personality and abilities by examining bumps on a person's skull. The theory was that each part of the brain was responsible for a particular human characteristic. Larger brain areas were said to be related to stronger characteristics, and they raised the skull over those areas into a bump. Researchers showed this early version of the mosaic theory to be wrong in detail but correct in that different brain areas have specialized functions. Those who believed that all brain areas are equal and unspecialized, however, resisted the mosaic idea. Data from all over the world gathered for more than a hundred years have illustrated not only that different regions of the brain are specialized but also how they are specialized.

There are three particularly influential models of brain organization. Paul Mac-Lean developed the theory of the triune brain to help researchers think about the overall functions of brain regions in man. This model helps explain that primitive brain areas do not vanish when more advanced structures evolve; rather, they interact with the more recent structures that lie on top of them. First there was the reptilian brain—the primitive structures making up the bulk of the most developed part of a reptile's brain. These consist of the swollen ending of the spinal cord before it ends, called the brain stem, and primitive structures sitting on top of the brain stem. The most noticeable of these structures are called the thalamus and hypothalamus. A lizard normally responds to immediate stimulation; when there is neither food nor an enemy, it usually does nothing. The human brain stem, thalamus, and hypothalamus perform similar functions.

In early mammals, a new structure called the cerebrum evolved on top of the thalamus. The cerebrum has neurons only on its outer surface, or cortex. The fibers carrying messages from those neurons are inside, in the medulla. The earliest cortex consisted of three to five layers of neurons and is called the paleocortex ("old cortex") and intermediate cortex. Later cortical areas six neurons thick, called the neocortex, evolved and covered the entire outer surface of the cerebrum. The paleocortex was relegated to the places where the two cerebral hemispheres come together and to clumps in the medulla of the cerebrum. These paleocortical and transitional areas, often collectively called the limbic system, control emotional responding and make behavior more flexible. When a mammal has no immediate stimulation, it rarely remains motionless, as does a lizard. Instead, it may go exploring for old enemies, old lovers, or simply knowledge about its environment. MacLean called the limbic system the paleomammalian brain.

The neocortex is the most prominent brain structure seen when one examines a mammalian brain. It inhibits impulsive behaviors that would otherwise result from motives and feelings arising from the lower centers. Having a conscience, for example, depends on the parts of these areas in the front of the brain in humans. MacLean called these areas the neomammalian brain.

Aleksandr Luria, a noted Russian neuropsychologist famous for his work diagnosing and helping brain-damaged soldiers, proposed another three-part model of brain function. Subcortical and limbic structures, basically MacLean's reptilian and paleomammalian brain, serve reflexes, motives, emotions, and arousal. The cerebral cortex, or MacLean's neomammalian brain, can be divided. The front part consists of the frontal lobes, and the hind part consists of the temporal, occipital, and parietal lobes. The front part plans and executes actions. There is a gradient from abstract to concrete functions within the frontal lobes, running from the prefrontal structures that lie behind the forehead back to areas controlling talking and eye movement to areas in the back of the frontal lobes controlling voluntary muscle control.

The hind portion of the cerebral cortex processes sensory information and stores memories. It consists of three lobes with their own specializations. The temporal lobes specialize in hearing and higher-order processing of emotional information from the paleomammalian brain. The parietal lobes process information about touch, muscle position, and location in space. The occipital lobes process visual information. The place in the center of each side of the back part of the brain where all three lobes touch includes a fold of cortical surface called the angular gyrus and the parietal, occipital, and temporal (POT) association areas. A human processes sequences of information there, including the orders of words in sentences, and integrates information from multiple senses.

A last theory that helps in understanding the brain is the right brain-left brain model. At one time, it was thought that the two hemispheres of the cerebral cortex were bilateral mirror images of each other. Today it is known that they have slightly different shapes and internal organizations, and they do somewhat different things. Roger Sperry from the California Institute of Technology in Pasadena, California, cut the bundles of nerves connecting the two hemispheres of cats, including the largest bundle, the corpus callosum. He found that each hemisphere could process information independently and suggested that this operation might help humans with epileptic seizures. When the operation was performed on humans, it was successful in reducing the severity of epileptic seizures. Sperry found that the two hemispheres could each process information individually. Each developed its own memory and had special skills. Sometimes the hemispheres conflicted when researchers gave each side of the brain different information. If the information was visual, such as matching pictures of faces, the right hemisphere would win; if it was verbal, the left would dominate.

Hemispheric specialization is called lateralization. Most control of the muscles is lateralized, with the left hemisphere controlling the right hand and the right hemisphere controlling the left hand. The left hemisphere is best at verbal, detail, and sequential processing. For example, finding one's way around by sequences of right and left turns usually requires the left hemisphere. Strokes damaging the left hemisphere are more likely to cause loss of speech. The expression of speech is controlled by Broca's area in the left frontal lobe. Understanding speech requires Wernicke's area, located where the three hind cerebral lobes meet. A large nerve bundle called the arcuate fasciculus connects the two types of speech centers. Because the left hemisphere usually controls language and movements of the right hand, most people write with their right hand.

Damage to the right hemisphere causes problems in assembling puzzles, recognizing people, playing music, and painting. Finding one's way around by maps or landmarks requires the right hemisphere. Looking at someone's face and naming them requires both hemispheres. Each hemisphere has some abilities of the other; this has been found to be most apparent in females and in left-handed people.

## Applications

Understanding the relationships between specialized skills, actions, and the specialization of the brain has been very helpful in diagnosing the location of brain injuries and wounds, although today this is less important because of electronic brain-imaging techniques, such as computerized axial tomography (CAT) scans, that permit precise computerized localization.

On a theoretical level, there is a much better understanding of how the areas of the brain generate abilities and consciousness. Before they knew much about the specialization of many brain parts, scientists tried to identify functions by stimulating brain areas with electrodes or by removing brain areas. Some regions did not show obvious reactions to these techniques, and early researchers did not know that these were areas specialized for thinking and associating. They labeled the brain parts the silent areas and thought they had no functions. It is now known that there is no surplus or silent brain area. All parts of the brain perform vital functions; when any brain part is injured, modern techniques can identify deficits in the performance of those functions.

Studies of lateralized brain functions have raised the question of why bilaterally symmetrical brains evolved lateralization. Most current thinking is that use of tools and the beginnings of speech put a premium on processing rapid, precise sequences of actions or perception. The hemisphere controlling the dominant hand, which is usually the left hemisphere, already had some of these abilities. The development of speech centers in turn gave an evolutionary advantage to individuals with more specializations of the left hemisphere.

Being able to localize brain damage may help with designing the best kinds of tasks for a patient in a rehabilitation program. It can also help in detecting hidden, subtle problems. As scientists have learned more about the complex interrelationships of different brain parts, most attempts to solve problem behaviors by removing brain tissue have stopped. Before and after World War II, an operation called prefrontal lobotomy was common. The surgeon would either remove or damage the front-most part of the cerebral cortex or cut the connections between those areas and lower brain centers. Now it is known that damage to the left prefrontal lobe leaves a person unable to anticipate details and makes a person act as if depressed, but with no real sadness. Damage to the right prefrontal lobe leaves a person unable to anticipate patterns, and people with such damage do socially inappropriate things, such as public belching. Knowledge about these side effects helped make these operations rare.

In the 1970's, some prominent brain scientists proposed the theory that education centered on verbal lecture was only educating students' left hemispheres. They suggested that education of the dominated right hemispheres was needed to increase intuition, creativity, and other useful abilities. Books were written advocating learning to draw with the right brain, and claims were made about freeing the right hemisphere from the control of the left. As the right hemisphere is better understood, it is clear that its abilities are used even in a highly verbal culture. "Reading" facial expressions, for example, requires the right hemisphere, and when a person's expression does not match his or her words, people are more likely to believe the person's face. On the other hand, there is some recent evidence that after damage to the left hemisphere, some people (who are more likely to be left-handed or female) can perhaps develop some right hemisphere speech abilities. This may lead to better treatments for patients who lose language abilities, a condition called aphasia.

## Context

Physiological psychology developed within a classic experimental psychology model. Most early work was with animals, much of it with rats. Simultaneously, physicians working with brain-damaged patients began to generate a broad range of data about the relationship between human brain anatomy and behavioral deficits. Psychologists developed testing procedures more sophisticated than those developed by neurologists. As a result, many neurologists and neurosurgeons hired psychologists to administer psychological tests to their patients to detect subtle changes in abilities and behaviors. Today the best neurodiagnostic approaches combine psychological testing techniques with clinical medical techniques, including those developed by Aleksandr Luria in Russia.

Psychologists understand refined experimental and testing procedures; physicians can be authorized to do brain surgery. Once Roger Sperry found that cats appeared to have two minds after he separated their two cerebral hemispheres, the next step was for psychologists to work with doctors, who could perform medically justified human operations. The step after that was to use psychological techniques to understand the very subtle changes in behavior that resulted. Using experimental procedures developing in the study of perception, learning, and cognition, Sperry, Michael Gazzaniga, and others were able to show that each hemisphere understood the world in its own way. Later they were able to show lateralized abilities in people with intact brains.

Physiological psychology in American psychology departments is becoming less oriented toward animal experimentation and more oriented toward human clinical studies. The cooperative efforts of psychologists (sometimes called psychoneurodiagnosticians) and medical doctors generate more precise information about how human brains work. This means that there is less need for animal models of how human brains function. New data about brain functioning is being incorporated into current learning, cognitive, clinical, and computer-related psychology theories.

## Bibliography

Changeux, Jean-Pierre. *Neuronal Man: The Biology of Mind.* Translated by Laurence Garey. New York: Pantheon Books, 1985. This book was very popular when originally published in France, and the translated version shows this was deserved. The author reviews the history of human investigation of the nervous system and how ideas about mind and body have changed as a result of greater knowledge. It is written for the layperson. Educates about a wide range of current neurological and biochemical discoveries and philosophical issues.

Gardner, Howard. *The Shattered Mind: The Person After Brain Damage.* New York: Alfred A. Knopf, 1975. A very readable account of how brain damage to various regions and connections of the brain changes a person. Excellent clinical descriptions of symptoms and how these interact with the person. Teaches the anatomy of the cerebral hemispheres in a painless and accurate way.

Kolb, Bryan, and Ian Q. Whishaw. *Fundamentals of Human Neuropsychology.* 3d ed. New York: W. H. Freeman, 1990. An excellent text. This book logically guides the reader through the fundamentals of brain and neuron function to detailed descriptions of research on the purposes of all major brain areas. Provides a general model to understand the brain and functional systems like memory or language. The material is designed to be understood at different levels.

Luria, Aleksandr R. "The Functional Organization of the Brain." *Scientific American* 196 (March, 1970): 66-78. Luria was a dominant force in Russian neuropsychology. He worked extensively with brain damaged soldiers and developed a neurodiagnostic approach that has had a tremendous impact on American diagnostic techniques. In this classic article he presents a simple but profound model of the organization of the human brain. The frontal lobes involve action and planning, the hind parts of the cortex involve memory and sensation, and lower brain areas organize motivation, emotion, and reflex.

Springer, Sally P., and Georg Deutsch. *Left Brain, Right Brain.* Rev. ed. New York: W. H. Freeman, 1985. A good review of the literature and experimental work on lateralized brain functions. It is evenhanded and reviews the more speculative theories about special right-hemisphere abilities carefully and fairly. Most extreme ideas, such as claiming that the left hemisphere is the overly logical male brain and the right hemisphere the intuitive, female, artistic brain, are rejected. There is a very good section on the origins and meaning of left-handedness.

*Leland C. Swenson*

## Cross-References

Aphasias, 279; Brain Injuries: Concussions, Contusions, and Strokes, 448; Brain-Stem Structures, 461; Forebrain Structures, 1043; Hindbrain Structures, 1175; Psychosurgery, 1983; Split-Brain Studies, 2355.

# BRAIN-STEM STRUCTURES

*Type of psychology:* Biological bases of behavior
*Field of study:* Nervous system

*The brain stem can be described as the cornerstone of the central nervous system; it is responsible for such vital processes as respiration, circulation, blood pressure regulation, and some aspects of attention.*

### Principal terms

AUTONOMIC ACTIVITIES: tasks that are carried out automatically, without conscious intent (for example, blinking of the eyes)

CARDIOVASCULAR SYSTEM: the heart as well as the collection of veins, arteries, and capillaries that transport blood throughout the body

CENTRAL NERVOUS SYSTEM: the brain and spinal cord

CLASSICAL CONDITIONING: the process in which an originally neutral stimulus (cue) repeatedly paired with a reward comes to produce a behavior on its own

COGNITION: a general concept referring to mental processes such as sensing, perceiving, thinking, and remembering

MUSCULAR TONE: the amount of muscle tension appropriate for supporting the body or allowing it to carry out some physical act

NEURON: a nerve cell; the smallest unit of neural tissue in the central nervous system

## Overview

The central nervous system consists of two primary structures: the brain and the spinal cord. The spinal cord serves as a mediator between spinal nerves and the brain. It possesses nerve fibers that both send sensory (for example, visual, auditory) information to the brain and relay motor (movement) information from the brain to the rest of the body.

The brain can be subdivided into three basic structures: the cerebral cortex, the cerebellum, and the brain stem. The cortex (which literally means "bark") is so named because it resembles the bark of a tree. The cortex is the largest part of the brain and is anatomically divided into left and right hemispheres (halves). The left and right portions of the cortex can be further divided into four lobes, termed the occipital, parietal, temporal, and frontal, with each subserving slightly different cognitive functions. The cerebellum is a structure which looks somewhat like the cerebral cortex and resides immediately behind the brain stem at the back of the head. The cerebellum is principally involved with the initiation of very rapid movements of the arms and legs.

Lying at the top of the spinal cord and at the base of the brain is the brain stem.

The spinal cord enlarges and differentiates anatomically as it enters the skull to form the three major components of the brain stem: the medulla, pons, and midbrain. While the brain stem resembles the spinal cord in function as well as appearance, it is considerably more elaborate and complex.

An integral structure that runs through the entire brain stem is the reticular formation. Neurons within the reticular formation form a netlike configuration that mediates communication between the spinal cord, cerebellum, cerebral cortex, and other brain structures. A specific feature of the reticular formation is the reticular activating system. This system receives information from the various sensory systems (for example, touch, vision) and interfaces in the spinal cord (ascending reticular activating system). A second pathway originating in the frontal part of the cortex sends messages down to the brain stem and is termed the descending reticular activating system.

Together, these two mechanisms allow a person to be alerted by meaningful sights, sounds, or touches in the environment. It is the ascending system that allows a person to hear an intruder opening a window when the person is in the midst of a deep sleep. It is the descending system that permits the planning and reasoning part of the cortex to increase a person's attention and alertness during an important exam in school. Collectively, the ascending and descending reticular activating systems form a general monitoring apparatus which is crucial in the maintenance of wakefulness, consciousness, and attention.

While the entire brain stem is responsible for the effectiveness of the reticular activating system, other functions are the independent domain of one of the three components of the brain stem. The midbrain, for example, performs a number of unique and specialized functions. Visual information is initially relayed to the midbrain. While the visual details of what a person is viewing are ultimately processed in the rear portion of the cerebral cortex, various visual reflexes do originate in the midbrain. Specifically, blinking, dilation and contraction of the pupil, and certain eye movements are organized in the midbrain. Similarly, certain hearing reflexes, such as being startled by a loud or unfamiliar noise, are initiated in this region. Finally, the midbrain also organizes basic movement patterns such as walking or running. The midbrain does not contain systems that enable the individual to make a voluntary or deliberate decision to move or refrain from moving.

Immediately below the midbrain is the pons, a large bulge in the brain stem. The center of the pons contains a substantial portion of the reticular system, including some neurons that appear to be necessary for the regulation of the sleep-wake cycle. The upper portion of the pons plays a role in wakefulness, while a mechanism in the lower part of the pons permits a person to fall asleep. Studies in the early 1960's shed additional light on the role of the pons in sleep. This research indicated that the pons is responsible for the vital inhibition of motor activity that accompanies certain stages of sleep. Without this control, people would become highly active during sleep and possibly hurt themselves.

The anatomically lowest structure of the brain stem is the medulla oblongata (or simply the medulla). Along with including a segment of the reticular formation, the medulla controls life-sustaining functions such as the regulation of the cardiovascular system, breathing, and the maintenance of muscular tone in the skeletal muscles. While these functions are needed for people's very survival, they are quite primitive in nature. The medulla also contributes to other, subtler, processes. The medulla has been implicated as a mechanism that helps to reduce the body's sensitivity to pain. It was shown in the late 1960's that electrical stimulation of the medulla with a special probe could produce analgesia. This system is available to reduce chronic, unavoidable pain that might otherwise incapacitate a person. A final function of the medulla involves its contribution to some types of classical conditioning. For example, research in the early 1980's showed that damage to a region of the medulla, termed the inferior olive, prevented acquisition of a conditioned eye blink. Most simply, this suggests that the ability to associate some cue with a forthcoming puff of air directed to the eye is abolished by damage to a specific region of the medulla. The implication is that even this relatively primitive brain structure has some part in learning new responses.

## Applications

Increasing the knowledge base concerning the functions of the brain stem has generated solutions to a number of practical problems. It has assisted in the more effective clinical treatment of individuals with a variety of psychiatric, occupational, and behavioral difficulties. As knowledge regarding the brain stem as well as the entire central nervous system increases, mental health professionals have a growing number of diagnostic and treatment options at their disposal. Some disorders which were previously believed to be caused by stress or other socially based influences are now readily attributable to known physical damage or disease of brain tissue. Similarly, laboratory experimentation directed at the brain stem has also resulted in advances in diverse fields such as business, industry, education, and athletics. Most of these advances focus on the brain stem as a factor in emotional and motivational behavior, which influences nearly all forms of human behavior.

Research conducted in the early 1970's helped to establish the brain stem—specifically, the reticular activating system—as a major contributor to human emotional experience. While higher brain systems may be responsible for selecting which emotion will be experienced and exhibited, the reticular activating system may provide the activation or energy that drives the given emotion. Thus, while concern or anxiety may be emotional components that are generated at the level of the cerebral cortex, autonomic activities such as facial expression, muscle tension, or tremors may be initiated by the reticular system.

This increased awareness of the brain stem's unique contribution to complex human emotional experience has added to the understanding and application of what is termed optimal arousal theory. In general, optimal arousal theory states that people's best performances occur when they are not too unaroused (bored) or overaroused (nervous). Animal research has helped to implicate the role of the brain stem in monitoring arousal levels to provide optimal performances. This theory, and the brain mechanism underlying it, has been used to prepare Olympic athletes for competition as well as to improve the safety and productivity of industrial and business settings. It has also been employed to assist students who are preparing to take various entry examinations for college and graduate school to keep arousal levels at the most helpful point.

While the research discussed above has probably influenced most people's lives in a positive way, other applications have benefited a more selective population. The findings of neurologists (physicians specializing in disorders of the central nervous system) and clinical neuropsychologists (psychologists specializing in diagnosis and intervention of patients with physical damage to the brain) have enriched the lives of many people suffering from brain damage and disease.

The cooperative involvement of these professionals has allowed for the more effective medical and psychological treatment of patients with a variety of neurological disorders. One group of individuals assisted by the explosion of knowledge related to brain-stem functioning are those who have suffered a traumatic brain injury. Because of the force and direction of brain injuries sustained in automobile and motorcycle accidents, the brain stem is quite vulnerable. Typically, the brain is jarred against the rough, bony interior of the skull and compressed within the lower region of the brain. The mechanical forces of motor-vehicle accidents commonly suppress the life-sustaining functions of the brain stem, causing coma (sustained loss of awareness and cognitive functions) and probable death.

While many fatalities occur annually as a result of traumatic brain injury, more and more patients are surviving because of recent medical advances. Because of this increased survival rate, these patients need continued treatment to deal with residual cognitive and emotional deficits. Attentional mechanisms may be dramatically impaired after brain-stem damage. Because the ability to attend or concentrate allows for a variety of "higher" cognitive functions, attentional abilities are quite important. Specific difficulties emerge for the patient socially, vocationally, and psychologically. Difficulties may arise when the individual attempts to drive a car, return to work, or simply carry out the day-to-day tasks of living.

Thanks to the increased understanding of the brain stem, these patients are reaping the benefits of more diverse and effective treatment. The work of McKay Moore Sohlberg and Catherine Mateer in the late 1980's illustrates how increasing knowledge of the brain stem has enhanced treatment strategies. These authors consider attention to be a multidimensional cognitive function rather than a single, relatively uncomplicated process. This more sophisticated portrayal of the brain stem's attentional capacity has changed the way patients are treated. Specifically, there is a greater recognition of the brain stem's contribution to screening out unvaluable information, attending to several tasks at one time, or doing something repetitive or boring for an extended period of time. Psychologists who attempt to rehabilitate patients with brain-stem damage involve them in activities and tasks which demand all of the above abilities.

## Context

Perhaps the first legitimate discoveries concerning the function of the brain stem occurred in the middle nineteenth century. During that period, Pierre Flourens did experiments with animals in which he studied the behavior changes that occurred when specific parts of the brain were intentionally damaged. While he made several noteworthy contributions to the experimental study of the brain, his demonstration that damage to the medulla arrested respiration may be his most impressive. A number of similar studies followed which implicated other brain-stem structures in the various life-sustaining functions mentioned previously.

The theory of Aleksandr Luria, however, seemed to contribute more than isolated functions of specific brain-stem structures. Luria seemed to explain the function of the brain stem as it related to the workings of the entire central nervous system. For him, the brain stem was the physical correlate to one of three principal functional units of the brain. Most simply expressed, he believed that the lower brain structures (primarily the brain stem) were responsible for regulating cortical tone or waking. By cortical tone, Luria was referring to the fact that brain-stem structures could influence higher regions of the brain such as the cerebral cortex. The brain stem increasingly came to be viewed as a sophisticated structure capable of contributing to all forms of human activity. It was no longer seen as the structure that simply maintained life.

In the mid-1970's, laboratory experimentation began to suggest that the brain stem may also contribute to the regulation of emotional experience. Once again, the reticular activation system was shown to interact with parts of the cerebral cortex in producing emotions and motives involved in complex human endeavors such as ceremonial and religious rituals.

In general, the developments that have been made in the study of the human brain have dramatically changed the way psychologists explore human behavior. For example, a number of techniques are used to study the physical functioning of the brain as it is carrying out some cognitive task. This method often involves the placement of small electronic sensors on the surface of the skull which are capable of detecting electrical activity deep within the brain. With this technique, those who wish to determine which portion of the brain is utilized for tasks such as thinking, remembering, planning, or imagining can actually locate the active part of the brain.

This method of studying the physical and functional activity of the brain has offered psychology a revolutionary "window" on the study of human behavior. No longer is the field solely dependent on the verbal report of a research participant who is asked about the mental experience of some cognitive task. Undoubtedly, the understanding of the function of the brain stem, indeed the entire brain, will continue to advance the field of psychological science.

## Bibliography

Bloom, Floyd E., and Arlyne Lazerson. *Brain, Mind, and Behavior.* 2d ed. New York: W. H. Freeman, 1988. Deals with the entire brain but contains topic coverage that is relevant to brain-stem structures. Examples of these areas include behavioral rhythms, emotions, and motivational behavior. Clearly written; contains some beautiful and informative illustrations.

Carlson, Neil R. *Physiology of Behavior.* 3d ed. Boston: Allyn & Bacon, 1986. A very well-written introductory text in physiological psychology. Describes the function and structure of the entire brain, and includes subsections detailing the role of the brain stem in human behavior. Avoids confusing the reader with a surplus of technical jargon.

Luria, Aleksandr Romanovich. *The Working Brain.* London: Allen Lane, 1973. One of the most cohesive and integrative descriptions of the inner workings of the brain in the field. Brain-stem mechanisms are primarily discussed as they contribute to attention and concentration abilities. Includes sections dealing with the various symptoms seen in patients with brain damage.

MacLean, P. "The Triune Brain." *American Scientist* 66 (1978): 101-113. A significantly more complex and detailed account of the brain stem's role in emotional experience. One of the introductory texts referenced in this section should be consulted before attempting this article.

Sacks, Oliver O. *The Man Who Mistook His Wife for a Hat and Other Clinical Tales.* New York: Simon and Schuster, 1987. A splendidly written memoir of treating patients with various disorders. Sacks is both entertaining and informative. The man of the book's title, "Dr. P.," was suffering from a tumor in the right occipital lobe of the brain.

Thompson, Richard F. *The Brain: An Introduction to Neuroscience.* New York: W. H. Freeman, 1985. A particularly good introduction to the workings of the nervous system. Contains chapters about the basic brain mechanisms, sensory and motor systems, and changes that occur in the brain throughout an individual's life.

*Jeffery B. Allen*

## Cross-References

The Central and Peripheral Nervous Systems, 494; Emotion: Neurophysiology and Neuroanatomy, 914; Forebrain Structures, 1043; Hindbrain Structures, 1175; Neural Anatomy and Cognition, 1640; Optimal Arousal Theory, 1721; Reticular Formation, 2103.

# SURVEY
# OF
# SOCIAL
# SCIENCE

# ALPHABETICAL LIST

# CATEGORY LIST